# Free Spirits

# Free Spirits

## Feminist Philosophers on Culture

**Kate Mehuron**
Eastern Michigan University

**Gary Percesepe**
Cedarville College

PRENTICE HALL, Englewood Cliffs, New Jersey 07632

LIBRARY OF CONGRESS CATALOGING-IN-PUBLICATION DATA

Mehuron, Kate.
    Free spirits : feminist philosophers on culture / Kate Mehuron,
Gary Percesepe.
      p.  cm.
    ISBN 0-02-380135-2 (paper)
    1. Feminist theory.   2. Culture.   I. Percesepe, Gary John, 1954–
. II. Title.
HQ1190.M44   1995
306—dc20                                  94-6867
                                              CIP

Editor: Maggie Barbieri and Ted Bolen
Production Supervisor: Jeff Chen
Production Manager: Alex Odulak and Francesca Drago
Text Cover Designer: Robert Freese
Cover Art: Agnoula Peters
Photo Researcher: Clare Maxwell

© 1995 by Prentice-Hall, Inc.
A Division of Simon & Schuster, Inc.
Englewood Cliffs, New Jersey 07632

PRINTED IN THE UNITED STATES OF AMERICA

10  9  8  7  6  5  4  3  2  1

0-02-380135-2

Prentice-Hall International (UK) Limited, *London*
Prentice-Hall of Australia Pty. Limited, *Sydney*
Prentice-Hall Canada Inc., *Toronto*
Prentice-Hall Hispoanoamericana, S.A., *Mexico*
Prentice-Hall of India Private Limited, *New Delhi*
Prentice-Hall of Japan, Inc., *Tokyo*
Simon & Schuster Asia Pte. Ltd., *Singapore*
Editora Prentice-Hall do Brasil, Ltda., *Rio de Janiero*

# *Preface*

---

We are grateful to many students, friends, and colleagues who have inspired our work on *Free Spirits*. First, we are thankful to our readers for their fine criticisms and suggestions for revision that spurred this book to its completion. Lee Quinby, her friends and colleagues, and the library at Hobart and William Smith Colleges, have been invaluable as a source of inspiration and reference for many of the essays and films included in this book. We also thank the Lesbian, Gay, Bisexual Student Organization and the Gay Student Union at Eastern Michigan University for their influence, especially with regard to their cultural insights and activist aspirations. Colleagues and students in the Women's Studies Program and the feminist theory discussion group at Eastern Michigan University have provided many helpful references and have suggested the overall pedagogical direction of this textbook through sustained conversations over the past two years. We are grateful to Nancy Snyder and her staff in the History and Philosophy Department at Eastern Michigan University for their material support in expediting the completion of this book. We give special thanks to Agnoula M. Peters for her artistic design of the cover of *Free Spirits*, and for her sense of the "spirit" of this textbook.

Special thanks are also extended to Paige Wolfanger, Darla Kennedy, Sherrie Wood, and Ami Johnston for their valuable assistance in the preparation of the manuscript and their help with the permissions. The 6 P.M. Tuesday/Thursday Advanced Aerobics class at the Springfield Court Club occasioned many hours of useful and often hilarious discussion of a serious topic, the technology of the self—special thanks in this regard to Karen Brown, Charbe Weaver, Suzanne Percesepe, and you too, Steve.

Finally, we wish to extend thanks to our editor, Maggie Barbieri, whose vision for this book and enthusiasm in the making of it have been both admirable and unflagging.

K.M.
G.P.

# Contents

# Copyright Acknowledgments

## Chapter 1

## Chapter 2

## Chapter 3

## Chapter 4

## Chapter 5

## Chapter 6

## Chapter 7

Stoltenberg, from *Refusing to Be a Man: Essays on Sex and Justice* by John Stoltenberg, Penguin/Meridian, New York.

Patrick D. Hopkins, "Gender Treachery: Homophobia, Masculinity, and Threatened Identities," in *Rethinking Masculinity: Philosophical Explorations in Light of Feminism*, eds. Larry May and Robert Strikwerda (Lanham, MD: 1992). Reprinted with permission of Rowan and Littlefield, Lanham, MD.

Thomas W. Laqueur, "The Facts of Fatherhood," *Conflicts in Feminism*, eds. Marianne Hirsch and Evelyn Fox Keller (New York: Routledge, 1990). Reprinted with permission of Routledge, Chapman and Hall.

## Chapter 8

Ann Snitow, "Holding the Line at Greenham Common: Being Joyously Political in Dangerous Times," in *Women on War*, ed. Daniela Gioseffi (New York: Simon and Schuster, Inc., 1988). Reprinted with permission of Ann Snitow.

Rayna Green, "Culture and Gender in Indian America," in *Race, Class and Gender: An Anthology*, eds. Margaret L. Anderson and Patricia Hill Colling (Belmont, CA: Wadsworth Publishing Co.) Reprinted with permission of Rayna Green.

Fran Peavey, "American Willing to Listen," in *Heart Politics* (Philadelphia: New Society Publishers, 1986). Reprinted with permission of New Society Publishers, 4527 Springfield Avenue, Philadelphia, Pennsylvania, 19143. 1–800–333–9093.

Trinh T. Minh-ha, "Yellow Sprouts." Reprinted from *Framer Framed* by Trinh T. Minh-ha, 1992, with permission of Routledge, Chapman and Hall, Inc.

# Free Spirits

# Introduction

BY KATE MEHURON

To familiarize yourself with this book, imagine our culture as a vast band of static, buzzing white noise. To hear anything definite, a listener needs to sort out the frequencies, adjust the volume, and tune into certain wavelengths. At this point, the metaphor may appear naive because culture is far more than an auditory experience. Without our participation, culture seems an undifferentiated morass of individual and institutional practices and policies; natural catastrophes; political events; geographic regions; diverse ethnic, racial, and sexual groups; specific urban, suburban, and rural populations; and visual media bombardments.

Despite its obvious limitations, this high-frequency metaphor can help to understand the intentions behind our selections and organization of *Free Spirits*. Consider both the analytical categories that social and political philosophers traditionally apply to the cultural world, and the feminist frameworks that have been used to look at and evaluate women's specifically gendered experience. To use our sound-wave image, such categories are used by thinkers to tune into certain cultural wavelengths, and as a result they sift and relegate some frequencies to background white noise. This background is necessary, given the choice to focus on and to evaluate culture as it is experienced by specific groups of people. As a result, the task of feminist thought to offer a critical reflection on our social experience seems perpetually unfinished. Likewise, the potential philosophical categories that can be borrowed, invented, or applied by feminist philosophical and cultural criticism seem to be infinitely renewable.

## Why We Chose This Title

"Free spirits" is a phrase coined by the philosopher Friedrich Nietzsche to describe his ideal of a philosophical attitude unencumbered by dogmatic beliefs about the nature of good, evil, and reality.[1] The phrase "free spirits" in this textbook's title speaks to our hope in the open possibility of cultural experiences yet to be explored, in our ability to be inventive with our analytical categories and values, and in the experimental spirit by which we can reorganize and select the cultural topics to be evaluated from a feminist perspective. Such an attitude risks taking a new perspective as it questions the grounds of any abstract idea. According to Nietzsche, the free-spirited philosopher will seek alternative historical descriptions of a cultural situation or experience, and this search will transform our theoretical understanding of any such situation by unearthing previously excluded accounts of its significance. For example, some of the essays in this textbook question institutional Christianity and try to sift what may be socially liberating in that tradition from the aspects of Christianity that are manipulated by groups who want to enforce racial, sexual, and ethnic social hierarchies in this society.

Although his phrase is inspiring enough to appear in the title of this textbook, Nietzsche should not be interpreted as a feminist, nor as an advocate of democratic values, nor as a thinker who valued real women. Despite his own misogyny and elitist rejection of democratic principles, feminist philosophers have been and continue to be influenced by Nietzsche's call for a nondogmatic, free-spirited approach to cultural criticism. For instance, in one of her earlier books, Mary Daly calls for feminist thinkers to use Nietzsche's formulation of the "transvaluation of values."[2] The transvaluation of values is the practice of using words that are laden with derogatory traditional values in unconventional ways, to create a new cultural consensus among communities of people who are demanding social justice. They want to use language differently to support their newly achieved consciousness of their ideals and aspirations as a community. According to Daly, it is important for women to affirmatively transform words such as *hag* or *lesbian* in this way. These words traditionally have been used to insult or humiliate women, with dispiriting effects on women's self-esteem and with unjust political consequences.

Similar political uses of this transvaluative gesture are made by people of color in this country to achieve a more democratized inclusion of their interests and values in American social life. The words *black*, *Chicano*, and *African-American* are all terms whose value-laden meanings have been affirmatively transformed in our public awareness as a result of their transvaluation by politically astute constituencies. *Free Spirits* shows how feminist concerns can be intertwined with other contemporary political projects on behalf of democratic social change. Such projects are conducted by specific political constituencies that have been relegated to minority status by our cultural institutions, practices, and media images.

Given the free-spirited impetus of this textbook, perhaps you are wondering what "feminist" means in this context. To invoke our auditory metaphor once more, it is clear that the widely accepted feminist frameworks of liberal, socialist, radical, psychoanalytic, and postmodern categories have been able to tune into certain wavelengths of women's experiences of gender inequity and sex oppression. These feminist frameworks, clarified by feminist scholars such as Alison Jaggar and Rosemarie Tong, continue to demonstrate their power as explanatory and descriptive schemas that show in concrete and intelligible terms the ways in which male-dominated societies maintain gender and sex oppression.[3] The diversity of these feminist categories for understanding gender and sex inequities in our culture and in an international context indicates the dynamic, controversial quality of feminist thought. They show the diversity of feminist theoretical approaches and the enormity of the task involved in formulating prescriptive directions to be taken to overcome the oppressive conditions in which different groups of women remain bound.

Because these more familiar feminist frameworks have not exhausted our philosophical and political understanding of the many facets of women's experience under patriarchal conditions, *Free Spirits* is not designed to replace these categories of description and evaluation of gender and sex oppression. Readers who study this textbook's selections will find it helpful to bring these frameworks to their assessments of any of the essays. It is our belief, however, that the organization and selections in *Free Spirits* highlight other cultural frequencies and adjust the volume so that other voices can be heard. In doing so, this book gives the airwaves over to some political constituencies and cultural issues that our familiar feminist theoretical approaches have in the past relegated to white noise. By bringing such constituencies and issues into focus, *Free Spirits* is intended to inspire the further development and complexity of feminist efforts to describe and enact the democratization of everyday life.

Clearly, this textbook's endeavor does not occur in a vacuum. For example, the demand that we change the frequencies to which feminist analytical frameworks are conventionally tuned has been made by thinkers who call for the construction of social theories of oppression that are committed to feminist concerns yet seek other frameworks for comprehending the issues at stake. This "call for theory" interprets the most publicized feminist concerns to be usually articulated by socially privileged white women. The intention behind the call for theory is to supplement with other voices this inequitable intellectual situation. For example, bell hooks has called for feminist thought to take account of the white supremacist and privileged class assumptions of its own categories and of the broader culture as well.[4] As another example, Marilyn Frye has undertaken the task of describing the "arrogant perception" by which white middle-class feminists have excluded from their thought and thus contained the influence of marginalized perspectives and their political demands.[5]

Similarly, the focus of lesbian and gay theory by Gayle Rubin and Eve Sedgwick on the analytical and political distinctions between sex and gender, and the recent transvaluative claims made on the word *queer* by the work of Douglas Crimp and others have challenged feminists to develop further their accounts of the interconnections between homophobia, racism, and sexism.[6] Social theory produced by scholarly groups such as the Achilles Heel Collective propose to take masculinity as a multicultural object of ongoing social and political analysis.[7] In doing so they attempt to shift theoretical focus without excluding or erasing the feminist concerns associated with the oppressiveness of gender- and sex-related hierarchies and misogynist practices in our everyday institutions.

Finally, recent cultural criticism has focused on the ways in which public consensus and discriminatory attitudes are constructed or maintained in popular films, media trend stories, and the visual manipulations of the advertising and marketing industries.[8] Cultural criticism seeks to describe the ways in which, for example, militant, imperialist, or racist versions of "femininity" and "masculinity" are constructed by popular cultural images and resuscitated over and over in our cultural memory by the corporate domination of our mass media. Yet in these projects, the complicated interaction between the white supremacist, imperialist histories and colonialist practices of the British and American empires are also examined.

This brief look at the intellectual context of *Free Spirits* within the broader milieu of feminist thought, social theory, and cultural criticism can serve to clarify the phrase "Feminist Philosophers Diagnose Culture." The categories of philosophical thought—epistemological, political, ethical, aesthetic—have traditionally distinguished it as an academic discipline and have legitimated for professional philosophers their choices of topics, their methods, and the technical vocabulary by which they make themselves understood by other professional philosophers. Of course, the reality of philosophical inquiry has never been that simple, as witnessed by the ways in which feminist concerns and approaches have permeated all the traditional philosophical areas, and by the complexities of differences and similarities that are only coarsely grasped by labels such as "analytic" versus "continental" approaches. It is no wonder that "multicultural" philosophical approaches are not easy to classify, given the precariousness of traditional de-marcations already structuring the field. Even less understood, however ubiquitous, is the interaction between "feminist" philosophical approaches and the familiar philosophical taxonomies they have saturated.

Our claim to feature "feminist philosophy" in *Free Spirits* is premised on several articles of faith. The first article of faith is that philosophy begins in wonder, which in turn implies the disposition to take on a radically different perspective than one's own. Second, philosophical thinking strives to think the unthought, whether that be excluded catego-ries, unpopular ethical or political perspectives, implicit assumptions, or marginalized worldviews. Third, philosophical thinking often culminates in material changes in the way that social affairs are conducted. Fourth, when cultural institutions, events, and social commentaries on them become matter for philosophical reflection, the work of achieving conceptual clarity and the principled engagement with these subjects can begin anew. Philosophical reflection is vitalized by the encounter with its "unthought," and feminist theory is fueled by philosophical methods of critical engagement. The many cultural phenomena that vie for philosophical reflection in this textbook also implicitly harbor sex and gender issues that are approachable through these articles of faith.

# How We Organized the Book

## Chapter 1: Cultural Images

Do the visual and verbal narratives that bolster our mass-marketed cultural images pro-duce ideologies about race, sex, and gender? How powerful are such images and their accompanying cultural narratives in manufacturing public consensus about controversial political events? In Chapter 1, "Cultural Images," we have assembled essays that address these questions. Most draw on specific media images that are easily retrieved from short-term cultural memory by visiting your local video store or by perusing the latest *Victoria's Secret* catalog.

In "Reel Time, Real Justice," Kimberlé Crenshaw and Gary Peller examine the media manipulation of the videotaped version of the beating of Rodney King by Los Angeles police officers. They argue that the media narratives produced by this event functioned as a smokescreen to obscure the negative social effects of the contemporary legal ideal of racial neutrality. Crenshaw and Peller argue that if critically examined, the Rodney King trial can illuminate certain oppressive narrative structures and narrative techniques that are influential in shaping contemporary debates about "affirmative action."

In "Black Ladies, Welfare Queens, and State Minstrels," Wahneema Lubiano ex-pands the implications of this critical focus on the media's narratives of political events by scrutinizing the nationally televised Senate hearings of Anita Hill's sexual harassment charges against then-Supreme Court nominee Clarence Thomas. Lubiano argues that the debates exploited Anita Hill's testimony by mobilizing national stereotypes of the "welfare queen"; this stereotype has been used by special interest groups since the early 1970s to stigmatize welfare and affirmative action programs in this country. Crenshaw, Peller, and Lubiano demonstrate the connections among our nationally televised media narratives about political events, our racial ideologies, our gender stereotypes, and the public policy programs that directly affect socioeconomically disadvantaged people in this country.

A closer look at the way in which popular cultural images foster popular ideals of masculinity and femininity is offered by Andrew Ross, Susan Bordo, and Danae Clark. Ross in "Cowboys, Cadillacs, and Cosmonauts" shifts our focus by examining the ways this country's TV western genres have fostered a nostalgic ideology of the nuclear family that simultaneously obscures the real demographic picture of the U.S. family. Ross expands his critique by showing the nostalgic automobile film genre as a Hollywood-induced cultural memory that glorifies white masculine autonomy even as it erases from public view the factual narratives that could historically inform his audience about the real decline of the U.S. automobile industry. Ross finishes by describing the connections between the "engendering of men" through popular science fiction films and our imperialist as well as nationalistic narratives of space conquest.

In "'Material Girl': The Effacements of Postmodern Culture," Susan Bordo argues that Madonna's career exemplifies a disturbing metamorphosis from her early refusal to be defined as a desirable object by patriarchal constructions of feminine sexuality, to today's Madonna. Our latter-day Madonna supports the sculpted, hyper-thin, plasticized public image that reiterates for all Madonna "wannabes" the ideal of feminine beauty. Bordo frames her analysis by criticizing the postmodern style of conversation that is exemplified by talk shows, in which issues are emptied of political content and images that are politically pertinent to women are featured as mere individual choices. Meanwhile, according to Bordo the mass-marketing appeals to women by the fashion, aerobics, and body-building industries illustrate Foucault's observation that people's compliance with these contemporary forms of discipline are also how people internalize societal norms of gender identity. According to Bordo, Madonna contributes to this cultural compliance to patriarchal ideals of feminine beauty.

Finally, Danae Clark argues in "Commodity Lesbianism" that dual marketing strategies that appeal to lesbian as well as straight consumers in such venues as Calvin Klein ads, *Mirabella*, *Tweeds*, *J. Crew*, and *Victoria's Secret* are capitalizing on various reading styles practiced by lesbian spectators. Clark's essay provides a valuable overview of the ways in which lesbian communities have historically revised their countercultural relationship to cultural ideals of femininity, ranging from the 1970s dyke "anti-style" style to contemporary styles of the "lipstick lesbian," androgynous presentations of the self, and camp femme–butch aesthetics. Although these dual marketing strategies may have resulted in more pleasure for lesbian spectators and consumers, Clark questions whether the commodification of lesbian styles also promotes a liberal ideology of choice that ignores the ongoing coercive aspects of compulsory heterosexuality in this culture. If camp is commodified, does that signal the dilution of an important political resistance to heterosexism that has been historically exercised by lesbian "styles"?

## Chapter 2: Community

How do the prejudices allied with racism, sexism, anti-Semitism, drug addiction, the pandemic of AIDS, and ethnic difference continue to fracture relationships between people? What sorts of communities are possible, given the material realities of these social problems? How can communities become politicized, and what sort of structural and discursive obstacles do politicized communities face as they use democratic channels for social change on their own behalf? In Chapter 2, "Community," we have selected personal testimony, conversation, and theory by social change activists and scholars who address these questions.

bell hooks, Cornell West, and Barbara Smith demonstrate through conversation and personal testimony how personal relationships can be more than simply sites of bitterness and acrimony affected by racist, sexist, homophobic, and anti-Semitic sentiment. The intimate exchange of candid conversation and compassionate regard, and the ethical evaluation of the political influence of institutional Christianity on our community lives, can also invent paths that might lead to social reconciliation and the overcoming of hierarchies of personal value associated with race, sex, ethnicity, and religion.

In "Breaking Bread," hooks and West converse about their shared concerns: the class-based crisis of animosity between black men and women, the history of the vital connection between black Christian religious communities and black political power, and the threat of drug-related addictions to black communities. Their dialogue emphasizes black community needs for a revitalized ethic of partnership between black men and women and a shared spirituality. Acknowledged as well is the need by black communities for a sustained analysis of class-based competitiveness between black men and women in this corporate society; this competitiveness is a major obstacle to partnerships within a socially progressive community context.

Barbara Smith in "Between a Rock and a Hard Place: Relationships Between Black and Jewish Women" discusses the implications of the often overlooked personal relationships between black and Jewish women. Smith critiques a common assumption that seems to corrode feminist alliances between black and Jewish women: to be Christian is to be by definition anti-Semitic. Smith chooses to identify the commonalities and differences between the historical legacies of institutionalized oppressions of Jewish-American women by the Holocaust and of African-American women by American slavery. Class privilege, if unanalyzed, continues to obscure the differences experienced by Jewish, middle-class, white lesbians and lesbian, working-class women of color. Smith argues that a significant political issue that ought to be the focal point of women's coalitional efforts is the rise of the anti-Semitic, racist, and homophobic right-wing international political movement. She warns that in the United States the New Right uses Christian rhetoric to win public sentiment for support of its ultimate aim: to institutionalize race, sex, and religious discrimination.

María Lugones, the women AIDS activists at Bedford Hills Correctional Facility, and Nancy Fraser write of concrete cultural and structural obstacles to the formation of politicized communities of women, and each tells stories of partial successes in overcoming these obstacles. In "Playfulness, 'World'-Travelling, and Loving Perception," Lugones employs Marilyn Frye's concept of "arrogant perception" to explain how racism and ethnic chauvinism prevent white/Anglo feminists from achieving bonds of loving identification with women of color. The failure to love and to thus form community ties is exacerbated by the double erasure of some women's ethnic uniqueness as well as the specific oppressions experienced by lesbians of color within the white imperialist context of the United States. Thus the homogenous label "Hispanic" imposed by Anglo arrogant perception obscures the ethnic diversity of Latino, Chicano, black-Dominican, white Cuban, Korean-Columbian, or Italian-Argentinian ethnic identities. Lugones supplies an account of how American Anglo imperialism fractures the experience of people of color and sexual minorities into different ontological worlds. Her account helps to explain why her own identity cannot remain intact across all worlds, and thus offers a descriptive framework for achieving compassionate bonds between feminists as arrogant perception is deconstructed.

The Women of ACE (AIDS Counseling and Education) at Bedford Hills Correctional Facility testify to the collective effort by women in this facility to overcome the structural stigmatization in Bedford Hills against women inmates infected by HIV. This collectively written account provides concrete information about how an affirmative community of support and education evolved out of the structurally repressive, fearful, and discriminatory environment of this women's prison. You should read this testimony in conjunction with Nancy Fraser's, "Struggle over Needs: Outline of a Socialist–Feminist Critical Theory of Late Capitalist Political Culture," for the story of ACE confirms the descriptive power of Fraser's schema of "the politics of needs discourse" for our contemporary welfare state. In addition, Fraser tells informative narratives about coalitional communities of women: the feminist activism that changed the landscape of domestic violence, Carol Stacks's account of the domestic kinship networks among poor black AFDC recipients in a midwestern town, and Rains's studies of young black women's resistance to "mental health" interventions in family planning programs. The silence around AIDS-related race, sex, and gender stigmatization is broken by the Women of ACE as they collaboratively write the experiences and problems faced by women infected by HIV in ethnically and racially diverse communities. Political strategies useful to women who face multiple stigmatizations as a result of socioeconomic disenfranchisement are theorized and enumerated by Fraser.

## Chapter 3: Megalopolis

Feminists have criticized the patriarchal dichotomy between the private and the public, arguing that this institutionally reinforced binary has unjustly rendered the oppression of women in the domestic sphere beyond appeal. However, Chapter 3, "Megalopolis," shifts the focus and explores how intimate, ethnically specific symbols associated with "home" such as the Latino *altares* tradition, or women's personal erotic space, are commodified and sold in the international market of kitsch religious art and international sex tourism. In this chapter, we understand the "megalopolis" to be urban space without local borders. It is urban space colonized by international systems of humanly exploitative commerce, and space in which the public access of women and other minority groups to goods, services, and safety is a private privilege bought by the socioeconomically advantaged.

In her essay "Home Is Where the *Han* Is: A Korean American Perspective on the Los Angeles Upheveals," Elaine H. Kim argues that Korean-Americans are left with only the most minimal and anguished sense of home. This is a conclusion reached by the disillusioning experience of Korean-Americans in the wake of their unprotected victimization by the Los Angeles upheavals and by their own historical legacy as the turf for other nationalist movements' military conquests. Kim argues that *han*, the sorrow and anger that grow from the accumulated experiences of oppression, is the only home space left. *Han* is an emotional space out of which Korean-Americans must create a nationalism that can preserve their communities from the cultural genocide of assimilation and the discriminatory attitudes toward them by other Asian-American groups and the white majority. Kim leaves the reader with an open question: How can a Korean-American cultural nationalist movement avoid the pitfalls of sexist and racist ideologies toward other Asian-American and ethnic minorities?

Weisman turns to another home space, the urban neighborhood, the public space of supposedly equal access to all inhabitants. In "The Private Use of Public Space," Weisman shows that public space, although home to the homeless and disenfranchised, is safe only for the privileged few. She argues that our urban environments enact territorial dramas that reinforce sex-role stereotypes through the threat of sexual violence, class privilege, and the dehumanization of certain groups of disenfranchised persons such as prostitutes, PWAs (People With AIDS), and single women with children. The counternarrative to this is Toronto's METRAC project, which she describes as an excellent model for urban protection of women in urban landscapes. However, even successful activist projects exemplified by the METRAC project or the women's antinuclear Greenham Common Peace Camp are not enough, for the dehumanization of our urban landscapes is the result of concrete public policy decisions, and the restoration of a dignified urban life for the socioeconomically disenfranchised will occur only through enlightened public policy in the future.

Cynthia Enloe and Celeste Olalquiaga examine the international commodification of women's sexuality and the Latino *altares* tradition. In "On the Beach: Sexism and Tourism," Enloe begins by historically addressing the ethical and political dilemmas posed by the rise of international tourism to Euro-American feminist ideologies of the autonomous, privileged woman traveler. Enloe argues that if feminist emancipation is conflated with this sort of material autonomy and practice, then the Euro-American feminist lifestyle is directly implicated in two international issues: the imperialist practice of compromising the economic self-sufficiency of newly decolonized nations and Euro-American subsidization of decolonized nations' tourism industries. Further, Enloe demonstrates the interdependency between governmental and corporate sponsorship of sex tourism industries that exploit poor indigenous women, the nationalist movements by nations bent on decolonizing themselves from Euro-American domination, and the vicious transmission and spread of HIV, especially among women and children in this political context.

In "Holy Kitschen," although far from condemning the emotional vicariousness of urban kitsch appropriations of the Latino *altares* tradition, Olalquiaga does view this aesthetic and consumer trend as a loss of the intimate emotional memories represented by traditional home altars. Olalquiaga explains the conversion of Catholic religious Latino imagery into kitsch art forms that are commodified in the urban landscape by reference to Jean Baudrillard's theory of simulation. Olalquiaga argues that second- and third-generation Latino women artists' aesthetic recycling of home altars challenges the sex-role stereotypes enacted by the first-degree traditional religious imagery of their upbringing. In addition, their artistic achievements signal an exciting secularization of the *altares*, a trend that exalts the artist behind the creation.

## Chapter 4: Technologies of the Self

The title of Chapter 4, "Technologies of the Self," is borrowed from the philosopher Michel Foucault's understanding of the care of the self as a practice that can resist the ways personal identities are coercively imposed on people by external structures of power.[9] Gloria Anzaldúa, in "How to Tame a Wild Tongue," focuses attention on how writing in one's chosen ethnic dialects, occupying the linguistic "borderland conflicts" of Spanish-speaking groups in the south and midwest, can exemplify this sort of care of the self. Anzaldúa testifies that in this dominant North American culture, choosing to care for the self by the many borderland languages of standard Spanish, standard Mexican-Spanish, Chicano Spanish, Tex-Mex, or *pachuco*, is a practice of resistance to the homogeneous identity of "Spanish," "Mexican," or "Chicano" imposed on Anzaldúa's tongue. For example, chosen dialect can carry high or low estimations by one Chicana feminist of another; this is examined in the context of Anzaldúa's narrative account of her linguistic and ethnic identity.

Foucault considered self-reflective writing styles to be technologies by which one can produce a self that is resistant to practices that normalize, or conform the individual to dominant racist or heterosexist standards. However, most of his historical and philosophical inquiries took dominant institutions such as the medical clinic, the psychiatric hospital, and the penitentiary as his objects of study. The essays by Susan Ferraro, Sandra Bartky, and Linda Singer can be interpreted to criticize certain institutionalized technologies that directly affect the formation of women's identities, insofar as their health depends on the disciplinary health protocols that these technologies prescribe. For example, in "The Anguished Politics of Breast Cancer," Ferraro analyzes the effects of the medical establishment's rhetoric on the treatment and prevention of breast cancer. She compares the rates of women's mortality from breast cancer with the statistics on AIDS, and evaluates the National Cancer Institute's dismal record of its research priorities for the treatment and prevention of both diseases for women. The class-based inequities that affect women's differential access to treatment trials and medical care are elucidated, and the potential of advocacy groups united under the National Breast Cancer Coalition to inform the breast cancer activist movement is evaluated.

Sandra Bartky appropriates Foucault's account of disciplinary practices that produce the "docile bodies" of modernity in a radical way, extending the analysis to the constellation of social practices that work together to make women's embodiment in our culture more docile than men's. Citing "women's magazines," advertisements, and other sources, Bartky explores the logic of subjection that governs practices such as dieting, exercise, clothing, cosmetics, gesture, posture, movement, and general bodily comportment.

In "Bodies–Pleasures–Powers," Linda Singer expores the theme of motherhood as a biosocial experience, extending her analysis to include the infamous Baby M surrogate motherhood case. Singer locates such controversies within the context of the New Right's and media's exploitation of AIDS-related panic. She shows the contradictory messages conveyed by the New Right's efforts to "naturalize" motherhood with its revitalized politics on behalf of the nuclear family, and the capitalist trend toward the heterosexist commodification of women's bodies represented by recent reproductive technologies and the legal enfranchisement of surrogate motherhood and fetal rights.

## Chapter 5: Ecofeminism

One of the more contentious areas of feminist thought today revolves around the issue of global environmental degradation. Are the many types of earth-based, feminist spiritualities relevant or irrelevant to social activism that strives to heal the environment? To what degree can feminist theory explain and provide a schema to remedy environmental racism and species chauvinism? Chapter 5, "Ecofeminism," features essays by Starhawk, Ynestra King, Carol J. Adams, and Carolyn Merchant, who address these questions.

In "Power, Authority and Mystery: Ecofeminism and Earth-Based Spirituality," Starhawk describes the basic concepts of earth-based spirituality, which she has derived from a feminist pagan worldview that is directly critical of the apocalyptic and male-dominated worldview of institutional Christianity. On her terms, our relationship to the environment must be revisioned within an "ethics of integrity" that can justify our concerned efforts to heal the earth. Starhawk envisions environmental activism within a broader framework of connection to other international movements of liberation that exemplify a similar ethical stance toward the world.

Starhawk's earth-based pagan challenge to the institutionalized Christian worldview is deepened by Ynestra King's philosophical analysis of the conceptual dualisms that contribute to a subjugated environment. In "Healing the Wounds: Feminism, Ecology, and the Nature/Culture Dualism," King challenges cultural feminisms such as those presumed by Starhawk, arguing that feminist women of color require a socialist analysis of environmental subjugation. If such an analysis is pursued, the interconnections between environmental degradation and the racist oppression of indigenous peoples will be brought to light. King does not reject feminist spirituality so much as she demands that earth-based spiritualities integrate a commitment to dialectical, material change that will involve the confrontation of environmental racism. In addition to environmental racism, feminists who align their radical politics to environmental issues are formulating the political and theoretical connections between this and capitalist public policies that profit from the meat industry.

Carol J. Adams, in "The Feminist Traffic in Animals," takes her departure from Gayle Rubin's groundbreaking materialist analysis of the international capitalist traffic in and exploitation of women, and applies these insights to a similar phenomenon found in the commercial trade and consumption of animals. Adam's essay is rich in analogies that compare the language, assumptions, and practices of meat-eating humans with the ways that people dehumanize others through white-skin privilege, or through heterosexist or sexist privilege. Part of the persuasive effect of Adams's argument is that feminists must politicize their relation to animals, because to the degree that women relegate their practices of animal consumption to a privatized, "personal" sphere, they are repeating, hence complying, in the same gestures that have historically subjugated women, sexual minorities, and people of color.

A comprehensive overview of the international environmental movement and women's activist contributions in economically developing nations is offered by Carolyn Merchant in "Ecofeminism." Merchant places cultural and socialist feminism in context by describing the liberal feminist approach to environmental concerns as well. She defends socialist ecofeminism over other philosophical approaches because of its capacity to explain the economic factors and the distributive inequities that are operative in the global environmental crisis. One of the most valuable aspects of Merchant's essay is its historical overview of the origins of feminist environmentalism, and her factual and descriptive emphasis on the work of radical women environmentalists in Kenya, Canada, California, India, and Latin America. Merchant discusses on the intertwined effects of Euro-American colonization and capitalist exploitation on the environmental degradation witnessed by decolonizing nations. Feminist activists in these nations connect the struggle for autonomy over and qualitative improvements in their sexual and reproductive health to environmental issues as well.

## Chapter 6: Sexualities

Ecofeminism is not the only area of contentious debate. Unquestionably, sexuality is the topic that garners the most controversy among feminists, as well as between feminists and other emancipatory movements. Our selections in Chapter 6, "Sexualities," represent an effort to enrich these debates, which, first of all, include the controversy among feminists over the legal censorship of pornography. The censorship position is advocated by Catharine MacKinnon and is opposed by the Feminists Against Censorship Taskforce (FACT). The substance of that debate is thoroughly represented by other anthologies and resources.[10] Because of this coverage in other resources, we have chosen to explore hard-core pornography through Linda Williams's philosophical and aesthetic analysis, and her political prescriptions on behalf of women involved in the pornography industry. We have highlighted MacKinnon's recent advocacy on behalf of women victimized by wartime rape. Rape as a war crime haunts all women and presents an atrocity that must be globally confronted by feminist thinkers.

Our first selection, Katie Roiphe's "Date Rape's Other Victim," is a concise summary of arguments that are extensively developed in her book *The Morning After: Sex, Fear and Feminism on Campus*. Roiphe claims that the topic of campus rape has become a cottage industry on college campuses, resulting in patronizing campus policies that detail the appropriate behaviors, rhetoric, and meaning of sexual "consent" in the context of student–student and student–professor relationships. Roiphe's argument against the "rape hype" has been received with fury by feminist activists who have worked for over a decade to place sexual harassment and discrimination on the public agenda for concern and reform. Roiphe's indictment is taken by her opponents to be a trivialization of the power abuses experienced by women not only on college campuses, but also in the workplace and beyond. What do you think?

Patricia Hill Collins brings a historical and multicultural perspective to the problem of sexual violence and objectification of women of color in the United States. In "The Sexual Politics of Black Womanhood," Collins elucidates the contributions of African-American novelists, who show the links between our patriarchal sex/gender hierarchies and the sexualized inequalities of race and social class in the United States. Collins draws important historical connections between contemporary pornographic portrayals of black sexuality, our American history of slavery, and the racist biologies of the nineteenth century that continue to exist in contemporary right-wing neo-Nazi movements and the neoconservative rhetoric against the welfare state. This essay provides an important historical and theoretical framework that ought to be read in conjunction with Lubiano's analysis of the Hill–Thomas hearings, bell hooks and Cornel West's dialogue, and Barbara Smith's observations about the coalitional possibilities between black and Jewish women in the United States.

Another contemporary controversy concerns the compatibilities and differences between feminist theories of sexuality and lesbian, gay, bisexual theories. The latter have recently transvaluated and appropriated the word *queer* to affirmatively name a new field of study that is expanding into many multicultural directions, into every academic discipline, and is becoming acknowledged as a vital participant in every social movement dedicated to radically democratizing our everyday lives. This textbook cannot do justice to "queer studies" any more than it can fully represent the history of radical feminist theories of sexuality. However, we feature Walter L. Williams's "Of Religions and Dreams: The Spiritual Basis of the Berdache Tradition" because of its respectful, historical approach to a spiritual tradition that has been nearly annihilated by the genocidal policies of Euro-Americans toward Native American culture in this country.

Williams places the transgendered, cross-dressing practices of the Native American berdache tradition within an account of that tradition's metaphysical beliefs and within the history of the destructive effects of Christian missionary zeal on those beliefs. Williams's essay explains the interdependence between Native American attitudes toward gender and sexuality, and their communally held cosmologies that support a partnership ethic with the environment. This essay ought to be read in conjunction with the lesbian feminist "borderland" perspectives held by Lugones and Anzaldúa, and the pagan worldview advocated by Starhawk.

If we step back from that lively frequency that buzzes with the feminist pros and cons about the censorship of pornography, what will a close-up philosophical, cultural and aesthetic look at hard-core pornography yield? In this regard, Linda Williams's essay "Fetishism and Hard Core" is the most incisive look that we could find. She explicitly describes the evolution of that hard-core feature, the "money shot" from the 1970s to the 1990s. In doing so, Williams defines the visual fetishization of male ejaculation in the money shot as a commodified, recent version of what has been historically characterized as the "phallic economy of pleasure." Although feature-length pornography is obsessed with visually capturing the moment of sexual satisfaction, it is paradoxically limited by its own medium to capturing only the male moment of pleasure and fails to represent female pleasure. Although Williams believes, following Foucault, that the industry is thoroughly mobilized by broader cultural trends that sexualize every aspect of everyday life, including female forms of sexual pleasure, this industry can be subverted by exploiting the inadequacy of its medium to female pleasure. Williams calls for feminist sex workers in the industries of pornography, sexual performance art, and prostitution to take advantage of the failures of phallocentric, visual sexual economies, as well as of the popular cultural fascination with sexual pleasure in general. By what inventive narratives, media, and performances can feminists embrace the affirmative potential of our wider cultural fascination with perversion?

The media's report of wartime rape of Muslim and Croatian women in the Balkan conflict is viscerally repellent for many women. In the description of any woman's experience of rape or sexual abuse, this visceral reaction is common because of women's strong empathic identification with the physical violation of any one of their own kind. The case of wartime rape multiplies our sense of injury because it graphically illustrates a collective violation of one sex against another and provokes anew the radical feminist hypothesis that the sexual oppression of women is fundamental to all other oppressions. Catharine A. MacKinnon's essay "Crimes of War, Crimes of Peace" confronts the historical, philosophical, and legal context of this latest instance of wartime rape. MacKinnon explains the historical legal precedents that prevent international recognition of wartime rape as a collective human rights violation and genocidal practice against *women*, as distinct from persons of a particular nationality. She argues that because states are empowered to prosecute human rights violations, yet no nation-state fully recognizes human rights violations of women within its borders, then rape as a war crime and rights violation against women is not legitimately recognized as a state violation to be prosecuted in international courts of law. MacKinnon locates the flaws of Western equality theory in its legitimation of "difference" as a way to exclude certain populations from the human rights protective umbrella; this flaw has culminated, for example, in the "legalized" Nazi politics of genocide. The same flaw is exhibited in the failure of the protective net of international law to acknowledge the violation of the human rights of women, especially in cases of individual and collective sexual abuse and genocide. MacKinnon connects her argument to her well-known stance against the international pornography industry; this is an industry that she believes perpetrates a wrongful international consensus that the commodification, exploitation, and abuse of women's sexuality are simply sex, rather than human rights violations against women.

## Chapter 7: Masculinities

Social theorists are inventing new concepts and explanatory schemas to understand the ways in which sexual, ethnic, national, and racial identities "engender" masculine, feminine, and transgendered styles of human being, and their heterosexual, bisexual, and homosexual object choices. In other words, social theory represents the effort to bring a multicultural as well as materialist approach to our efforts to comprehend sexual and gender diversity.

Richard Rodriguez gives a personal account of how his own sense of masculinity is engendered by his ethnic upbringing in a Mexican-American family. You will find this account even more inspiring and thought-provoking if you read Rodriguez in conjunction with the discussions by Lugones and Anzaldúa of the ways in which dialect, class status, lesbian invisibility, and familial origins in the cultures of Mexico, Latin America, and the Caribbean interact with their sense of gender identity. Rodriguez's account furthers this discussion by acknowledging the symbolic ties between his own masculine identification with his father, the social status of clothes, the social significance of Hispanic men's manual labor as compared with intellectual labor, Hispanic macho attitudinal and behavioral norms, and finally Rodriguez's own sexual identity.

How can a man be a feminist? The essays by John Stoltenberg, Patrick D. Hopkins, and Thomas W. Laqueur are as complex as Rodriguez's reflections. Stoltenberg's address to a college audience is fascinating when read in conjunction with Roiphe's "Date Rape's Other Victim." His essay seeks to persuade men that the ways in which they conventionally choose to be sexual—privileging penile sensation, veering toward sexualized violence, ignoring the consensual and emotional dimensions of one's self and one's sex partner—can be politically evaluated. Men, Stoltenberg asserts, are conditioned to enjoy sex in these narrow ways, because our patriarchal social conditioning decrees that these ways of having a sex are what makes a man a "man." In this way, Stoltenberg argues that the idea of the male sex is like the idea of an Aryan race. It took a Nazi regime to repetitively enforce the idea that the Aryan race was something real and superior to all others.

Patrick D. Hopkins supports Stoltenberg's claim about the cultural enforcement of gender identity in "Gender Treachery: Homophobia, Masculinity, and Threatened Identities." Hopkins asserts that given the sex-class system, masculinity in this society must constantly monitor itself; it is a gendered performance that must remain stabilized for some persons to qualify for the superior designation of "manhood." Within this context, Hopkins defends an explanation for the motivations and orgins of homophobia and heterosexism. Discriminatory attitudes toward sexual minorities and the privileging of heterosexual object choice are mechanisms that ensure the stability of masculine gender identity. Without that stability, global male dominance is endangered. Both Stoltenberg and Hopkins are contributing in a substantive way to the notion that men are feminists insofar as they work to overcome a masculine identity complicitous with this sex-class system, and insofar as they advocate the pleasures and plurality of sexes and genders in an ideally egalitarian society. As Hopkins has stated, male feminists want to "betray gender."

Earlier we mentioned Linda Singer's approach to the Baby M case within her larger examination of the ways that capitalist commodification of reproductive technologies and patrilineal privilege are enshrined by legal precedent in this country. Thomas W. Laqueur in "The Facts of Fatherhood" returns to the issue of paternity and explicitly takes up the Baby M case, locating it within a history of fatherhood. Laqueur finds that the most notable feature of our available histories of fatherhood is the pathological lack of information or historic detail about its emotional bonds. Rather, the patriarchal ideologies of fatherhood reign in our historical discourses: ideological discourses that align the father to the sovereign master, governing body, domestic autocrat. Laqueur wants to dispense with the popular dilemma operative in discussions about the Baby M case that is a residue of this historical pathology: either valorize the sacred bond of the biological mother with the child or surrender all such relations to market forces and their complicity with patriarchal, patrilineal privilege. Rather, Laqueur opts to follow feminist perspectives that view neither fatherhood nor motherhood as "given" or natural relationships. Implied by this perspective is the value of an extended emotional economy. According to Laqueur, those who have the rights and obligations of parenthood ought to be those who invest the emotional, imaginative, material, and psychic capital in the impregnation, gestation, and subsequent life of the child. A fuller appreciation of the implications of Laqueur's argument can be gained by reading his essay in conjunction with Linda Singer's "Bodies–Pleasures–Powers."

## Chapter 8: The Politics of Hope

Chapter 8 gives voice to those whose poetic and experiential invocations of revolutionary change will linger in our awareness long after the study, analysis, and discussion of these selections are over. Trinh T. Minh-ha's essay is the most enigmatic selection in this chapter, and yet her beautifully crafted phrases about gender and revolutionary change continue to fascinate. However, all of these selections bear that quality of wonder that we have taken to be a signal of the possibility of renewed philosophical reflection about the world.

Ann Snitow narrates her own activist experience at the Greenham Common Peace Camp, which was described and admired by Weisman in her discussion of the feminist politics of space. Snitow relates her initial reservations about feminist efforts to oppose militarism, given the enormous needs of women for advocacy on behalf of specifically female issues. She notes that the feminist rationalization for direct action and civil disobedience, in alliance with thousands of women continuing over many years and extending to many other disarmament encampments, *follows* upon active resistance. Civil disobedience in the context of nuclear disarmament is also an act by all women against their own gender socialization and against the complicity of women with male violence. Their activism gives them the exhilarating discovery of a "new cosmopolitanism" for women that can inform and ignite the participation of feminism in other international movements for social change.

Rayna Green, in "Culture and Gender in Indian America," expresses solidarity with this discovery when she writes that Indians "can't simply function as vague, ghostly reminders of poverty index levels, of hunger and homelessness in America; that's irrelevant." According to Green, what *is* relevant is the metaphor of the Native American woman who waits in a specifically Indian manner, who dignifies the causes of others as well. The Native American anticipation of freedom and justice lies dormant and marginalized, waiting for the arrival of a just public consciousness; a consciousness that many Native Americans have already achieved. Such achievements in consciousness include the awareness and affirmation of our essentially hybrid identities, the respect accorded to others' stories, the honor of women's presence within the sphere of public decisions, the gift of giving itself, and the infinite extension of the concept of family among our own species and beyond species chauvinism.

Fran Peavey, known as the "atomic comic" and as a social change consultant, created her "American Willing to Listen" project to listen to what non-American people have to say about the United States' involvement in the nuclear arms buildup, colonization, international tourism, the sex industry, and environmental degradation. Her project is dedicated to traveling in a way that is different from the Euro-American tourist's emotionally detached, ready-to-be-served attitudes that Cynthia Enloe has described. Rather, Peavey lingers on Bangkok street corners and in the coffeehouses serviced by women sex workers and waits for their stories to come forth. They tell of the economic anxieties associated with nationalist policies of decolonization, the frightening presence of U.S. military bases in local territories, the hardships of balancing child care and gaining access to an education for their children. Peavey learns of the racism experienced by Koreans in Japan; of the environmental damage in Varanasi, India; and of the alternative schools in Bangkok. Peavey writes, "My listening project is a kind of tuning-up of my heart to the affairs of the world. I hear the news in a very different way now, and I act with a larger context in mind." It is clear that Peavey's project does not simply confirm that poverty, various kinds of discrimination, and environmental damage are universal. Rather, she proposes that philosophies of resistance and direct action require the empathic wisdom associated with apprehending the broader social and political context in its personal and concrete specificity.

To what sort of frequency is Trinh's "Yellow Sprouts" tuned? We often decide that a thought has less value if it is not immediately comprehensible. That sort of judgment call is overruled by the goals of this text, which is explicitly designed to stretch the reader's imagination to hear wavelengths different from those perhaps more familiar in our Western Eurocentric culture. In listening to Trinh, it helps to realize that she is drawing on Taoist imagery of the waxing and waning moonlight to think about the processes of political change from a Taoist perspective. This means that she is not thinking of the moon in the stereotypical modes of Western culture. Western culture tends to mythologize the moon according to strict gender polarities: The moon is female in its passive receptivity and in its sensuality and changing forms. The Taoist point of view rejects all static polarities in favor of a metaphysical view of the changing nature of all things. Although Trinh writes that in Chinese poetry the moon expresses feminine beauty and its carnal presence, she reminds the reader that the moon is the day in the night and thus the feminine and the masculine contain one another. This sense of the fluidity of all dualisms is the Taoist ground of political hope and revolutionary change. Thus Trinh writes, "Politics waxes and wanes, and like a lunar eclipse, it vanishes only to return rejuventating itself as it reaches its full intensity." If you keep these key ideas in mind as you read Trinh's poetic invocation of revolutionary change, you will be able to discern a very strong political and theoretical position in her essay. Trinh stays closely involved in a conversation with Western thinkers during the course of her meditation.

## Instructional Uses of This Textbook

*Free Spirits* is designed for use on both the graduate and the undergraduate levels. In nearly all of the chapters, the selections are arranged so that the most concrete and personal essays are first, and the most abstract and theoretical essays last. At the end of each essay, we have recommended helpful background reading for students' research and instructors' instructional supplementation. You will also find recommended audiovisual resources listed and briefly annotated at the end of each essay. Our recommendations highlight for classroom discussion interesting connections between our selected essays and the visual images produced by social change activists, Hollywood, or the popular media. Those films and videos that are listed without further references can be found in most video stores. A list of the addresses and phone numbers for some of the audiovisual resources found in this book is included at the back of the book.

The selections in *Free Spirits* need not be used in the order in which they are presented in this book. The following are some alternative ways of organizing the readings in *Free Spirits* for classroom use. Although these suggestions are not exhaustive, it is hoped that they will provide inspiration for undergraduate and graduate course preparation. The whole text is useful in philosophy and culture courses. In addition, it can be used in courses on multicultural approaches to Christianity, women's studies courses, gender studies courses, courses in multicultural social and political theory, and courses in queer theory.[11]

*Multicultural Approaches to Christianity*

hooks and West, "Breaking Bread"
Barbara Smith, "Between a Rock and a Hard Place: Relationships Between Black and
    Jewish Women"
Celeste Olalquiaga, "Holy Kitchen: Collecting Religious Junk from the Street"

Linda Singer, "Bodies–Pleasures–Powers"

Starhawk, "Power, Authority and Mystery: Ecofeminism and Earth-Based Spirituality"

Ynestra King, "Healing the Wounds: Feminism, Ecology, and the Nature/Culture Dualism"

Walter L. Williams, "Of Religions and Dreams: The Spiritual Basis of the Berdache Tradition"

Thomas W. Laqueur, "The Facts of Fatherhood"

Rayna Green, "Culture and Gender in Indian America"

Trinh T. Minh-ha, "Yellow Sprouts"

*Women's Studies*

Wahneema Lubiano, "Black Ladies, Welfare Queens, and State Minstrels"

Susan Bordo, "'Material Girl': The Effacements of Postmodern Culture"

Danae Clark, "Commodity Lesbianism"

Barbara Smith, "Between a Rock and a Hard Place: Relationships Between Black and Jewish Women"

María Lugones, "Playfulness, 'World'-Travelling, and Loving Perception"

Women of ACE (AIDS Counseling and Education): "Voices"

Nancy Fraser, "Struggle over Needs: Outline of a Socialist–Feminist Critical Theory of Late Capitalist Political Culture"

Leslie Kanes Weisman, "The Private Use of Public Space"

Cynthia Enloe, "On the Beach: Sexism and Tourism"

Gloria Anzaldúa, "How to Tame a Wild Tongue"

Susan Ferraro, "The Anguished Politics of Breast Cancer"

Sandra Bartky, "Foucault, Femininity, and the Modernization of Patriarchal Power"

Linda Singer, "Bodies–Pleasures–Powers"

Starhawk, "Power, Authority and Mystery: Ecofeminism and the Nature/Culture Dualism"

Carol J. Adams, "The Feminist Traffic in Animals"

Carolyn Merchant, "Ecofeminism"

Katie Roiphe, "Date Rape's Other Victim"

Patricia Hill Collins, "The Sexual Politics of Black Womanhood"

Linda Williams, "Fetishism and Hard Core"

Catharine A. MacKinnon, "Crimes of War, Crimes of Peace"

Patrick D. Hopkins, "Gender Treachery: Homophobia, Masculinity, and Threatened Identities"

Thomas W. Laqueur, "The Facts of Fatherhood"

Ann Snitow, "Holding the Line at Greenham Common: Being Joyously Political in Dangerous Times [Feb. 1985]"

Rayna Green, "Culture and Gender in Indian America"

Fran Peavey, "American Willing to Listen"

Trinh T. Minh-ha, "Yellow Sprouts"

*Gender Studies*

Andrew Ross, "Cowboys, Cadillacs, and Cosmonauts: Families, Film Genres, and Technocultures"

Susan Bordo, "'Material Girl': The Effacements of Postmodern Culture"

Danae Clark, "Commodity Lesbianism"
hooks and West, "Breaking Bread"
Barbara Smith, "Between a Rock and a Hard Place: Relationships Between Black and
    Jewish Women"
María Lugones, "Playfulness, 'World'-Travelling, and Loving Perception"
Cynthia Enloe, "On the Beach: Sexism and Tourism"
Gloria Anzaldúa, "How to Tame a Wild Tongue"
Sandra Bartky, "Foucault, Femininity, and the Modernization of Patriarchal Power"
Linda Singer, "Bodies–Pleasures–Powers"
Patricia Hill Collins, "The Sexual Politics of Black Womanhood"
Walter L. Williams, "Of Religions and Dreams: The Spiritual Basis of the Berdache
    Tradition"
Linda Williams, "Fetishism and Hard Core"
Catharine A. MacKinnon, "Crimes of War, Crimes of Peace"
Richard Rodriguez, "Complexion"
John Stoltenberg, "How Men Have (a) Sex"
Patrick D. Hopkins, "Gender Treachery: Homophobia, Masculinity, and Threatened
    Identities"
Thomas W. Laqueur, "The Facts of Fatherhood"
Rayna Green, "Culture and Gender in Indian America"
Trinh T. Minh-ha, "Yellow Sprouts"

*Social and Political Theory*

Crenshaw and Peller, "Reel Time, Real Justice"
Wahneema Lubiano, "Black Ladies, Welfare Queens, and State Minstrels"
Andrew Ross, "Cowboys, Cadillacs, and Cosmonauts: Families, Film Genres, and
    Technocultures"
Susan Bordo, " 'Material Girl': The Effacements of Postmodern Culture"
Danae Clark, "Commodity Lesbianism"
Women of ACE (AIDS Counseling and Education): "Voices"
Nancy Fraser, "Struggle over Needs: Outline of a Socialist–Feminist Critical Theory of
    Late Capitalist Political Culture"
Elaine H. Kim, "Home Is Where the *Han* Is: A Korean American Perspective on the Los
    Angeles Upheavals"
Leslie Kanes Weisman, "The Private Use of Public Space"
Celeste Olalquiaga, "Holy Kitschen: Collecting Religious Junk from the Street"
Cynthia Enloe, "On the Beach: Sexism and Tourism"
Gloria Anzaldúa, "How to Tame a Wild Tongue"
Susan Ferraro, "The Anguished Politics of Breast Cancer"
Sandra Bartky, Foucault, Femininity, and the Modernization of Patriarchal Power"
Linda Singer, "Bodies–Pleasures–Powers"
Ynestra King, "Healing the Wounds: Feminism, Ecology, and the Nature/Culture
    Dualism"
Carol J. Adams, "The Feminist Traffic in Animals"
Carolyn Merchant, "Ecofeminism"

Patricia Hill Collins, "The Sexual Politics of Black Womanhood"
Catharine A. MacKinnon, "Crimes of War, Crimes of Peace"
Thomas W. Laqueur, "The Facts of Fatherhood"
Ann Snitow, "Holding the Line at Greenham Common: Being Joyously Political in Dangerous Times [Feb. 1985]"

*Queer Theory*

Danae Clark, "Commodity Lesbianism"
Barbara Smith, "Between a Rock and a Hard Place: Relationships Between Black and Jewish Women"
María Lugones, "Playfulness, 'World'-Travelling, and Loving Perception"
Women of ACE (AIDS Counseling and Education): "Voices"
Gloria Anzaldúa, "How to Tame a Wild Tongue"
Linda Singer, "Bodies–Pleasures–Powers"
Walter L. Williams, "Of Religions and Dreams: The Spiritual Basis of the Berdache Tradition"
Linda Williams, "Fetishism and Hard Core"
Richard Rodriguez, "Complexion"
John Stoltenberg, "How Men Have (a) Sex"
Patrick D. Hopkins, "Gender Treachery: Homophobia, Masculinity, and Threatened Identities"
Thomas W. Laqueur, "The Facts of Fatherhood"

# Notes

1. Friedrich Nietzsche, "The Free Spirit," *Beyond Good and Evil: Prelude to a Philosophy of the Future*, trans. Walter Kaufmann (New York: Random House, 1966).
2. Mary Daly, *Gyn/Ecology: The Metaethics of Radical Feminism* (Boston: Beacon, 1978).
3. Alison M. Jaggar, *Feminist Politics and Human Nature* (Totowa, NJ: Rowman & Littlefield, 1988); Rosemarie Tong, *Feminist Thought: A Comprehensive Introduction* (Boulder: Westview, 1989); *Feminist Philosophies: Problems, Theories, and Applications*, eds. Janet A. Kourany, James P. Sterba, and Rosemarie Tong (Englewood Cliffs, NJ: Prentice-Hall, 1992).
4. bell hooks, *Feminist Theory from Margin to Center* (Boston: South End Press, 1984).
5. Marilyn Frye, *The Politics of Reality: Essays in Feminist Theory* (Freedom, CA: The Crossing Press, 1983).
6. Gayle Rubin, "Thinking Sex: Notes for a Radical Theory of the Politics of Sexuality," *The Lesbian and Gay Studies Reader*, eds. Henry Abelove, Michele Aina Barale, and David M. Halperin (New York: Routledge, 1993); Eve Kosofsky Sedgwick, *Tendencies* (Durham, NC: Duke University Press, 1993); Douglas Crimp, "Right On, Girlfriend!" *Fear of a Queer Planet: Queer Politics and Social Theory*, ed. Michael Warner (Minneapolis, MN: University of Minnesota Press, 1993).
7. *The Achilles Heel Reader: Men, Sexual Politics and Socialism* (New York: Routledge, 1991).
8. Lawrence Grossberg, Cary Nelson, and Paula Treichler, eds., *Cultural Studies* (New York: Routledge, 1992).
9. Michel Foucault, "The Ethic of Care for the Self as a Practice of Freedom," *The Final Foucault*, eds. James Bernauer and David Rasmussen (Cambridge, MA: MIT Press, 1988).
10. Catharine MacKinnon, "Not a Moral Issue," *Feminism Unmodified* (Cambridge, MA: Harvard University Press, 1987); J. Ralph Lindgren and Nadine Taub, "Pornography," *The Law of Sex Discrimination* (St Paul, MN: West, 1988); Rosemarie Tong, "Radical Feminism on Gender and Sexuality," *Feminist Thought* (Boulder, CO: Westview, 1989), 111–123.
11. We have borrowed this idea for instructional use from *The Lesbian and Gay Studies Reader* (see item 6), pp. xx–xxii. They in turn borrowed from *Cultural Studies* (item 8), pp. 17–22.

# CHAPTER 1

# Cultural Images

Anita Hill is hugged by her mother, Irma Hill, as she sits in the witness chair before the Senate Judiciary Committee. [Rick Wilking/Reuters/Bettman]

# Reel Time/Real Justice

## KIMBERLÉ CRENSHAW and GARY PELLER

Kimberlé Crenshaw teaches law at UCLA. Gary Peller teaches law at Georgetown University. "Reel Time/Real Justice" is a condensed version of a piece forthcoming in the *Denver Law Journal*.

Like the Anita Hill/Clarence Thomas hearings a few months before, the Rodney King beating, the acquittal of the Los Angeles police officers who "restrained" him, and the subsequent civil unrest in L.A. flashed Race across the national consciousness, and the gaze of American culture momentarily froze there. Pieces of everyday racial dynamics seemed briefly clear, then faded from view, replaced by presidential politics and natural disasters.

In this essay, we want to examine in more depth what was exposed during the brief national focus on Rodney King. We take two main events, the acquittal of the police officers who beat King and the civil unrest in Los Angeles following the verdict, as starting points for an analysis of the ideological and symbolic intertwining of race and power in American culture. Along the way, we explicate the outlines of a "Critical Race Theory" focused not solely on the Rodney King "incident," but more broadly on a consideration of how racial power generally is produced, mediated, and legitimated, an approach that seeks to connect developments in diverse arenas in which race and power are contested.

As we see it, there is a deep connection between the various ideological conflicts that become apparent in the way Rodney King events played in national consciousness. The techniques utilized to convince the Simi Valley jury of the "reasonableness" of the use of force on Rodney King are linked to the struggle, in a quite different legal arena, over whether to permit race-conscious, affirmative-action programs, and both those arenas are in turn related to the conflict over whether to see the events in South Central L.A. as an "insurrection," as Representative Maxine Waters characterized it, or as a "riot" of the "mob," the official version presented in dominant media and by the president of the United States. At stake at each axis of conflict is a contest over which, and whose, narrative structure will prevail in the interpretation of events in the social world. And exposed at each conflict is the inability of concepts like "the rule of law," or "reason," or even the technology of video, to mediate these conflicts in a neutral, aracial way.

We believe that the realm of interpretation, ideology, and narrative is a critical site in the production of American racial domination. The Rodney King episode is particularly challenging for our approach because it seems so easily assimilable to more conventional models of the way that power works. Rather than imagine racial power being produced in the soft space of ideological "superstructure," the world saw it exercised at another point of production—at the material "base" where the nightstick met the skull. And unlike 1980s and 1990s racial controversies over affirmative action, ethnocentrism, and multi-culturalism, the King beating bore the familiar markings of the 1950s and 1960s—rather

than being encased carefully in definitions of merit and neutrality, old-time white supremacy was boldly and crudely inscribed on the body of King. You don't need any fancy
theory to figure out what went on between the L.A. police and Rodney King. That's true.
But the Rodney King events are also particularly illuminating for an approach that focuses
on the ideological, because part of what was revealed in the Rodney King saga was the
need for an account of how racial power continues to work, blatantly in the King case,
decades after it has been outlawed as a matter of formal decree, cultural convention, and
elite preference.

To get a picture of how various structures of interpretation played out after the verdict,
first remember the reaction in most sectors of American culture when the famous videotape of L.A. police officers beating King was initially broadcast on network television.
There was a broad national outrage shared by African Americans and most whites and
minorities, with the only fairly visible exception being the fringe (but becoming stronger)
white protofascists of the Patrick Buchanan/David Duke camps. This was an easy event for
the entire mainstream of American culture to abhor; it didn't present any of the "hard
questions" of the 1990s' controversies over race—like the "dilemma" of affirmative
action, say. And the videotape lent objectivity to the charge of police brutality—there was
no question of interpretation and subjective bias clouding the issue.

This wide consensus was actually based on the congruence of various ideological
positions around the "proof" of the videotape, as became apparent in the verdict's after-
math. But for most people, including most political conservatives, there was no difficulty
"seeing" what the tape represented: old-style, garden-variety racist power exemplified by
the Bull Connor/Pretorialike images of heavily armed white security officers beating a
defenseless Black man senseless. Part of the progress that African Americans have made
in terms of the achievement of formal legal equality and its cultural analogs was manifest
in the circumstance that, unlike the 1950s and 1960s, there was no voice anywhere near
the mainstream of American life saying that this kind of police practice was legitimate. In
the 1990s, the moderate white Right also defines itself in terms of the repudiation of the
backward doctrines of white supremacy. The breadth of the wide social consensus over the
King videotape was rooted in the sense that how one understood what happened to
Rodney King was not linked to how one understood the "murkier" issues of contemporary
racial conflict; in political terms, the King videotape gave the moderate Right the opportunity to oppose clear-cut racism and thus to demonstrate that its opposition to affirmative
action, say, is not linked to interests in racial supremacy.

But this broad consensus was misleading to the extent it made it appear that the video
meant the same thing to everyone; subsequent events would reveal the deep cleavages in
how the tape was understood. In our view, the differentiation that underlay the consensus
around the King tape—between "old" ideologies of racial supremacy and contemporary
"dilemmas" of race—was too quick, and obscured the ways that, in fact, the acquittal of
the L.A. police officers of using excessive force was intertwined with narrative structures
that prevail in debates about "affirmative action." Part of understanding the failure of the
formal legal equality achieved by African Americans to protect Rodney King means
understanding how formal prohibitions like those against police brutality and against
racial discrimination are necessarily always mediated through narrative structures, of
which the Simi Valley jury's verdict is a particularly striking example but not different in

kind from the more rarified ideologies of Supreme Court justices—that is, from the racial ideologies of the "moderates." When the cultural consensus over the meaning of the videotape blew apart in the violence of South Central L.A., the limits of formal legal equality also became apparent.

It is useful to pause here to consider how the initial, widespread, "common-sense" consensus about what the King video showed was confronted by the defense attorneys in the courtroom. They had frame-by-frame stills made of the video, which were mounted on clean white illustration board, and then used as the basis for questions to "experts" on prisoner restraint. Each micromoment of the beating of King was broken down into a series of frozen images. As to each one, the experts were asked whether it was clear that King had assumed a compliant posture, or might a police officer have reasonably concluded that he still was a threat to resist. Once the video was broken up like this, each still picture could then be rewoven into a different narrative about the restraint of King, one in which each blow to King represented, not beating one of the "gorillas in the mist," but a police-approved technique of restraint complete with technical names for each baton strike (or "stroke"). The videotape images were *physically* mediated by the illustration board upon which the still pictures were mounted, and in the same moment of *disaggregation*, they were *symbolically* mediated by the new narrative backdrops of the technical discourse of institutional security and the reframing of King as a threat rather than a victim.

The eighty-one-second video was, in short, broken into scores of individual still pictures, each of which was then subject to endless reinterpretation. Then, since no single picture taken by itself could constitute excessive force, taken together, the video tape as a whole said something different—not incredibly clear evidence of racist police brutality, but instead ambiguous slices of time in a tense moment that Rodney King had created for the police.

There are many "explanations" for the King verdict. Most center around the image of jury lawlessness—the idea that what the jury did was in a way corrupt, because they ignored the clear evidence of brutality to acquit the police. They didn't follow the rules. Along these lines, there are some who claim to have expected the verdict, because you just can't get justice out of the "system" controlled by "them." Others have located the pivotal turning point at the granting of the defense motion for a change of venue, resulting in the case being tried in an area dominated by law-and-order white conservatives, and, ironically, an area disproportionately the home of LAPD officers and retirees. Another view places responsibility on an inept (or worse) prosecution that failed to humanize Rodney King to counter the defense continually objectifying him.

There is some truth in each of these explanations. The problem we see, however, is that they either differentiate the King verdict too sharply from the other sites for the production and exercise of American racial power—that is, suggesting that, but for these "quirks" of the case and the irrationality of the jurors, the legal system would respond to an event like the beating of Rodney King—or, at the opposite pole, they too quickly make the particular way that the King judgment was reached subordinate to an overly instrumental view of the way that law and other mediating ideologies serve power.

In our view, law, in general, and the courtroom, in particular, are arenas where narratives are contested, and the power of interpretation exercised. In that sense, the legal realm is a political realm. But it would be a mistake to see narratives simply as some after-the-fact story about events concocted after the *real* power has already been exercised; the story lines developed in law "mediate" power in the sense that they both "translate" power as nonpower (the beating of King becomes the "reasonable exercise of force necessary to restrain a prisoner"); and they also *constitute* power, in the sense that the narrative lines shape what and how events are perceived in the first place. Understanding these relationships between law, power, and ideology is necessary to comprehending that, in many ways, the King verdict was *typical*, not extraordinary.

To develop this idea, it is helpful to turn from the King verdict to a very different legal arena, the issuance of Supreme Court opinions. Our point here is to draw connections between the narrative structure presented by the defense attorneys in the police-brutality trial—breaking the videotape up into scores of single, still images—and the narrative structure utilized in the more academic and "rational" atmosphere of the Supreme Court.

We will discuss in brief outline the case of *Richmond vs. Croson*,[1] where a Supreme Court majority struck down as unconstitutional Richmond, Virginia's municipal policy of awarding construction contracts on a race-conscious, affirmative-action basis. Under Richmond's program, prime contractors were required to "set aside" 30 percent of their work to be performed by minority subcontractors. As matter of legal doctrine, *Croson* is an important refinement of the meaning of "equal protection" in the Fourteenth Amendment; it is the first case in which a majority of the Court applied "strict scrutiny" (meaning stringent requirements of a policy's importance and fit), the traditional test for "malign" racial classifications that burden Blacks, to a "benign" affirmative-action plan burdening whites. The symbolic message of this doctrinal development is that the problem of racism is a symmetrical one—both Blacks and whites can suffer when racial classifications are utilized, and therefore the same level of scrutiny is warranted whether a racial classification benefits Blacks or whites. From this vantage point, racism consists of the failure to treat people on an individual basis according to terms that are neutral to race. In the Richmond context, this embrace of "color blindness" as the norm of equal protection meant that the Court could plausibly equate the legal significance of the City of Richmond benefiting white contractors through the contracting system (say, by excluding Blacks) with the legal consequences of a decision to benefit Black contractors (by requiring set-asides).[2]

In this doctrinal setting, the legal issue in *Croson* was whether the Richmond affirmative-action policy was constitutional—could it survive "strict scrutiny"?—as a policy serving the compelling aim of remedying past discrimination against Blacks. According to the Court such an aim was in fact compelling, but only as the remedy for "particular" discrimination, lest the "remedy" constitute a new instance of racial discrimination. The problem in *Croson* was that there had been no "proof" that there had been significant racial discrimination in the Richmond construction industry that needed remedying.

The analog to the videotape of Rodney King's beating that failed to "prove" unreasonable and excessive force was the familiar picture of Black economic exclusion suggested by the formal record before the Supreme Court in *Croson*. The record included: Congressional findings that there had been massive discrimination in the construction industry across the country; the 50 percent Black population of Richmond; the fact that .67 percent of the city's prime contracting dollars went to minority-owned businesses; and the testimony of the mayor, the city manager, and two councilmen as to the long and thorough history of racial discrimination that the City of Richmond had officially sanctioned and practiced in education, voting, and housing.

Like the Simi Valley jury, the Supreme Court was confronted with a picture—the near-total dominance of white firms in the contracting business of Richmond, Virginia, in the one case, the videotape in the other—and asked to determine if illegitimate power had been exercised. And like the attorneys for the L.A. police officers, the Court utilized the process of *disaggregation* to conclude that racial discrimination was not proven to be the cause of the huge disparity between the racial composition of Richmond's population and the racial composition of recipients of prime construction contracts.[3] Just as the defense attorneys directed the jury's consideration from the reel time of the video to the disaggregated stills of the L.A. police and Rodney King, the Court freeze-framed each element of the Richmond setting and isolated it from its meaning-giving context—the history of racial subordination in Richmond, Virginia, the former capital of the Confederacy and one of the central sites of "massive resistance" to desegregation orders in the 1960s. The Court's opinion considered each piece of evidence individually, determining that, by itself, each wasn't sufficient to conclude that there had been discrimination, and therefore ruling that there was no "proof" that the Richmond construction industry had been the site of racial discrimination that could now be remedied legally by affirmative-action set-asides.

Once the Court disaggregated each factor from its context in the full picture of the racial history of Richmond, it was still left with the glaring statistical evidence that Blacks had been shut out of the construction contracting business. And, as with the L.A. policemen's defense at trial, once meaning was divorced from context, it was possible to weave the disaggregated images together with new, alternative narratives. In the Rodney King brutality case, the stills were reconnected through a story of King's power and agency—his body could become "cocked" and could appear "in a trigger position." In the *Croson* affirmative-action case, a new narrative was also created, one which implicitly explained the lack of minority contractors in terms of the (lack of) skill, initiative, and choice of Blacks—rather than the exclusionary power exercised by whites.

Part of the great appeal of what we have been calling "formal legal equality"—the blanket legal prohibitions against racial discrimination that were achieved in the 1960s—is the belief that the identification of the grossest forms of racial discrimination is straightforward and objective. Rather than leave protection to the whim of politics or the discretion of power, the imagery of the "rule of law" suggests that the prohibition against racial discrimination is clear and determinate. It doesn't depend on "subjective" evaluation. And from this frame, what's so enraging about the King verdict is that it seems to show that even such clear, objective prohibitions can be subverted by racial power, like that embodied in the Simi Valley jury.

Our first point in drawing out the structural similarities in the ways that narratives were constructed in the Rodney King trial and the Supreme Court's *Croson* opinion is to question this kind of thinking about the protections of formal equality. In other words, we are not saying that the Supreme Court is like the Rodney King jury in the sense that they, too, are acting lawlessly or corruptly by violating some objectively identifiable "reality" about race in America, or in Richmond. Rather, our point is to examine critically how ideological narratives work as a form of social power, to show how a belief in formal legal equality, in the objectivity of "the rule of law," can help obscure the everyday character of racial power.

As we see it, an important image underlying the initial consensus in American culture about the videotape and ultimate acquittal of the L.A. police officers who beat Rodney King was that the videotape exemplified an old-style mode of racial domination that, today, virtually the entire American culture opposes. The videotape reverberated with the skeletons of American apartheid. And on issues of "basic civil rights," a wide spectrum has embraced the morality of 1960s race reforms ensuring formal equality "regardless" of race. On the other hand, the "disagreements" over affirmative action, or multicultural-ism, seem less clearly focused, less objective, and more political.

But this way of perceiving these two arenas of race is, to our minds, already a product of a particular narrative, a particular way of articulating the meaning of race within which the granting of legal rights to formal equality—to being treated the same as everyone else regardless of race—is taken as an intrinsically meaningful and compre-hensible goal separate from the "murkiness" that's supposed to be involved in the morally "tougher" 1990s issues of race. The prohibition of explicit racial discrimination is seen as a formally realizable goal, in the sense that it can be applied without any more elaboration of controversial value choices. That's how come we can be so sure the Simi Valley jury acted "lawlessly," or "fraudulently," in a way that seems at first so different from the careful, reasoned, philosophical arguments of Supreme Court opinions. There appears to be a qualitative difference between what the Simi Valley jury did and what the Supreme Court does. In the cultural imagination, it's like the difference between rednecks and the gentry.

As we have suggested, this contrast between arenas of racial controversy is ideologically constructed: from another perspective, that of "narrative" and "disaggregation," the sharp difference between issues of "formal equality" as opposed to "special treatment" fades as the identification of each is seen to depend, ultimately, on which pictures of the world are believed, and which are disbelieved. The sharp distinction usually drawn between formal equality and affirmative action suggests that formal equality can be achieved outside the realm of power and interpretation because it can be identified objectively by law. But to us, what the King verdict represents is not the corrupt subversion of the values of the rule of law, but rather the ideological power of belief in the rule of law itself.

Through the description of "disaggregation," we have tried to describe features of what we see as the dominant form of contemporary race ideology, linking the Simi Valley jury's acquittal of the police with the race narratives of moderate, mainstream legal culture. Through the typical process of "disaggregation," a narrative is created within which racial power has been "mediated" out, like the anesthetic effect of mounting stills on clinically white illustration board. In both the Simi Valley police-brutality trial and the *Croson* case, a narrative mediates the representation of the world by divorcing the effects of racial power—the number of Black contractors in Richmond, the curled body of Rodney King—from their social context and from their historic meaning. In the compulsive legal search for the clearly defined, objectively verifiable, perpetrating act of illegitimate power—the single, particular offending blow in the frame-by-frame representation of King and the L.A. police; the particular acts of discrimination that directly caused white economic hegemony in Richmond, Virginia—social events are decontextualized in both *space*—where things happened, and between whom—and *time*—what larger forces operated to give events their meaning.

Hence the symmetry of the idea of "racism" in mainstream American culture: once race is divorced from its social meaning in schools, workplaces, streets, homes, prisons, and paychecks and from its historic meaning in terms of the repeated American embrace of white privilege, then all that's left, really, is a hollow, analytic norm of "color-blind"—an image of racial power as embodied in abstract classifications by race that could run either way, against whites as easily as against Blacks. And finally, this kind of disaggregation also, oddly, seems like the very definition of what's neutral and objective, a narrative that doesn't depend on point of view, a tape of social world with the images so enlarged and slowed down that it could say anything.

Rather than see the jury acquittal as an aberration by some low-down, Simi Valley redneck consciousness, consider it the reigning ideological paradigm of how to identify illegitimate racial power, vivid precisely because of the extremity of the conclusion that only "reasonable force" had been used on Rodney King. The virtue of formal equality is that there is something important in the fact that power wielders can no longer justify conditions in the social world based on the supposed natural inferiority of Blacks. But the problem of formal equality is that it is appealing precisely because it seems to be able to do what it cannot do—resolve issues of social power, racial power, once and for all, according to some neutral and objective rules.

Our point here is that Rodney King did, in a sense, get the fruits of formal equality. But the terms that embody the guarantee of the rule of law—terms like "reasonable force" or "equal protection"—are necessarily indeterminate. Their meaning must be socially constructed—through narratives of place and time—for there to be any meaning to them at all. What the Simi Valley jury did is not so different from what the Supreme Court does. In neither realm is the rule of law being subverted; the "law" and the "facts" of the social world do not exist in any objective, ready-made form. They must always be interpreted according to politics, ideology, and power.

The belief in what we've called formal equality resulted in one particularly intense set of reactions to the verdict—the extreme disillusionment felt by many (particularly integrationist-oriented) Blacks who had invested more than symbolic meaning in the guarantees of objectivity presented by law, in particular, and the wider cultural rhetoric, in general. Like the white cultural mainstream, many Blacks believed that the baton against Rodney King's skull would speak for itself, just as many have believed that principles of color blindness and other varieties of formal equality provide a clear, almost self-generating protection against racial discrimination. What many people did not comprehend was that police brutality, just like discrimination, does not speak for itself. This very struggle over meaning is precisely what the intense contestations about race in the law are really about. Rather than providing some kind of firm ground to challenge racist institutional practices, notions of formal equality, objectivity, neutrality, and the like tend to obscure the way that race is experienced by the vast majority of African Americans in this society.

We have described "disaggregation" as a narrative technique that narrows the perception of the range of illegitimate racial power by divorcing particular episodes from their larger social context. We have relied implicitly on a contrast between this kind of "distortion" and "real" time, considering things as they "are" rather than freeze-framing space and time into isolated stills that can be reinterpreted through a benign narrative of justification. The part of our argument that seeks to identify "disaggregation" as part of a conservative ideology is made easier by the image we all share of Rodney King being beaten, and the confident sense we have that we see the *meaning* of the videotape. It is by implicit reference to this "real" time that the disaggregation technique looks like a distortion.

Here we want to question the "real" time we have to this point assumed, and consider the implications of thinking that we can identify the corruption of the Simi Valley jury by contrasting its verdict with the reality depicted on the videotape. Consider the possibility that even the videotape itself has no special, objective status—what we progressives "see" in the images is the product of mediating narratives in much the same way as what the Simi Valley jury "saw" depended on the technique of disaggregation that we have been discussing.

People invested very different meanings in the Rodney King videotape. For many, the existence of the videotape was a source of excitement that technology was finally utilized in service of the masses, so that "they" (the authorities) couldn't say that people were just making up charges of police brutality. The underlying assumption for a lot of people was that such conduct is a more or less regular feature of many police encounters with Blacks, particularly in L.A. The underlying frustration has been over not being able to put a stop to these practices through the creation of formal legal prohibitions because of the inability to "prove" what happened. When the tape was first broadcast, in addition to the pain of seeing such brutality, there was also exhilaration that the videotape would solve the problem of proof so that the police would finally be disciplined. Simply put, the significance of the video was not that it proved to masses of Blacks and others that the L.A. police are brutally racist, but rather that it was projected as what would satisfy "the law" that brutality against Blacks occurred.

But also within the initial national outrage at the King videotape were many who saw the brutality depicted in the videotape as awful but exceptional, as part of another era which reared its ugly head only occasionally and happened to be caught on videotape. The videotape "proved" brutality, but the brutality and the fortuity that it recorded were experienced as popping out of the same random, chaotic sea.

In short, a gulf of incomprehension existed underneath the broad American consensus that the videotape depicted outrageous police behavior. For some, the existence of the videotape was critical to comprehending that this kind of racist brutality "still" occurs in American society, because the videotape presented "objective" proof. In other words, without the tape, they would have had no outrage, indeed no consciousness, of the conditions of police-and-community relations in L.A. For others, the videotape didn't serve to *establish* this kind of police behavior, but rather simply to document it and thus satisfy the powers that be.

There is a deep, ideological connection between the kind of need for, and embrace of, "objective" proof and the more general ways that race is understood in American culture. The special status that was accorded the King videotape as objective proof was, we believe, a social construct, just as the particular interpretation of the tape embraced by the Simi Valley jury was constructed. *Both* the perception of the tape as showing a "reasonable exercise of force" *and* the perception of the tape as showing "racist brutality" depend, not simply on the physiology of visual perception, but rather on *interpretation*, on the mediation of perception with background narratives that give visual images meaning.

Valorizing the so-called "objective proof" of the videotape is problematic, because, to the extent that the videotape was understood to "prove" the racist brutality of the LAPD, such a conclusion implicitly rested on the idea that, but for the tape, no "objective" proof was available. Yet an important piece of the background context to the Rodney King events was that there has always been available the witness and testimony of hundreds of thousands of victims of police brutality who can attest to the practices of the L.A. police, as well as those of many other departments. Typically, such victims are arrested for "disorderly conduct" after they have been beaten, and so deep is the street-level understanding of the uselessness of the processes of the "rule of law" that, in the overwhelming run of cases, no complaint is ever made. The emphasis on the objective proof of the videotape, in short, marginalizes as merely subjective all those whose reality is devalued because there was no tape, only their word and the community's long-standing experience of the LAPD.

Underlying the elevation of the videotape as objective proof of the racist brutality of the LAPD is a hierarchy of evidence and meaning, a hierarchy that distinguishes between objective proof and subjective assertion, fact and opinion, disinterest and bias. These categories are neither natural nor independent criteria with which to evaluate various narratives about the world; they, themselves, form the vocabulary for a particular narrative, one that assumes the possibility of a vantage point of "objectivity" that could exist outside of any particular vision or interpretation, a vantage point that is seductive because it seems to transcend the partialities of history and geography, of time and space. But the images of objectivity and impersonality, like the allied distinctions between fact and opinion, between color blindness and discrimination—and between law and politics— are, in our social context, the terms of a particular discourse of power, here the power that's manifest in the inability of Black people in L.A. to get redress when the police beat them unless they have what will satisfy others as "proof."

To see how the hierarchies of objectivity and subjectivity work as a discourse of power to marginalize the victims of these racist police practices, consider that it is not the videotape, the disinterestedness of technology, that makes us "see" what happened to Rodney King. The videotape images of the L.A. police officers and Rodney King do not mean what they mean for us as a matter of objectivity, but rather as a matter of social construction. We must, necessarily, weave narratives into the images to give them a life in some time and space. Just as the legal concepts of formal equality are indeterminate and only acquire meaning in a social struggle over describing the world, as the *Croson* case reveals, so the video images are clear to us because we bring our own narratives to them, and we see in them the images of Bull Connor and Soweto and various episodes of the long story of racial apartheid being brutally enforced, images and narrative lines that we carry around in our collective memory. In this sense, our judgment, like that of the Simi Valley jury and the Supreme Court in *Croson*, is mediated by background narratives that tie together what otherwise would be a random set of images.

These different images underlying people's first impressions of the King videotape help make sense of the various reactions to the verdict. Of course, the sharpest contrast was between those who responded to the verdict by taking to the streets in Pico and South Central and, at the opposite pole, the police-department personnel who cheered the news. But most across the spectrum of mainstream culture who deplored the "rioting" didn't do so because they agreed with the verdict or with the cheering police. To the contrary, for the most part, they sought to preserve the very value that they thought the Simi Valley jury had impugned—the value of the rule of law. The dominant public discourse of the "L.A. riots" quickly became articulated as an opposition between those urging restraint and advocating respect for the "rule of law" and those articulating an alternative first principle of "no justice, no peace." The contrast between the rhetoric of "rule of law" and "no justice, no peace" was soon translated by the dominant culture into a contest between an objective, reasoned, responsible reaction and an emotional, passionate, irresponsible one. These strands of narrative culminated in the symbolic conflict between whether the people out in the streets should be seen as a "mob" "rioting" or as part of an "insurrection."

It didn't seem ironic that many people who deplored the Simi Valley verdict also deplored the "rioting." In fact, from within the discourse of objectivity and respect for "the rule of law," it seemed obvious that there was a deep link between the jurors who acquitted the police who "restrained" Rodney King and the rioters on the street. In the dominant cultural narrative, both embodied a form of irrationality, of emotion-driven distortion. In the case of the jurors, their irrationality with respect to the videotape was seen in terms of white racism and fear of Black crime. And the people on the streets looked simply like a chaotic, emotional reaction, one without "reason," in the burning of neighborhoods, stores, and the like.

The language of an "insurrection" that Rep. Maxine Waters and others employed suggests, however, a counternarrative, one which implicitly rejects the various rhetorical clusters that came to define the way that the Rodney King events were incorporated into mainstream discourse—including the reference points of objectivity, rationality, color-blindness, and legalism. The narrative of insurrection suggests a competing view of the whole Rodney King episode.

Rather than view the beating of King as an aberration from a legal norm of the "reasonable" use of force, the insurrection narrative implies a focus on the power relations and dynamics that exist between the "rioters" and the police. While the image of "riot" suggests a kind of instantaneous, emotional reaction to the verdict, the image of an insurrection directs attention from the "shock" of the verdict to the day-to-day subordination of the L.A. African-American community. Rather than see the beating of King as an outrageous deviation from the norm of police objectivity, the image of community subordination comprehends a systematic set of social dynamics—including a geographic context in which a largely Anglo police force with enforcement responsibility for the sprawling metropolis of L.A. speeds through Black neighborhoods in fortified, heavily armed cruisers dispatched from some remote location, and a historical context in which police brutality toward Blacks has been common and repeatedly the subject of investigation, expert commission report, and inaction. In contrast to the image of the uprising as an explosive reaction to a disappointing verdict, the language of insurrection conceives of the uprising as a communal response to a much larger set of issues of social power.

The image of insurrection, in short, is part of a narrative that sees the relations of police and Blacks in L.A., not as the disaggregated dyad of state official and private citizen, mediated by neutral legal norms of reasonableness and nondiscrimination, but instead in terms of the power-laden relationship of communities defined by race, within which whites, through the police, exercise a kind of occupying power, and within which Black neighborhoods appear as something like colonies. In these terms, an "insurrection" is not the blindly irrational acts of "rioters" (who, in the dominant narrative, should be expected to protest peacefully), but the concerted action of a community determined to raise the cost of peace to the colonizers, and thereby to increase its leverage on the continuing power relations.

Following the widespread urban unrest of the 1960s the Kerner Commission concluded that the "riots" expressed an angry frustration with the slow pace of racial integration.[4] To reach that conclusion, the Commission had to misinterpret the Black Nationalist rhetoric of many rioters themselves, and impose an integrationist view of racial justice. The dominant reaction to the recent disorder in L.A. evidences the same ideological framing of the issue. But like the disciples of Malcolm X in the 1960s, the narrative of insurrection challenges the vision of race and racial power implicit in the conventional idea that racial justice means the end of "discrimination" and the achievement of formal equality and integration into the dominant community. Instead, the imagery of occupation and subordination points to a wholly different comprehension of race relations, one which looks to the power relations between historically defined racial communities, rather than away from race and toward colorblindness. And accordingly, rather than see justice in terms of achieving police colorblindness, a race-conscious focus on power between communities focuses attention on the legitimacy of the dominant community administering the "colony" in the first place. Most who deplored the L.A. riots assumed a Vegalist model of racial justice in which the norms of objectivity and neutrality are central to the achievement of racial integration. From within that kind of ideology, there is simply no place for ideas like community control over police, education, and other public services, because the Black community, say, is no longer even perceived—there are just people who "happen to be Black."

Rejecting the proposed "grounds" for determining the "real" in "objective" and "impartial" fashion, we believe that relations between communities cannot be mediated in a neutral fashion through the recognition of formal legal rights. Accordingly, the problem in the Simi Valley verdict acquitting the L.A. police was not that it deviated corruptly from some objective norm of legality of objectivity; instead, those "norms" themselves constitute a narrative, an ideology for understanding race that excludes from vision the political and power-laden terms of race relations.

But believing that issues—like the meaning of the Rodney King videotape or the racial composition of Richmond's construction contractors—are necessarily and always subject to interpretation rather than "objective" proof does not mean that we are any less outraged by the verdict. The identification and enforcement of legal rights require acts of meaning attribution, of narration. So does comprehending the "meaning" of a videotape. But that doesn't mean that everything is therefore relative, that anything goes since it's all power anyway. To the contrary, once the narratives became so disparate between a community and the police, or the legal system, it seems to us that it is time to recognize that, in a deep sense, Blacks in L.A. live in a different world from whites, in something like a different nation. They and the police are like foreigners to each other. And understanding this distance means comprehending relations, not according to norms of universal equality and equal treatment, but as the rule of one community over another.

From this counternarrative, what is needed is not color blindness on the part of the police force, but the redistribution of power so that the police force is not an outside occupier, but rather a part of the community itself, subject to regulation by the Black community in L.A. The community doesn't need formal equality from the police, but actual control *over* the police—as well as other public institutions.

# Reading Questions

1. According to the authors, what is the difference between an "insurrection" and a "riot"?
2. Why is the concept of disaggregation important to the author's description of the narrative structure of the Rodney King beating?
3. How, according to the authors, do the story lines in law "mediate" power? Why is the legal case of *Richmond vs. Croson* analogized to the Rodney King case?
4. According to the authors, how do ideological narratives informed by the belief in formal, race-neutral legal equality obscure the everyday character of racial power?
5. What is the difference between understanding the Rodney King videotape as "objective proof" rather than as a "social construction"?
6. What kind of redistributions of power are called for by counternarratives of the videotape?

# Recommended Reading

D. Bell, *Race, Racism and American Law,* 2nd ed. (Boston: Little, Brown, 1980)

Derrick Bell, *Faces from the Bottom of the Well* (New York: Harper Collins, 1992)

E. Cashmore, *The Logic of Racism* (London: Allen & Unwin, 1987)

Mike Davis, *City of Quartz: Excavating the Future of Los Angeles.* (New York: Routledge, 1992)

H. L. Gates, Jr., and D. La Capra, eds., *The Bounds of Race* (Ithaca: Cornell University Press, 1989)

J. Solomos, *Black Youth, Racism and the State* (Cambridge: Cambridge University Press, 1988)

Patricia Williams, *The Alchemy of Race and Rights: Diary of a Law Professor* (Cambridge: Harvard University Press, 1991)

# Recommended Audiovisual Resources

Any home videotape of the Rodney King beating.

For specific documentaries analyzing the Rodney King episode, write or call Insight Media. Request its specific catalog listing social and political documentaries. (For the contact information of Insight Media and other audiovisual resources mentioned in this book, see "Audiovisual Resources" at the back of the book.)

*Boyz N the Hood.* 1991. Directed by John Singleton. Power drama about gang violence in south-central Los Angeles.

*Street Gangs of Los Angeles.* 1993. Directed by Hans Albert. Produced by ZDS German Television. Documentary on Los Angeles street gangs. Films for the Humanities & Sciences.

*L.A. Justice.* 1992. Produced by Eric Shapiro, Catherine Lasiewicz, Al Briganti, and Steve Glauber. Reports on the court system of Los Angeles County, California. Films for the Humanities & Sciences.

# Black Ladies, Welfare Queens, and State Minstrels

## Ideological War by Narrative Means*

### WAHNEEMA LUBIANO

Wahneema Lubiano teaches in the English Department at Princeton University. She is a contributor to *Race-ing Justice, En-gendering Power*, from which this selection is taken.

---

Let's face it. I am a marked woman, but not everybody knows my name. . . . "Sapphire" . . . or "Black Woman at the Podium": I describe a locus of confounded identities, a meeting ground of investments and privations in the national treasury of rhetorical wealth. My country needs me, and if I were not here, I would have to be invented.

—Hortense Spillers

A society is possible in the last analysis because the individuals in it carry around in their heads some sort of picture of that society.

—Karl Mannheim

There are pictures that function as *cover stories* in and of themselves; they (both the pictures and cover stories) simultaneously mask and reveal political power and its manipulations. Cover stories cover or mask what they make invisible with an alternative presence; a presence that redirects our attention, that covers or makes absent what has to

---

* I believe Anita Hill's account. This reading of the discourse around Hill's allegations, however, is not dependent upon believing her. I am deconstructing here the ways that meanings are constructed and/or influenced by power in the debate that went on as a result of her charges, the ways that public discourse is influenced by activating salient and preexisting narratives. My essay turns textual analysis into a lens focusing on the overlap of political, economic, and cultural issues. One does not have to believe Hill, or to see her as a feminist, a worker–saint, or another Rosa Parks in order to think about, recognize, or map the workings of power, or to examine the ways in which the engine of the United States' political economy runs, as I argue here, on the fuel of certain cultural politics. Hill did not choose to quit her job and wait tables, to be a word processor, or to do anything else that might have made her a more politically sympathetic, "attractive," or "authentic" victim. That she didn't does not preclude our attending to the operations of power in this historical moment, or our examining how narratives of race and gender undergird the political economy of the United States; how those narratives appeared during and in the hearings; and how they continue to allow the political status quo to resist change. Clarence Thomas's position and repositionings were the manifestation of a sophisticated set of power deployments. Notwithstanding Hill's much-discussed "ambition" and notwithstanding what might be her complicity in the Reagan and Bush administrations' hamstringing of the EEOC, in this historical moment Anita Hill is not the articulation of state power. Clarence Thomas is.

remain unseen if the *seen* is to function as the *scene* for a different drama. One story provides a cover that allows another story (or stories) to slink out of sight. Like the "covers" of secret agents, cover stories are faces for other texts, different texts. They are pretexts that obscure context, fade out subtexts, and, in the case of the Clarence Thomas hearings, protect the texts of the powerful.

On the twelfth and thirteenth of October, the *New York Times* juxtaposed photographs of Anita Hill and Clarence Thomas. The chronology and context of these juxtapositions were important. They articulated a particular ideological salience, not the least because of the subliminal effect of the placements—occurring at the particular points in the hearing when they did—as narrative shorthand for, first, pretense of thematic balance, and then, reassertion of business as usual:

1. October 12, when the outcome of the second hearings seemed undecided, at least in the media's explicit discussions, photographs of the two ran side by side. Identically posed, Hill and Thomas were pictured with their right hands raised for the swearing-in. The placement of the photographs suggested their equality before the sight of those watching this spectacle taking place before some bar of justice, in front of an oversight committee.

The side-by-side visual equality of representation obscured the dramatic disparity of power hidden by the juxtaposition: Thomas, head of EEOC, judge, and friend of powerful men, chosen for his position and admired by our head of state, beneficiary of the apparatuses of state power—and a man who would be among the most powerful if confirmed by the Senate, next to a woman professor of law, holding a faculty position at a state university, and whose photograph was reproduced in the newspaper because of Thomas's alleged transgressions. This insistence on foregrounding the *individual* nature of accusation and response—regardless of where one lays the blame—was characteristic of much of the media's discussion of these proceedings.*

2. Twenty-four hours later, pictures of Hill and Thomas were again juxtaposed, only by then much had changed. Thomas had declared himself to be the victim of a "high-tech lynching" and the two photographs ran after calls responding to the televised hearings had begun to come into CNN, other television stations, and various radio talk shows around the country. This time the photographs were placed on the page next to the headline "Theater of Pain." Discussion, at least as the corporate and/or mainstream press was recording it, seemed to be cohering around the idea of Thomas as the central figure in that "theater." In this photographic arrangement, the missionary position is assumed, or resumed, male on top, female on bottom. *This* placement, a representation of gendered power relations, was the visual harbinger of the newly, if only implicitly, established discovery of a new "American" hero: Clarence Thomas, man under siege and warrior for the reassertion of order and law.

These pictures, through their timing and their spatial arrangement, were signposts for

---

* I use "individual" pejoratively here because I am examining the problem of discussions of this moment that insisted on seeing individuals outside of political power. Individuals are always wrapped in larger world narrative contexts. The problem with constructions of mythic individualism is that their ties to power go unnoted.

Left: Clarence Thomas. Right: Anita Hill. [Rick Wilking/Reuters/Bettman] Editors' note: These photographs do not directly correspond to Lubiano's specific references.

a successful set of narrative constructions, activations, and deployments by the state*— including what people are reminded of when certain categories, phrases, and abstract figures with political resonance are evoked. State power did its work by virtue of its invisibility and because it is embedded in the public's understanding of everyday occur-

* By "state," I mean both the system of formal governmental and economically influential entities of executive mandate, legislation, policy-making, and regulation—the president, his Cabinet, administration—and economically and politically powerful legislators, as well as the "common ideological and cultural construct" that "occurs not merely as a subjective belief, incorporated in the thinking and action of individuals [but] represented and reproduced in visible everyday forms" (Timothy Mitchell, "The Limits of the State: Beyond Statist Approaches and Their Critics," *American Political Science Review*, vol. 85, no. 1 [March 1991], p. 81). Among those "everyday forms" I include things like the constantly evoked concerns over categories of thought like "threats to national well-being" or "American-ness," or, clichéd and (often conservative) commonsense understandings about gender and race.

In other words, when I speak of state power in regard to Thomas's position in the confirmation hearings, I'm bringing together, for example, the actual workings of the executive branch of the government—concretized here in my use of "President Bush" or "the state"—on behalf of Thomas; the various connections that Thomas's career has had to powerful and influential government and economic entities and individuals; *and* the ways that the national public reproduced state concerns and interests in their understandings of and responses to the Thomas–Hill events.

rences and beliefs. Photographs, such as those I discuss here, and other salient narratives, are the means by which sense is made in and of the world; they also provide the means by which those who hold power (or influence the maintenance of power) make or attempt to make sense of the world *for others*. Such narratives are so naturalized, so pushed by the momentum of their ubiquity, that they seem to be reality.[1] That dynamic is the work of ideology.

As a result of the "work" done by such narratives, Thomas's own power was masked; that power and the state power that supported him throughout the debate were naturalized as his "dignity," "character," and "integrity."* Those three words, used as descriptions of his basic essence, were divorced from any sustained attention to the history of his behavior, career record, or written philosophy. His "integrity"—which seemed to be based largely on some historical integrity accorded his grandfather's occupation as sharecropper, for example—was simply and unquestioningly accepted. Because the interrogation of his actually existing judicial and political record was muted, no mechanism existed that would have supported a challenge to this integrity.

Newspapers, radio programs, and television networks, stations, and programs, need not deliberately contrive to make absent certain narratives by presenting others; it is unnecessary that the work of (or on behalf of) power go on via conspiratorial agreement or arrangement. Such work goes on because the media, along with other public and private entities (including institutions, churches, schools, families, and civic organizations, among others), constantly make available particular narratives and not others. In turn, such consistently reinforced presences reproduce the world in particular ways: what we see becomes what we "get," what we believe. The photographs I refer to above represent visually, first, the seemingly equal position of accuser and accused, and then, the reassertion of the customary dominance of male and institutional authority back in its rightful place: order in the court, here comes the judge. Thomas was the cover text and the pretext. Here the subtext—the disappeared, the absent—was the narrative of power. Those photographs, however, are only the surface manifestation of narrative ideological battle.

A particular set of narratives did battle for this confirmation. A specifically nuanced "blackness"† was constructed and strengthened by narratives preexisting in the national historical memory around two figures, the "black lady" and the "welfare mother" or "queen" in such a way as to do battle on behalf of power.[2] Categories like "black woman," "black women," or particular subsets of those categories, like "welfare mother/queen," are not simply social taxonomies, they are also recognized by the national public as stories that describe the world in particular and politically loaded ways—and that is exactly why

---

* There were honorable exceptions to this general silence on Thomas's history; much of the alternative, noncorporate (and nondaily) press and their writers (e.g., *The Nation*, *The Village Voice*, *The Progressive*, *In These Times*, *Extra*, *Lies of Our Times*, and *Z Magazine*) were consistent in their depth, comprehensive and insightful in their analysis and their reportage. Additionally, at least one electronic network, the Activists Mailing List, was active in disseminating information about Thomas and his background.

† Here, by "blackness," I mean conscious awareness by an individual of being part of a group—Negroes, black Americans, Afro- or African Americans—with a particular place in history and a political relationship to other groups within the geopolitical site of the United States. Blackness is also a way of referring to the existence, as a socially constructed fact, of that group.

they are constructed, reconstructed, manipulated, and contested. They are, like so many other social narratives and taxonomic social categories, part of the building blocks of "reality" for many people; they suggest something about the world; they provide simple, uncomplicated, and often wildly (and politically damaging) inaccurate information about what is "wrong" with some people, with the political economy of the United States. They even stand for threats to ideas about what the relationship of the family to the state ought to be.* Welfare queen and black lady were and are cover stories that shielded the text of power—by being extravagantly displayed narratives already in circulation and engaging our attention—before, during, and since the Thomas hearings. And against that backdrop, Thomas functioned as a minstrel—not as an unwitting or ignorant dupe but as a power figure who drew on and articulated—from behind his black skin surface—white state power.

I argue that the narrative, or the cathected set of narratives signaled by the category "black women," or represented by the place of individual black women as they are figured in the arena of cultural politics, is what made it possible to mobilize wider support for Thomas. More, I suggest that those narratives can work and did work as a form of shorthand, functioning effectively even when their content was and is not explicitly spelled out. As is the case with words such as "woman," "character," "merit," or "decline in the American way of life," these particular narratives' contents have been constructed over time and transformed to fit the requirements of maintaining the present terms of the U.S. political economy.

Because of their historical and political salience, the welfare queen and the black lady are two figures who exist as narratives guaranteed to mobilize support for Thomas's confirmation from almost every sector of U.S. society. Those figures constitute a constellation of ideas about women, family, economics, and cultural well-being; and their narrative deployments in the interests of maintaining the status quo dissolve the line between "real" and "cultural" politics. The most immediately recognizable figure, the welfare queen, is omnipresent in the media—even when (and perhaps especially when) she is not explicitly named. Given a couple of centuries (and, in the corporate and/or mainstream press, an especially intense couple of decades) of seeing and hearing the behaviors and economic position of poor African Americans laid at the door of their "problematic" family structure and/or culture, given the various ways in which every large urban newspaper and most small-town newspapers remind us of the "blight" (political, social, and economic) of the cities, and given the ubiquity of political and community figures whose commentary focuses on attributing the "decline of the nation" to the urban poor and the inappropriateness or inadequacy (take your choice) of state intervention against those problems, the welfare queen is omnipresent in discussions about "America's" present or future even when unnamed. All of those things are constantly in the news (not that welfare queens were ever much out of the news)—urban crime, the public

---

* Kimberlé Crenshaw also notes that the plight of the welfare queen is "solely rooted in her dependence on the state" ("Round-table: Doubting Thomas," *Tikkun*, vol. 6, no. 5 [September–October 1991], p. 27). But my intention here is to map the ways in which mere economic dependence gets figured in narrative terms as an allegorical cover story of moral or character failing and draws our attention away from the political economy to a different "spectacle" altogether.

schools, the crack trade, teenage pregnancy are all narratives in which "welfare queen" is writ large.* (Recently the *Moynihan Report* is itself back in the news.)

It is difficult to conceive of a "normal," an unproblematic, space in our historical moment for black women outside of the demonic-narrative economy of the welfare queen or the betrayal-narrative economy of the black-lady overachiever—both figures about which Moynihan warns. And deploying the two narratives does double duty for the machinations of the powerful. What comes out of and is supported by the *Moynihan Report* is alarm at the existence of two problems: the single black female parent (more explicitly central as a policy problem) and the (less central and, thus, meriting less *explicit* attention) black female overachiever. The two figures' pernicious hold on the national imagination constantly springs to devastating life in the service of ideology. What seems to "threaten" the individual Clarence Thomas? What is used, finally, to discredit both Anita Hill and Emma Mae Martin as individuals? Their existence as social narratives. How do the two function as narratives? What constantly invigorates them? Those narratives work not simply by virtue of what is said within the narratives themselves, but by what is called on that is connected to them. What, then, are we being asked to remember? In the economy of the Thomas–Hill discourse, a set of tropes were mobilized on Thomas's behalf, among them the culture-of-poverty discourse. How might those tropes have been tacked onto Hill and Martin, the other, less-discussed woman?

The ways in which narratives that mark those figures were embedded in the debates around Hill and Thomas are complex. For many people, Thomas occupied almost mythic ground in this discourse; he articulated and seemed to embody the Horatio Alger success myth, the ultimate American individual—and lest we forgot that he embodied the myth, countless media commentators reminded us that he did. His story moved along three equally salient axes: (1) he was proof that anyone, any individual, can succeed who tries hard enough; (2) he was just an individual with a right to privacy like anyone else; and (3) he represented, in fact embodied, an entire history of black men oppressed by a more powerful group. Against that background, Thomas's much less visible, and certainly unarticulated (in most forums), connections with powerful people, and the differences between Thomas's treatment within his family and that of his sister, were "disappeared."

Thomas and his grandfather became, within the economy of those myths, the bringers of order, of law—against chaos, against anarchy—the male figures so desperately needed in (and missing from) Moynihan's "black family." Thomas's mention of his grandfather functioned to invoke nostalgia for a golden age when black men were real men (and present in their families), a nostalgia that could find its desired object in Thomas himself, the present-day embodiment of that age. Thomas made of himself not a "man" but an empty mythical vessel into which the state could pour what it needed and then attempt to make all of us consume it as blackness, an ineffable "blackness," in order to draw attention away from what we were actually consuming: yet another narrative of state power.

---

*In other words, "welfare queen" and "black lady" are socially constructed categories, similar to those that Spillers describes as "markers so loaded with mythical prepossession that there is no easy way for the agents buried beneath them to come clean" (p. 65).

The lesson implied by the *Moynihan Report* (as well as the vicious "common sense" of certain policy-makers and social commentators), in many ways the Ur-text for the simplistic "culture of poverty" discussions as they are represented in the media,[3] is that the welfare-dependent single mother is finally the synecdoche, the shortest possible short-hand, for the pathology of poor, urban, black culture. Responsible for creating and maintaining a family that can only be perceived as pathological compared to the norma-tive (and thus allegedly "healthy") family structure in the larger society, the welfare mother is the root of greater black pathology. But the flip side of the pathological welfare queen, as Moynihan's own language tells us, is the other kind of black woman—the black lady, the one whose disproportionate overachievement stands for black cultural strange-ness and who ensures the underachievement of "the black male" in the lower classes because "ours [the U.S.] is a society which presumes male leadership in private and public affairs."[4] And because the culture of African Americans seems not to fit into this pattern, Moynihan tells us, it "is placed at distinct disadvantage."[5] There we have it. Whether by virtue of *not achieving* and thus passing on bad culture as welfare mothers, or by virtue of *managing to achieve* middle-class success via education, career, and/or economic successes (and thus, I suppose, passing on genes for autonomous female success?), black women are responsible for the disadvantaged status of African Amer-icans.

Make no mistake about it: in the grip of a recession, with political figures outdoing each other to shift the blame away from the structural inadequacies of the political economy and its effect on all of the poor, most of the working class, and an increasingly larger share of the middle class, the lines between real and cultural politics disappear in the creation of all-purpose scapegoats. Before, during, and since the Thomas hearings, the decline of "America" has been linked somehow to the popularly despised vision of its being or threatening to become a "welfare state." With that specter constantly before U.S. citizens, the adjective "welfare" demonizes anything that follows it, something that David Duke—only the most extreme and dramatic articulator of a narrative that we can read in any newspaper almost any day of the week—learned and recently manipulated in Lou-isiana very well (even if he was ultimately unsuccessful in getting himself elected). What welfare mothers/queens and black ladies—as cover stories that draw our attention away from the abuses and failures of our political-economic structure—also do is to under-mine the notion of family (actually existing families as well as normative ideas about the family) as entirely private, individual, and not connected to the state or the collective public.

Between the specters of Emma Mae Martin—denounced by Thomas as an example of "welfare dependency" (read: welfare queen)—on the one hand, and Anita Hill—embodiment of black-lady status—on the other hand, the confirmation of Thomas could be viewed as necessary to help save the life of the nation, which might otherwise go down the tubes trying to fight the pathology of the urban black poor dragging at its heels. Here, as in other times, black women function as the narrative means by which the country can make up its mind yet again about a whole set of issues. Of course, that Hill was single (as well as middle-class) helped; in that way she could be painted as the ultimate threatening outlaw—a loose cannon, out to subvert the "family," the "American" family. What Thomas's confirmation process needed was just that kind of "outlaw" to make an appear-ance so that the "hero" could emerge. To many African Americans, Thomas's distortion of his less fortunate sister's situation was a mean-spirited and unheroic action; thus, without Hill's outlawness, Thomas could not have become a hero.* Her appearance, and especially the thematic use made of her by Thomas's supporters and the state, made his confirmation much more certain.

Within the terms specifically of, or influenced by, the *Moynihan Report* and generally of the discourse on the "culture of poverty," "welfare queen" is a phrase that describes economic dependency—the lack of a job and/or income (which equals degeneracy in the Calvinist United States); the presence of a child or children with no father and/or husband (moral deviance); and, finally, a charge on the collective U.S. treasury—a human debit. The cumulative totality, circulation, and effect of these meanings in a time of scarce resources among the working class and the lower middle class is devastatingly intense. The welfare queen represents moral aberration and an economic drain, but the figure's problematic status becomes all the more threatening once responsibility for the destruction of the "American way of life" is attributed to it. Demonic is not too strong a word to describe the politics of that narrative. Emma Mae Martin embodied that narrative; she, as Thomas described her,[6] was one of those drawing the nation down into the depths of despair. This narrative is not new: not only was it useful to Duke, it has been explicitly reinvigorated by the *New York Times*'s recent attempts to breathe new life into Moynihan and his report, and by the governors, state legislatures, and presidential candidates who have declared war on the welfare poor, epitomized as welfare mothers and AFDC (Aid to Families with Dependent Children) families, *not*, for example, as government-subsidized corporations or upper-class individuals and families subsidized by tax cuts and credits.†

Read the newspapers, watch television, or simply listen to people talk: among other things, welfare queens are held responsible for the crack trade and crack babies. And they combine that with moral degeneracy within their families—for example, they trade sex for crack in front of their children. (Within the economy of this narrative the crack dealer is also demonized, but he is the creation of his pathological "nurturer" because it is she who reproduces the culture.) Behind the bland and leaden policy language that paints her as simply incapable is something more vicious, which finds its outlet in other ugly images and language. She is the agent of destruction, the creator of the pathological, black, urban, poor family from which all ills flow; a monster creating crack dealers, addicts,

---

* On the other hand, both Lisa Jones (*Village Voice*, November 12, 1991, pp. 27–28) and Crenshaw wrote about the *lack* of critical response to Thomas's distortions about his sister by many African Americans. Crenshaw argues that Thomas's misrepresentations did *not* constitute a stumbling block for their support, that "Thomas reflects a very specific ideology about Black women—an ideology of put-down that is a growing phenomenon within the Black community" (p. 27). While I don't completely disagree with Jones and Crenshaw, still, I think, given the letters in newspapers around the country, and the calls from African Americans to radio talk shows, that enough African Americans (even though a minority) were troubled by his distortions that their (and others') disapproval was a factor that made a counternarrative necessary.

† The *Report* has more lives than a cat and it continues to heavily influence discussions in the corporate and mainstream media about the urban poor. The theme of the destructive "underclass" has a place in our collective memory that is being dusted off for yet more work as various states cut welfare benefits and newspapers print additional descriptions of the depreciations of the poor—welfare recipients prominent among them, as always—on "attractive welfare states" like California. Politicians gain credibility for themselves by coming out against the notion of the United States as a welfare state.

muggers, and rapists—men who become those things because of being immersed in *her* culture of poverty.

Such women are totally unlike Thomas, whose story about his grandfather resonates so thoroughly across a public imagination accustomed to myths about heroic male individuals that his mother's history and that of any other women in his family—and their own particularity—are erased. His grand*father* was the proper nurturer—the stand-in for the law's order at home. Unlike Thomas's sister.

Hill, about whom I will say more below, is the narrative constituted by the other Moynihan trope—the black female overachiever and betrayer of a possible black patriarchy—but whose existence is noted at least as far back as the eighteenth century in David Walker's *Appeal . . . to the Coloured Citizens of the World.*[7] Both she and Martin can be seen as exemplifying the pathology of the category "black women." And the attacks on the two women were exercises of state power by means of invoking racist and sexist stereotypes passing themselves off as social-science–supported policy.

What is a welfare state, finally, but a government that assumes responsibility for its citizens' well-being; theoretically, at least, it takes care of those who cannot take care of themselves: children, for example. And according to narratives about welfare queens, what is the reason such children need care? The misbehavior of their mothers, who either never had or cannot keep their husbands. So what is going to destroy America? Black welfare queens in particular and black female misbehavior in general. And it does not matter that all such children needing state care are not black, or that poverty and unemployment are reasons that they need state care; what matters, what resonates in the national mind's eye, is the constant media-reinforced picture of the welfare queen—always black. Within the terms of this narrative, however, Thomas not only neutralizes his sister early by caricaturing her, or by reminding his listening and watching audience of her existence as a caricature, he triumphs over her. But after that, who almost destroys the state's standard-bearer in these hearings? An overachieving black lady. The flip side of the pathology coin, the welfare queen's more articulate sister.

The two of them—threatening to bring down further destruction on all normal Americans (as J. C. Alvarez so loved saying)—have to be contained. The attack that focuses on them comes together in particular kinds of ways. When Hill, already aberrant by virtue of her class status, is referred to as a lunatic—someone who fantasizes; when she's referred to as a lesbian—someone whom we are to see as unnatural in a heterosexual family romance, or as someone telling a story that ought to be kept away from children; when her very "ladylike" (another word for "middle-class") behavior is read as an aberration because a black lady is either an oxymoron, or yet another indication of the pathology of African-American culture; then she's as demonized (although differently so) as the welfare queen.

Hill is a threat either because she's *not* a real lady (not "ladylike")—she's a debater, she holds her own aggressively in an argument, and she's ambitious—or because she *is* a real lady—by virtue of her class standing. In either case she is dangerous. In a way, she is even more of a threat to male dominance than Thomas's sister—the welfare queen—because the national public "recognizes" his sister but does not know as easily and as consciously how to recognize the lady. We're accustomed to thinking of the welfare queen as pathological because we've "learned" the story of the culture of underdevelopment; Hill is demonized because we don't *know* who she is.* And her quiet, direct, and tearless (read: unfeminine) delivery worked against her.

Class position and status came into play to marginalize Hill at the same time that the class position of the powerful male (Thomas) was ignored. According to the statement of J. C. Alvarez, a self-described "real American,"† Hill's education and career trajectory discredited her because, for Alvarez, an educated Yale Law School graduate has no victim "authenticity," no right to fears about her relationship to a powerful man or to the marketplace.[8] Alvarez's assessment of Hill's inauthenticity as a victim was echoed by numerous callers to CNN and radio talk shows who indicated that they didn't believe Hill because, unlike an uneducated person—a factory worker, for example—Hill had options; she could get another job. The upward mobility demonstrated by Thomas's career—and celebrated in the media and on the Senate floor—became in Hill's case simply more reason for distrust of her. The suspicious anti-Hill callers, aware of Hill's class position and relative labor flexibility, were completely blind to Thomas's class position and power.

The logic of narratives that demonized Hill didn't seem to require rational defense whether or not such narratives were vulnerable to rational critique. Think of the casual linkages—so beloved of Orrin Hatch, Strom Thurmond, and Alan Simpson: lesbian, spurned woman. It doesn't matter that no one was ever lynched on behalf of a lesbian, or that being a woman spurned by a man implies heterosexuality. That lesbian and spurned woman cannot be rationally linked together simply means that a debased discourse doesn't care whether the terms of "othering" are logical or not. Any demonic narrative will do in a pinch, even two or three, it simply depends upon what demon is most effective in making the sense of the world that power requires.

The final, most devastating subtext, however, of the black-lady narrative is affirmative action—everybody's football. And there were code words that linked Hill with affirmative action: J. C. Alvarez's remarks about corporations looking for "women like [Hill]," for example, a possible corporate search that provided reason for Alvarez and the general public to doubt Hill's credibility. How did affirmative action and Hill function together as demonic narratives that worked on behalf of Thomas's confirmation? Regardless of whatever arguments could be and have been made on behalf of affirmative action, whether or not Hill went to school as an affirmative-action student, whether or not she got any of her positions as a result of affirmative action or equal-opportunity programs, she's tarred with the affirmative-action brush by virtue of the salience of affirmative action in the news and the political game-playing that went on around the civil rights bill. Affirmative action then became another powerful (and largely unspoken) reason that the public could not trust Anita Hill's story—because affirmative action is the reason that the

---

* Recently, Susan Douglas noted that Hill looked and acted prim, even prudish (*In These Times*, November 6–12, 1991, p. 18), behavior seen as deviant because it wasn't exuberant, earthy, physically expressive. It went against the grain of media, especially television, portraits of black women. This is a media criticism, of course, that countless African-American feminists and cultural commentators have made for decades.

† Ironically, the self-described "John Q. Public" and "ordinary American" J. C. Alvarez is herself a Princeton University graduate (class of '77). Howard Taylor, Princeton University, brought this information to my attention.

national public thinks it *knows* she could have gotten another job and therefore should have left the one she had. Thus, the public was given yet another sin to lay at the feet of affirmative action: Anita Hill. And such is the horrible double edge of that particular blade, that another sin was laid (simultaneously) at *Hill's* feet: her potential employment attractiveness in affirmative-action terms.

Affirmative action created the monster Hill, who then came forward to do battle against the white knight (or the black knight on behalf of white state power), Clarence Thomas, who intended to do away with the dragon of affirmative action. Despite the *fact* of his affirmative-action-aided education, he proudly articulated antiaffirmative-action credentials and experience. And for those looking for additional reasons to support Thomas, Hill's performance before the Senate committee made it clear why affirmative action is a bad idea: affirmative action means that U.S. children will have to hear educated African Americans talk about pubic hair, long dongs, big breasts, and bestiality in Senate chambers!

Affirmative action, welfare state, and welfare queen have become a mantra, evoked as single (albeit complicated) signs for and of everything wrong with the United States; those words do yeoman duty, especially in a debased discourse that seeks to undermine the need for state assistance: i.e., people don't need jobs to prosper—never mind that the industrial basis for most African-American (and other working-class) conventionally male employment has fled the country to farther-flung and cheaper sites—people only need the right kind of moral nurturing and socialization to succeed. And if they don't get the right kind of moral training, then of course the country will go to the dogs. Within the terms of the convergent narratives of the Thomas hearings, the message was clear: at the end of history, with the smoking gun in her hand, stands a two-faced figure: Ms. Black Professional/the welfare queen. Only Thomas's confirmation could avert the end of civilization as we know it.

Within the economy of that simplistic narrative, how could the state not win? And Thomas was its linchpin.

In this debate "Anita Hill" and "Emma Mae Martin" were not actually existing individuals as much as they were narrative stand-ins for certain properties of the mythic black-lady and welfare-queen categories. The names of the two actually existing women became increasingly unimportant as the "names" for their "types" took over the discourse. The existence of those names—black lady and welfare queen, even unspoken—saved Thomas's name and his *nomination*, or his *naming*, to the Supreme Court. Given the fact that some people were paying attention to criticism of Thomas's EEOC record, his connection to lobbyists for South Africa, his improper behavior in overturning a $10.4 million damage award against Ralston Purina, and his attacks on his sister, the state might not have managed to pull off his confirmation or to make it as publicly popular as it turned out to be.

The particular confluence of these narratives (and the political work they did) demanded that Thomas (as Alisa Solomon also notes in the *Village Voice*)[9] *become* "black," have a public racial "conversion experience," but I would add that the conversion experience was even more necessary in order for the *state* to "pass" as black. Blackness, as an abstraction, did battle for Thomas because few people actually belonging to the group "black" or "African-American"* would have gone to war on behalf of Thomas the corrupt judge, Thomas the bigot, Thomas the incompetent and inadequate head of EEOC. But for Thomas the black male victim of "Sapphire"—black female emasculator and betrayer of black men and carrier of black family pathology—well, the African-American legions would and did rise to battle against her. Out of the ooze of his past record climbed Thomas, the *real* black thing.

As necessary as it was to the state, however, that the African-American community be seen to support this nomination, such support was not in and of itself sufficient to secure Thomas's confirmation. The whole country had to be engaged in the making and marking of Thomas as hero, especially given the media attention to critiques of, and pressure brought to bear by, feminists of various races and ethnicities; thus the need for the welfare queen/black lady narratives.

Nonetheless, what of blackness?† Under what conditions? In our attention to the history of racism in the United States, African Americans have learned to keep in our memory the unrelenting attacks on our existence as a group regardless of whatever else might be at stake. But blackness is simply too large and unelaborated a category to carry the weight of analysis in this case. Thomas has class allegiances and alliances that are inimical to the interests of most of the group in this country. He has made a political career arguing against racism as a constitutive element of material existence for black people, and working against the interests of black people of both genders and women of all races. Nonetheless, Thomas's conservatism disappeared, covered over by the soothing balm of black common sense.

What are we to make of many African Americans' insistence on seeing Thomas simply as a black person being attacked by white people? Both Thomas's and the right's abilities to buffer him by taking advantage of black rage and white-liberal guilt depended on the construction of a mythic blackness as a category emptied of history and female gendering. In such discussions "woman"—as in a woman scorned or spurned, a vicious liar or deluded psychotic—is timeless and colorless. Such a dynamic ensures the rhetorical slippage embodied in the travesty of his use of lynching as metaphor; its historical baggage is elided in the hysteria of the moment.‡

This means that certain kinds of black individuals were constituted as needing protection from other members of the group: "Any black person who goes against what people think black people should do or think becomes the object of attack," according to the testimony of Dr. Nancy Fitch (formerly of Thomas's staff). Her assertion, which wrongly

---

* While I make no claims about racial biology, given the political reality of twentieth-century U.S. life and more than three hundred years of history, here I refer to the idea of "blackness" as a social fact if not a biological reality.

† Here I refer to both the social construction and political consciousness senses of blackness as defined in the footnote on p. 37.

‡ Some metaphorical uses of lynching and abuses of its historical specificity were arrogantly transparent in their deployment. Peggy Noonan wrote (in an op-ed piece in the October 15, 1991, *New York Times*) that "regular Americans" did think Thomas was being lynched, "not because he's a black man—*they saw Robert Bork swinging from the same tree*—but because he's a conservative" (my emphasis). If Thomas's evocation of lynching as a defense against the Senate committee's feeble interrogation of his past behaviors was cynical, then Noonan's attempt to wrap lynching, with its specific and racist history, around Bork was obscene.

and ahistorically insists that criticism within the group has the power to silence dissent, echoes the right's assertions that only black conservatives are the *real* dissenters, the real rugged individuals and, as such, are objects of black "political correctness." Within the terms of this narrative economy Thomas becomes like black lynching victims of old—a black threat to be neutralized by, well, by whom, really? To whom does Thomas pose a threat? Certainly *not* to white and powerful men, not to the state.

Further, if lynching, like the lash of the whip or scars on the slave's back, is the most concrete enactment of race oppression, then the narratives of "grandfather, the share-cropper," lynching, and endangered black manhood all came together in a devastating way. Against this scenario, a critique of a black conservative is transformed into a threat to individualism, becomes un-American, and it does so despite the fact that Hill is conservative (although less so than Thomas), that most of the people supporting her on the committee floor were identifiable as conservatives. Hill's conservatism disappears also, but not in the way that Thomas's does—hers disappears without the balm of blackness. Instead, she becomes the embodiment of black female betrayal or "white" (by fiat) feminist cat's-paw.

The efficacy of the lynching metaphor is due to problematic recourse to black common sense that reasons thusly: they (whites) are out to get us. Such common sense, of course, has much past and present evidence to buttress it. Unfortunately, impelled by the strength and general historical accuracy of that common sense, African Americans who moved uncritically over to (or were always on) Thomas's side protected "white" state power and upper-class privilege in the name of blackness and out of concern for black manhood. Such was the metaphysical dilemma posed by regarding the social fact of blackness and its political and cultural significance from too crude a common-sense vantage point.* And because when the chips were down, and blackness from this common-sense per-spective equals only black *man*hood, Hill's race became both hypervisible and invisible at the same time. That it "disappeared" and "reappeared" is important, but more important is how it disappeared and reappeared at the same time. With no check on Thomas's evocation of his blackness, with no real check by Democrats or the mainstream press, Hill got whiter.

Blackness as a mobilizing rhetorical resource for Thomas was enhanced for African Americans by narrative presentation of a "Sapphire" figure. Nonetheless, as I asserted earlier, while mobilizing blackness was necessary to turn Thomas (the racial conservative who does not believe in or exhibit racial solidarity) into a black hero for African Amer-icans, doing so was insufficient to guarantee popular acceptance of his confirmation among the larger population. It was the political work done by the tainted presence of the black lady—with her class privilege so consistently recognized, evoked, and articulated—and the equally but differently tainted and powerfully present figure, the welfare queen,

---

* One recurrent form of patriarchal idiocy that relied on knee-jerk allegiance to blackness as masculine terrain was articulated in the language of Ishmael Reed: "White feminists will go to any means to advance *their* cause, Thomas is right about being lynched" (my emphasis; *In These Times*, October 23–29, 1991, quoted by Salim Muwakkil). With this stunningly reductionist insight, Reed erased Hill's own agenda, her conservatism, and the vitality of black feminism, while allying himself with the mouthpiece of white state power.

that constituted the vehicle by which Thomas could ride both from and into history as the black hero fighting the forces of U.S. entropy and bad women. *

Further, this narratively constructed pathology of black women reasserted *America's* health in the minds of much of its citizenry. State power is patriarchal power whether it is externally imposed or produced and reproduced within the individual, private, and domestic realms of black communities. The state's manipulation of narratives like the poverty-produced "welfare queen" and the affirmative-action–produced "black lady" not only perpetuate racism and sexism but guarantee the continued unequal distribution of economic resources. And that is precisely what I mean by ideological war by narrative means. Understanding those operations is how we can recognize the blurring of the line between real and cultural politics. These narratives masked the general but more elusive operations of power. They forced our attention away from power, from the selection of political elites, from the failures of the U.S. political economy, and toward a particular individual drama. At the same time that the second set of Thomas confirmation hearings were going on: (1) President Bush vetoed legislation that would have added more weeks of unemployment benefits to people out of work more than six months; (2) Bush "worried" (at least according to the *New York Times*) about banks, their loans, and a sluggish economy—he "approved" some "measures" and spoke of taking "more steps" to help "stabilize" the economy; and (3) at the same time, Haitian demonstrators marched at different locations in the country in support of Haiti's deposed President Aristide.

In those moments the state withheld bread and put on a media "circus" instead of alleviating any of the abuses of its economy. Meanwhile, news of yet another geopolitical site where the relation between raw events of power and ideological contestation, in a part of the hemisphere in which U.S. economic and political policy and interests are heavily involved, was being written in the margins of newsprint framing the "spectacle" being played out on CNN. The political economy of the United States was being reconstructed in narrative terms that placed discussion of poor unemployed people, banks, and Haiti on

---

* Various journalists, political analysts, and cultural critics have delineated ways in which we can understand the moment of these hearings and the discourse surrounding them in ways that allow us to see genuine gendered and racialized challenges to the successful and multifaceted operations of power. And those of us who opposed Thomas did what we could with the evidence available about Thomas and his record—in scattered spaces in the media, in groups that lobbied the Senate and the committee, in networks that provided information to the Senate committee, and under unenviable circumstances. But while we challenged the workings of conservative narratives of race and gender, we were unable to interrupt the workings of such ideas as they took flesh in a particular moment. Specific cultural politics did the work of stabilizing the U.S. political economy in this moment as it has in the past.

The slogan "Men have to listen to women" (something people said over and over again when they wrote in the newspaper or talked on television) used as a political imperative was a very good place to begin, but the complications inherent in the constitutive elements of that phrase surfaced quickly. What women? The question arose because women who were supporters of a very powerful man (who will be even more powerful) came forward to do battle on behalf of the continued operation of uncritiqued power. Women like J. C. Alvarez, who defined "real" womanhood and told us what a "real" victim of sexual harassment would do, seized the category "woman" in order to make it impossible for other women, or at least one woman in particular, to be heard.

And of course some men did listen to women. In fact, they rushed to listen to particular women: Senator Simpson, who found it impossible to believe anything Hill and her supporters had to say, found that he could listen to the string of women defending Thomas and attacking Hill; he listened and begged for more.

the margins of the newspaper pages—*outside* the frame of the Thomas–Hill controversy. The spectacle around Hill's charges covered over the overlap between what seem to be private matters and the public abuse of male power and obscured the ways in which the realm of the private is permeated with real or public politics. None of this was new. Approval for the Persian Gulf War, for example, was sustained in considerable part by the consistent demonic spectacle of Saddam Hussein, alternately cast as a madman, a rapist, and/or a homosexual via T-shirts, novelties, radio shows, television, and the print media. Visually, textually, politically, the operation of a powerful state exercised and maintained its power by any means available to it, with the connivance of much of the press, the broadcast media, and the national public. And those places where power was least visible might well be where it was most present.

Photographic placement was not the only means by which power was hidden: textual examples abounded. One of the most egregious was written by R. W. Apple, Jr., in the *New York Times:*[10] "The Senators who must vote on Tuesday were left with only two options: Either she was telling the truth or she is a sociopath; either these horrifying events took place or she, for some reason invented them." One would have to look long and hard for a better example of a syntax mugging on behalf of the more powerful figure in these hearings: Thomas as agent is absent from this sentence. On the other hand, Hill, as syntax agent, makes three appearances: (1) possible truth-teller, (2) sociopath, or (3) inventor of events. But there is no Thomas agency even where, in term of syntactic parallelism, one might most expect to see him (or it) as in "horrifying events took place."* No Thomas there; even if the events *happened*, they did so passively, they took place without his doing. To see more clearly how this piece of a sentence protects the more powerful figure, consider how else the reporter *could have* written this part of the sentence: "Either he is a liar, or she is a sociopath; either he is guilty of horrifying abuses of power or she is guilty of inventing them."

Further into the same article, Apple's protection of power was extended from Thomas in particular to cover, generally, those powerful institutional sites that are, apparently for him, never contaminated with abusive language and/or behaviors: "Either he said these wretched things to her—things that one associates with the seamiest of criminal cases or the raunchiest of locker rooms, not with the *Senate* or *Supreme Court*—or he did not" (my emphasis).

Thomas is the state incubus returning as the masque† of blackness within the sanctity of the Senate. The spectacle of the Thomas hearings did not just mask the operation of state power in the political economy; it did the work. In so far as the state-assisted Thomas was able to "make" himself and to be made the mythological black patriarchal male figure—and thereby marginalize Martin and Hill both as real people and as the categories they represent—then the political economy was made flesh. Thomas's elevation through

---

* This distortion of language belongs up there with another hall of fame example of passive political "guiltspeak": "Mistakes were made."

† I use "masque" here in the Renaissance sense: "An entertainment in which a procession of masqued or otherwise disguised figures represented a highly imaginative action. . . . the spectacle was of the greatest importance to the presentation of the mythological or similarly fantastic subjects" (taken from Alex Preminger, ed., *The Princeton Handbook of Poetic Terms* [Princeton: Princeton University Press, 1986]). In short, my reference to Thomas and his confirmation process as a masque means that his spectacle of blackness was a disguised display of power.

the second hearings to his place as exemplar of solid American heroism and virtuous blackness laundered the state's relationship to racism, to the economic and political abuse of poor people generally, poor black people specifically, and to black women of whatever economic level. His elevation put a black face on patriarchal and oligarchic business as usual. But state power does not act on its own—the narratives deployed here were effective precisely because they circulate, with the considerable help of the corporate and/or mainstream media, through the culture.

Across history, and certainly in this moment, one of the most reliable all-purpose scapegoats has been the black woman. In this moment both the "welfare queen" and the "black lady" are pathologies created by an erring state: welfare queens are poor and pathologically dependent because of state welfare handouts, and black ladies are pathologically independent because state-influenced or -assisted affirmative-action programs keep such ladies from what they might otherwise become: the spousal appendages of successful black patriarchs. Thomas, on the other hand, was constructed as the quintessential self-made man. If he could be seen as essentially self-made (i.e., without the help of the state), then Hill and Martin could be seen to represent the bad results of state intervention. The state thus makes its own interventions (however inadequate and attenuated) on behalf of poor and middle-class black women look like mistakes it needs to rectify. (Tougher times ahead for the disadvantaged for their own good!) With Thomas's ascension to the Supreme Court, it disavows its bad progeny—the two women—and claims its good progeny—the self-made, as opposed to state-made, man.

By confirming Thomas, by affirming the black father, the stand-in for state power, not only did the state and Senate do business as usual, but the black-female threat to what "America" means was wrestled to the ground. No wimps here: the black-female "troubles" are over for now; America is back and standing tall. Bush is in control again, standing firmly on the nation-threatening black-female "thing." The imaginary demons were contained while the latest embodiment of the eternal "undead" of state power (or the *real thing*) moved on to his seat in Washington, D.C. The first pair of pictures I described at the beginning of this essay "hid" real power inequities by flaunting visual egalitarianism; the second pair simply used spatial placement to reassert unarticulated hierarchy. Consider three other pictures given prominent place in the *New York Times*.

1. On October 11, a front-page photograph of Thomas striding across his lawn was placed directly above an article about Hill entitled "A Private Person in a Storm." Perhaps the *Times* (perversely?) thought that Hill was so very private that a photograph of her adversary could stand in for her, or perhaps the newspaper was simply hedging its bets, or—even more frighteningly—the editor never noticed that a picture of Thomas was marginalizing yet another narrative about Hill. Whatever. Still, Thomas (and his privacy) were clearly on view and on top. And Hill (and her privacy) were disappeared, or were at least subordinated to Thomas—on the bottom.

2. On October 10 a picture of Thomas and Bush sitting together somewhere in the White House ran on the front page. The two men are seated together; Thomas is smiling and looking at Bush; Bush is looking solemnly toward the camera. The "great white father" embodies—in his presence in that picture and by his proximity to Thomas—the presence of state power and determination. Seeming to lean slightly closer to the camera, Bush is out front in every sense of the phrase. This picture ran before the second hearing began, when state power was more obviously making itself explicit; before the push began

to represent Thomas as an individual about to be attacked by the big bad Senate committee. It was the last time during these hearings that the photographic spotlight (in the *Times*) was on Bush.

3. On October 13, the same day as the "Theater of Pain" picture I referred to earlier, a photograph of Thomas and Senator Danforth ran inside the *Times*. Thomas is gazing down at the floor following the end of the hearing after his "I would have preferred an assassin's bullet" speech. Danforth, his friend and advisor, is touching Thomas's shoulder with his hand. Again, Thomas is in the presence of power and being comforted by it. This picture reinforced the narrative of a hurt and suffering Thomas. In fact, by then, "he has suffered enough" was the common and constant refrain. Compared to all those he harmed as head of EEOC, or those who sought and did not receive help through the EEOC? Compared to those who might be in a position to be harmed by his elevation to the Supreme Court bench?

# Coda

There are questions that this essay has tried to address: What does it mean to see or hear power so constantly elided or treated as if separable from gender or racial dynamics? What is a black politics—absent class and/or gender specificity? What is being coerced when "woman" is used in specific ways—especially when categories like "black woman" are not explicitly articulated but are, nonetheless, overwhelmingly present? Where are women in relation to class and/or power? What of specific women (powerless in and of themselves) acting as articulators of power positions? How did pro-Thomas voices mobilize "history" onto their side and why did it work? What are the drawbacks for civic debate and political process when historical themes are used as a shorthand to dramatize crises and manipulate or motivate sympathies—a kind of persuasion by evocation and recognition of congruence?[11]

Because of the relative success of the state in this moment, I have written an alarmist critique. But in the end I stave off despair by remembering some expressions of skepticism that undermined the process against which this essay warns. Some cut through this ugliness by contesting the narratives in circulation throughout this hearing: the alternative press generally, and specific writers in the corporate and mainstream press; and various people who called into CNN and radio talk shows around the country who articulated their suspicion about the absence of discussion about President Bush's work in all of this, or who spoke of their anger over the ways in which race was being deployed, or who wondered out loud about what this spectacle meant in the middle of a recession. Some made use of the media to question the workings of power—for example, Democratic Representative Craig Washington, speaking for the Congressional Black Caucus, responded to telephone callers during a segment on CNN and shed heavily Texas-inflected light on the darkness.

One finds hope where one can and sometimes in unexpected places. *People* magazine ran stories on Anita Hill and on Clarence and Virginia Thomas. In the short (two-page) article (October 28, 1991) on Anita Hill, they seemed to adhere to their customary human-interest structure. But that article was written apparently without her participation; there were no new pictures of Hill with her family—all the photographs used were pictures from her past, of her parents at the hearing, and of their home. There was no interview with her, no new quotes from her; in short, it was human interest without the presence of the private or "human" Hill. However, surprisingly (for me at least), the article was appended with five pages of women's narratives (complete with pictures), all of whose experiences supported the credibility, at least, of Hill's reasons for not coming forward at the time of the harassment. *People* followed those five pages with separate boxes on Catharine MacKinnon and Deborah Tannen talking about sexual harassment.

The second article (November 11, 1991) was a long interview with Virginia Thomas. The article ran multiple photographs of both of the Thomases, including one picture of the two reading a Bible on the couch. What a cover story, I thought. How could it not work, especially in conjunction with the "wife," the legitimate woman, narrating her story? I assumed that its effect would be a replay of the two panels of women who supported Thomas in the second hearings, that the picture of Virginia Thomas sitting so comfortably in (and so much of) the domestic sphere with her husband—and holding on to one of the most widely circulated texts in the nation—would speak so loudly against Hill's "outlaw" position that Hill's own narrative would vanish from view. I was certain that support for the Thomases would explode all over the letters-to-the-editor page of a later issue. In the issue (three weeks later) that carried the responses, however, while *People* indicated that "Virginia Thomas's account . . . brought more letters than any other story this year," most of the mail was *negative*, many of the letters printed (from people who might well be Christians but were clearly not taken in by the picture—and yet another cover story—of Bible-holding domesticity) were cogently contemptuous; to wit:

> It would appear from Virginia Thomas's story that Justice Clarence Thomas should have been nominated for sainthood instead of the Supreme Court.
>
> When I was a kid, taking the Lord's name in vain meant swearing or cursing. These days I'm inclined to think it means tossing around the name of God to protect or promote one's public image. I still believe Anita Hill. (*People*, December 2, 1991)

These examples, appearing in such a forum, made it a little easier for me to believe something that is a necessary tenet of faith for those engaged in criticizing and fighting undemocratic operations of power: power is never completely successful.

## Reading Questions

1. What, according to Lubiano, is objectionable about the media's tendency to focus on the *individual* nature of accusation and response in the Hill–Thomas hearings?
2. What does Lubiano mean by "state power"?
3. What does Lubiano mean by her criticism that certain aspects of the Hill–Thomas hearings were "naturalized"?
4. What seems to be the current Administration's policy stance toward the welfare state? Are the figures of the "welfare queen" used by the media or the Administration in ways that stigmatize welfare, affirmative action, or health policies?

## Recommended Reading

M. Cross and M. Johnson, *Race and the Urban System* (Cambridge: Cambridge University Press, 1989)

P. J. M. Essed, *Everyday Racism* (Claremont, CA: Hunter House, 1988)

R. Jenkins and J. Solomos, *Racism and Equal Opportunity in the 1980s* (Cambridge: Cambridge University Press, 1987)

Lee Rainwater and W. L. Yancey, eds., *The Moynihan Report*

*and the Politics of Controversy* (Cambridge: MIT Press, 1967)

W. J. Wilson, *The Truly Disadvantaged: The Inner City, the Underclass, and Public Policy* (Chicago: University of Chicago Press, 1987)

## Recommended Audiovisual Resources

*The Hill–Thomas Hearings.* 1993. Documentary narrated by Gloria Steinem. Contact *Ms.* magazine.

Contact Insight Media for additional videos that analyze the Hill–Thomas hearings.

# Cowboys, Cadillacs, and Cosmonauts

## Families, Film Genres, and Technocultures

### ANDREW ROSS

Andrew Ross is the director of American Studies at New York University. He is the author of *No Respect: Intellectuals and Popular Culture,* and numerous other books and articles in cultural criticism.

---

"I feel just like a guy at the shopping center with the groceries waiting for his wife."

—Pete Conrad, waiting to store equipment on the lunar module of *Apollo XII*

In Barry Levinson's 1987 film *Tin Men*, set in Baltimore in 1962, the lunchtime banter of four aluminum siding salesmen (the tin men of the title) often revolves around the shared suspicion that "*Bonanza* is not an accurate depiction of the West." One of the characters, who claims that ordinarily he isn't "too picky" about such details, says that he "is beginning to think that the show doesn't have too much realism." Why? Because it depicts "a fifty-year-old father with three forty-seven-year-old sons." A companion who points out, with mock humility, that he is no "authority" on the TV show, casts further suspicion on the Ben Cartwright patriarch, who must, he says, possess "the kiss of death" to have had three children from "three different wives who all die at childbirth." In addition, they agree that the characters seldom show any interest in the topic of women. No one, not even Little Joe or Hoss, ever talks about getting horny or getting laid.

In recent years, we have seen a rising tide of complaints about standardized depictions, in media and advertising, of a nuclear family model that bears little resemblance to real, demographic families in the United States, where, it is pointed out, the nuclear family has long been in decline. While the ideology of familialism is everywhere, the families themselves are increasingly hard to find. The complaint of Levinson's tin men about *Bonanza*'s weird, one-parent family expresses some of this current critical anxiety, but the comments of these characters are also set within a conventional filmic context that invokes a number of historical perspectives about the apparent incoherence of the nuclear family unit.

*Tin Men*, as I will show later, bristles with references to the generic codes of the classic Western, especially those that demarcate the genre's obsession with masculinity and its technological extensions. But the film is also a 1980s nostalgia film, depicting the innocent, prelapsarian conditions of 1962, which are nonetheless seen to contain the seeds of the oncoming decline of the United States' postwar social stability and economic prosperity. As in the classic Western, an ideal masculine way of life on the New Frontier is shown to be threatened with extinction. While the film tries to establish the threat objectively, in economic terms, I would argue that it is more fully displayed in a reconfiguration of courtship and marital relations that interrupts the utopian temporality of male camaraderie so shrewdly and passionately described in Levinson's films generally. Consequently, the debate in the diner about *Bonanza* takes on an added significance, not only for the film's own play of narratives, but also for the historical timespan—1962–1987—that the film mediates.

The *Bonanza* family debate can be seen, then, in the context of the messages it bears about the structural conventions of the Western itself, straining, by now, under the historical burden of recalling the days of frontier settlement and the origin of American imperialist expansionism in the nineteenth century. In particular, this strain is increasingly manifest in the genre's difficulties in resolving the contradiction between, on the one hand, the opportunistic brand of male self-reliance that is often referred to as "rugged individualism" and, on the other, the communal domesticity represented by the settlement family, each threatened in different ways by the arrival from the East of technological development and government regulation. As a cultural genre, the Western does not hold the copyright on telling this story, anymore than the Old West should always be invoked as a privileged site of the nation's foundational mythologies. If the Revolutionary War would seem a more likely candidate for mythologizing masculine and national identity, it is nonetheless clear that there are ideological risks involved in dwelling upon armed resistance to colonial vassalage. More well known to us, largely as a result of the cultural work done by the Western, are the advantages of focusing upon a period of territorial aggrandisement—the exploitation of land and labor through the codes of "lawlessness," the justification of genocide through the codes of "manifest destiny," and the legitimation of wild misogyny through the codes of maverick male autonomy. What has been repressed, of course, is the debt of the Southwestern cowboy mythology to the Mexican *vaquero* culture of cattlemen, which it appropriated wholesale, along with the culturally specific macho codes of the *rancheros*: "everything that served to characterize the American cowboy as a type was taken over from the Mexican *vaquero*: utensils and language, methods and equipment."[1]

In the pages that follow, I will track the logic of the Western codes governing masculinity (and its technological extensions) and nuclear familialism (in its successive management of crises) as their legacy is rearticulated in other film genres—the oil melodrama, the automobile nostalgia film, and science fiction, both naive and postmodern.

# Ponderosa Lost

Although weakened by genre burnout in print, on film, and now on TV, the Western, by the 1960s, was still a convenient vehicle for playing out the conflict between male restlessness and familial domesticity.[2] With the Cartwrights' baronial settlement, the Ponderosa, playing a starring role, *Bonanza* had become the most successful of the TV "property Westerns" in which social and kinship affinities governed solely by property relations had come to replace the codes of gunmanship as a determining structural feature of the genre's preoccupation with possessive individualism. Since Hollywood made its first horizontal penetration of the television industry in the mid-1950s with shows starring already established Western stars like Gene Autry, Roy Rogers, and William Boyd, the development of the TV Western had managed to reflect, over the course of ten years, each successive historical stage in the violent settlement of the Western states:[3] from the genteel frontiersman to the mercenary hired gun; from the bustling cattle boom of the 1880s to the schlocky performance art of Buffalo Bill Cody's Wild West Shows; from the glorification of outlawed prole desperadoes like Billy the Kid and the James Gang to the style fetishism of the rodeo dudes.

In the space of that TV decade, then, the atomistic rituals of the roving cowboy, bound to early libertarian codes of social action, had first been augmented by family or spouse substitutes in the form of celebrity horses like Trigger, Silver, and Champion, each famed for selfless loyalty and trust, and by "ethnic" sidekicks like Tonto and Pancho, equally valued for their unquestioning obedience. Subsequently, the introduction of advanced gun technology and the heyday of the independent, maverick gunfighter in *Gunsmoke*, *Wyatt Earp*, and *Colt 45* reinforced a typical male ambivalence about the values of domestic settlement, even as the rationale for the gunfighter's presence was to secure moral and territorial space for the settlement of families. In turn, the advent of the drover team or herd Westerns, like *Rawhide* and *Wagon Train*, celebrated the trail life of ideal male communities, paternalized by the wagon master, and serviced by a stereotypical cook whose sexually ambiguous associations are still perpetuated in ads like the recent homophobic Nut 'n Honey TV commercial. By the time of *Bonanza* and other property Westerns like *High Chaparral* and *The Virginian*, the domestic cook is Chinese.

The guidelines for *Bonanza* scriptwriters show how strict taboos were enforced to keep intact the show's formulaic view of family, property, and race relations:

> We often have a surfeit of Indian stories. Forget, too, any stories concerning a "wife" showing up, or someone claiming to own the Ponderosa, or the young, misunderstood rebel who regenerates because of the Cartwrights' tolerance and example.[4]

As is clear from these and other guidelines, the trajectory of the TV Western was one that safely bypassed the history of Native American genocide and the appropriation of Mexican culture and lands, just as it sweetened the history of the brutal carving out and baronial colonization of cattle kingdoms at the expense of small homesteaders.[5] With the cumulative popular appeal of the genre behind it, *Bonanza* might have soldiered on for much longer without taking account of either of these histories. It was the structural absence of a Cartwright wife, however, that finally sealed the fate of the new "suburban" phase of this genre, just as this absence had underscored the show's continuity with the atomistic characterology of the early Western. Even if the thrice-widowed Ben's paternalism mel-

lowed visibly over the years, the crisis of filiation under which the three absurdly infantilized sons labored was too much to bear for a consistently persuasive representation of
this one-parent family for a modern TV audience. One son left, another died, and the
series, increasingly confused about the nonmarital status of its characters, ended amid a
controversy over the representation of the murder of Alice Cartwright, Little Joe's bride.
On the other hand, the popularity of the show's nonnuclear family over the course of its
thirteen-year run (1959–1973) might still attest to its success in somehow representing
values that are invariably associated with the nuclear 1950s TV family as depicted in their
suburban form by *Father Knows Best* and *Ozzie and Harriet* or in the regional homilies
offered in the 1970s by *The Waltons*: the close-knit, property-owning family as the
privileged site of caring, stability, moral authority, and emotional security. While the
nuclear, two-parent family has no ultimate rights over such values, my examples intend
to suggest that the ideology of familialism is so closely identified with these values that any
set of alternative living arrangements that seeks to claim them is still obliged to define itself
as a "family," whether extended and thus tribal/communal, or else reduced to essential,
dyadic bonding. The popularity of a show like *Bonanza* showed, perhaps, how pliant that
ideology was, while the reinforced familialism of the 1980s proves how efficiently it has
absorbed and contained the powerful countercultural challenge to traditional family
structures in the late 1960s and early 1970s, which ran the gamut from decentered hippie
communities, modeled on the egalitarian Native American tribe, to the nomadic feudal
patriarchalism of the thirty-five-member Manson "family."[6]

Arguably the most successful, and problematic, of the 1960s' attempts to romanticize
pre-industrial kinship values were those made *in the service* of postindustrial ideology.
None were more persuasive than those of Marshall McLuhan, who advocated an "Ori-
entalization" and "retribalization" of families in advanced industrial societies through the
medium of new cultural technologies like television. The chief obstacle in the path of
postindustrial utopia, as McLuhan saw it, was the tendency of its new technological
environments simply to reflect the content of outdated environments, a phenomenon he
called "rear-view mirrorism." Writing in 1966 at the height of U.S. domination of the
world's media markets, McLuhan cited *Bonanza*'s popularity as an example of this contradictory face of technologist ideology:

> *Bonanza* is not our present environment, but the old one; and in darkest suburbia we latch
> onto this image of the old environment. This is normal. While we live in the television
> environment, we cannot see it. . . . Anyone who talks about centralism in the twentieth
> century is looking at the old technology—*Bonanza*—not the new technology—electric
> technology. . . . Our thinking is all done still in the old nineteenth-century world because
> everyone always lives in the world just behind—the one they can see, like *Bonanza*.
> *Bonanza* is the world just behind, where people feel safe. Each week 350 million people
> see *Bonanza* in sixty-two different countries. They don't all see the same show, obviously.
> In America, *Bonanza* means "way-back-when." And to many of the other sixty-two
> countries it means a-way-forward when we get there.[7]

Here McLuhan proposed a cultural parable for advanced technological societies. As I
have elsewhere pointed out, it is also "a parable about underdevelopment in many of the
sixty-two countries (almost a hundred finally, in *Bonanza*'s case) in which a technologically advanced culture's own imaginary and anachronistic relation to its past develop-

ment is being introduced."[8] In imagining the point of view of consumers in the foreign media markets upon which Hollywood film and network TV programming were being dumped, McLuhan saw only the witty, anachronistic side of culture shock, predicated upon assumptions about the inevitable linear shape ("when we get there") of technological progress along the Western model, assumptions that would not go uncontested in the decade ahead.

McLuhan's working concept of technological environments is nonetheless a useful one if we do not attribute to it the functional homogeneity and absolute determinist power that he does. It can be understood instead as a set of discursive rules, and in this respect it is similar to the concept of the genre, which, however imprecisely defined, impure, and variable in its permutation of rules and conventions, is still a model of efficiency, rather like the Colt revolver, the result of the first "American" production system of interchangeable parts. Genres are like technological environments inasmuch as their uneven influence, over a period of time, helps to shape our collective responses to perceived social contradictions. The cultural work that they perform serves to transform a set of material conditions into a narrative economy.

## The Oil Crisis

If McLuhan had chosen to consider that the sponsor of *Bonanza* was General Motors—it was a highly visible sponsorship—then a different kind of political economy and a different understanding of technological environments might have underscored his comments about the show. It would be a story that looked backwards to the "heritage" of empire and settlement in the Old West but that drew, for its current cultural and economic sense, upon the iconography and the oil-rich resources of the New West. At the time when McLuhan was writing and *Bonanza*'s ratings were at their peak, the oil-dependent automobile industry, economic guarantor of the postwar Pax Americana, accounted for 10 percent of all manufacturing and one out of every six jobs. No single product before or since is ever likely to dominate the economic base and imagination of a world power to the same extent as the automobile did in the postwar age of consensus. The decline of the U.S. auto industry was completely synonymous with deindustrialization and the flight of U.S. capital overseas.

Just as there is an economic narrative that puts cowboys and Cadillacs together without too much in the way of contradictions, the cattle-rich base of the Cartwrights' property wealth rests uneasily, but not anachronistically, alongside the new social organization of the Western oil family dynasty. Cattle ranching is a labor-intensive business in principle—though not always on TV (the Ponderosa's 600,000 acre spread was worked by no more than four hired hands). On the oil ranch, there isn't much to do, except spend more time with the family. Hence the great Western melodramas like *Written on the Wind*, *Hud*, *Giant*, and the long-running TV equivalent *Dallas*, each of which focused on internal family tensions, on crises of filial succession and inheritance, and on the moral dissolution and decadence of a leisure class—all of the problems, in short, of that specific North American type of late capitalism, the aristocratic family with a suburban imagination. But if oil wells had become a dishonorable replacement for ranching and the dissolute dynasty represented a falling off from the close-knit cattle clan, the West and the

Western were still ideological places for working out what exactly it is that a man "has to do."

This enduring legacy is quite evident in Levinson's *Tin Men*, a film that has fully absorbed the popular consciousness about the meaning of these Western narratives and oppositions. At the same time, it presents a clever reframing of the conflict between technological environments that helps to define masculine identity inside and outside the family. Punctuated with references to all of the generic phases of the Western, *Tin Men* dramatizes the end of an equally mythical period when North American men's relation to both their independent and familial identity was mediated across the lavishly styled surfaces of their new Cadillacs. The central action is provided by a prolonged conflict between two tin men: BB, a natty, maverick type, single and enterprising, and Tilley, a frustrated citizen type, married and unimaginative. This conflict involves several show-downs, involving destructive attacks on their respective cars, at, among other sites, a local race track and a bar called the Corral Club and against the backdrop of a Western shoot-out on a drive-in screen. Revenge, for the rogue male BB, takes the form of "stealing" Tilley's wife, Nora, but she ends up outlawing the cowboy in him with a series of speeches and actions that displays her protofeminism. Investigating evidence of their hustling, fraud, and misrepresentations as a aluminum-siding salesmen, a government Home Improvements Commission revokes both of their licenses. Tilley, the populist "small man" victim, who is everywhere harried by the IRS, views this as a McCarthy-style outrage, while BB, the shrewd sharpie, sees it as a symptom of "the future," otherwise depicted throughout the film by BB's close attention to the humble appearances on Baltimore streets of the Volkswagen Beetle. The closing scene ends with a reconciliation that leads the spectator to assume that the enemies might romantically team up and seek their fortune together in the new business of selling Volkswagen automobiles. Nat King Cole croons over the credits: "Now I've found my joy/I'm as happy as a baby boy/With another brand new choo-choo toy/When I met sweet Lorraine, Lorraine, Lorraine."

Like the classic Western, the film registers the end of a golden age of male autonomy: the Law has moved in to cramp the male style, and suddenly, the world, like its new automobiles, is a smaller and more restricted vehicle in which to maneuver. In the home improvements business, selling, in which each man had a style all of his own, had nonetheless been a story of hucksterism, of livelihoods dependent upon hoodwinking women about how to "beautify" the exterior of their homes. In the business of male bonding and male rivalry, it had been a story that posited the economy of the automobile, with its own "beautified" and feminized exterior, against the economy of the home and the family—an opposition in which a dented car, equated with a dented virility, could arbitrarily determine the fate of the family. The causes and symptoms of decline are manifest everywhere; the interventionist state is clamping down on the old, unregulated enterprise, the appearance of "economical" import cars on North American streets her-alds the end of the Golden Age of Detroit-style production and consumption, and women aren't going to stand by their men anymore. If, in the face of all of these threatening horizons, *Tin Men* is a "nostalgia" film, it is because it is typically Western—it says that white males, even if they have the right stuff, will never be able to get up to the same tricks again, while enjoying the technological legitimacy and confidence they shared along with Detroit's latest hurrah or the feudal allegiances they could once expect from their families. For these tin men, struggling to survive the coming shift in technological environments, both economic and sexual, the contours of their masculinity may have to be redesigned, for life on the Ponderosa will never be quite the same again.

Francis Ford Coppola's *Tucker* (1988) offers a more conscious narrative about U.S. economic decline through the vehicle of the automobile nostalgia genre. Here, the typical Coppola opposition between the utopian family community and the ruthlessly anonymous face of big business is economically posed as a contest over the technological definition of "the family car," that benign, iconic model of Fordist production in the immediate postwar period. A visionary techno-entrepreneur, Tucker plans and designs an authentic "family car" that will truly embody family values—a safe, caring, ethical car that looks the future confidently in the face, just as it respectfully pays tribute to the decor and furnishings of a less streamlined past. The production of this car becomes a family business in every sense, strongly identified in promotional events with Tucker's own happy family and based on a small, close-knit production team that militates against the big Fordist ethic of Detroit. In his inclusion (daring in the postwar years) of a Japanese-American engineer in the production team, Tucker unconsciously but symbolically gestures toward a future in which the struggle for technological innovation and supremacy, just recently waged against imperial Japan, will be lost.

Tucker's family enterprise falls victim to the corruptions of power generated by the Detroit manufacturers' influence in Washington, and Coppola's film embraces its small-guy Capraesque logic in full consciousness of the future decline of the auto industry. Complaining in the classical rhetoric of populist nostalgia that he has been a "generation too late," Tucker's courtroom speech appeals to what appear to be embryonic (but are, in fact, long-established) resentments about a technologically administered society: "Bureaucrats would squash Benjamin Franklin. . . . Let's not close out the small guy. One day, we'll be buying cars from our former enemies. That's what happens if the bureaucrats squash the innovators."

In contrast to the fantasmatic historical sense of Rockwellian films like *Back to the Future*, *Tucker*'s idealistic picture of the happy 1950s family is at least technologically grounded. By this I mean that it takes to the letter many of the mythical values and meanings now associated with the iconic "family car" of the 1950s and seriously attempts to ground them within a more or less credible world of representations. In the benign picture of the household economy associated with Tucker's car, Coppola offers a productionist version of the atomized family utopias of the new suburban landscapes that had been organized around consumerism in the 1950s. Like the covered wagon and the "iron horse," the automobile was linked to the creation of "pioneer" suburban communities, whose domestic technological environments were similarly organized around privatized mobility. But while Tucker's tight-knit household economy emphasizes the cohering effects of the automobile on family life, it ignores the dispersing effects. The intrusion of the car on family life just as often facilitated an escape from repressive family rituals and habits, while it provided an alternative domestic space for more adventurous teenage family romances; youth films from *Rebel Without a Cause* to *American Graffiti* celebrate this other, liberating side of automobile culture.

Similarly one-sided is the film's representation of the family not as a consumerist economy whose source of authority and power lies ultimately in the home, but rather in terms of a (male) productionist unit that takes over, and subsequently masquerades as, a gendered household economy. In the former, alternative version, the mother would have had to play much more of a leading role, if only in fostering and shaping the redeeming values of the family through its members. In fact, the culture of consumerism was organized around this very premise, just as the nineteenth-century cult of domesticity and its ideological blueprint, preached in the manuals of persuasion, for a Christian "family state" centered in the home, had earlier presented the female-dominated household economy as a utopian alternative to the world of trade, manufacturing, and government.[9] As a result of its conflation of these two economies, *Tucker* manages to resolve the contradictions between market individualism and domestic collectivity that are present in a conservative ideology of the family—an ideology where the *market ideal* of the self-supporting (male) individual must somehow be reduced to the *moral ideal* of a collective family unit, supported, of course, by a single male breadwinner.[10] Given the recent contribution of women to factory wartime production, Mrs. Tucker's intimate role in the "production" of the automobile, even if she figures mostly in a promotional context, tells yet another tale about the containing, or incorporative, power of familialist ideology in the film.

## Empire of the Son

One might still be surprised, however, by the extent to which Coppola commits himself so fanatically to a cohesive family ideology, even in the light of his long obsession with the family, from *The Godfather* to *Peggy Sue Got Married*. But Coppola's stories, and his obsessions, are as much an outcropping of the Hollywood imagination as they are an ideological critique of the Hollywood system. Coppola's own Hollywood reputation as an outlawed, visionary techno-entrepreneur is itself heavily overlaid with paternalistic features. In his dual role as technological pioneer and paternal protector of his film "people," he embodies the contradictions of familialism as seamlessly as his Tucker. So too, in the mythology of the new Hollywood genre cinema devoted to techno-worship, Coppola might take his place as father, godly or not, within the holy trinity completed by Stephen Spielberg and George Lucas. Within this canonically motherless family, Spielberg is cast in the filial role of the eternal *Wunderkind*, and Lucas is the Holy Ghost in the machine, the facilitator, the brother of invention.

The naive science-fiction genres favored by Spielberg and Lucas (children's films made for adults, or, as the marketing slogan goes, "for kids of all ages") have all but replaced the Western as the dominant Hollywood genre for speaking about the foundational myths of masculine and national identity. As modern narratives of empire, science-fiction films today increasingly borrow more conventions from the Western than from the horror genres that were their primary source in the 1950s. If they no longer speak to the history of an internally colonized settlement, their concern has been with external conquests in space, the "final frontier." On the other hand, they share the xenophobia and the euphoric nostalgia of the classic Western, providing, in the figure of the "alien" (as the *unfamiliar*, and thus outside the family), one of the most fully articulated image repertoires of racist and racially marked types in North American culture.

The figure of the alien is now so current in the Hollywood imaginary that the semantic distance it has maintained with respect to the typology of the "alien" generated by the U.S. Immigration Service has collapsed upon itself. For example, the 1988 film *Alien Nation*, directed by Graham Baker, is the story of the absorption of a stray alien population, genetically altered for slavery, into the U.S. labor force as a new underclass, working with methane and other poisonous substances to which the aliens are immune.[11] ACLU lawyers defend the newcomers' rights, but discrimination is rife, alien ghetto crime proliferates, and racist jokes abound. With all the promise of a bad cop-buddy movie, the film depicts the course of bonding between a white hard-ass bigot officer and the first alien to achieve the rank of detective in the Los Angeles Police Department (indeed, it is the alien who has an "Ozzie and Harriet" family and who helps to bring together the separated family of his new buddy). Presented explicitly as an allegory of immigration racism and primitive capitalist exploitation in Southern California, the film recycles too many familiar racist moves, however, to render it critical. The *Alien National Inquirer*, a promotional newspaper distributed at theaters where the film showed, reproduces uncomfortable racist mythologies in its advertising section: lazy aliens (the La-Z-Alien Recliner), the well endowed alien (Chippenaliens), alien hair obsessions, "exotic" foods (Chief Boyar Dee's Beaveroni), and so forth.

But for all its troubled intimacy with the discourses of racism, *Alien Nation* is symptomatic of a new wave of *domestic* alien pictures that overtly address questions of race and class, a tendency brilliantly heralded by John Sayles' *Brother from Another Planet* and figured, more indirectly, in Julian Temple's *Earth Girls Are Easy*, where a racially diverse trio of aliens are freely and easily submerged into the hedonistic subcultures of valley life in Southern California. This tendency, however, is far removed from the ideology of science-fiction promoted by the Spielberg-Lucas school, whose most domesticated alien has been E.T., a charmingly deformed infant-savant, and whose most xenophobic productions have been spectacular theological sagas about final conflicts and crusades against dark, totalitarian empires. Much has been written about the close association of *Star Wars'* Cold War mysticism with the global agenda of the North American New Right. The critique has been so accurate, in fact, that the popularity of the Lucas films has sufficiently blurred the line between imperial fiction and technological reality for it to have helped to legitimize the plans for SDI (Strategic Defense Initiative), a new permanent arms economy linked to the industrialization and militarization of the space frontier.

More problematic for critics of the Spielberg–Lucas school has been the phenomenon of the infantilization of the spectator. This is an effect inscribed within the films not only in terms of the Oedipal configurations worked out around the usually centralized family milieu, but also in relation to the wondrous gee-whizzery of magically clean technology. Robin Wood has described these films' appeal in terms both of a regression to childhood and of the narrative of the restoration of the father in Hollywood cinema.[12] Vivian Sobchak extends this analysis by pointing to the born-again father-as-child as a figure for resolving the crisis of patriarchy.[13] Historically speaking, in these parables about science-fiction technology, which regularly evoke as their frames of reference a 1950s TV boyhood, the narrative of "going back to the future" is a powerful conservative recuperation of the postlapsarian present. It is a familiar way of imaginatively predating the less-than-mythical breaks that divide us historically from the 1950s: post-Oedipal maturity, the real economic decline of U.S. supremacy, the erosion of the nuclear family, the loss of the political "innocence" of the postwar "youth culture," the breakup of the liberal middle-class consensus, the ignominy of U.S. interventionism, and so on.

In fact, the postimperial nostalgia espoused by Spielberg and Lucas has taken on a visibly generational form, comprising a narrative that can be told in the space of a single generation—specifically, their own generation—which spans the postwar period of the rise and fall of "American" empire. The generational framing of this narrative is not yet explicitly moral; it has not become a conventional feature of the filmic narrative itself, as it is in, say, the most nostalgic of classic Westerns.[14] Lacking the historical distance provided by the Western, Spielberg–Lucas nostalgia has been interpreted as a much more personalized and Oedipalized investment on the part of the directors themselves, especially in the case of Spielberg, whose valorization of the infantile presexual male and the restored nuclear family, with or without a *real* father, has been an invariable feature of his films.

When Spielberg does address real historical conditions and events, it is symptomatically in the context of two films, *1941* and *Empire of the Sun*, that relate to Japanese imperial power and the U.S.–Japanese military struggle for aerial supremacy. *1941* is a forgettable slapstick farce set in a hysterical California weeks after Pearl Harbor, during the violently racist "zoot suit riots," in which U.S. servicemen attacked Mexican-Americans wearing fashions pioneered by black jazz musicians. The sexual angle of the farce is developed through a female character who is turned on by airplane technology; she "has a serious interest in strategic bombers." This identification with phallic, aerial firepower was to find its vintage Spielbergian formulation in *Empire of the Sun*.

*Empire of the Sun* (1987) transforms J. G. Ballard's bleak memoir of a neocolonial childhood in Shanghai into an astonishing story about a boy's education in what Walter Benjamin saw as the specifically fascist aestheticization of technology and power. Jamie Graham, the precocious and resourceful boy-hero of the film, is growing up in an idealized British bourgeois family setting in a Shanghai that is threatened by the imperial Japanese invasion. Having abandoned the God of Anglicanism and lacking any sense of patriotic affiliation, his sympathies in the coming conflict are becoming quite clear; at the age of ten, he is "thinking of joining the Japanese air force" because they have the better pilots and the superior technology that his comic books valorize. Separated from his parents in the confusion of the invasion, his male survivalist education in the hard school of wartime labor camps is governed by a series of affiliatory maneuvers and deals that he negotiates with representatives of different nationalities in the labor camp. He has little patience for the old paternalistic British code of decency, fair play, and humanistic respect for elders and finds the tough camaraderie and competitive individualism of the U.S. community more attractive and exciting; he becomes an honorary North American, with an Americanized name, Jim, a flying jacket, baseball cap, and entrepreneurial manner to accompany these acquisitions. His ultimate respect, however, is reserved for the "honorable" militaristic codes of the Japanese pilots whose airfield abuts the labor camp.

Between his schooling in unprincipled North American male pragmatism and his training in the deferential master–slave code demanded by the Japanese camp commander, his education as a protofascist youth looks to be almost complete. During a bombing raid on the airfield, in which the smell of cordite overexcites his imagination and his body, he is struck by the thought that he cannot remember what his parents look like. The rest of the film looks toward the final restoration of the family. The Americans betray him, and the Japanese are humiliated in war. But there is no real satisfaction for him in the reunion with his parents at the close of the film. Instead, gratification is provided by a rejuvenation of his faith in aerial military technology, this time as a result of his mystical, proto-orgasmic encounter with the moment of origin of a new empire of the sun, the artificial sun of the atom bomb's white light on the horizon. In Ballard's autobiography, this is a gloomy if not nihilistic scenario. In Spielberg's version it is an altar scene of awe and techno-worship; for Jim, the explosion is "like God taking a photograph."

If only because of its explicit historical setting, *Empire of the Sun* is the most politically clearcut of Spielberg's allegories of born-again boyhood. Structurally, the hero is faced with a difficult choice among a number of imperialist lifestyles: the bankrupt British code of being a "decent chap," the busy commercial Darwinism of North American "pragmatism," or the rigorously demanding ideology of Japanese "honor." His Oedipal choice à la Spielberg proves to be a disinterested, disembodied one, a mystical identification with the new atomic technology that is posed as beyond sexuality, race, class, and nationality, after which choice his parents can then reappear as the *familia ex machina*. The "West," then, with its outdated codes of masculine ethics, is no longer the natural site of the Spielbergian *Bildungsroman*. It is an "empire of the son" in aerospace that Jim chooses, an empire of promise that has yet to commit atrocities and fail expectations and that is offered its own originary code of manifest destiny by the appearance of the atomic omen in the sky.

## (Not) Lost in Space

The technological miracle in the skies that so inspires Spielberg's Jim is the barbaric origin, not just of the Cold War and the United States' permanent arms economy, but also of what Dale Carter has called the Rocket State, which is imaginatively aimed at realizing a technological environment for the colonization of space.[15] The backdrop to all postwar science fiction, from the germophobic, anti-Communist films of the Cold War to the clean, wonderworld technology of *Star Wars*, was the development of an aerospace industry to meet the national challenge of world supremacy. The aerospace imaginary fostered its own folk heroes in astronauts with a national iconic function, even though they were eventually exposed as "tin men," with little opportunity, within the strict operational environment of the space program, to prove that they had the "right stuff" of frontiersmanship.

In the development of the Rocket State, partial erosion of the sexual division of labor has given rise to the need for representations of women in iconic, pioneering roles hitherto exclusively reserved for men, and it is through these roles that the near future of postmodern familialism is being introduced. Consequently, the *Challenger* disaster that involved Christa McAuliffe in 1986 was a difficult event for liberal narratives about equal opportunity to absorb and contain. The McAuliffe mission was planned in every respect as an "ultimate field trip" and also as a gender-blind history lesson in national identity for students. McAuliffe herself had underscored the continuity of colonialist history when she compared her mission to that of the pioneering women of the Old West who had traveled across the Plains in Conestoga wagons, keeping personal journals of their experiences and writing letters back East.[16] So too, the multi-ethnic family that made up the *Challenger* crew—a black, a Jew, and an Asian-American from Hawaii, in addition to two women— was a *Star Trek* melting pot community, boasting a range of cultural diversity that would be conspicuously absent from the all-white, male makeup of the next shuttle crew.[17]

Beyond its many resonances with Western and science-fiction genres, the Christa McAuliffe story could also be told as the story of what happens when Mother leaves the family to go out and work. (Her job, in this case, was not a skilled job; much of her training "consisted of stern admonitions to 'never touch those switches.'"[18]) In this respect, the McAuliffe story was shot through with symptoms of the new national anxiety about mothers in the workforce. Forget the pioneering women in the covered wagons. Self-supporting individualism of the sort valorized by a conservative ideology of the family depends today upon easy access to day care, and this is not the stuff of which pioneering legends are easily made. No more helpful toward a successful representation of the space family was the overplanned control technology of the space program, notoriously responsible for casting its astronauts as helplessly passive, even as victims, rather than sovereign rulers of their interplanetary fates.

The tragic failure of the McAuliffe mission, then, inadvertently called attention to the difficulties involved in presenting "pioneer" women in ways that appeal to equal opportunity and to sexual difference alike. Time-honored codes that had served to resolve the contradictions, rooted in the Western genre, between male individualism and familialism could not perform the same effortless role for women in a similar position. Between femininity and familialism lay the technologies of reproduction; there was no clean technological break or separation of public and private environments. Nowhere was this difference more fully addressed than in science-fiction film, from the naive narratives about body-invading mutant offspring of science-out-of-control experiments to the more lovable aliens of recent control technology environments. If, as Vivian Sobchak has argued, the pressure of conservative patriarchalism à la Spielberg and Lucas has produced a number of successful if unstable narratives in the born-again-father mold, a similar story might be told within Hollywood film about attempts to rewrite the relation of women to the new reproductive technologies. For it is in the new technological environments of human reproduction, more germane to femininity than to masculinity, that the contest over definitions of familialism is currently being waged. Consider, then, the case of Ripley, the most famous heroine of modern science fiction, whose adventures in *Alien* and *Aliens*, respectively, tell a disturbing story about a woman who is professionally trained in the use of aerospace technology but who is consequently an amateur or "natural" when faced with a crisis involving reproductive technology.

When it appeared in 1979, *Alien* was almost immediately recognized as a film that stretched the limits of modern science-fiction and naive horror genres in order to comment explicitly on *commercial* and *patriarchal* attempts to colonize female control over reproduction. The film starts out by presenting a gender-coded dialogue between the technological environment of the Nostromo and that of the alien spaceship.[19] Because it is a dystopian film, the surfaces are not friendly and appealing: the grungy, hardware-confining spaces of the Nostromo prove to be unsafe and claustrophobic, while the fossilized, biomechanoid design of the Alien's terrain, gestating even as it wears the look of death, is replete with female reproductive imagery, which the film, in line with classical science-fiction codes, presents as threatening. In using a human male body as an incubator for part of its life cycle, the alien environment manages to reproduce itself with all of the iconographic trappings of a destructive rapist. This dystopian picture of reproductive technologies is set within a sharp critique of the capitalist logic that is sending pioneer families and mining crews out into space to colonize mineral resources and whose android agent and computer are programmed to decide that human lives are expendable in the Company's pursuit of new organic technologies for its bioweapons division.

In *Alien*, Ripley is the only character who is able to survive the Alien's rampage. She survives not because she is a true professional, responsibly in control of the technologies of control, and not because, in the confrontation scene, she evokes "feminine intuition" by wishing on a "lucky star." She survives because she alone is in a position to recognize the logic of the film's narrative about reproductive technology; she is in a position to greet the Alien as a "son of a bitch," just moments after she has named the Company's computer "Mother, you Bitch" for failing to deactivate the self-destruct program. She alone can see that the Alien's blend of autogenetic self-sufficiency and aggressive individualism—"a perfect organism, whose structural perfection is matched only by its hostility" in the admiring words of Ash, the Company's android—is perfectly complicit with the patriarchal logic of the Company that allows the Alien free destructive rein over her companions' bodies. From her point of view, the Alien technoculture can be seen as the full embodiment of the dream of womanless reproduction, since its autogenesis is dependent upon the colonization of other *male* bodies—the only bodies that the film wants us to see being used in this way.

In *Aliens*, the militaristic, nationalistic sequel, Ripley's position and her lucidly critical point of view are realigned and rewritten to meet the demands of more conservative narratives of gender and race. The Aliens' colonization of other bodies is more indiscriminate than in the original film, and indeed we actually *see* female bodies being colonized. So too, *Alien*'s precise critique of the Company's capitalist logic has dissipated; exploitation is personified in the individual figure of the Company agent, Burke, the bad guy who acts independently of his employers. As a result, when Ripley criticizes the motives behind the Company's appropriation of alien technologies, she can only blame the human species as a whole; she says, "at least the aliens don't fuck each other over for a percentage."

In contrast to her role in *Alien*, Ripley's role in the sequel is not only clearly gender-coded as female, but is also marked from the very beginning of the film as maternal. The opening scenes establish Jonesy the cat as her surrogate child, and her nightmare birthing dreams indicate unresolved maternal anxieties and desires. We are also offered the spectacle of our heroine going weak at the knees at the thought of the endangered colonist families on the terraformed planet. *Alien*'s clear critique of corporate logic is bypassed by the way in which the sequel takes up the question of motherhood, surrogate or otherwise, in order to establish a mythical showdown, *High Noon*–style, between good and bad mothers. In the final analysis, personalizing the queen Alien as a "bitch," as Ripley does in the confrontation scene, is arguably less of a critical perception than a recognition (as in the original film when she reserves the term *bitch* for Mother, the name of the company computer) of the common logic of aggressive colonization shared by the Company and the Alien offspring. In effect, the "natural" vengeance of the grieving Alien mother comes to displace the logic of genocide, colonization, and the dream of womanless reproduction as motives for aggression. If Ripley ends up with a strange kind of one-parent family to look after—the adopted, feral child, Newt, and two castrated men, Bishop, the decapitated android, and Hicks, the wounded lieutenant—it is nonetheless the best that the film can offer in the way of solutions to the crisis of the family.

As part of the final, Western showdown between the good and bad mother, *destructive* "human" technology in the shape of Ripley's appropriation of the marines' arsenal of firepower is seen as justified in the fight against *reproductive* "alien" technology. The film's move to make Ripley into a female Rambo, bristling with state-of-the-art weaponry while recklessly but heroically protecting her adopted child, can and has been read as one way of taking technology into one's own hands, an unavoidable move if we are to have strong female heroines looking after their own. But what may prove, I think, to be more important about the film's dominant image of Ripley—guns, flamethrowers and cannons blazing—is not that she is a woman or a (step)mother, but rather that she is a *North American*, and a white North American at that. Nor does it really matter what she is firing at, anymore than it matters whom Stallone, Schwarzenegger, Bronson, or Eastwood are firing at. What she does when she strikes this pose is to take on a recognizably national identity, marked by the gesture of *shooting from the hip*, the properly casual North American style of blowing away an adversary.

For whom, finally, is Ripley pulling the trigger of her Peacemaker? Not for some universal good mother, not for the protection of her otherwise defenseless adopted family, but for a particular audience, constructed within the national imaginary as defined by the history of Hollywood genre film, especially the Western, and as responsive as ever to a trigger-happy technological environment. The iconography of this pose is quite culture-specific; it belongs to a rhetoric of violence spoken, in film theaters around the world, in a North American accent and acted out with the deathless swagger of empire. The story of the assimilation of Ripley into this Western–masculinist posture is thus a remarkable example of the conservative power of generic narratives to tailor the representation of technological environments to fit a body that is as much untroubled by sexual difference as it is secure in its assumption of a national identity founded on the genocide of aliens. In fact, Ripley's story shows some of the moves by which women can be, and increasingly will be, presented as accomplices, unwilling or not, in the particular national tradition of "engendering men" that I have been describing here.

## Reading Questions

1. What does Ross mean by the "ideology of familialism" in his section "Ponderosa Lost"?
2. What sorts of masculine ambivalences does Ross claim are illustrated by TV westerns?
3. How, according to Ross, does the demise of the oil-dependent automobile industry featured in Coppola's *Tucker* show the contradictions between market individualism and domestic collectivity?
4. How, according to Ross, did the U.S. oil crisis remythologize masculine and national identity?
5. What kind of relationship holds between the popularity of science fiction films and the legitimation of the U.S. Strategic Defense Initiative?
6. What does Ross mean by his claim that the militaristic, nationalistic, and imperialistic narratives of contemporary science fiction films "engender" men?

## Recommended Reading

Paul Buhle, ed., *Popular Culture in America* (Minneapolis: University of Minnesota Press, 1987)

Stuart Ewen and Elizabeth Ewen, *Channels of Desire: Mass Images and the Shaping of American Culture* (Minneapolis: University of Minnesota Press, 1992)

E. Gellner, *Nations and Nationalism* (Oxford: Basil Blackwell, 1983)

J. M. Mackenzie, *Imperialism and Popular Culture* (Manchester: Manchester University Press, 1986)

Elayne Rapping, *The Movie of the Week: Private Stories, Public Events* (Minneapolis: University of Minnesota Press, 1993)

Andrew Ross, *No Respect: Intellectuals and Popular Culture* (New York: Routledge, 1989)

## Recommended Audiovisual Resources

Any of the films mentioned in Ross's essay. Nearly all of them are available at any well-stocked video store.

# "Material Girl"

## The Effacements of Postmodern Culture

### SUSAN BORDO

Susan Bordo is the Ashland Chair at the University of Kentucky, Lexington. She is the author of *The Flight to Objectivity* and *Unbearable Weight: Feminism, Western Culture, and the Body*.

## Plasticity as Postmodern Paradigm

In a culture in which organ transplants, life-extension machinery, microsurgery, and artificial organs have entered everyday medicine, we seem on the verge of practical realization of the seventeenth-century imagination of body as machine. But if we have technically and technologically realized that conception, it can also be argued that metaphysically we have deconstructed it. In the early modern era, machine imagery helped to articulate a totally determined human body whose basic functionings the human being was helpless to alter. The then-dominant metaphors for this body—clocks, watches, collections of springs—imagined a system that is set, wound up, whether by nature or by God the watchmaker, ticking away in predictable, orderly manner, regulated by laws over which the human being has no control. Understanding the system, we can help it to perform efficiently, and we can intervene when it malfunctions. But we cannot radically alter its configuration.

Pursuing this modern, determinist fantasy to its limits, fed by the currents of consumer capitalism, modern ideologies of the self, and their crystallization in the dominance of United States mass culture, Western science and technology have now arrived, paradoxically but predictably (for it was an element, though submerged and illicit, in the mechanist conception all along), at a new, postmodern imagination of human freedom from bodily determination. Gradually and surely, a technology that was first aimed at the replacement of malfunctioning parts has generated an industry and an ideology fueled by fantasies of rearranging, transforming, and correcting, an ideology of limitless improvement and change, defying the historicity, the mortality, and, indeed, the very materiality of the body. In place of that materiality, we now have what I will call cultural plastic. In place of God the watchmaker, we now have ourselves, the master sculptors of that plastic. This disdain for material limits and the concomitant intoxication with freedom, change, and self-determination are enacted not only on the level of the contemporary technology of the body but in a wide range of contexts, including much of contemporary discourse on the body, both popular and academic. In this essay, looking at a variety of these discursive contexts, I attempt to describe key elements of this paradigm of plasticity and expose some of its effacements—the material and social realities it denies or renders invisible.

# Plastic Bodies

"Create a masterpiece, sculpt your body into a work of art," urges *Fit* magazine. "You visualize what you want to look like, and then you create that form." "The challenge presents itself: to rearrange things."[1] The precision technology of body-sculpting, once the secret of the Arnold Schwarzeneggers and Rachel McLishes of the professional body-building world, has now become available to anyone who can afford the price of membership in a gym. "I now look at bodies," says John Travolta, after training for the movie *Staying Alive*, "almost like pieces of clay that can be molded."[2] On the medical front, plastic surgery, whose repeated and purely cosmetic employment has been legitimated by Michael Jackson, Cher, and others, has become a fabulously expanding industry, extending its domain from nose jobs, face lifts, tummy tucks, and breast augmentations to collagen-plumped lips and liposuction-shaped ankles, calves, and buttocks. In 1989, 681,000 procedures were done, up 80 percent over 1981; over half of these were performed on patients between the ages of eighteen and thirty-five.[3] The trendy *Details* magazine describes "surgical stretching, tucking and sucking" as "another fabulous [fashion] accessory" and invites readers to share their cosmetic-surgery experiences in their monthly column "Knife-styles of the Rich and Famous." In that column, the transportation of fat from one part of the body to another is described as breezily as changing hats might be:

> Dr. Brown is an artist. He doesn't just pull and tuck and forget about you. . . . He did liposuction on my neck, did the nose job and tightened up my forehead to give it a better line. Then he took some fat from the side of my waist and injected it into my hands. It goes in as a lump, and then he smooths it out with his hands to where it looks good. I'll tell you something, the nose and neck made a big change, but nothing in comparison to how fabulous my hands look. The fat just smoothed out all the lines, the veins don't stick up anymore, the skin actually looks soft and great. [But] you have to be careful not to bang your hands.[4]

Popular culture does not apply any brakes to these fantasies of rearrangement and self-transformation. Rather, we are constantly told that we can "choose" our own bodies. "The proper diet, the right amount of exercise and you can have, pretty much, any body you desire," claims Evian. Of course, the rhetoric of choice and self-determination and the breezy analogies comparing cosmetic surgery to fashion accessorizing are deeply mystifying. They efface, not only the inequalities of privilege, money, and time that prohibit most people from indulging in these practices, but the desperation that characterizes the lives of those who do. "I will do anything, *anything*, to make myself look and feel better," says Tina Lizardi (whose "Knife-styles" experience I quoted from above). Medical science has now designated a new category of "polysurgical addicts" (or, in more casual references, "scalpel slaves") who return for operation after operation, in perpetual quest of the elusive yet ruthlessly normalizing goal, the "perfect" body.[5] The dark underside of the practices of body transformation and rearrangement reveals botched and sometimes fatal operations, exercise addictions, eating disorders. And of course, despite the claims of the Evian ad, one cannot have *any* body that one wants—for not every body will *do*. The very advertisements whose copy speaks of choice and self-determination visually legislate the effacement of individual and cultural difference and circumscribe our choices.

That we are surrounded by homogenizing and normalizing images—images whose content is far from arbitrary, but is instead suffused with the dominance of gendered, racial, class, and other cultural iconography—seems so obvious as to be almost embarrassing to be arguing here. Yet contemporary understandings of the behaviors I have been describing not only construct the situation very differently but do so in terms that preempt precisely such a critique of cultural imagery. Moreover, they reproduce, on the level of discourse and interpretation, the same conditions that postmodern bodies enact on the level of cultural practice: a construction of life as plastic possibility and weightless choice, undetermined by history, social location, or even individual biography. A 1988 *Donahue* show offers my first illustration.

The show's focus was a series of television commercials for DuraSoft colored contact lenses. In these commercials as they were originally aired, a woman was shown in a dreamlike, romantic fantasy—for example, parachuting slowly and gracefully from the heavens. The male voiceover then described the woman in soft, lush terms: "If I believed in angels, I'd say that's what she was—an angel, dropped from the sky like an answer to a prayer, with eyes as brown as bark." [Significant pause] "No . . . I *don't think so*." [At this point, the tape would be rewound to return us to:] "With eyes as violet as the colors of a child's imagination." The commercial concludes: "DuraSoft colored contact lenses. Get brown eyes a second look."

The question posed by Phil Donahue: Is this ad racist? Donahue clearly thought there was controversy to be stirred up here, for he stocked his audience full of women of color and white women to discuss the implications of the ad. But Donahue was apparently living in a different decade from most of his audience, who repeatedly declared that there was nothing "wrong" with the ad, and everything "wrong" with any inclinations to "make it a political question." Here are some comments taken from the transcript of the show:

> "Why does it have to be a political question? I mean, people perm their hair. It's just because they like the way it looks. It's not something sociological. Maybe black women like the way they look with green contacts. It's to be more attractive. It's not something that makes them—I mean, why do punk rockers have purple hair? Because they feel it makes them feel better." [white woman]
> "What's the fuss? When I put on my blue lenses, it makes me feel good. It makes me feel sexy, different, the other woman, so to speak, which is like fun." [black woman]
> "I perm my hair, you're wearing make-up, what's the difference?" [white woman]
> "I want to be versatile . . . having different looks, being able to change from one look to the other." [black female model]
> "We all do the same thing, when we're feeling good we wear new makeup, hairstyles, we buy new clothes. So now it's contact lenses. What difference does it make?" [white woman]
> "It goes both ways . . . Bo Derek puts her hair in cornstalks, or corn . . . or whatever that thing is called. White women try to get tan." [white woman]
> "She's not trying to be white, she's trying to be different." [about a black woman with blue contact lenses]
> "It's fashion, women are never happy with themselves."
> "I put them in as toys, just for fun, change. Nothing too serious, and I really enjoy them." [black woman][6]

Some points to note here: first, putting on makeup, styling hair, and so forth are conceived of only as free *play*, fun, a matter of creative expression. This they surely are.

But they are also experienced by many women as necessary before they will show themselves to the world, even on a quick trip to the corner mailbox. The one comment that hints at women's (by now depressingly well documented) dissatisfaction with their appearance trivializes that dissatisfaction and puts it beyond the pale of cultural critique: "It's fashion." What she means is, "It's *only* fashion," whose whimsical and politically neutral vicissitudes supply endless amusement for women's eternally superficial values. ("Women are never happy with themselves.") If we are never happy with ourselves, it is implied, that is due to our female nature, not to be taken too seriously or made into a political question. Second, the content of fashion, the specific ideals that women are drawn to embody (ideals that vary historically, racially, and along class and other lines) are seen as arbitrary, without meaning; interpretation is neither required nor even appropriate. Rather, all motivation and value come from the interest and allure — the "sexiness" — of change and difference itself. Blue contact lenses for a black woman, it is admitted, make her "other" ("the other woman"). But that "other" is not a racial or cultural "other"; she is sexy because of the piquancy, the novelty, the erotics of putting on a different self. *Any* different self would do, it is implied.

Closely connected to this is the construction of *all* cosmetic changes as the same: perms for the white women, corn rows on Bo Derek, tanning, makeup, changing hairstyles, blue contacts for black women — all are seen as having equal political valence (which is to say, *no* political valence) and the same cultural meaning (which is to say, *no* cultural meaning) in the heterogeneous yet undifferentiated context of the things "all" women do "to be more attractive." The one woman in the audience who offered a different construction of this behavior, who insisted that the styles we aspire to do not simply reflect the free play of fashion or female nature — who went so far, indeed, as to claim that we "are brainwashed to think blond hair and blue eyes is the most beautiful of all," was regarded with hostile silence. Then, a few moments later, someone challenged: "Is there anything *wrong* with blue eyes and blond hair?" The audience enthusiastically applauded this defender of democratic values.

This "conversation" — a paradigmatically postmodern conversation, as I will argue shortly — effaces the same general elements as the rhetoric of body transformation discussed earlier. First, it effaces the inequalities of social position and the historical origins which, for example, render Bo Derek's corn rows and black women's hair-straightening utterly noncommensurate. On the one hand, we have Bo Derek's privilege, not only as so unimpeachably white as to permit an exotic touch of "otherness" with no danger of racial contamination, but her trend-setting position as a famous movie star. Contrasting to this, and mediating a black woman's "choice" to straighten her hair, is a cultural history of racist body-discriminations such as the nineteenth-century comb-test, which allowed admission to churches and clubs only to those blacks who could pass through their hair without snagging a fine-tooth comb hanging outside the door. (A variety of comparable tests — the pine-slab test, the brown bag test — determined whether one's skin was adequately light to pass muster.)[7]

Second, and following from these historical practices, there is a disciplinary reality that is effaced in the construction of all self-transformation as equally arbitrary, all variants of the same trivial game, without differing cultural valence. I use the term *disciplinary* here in the Foucauldian sense, as pointing to practices that do not merely transform but *normalize* the subject. That is, to repeat a point made earlier, not every body will do. A 1989 poll of *Essence* magazine readers revealed that 68 percent of those who responded wear their hair straightened chemically or by hot comb.[8] "Just for fun"? For the kick of being "different"? When we look at the pursuit of beauty as a normalizing discipline, it becomes clear that not all body transformations are the same. The general tyranny of fashion—perpetual, elusive, and instructing the female body in a pedagogy of personal inadequacy and lack—is a powerful discipline for the normalization of *all* women in this culture. But even as we are all normalized to the requirements of appropriate feminine insecurity and preoccupation with appearance, more specific requirements emerge in different cultural and historical contexts, and for different groups. When Bo Derek put her hair in corn rows, she was engaging in normalizing feminine practice. But when Oprah Winfrey admitted on her show that all her life she has desperately longed to have "hair that swings from side to side" when she shakes her head, she revealed the power of racial as well as gender normalization, normalization not only to "femininity," but to the Caucasian standards of beauty that still dominate on television, in movies, in popular magazines. (When I was a child, I felt the same way about my thick, then curly, "Jewish" hair as Oprah did about hers.) Neither Oprah nor the *Essence* readers nor the many Jewish women (myself included) who ironed their hair in the 1960s have creatively or playfully invented themselves here.

DuraSoft knows this, even if Donahue's audience does not. Since the campaign first began, the company has replaced the original, upfront magazine advertisement with a more euphemistic variant, from which the word *brown* has been tastefully effaced. (In case it has become too subtle for the average reader, the model now is black—although it should be noted that DuraSoft's failure to appreciate brown eyes also renders the eyes of most of the world not worth "a second look.") In the television commercial, a comparable "brownwash" was effected; here "eyes as brown as . . ." was retained, but the derogatory nouns—"brown as boots," "brown as bark"—were eliminated. The announcer simply was left speechless: "eyes as brown as . . . brown as . . .," and then, presumably having been unable to come up with an enticing simile, shifted to "violet." As in the expurgated magazine ad, the television commercial ended: "Get *your* eyes a second look."

When I showed my students these ads, many of them were as dismissive as the *Donahue* audience, convinced that I was once again turning innocent images and practices into political issues. I persisted: if racial standards of beauty are not at work here, then why no brown contacts for blue-eyed people? A month later, two of my students triumphantly produced a DuraSoft ad for brown contacts, appearing in *Essence* magazine, and with an advertising campaign directed solely at *already* brown-eyed consumers, offering the promise *not* of "getting blue eyes a second look" by becoming excitingly darker, but of "subtly enhancing" dark eyes, by making them *lighter* brown. The creators of the DuraSoft campaign clearly know that not all differences are the same in our culture, and they continue, albeit in ever more mystified form, to exploit and perpetuate that fact.[9]

## Plastic Discourse

The *Donahue* DuraSoft show (indeed, any talk show) provides a perfect example of what we might call a postmodern conversation. All sense of history and all ability (or inclination) to sustain cultural criticism, to make the distinctions and discriminations that would permit such criticism, have disappeared. Rather, in this conversation, "anything goes"—

and any positioned social critique (for example, the woman who, speaking clearly from consciousness of racial oppression, insisted that the attraction of blond hair and blue eyes has a cultural meaning significantly different from that of purple hair) is immediately destabilized. Instead of distinctions, endless *differences* reign—an undifferentiated pastiche of differences, a grab bag in which no items are assigned any more importance or centrality than any others. Television is, of course, the great teacher here, our prime modeler of plastic pluralism: if one *Donahue* show features a feminist talking about battered wives, the next show will feature mistreated husbands. Women who love too much, the sex habits of priests, disturbed children of psychiatrists, daughters who have no manners, male strippers, relatives who haven't spoken in ten years all have their day alongside incest, rape, and U.S. foreign policy. All are given equal weight by the great leveler—the frame of the television screen.

This spectacle of difference defeats the ability to sustain coherent political critique. Everything is the same in its unvalenced difference. ("I perm my hair, you're wearing makeup, what's the difference?") Particulars reign, and generality—which collects, organizes, and prioritizes, suspending attention to particularity in the interests of connection, emphasis, and criticism—is suspect. So, whenever some critically charged generalization was suggested on Donahue's DuraSoft show, someone else would invariably offer a counterexample—I have blue eyes, and I'm a black woman; Bo Derek wears corn rows—to fragment the critique. What is remarkable is that people accept these examples as *refutations* of social critique. They almost invariably back down, utterly confused as to how to maintain their critical generalization in the face of the destabilizing example. Sometimes they qualify, claiming they meant some people, not all. But of course they meant neither all nor some. They meant *most*—that is, they were trying to make a claim about social or cultural *patterns*—and that is a stance that is increasingly difficult to sustain in a postmodern context, where we are surrounded by endlessly displaced images and are given no orienting context in which to make discriminations.

Those who insist on an orienting context (and who therefore do not permit particulars to reign in all their absolute "difference") are seen as "totalizing," that is, as constructing a falsely coherent and morally coercive universe that marginalizes and effaces the experiences and values of others. ("Is there anything *wrong* with blue eyes and blond hair?") As someone who is frequently interviewed by local television and newspaper reporters, I have often found my feminist arguments framed in this way, as they were in an article on breast-augmentation surgery. After several pages of "expert" recommendations from plastic surgeons, my cautions about the politics of female body transformation (none of them critical of individuals contemplating plastic surgery, all of them of a cultural nature) were briefly quoted by the reporter, who then went on to end the piece with a comment on *my* critique—from the director of communications for the American Society of Plastic and Reconstructive Surgery:

> Those not considering plastic surgery shouldn't be too critical of those who do. It's the hardest thing for people to understand. What's important is if it's a problem to that person. We're all different, but we all want to look better. We're just different in what extent we'll go to. But none of us can say we don't want to look the best we can.[10]

With this tolerant, egalitarian stroke, the media liaison of the most powerful plastic surgery lobby in the country presents herself as the protector of "difference" against the homogenizing and stifling regime of the feminist dictator.

Academics do not usually like to think of themselves as embodying the values and preoccupations of popular culture on the plane of high theory or intellectual discourse. We prefer to see ourselves as the demystifyers of popular discourse, bringers-to-conscious-ness-and-clarity rather than unconscious reproducers of culture. Despite what we would *like* to believe of ourselves, however, we are always within the society that we criticize, and never so strikingly as at the present postmodern moment. All the elements of what I have here called postmodern conversation—intoxication with individual choice and creative *jouissance*, delight with the piquancy of particularity and mistrust of pattern and seeming coherence, celebration of "difference" along with an absence of critical perspective differentiating and weighing "differences," suspicion of the totalitarian nature of generalization along with a rush to protect difference from its homogenizing abuses— have become recognizable and familiar in much of contemporary intellectual discourse. Within this theoretically self-conscious universe, moreover, these elements are not merely embodied (as in the *Donahue* show's DuraSoft conversation) but explicitly the-matized and *celebrated*, as inaugurating new constructions of the self, no longer caught in the mythology of the unified subject, embracing of multiplicity, challenging the dreary and moralizing generalizations about gender, race, and so forth that have so preoccupied liberal and left humanism.

For this celebratory, academic postmodernism, it has become highly unfashionable— and "totalizing"—to talk about the grip of culture on the body. Such a perspective, it is argued, casts active and creative subjects as passive dupes of ideology; it gives too much to dominant ideology, imagining it as seamless and univocal, overlooking both the gaps which are continually allowing for the eruption of "difference" and the poly-semous, unstable, open nature of all cultural texts. To talk about the grip of culture on the body (as, for example, in "old" feminist discourse about the objectification and sexualization of the female body) is to fail to acknowledge, as one theorist put it, "the cultural work by which nomadic, fragmented, active subjects confound dominant dis-course."[11]

So, for example, contemporary culture critic John Fiske is harshly critical of what he describes as the view of television as a "dominating monster" with "homogenizing power" over the perceptions of viewers. Such a view, he argues, imagines the audience as "powerless and undiscriminating" and overlooks the fact that:

> Pleasure results from a particular relationship between meanings and power. . . . There is no pleasure in being a "cultural dope." . . . Pleasure results from the production of meanings of the world and of self that are felt to serve the interests of the reader rather than those of the dominant. The subordinate may be disempowered, but they are not powerless. There is a power in resisting power, there is a power in maintaining one's social identity in opposition to that proposed by the dominant ideology, there is a power in asserting one's own subcultural values against the dominant ones. There is, in short, a power in being different.[12]

Fiske then goes on to produce numerous examples of how *Dallas*, *Hart to Hart*, and so forth have been read (or so he argues) by various subcultures to make their own "socially pertinent" and empowering meanings out of "the semiotic resources provided by tele-vision."

Note, in Fiske's insistent, repetitive invocation of the category of power, a characteristically postmodern flattening of the terrain of power relations, a lack of differentiation between, for example, the power involved in creative *reading* in the isolation of one's own home and the power held by those who control the material production of television shows, or the power involved in public protest and action against the conditions of that production and the power of the dominant meanings—for instance, racist and sexist images and messages—therein produced. For Fiske, of course, there *are* no such dominant meanings, that is, no element whose ability to grip the imagination of the viewer is greater than the viewer's ability to "just say no" through resistant reading of the text. That ethnic and subcultural meaning *may* be wrested from *Dallas* and *Hart to Hart* becomes for Fiske proof that dominating images and messages are only in the minds of those totalitarian critics who would condescendingly "rescue" the disempowered from those forces that are in fact the very medium of their creative freedom and resistance ("the semiotic resources of television").

Fiske's conception of power—a terrain without hills and valleys, where all forces have become "resources"—reflects a very common postmodern misappropriation of Foucault. Fiske conceives of power as in the *possession* of individuals or groups, something they "have"—a conception Foucault takes great pains to criticize—rather than (as in Foucault's reconstruction) a dynamic of noncentralized forces, its dominant historical forms attaining their hegemony, not from magisterial design or decree, but through multiple "processes, of different origin and scattered location," regulating and normalizing the most intimate and minute elements of the construction of time, space, desire, embodiment.[13] This conception of power does *not* entail that there are no dominant positions, social structures, or ideologies emerging from the play of forces; the fact that power is not held by any *one* does not mean that it is equally held by *all*. It is in fact not "held" at all; rather, people and groups are positioned differentially within it. This model is particularly useful for the analysis of male dominance and female subordination, so much of which is reproduced "voluntarily," through our self-normalization to everyday habits of masculinity and femininity. Within such a model, one can acknowledge that women may indeed contribute to the perpetuation of female subordination (for example, by embracing, taking pleasure in, and even feeling empowered by the cultural objectification and sexualization of the female body) without this entailing that they have power in the production and reproduction of sexist culture.

Foucault does insist on the *instability* of modern power relations—that is, he emphasizes that resistance is perpetual and unpredictable, and hegemony precarious. This notion is transformed by Fiske (perhaps under the influence of a more deconstructionist brand of postmodernism) into a notion of resistance as *jouissance*, a creative and pleasurable eruption of cultural "difference" through the "seams" of the text. What this celebration of creative reading as resistance effaces is the arduous and frequently frustrated historical struggle that is required for the subordinated to articulate and assert the value of their "difference" in the face of dominant meanings—meanings which often offer a pedagogy directed at the reinforcement of feelings of inferiority, marginality, ugliness. During the early fifties, when *Brown v. the Board of Education* was wending its way through the courts, as a demonstration of the destructive psychological effects of segregation black children were asked to look at two baby dolls, identical in all respects except color. The children were asked a series of questions: which is the nice doll? which is the bad doll? which doll would you like to play with? The majority of black children, Kenneth Clark reports, attributed the positive characteristics to the white doll, the negative characteristics to the black. When Clark asked one final question, "Which doll is like you?" they looked at him, he says, "as though he were the devil himself" for putting them in that predicament, for forcing them to face the inexorable and hideous logical implications of their situation. Northern children often ran out of the room; southern children tended to answer the question in shamed embarrassment. Clark recalls one little boy who laughed, "Who am I like? That doll! It's a nigger and I'm a nigger!"[14]

Failing to acknowledge the psychological and cultural potency of normalizing imagery can be just as effective in effacing people's experiences of racial oppression as lack of attentiveness to cultural and ethnic differences—a fact postmodern critics sometimes seem to forget. This is not to deny what Fiske calls "the power of being different"; it is, rather, to insist that it is won through ongoing political *struggle* rather than through an act of creative interpretation. Here, once again, although many postmodern academics may claim Foucault as their guiding light, they differ from him in significant and revealing ways. For Foucault, the metaphorical terrain of resistance is explicitly that of the "battle"; the "points of confrontation" may be "innumerable" and "instable," but they involve a serious, often deadly struggle of embodied (that is, historically situated and shaped) forces.[15] Barbara Kruger exemplifies this conception of resistance in a poster that represents the contemporary contest over reproductive control through the metaphor of the body as battleground. Some progressive developers of children's toys have self-consciously entered into struggle with racial and other forms of normalization. The Kenya Doll comes in three different skin tones ("so your girl is bound to feel pretty and proud") and attempts to create a future in which hair-straightening *will* be merely one decorative option among others. Such products, to my mind, are potentially effective "sites of resistance" precisely because they recognize that the body is a battleground whose self-determination has to be fought for.

The metaphor of the body as battleground, rather than postmodern playground, captures, as well, the *practical* difficulties involved in the political struggle to empower "difference." *Essence* magazine has consciously and strenuously tried to promote diverse images of black strength, beauty, and self-acceptance. Beauty features celebrate the glory of black skin and lush lips; other departments feature interviews with accomplished black women writers, activists, teachers, many of whom display styles of body and dress that challenge the hegemony of white Anglo-Saxon standards. The magazine's advertisers, however, continually play upon and perpetuate consumers' feelings of inadequacy and insecurity over the racial characteristics of their bodies. They insist that, in order to be beautiful, hair must be straightened and eyes lightened; they almost always employ models with fair skin, Anglo-Saxon features, and "hair that moves," insuring association of their products with fantasies of becoming what the white culture most prizes and rewards.

This ongoing battle over the black woman's body and the power of its "differences" ("differences" which actual black women embody to widely varying degrees, of course) is made manifest in the twentieth-anniversary issue, where a feature celebrating "The Beauty of Black" faced an advertisement visually legislating virtually the opposite (and offering, significantly, "escape"). This invitation to cognitive dissonance reveals what *Essence* must grapple with, in every issue, as it tries to keep its message of African

American self-acceptance clear and dominant, while submitting to economic necessities on which its survival depends. Let me make it clear here that such self-acceptance, not the reverse tyranny that constructs light-skinned and Anglo-featured African Americans as "not black enough," is the message *Essence* is trying to convey, against a culture that *denies* "the Beauty of Black" at every turn. This terrain, clearly, is not a playground but a minefield that constantly threatens to deconstruct "difference" *literally* and not merely literarily.

## "Material Girl": Madonna as Postmodern Heroine

John Fiske's conception of "difference," in the section quoted above, at least imagines resistance as challenging specifiable historical forms of dominance. Women, he argues, connect with subversive "feminine" values leaking through the patriarchal plot of soap operas; blacks laugh to themselves at the glossy, materialist-cowboy culture of *Dallas*. Such examples suggest a resistance directed against *particular* historical forms of power and subjectivity. For some postmodern theorists, however, resistance is imagined as the refusal to embody *any* positioned subjectivity at all; what is celebrated is continual creative escape from location, containment, and definition. So, as Susan Rubin Suleiman advises, we must move beyond the valorization of historically suppressed values (for example, those values that have been culturally constructed as belonging to an inferior, female domain and generally expunged from Western science, philosophy, and religion) and toward "endless complication" and a "dizzying accumulation of narratives."[16] She appreciatively (and perhaps misleadingly) invokes Derrida's metaphor of "incalculable choreographies"[17] to capture the dancing, elusive, continually changing subjectivity that she envisions, a subjectivity without gender, without history, without location. From this perspective, the truly resistant female body is, not the body that wages war on feminine sexualization and objectification, but the body that, as Cathy Schwichtenberg has put it, "uses simulation strategically in ways that challenge the stable notion of gender as the edifice of sexual difference . . . [in] an erotic politics in which the female body can be refashioned in the flux of identities that speak in plural styles."[18] For this erotic politics, the new postmodern heroine is Madonna.

This celebration of Madonna as postmodern heroine does not mark the first time Madonna has been portrayed as a subversive culture-figure. Until the early 1990s, however, Madonna's resistance has been interpreted along "body as battleground" lines, as deriving from her refusal to allow herself to be constructed as a passive object of patriarchal desire. John Fiske, for example, argues that this was a large part of Madonna's original appeal to her "wanna-bes"—those hordes of middle-class pre-teeners who mimicked Madonna's moves and costumes. For the "wanna-bes," Madonna demonstrated the possibility of female heterosexuality that was independent of patriarchal control, a sexuality that defied rather than rejected the male gaze, teasing it with her own gaze, deliberately trashy and vulgar, challenging anyone to call her a whore, and ultimately not giving a damn how she might be judged. Madonna's rebellious sexuality, in this reading, offered itself, not as coming into being through the look of the "other," but as self-defining and in love with, happy with itself—an attitude that is rather difficult for women to achieve in this culture and that helps to explain, as Fiske argues, her enormous appeal for pre-teen girls.[19] "I like the way she handles herself, sort of take it or leave it; she's sexy but she doesn't need men. . . . she's kind of there all by herself," says one. "She gives us ideas. It's really women's lib, not being afraid of what guys think," says another.[20]

Madonna herself, significantly and unlike most sex symbols, has never advertised herself as disdainful of feminism or constructed feminists as man-haters. Rather, in a 1985 *Time* interview, she suggests that her lack of inhibition in "being herself" and her "luxuriant" expression of "strong" sexuality constitute her brand of feminist celebration.[21] Some feminist theorists would agree. Molly Hite, for example, argues that "asserting female desire in a culture in which female sexuality is viewed as so inextricably conjoined with passivity" is "transgressive":

> Implied in this strategy is the old paradox of the speaking statue, the created thing that magically begins to create, for when a woman writes—self-consciously from her muted position as a woman and not as an honorary man—about female desire, female sexuality, female sensuous experience generally, her performance has the effect of giving voice to pure corporeality, of turning a product of the dominant meaning-system into a producer of meanings. A woman, conventionally identified with her body, writes about that identification, and as a consequence, femininity—silent and inert by definition—erupts into patriarchy as an impossible discourse.[22]

Not all feminists would agree with this, of course. For the sake of the contrast I want to draw here, however, let us grant it, and note, as well, that an argument similar to Fiske's can be made concerning Madonna's refusal to be obedient to dominant and normalizing standards of female *beauty*. I am now talking, of course, about Madonna in her more fleshy days. In those days, Madonna saw herself as willfully out of step with the times. "Back in the fifties," she says in the *Time* interview, "women weren't ashamed of their bodies." (The fact that she is dead wrong is not relevant here.) Identifying herself with her construction of that time and what she calls its lack of "suppression" of femininity, she looks down her nose at the "androgynous" clothes of our own time and speaks warmly of her own stomach, "not really flat" but "round and the skin is smooth and I like it." Contrasting herself to anorectics, whom she sees as self-denying and self-hating, completely in the thrall of externally imposed standards of worthiness, Madonna (as she saw herself) stood for self-definition through the assertion of her own (traditionally "female" and now anachronistic) body-type.

Of course, this is no longer Madonna's body type. Shortly after her 1987 marriage to Sean Penn she began a strenuous reducing and exercise program, now runs several miles a day, lifts weights, and has developed, in obedience to dominant contemporary norms, a tight, slender, muscular body. Why did she decide to shape up? "I didn't have a flat stomach anymore," she has said. "I had become well-rounded." Please note the sharp about-face here, from pride to embarrassment. My goal here, however, is not to suggest that Madonna's formerly voluptuous body was a nonalienated, freely expressive body, a "natural" body. While the slender body is the current cultural ideal, the voluptuous female body is a cultural form, too (as are all bodies), and was a coercive ideal in the fifties. My point is that in terms of Madonna's own former lexicon of meanings—in which feminine voluptuousness and the choice to be round in a culture of the lean were clearly connected to spontaneity, self-definition, and defiance of the cultural gaze—the terms set by that gaze have now triumphed. Madonna has been normalized; more precisely, she has self-normalized. Her "wanna-bes" are following suit. Studies suggest that as many as 80 percent of nine-year-old suburban girls (the majority of whom are far from overweight) are making rigorous dieting and exercise the organizing discipline of their lives.[23] They do not require Madonna's example, of course, to believe that they must be thin to be acceptable. But Madonna clearly no longer provides a model of resistance or "difference" for them.

None of this "materiality"—that is, the obsessive body-praxis that regulates and disciplines Madonna's life and the lives of the young (and not so young) women who emulate her—makes its way into the representation of Madonna as postmodern heroine. In the terms of this representation (in both its popular and scholarly instantiations) Madonna is "in control of her image, not trapped by it"; the proof lies in her ironic and chameleon-like approach to the construction of her identity, her ability to "slip in and out of character at will," to defy definition, to keep them guessing.[24] In this coding of things, as in the fantasies of the polysurgical addict (and, as I argue elsewhere in [the book from which this reading is taken], the eating-disordered woman), *control* and *power*, words that are invoked over and over in discussions of Madonna, have become equivalent to *self-creating*. Madonna's new body has no material history; it conceals its continual struggle to maintain itself, it does not reveal its pain. (Significantly, Madonna's "self-exposé," the documentary *Truth or Dare*, does not include any scenes of Madonna's daily workouts.) It is merely another creative transformation of an ever-elusive subjectivity. "More Dazzling and Determined Not to Stop Changing," as *Cosmopolitan* describes Madonna: ". . . whether in looks or career, this multitalented dazzler will never be trapped in *any* mold!"[25] The plasticity of Madonna's subjectivity is emphasized again and again in the popular press, particularly by Madonna herself. It is how she tells the story of her "power" in the industry: "In pop music, generally, people have one image. You get pigeonholed. I'm lucky enough to be able to change and still be accepted . . . play a part, change characters, looks, attitudes."[26]

Madonna claims that her creative work, too, is meant to escape definition. "Everything I do is meant to have several meanings, to be ambiguous," she says. She resists, however (in true postmodern fashion), the attribution of serious artistic intent; rather (as she told *Cosmo*), she favors irony and ambiguity, "to entertain myself" and (as she told *Vanity Fair*) out of "rebelliousness and a desire to fuck with people."[27] It is the postmodern nature of her music and videos that has most entranced academic critics, whose accolades reproduce in highly theoretical language the notions emphasized in the popular press. Susan McClary writes:

> Madonna's art itself repeatedly deconstructs the traditional notion of the unified subject with finite ego boundaries. Her pieces explore . . . various ways of constituting identities that refuse stability, that remain fluid, that resist definition. This tendency in her work has become increasingly pronounced; for instance, in her recent controversial video "Express Yourself" . . . she slips in and out of every subject position offered within the video's narrative context . . . refusing more than ever to deliver the security of a clear, unambiguous message or an "authentic" self.[28]

Later in the same piece, McClary describes "Open Your Heart to Me," which features Madonna as a porn star in a peep show, as creating "an image of open-ended *jouissance*—an erotic energy that continually escapes containment."[29] Now, many feminist viewers may find this particular video quite disturbing, for a number of reasons. First,

Do cultural images of Madonna show a resistant female body that wages war on feminine sexualization and objectification? Or is this just more of the same mind/body dualism that "reinforces patriarchy"?
[Left: UPI/Bettman. Right: Richard Harbus/UPI/Bettmann]

unlike many of Madonna's older videos, "Open Your Heart to Me" does not visually emphasize Madonna's subjectivity or desire—as "Lucky Star," for example, did through frequent shots of Madonna's face and eyes, flirting with and controlling the reactions of the viewer. Rather, "Open Your Heart to Me" places the viewer in the position of the voyeur by presenting Madonna's body as object, now perfectly taut and tightly managed for display. To be sure, we do not identify with the slimy men, drooling over Madonna's performance, who are depicted in the video; but, as E. Ann Kaplan has pointed out, the way men view women *in* the filmic world is only one species of objectifying gaze. There is also the viewer's gaze, which may be encouraged by the director to be either more or less objectifying.[30] In "Open Your Heart to Me," as in virtually all rock videos, the female body is offered to the viewer purely as a spectacle, an object of sight, a visual commodity to be consumed. Madonna's weight loss and dazzling shaping-up job make the spectacle of her body all the more compelling; we are riveted to her body, fascinated by it. Many men and women may experience the primary reality of the video as the elicitation of

Hillary Rodham Clinton has changed her hairstyle continuously since the 1992 presidential campaign (left). Did her work on health care reform help to change America's image of what a "First Lady" should be? What does her hair have to do with it? [Left: Reuters/Bettmann. Right: Sue Ogrocki/Reuters/Bettmann]

desire *for* that perfect body; women, however, may also be gripped by the desire (very likely impossible to achieve) to *become* that perfect body.

These elements can be effaced, of course, by a deliberate abstraction of the video from the cultural context in which it is historically embedded—the continuing containment, sexualization, and objectification of the female body—and in which the viewer is implicated as well and instead treating the video as a purely formal text. Taken as such, "Open Your Heart to Me" presents itself as what E. Ann Kaplan calls a "postmodern video": it refuses to "take a clear position vis-à-vis its images" and similarly refuses a "clear position for the spectator within the filmic world . . . leaving him/her decentered, confused."[31] McClary's reading of "Open Your Heart to Me" emphasizes precisely these postmodern elements, insisting on the ambiguous and unstable nature of the relationships depicted in the narrative of the video, and the frequent elements of parody and play. "The usual power relationship between the voyeuristic male gaze and object" is "destabilized," she claims, by the portrayal of the male patrons of the porno house as leering and pathetic. At the same time, the portrayal of Madonna as porno queen–object is deconstructed, McClary argues, by the end of the video, which has Madonna changing her clothes to those of a little boy and tripping off playfully, leaving the manager of the house sputtering behind her. McClary reads this as "escape to androgyny," which "refuses essentialist gender categories and turns sexual identity into a kind of play." As for the gaze of the viewer, she admits that it is "risky" to "invoke the image of porn queen in order to perform its deconstruction," but concludes that the deconstruction is successful: "In this video, Madonna confronts the most pernicious of her stereotypes and attempts to channel it into a very different realm: a realm where the feminine object need not be the object of the patriarchal gaze, where its energy can motivate play and nonsexual pleasure."[32]

I would argue, however, that despite the video's evasions of clear or fixed meaning there *is* a dominant position in this video: it is that of the objectifying gaze. One is not *really* decentered and confused by this video, despite the "ambiguities" it formally contains. Indeed, the video's postmodern conceits, I would suggest, facilitate rather than deconstruct the presentation of Madonna's body as an object on display. For in the absence of a coherent critical position telling us how to read the images, the individual images themselves become preeminent, hypnotic, fixating. Indeed, I would say that ultimately this video is entirely about Madonna's body, the narrative context virtually irrelevant, an excuse to showcase the physical achievements of the star, a video centerfold. On this level, any parodic or destabilizing element appears as cynically, mechanically tacked on, in bad faith, a way of claiming trendy status for what is really just cheesecake—or, perhaps, soft-core pornography.

Indeed, it may be worse than that. If the playful "tag" ending of "Open Your Heart to Me" is successful in deconstructing the notion that the objectification, the sexualization of women's bodies is a serious business, then Madonna's *jouissance* may be "fucking with" her youthful viewer's perceptions in a dangerous way. Judging from the proliferation of rock and rap lyrics celebrating the rape, abuse, and humiliation of women, the message—not Madonna's responsibility alone, of course, but hers among others, surely—is getting through. The artists who perform these misogynist songs also claim to be speaking playfully, tongue-in-cheek, and to be daring and resistant transgressors of cultural structures that contain and define. Ice T, whose rap lyrics gleefully describe the gang rape of a woman—with a flashlight, to "make her tits light up"—claims that he is only "telling it like it is" among black street youth (he compares himself to Richard Wright), and he scoffs at feminist humorlessness, implying, as well, that it is racist and repressive for white feminists to try to deny him his indigenous "style." The fact that Richard Wright embedded his depiction of Bigger Thomas within a critique of the racist culture that shaped him, and that *Native Son* is meant to be a *tragedy*, was not, apparently, noticed in Ice T's postmodern reading of the book, whose critical point of view he utterly ignores. Nor does he seem concerned about what appears to be a growing fad—not only among street gangs, but in fraternity houses as well—for gang rape, often with an unconscious woman, and surrounded by male spectators. (Some of the terms popularly used to describe these rapes include "beaching"—the woman being likened to a "beached whale"—and "spectoring," to emphasize how integral a role the onlookers play.)

My argument here is a plea, not for censorship, but for recognition of the social contexts and consequences of images from popular culture, consequences that are frequently effaced in postmodern and other celebrations of "resistant" elements in these images. To turn back to Madonna and the liberating postmodern subjectivity that Mc-Clary and others claim she is offering: the notion that one can play a porno house by night and regain one's androgynous innocence by day does not seem to me to be a refusal of essentialist categories about gender, but rather a new inscription of mind/body dualism. What the body does is immaterial, so long as the imagination is free. This abstract, unsituated, disembodied freedom, I have argued in this essay, glorifies itself only through the effacement of the material praxis of people's lives, the normalizing power of cultural images, and the continuing social realities of dominance and subordination.

## Reading Questions

1. How, according to Bordo, is the "postmodern imagination from bodily determination" oppressive to women?
2. What does Bordo mean by the "hegemonic power of normalizing images"?
3. Why does Bordo claim that "postmodern conversations" efface social privilege and social inequalities? Do you agree that such conversations ought to be eliminated?
4. How, according to Bordo, should feminists understand and use Foucault's view of power in cultural analysis?
5. What does Bordo mean by her claim that the media uses a "paradigm of plasticity"?

## Recommended Reading

Susan Bordo, *Unbearable Weight: Feminism, Western Culture, and the Body* (Berkeley: University of California Press, 1993)

Jacques Derrida and Christie McDonald, "Interview: Choreographies," *The Ear of the Other: Otobiography, Transference, Translation*, ed. Christie McDonald, trans. Peggy Kamuf (New York: Schocken Books, Inc., 1985)

John Fiske, *Television Culture* (New York: Methuen, 1987)

Hal Foster, ed., *The Anti-Aesthetic; Essays on Postmodern Culture* (Port Townsend, WA: Bay Press, 1983)

Michel Foucault, *Discipline and Punish* (New York: Vintage Press, 1979)

Ann Hollander, *Seeing Through Clothes* (New York: Viking Press, 1978)

bell hooks, "Madonna" and "Is Paris Burning?" in *Black Looks* (Boston: South End Press, 1992)

## Recommended Audiovisual Resources

*The Immaculate Collection*. Madonna. 1990. Contains music videos of "Open Your Heart," "Like a Prayer," and "Express Yourself," among others.

*Truth or Dare*. 1991. Directed by Alex Keshishian. Full-length documentary about Madonna and her career.

*Paris Is Burning*. 1990. Directed by Jennie Livingston. Documentary about the practices of black and Hispanic gays in New York City. Personal interviews and footage about voguing and dance balls in Harlem.

*Eating*. 1991. Directed by Henry Jaglom. A group of women talk about food, sex, and self-esteem.

*My Mother Thought She Was Audrey Hepburn*. 1992. Directed by Sharon Jue. A personal statement about growing up Asian American in a white society. Filmakers Library.

*Too Much, Too Soon*. 1987. Directed by Mark Schwartz. Focuses on Sue Ann McKean, who explains that bodybuilding for women does not diminish their femininity, but develops self-esteem. Cinema Guild.

# Commodity Lesbianism

## DANAE CLARK

Danae Clark teaches in the Department of Communications at the University of Pittsburgh.

A commodity appears, at first sight, a very trivial thing, and easily understood. Its analysis shows that it is, in reality, *a very queer thing.* . . .

Karl Marx, *Capital*[1]

In an effort to articulate the historical and social formation of female subjectivity under capitalism, feminist investigations of consumer culture have addressed a variety of complex and interrelated issues, including the construction of femininity and desire, the role of consumption in media texts, and the paradox of the woman/commodity relationship. Implicit in these investigations, however, has been an underlying concern for the heterosexual woman as consuming subject.[2] Perhaps because, as Jane Gaines notes, "consumer culture thrives on heterosexuality and its institutions by taking its cues from heterosexual 'norms,'"[3] theories *about* consumerism fall prey to the same normalizing tendencies. In any event, analyses of female consumerism join a substantial body of other feminist work that "assumes, but leaves unwritten, a heterosexual context for the subject" and thus contributes to the continued invisibility of lesbians.[4]

But lesbians too are consumers. Like heterosexual women they are major purchasers of clothing, household goods and media products. Lesbians have not, however, been targeted as a separate consumer group within the dominant configuration of capitalism, either directly through the mechanism of advertising or indirectly through fictional media representations; their relation to consumerism is thus necessarily different. This "difference" requires a careful look at the relation between lesbians and consumer culture, representations of lesbianism and consumption in media texts, and the role of the lesbian spectator as consuming subject. Such an investigation is especially timely since current trends in both advertising and commercial television show that lesbian viewers (or at least some segments of the lesbian population) are enjoying a certain pleasure as consumers that was not available to them in the past. An analysis of these pleasures should therefore shed light not only on the place that lesbians occupy within consumer culture, but on the identificatory processes involved in lesbian reading formations.

## Dividing the Consumer Pie

Lesbians have not been targeted as consumers by the advertising industry for several historical reasons. First, lesbians as a social group have not been economically powerful; thus, like other social groups who lack substantial purchasing power (for example, the elderly), they have not been attractive to advertisers. Second, lesbians have not been easily identifiable as a social group anyway. According to the market strategies commonly used by advertisers to develop target consumer groups, four criteria must be met. A group must be: (1) identifiable, (2) accessible, (3) measurable, and (4) profitable.[5] In other words, a particular group must be "knowable" to advertisers in concrete ways. Lesbians present a problem here because they exist across race, income and age (three determinants used by advertisers to segment and distinguish target groups within the female population). To the extent that lesbians are not identifiable or accessible, they are not measurable and, therefore, not profitable. The fact that many lesbians prefer not to be identified because they fear discrimination poses an additional obstacle to targeting them. Finally, most advertisers have had no desire to identify a viable lesbian consumer group. Advertisers fear that by openly appealing to a homosexual market their products will be negatively associated with homosexuality and will be avoided by heterosexual consumers.[6] Thus, although homosexuals (lesbians and gay men) reputedly comprise 10% of the overall U.S. market population—and up to 20–22% in major urban centers such as New York and San Francisco—advertisers have traditionally stayed in the closet when it comes to peddling their wares.[7]

Recently, however, this trend has undergone a visible shift—especially for gay men. According to a 1982 review in *The New York Times Magazine* called "Tapping the Homosexual Market," several of today's top advertisers are interested in "wooing . . . the white, single, well-educated, well-paid man who happens to be homosexual."[8] This interest, prompted by surveys conducted by *The Advocate* between 1977 and 1980 that indicated that 70% of their readers aged 20–40 earned incomes well above the national median, has led companies such as Paramount, Seagram, Perrier, and Harper & Row to advertise in gay male publications like *Christopher Street* and *The Advocate*.[9] Their ads are tailored specifically for the gay male audience. Seagram, for example, ran a "famous men of history" campaign for Boodles Gin that pictured men "purported to be gay."[10]

A more common and more discreet means of reaching the gay male consumer, however, is achieved through the mainstream (predominately print) media. As one marketing director has pointed out, advertisers "really want to reach a bigger market than just gays, but [they] don't want to alienate them" either.[11] Thus, advertisers are increasingly striving to create a dual marketing approach that will "speak to the homosexual consumer in a way that the straight consumer will not notice."[12] As one observer explains:

> It used to be that gay people could communicate to one another, in a public place, if they didn't know one another, only by glances and a sort of *code behavior* . . . to indicate to the other person, but not anybody else, that you, too, were gay. Advertisers, if they're smart, can do that too (emphasis added).[13]

One early example of this approach was the Calvin Klein jeans series that featured "a young, shirtless blond man lying on his stomach" and, in another ad, "a young, shirtless blond man lying on his side, holding a blue-jeans jacket." According to Peter Frisch, a gay marketing consultant, one would "have to be comatose not to realize that it appeals to gay men" (I presume he is referring to the photographs' iconographic resemblance to gay pornography).[14] Calvin Klein marketing directors, however, denied any explicit gay element:

> We did not try *not* to appeal to gays. We try to appeal, period. With healthy, beautiful people. If there's an awareness in that community of health and grooming, they'll respond to the ads.[15]

This dual marketing strategy has been referred to as "gay window advertising."[16] Generally, gay window ads avoid explicit references to heterosexuality by depicting only one individual or same-sexed individuals within the representational frame. In addition, these models bear the signifiers of sexual ambiguity or androgynous style. But "gayness" remains in the eye of the beholder: gays and lesbians can read into an ad certain subtextual elements that correspond to experiences with or representations of gay/lesbian subculture. If heterosexual consumers do not notice these subtexts or subcultural codes, then advertisers are able to reach the homosexual market along with the heterosexual market without ever revealing their aim.

The metaphor of the window used by the advertising industry to describe gay marketing techniques is strikingly similar to feminist descriptions of women's relation to consumer culture and film representation. Mary Ann Doane, for example, remarks that "the film frame is a kind of display window and spectatorship consequently a form of window shopping."[17] Jane Gaines likewise suggests that cinemagoing is "analogous to the browsing-without-obligation-to-buy pioneered by the turn-of-the-century department store, where one could, with no offense to the merchant, enter to peruse the goods, exercising a kind of *visual connoisseurship*, and leave without purchase" (emphasis added).[18] Gaines further argues that the show window itself is "a medium of circulation" and that "commodification seems to facilitate circulation by multiplying the number of possible contexts."[19] The metaphor of the window, in other words, posits an active reader as well as a multiple, shifting context of display.

The notion of duality that characterizes gay window advertising's marketing strategy is also embodied in various theoretical descriptions and approaches to consumer culture in general. Within the Frankfort School, for example, Adorno speaks of the dual character or dialectic of luxury that "opens up consumer culture to be read as its opposite," and Benjamin suggests that consumer culture is a dual system of meaning whereby "the economic life of the commodity imping[es] upon its life as an object of cultural significance."[20] More recently, a duality has been located in feminist responses to consumer culture and fashion culture in particular. As Gaines notes, the beginning of the Second Wave of feminist politics and scholarship was marked by a hostility toward fashion, perceiving it as a patriarchal codification and commodification of femininity that enslaved women and placed their bodies on display. But this "anti-fashion" position is now joined by a feminist perspective that sees fashion culture as a site of female resistance, masquerade and self-representation.[21] At the heart of this "fabrication," says Gaines, is a gender confusion and ambiguity that disrupts and confounds patriarchal culture.[22]

Lesbians have an uneasy relationship to this dual perspective on fashion. First of all, lesbians have a long tradition of resisting dominant cultural definitions of female beauty and fashion as a way of separating themselves from heterosexual culture politically and as a way of signaling their lesbianism to other women in their subcultural group. This resistance to or reformulation of fashion codes thus distinguished lesbians from straight women at the same time that it challenged patriarchal structures. As Arlene Stein explains in a recent article on style in the lesbian community:

Lesbian-feminist anti-style was an emblem of refusal, an attempt to strike a blow against the twin evils of capitalism and patriarchy, the fashion industry and the female objectification that fueled it. The flannel-and-denim look was not so much a style as it was anti-style—an attempt to replace the artifice of fashion with a supposed naturalness, free of gender roles and commercialized pretense.[23]

Today, however, many lesbians, particularly younger, urban lesbians, are challenging this look, exposing the constructedness of "natural" fashion, and finding a great deal of pleasure in playing with the possibilities of fashion and beauty.

This shift, which is not total and certainly not without controversy, can be attributed to a number of factors. First of all, many lesbians are rebelling against a lesbian-feminist credo of political correctness that they perceive as stifling. As a *Village Voice* writer observes:

> A lesbian can wag her fingers as righteously as any patriarchal puritan, defining what's acceptable according to what must be ingested, worn, and especially desired. . . . In a climate where a senator who doesn't like a couple of photographs tries to do away with the National Endowment for the Arts, censorious attacks within the lesbian community begin to sound a lot like fundamentalism. . . . They amount to a policing of the lesbian libido.[24]

Stein thus notes that while the old-style, politically correct(ing) strain of lesbian feminism is on the wane, "life style" lesbianism is on the rise. Lifestyle lesbianism is a recognition of the "diverse subcultural pockets and cliques—corporate dykes, arty dykes, dykes of color, clean and sober dykes—of which political lesbians are but one among many."[25] But it may also be a response to the marketing strategies of consumer culture.

The predominate research trend in U.S. advertising for the past two decades has been VALS (values and life styles) research. By combining information on demographics (sex, income, educational level), buying habits, self-image, and aspirations, VALS research targets and, in the case of yuppies, effectively *creates* consumer lifestyles that are profitable to advertisers.[26] Given lesbian-feminism's countercultural, anti-capitalist roots, it is not surprising that lesbians who "wear" their lifestyles or flaunt themselves as "material girls" are often criticized for trading in their politics for a self-absorbed materialism. But there is more to "lipstick lesbians" or "style nomads" than a freewheeling attitude toward their status as consumers or a boredom with the relatively static nature of the "natural look" (fashion, after all, implies change). Fashion-conscious dykes are rebelling against the idea that there is a clear one-to-one correspondence between fashion and identity. As Stein explains:

> You can dress as a femme one day and a butch the next. You can wear a crew-cut along with a skirt. Wearing high heels during the day does not mean you're femme at night, passive in bed, or closeted on the job.[27]

Seen in this light, fashion becomes an assertion of personal freedom as well as political choice.

The new attitudes of openness toward fashion, sexuality and lifestyle would not have been possible, of course, without the lesbian-feminist movement of recent decades. Its emergence may also have an economic explanation. According to a recent survey in

OUT/LOOK, a national gay and lesbian quarterly, the average annual income for individual lesbians (who read OUT/LOOK) is $30,181; the average lesbian household income is approximately $58,000.[28] Since lesbians as a group are beginning to raise their incomes and class standing, they are now in a position to afford more of the clothing and "body maintenance" that was once beyond their financial capabilities. Finally, some credit for the changing perspectives on fashion might also be given to the recent emphasis on masquerade and fabrication in feminist criticism and to the more prominent role of camp in lesbian criticism. At least within academic circles these factors seem to affect, or to be the effect of, lesbian theorists' fashion sensibilities.

But regardless of what has *caused* this shift, or where one stands on the issue of fashion, advertisers in the fashion industry have begun to capitalize upon it. Given the increasing affluence and visibility of one segment of the lesbian population—the predominantly white, predominantly childless, middle-class, educated lesbian with disposable income—it appears that advertisers are now interested in promoting "lesbian window advertising." (Even while recognizing the highly problematic political implications of such a choice, I will continue to use the term "gay" instead of "lesbian" when referring to this marketing strategy since "gay window advertising" is the discursive phrase currently employed by the advertising industry.) In fashion magazines such as *Elle* and *Mirabella*, and in mail-order catalogs such as *Tweeds, J. Crew* and *Victoria's Secret*, advertisers (whether knowingly or not) are capitalizing upon a dual market strategy that packages gender ambiguity and speaks, at least indirectly, to the lesbian consumer market. The representational strategies of gay window advertising thus offer what John Fiske calls "points of purchase" or points of identification that allow readers to make sense of cultural forms in ways that are meaningful or pleasurable to them.[29] The important question here is how these consumer points of purchase become involved in lesbian notions of identity, community, politics, and fashion.

## When Dykes Go Shopping . . .

In a recent issue of *Elle*, a fashion layout entitled "Male Order" shows us a model who, in the words of the accompanying ad copy, represents "the zenith of masculine allure." In one photograph the handsome, short-haired model leans against the handlebars of a motorcycle, an icon associated with bike dyke culture. Her man-styled jacket, tie, and jewelry suggest a butch lesbian style that offers additional points of purchase for the lesbian spectator. In another photograph from the series, the model is placed in a more neutral setting, a cafe, that is devoid of lesbian iconography. But because she is still dressed in masculine attire and, more importantly, exhibits the "swaggering" style recommended by the advertisers, the model incorporates aspects of lesbian style. Here, the traditional "come on" look of advertising can be read as the look or pose of a cruising dyke. Thus, part of the pleasure that lesbians find in these ads might be what Elizabeth Ellsworth calls "lesbian verisimilitude," or the representation of body language, facial expression, and general appearance that can be claimed and coded as "lesbian" according to current standards of style within lesbian communities.[30]

A fashion layout from *Mirabella*, entitled "Spectator," offers additional possibilities for lesbian readings. In this series of photographs by Deborah Turbeville, two women (not always the same two in each photograph) strike poses in a fashionable, sparsely decorated apartment. The woman who is most prominently featured has very short, slicked-back hair and, in three of the photographs, she is wearing a tank top (styled like a man's undershirt) and baggy trousers. With her confident poses, her broad shoulders and strong arms (she obviously pumps iron), this fashion model can easily be read as "highstyle butch." The other women in the series are consistently more "femme" in appearance, though they occasionally wear masculine-style apparel as well. The lesbian subtext in this fashion layout, however, is not limited to the models' appearances. The adoption of butch and femme *roles* suggests the possibility of interaction or a "playing out" of a lesbian narrative. Thus, while the women are physically separated and do not interact in the photographs, [31] their stylistic role-playing invites the lesbian spectator to construct a variety of (butch–femme) scenarios in which the two women come together. The eroticism of these imaginary scenes is enhanced by compositional details such as soft lighting and a rumpled bedsheet draped over the apartment window to suggest a romantic encounter. The variation of poses and the different combination of models also invites endless possibilities for narrative construction. Have these two women just met? Are they already lovers? Is there a love triangle going on here?, and so on.

Much of what gets negotiated, then, is not so much the contradictions between so-called "dominant" and "oppositional" readings, but the details of the subcultural reading itself. Even so, because lesbians (as members of a heterosexist culture) have been taught to read the heterosexual possibilities of representations, the "straight" reading is never entirely erased or replaced. Lesbian readers, in other words, know that they are not the primary audience for mainstream advertising, that androgyny is a fashionable and profitable commodity, and that the fashion models in these ads are quite probably heterosexual. In this sense, the dual approach of gay window advertising can refer not only to the two sets of readings formulated by homosexuals and heterosexuals, but to the dual or multiple interpretations that exist *within* lesbian reading formations. The straight readings, however, do not simply exist alongside alternative readings, nor do they necessarily diminish the pleasure found in the alternate readings. As "visual connoisseurs" lesbians privilege certain readings (styles) over others, or, in the case of camp readings, the straight reading itself forms the basis of (as it becomes twisted into) a pleasurable interpretation.

Here, as Sue-Ellen Case might argue, is the locus of a true masquerade of readership. [32] Lesbians are accustomed to playing out multiple styles and sexual roles as a tactic of survival and thus have learned the artifice of invention in defeating heterosexual codes of naturalism:

> The closet has given us the lie; and the lie has given us camp—the style, the discourse, the *mise-en-scène* of butch–femme roles. The survival tactic of hiding and lying [has] produced a camp discourse . . . in which gender referents are suppressed, or slip into one another, fictional lovers are constructed, [and] metaphors substitute for literal descriptions. [33]

I would not argue, as Case does, that "the butch–femme couple inhabit the [lesbian] subject position together" [34] since the butch–femme aesthetic is a historically specific (and even community and lifestyle specific) construct that ranges from the rigid butch–femme roles of the 1950s to the campy renaissance of today's butch–femme role-playing, and thus cannot represent a consistent subject position. But a lesbian subject's recognition of the butch–femme binarism, as it has been historically styled by lesbian communities, is an essential component of a reading practice that distances, subverts and plays with both heterosexist representations and images of sexual indeterminacy. Another aspect of reading that must be considered is the pleasure derived from seeing the dominant media "attempt, but fail, to colonize 'real' lesbian space."[35] Even in representations that capitalize upon sexual ambiguity there are certain aspects of lesbian subculture that remain (as yet) inaccessible or unappropriated. By claiming this unarticulated space as something distinct and separable from heterosexual (or heterosexist) culture, lesbian readers are no longer outsiders, but insiders privy to the inside jokes that create an experience of pleasure and solidarity with other lesbians "in the know." Thus, as Ellsworth notes, lesbians "have responded to the marginalization, silencing and debasement" found in dominant discourse "by moving the field of social pleasures . . . to the center of their interpretive activities" and reinforcing their sense of identity and community.[36]

This idea assumed concrete dimensions for me during the course of researching and presenting various versions of this paper. Lesbians across the country were eager to talk about or send copies of advertisements that had "dyke appeal" (and there was a good deal of consensus over how that term was interpreted). A number of lesbians admitted to having an interest in *J. Crew* catalogs because of a certain model they looked forward to seeing each month. Another woman told me of several lesbians who work for a major fashion publication as if to reassure me that gay window fashion photography is not an academic hallucination or a mere coincidence. Gossip, hearsay and confessions are activities that reside at the center of lesbian interpretive communities and add an important discursive dimension to lesbians' pleasure in looking.

This conception of readership is a far cry from earlier (heterosexist) feminist analyses of advertising that argued that "advertisements help to endorse the powerful male attitude that women are passive bodies to be endlessly looked at, waiting to have their sexual attractiveness matched with *active* male sexual desire," or that women's relation to advertisements can only be explained in terms of anxiety or "narcissistic damage."[37] These conclusions were based on a conspiracy theory that placed ultimate power in the hands of corporate patriarchy and relegated no power or sense of agency to the female spectator. Attempts to modify this position, however, have created yet another set of obstacles around which we must maneuver with caution. For in our desire and haste to attribute agency to the spectator and a means of empowerment to marginal or oppressed social groups, we risk losing sight of the interrelation between reading practices and the political economy of media institutions.

In the case of gay window advertising, for example, appropriation cuts both ways. While lesbians find pleasure (and even validation) in that which is both accessible and unarticulated, the advertising industry is playing upon a material and ideological tension that simultaneously appropriates aspects of lesbian subculture and positions lesbian reading practices in relation to consumerism. As John D'Emilio explains: "This dialectic—the constant interplay between exploitation and some measure of autonomy—informs all of the history of those who have lived under capitalism."[38] According to D'Emilio's argument that capitalism and the institution of wage labor have created the material conditions for homosexual desire and identity, gay window advertising is a logical outgrowth of capitalist development, one which presumably will lead to more direct forms of marketing in the future. But the reasons behind this development can hardly be attributed to a growing acceptance of homosexuality as a legitimate lifestyle. Capitalist enterprise creates a tension: materially it "weakens the bonds that once kept families together," but ideologically it "drives people into heterosexual families." Thus, "while capitalism has knocked the material foundations away from family life, lesbians, gay men, and heterosexual feminists have become the scapegoats for the social instability of the system."[39] The result of this tension is that capitalists welcome homosexuals as consuming subjects but not as social subjects. Or, as David Ehrenstein remarks, "the market is there for the picking, and questions of 'morality' yield ever so briefly to the quest for capital."[40]

The sexual indeterminacy of gay window advertising's dual market approach thus allows a space for lesbian identification, but must necessarily deny the representation of lesbian identity politics. This is a point that has so far been overlooked in the ongoing feminist and lesbian/gay debates over the issue of identity politics.[41] At the core of these debates is the post-structuralist challenge to essentialist definitions of identity. While theorists and activists alike agree that some shared sense of identity is necessary to build a cohesive and visible political community, some theorists argue that any unified conception of gay/lesbian identity is reductive and ahistorical. They thus opt for a historically constructed notion of *identities* that is contradictory, socially contingent, and rooted in progressive sexual politics. But while the controversies are raging over whether gay/lesbian identity is essential or constructed, media industries are producing texts that deny the very politics feminists and lesbians are busy theorizing.

Mainstream media texts employ representational strategies that generally refer to gays and lesbians in *anti-essentialist* terms. That is, homosexuals are not depicted as inherently different from heterosexuals; neither does there exist a unified or authentic "gay sensibility." As Mark Finch observes, "[t]he most recuperable part of the gay movement's message is that gay people are individuals."[42] The result is a liberal gay discourse that embraces humanism while rejecting any notion of a separate and authentic lesbian/gay subject. The homosexual, says John Leo, is thus "put together from disarticulating bits and pieces of the historical discourse on homosexual desire, which become a narrative pastiche for middle-class 'entertainment.'"[43] As a mode of representation that lacks any clear positioning toward what it shows, pastiche embodies "the popular" in the sense that people are free to make their own meanings out of the cultural bits and ideological pieces that are presented to them.

But this postmodern, anti-essentialist (indeed, democratic) discourse could also be interpreted as homophobic response. As Jeffrey Weeks ironically points out, "The essentialist view lends itself most effectively to the defence of minority status."[44] (For example, if homosexuality were to be classified by the courts as biologically innate, discrimination would be more difficult to justify. By contrast, when a sense of lesbian or gay identity is lost, the straight world finds it easier to ignore social and political issues that directly affect gays and lesbians as a group.) The constructionist strategies of the media are thus not as progressive as anti-essentialist theorists (or media executives) might have us believe. The issue is not a matter of choosing between constructionism or essentialism, but a matter of examining the political motivations involved in each of these approaches—whether they appear in theory or media texts.

If we take politics as our starting point, then media and advertising texts can be analyzed in terms of their (un)willingness or (in)ability to represent the identity politics of current lesbian communities. Gay window advertising, as suggested earlier, consciously disavows any explicit connection to lesbianism for fear of offending or losing potential customers. At the same time, an appropriation of lesbian styles or appeal to lesbian desires can also assure a lesbian market. This dual approach is effective because it is based on two key ingredients of marketing success: style and choice. As Dick Hebdige has noted, "it is the subculture's stylistic innovations which first attract the media's attention."[45] Because style is a cultural construction, it is easily appropriated, reconstructed and divested of its original political or subcultural signification. Style as resistance becomes commodifiable as chic when it leaves the political realm and enters the fashion world. This simultaneously diffuses the political edge of style. Resistant trends (such as wearing men's oversized jackets or oxford shoes—which, as a form of masquerade, is done in part for fun, but also in protest against the fashion world's insistence upon dressing women in tightly-fitted garments and dangerously unstable footwear) become restyled as high-priced fashions.

In an era of "outing" (the practice of forcing gay and lesbian public figures to come out of the closet as a way to confront heterosexuals with our ubiquity as well as our competence, creativity or civicmindedness), gay window advertising can be described as a practice of "ining." In other words, this type of advertising invites us to look *into* the ad to identify with elements of style, invites us *in* as consumers, invites us to be part of a fashionable "*in* crowd," but negates an identity politics based on the act of "coming out." Indeed, within the world of gay window advertising, there is no lesbian community to come out to, no lesbian community to identify with, no indication that lesbianism or "lesbian style" is a political issue. This stylization furthermore promotes a liberal discourse of choice that separates sexuality from politics and connects them both with consumerism. Historically, this advertising technique dates back to the 1920s, as Roland Marchand explains:

> The compulsion of advertising men to relegate women's modernity to the realm of consumption and dependence found expression not only in pictorial styles but also in tableaux that sought to link products with the social and political freedoms of the new woman. Expansive rhetoric that heralded women's march toward freedom and equality often concluded by proclaiming their victory only in the narrower realm of consumer products.[46]

Just as early twentieth-century advertisers were more concerned about women's votes in the marketplace than their decisions in the voting booth, contemporary advertisers are more interested in lesbian consumers than lesbian politics. Once stripped of its political underpinnings, lesbianism can be represented as a style of consumption linked to sexual preference. Lesbianism, in other words, is treated as merely a sexual style that can be chosen—or not chosen—just as one chooses a particular mode of fashion for self-expression.

But within the context of consumerism and the historical weight of heterosexist advertising techniques, "choice" is regulated in determinate ways. For example, gay window advertising appropriates lesbian subcultural style, incorporates its features into commodified representations, and offers it back to lesbian consumers in a packaged form cleansed of identity politics. In this way, it offers lesbians the opportunity to solve the "problem" of lesbianism: by choosing to clothe oneself in fashionable ambiguity, one can pass as "straight" (in certain milieux) while still choosing lesbianism as a sexual preference; by wearing the privilege of straight culture, one can avoid political oppression. Ironically, these ads also offer heterosexual women an alternative as well. As Judith Williamson notes, "[t]he bourgeois always wants to be in disguise, and the customs and habits of the oppressed seem so much more fascinating than his (sic) own."[47] Thus, according to Michael Bronski, "when gay sensibility is used as a sales pitch, the strategy is that gay images imply distinction and non-conformity, granting straight consumers a longed-for place outside the humdrum mainstream."[48] The seamless connections that have traditionally been made between heterosexuality and consumerism are broken apart to allow straight and lesbian women alternative choices. But these choices, which result in a rearticulated homogenized style, deny the differences among women as well as the potential antagonisms that exist between straight and lesbian women over issues of style, politics, and sexuality. As Williamson might explain, "femininity needs the 'other' in order to function . . . even as politically [it] seek[s] to eliminate it."[49]

Similar contradictions and attempts at containment occur within the discourses surrounding women's bodybuilding. As Laurie Schulze notes, "The deliberately muscular woman disturbs dominant notions of sex, gender, and sexuality, and any discursive field that includes her risks opening up a site of contest and conflict, anxiety and ambiguity."[50] Thus, within women's fashion magazines, bodybuilding has been recuperated as a normative ideal of female beauty that promotes self-improvement and ensures attractiveness to men. This discourse

> also assures women who are thinking about working out with weights that they need not fear a loss of privilege or social power; despite any differences that may result from lifting weights, they will still be able to "pass."[51]

The assurances in this case are directed toward heterosexual women who fear that bodybuilding will bring the taint of lesbianism. The connection between bodybuilding and lesbianism is not surprising, says Schulze, for "the ways in which female bodybuilders and lesbians disturb patriarchy and heterosexism . . . draw very similar responses from dominant culture."[52] Both the muscular female and the butch lesbian are accused of looking like men or wanting to be men. As Annette Kuhn puts it, "Muscles are rather like drag."[53] Lesbian style, too, tends toward drag, masquerade and the confusion of gender. Thus, both are subjected to various forms of control that either refuse to accept their physical or sexual "excesses" or otherwise attempt to domesticate their threat and fit them into the dominant constructions of feminine appearances and roles.

Both bodybuilders and lesbians, in other words, are given opportunities to "pass" in straight feminine culture. For body builders, this means not flexing one's muscles while walking down the street or, in the case of competitive bodybuilders, exhibiting the signs of conventional feminine style (for example, makeup, coiffed hair and string bikinis) while flexing on stage.[54] For lesbians, as discussed earlier, this means adopting more traditionally feminine apparel or the trendy accoutrements of gender ambiguity. But within these passing strategies are embodied the very seeds of resistance. As Schulze argues, muscle culture is a "terrain of resistance/refusal" as well as a "terrain of control."[55] It's simply a matter of how much muscle a woman chooses to flex. Within bodybuilding subculture, flexing is encouraged and admired; physical strength is valorized as a new form of femininity. Lesbians engage in their own form of "flexing" within lesbian subcultures (literally so for those lesbians who also pump iron) by refusing to pass as straight.

This physical and political flexing calls the contradictions of women's fashion culture into question and forces them out of the closet. It thus joins a long history of women's subversive and resistant responses to consumer culture in general. Although consumer culture has historically positioned women in ways that benefit heterosexist, capitalist patriarchy, women have always found ways to exert their agency and create their own pleasures and spaces. Fiske, for example, discusses the way that shopping has become a "terrain of guerrilla warfare" where women change price tags, shoplift or try on expensive clothing without the intent of purchase.[56] The cultural phenomenon of shopping has also provided a homosocial space for women (for example, mothers and daughters, married and single adult women, teenage girls) to interact and bond. Lesbians have been able to extend this pleasure by shopping with their female lovers or partners, sharing the physical and erotic space of the dressing room, and, afterwards, wearing/exchanging the fashion commodities they purchase. Within this realm, the static images of advertising have even less control over their potential consumers. Gay window advertising, for example, may commodify lesbian masquerade as legitimate high-style fashion, but lesbians are free to politicize these products or reappropriate them in combination with other products/fashions to act as new signifiers for lesbian identification or ironic commentaries on heterosexual culture.

This is not to suggest that there exists an authentic "lesbian sensibility" or that all lesbians construct the same, inherently progressive, meanings in the realm of consumption. One must be wary of the "affirmative character" of a cultural study that leans toward essentialist notions of identity at the same time as it tends to overestimate the freedom of audience reception.[57] Since lesbians are never simply lesbians but also members of racial groups, classes, and so on, their consumption patterns and reading practices always overlap and intersect those of other groups. In addition, there is no agreement within lesbian communities on the "proper" response or relationship to consumer culture. This is precisely why the lesbian "style wars" have become a topic of such heated debate. Arlene Stein pinpoints the questions and fears that underlie this debate:

> Are today's lesbian style wars skin-deep, or do they reflect a changed conception of what it means to be a dyke? If a new lesbian has in fact emerged, is she all flash and no substance, or is she at work busily carving out new lesbian politics that strike at the heart of dominant notions of gender and sexuality?[58]

The answers are not simple, not a matter of binary logic. Some lesbians choose to mainstream. Others experience the discourse of fashion as an ambivalence—toward power, social investment, and representation itself.[59] Still others engage a camp discourse or masquerade that plays upon the lesbian's ambivalent position within straight culture. These responses, reading practices, interpretive activities—whatever one might call them—are as varied as the notions of lesbian identity and lesbian community.

Given the conflicts that lesbians frequently experience within their communities over issues of race, class and life style, lesbians are only too aware that a single, authentic identity does not exist. But, in the face of these contradictions, lesbians are attempting to forge what Stuart Hall calls an *articulation*, "a connection, a linkage that can establish a unity among different elements within a culture, under certain conditions."[60] For lesbians, the conditions are *political*. Lesbian identity politics must therefore be concerned with constructing political agendas and articulating collective identities that take into account our various needs and differences as well as our common experiences and oppressions *as a social group*. So too a theory of lesbian reading practices rooted in identity politics must stretch beyond analyses of textual contradictions to address the history of struggle, invisibility and ambivalence that positions the lesbian subject in relation to cultural practices.

Ironically, now that our visibility is growing, lesbians have become the target of "capitalism's constant search for new areas to colonize."[61] This consideration must remain central to the style debates. For lesbians are not simply forming a new relationship with the fashion industry, *it* is attempting to forge a relationship with us. This imposition challenges us and is forcing us to renegotiate certain aspects of identity politics. (I can't help but think, for example, that the fashion controversy may not be about "fashion" at all but has more to do with the fact that it is the femmes who are finally asserting themselves.) In the midst of this challenge, the butch–femme aesthetic will undoubtedly undergo realignment. We may also be forced to reconsider the ways in which camp can function as a form of resistance. For once "camp" is commodified by the culture industry, how do we continue to camp it up?

The only assurance we have in the shadow of colonization is that lesbians *as lesbians* have developed strategies of selection, (re)appropriation, resistance, and subversion in order to realign consumer culture according to the desires and needs of lesbian sexuality, subcultural identification, and political action. Lesbian reading/social practices, in other words, are informed by an identity politics, however that politics may be formulated historically by individuals or by larger communities. This does not mean that the readings lesbians construct are always "political" in the strictest sense of the term (for example, one could argue that erotic identification is not political, and there is also the possibility that lesbians will identify with mainstreaming). Nonetheless, the discourses of identity politics—which arise out of the lesbian's marginal and ambivalent social position—have *made it possible* for lesbians to consider certain contradictions in style, sexual object choice and cultural representation that inform their reading practices, challenge the reading practices of straight culture, and potentially create more empowered, or at least pleasurable, subject positions as lesbians. Because identities are always provisional, lesbians must also constantly assert themselves. They must replace liberal discourse with camp discourse, make themselves visible, foreground their political agendas and their politicized subjectivities.

This may explain why feminists have avoided the issue of lesbian consumerism. Lesbians may present too great a challenge to the heterosexual economy in which they are invested, or lesbians may be colonizing the theoretical and social spaces they wish to inhabit. As long as straight women focus on the relation between consumer culture and women in general, lesbians remain invisible, or are forced to pass as straight, while heterosexual women can claim for themselves the oppression of patriarchal culture or the pleasure of masquerade that offers them "a longed for place outside the humdrum mainstream." On the other hand, straight feminists may simply fear that lesbians are better shoppers. When dykes go shopping in order to "go camping," they not only subvert the mix 'n' match aesthetic promoted by dominant fashion culture, they do it with very little credit.

# Reading Questions

1. Explain the stated and implied goals of "gay window advertising" as used in contemporary marketing strategies.
2. How do lesbian reading practices subvert consumer marketing ploys?
3. Why does Clark assert that "capitalists welcome homosexuals as consuming subjects but not as social subjects"?
4. Discuss the debate between lesbians who perceive the discourse of fashion as resistance to cultural oppression and consumer culture, and those who consider it as merely superficial "style wars."

# Recommended Reading

Bad Object-Choices, ed., *How Do I Look? Queer Film and Video* (Seattle, WA: Bay Press, 1991)

Sue-Ellen Case, "Towards a Butch—Femme Aesthetic," *The Lesbian and Gay Studies Reader*, ed. Henry Abelove, Michele Aina Barale, David M. Halperin (New York: Routledge, 1993)

Madeline Davis and Elizabeth Lapovsky Kennedy, *Boots of Leather, Slippers of Gold: The History of a Lesbian Community* (New York: Routledge, 1993)

Lillian Faderman, *Odd Girls and Twilight Lovers: A History of Lesbian Life in Twentieth Century America* (New York: Penguin Books, 1991)

Marilyn Frye, *The Willful Virgin: Essays in Feminism 1976—1992* (Freedom, CA: The Crossing Press, 1992)

Marjorie Garber, *Vested Interests: Cross Dressing and Cultural Anxiety* (New York: Routledge, 1992)

Tracy Morgan, "Butch—Femme and the Politics of Identity," *Sisters, Sexperts, Queers: Beyond the Lesbian Nation*, ed. Arlene Stein (New York: Penguin Books, 1993)

Joan Nestle, ed., *The Persistent Desire: A Femme—Butch Reader* (Boston: Alyson, 1992)

Alisa Solomon, "Not Just a Passing Fancy: Notes on Butch," *Theater* 24:2 (1993)

# Recommended Audiovisual Resources

*The Ballad of Little Jo*. 1993. Directed by Maggie Greenwald. Recent fiction film portraying a woman who cross-dresses in the effort to "pass" as a man in the wild west.

*Basic Instinct*. 1992. Directed by Paul Verhoeven. Controversial portrayal of bisexual and "lipstick lesbian" styles within the context of a brutal ice-pick murder mystery.

*Forbidden Love*. 1993. Directed by Aerlyn Weissman and Lynne Fernie. Fascinating documentary featuring interviews with Canadian and American lesbians who tell their stories of the pre-Stonewall femme—butch bar scene culture of the 1950s and 1960s. Women Make Movies.

*She Must Be Seeing Things*. 1987. Directed by Sheila McLaughlin. Story of the erotic fascination between a filmmaker and her friend. Women Make Movies.

# CHAPTER 2

# Community

Haitian emigré at an Easter service in Brooklyn, New York. © 1984 Kathleen Foster/Impact Visuals.

# Breaking Bread

## BELL HOOKS and CORNEL WEST

bell hooks is the pen name of Gloria Watkins, who teaches at Oberlin College. She is the author of many books on feminism, race, and culture, including *Feminist Theory: From Margin to Center* and *Yearning: Race, Gender, and Cultural Politics.* Cornel West is professor of religion and the director of the African-American Studies program at Princeton University. He is the author of *The American Evasion of Philosophy, Race Matters,* and many other works on race and cultural criticism.

**b.h.**  I requested that Charles sing "Precious Lord" because the conditions that led Thomas Dorsey to write this song always make me think about gender issues, issues of black masculinity. Mr. Dorsey wrote this song after his wife died in childbirth. That experience caused him to have a crisis of faith. He did not think he would be able to go on living without her. That sense of unbearable crisis truly expresses the contemporary dilemma of faith. Mr. Dorsey talked about the way he tried to cope with this "crisis of faith." He prayed and prayed for a healing and received the words to this song. This song has helped so many folk when they are feeling low, feeling as if they can't go on. It was my grandmother's favorite song. I remembered how we sang it at her funeral. She died when she was almost ninety. And I am moved now as I was then by the knowledge that we can take our pain, work with it, recycle it, and transform it so that it becomes a source of power.

Let me introduce to you my "brother," my comrade Cornel West.

**C.W.**  First I need to just acknowledge the fact that we as black people have come together to reflect on our past, present, and objective future. That, in and of itself, is a sign of hope. I'd like to thank the Yale African-American Cultural Center for bringing us together. bell and I thought it would be best to present in dialogical form a series of reflections on the crisis of black males and females. There is a state of siege raging now in black communities across this nation linked not only to drug addiction but also consolidation of corporate power as we know it, and redistribution of wealth from the bottom to the top, coupled with the ways with which a culture and society centered on the market, preoccupied with consumption, erode structures of feeling, community, tradition. Reclaiming our heritage and sense of history are prerequisites to any serious talk about black freedom and black liberation in the twenty-first century. We want to try to create that kind of community here today, a community that we hope will be a place to promote understanding. Critical understanding is a prerequisite for any serious talk about coming together, sharing, participating, creating bonds of solidarity so that black people and other progressive people can continue to hold up the blood-stained banners that were raised when that song was sung in the civil rights movement. It was one of Dr. Martin Luther King's favorite songs, reaffirming his own struggle and that of many others who have tried to link some sense of faith, religious faith, political faith, to the struggle for freedom. We thought it would be best to have a dialogue to put forth analysis and provide a sense of what form a praxis would take. That praxis will be necessary for us to talk seriously about black power, black liberation in the twenty-first century.

**b.h.**  Let us say a little bit about ourselves. Both Cornel and I come to you as individuals who believe in God. That belief informs our message.

**C.W.**  One of the reasons we believe in God is due to the long tradition of religious faith in the black community. I think, that as a people who have had to deal with the absurdity of being black in America, for many of us it is a question of God and sanity, or God and suicide. And if you are serious about black struggle you know that in many instances you will be stepping out on nothing, hoping to land on something. That is the history of black folks in the past and present, and it continually concerns those of us who are willing to speak out with boldness and a sense of the importance of history and struggle. You speak knowing that you won't be able to do that for too long because America is such a violent culture. Given those conditions you have to ask yourself what links to a tradition will sustain you given the absurdity and insanity we are bombarded with daily. And so the belief in God itself is not to be understood in a noncontextual manner. It is understood in relation to a particular context, to specific circumstances.

**b.h.**  We also come to you as two progressive black people on the left.

**C.W.**  Very much so.

**b.h.**  I will read a few paragraphs to provide a critical framework for our discussion of black power, just in case some of you may not know what black power means. We are gathered to speak with one another about black power in the twenty-first century. In James Boggs's essay, "Black Power: A Scientific Concept Whose Time Has Come," first published in 1968, he called attention to the radical political significance of the black power movement, asserting: "Today the concept of black power expresses the revolutionary social force which must not only struggle against the capitalist but against the workers and all who benefit by and support the system which has oppressed us." We speak of black power in this very different context to remember, reclaim, revision, and renew. We remember first that the historical struggle for black liberation was forged by black women and men who were concerned about the collective welfare of black people. Renewing our commitment to this collective struggle should provide a grounding for new direction in contemporary political practice. We speak today of political partnership between black men and women. The late James Baldwin wrote in his autobiographical preface to *Notes of a Native Son*: "I think that the past is all that makes the present coherent and further that the past will remain horrible for as long as we refuse to accept it honestly." Accepting the challenge for this prophetic statement as we look at our contemporary past as black people, the space between the sixties and the nineties, we see a weakening of political solidarity between black men and women. It is crucial for the future black liberation struggle that we remain ever mindful that ours is a shared struggle, that we are each other's faith.

**C.W.**  I think we can even begin by talking about the kind of existentialist chaos that exists in our own lives and our inability to overcome the sense of alienation and frustration we experience when we try to create bonds of intimacy and solidarity with one another. Now part of this frustration is to be understood again in relation to structures and institutions. In the way in which our culture of consumption has promoted an addiction to stimulation—one that puts a premium on bottled commodified stimulation. The market does this in order to convince us that our consumption keeps oiling the economy in order for it to reproduce itself. But the effect of this addiction to stimulation is an undermining, a waning of our ability for qualitatively rich relationships. It's no accident that crack is the postmodern drug, that it is the highest form of addiction known to humankind, that it provides a feeling ten times more pleasurable than orgasm.

**b.h.**  Addiction is not about relatedness, about relationships. So it comes as no surprise that as addiction becomes more pervasive in black life it undermines our capacity to experience community. Just recently, I was telling someone that I would like to buy a little house next door to my parent's house. This house used to be Mr. Johnson's house but he recently passed away. And they could not understand why I would want to live near my parents. My explanation that my parents were aging did not satisfy. Their inability to understand or appreciate the value of sharing family life intergenerationally was a sign to me of the crisis facing our communities. It's as though as black people we have lost our understanding of the importance of mutual interdependency, of communal living. That we no longer recognize as valuable the notion that we collectively shape the terms of our survival is a sign of crisis.

**C.W.**  And when there is crisis in those communities and institutions that have played a fundamental role in transmitting to younger generations our values and sensibility, our ways of life and our ways of struggle, we find ourselves distanced, not simply from our predecessors but from the critical project of black liberation. And so more and more we seem to have young black people who are very difficult to understand, because it seems as though they live in two very different worlds. We don't really understand their music. Black adults may not be listening to NWA (Niggers With Attitude) straight out of Compton, California. They may not understand why they are doing what Stetsasonic is doing, what Public Enemy is all about, because young people have been fundamentally shaped by the brutal side of American society. Their sense of reality is shaped on the one hand by a sense of coldness and callousness, and on the other hand by a sense of passion for justice, contradictory impulses which surface simultaneously. Mothers may find it difficult to understand their children. Grandparents may find it difficult to understand us—and it's this slow breakage that has to be restored.

**b.h.**  That sense of breakage, or rupture, is often tragically expressed in gender relations. When I told folks that Cornel West and I were talking about partnership between black women and men, they thought I meant romantic relationships. I replied that it was important for us to examine the multi-relationships between black women and men, how we deal with fathers, with brothers, with sons. We are talking about all our relationships across gender because it is not just the heterosexual love relationships between black women and men that are in trouble. Many of us can't communicate with parents, siblings, etc. I've talked with many of you and asked, "What is it you feel should be addressed?" And many of you responded that you wanted to talk about black men and how they need to "get it together."

Let's talk about why we see the struggle to assert agency—that is, the ability to act in one's best interest—as a male thing. I mean, black men are not the only ones among us who need to "get it together." And if black men collectively refuse to educate themselves for critical consciousness, to acquire the means to be self-determined, should our communities suffer, or should we not recognize that both black women and men must struggle for self-actualization, must learn to "get it together"? Since the culture we live in continues to equate blackness with maleness, black awareness of the extent to which our survival depends on mutual partnership between women and men is undermined. In renewed black liberation struggle, we recognize the position of black men and women, the tremendous role black women played in every freedom struggle.

Certainly Septima Clark's book *Ready from Within* is necessary reading for those of us who want to understand the historical development of sexual politics in black liberation struggle. Clark describes her father's insistence that she not fully engage herself in civil rights struggle because of her gender. Later, she found the source of her defiance in religion. It was the belief in spiritual community, that no difference must be made between the role of women and that of men, that enabled her to be "ready within." To Septima Clark, the call to participate in black liberation struggle was a call from God. Remembering and recovering the stories of how black women learned to assert historical agency in the struggle for self-determination in the context of community and collectivity is important for those of us who struggle to promote black liberation, a movement that has at its core a commitment to free our communities of sexist domination, exploitation, and oppression. We need to develop a political terminology that will enable black folks to talk deeply about what we mean when we urge black women and men to "get it together."

C.W.  I think again that we have to keep in mind the larger context of American society, which has historically expressed contempt for black men and black women. The very notion that black people are human beings is a new notion in western civilization and is still not widely accepted in practice. And one of the consequences of this pernicious idea is that it is very difficult for black men and women to remain attuned to each other's humanity, so when bell talks about black women's agency and some of the problems black men have when asked to acknowledge black women's humanity, it must be remembered that this refusal to acknowledge one another's humanity is a reflection of the way we are seen and treated in the larger society. And it's certainly not true that white folks have a monopoly on human relationships. When we talk about a crisis in western civilization, black people are a part of that civilization even though we have been beneath it, our backs serving as a foundation for the building of that civilization, and we have to understand how it affects us so that we may remain attuned to each other's humanity, so that the partnership that bell talks about can take on real substance and content. I think partnerships between black men and black women can be made when we learn how to be supportive and think in terms of critical affirmation.

b.h.  Certainly black people have not talked enough about the importance of constructing patterns of interaction that strengthen our capacity to be affirming.

C.W.  We need to affirm one another, support one another, help, enable, equip, and empower one another to deal with the present crisis, but it can't be uncritical, because if it's uncritical then we are again refusing to acknowledge other people's humanity. If we are serious about acknowledging and affirming other people's humanity then we are committed to trusting and believing that they are forever in process. Growth, development, maturation happens in stages. People grow, develop, and mature along the lines in which they are taught. Disenabling critique and contemptuous feedback hinders.

**b.h.** We need to examine the function of critique in traditional black communities. Often it does not serve as a constructive force. Like we have that popular slang word "dissin'" and we know that "dissin'" refers to a kind of disenabling contempt—when we "read" each other in ways that are so painful, so cruel, that the person can't get up from where you have knocked them down. Other destructive forces in our lives are envy and jealousy. These undermine our efforts to work for a collective good. Let me give a minor example. When I came in this morning I saw Cornel's latest book on the table. I immediately wondered why my book was not there and caught myself worrying about whether he was receiving some gesture of respect or recognition denied me. When he heard me say "where's my book?" he pointed to another table.

Often when people are suffering a legacy of deprivation, there is a sense that there are never any goodies to go around, so that we must viciously compete with one another. Again this spirit of competition creates conflict and divisiveness. In a larger social context, competition between black women and men has surfaced around the issue of whether black female writers are receiving more attention than black male writers. Rarely does anyone point to the reality that only a small minority of black women writers are receiving public accolades. Yet the myth that black women who succeed are taking something away from black men continues to permeate black psyches and inform how we as black women and men respond to one another. Since capitalism is rooted in unequal distribution of resources, it is not surprising that we as black women and men find ourselves in situations of competition and conflict.

**C.W.** I think part of the problem is deep down in our psyche we recognize that we live in such a conservative society, a society of business elites, a society in which corporate power influences are assuring that a certain group of people do get up higher.

**b.h.** Right, including some of you in this room.

**C.W.** And this is true not only between male and female relations but also black and brown relations and black and Korean, and black and Asian relations. We are struggling over crumbs because we know that the bigger part of lower corporate America is already received. One half of one percent of America owns twenty-two percent of the wealth, one percent owns thirty-two percent, and the bottom forty-five percent of the population has twenty percent of the wealth. So, you end up with this kind of crabs-in-the-barrel mentality. When you see someone moving up you immediately think they'll get a bigger cut in big-loaf corporate America and you think that's something real because we're still shaped by the corporate ideology of the larger context.

**b.h.** Here at Yale many of us are getting a slice of that mini-loaf and yet are despairing. It was discouraging when I came here to teach and found in many black people a quality of despair which is not unlike that we know is felt in "crack neighborhoods." I wanted to understand the connection between underclass black despair and that of black people here who have immediate and/or potential access to so much material privilege. This despair mirrors the spiritual crisis that is happening in our culture as a whole. Nihilism is everywhere. Some of this despair is rooted in a deep sense of loss. Many black folks who have made it or are making it undergo an identity crisis. This is especially true for individual black people working to assimilate into the "mainstream." Suddenly, they may feel panicked, alarmed by the knowledge that they do not understand their history, that life is without purpose and meaning. These feelings of alienation and estrangement create suffering. The suffering many black people experience today is linked to the suffering of the past, to "historical memory." Attempts by black people to understand that suffering, to come to terms with it, are the conditions which enable a work like Toni Morrison's *Beloved* to receive so much attention. To look back, not just to describe slavery but to try and reconstruct a psycho-social history of its impact has only recently been fully understood as a necessary stage in the process of collective black self recovery.

**C.W.**  The spiritual crisis that has happened, especially among the well-to-do blacks, has taken the form of the quest for therapeutic release. So that you can get very thin, flat, and uni-dimensional forms of spirituality that are simply an attempt to sustain the well-to-do black folks as they engage in their consumerism and privatism. The kind of spirituality we're talking about is not the kind that remains superficial just physically but serves as an opium to help you justify and rationalize your own cynicism vis-à-vis the disadvantaged folk in our community. We could talk about churches and their present role in the crisis of America, religious faith as the American way of life, the gospel of health and wealth, helping the bruised psyches of the black middle class make it through America. That's not the form of spirituality that we're talking about. We're talking about something deeper—you used to call it conversion—so that notions of service and risk and sacrifice once again become fundamental. It's very important, for example, that those of you who remember the days in which black colleges were hegemonic among the black elite remember them critically but also acknowledge that there was something positive going on there. What was going on was that you were told every Sunday, with the important business of chapel, that you had to give service to the race. Now it may have been a petty bourgeois form, but it created a moment of accountability, and with the erosion of the service ethic the very possibility of putting the needs of others alongside of one's own diminishes. In this syndrome, me-ness, selfishness, and egocentricity become more and more prominent, creating a spiritual crisis where you need more psychic opium to get you over.

**b.h.**  We have experienced such a change in that communal ethic of service that was so necessary for survival in traditional black communities. That ethic of service has been altered by shifting class relations. And even those black folks who have little or no class mobility may buy into a bourgeois class sensibility; TV shows like *Dallas* and *Dynasty* teach ruling class ways of thinking and being to underclass poor people. A certain kind of bourgeois individualism of the mind prevails. It does not correspond to actual class reality or circumstances of deprivation. We need to remember the many economic structures and class politics that have led to a shift of priorities for "privileged" blacks. Many privileged black folks obsessed with living out a bourgeois dream of liberal individualistic success no longer feel as though they have any accountability in relation to the black poor and underclass.

**C.W.**  We're not talking about the narrow sense of guilt privileged black people can feel, because guilt usually paralyzes action. What we're talking about is how one uses one's time and energy. We're talking about the ways in which the black middle class, which is relatively privileged vis-à-vis the black working class, working poor, and underclass, needs to acknowledge that along with that privilege goes responsibility. Somewhere I read that for those to whom much is given, much is required. And the question becomes, "How do we exercise that responsibility given our privilege?" I don't think it's a credible notion to believe the black middle class will give up on its material toys. No, the black middle class will act like any other middle class in the human condition; it will attempt to maintain its privilege. There is something seductive about comfort and convenience. The black middle class will not return to the ghetto, especially given the territorial struggles going on with gangs and so forth. Yet, how can we use what power we do have to be sure more resources are available to those who are disadvantaged? So the question becomes "How do we use our responsibility and privilege?" Because, after all, black privilege is a result of black struggle.

I think the point to make here is that there is a new day in black America. It is the best of times and the worst of times in black America. Political consciousness is escalating in black America, among black students, among black workers, organized black workers and trade unions, increasingly we are seeing black leaders with vision. The black church is on the move, black popular music, political themes and motifs are on the move. So don't think in our critique we somehow ask you to succumb to a paralyzing pessimism. There are grounds for hope and when that corner is turned, and we don't know what particular catalytic event will serve as the take-off for it (just like we didn't know December 1955 would be the take-off), but when it occurs we have got to be ready. The privileged black folks can play a rather crucial role if we have a service ethic, if we want to get on board, if we want to be part of the progressive, prophetic bandwagon. And that is the question we will have to ask ourselves and each other.

**b.h.**  We also need to remember that there is a joy in struggle. Recently, I was speaking on a panel at a conference with another black woman from a privileged background. She mocked the notion of struggle. When she expressed, "I'm just tired of hearing about the importance of struggle; it doesn't interest me," the audience clapped. She saw struggle solely in negative terms, a perspective which led me to question whether she had ever taken part in any organized resistance movement. For if you have, you know that there is joy in struggle. Those of us who are old enough to remember segregated schools, the kind of political effort and sacrifice folks were making to ensure we would have full access to educational opportunities, surely remember the sense of fulfillment when goals that we struggled for were achieved. When we sang together "We shall overcome" there was a sense of victory, a sense of power that comes when we strive to be self determining. When Malcolm X spoke about his journey to Mecca, the awareness he achieved, he gives expression to that joy that comes from struggling to grow. When Martin Luther King talked about having been to the mountain top, he was sharing with us that he arrived at a peak of critical awareness, and it gave him great joy. In our liberatory pedagogy we must teach young black folks to understand that struggle is process, that one moves from circumstances of difficulty and pain to awareness, joy, fulfillment. That the struggle to be critically conscious can be that movement which takes you to another level, that lifts you up, that makes you feel better. You feel good, you feel your life has meaning and purpose.

**C.W.** A rich life is fundamentally a life of serving others, a life of trying to leave the world a little better than you found it. That rich life comes into being in human relationships. This is true at the personal level. Those of you who have been in love know what I am talking about. It is also true at the organizational and communal level. It's difficult to find joy by yourself even if you have all the right toys. It's difficult. Just ask somebody who has got a lot of material possessions but doesn't have anybody to share them with. Now that's at the personal level. There is a political version of this. It has to do with what you see when you get up in the morning and look in the mirror and ask yourself whether you are simply wasting time on the planet or spending time in an enriching manner. We are talking fundamentally about the meaning of life and the place of struggle. bell talks about the significance of struggle and service. For those of us who are Christians there are certain theological foundations on which our commitment to serve is based. Christian life is understood to be a life of service. Even so, Christians have no monopoly on the joys that come from service and those of you who are part of secular culture can also enjoy this sense of enrichment. Islamic brothers and sisters share in a religious practice which also places emphasis on the importance of service. When we speak of commitment to a life of service we must also talk about the fact that such a commitment goes against the grain, especially the foundations of our society. To talk this way about service and struggle we must also talk about strategies that will enable us to sustain this sensibility, this commitment.

**b.h.** When we talk about that which will sustain and nurture our spiritual growth as a people, we must once again talk about the importance of community. For one of the most vital ways we sustain ourselves is by building communities of resistance, places where we know we are not alone. In *Prophetic Fragments*, Cornel began his essay on Martin Luther King by quoting the lines of the spiritual, "He promised never to leave me, never to leave me alone." In black spiritual tradition the promise that we will not be alone cannot be heard as an affirmation of passivity. It does not mean we can sit around and wait for God to take care of business. We are not alone when we build community together. Certainly there is a great feeling of community in this room today. And yet when I was here at Yale I felt that my labor was not appreciated. It was not clear that my work was having meaningful impact. Yet I feel that impact today. When I walked into the room a black woman sister let me know how much my teaching and writing had helped her. There's more of the critical affirmation Cornel spoke of. That critical affirmation says, "Sister, what you're doing is uplifting me in some way." Often folk think that those folks who are spreading the message are so "together" that we do not need affirmation, critical dialogue about the impact of all that we teach and write about and how we live in the world.

**C.W.** It is important to note the degree to which black people in particular, and progressive people in general, are alienated and estranged from communities that would sustain and support us. We are often homeless. Our struggles against a sense of nothingness and attempts to reduce us to nothing are ongoing. We confront regularly the question "Where can I find a sense of home?" That sense of home can only be found in our construction of those communities of resistance bell talks about and the solidarity we can experience within them. Renewal comes through participating in community. That is the reason so many folks continue to go to church. In religious experience they find a sense of renewal, a sense of home. In community one can feel that we are moving forward, that struggle can be sustained. As we go forward as black progressives, we must remember that community is not about homogeneity. Homogeneity is dogmatic imposition, pushing your way of life, your way of doing things onto somebody else. That is not what we mean by community. Dogmatic insistence that everybody think and act alike causes rifts among us, destroying the possibility of community. That sense of home that we are talking about and searching for is a place where we can find compassion, recognition of difference, of the importance of diversity, of our individual uniqueness.

**b.h.**  When we evoke a sense of home as a place where we can renew ourselves, where we can know love and the sweet communion of shared spirit, I think it's important for us to remember that this location of well-being cannot exist in a context of sexist domination, in a setting where children are the objects of parental domination and abuse. On a fundamental level, when we talk about home, we must speak about the need to transform the African-American home, so that there, in that domestic space, we can experience the renewal of political commitment to the black liberation struggle. So that there in that domestic space we learn to serve and honor one another. If we look again at the civil rights, at the black power movement, folks organized so much in homes. They were the places where folks got together to educate themselves for critical consciousness. That sense of community, cultivated and developed in the home, extended outward into a larger more public context. As we talk about black power in the twenty-first century, about political partnership between black women and men, we must talk about transforming our notions of how and why we bond. In *Beloved*, Toni Morrison offers a paradigm for relationships between black men and women. Sixo describes his love for Thirty-Mile Woman, declaring, "She is a friend of mind. She gather me, man. The pieces I am, she gather them and give them back to me in all the right order. It's good, you know, when you got a woman who is a friend of your mind." In this passage Morrison evokes a notion of bonding that may be rooted in passion, desire, even romantic love, but the point of connection between black women and men is that space of recognition and understanding, where we know one another so well, our histories, that we can take the bits and pieces, the fragments of who we are, and put them back together, re-member them. It is this joy of intellectual bonding, or working together to create liberatory theory and analysis that black women and men can give one another, that Cornel and I give to each other. We are friends of one another's mind. We find a home with one another. It is that joy in community we celebrate and share with you this morning.

# Reading Questions

1. According to hooks and West, what is the crisis between black men and women, and how is the consolidation of corporate power related to it?
2. What, according to the authors, is the connection between the tradition of religious faith in the black community and black power?
3. What do the authors mean by "addiction" and why is it considered a threat to black communities?
4. What are some of the specific factors the authors understand to estrange black women and men from constructive partnerships?
5. What are some examples of how the service ethic in black as well as other minority communities is corroded by shifting class relations?

# Recommended Reading

M. Banton, *Racial and Ethnic Competition* (Cambridge: Cambridge University Press, 1983)

Franz Fanon, *Black Skin White Masks*, trans. Charles Lam Markmann (New York: Grove Press, Inc., 1967)

bell hooks, "Homophobia in Black Communities," *Talking Back: Thinking Feminist, Thinking Black* (Boston: South End, 1989)

bell hooks, *Sisters of the Yam: Black Women and Self-Recovery* (Boston: South End, 1993)

Kesho Yvonne Scott, *The Habit of Surviving: Black Women's Strategies for Life* (New Brunswick, NJ: Rutgers University Press, 1991)

Cornel West, *Prophetic Thought in Postmodern Times: Beyond Eurocentrism and Multiculturalism*, Vols. 1 and 2 (Monroe, ME: Common Courage Press, 1993)

# Recommended Audiovisual Resources

*Are We Different?* 1993. Produced by John Arthos. Gives voice to African-American students around the country concerning the tacit code of silence on matters of race. Filmakers Library.

*Dealing with Drugs: Re-evaluating the "War on Drugs."* 1994. Produced by Canadian Broadcasting Corporation. Documentary and public policy analysis of the interaction of drug abuse and AIDS in our urban areas. Filmakers Library.

*No Regret.* 1992. Directed by Marlon Riggs. Riggs's documentary records the strength, humor, and courage of five black, gay, HIV-positive men as they come to terms with their illness. Frameline Release.

*Tongues Untied.* 1989. Directed by Marlon Riggs. Riggs's personal interviews with gay African-American men, about their gay and cross-dressing experiences in the United States. Frameline Release.

# Between a Rock and a Hard Place
## Relationships Between Black and Jewish Women

### BARBARA SMITH

Barbara Smith is the editor of *Home Girls: A Black Feminist Anthology* and coeditor of *All the Women Are White, All the Blacks Are Men, but Some of Us Are Brave.* She has authored numerous articles on feminism, race, and queer theory, and has served on the editorial board of Kitchen Table: Women of Color Press, in New York City.

Our strategy is how we cope—how we measure and weigh what is to be said and when, what is to be done and how, and to whom and to whom and to whom, daily deciding/risking who it is we can call an ally, call a friend (whatever that person's skin, sex, or sexuality). We are women without a line. We are women who contradict each other.[1]

—Cherríe Moraga

I have spent the better part of a week simply trying to figure out how to begin. Every day, I've asked myself, as I sifted through files and pages of notes that were not getting me one bit closer to a start, "Why in hell am I doing this?" and when most despairing, "Why me?" Despair aside, I knew that if I could remember not just the reasons, but the feelings that first made me want to speak about the complicated connections and disconnections between Black and Jewish women, racism and anti-Semitism, I might find my way into this piece.

The emergence in the last few years of a Jewish feminist movement has of course created the context for this discussion. Jewish women have challenged non-Jewish women, including non-Jewish women of color, to recognize our anti-Semitism and in the process of building their movement Jewish women have also looked to Third World feminists for political inspiration and support. Not surprisingly, as these issues have been raised, tensions that have characterized relationships between Black and Jewish people in this country have also surfaced within the women's movement. Jewish women's perception of Black and other women of color's indifference to or active participation in anti-Semitism and Third World women's sense that major segments of the Jewish feminist movement have failed to acknowledge the weight of their white-skin privilege and capacity for racism, have inevitably escalated suspicion and anger between us.

To be a Black woman writing about racism and anti-Semitism feels like a no-win situation. It's certainly not about pleasing anybody, and I don't think it should be. I worry, however, that addressing anti-Semitism sets me up to look like a woman of color overly concerned about "white" issues. What I most fear losing, of course, is the political support and understanding of other women of color, without which I cannot survive.

This morning, for guidance, I turned to Bernice Johnson Reagon's "Coalition Politics: Turning the Century," because besides all the pain that has led me to examine these issues, there is also the positive motivation of my belief in coalitions as the only means we have to accomplish the revolution we so passionately want and need. She writes:

> I feel as if I'm gonna keel over any minute and die. That is often what it feels like if you're *really* doing coalition work. Most of the time you feel threatened to the core and if you don't you're not really doing no coalescing. . . . You don't go into coalition because you just *like* it. The only reason you would consider trying to team up with somebody who could possibly kill you, is because that's the only way you can figure you can stay alive.[2]

It helps to be reminded that the very misery that I and all of us feel when we explore the volatile links between our identities and the substance of our oppressions is only to be expected. If we weren't upset about the gulfs between us, if we weren't scared of the inherent challenge to act and change that the recognition of these gulfs requires, then we wouldn't "really [be] doing no coalescing."

What follows is one Black woman's perspective, necessarily affected by the generally complicated character of Black and Jewish relations in this country. This is not pure analysis. Far from it. I am focusing on relationships between Black and Jewish women, because in my own life these relationships have both terrorized me and also shown me that people who are not the same not only can get along, but at times can work together to make effective political change. Although this discussion may be applicable to dynamics between other women of color and Jewish women, I am looking specifically at Black–Jewish relationships because of the particular history between the two groups in the U.S. and because as an Afro-American woman this is the set of dynamics I've experienced first hand. Although the subject of Black and Jewish relationships cannot help but make reference to systematically enforced racism and anti-Semitism, I am emphasizing interactions between us because that feels more graspable to me, closer to the gut and heart of the matter.

Because of the inherent complexities of this subject, one of the things I found most overwhelming was the sense that I had to be writing for two distinct audiences at the same time. I was very aware that what I want to say to other Black women is properly part of an "in-house" discussion and it undoubtedly would be a lot more comfortable for us if somehow the act of writing did not require it to go public. With Jewish women, on the other hand, although we may have a shared bond of feminism, what I say comes from a position outside the group. It is impossible for me to forget that in speaking to Jewish women I am speaking to white women, a role complicated by a racist tradition of Black people repeatedly having to teach white people about the meaning of oppression. I decided then to write sections that would cover what I need to say to Black women and what I need to say to Jewish women, fully understanding that this essay would be read in its entirety by both Black and Jewish women, as well as by individuals from a variety of other backgrounds.

## Embedded in the Very Soil

I am anti-Semitic. I am not writing this from a position of moral exemption. My hands are not clean, because like other non-Jews in this society I have swallowed anti-Semitism simply by living here, whether I wanted to or not. At times I've said, fully believing it, that I was not taught anti-Semitism at home growing up in Cleveland in the 1950's. In comparison to the rabid anti-Semitism as well as racism that many white people convey to their children as matter-of-factly as they teach them the alphabet and how to tie their shoes, my perception of what was going on in my house is relatively accurate. But only relatively.

On rare occasions things were said about Jews by members of my family, just as comments were made about white people in general, and about Cleveland's numerous European immigrant groups in particular. My family had "emigrated" too from the rural South during the 1920's, 30's, and 40's and their major observation about Jewish and other white people was that they could come to this country with nothing and in a relatively short period "make it." Our people, on the other hand, had been here for centuries and continued to occupy a permanent position on society's bottom. When I was growing up there were Jewish people living in Shaker Heights, one of the richest suburbs in the U.S., where Blacks were not allowed to purchase property even if they had the money, which most, of course, did not. The fact that Jews were completely barred from other suburbs and perhaps restricted to certain sections of Shaker Heights was not of great import to us. I remember vividly when my aunt and uncle (my mother's sister and brother) were each trying to buy houses in the 1950's. They searched for months on end because so many neighborhoods in the inner city including working-class ones were also racially segregated.[3] I was six or seven, but I remember their exhausted night-time conversations about the problem of where they might be able to move, I felt their anger, frustration, and shame that they could not provide for their families on such a basic level. The problem was white people, segregation, and racism. Some Jews were, of course, a part of that, but I don't remember them being especially singled out. I did not hear anti-Semitic epithets or a litany of stereotypes. I do remember my uncle saying more than once that when they didn't let "the Jew" in somewhere, he went and built his own. His words were edged with both envy and admiration. I got the message that these people knew how to take care of themselves, that we could learn a lesson from them and stop begging the white man for acceptance or even legal integration.

Despite how I was raised, what I've come to realize is that even if I didn't learn anti-Semitism at home, I learned it. I know all the stereotypes and ugly words not only for Jews, but for every outcast group including my own. Such knowledge goes with the territory. Classism, racism, homophobia, anti-Semitism, and sexism float in the air, are embedded in the very soil. No matter how cool things are at home, you catch them simply by walking out of the house and by turning on the t.v. or opening up a newspaper inside the house. In the introduction to *Home Girls*, I wrote about this unsettling reality in relationship to how I sometimes view other women of color:

> Like many Black women, I know very little about the lives of other Third World women. I want to know more and I also want to put myself in situations where I have to learn. It isn't easy because, for one thing, I keep discovering how deep my own prejudice goes. I feel so very American when I realize that simply by being Black I have not escaped the typical American ways of perceiving people who are different from myself.[4]

I never believe white people when they tell me they aren't racist. I have no reason to. Depending on the person's actions I might possibly believe that they are actively engaged in opposing racism, are anti-racist, at the very same time they continue to be racially ignorant and cannot help but be influenced as white people by this system's hatred of people of color. Unwittingly, anti-racist whites may collude at times in the very system they are trying to fight. In her article "Racism and Writing: Some Implications for White Lesbian Critics," Elly Bulkin incisively makes the distinction between the reality of being *actively* anti-racist and the illusion of being non-racist—that is, totally innocent.[5] She applies to racism, as I do here to anti-Semitism, the understanding that it is neither possible nor necessary to be morally exempt in order to stand in opposition to oppression. I stress this point because I want everybody reading this, and particularly Black women, to know that I am not writing from the position of having solved anything and because I have also heard other Black women, white non-Jewish women, and at times myself say, "But I'm not anti-Semitic." This kind of denial effectively stops discussion, places the burden of "proof" upon the person(s) experiencing the oppression, and makes it nearly impossible ever to get to the stage of saying: "This is an intolerable situation. What are we going to do about it?"

## A Love–Hate Relationship

If somebody asked me to describe how Black and Jewish feminists, or Blacks and Jews in general, deal with each other I would say what we have going is a love–hate relationship. The dynamic between us is often characterized by contradictory and ambivalent feelings, both negative and positive, distrust simultaneously mixed with a desire for acceptance; and deep resentment and heavy expectations about the other group's behavior. This dynamic is reflected in the current dialogue about Jewish identity and anti-Semitism in the feminist movement, when Jewish women seem to have different expectations for Black and other women of color than they do for white non-Jewish women. Often more weight is placed upon the anti-Jewish statements of women of color than upon the anti-Semitism of white non-Jewish feminists, although they are the majority group in the women's movement and in the society as a whole, and have more direct links to privilege and power.

I think that both Black and Jewish people expect more from each other than they do from white people generally or from gentiles generally. Alice Walker begins a response to Letty Cottin Pogrebin's article "Anti-Semitism in the Women's Movement" by writing:

> There is a close, often unspoken bond between Jewish and black women that grows out of their awareness of oppression and injustice, an awareness many Gentile women simply do not have.[6]

Our respective "awareness of oppression" leads us to believe that each other's communities should "know better" than to be racist or anti-Semitic because we have first-hand knowledge of bigotry and discrimination. This partially explains the disproportionate anger and blame we may feel when the other group displays attitudes much like those of the larger society.

It's true that each of our groups has had a history of politically imposed suffering. These histories are by no means identical, but at times the impact of the oppression has been brutally similar—segregation, ghettoization, physical violence, and death on such a massive scale that it is genocidal. Our experiences of racism and anti-Semitism, suffered at the hands of the white Christian majority, have sometimes made us practical and ideological allies. Yet white Jewish people's racism and Black gentile people's anti-Semitism have just as surely made us view each other as enemies. Another point of divergence is the fact that the majority of Jewish people immigrated to the United States to escape oppression in Europe and found a society by no means free from anti-Semitism, but one where it was possible in most cases to breathe again. For Black people, on the other hand, brought here forcibly as slaves, this country did not provide an escape. Instead, it has been the very locus of our oppression. The mere common experience of oppression does not guarantee our being able to get along, especially when the variables of time, place, and circumstance combine with race and class privilege, or lack of them, to make our situations objectively different.

The love–hate dynamic not only manifests itself politically, when our groups have functioned as both allies and adversaries, but also characterizes the more daily realm of face-to-face interactions. I think that women of color and Jewish women sometimes find each other more "familiar" than either of our groups find Christian majority W.A.S.P.s. A Black friend tells me, when I ask her about this sense of connectedness, "We don't come from quiet cultures." There are subliminal nuances of communication, shared fixes on reality, modes of expressing oneself, and ways of moving through the world that people from different groups sometimes recognize in each other. In his collection of interviews, *Working*, Studs Terkel uses the term the "feeling tone."[7] I think that Black and Jewish people sometimes share a similar "feeling tone." Melanie Kaye/Kantrowitz corroborates this perception in her instructive article, "Some Notes on Jewish Lesbian Identity." She describes the difficulties a group of non-Jewish women had with her "style" during the process of interviewing her for a job:

> Most of the women troubled by me had been sent to expensive colleges by their fathers, they spoke with well-modulated voices, and they quaked when I raised mine. They didn't understand that to me anger is common, expressible, and not murderous. They found me "loud" (of course) and "emotional." Interestingly, I got along fine with all the women of color in the group. . . .[8]

In a different situation a woman of color might very well feel antagonism toward a Jewish woman's "style," especially if she associates that "style" with a negative interaction—for example, if she experiences racist treatment from a Jewish woman or if she has to go through a rigorously unpleasant job interview with someone Jewish.

Nevertheless, Black and Jewish women grow up knowing that in relationship to the dominant culture, we just don't fit in. And though the chances of a Jewish woman being accepted by the status quo far exceed my own, when I'm up against the status quo I may turn to her as a potential ally. For example, on my way to an all white writer's retreat in New England, I'm relieved to find out that the female director of the retreat is Jewish. I think she might understand the isolation and alienation I inevitably face as the only one. Feelings of outsiderness cover everything from self-hatred about features and bodies that don't match a white, blue-eyed ideal, to shame about where your father works, or how your mother talks on the telephone. These feelings of shame and self-hatred affect not just Black and Jewish women, but other women of color and white ethnic and poor women. Class can be as essential a bond as ethnicity between women of color and white women, both Jewish and non-Jewish. Chicana poet Cherríe Moraga describes her differing levels of awareness about Jewish and Black genocide in "Winter of Oppression, 1982," and also remarks on the positive link that she has felt to Jewish people:

> . . . I already understood
> that these people were killed
> for the spirit-blood
> that runs through them.
>
> They were like us in this.
> Ethnic people with long last names
> with vowels at the end or the wrong
> type of consonants
> combined     a colored kind of white people[9]

There are ways that we recognize each other, things that draw us together. But feelings of affinity in themselves are not sufficient to bridge the culture, history, and political conditions that separate us. Only a conscious, usually politically motivated desire to work out differences, at the same time acknowledging commonalities, makes for more than superficial connection.

## To Jewish Women

I was concerned about anti-Semitism long before I called myself a feminist, indeed long before there was a feminist movement in which to work. Perhaps because I was born a year after World War II ended, that whole era seems quite vivid to me, its essence conveyed by members of my family. I got a basic sense about the war years and about what had happened to Jewish people because people around me, who had been greatly affected by those events, were still talking about them. Books, films, and history courses provided facts about Jewish oppression. Being friends with Jewish kids in school provided me with another kind of insight, the perception that comes from emotional connection.

My problems with recent explorations of Jewish identity and anti-Semitism in the women's movement do not result from doubting whether anti-Semitism exists or whether it is something that all people, including people of color, should oppose. What concerns me are the ways in which some Jewish women have raised these issues that have contributed to an atmosphere of polarization between themselves and women of color. My criticisms are not of Jewish feminism in general, but of specific political and ideological pitfalls that have led to the escalation of hostility between us, and that cannot be explained away as solely Black and other women of color's lack of sensitivity to anti-Semitism.

These polarizations have directly and painfully affected me and people close to me. One major problem (which I hope this essay does not contribute to) is that far too often these battles have been fought on paper, in published and unpublished writing. Besides the indirectness of this kind of confrontation, I want to say how sick I am of paper wars, when we are living on a globe that is literally at war, where thousands of people are dying every day, and most of the rest of the world's people still grapple for the barest human necessities of food, clothing, and shelter. In *Home Girls* I wrote the following to Black women about negative dynamics between Black and Jewish women in the movement:

> . . . I question whom it serves when we permit internal hostility to tear the movement we have built apart. Who benefits most? Undoubtedly, those outside forces that will go to any length to see us fail.[10]

I ask the same question here of Jewish women.

One of the most detrimental occurrences during this period has been the characterizing of Black and/or other women of color as being more anti-Semitic and much less concerned about combatting anti-Semitism than white non-Jewish women. Letty Cottin Pogrebin's article "Anti-Semitism in the Women's Movement" which appeared in *Ms.* magazine in June, 1982, and which was widely read, exemplifies this kind of thinking. She cites "Black–Jewish Relations" as one of ". . . the five problems basic to Jews and sisterhood," and then uses a number of quotes from Black women who are unsupportive of Jewish issues, but who also are not apparently active in the women's movement.[11] I have already referred to the social and historical circumstances that have linked our two groups and that might lead to our higher expectations for commitment and understanding of each other's situations. The desire for recognition and alliances, however, does not justify the portrayal of Black women, in particular, as being a bigger "problem" than white non-Jewish women or, more significantly, than the white male ruling class that gets to enforce anti-Semitism via the system. Black women need to know that Jewish women can make distinctions between the differing impact, for example, of a woman of color's resentment against Jews, her very real anti-Semitism, and that of the corporate giant, the government policy maker, or even the Ku Klux Klan member. Jewish women need to acknowledge the potential for racism in singling out Black and other women of color and that racism has already occurred in the guise of countering anti-Semitism. I expect Jewish women to confront Black women's anti-Semitism, but I am more than a little suspect when such criticism escalates time and again into frontal attack and blame.

I think Jewish women's desire for support and recognition has also resulted at times in attempts to portray our circumstances and the oppressions of racism and anti-Semitism as parallel or even identical. The mentality is manifested at its extreme when white Jewish women of European origin claim Third World identity by saying they are not white but Jewish, refusing to acknowledge that being visibly white in a racist society has concrete benefits and social-political repercussions. How we are oppressed does not have to be the same in order to qualify as real. One of the gifts of the feminist movement has been to examine subtleties of what comprises various oppressions without needing to pretend that they are all alike. As a Third World Lesbian I know, for example, that although her day-to-day circumstances may look nothing like my own, a white heterosexual middle-class woman experiences sexual oppression, that she can still be raped, and that class privilege does not save her from incest.

Trying to convince others that one is legitimately oppressed by making comparisons can either result from or lead to the ranking of oppressions, which is a dangerous pitfall in and of itself. In a letter responding to the Pogrebin article, a group of Jewish women write: "We sense a competition for victim status in Pogrebin's article and elsewhere. . . ."[12] I have sensed the same thing and I know it turns off women of color quicker than anything.

In a white dominated, capitalist economy, white skin, and if you have it, class privilege, definitely count for something, even if you belong at the very same time to a group or to groups that the society despises. Black women cannot help but resent it when people who have these privileges try to tell us that "everything is everything" and that their oppression is every bit as pervasive and dangerous as our own. From our frame of reference, given how brutally racism has functioned politically and historically against people of color in the U.S., such assertions are neither experientially accurate nor emotionally felt.

The fact that we have differing amounts of access to privilege and power can't help but influence how we respond to Jewish women's assertions of their cultural and political priorities. For example, in the last section of "Some Notes on Jewish Lesbian Identity," Melanie Kaye/Kantrowitz names Jewish women who resisted inside the concentration camps and in the Warsaw Ghetto, usually at the price of their lives. She concludes her article:

> Those were Jewish women. I come from women who fought like that.
> I want a button that says *Pushy Jew Loud Pushy Jew Dyke.*[13]

Despite the fact that this is a proud affirmation, reading the last sentence makes me wince, not because I don't understand the desire to reshape the negative words and images the society uses against those of us it hates, but because my gut response is, "I don't want to be treated like that." The positive image of Jewish women, who, like many Black women, refuse to disappear, who are not afraid to speak up, and who fight like hell for freedom, comes up against my experience as a Black woman who has, at times, felt pushed around and condescended to by women who are not just Jewish, but, more significantly, white. Because I come from a people who have historically been "pushed" around by all kinds of white people, I get upset that a traditional way of behaving might in fact affect me differently than it does a white non-Jewish woman.

Black and other women of color are much more likely to take seriously any group which wants their political support when that group acknowledges its privilege, at the same time working to transform its powerlessness. Privilege and oppression can and do exist simultaneously. I know, because they function together in my own life. As a well educated, currently able-bodied individual from a working-class family, who is also Black, a woman, and a Lesbian, I am constantly aware of how complex and contradictory these intersections are. Being honest about our differences is painful and requires large doses of integrity. As I've said in discussions of racism with white women who are sometimes overwhelmed at the implications of their whiteness, no one on earth had any say whatsoever about who or what they were born to be. You can't run the tape backward and start from scratch, so the question is, what are you going to do with what you've got? How are you going to deal responsibly with the unalterable facts of who and what you are, of having or not having privilege and power? I don't think anyone's case is inherently hopeless. It depends on what you decide to *do* once you're here, where you decide to place yourself in relationship to the ongoing struggle for freedom.

Another extremely negative wedge that has been driven between women of color and Jewish women is the notion that white Jewish and non-Jewish women have been "forced" to confront racism while women of color have not been required to, or have been completely unwilling to confront anti-Semitism. This is, of course, untrue. There are Black and other women of color who have taken definite stands against anti-Semitism (and our commitment to this issue cannot be measured, as I suspect it probably has been, by what is available in print). On the other hand, obviously not all white feminists or white people have sufficiently challenged racism, because if they had, racism would be a thing of the past. The implied resentment at having been "forced" to confront racism, is racist in itself. This kind of statement belies a weighing mentality that has no legitimate place in progressive coalition politics. Our support for struggles that do not directly encompass our own situations cannot be motivated by an expectation of pay-back. Of course we're likely to choose ongoing political allies on the basis of those groups and individuals who recognize and respect our humanity and issues, but the bottom line has got to be a fundamental opposition to oppression, period, not a tit-for-tat of "I'll support 'your' issue if you'll support 'mine'." In political struggles there wouldn't be any "your" and "my" issues, if we saw each form of oppression as integrally linked to the others.

A final matter that I want to discuss that can be offensive to Black and other women of color is the idea put forth by some Jewish feminists that to be or to have been at any time a Christian is to be by definition anti-Semitic. Traditional, institutionalized Christianity has, of course, had as one of its primary missions the destruction and invalidation of other systems of religious belief, not only Judaism, but Islam, Buddhism, Hinduism, and all of the indigenous religions of people of color. Holy wars, crusades, and pogroms qualify, I suppose, as "Christian totalitarianism,"[14] but I have great problems when this term is applied to the mere practice of Christianity.

In the case of Black people, the Christian religion was imposed upon us by white colonizers in Africa and by white slaveowners in the Americas. We nevertheless reshaped it into an a entirely unique expression of Black spirituality and faith, which has been and continues to be a major source of sustenance and survival for our people. Being Christian hardly translates into "privilege" for Black people, as exemplified by the fact that most white churches do not encourage Black membership and many actually maintain tacit or official policies of racial segregation. Christian privilege becomes a reality when it is backed up by race and class privilege. It is demoralizing and infuriating to have Black and other people of color's religious practices subsumed under the catch-all of white Christianity or Christian "totalitarianism." If anything has been traditionally encouraged in Afro-American churches, it is an inspirational identification with the bondage of "the Children of Israel" as recounted in the Old Testament. This emphasis did not, of course, prevent anti-Semitism (during slavery there was virtually no contact between Black and Jewish people in this country), but there needs to be some distinction made between being raised as a Christian, being anti-Semitic, and the historical role of the institutionalized Christian church in promoting anti-Semitism when its powers and goals have been directly tied to the power and interests of the state.

## To Black Women

Why should anti-Semitism be of concern to Black women? If for no other reason, anti-Semitism is one aspect of an intricate system of oppression that we by definition oppose when we say we are feminist, progressive, political. The Ku Klux Klan, the Christian right wing, and the American Nazi Party all promote anti-Semitism as well as racism. Lack of opposition to anti-Semitism lines us up with our enemies. People of color need to think about who our cohorts are when we express attitudes and take stands similar to those of the most dangerous and reactionary elements in this society. I'm talking here out of political principles, which can be a useful guide for approaching complicated questions. But needless to say, principles are not what any of us operate out of one-hundred percent of the time.

Certainly principles have only taken me so far in trying to deal with my gut responses to the ways that issues of anti-Semitism and Jewish identity have been raised in the women's movement. Like many Black feminists I could not help but notice how Jewish feminism arose just at the point that Third World feminist issues were getting minimal recognition from the movement as a whole. I saw how the feminism of women of color helped to lay the groundwork for Jewish feminists to name themselves, often without acknowledgment. I've seen how easy it has been for some Jewish women to make the shift from examining their role as racist oppressors, to focusing solely on their position as victims of oppression. I've also found the uncritical equating of the impact of anti-Semitism in the U.S. with the impact of racism absolutely galling.

If such "oversights" have made it difficult for us to get to the issue of anti-Semitism, continuing to experience racism from those women who seemingly want us to ignore their treatment of us and instead put energy into opposing an oppression which directly affects them has made commitment to the issue feel nearly impossible. The history of Black people in this country is a history of blood. It does not always dispose us to being altruistic and fair, because history has not been fair. Our blood is still being spilled. I know with what justification and fury we talk among ourselves about white people, Jews and non-Jews alike, and we will undoubtedly continue to talk about them as long as racism continues to undermine our lives.

In the case of racist Jewish people, we have something to throw back at them—anti-Semitism. Righteous as such comebacks might seem, it does not serve us, as feminists and political people, to ignore or excuse what is reactionary in ourselves. Our anti-Semitic attitudes are just that, both in the political sense and in the sense of reacting to another group's mistreatment of us. Although it isn't always possible or even logical for us to be "fair," being narrowminded and self-serving is not part of our Black ethical tradition either. Trying as it may seem, I think we are quite capable of working through our ambivalent or negative responses to arrive at a usable Black feminist stance in opposition to anti-Semitism.

A major problem for Black women, and all people of color, when we are challenged to oppose anti-Semitism, is our profound skepticism that white people can actually be oppressed. If white people as a group are our oppressors, and history and our individual experiences only verify that in mass they are, how can we then perceive some of these same folks as being in trouble, sometimes as deep as our own? A white woman with whom I once taught a seminar on racism and sexism told me about a friend of hers, also a teacher, who used John Steinbeck's *The Grapes of Wrath* in a class that had a large number of Black students. She told me how these students were absolutely convinced that the characters in the novel were Black because their situation was so terrible. It had never occurred to them that white people could suffer like that and the instructor had quite a job to do to get them to believe otherwise. I think it was in many ways an understandable mistake on the Black students' part, given how segregated Black life still is from white life in this country; the extreme arrogance and romanticism with which white people usually portray themselves in the media; and also how lacking all North Americans are in a class analysis (economic exploitation was the major force oppressing Steinbeck's characters).

On the other hand, this incident points to a basic attitude among us that I think often operates when the issue of anti-Semitism is raised. Almost all Jews in the United States are white people of European backgrounds, and therefore benefit from white-skin privilege, which is often combined with class privilege. Our frequent attitude when this particular group of white people tells us they're oppressed is (in the words of Ma Rainey) "Prove it on me!"[15] Many Black women who I've either talked to directly or who I've heard talk about the subject of anti-Semitism simply do not believe that Jews are now or ever have been oppressed. From our perspective it doesn't add up, because in those cases where Jewish people have white skin, high levels of education, economic privilege, and political influence, they are certainly not oppressed like us. I have to admit that this is certainly the aspect of the position of Jewish people in this country that I have the most problems with and I think many other people of color do too. White skin and class privilege make assimilation possible and provide a cushion unavailable to the majority of people of color. Sometimes I actually get disgusted when I see how good other people can have it and still be oppressed. When white, economically privileged Jews admit to their privilege, as opposed to pretending that it either doesn't exist or that it has no significant impact upon the quality of their lives, then I don't feel so envious and angry.

Jewish oppression is not identical to Black oppression, but it is oppression brought to bear by the same white-male ruling class which oppresses us. An investigation of Jewish history, as well as of the current situation of Jews in countries such as Russia, reveals centuries of abuse by traditionally Christian dominated states. Anti-Semitism has taken many forms, including physical segregation, sanctions against the practice of the Jewish religion, exclusion from certain jobs and professions, violent attacks by individuals, state co-ordinated pogroms (massacres), and the Nazi-engineered Holocaust which killed one-third of the world's Jews between 1933 and 1945. Anti-Semitism has been both more violent and more widespread in Europe than in the U.S., but it is currently on the increase as the political climate grows ever more reactionary. Because it is not point-for-point identical to what we experience doesn't mean it is not happening or that it is invalid for people to whom it is happening to protest and organize against it.

Another instance of skepticism about whether white people can actually be oppressed sometimes occurs when Black people who do not identify with feminism are asked to consider that sexual politics affect all women. Their disbelief leads to at least two equally inaccurate responses. The first is that sexism is a white woman's thing and Black women are, of course, already liberated. The other is that it is not possible for a rich white woman, "Miss Ann type" to be oppressed in the first place. In neither response is sexual oppression taken seriously or seen as an independently operating system. White-skin privilege is assumed to compensate for lack of power and privilege in every other sphere. All white women are assumed to be exactly alike, a monolithic group who are wealthy, pampered, and self-indulgent. However, as Third World feminists we know that sexual oppression cuts across all racial, class, and nationality lines, at the same time we understand how race, class, ethnicity, culture and the political system under which one lives determine the specific content of that oppression. The ability to analyze complicated intersections of privilege and oppression can help us to grasp that having white skin does not negate the reality of anti-Semitism. As long as opposing anti-Semitism is narrowly viewed as defending white people's interests, we will undoubtedly be extremely reluctant to speak about it.* We need to understand that we can oppose anti-Semitism at the very same time that we oppose white racism, including white Jewish people's racism.

---

*It is also important to know that significant numbers of Jews outside the U.S. are people of color, including Jews from Ethiopia, China, India, Arab countries, and elsewhere.

In political dialogue and in private conversation, it is more than possible to attack and criticize racism and racist behavior without falling back on the stereotypes and ideology of another system of oppression. The bankruptcy of such tactics is exemplified by a front page headline in *The Black American* newspaper (notable for its reactionary stances on just about everything) which derisively referred to New York's mayor, Edward Koch, as a faggot.[16] Koch's general misrule and countless abuses against people of color in New York are a matter of public record. Homophobia aimed at him did not directly confront these abuses, however; his racism in no way justified a homophobic put-down; and finally such tactics were transparently the weapons of the weak and weakminded. The self-righteousness with which some individuals express homophobia parallels the self-righteousness with which some of these same individuals and others express anti-Semitism. In both instances, such attacks are not even perceived as wrong, because of the pervasive, socially sanctioned contempt for the group in question. I'm not suggesting that people merely talk nice to each other for the sake of talking nice, but that as progressive women of color it is our responsibility to figure out how to confront oppression directly. If we are not interested in being called out of our names, we can assume that other people don't want to be called out of theirs either, even when the larger white society thoroughly condones such behavior.

The disastrous situation in the Middle East is used as yet another justification for unbridled anti-Semitism, which crops up in political groupings ranging from the most reactionary to the most ostensibly radical. The fact that the left, including some Third World organizations, frequently couches its disagreements with Israel's politics in anti-Semitic terms further confuses us about how to state our criticisms effectively and ethically.[17] Too often when I've brought up the problem of anti-Semitism, a woman of color responds, "But what about the Middle East?" as if opposition to Israeli actions and support for the Palestinians' right to a homeland can only be expressed by making anti-Semitic remarks to reinforce valid political perspectives. This tactic "works" all too often because so many non-Jews do not perceive verbalized anti-Semitism as unacceptable or when confronted, they act as if it has not even occurred.

Without delving into the pros and cons of the convoluted Middle East situation, I think that it is essential to be able to separate what Israel does when it functions as a white male-run imperialist state from what individual Jewish people's responsibility in relation to that situation can be. What do Jewish people who are not the people who run that state, by and large, actually want and stand for? There is a peace movement in Israel of which Israeli feminists are a significant part. In this country progressive groups like the New Jewish Agenda are defining a more complex political stance of supporting the continued existence of the state of Israel, while voicing grave criticisms of current policies and recognizing the rights of Palestinians to a homeland. Black and other Third World women must express our opposition to Israeli actions in the Middle East, if in fact we are opposed, without assuming that every Jewish person both there and here uncritically agrees with Israeli actions and colludes with those policies. Can criticisms be expressed without throwing in the "obligatory" anti-Semitic remarks and attitudes? Can Jewish women hear criticisms of Israeli actions not only from women of color but also from white non-Jewish women without assuming that their rights as Jews and as human beings to continue to survive are being questioned?

Of course, there is an emotional layer to Black and Jewish women's attitudes about the Israeli–Palestinian conflict that is directly linked to who we are. Many Jewish women view Israel as a place of refuge. They support it as the only existing Jewish state, the one place where Jews were allowed to emigrate freely following the Holocaust, and where most Jews are still granted automatic citizenship.* Often Black and other women of color feel a visceral identification with the Palestinians, because like the Vietnamese, Nicaraguans, and Black South Africans, they are a colored people struggling for the liberation of their homeland. Our two groups very often have differing responses to the Middle East situation and I am not so naive as to expect total agreement between us about the best course for rectifying what has been up to now an intractable and violent situation. I am only asserting that our anti-Semitic or Jewish people's racist attacks do not comprise legitimate "criticisms" of the other group's point of view.

How we deal as Black women with anti-Semitism and with Jewish women ultimately boils down to how we define our politics which are admittedly diverse. What I've written here are some ways to think about these vastly complicated issues, growing out of my particular political perspective. As a Black feminist I believe in our need for autonomy in determining where we stand on every issue. I also believe in the necessity for short and long term coalitions when it is viable for various groups to get together to achieve specific goals. Finally, there is my personal belief that political interactions and all other human connections cannot work without some basic level of ethics and respect. We don't oppose anti-Semitism because we owe something to Jewish people, but because we owe something very basic to ourselves.

## Between a Rock and a Hard Place

Some of the pitfalls that have characterized the growth of Jewish feminism can be traced to ideological tendencies in the women's movement as a whole. I want to outline several of these here, because of the effect they have had upon relationships between Black and Jewish women, as well as upon relationships between other women of different cultures, classes, and races. These tendencies have also led to numerous misunderstandings within feminism, generally, about the nature of oppression and how to fight it.

The concept of identity politics has been extremely useful in the development of Third World feminism. It has undoubtedly been most clarifying and catalytic when individuals do in fact have a combination of non-mainstream identities as a result of their race, class, ethnicity, sex, and sexuality; when these identities make them direct targets of oppression; and when they use their experiences of oppression as a spur for activist political work. Identity politics has been much less effective when primary emphasis has been placed upon exploring and celebrating a suppressed identity within a women's movement context, rather than upon developing practical political solutions for confronting oppression in the society itself.

A limited version of identity politics often overlaps with two other currents within the movement: Lesbian separatism and cultural feminism (which emphasizes the development of a distinct women's culture through such vehicles as music, art, and spirituality). These approaches to dealing with being social-cultural outsiders only work when the more stringent realities of class and race are either not operative (because everybody involved is white and middle-class) or when these material realities are ignored or even forcibly

---

*Jewish Lesbians and gay men are excluded from the Law of Return.

denied. Lesbian separatism, which might be thought of as an extreme variety of identity politics, has seldom been very useful for poor and working-class white women or for the majority of women of color, because in attributing the whole of women's oppression to one cause, the existence of men (or of patriarchy), it has left out myriad other forces that oppress women who are not economically privileged and/or white. When Jewish feminism has subscribed to or been influenced by cultural feminism, separatism, or a narrow version of identity politics, it has been limited in both analysis and strategy, since, for example, anti-Semitism does not manifest itself solely as attacks upon individuals' identities, nor does it only affect Jewish women.

Another major misunderstanding within feminism as a whole that has affected the conception of Jewish feminism is the notion that it is politically viable to work on anti-Semitism, racism, or any other system of oppression solely *within* a women's movement context. Although all the systems of oppression cannot help but manifest themselves inside the women's movement, they do not start or end there. It is fallacious and irresponsible to think that working on them internally only with other feminists is ultimately going to have a substantial, permanent effect on the power structure from which they spring. I don't live in the women's movement, I live on the streets of North America. Internal women's movement solutions are just that. They have only fractional impact on the power of the state which determines the daily content of my life.

Although I've focused on relationships between Black and Jewish women, I do not think for a moment that the whole of our respective oppressions can be reduced to how we treat each other, which is yet another mistaken notion afloat in the movement. Yes, it helps for us as feminists to respect each other's differences and to attempt to act decently, but it is ultimately much more "helpful" to do organizing that confronts oppression at its roots in the political system as a whole.

There is a last point I want to make about the political work we do and the people we are able to do it with. My intention in addressing the issues of Black and Jewish relationships, racism and anti-Semitism has been to encourage better understanding between us and to support the possibility of coalition work. It is obvious, however, that there are substantial political differences and disagreements between us and that some of these, despite efforts to alleviate them, will no doubt remain. Ongoing coalitions are formed, in truth, not on the basis of political correctness or "shoulds," but on the pragmatic basis of shared commitments, politics, and beliefs. Some Jewish women and some women of color are not likely to work together because they are very much in opposition to each other *politically*. And that's all right, because there are other Jewish women and women of color who are already working together and who will continue to do so, because they have some basic political assumptions and goals in common.

Relationships between Black and Jewish women are the very opposite of simple. Our attempts to make personal/political connections virtually guarantee our being thrust between "the rock" of our own people's suspicion and disapproval and "the hard place" of the other group's antagonism and distrust. It is a lot easier to categorize people, to push them into little nastily-labelled boxes, than time and again to deal with them directly, to make distinctions between the stereotype and the substance of who and what they are. It's little wonder that so often both Black and Jewish women first label and then dismiss each other. All of us resort to this tactic when the impact of our different histories, cultures, classes, and skins backs us up against the wall and we do not have the courage or desire to examine what, if anything, of value lies between us. Cherríe Moraga writes, "Oppression does not make for hearts as big as all outdoors. Oppression makes us big and small. Expressive and silenced. Deep and dead."[18] We are certainly damaged people. The question is, finally, do we use that damage, that first-hand knowledge of oppression, to recognize each other, to do what work we can together? Or do we use it to destroy?

## Reading Questions

1. What are some examples of white-skin privilege, and how is it different from class privilege?
2. Why does Smith claim that she is anti-Semitic?
3. What, according to Smith, are the major differences between the politically imposed suffering of white American Jewish people and American people of color?
4. What is coalitional politics, and why, according to Smith, are competitions for victim status destructive of coalitions?
5. Why does Smith argue against the idea that to be a practicing Christian is to be anti-Semitic? How does she distinguish Christianity as it is practiced by the white majority in the United States, as compared to how it has been traditionally practiced by African Americans?
6. What is "assimilation"? And why is Smith occasionally disgusted by it?
7. What position does Smith take toward the Israeli–Palestinian conflict in the Middle East? Why is this conflict significant for American feminism?

## Recommended Reading

Gloria Anzaldúa and Cherríe Moraga, eds., *This Bridge Called My Back: Writings by Radical Women of Color* (New York: Kitchen Table, Women of Color Press, 1983)

Evelyn Torton Beck, "From 'Kike' to 'Jap': How Misogyny, Anti-Semitism, and Racism Construct the 'Jewish American Princess,' " *Sojourner: The Women's Forum* (September 1988)

Elly Bulkin, "Hard Ground: Jewish Identity, Racism and Anti-Semitism," *Yours in Struggle: Three Feminist Perspectives on Anti-Semitism and Racism*, ed. Elly Bulkin, Minnie Bruce Pratt, and Barbara Smith (Ithaca, NY: Firebrand Books, 1984)

Audre Lorde, *Sister Outsider: Essays and Speeches* (Trumansburg, NY: Crossing Press, 1984)

Judith Plaskow, *Women and Judaism: Judaism from a Feminist Perspective* (New York: HarperCollins, 1991)

Letty Pogrebin, *Deborah, Golda and Me: Being Female and Jewish in America* (New York: Doubleday, 1992)

Edward Said, *The Question of Palestine* (New York: Columbia University Press, 1979)

Edward Said, *Culture and Imperialism* (New York: Knopf, 1993)

## Recommended Audiovisual Resources

*The New Politics of Race: The New David Duke*. 1992. Phil Donahue interviews David Duke. Films for the Humanities & Sciences.

*A Question of Color*. 1992. Directed by Kathe Sandler. Sandler's documentary confronts color consciousness among African Americans, through the 1960s "black is beautiful" movement and the ongoing struggle of black women to redefine European standards of beauty that affect their sense of self-worth today. A Frameline release.

# Playfulness, "World"-Travelling, and Loving Perception

## MARÍA LUGONES

María Lugones teaches philosophy and cultural studies at the State University of New York at Binghamton and is active in radical grassroots politics at Escuela Popular Nortena.

## "Worlds" and "World" Travelling

Some time ago I came to be in a state of profound confusion as I experienced myself as both having and not having a particular attribute. I was sure I had the attribute in question and, on the other hand, I was sure that I did not have it. I remain convinced that I both have and do not have this attribute. The attribute is playfulness. I am sure that I am a playful person. On the other hand, I can say, painfully, that I am not a playful person. I am not a playful person in certain worlds. One of the things I did as I became confused was to call my friends, far away people who knew me well, to see whether or not I was playful. Maybe they could help me out of my confusion. They said to me, "Of course you are playful" and they said it with the same conviction that I had about it. Of course I am playful. Those people who were around me said to me, "No, you are not playful. You are a serious woman. You just take everything seriously." They were just as sure about what they said to me and could offer me every bit of evidence that one could need to conclude that they were right. So I said to myself: "Okay, maybe what's happening here is that there is an attribute that I do have but there are certain worlds in which I am not at ease and it is because I'm not at ease in those worlds that I don't have that attribute in those worlds. But what does that mean?" I was worried both about what I meant by "worlds" when I said "in some worlds I do not have the attribute" and what I meant by saying that lack of ease was what led me not to be playful in those worlds. Because you see, if it was just a matter of lack of ease, I could work on it.

I can explain some of what I mean by a "world." I do not want the fixity of a definition at this point, because I think the term is suggestive and I do not want to close the suggestiveness of it too soon. I can offer some characteristics that serve to distinguish between a "world," a utopia, a possible world in the philosophical sense, and a world view. By a "world" I do not mean a utopia at all. A utopia does not count as a world in my sense. The "worlds" that I am talking about are possible. But a possible world is not what I mean by a "world" and I do not mean a world-view, though something like a world-view is involved here.

For something to be a "world" in my sense it has to be inhabited at present by some flesh and blood people. That is why it cannot be a utopia. It may also be inhabited by some imaginary people. It may be inhabited by people who are dead or people that the inhabitants of this "world" met in some other "world" and now have in this "world" in imagination.

A "world" in my sense may be an actual society given its dominant culture's description and construction of life, including a construction of the relationships of production, of gender, race, etc. But a "world" can also be such a society given a non-dominant construction, or it can be such a society or *a* society given an idiosyncratic construction. As we will see it is problematic to say that these are all constructions of the same society. But they are different "worlds."

A "world" need not be a construction of a whole society. It may be a construction of a tiny portion of a particular society. It may be inhabited by just a few people. Some "worlds" are bigger than others.

A "world" may be incomplete in that things in it may not be altogether constructed or some things may be constructed negatively (they are not what 'they' are in some other "world"). Or the "world" may be incomplete because it may have references to things that do not quite exist in it, references to things like Brazil, where Brazil is not quite part of that "world." Given lesbian feminism, the construction of 'lesbian' is purposefully and healthily still up in the air, in the process of becoming. What it is to be a Hispanic in this country is, in a dominant Anglo construction purposefully incomplete. Thus one cannot really answer questions of the sort "What is a Hispanic?", "Who counts as a Hispanic?", "Are Latinos, Chicanos, Hispanos, black dominicans, white cubans, korean-colombians, italian-argentinians, hispanic?" What it is to be a 'hispanic' in the varied so-called hispanic communities in the U.S. is also yet up in the air. We have not yet decided whether there is something like a 'hispanic' in our varied "worlds." So, a "world" may be an incomplete visionary non-utopian construction of life or it may be a traditional construction of life. A traditional Hispano construction of Northern New Mexican life is a "world." Such a traditional construction, in the face of a racist, ethnocentrist, money-centered anglo construction of Northern New Mexican life is highly unstable because Anglos have the means for imperialist destruction of traditional Hispano "worlds."

In a "world" some of the inhabitants may not understand or hold the particular construction of them that constructs them in that "world." So, there may be "worlds" that construct me in ways that I do not even understand. Or it may be that I understand the construction, but do not hold it of myself. I may not accept it as an account of myself, a construction of myself. And yet, I may be *animating* such a construction.

One can "travel" between these "worlds" and one can inhabit more than one of these "worlds" at the very same time. I think that most of us who are outside the mainstream of, for example, the U.S. dominant construction or organization of life are "world travellers" as a matter of necessity and of survival. It seems to me that inhabiting more than one "world" at the same time and "travelling" between "worlds" is part and parcel of our experience and our situation. One can be at the same time in a "world" that constructs one as stereotypically latin, for example, and in a "world" that constructs one as latin. Being stereotypically latin and being simply latin are different simultaneous constructions of persons that are part of different "worlds." One animates one or the other or both at the same time without necessarily confusing them, though simultaneous enactment can be confusing if one is not on one's guard.

In describing my sense of a "world," I mean to be offering a description of experience, something that is true to experience even if it is ontologically problematic. Though I would think that any account of identity that could not be true to this experience of outsiders to the mainstream would be faulty even if ontologically unproblematic. Its ease would constrain, erase, or deem aberrant experience that has within it significant insights into non-imperialistic understanding between people.

Those of us who are "world"-travellers have the distinct experience of being different in different "worlds" and of having the capacity to remember other "worlds" and ourselves in them. We can say "That is me there, and I am happy in that 'world.'" So, the experience is of being a different person in different "worlds" and yet of having memory of oneself as different without quite having the sense of there being any underlying "I." So I can say "That is me there and I am so playful in that 'world.'" I say "That is *me* in that 'world'" not because I recognize myself in that person, rather the first person statement is non-inferential. I may well recognize that that person has abilities that I do not have and yet the having or not having of the abilities is always an "I have . . ." and "I do not have . . .," i.e. it is always experienced in the first person.

The shift from being one person to being a different person is what I call "travel." This shift may not be willful or even conscious, and one may be completely unaware of being different than one is in a different "world," and may not recognize that one is in a different "world." Even though the shift can be done willfully, it is not a matter of acting. One does not pose as something else, one does not pretend to be, for example, someone of a different personality or character or someone who uses space or language differently than the other person. Rather one is someone who has that personality or character or uses space and language in that particular way. The "one" here does not refer to some underlying "I." One does not *experience* any underlying "I."

## Being at Ease in a "World"

In investigating what I mean by "being at ease in a 'world'," I will describe different ways of being at ease. One may be at ease in one or in all of these ways. There is a maximal way of being at ease, viz. being at ease in all of these ways. I take this maximal way of being at ease to be somewhat dangerous because it tends to produce people who have no inclination to travel across "worlds" or have no experience of "world" travelling.

The first way of being at ease in a particular "world" is by being a fluent speaker in that "world." I know all the norms that there are to be followed, I know all the words that there are to be spoken. I know all the moves. I am confident.

Another way of being at ease is by being normatively happy. I agree with all the norms, I could not love any norms better. I am asked to do just what I want to do or what I think I should do. At ease.

Another way of being at ease in a "world" is by being humanly bonded. I am with those I love and they love me too. It should be noticed that I may be with those I love and be at ease because of them in a "world" that is otherwise as hostile to me as "worlds" get.

Finally one may be at ease because one has a history with others that is shared, especially daily history, the kind of shared history that one sees exemplified by the response to the "Do you remember poodle skirts?" question. There you are, with people you do not know at all. The question is posed and then they all begin talking about their poodle skirt stories. I have been in such situations without knowing what poodle skirts, for example, were and I felt so ill at ease because it was not *my* history. The other people did not particularly know each other. It is not that they were humanly bonded. Probably they did not have much politically in common either. But poodle skirts were in their shared history.

One may be at ease in one of these ways or in all of them. Notice that when one says meaningfully "This is *my* world," one may not be at ease in it. Or one may be at ease in it only in some of these respects and not in others. To say of some "world" that it is "*my* world" is to make an evaluation. One may privilege one or more "worlds" in this way for a variety of reasons: for example because one experiences oneself as an agent in a fuller sense than one experiences "oneself" in other "worlds." One may disown a "world" because one has first person memories of a person who is so thoroughly dominated that she has no sense of exercising her own will or has a sense of having serious difficulties in performing actions that are willed by herself and no difficulty in performing actions willed by others. One may say of a "world" that it is "my world" because one is at ease in it, i.e. being at ease in a "world" may be the basis for the evaluation.

Given the clarification of what I mean by a "world," "world"-travel, and being at ease in a "world," we are in a position to return to my problematic attribute, playfulness. It may be that in this "world" in which I am so unplayful, I am a different person than in the "world" in which I am playful. Or it may be that the "world" in which I am unplayful is constructed in such a way that I could be playful in it. I could practice, even though that "world" is constructed in such a way that my being playful in it is kind of hard. In describing what I take a "world" to be, I emphasized the first possibility as both the one that is truest to the experience of "outsiders" to the mainstream and as ontologically problematic because the "I" is identified in some sense as one and in some sense as a plurality. I identify myself as myself through memory and I retain myself as different in memory. When I travel from one "world" to another, I have this image, this memory of myself as playful in this other "world." I can then be in a particular "world" and have a double image of myself as, for example, playful and as not playful. But this is a very familiar and recognizable phenomenon to the outsider to the mainstream in some central cases: when in one "world" I animate, for example, that "world's" caricature of the person I am in the other "world." I can have both images of myself and to the extent that I can materialize or animate both images at the same time I become an ambiguous being. This is very much a part of trickery and foolery. It is worth remembering that the trickster and the fool are significant characters in many non-dominant or outsider cultures. One then sees any particular "world" with these double edges and sees absurdity in them and so inhabits oneself differently. Given that latins are constructed in Anglo "worlds" as ste-reotypically intense—intensity being a central characteristic of at least one of the anglo stereotypes of latins—and given that many latins, myself included, are genuinely intense, I can say to myself, "I am intense" and take a hold of the double meaning. And further-more, I can be stereotypically intense or be the real thing and, if you are Anglo, you do not know when I am which *because* I am Latin-American. As Latin-American I am an ambiguous being, a two-imaged self: I can see that gringos see me as stereotypically intense because I am, as a Latin-American, constructed that way but I may or may not *intentionally* animate the stereotype or the real thing knowing that you may not see it in anything other than in the stereotypical construction. This ambiguity is funny and is not just funny, it is survival-rich. We can also make the picture of those who dominate us funny precisely because we can see the double edge, we can see them doubly constructed, we can see the plurality in them. So we know truths that only the fool can speak and only the trickster can play out without harm. We inhabit "worlds" and travel across them and keep all the memories.

Sometimes the "world"-traveller has a double image of herself and each self includes as important ingredients of itself one or more attributes that are *incompatible* with one or more of the attributes of the other self: for example being playful and being unplayful. To the extent that the attribute is an important ingredient of the self she is in that "world," i.e., to the extent that there is a particularly good fit between that "world" and her having that attribute in it and to the extent that the attribute is personality or character central, that "world" would have to be changed if she is to be playful in it. It is not the case that if she could come to be at ease in it, she would be her own playful self. Because the attribute is personality or character central and there is such a good fit between that "world" and her being constructed with that attribute as central, *she* cannot become playful, she is unplayful. To become playful would be for her to become a contradictory being. So I am suggesting that the lack of ease solution cannot be a solution to my problematic case. My problem is not one of lack of ease. I am suggesting that I can understand my confusion about whether I am or am not playful by saying that I am both and that I am different persons in different "worlds" and can remember myself in both as I am in the other. I am a plurality of selves. This is to understand my confusion because *it is to come to see it as a piece* with much of the rest of my experience as an outsider in some of the "worlds" that I inhabit and of a piece with significant aspects of the experience of non-dominant people in the "worlds" of their dominators.

So, though I may not be at ease in the "worlds" in which I am not constructed playful, it is not that I am not playful *because* I am not at ease. The two are compatible. But lack of playfulness is not caused by lack of ease. Lack of playfulness is not symptomatic of lack of ease but of lack of health. I am not a healthy being in the "worlds" that construct me unplayful.

## Playfulness

I had a very personal stake in investigating this topic. Playfulness is not only the attribute that was the source of my confusion and the attitude that I recommend as the loving attitude in travelling across "worlds," I am also scared of ending up a serious human being, someone with no multi-dimensionality, with no fun in life, someone who is just someone who has had the fun constructed out of her. I am seriously scared of getting stuck in a "world" that constructs me that way. A world that I have no escape from and in which I cannot be playful.

I thought about what it is to be playful and what it is to play and I did this thinking in a "world" in which I only remember myself as playful and in which all of those who know me as playful are imaginary beings. A "world" in which I am scared of losing my memories of myself as playful or have them erased from me. Because I live in such a "world," after I formulated my own sense of what it is to be playful and to play I decided that I needed to "go to the literature." I read two classics on the subject: Johan Huizinga's *Homo Ludens* and Hans-Georg Gadamer's chapter on the concept of play in his *Truth and Method*. I discovered, to my amazement, that what I thought about play and playfulness, if they were right, was absolutely wrong. Though I will not provide the arguments for this interpretation of Gadamer and Huizinga here, I understood that both of them have an agonistic sense of "play." Play and playfulness have, ultimately, to do with contest, with winning, losing, battling. The sense of playfulness that I have in mind has nothing to do with those things. So, I tried to elucidate both senses of play and playfulness by contrasting them to each other. The contrast helped me see the attitude that I have in mind as the loving attitude in travelling across "worlds" more clearly.

An agonistic sense of playfulness is one in which *competence* is supreme. You better know the rules of the game. In agonistic play there is risk, there is *uncertainty*, but the uncertainty is about who is going to win and who is going to lose. There are rules that inspire hostility. The attitude of *playfulness is conceived as secondary to or derivative from play*. Since play is agon, then the only conceivable playful attitude is an agonistic one (the attitude does not turn an activity into play, but rather presupposes an activity that is play). One of the paradigmatic ways of playing for both Gadamer and Huizinga is role-playing. In role-playing, the person who is a participant in the game has a *fixed conception of him or herself*. I also think that the players are imbued with *self-importance* in agonistic play since they are so keen on winning given their own merits, their very own competence.

When considering the value of "world"-travelling and whether playfulness is the loving attitude to have while travelling, I recognized the agonistic attitude as inimical to travelling across "worlds." The agonistic traveller is a conqueror, an imperialist. Huizinga, in his classic book on play, interprets Western civilization as play. That is an interesting thing for Third World people to think about. Western civilization has been interpreted by a white western man as play in the agonistic sense of play. Huizinga reviews western law, art, and many other aspects of western culture and sees agon in all of them. Agonistic playfulness leads those who attempt to travel to another "world" with this attitude to failure. Agonistic travellers fail consistently in their attempt to travel because what they do is to try to conquer the other "world." The attempt is not an attempt to try to erase the other "world." That is what assimilation is all about. Assimilation is the destruction of other people's "worlds." So, the agonistic attitude, the playful attitude given western man's construction of playfulness, is not a healthy, loving attitude to have in travelling across "worlds." Notice that given the agonistic attitude one *cannot* travel across "worlds," though one can kill other "worlds" with it. So for people who are interested in crossing racial and ethnic boundaries, an arrogant western man's construction of playfulness is deadly. One cannot cross the boundaries with it. One needs to give up such an attitude if one wants to travel.

So then, what is the loving playfulness that I have in mind? Let me begin with one example: We are by the river bank. The river is very, very low. Almost dry. Bits of water here and there. Little pools with a few trout hiding under the rocks. But mostly is wet stones, grey on the outside. We walk on the stones for awhile. You pick up a stone and crash it onto the others. As it breaks, it is quite wet inside and it is very colorful, very pretty. I pick up a stone and break it and run toward the pieces to see the colors. They are beautiful. I laugh and bring the pieces back to you and you are doing the same with your pieces. We keep on crashing stones for hours, anxious to see the beautiful new colors. We are playing. The playfulness of our activity does not presuppose that there is something like "crashing stones" that is a particular form of play with its own rules. Rather *the attitude that carries us through the activity, a playful attitude, turns the activity into play.* Our activity has no rules, though it is certainly intentional activity and we both understand what we are doing. The playfulness that gives meaning to our activity includes uncertainty, but in this case the uncertainty is an *openness to surprise*. This is a particular metaphysical attitude that does not expect the world to be neatly packaged, ruly. Rules may fail to explain what we are doing. We are not self-important, we are not fixed in particular constructions of ourselves, which is part of saying that we are *open to self-construction*. We may not have rules, and when we do have rules, *there are no rules that are to us sacred*. We are not worried about competence. We are not wedded to a particular way of doing things. While playful we have not abandoned ourselves to, nor are we stuck in, any particular "world." We *are there creatively*. We are not passive.

Playfulness is, in part, an openness to being a fool, which is a combination of not worrying about competence, not being self-important, not taking norms as sacred and finding ambiguity and double edges a source of wisdom and delight.

So, positively, the playful attitude involves openness to surprise, openness to being a fool, openness to self-construction or reconstruction and to construction or reconstruction of the "worlds" we inhabit playfully. Negatively, playfulness is characterized by uncertainty, lack of self-importance, absence of rules or a not taking rules as sacred, a not worrying about competence and a lack of abandonment to a particular construction of oneself, others and one's relation to them. In attempting to take a hold of oneself and of one's relation to others in a particular "world," one may study, examine and come to understand oneself. One may then see what the possibilities for play are for the being one is in that "world." One may even decide to inhabit that self fully in order to understand it better and find its creative possibilities. All of this is just self-reflection and it is quite different from resigning or abandoning oneself to the particular construction of oneself that one is attempting to take a hold of.

# Conclusion

There are "worlds" we enter at our own risk, "worlds" that have agon, conquest, and arrogance as the main ingredients in their ethos. These are "worlds" that we enter out of necessity and which would be foolish to enter playfully in either the agonistic sense or in my sense. In such "worlds" *we* are not playful.

But there are "worlds" that we can travel to lovingly and travelling to them is part of loving at least some of their inhabitants. The reason why I think that travelling to someone's "world" is a way of identifying with them is because by travelling to their "world" we can understand *what [it] is to be them and what it is to be ourselves in their eyes*. Only when we have travelled to each other's "worlds" are we fully subjects to each other (I agree with Hegel that self-recognition requires other subjects, but I disagree with his claim that it requires tension or hostility).

Knowing other women's "worlds" is part of knowing them and knowing them is part of loving them. Notice that the knowing can be done in greater or lesser depth, as can the loving. Also notice that travelling to another's "world" is not the same as becoming intimate with them. Intimacy is constituted in part by a very deep knowledge of the other self and "world" travelling is only part of having this knowledge. Also notice that some people, in particular those who are outsiders to the mainstream, can be known only to the extent that they are known in several "worlds" and as "world"-travellers.

Without knowing the other's "world," one does not know the other, and without knowing the other one is really alone in the other's presence because the other is only dimly present to one.

Through travelling to other people's "worlds" we discover that there are "worlds" in which those who are the victims of arrogant perception are really subjects, lively beings, resistors, constructors of visions even though in the mainstream construction they are animated only by the arrogant perceiver and are pliable, foldable, file-awayable, classifiable. I always imagine the Aristotelian slave as pliable and foldable at night or after he or she cannot work anymore (when he or she dies as a tool). Aristotle tells us nothing about the slave *apart from the master*. We know the slave only through the master. The slave is a tool of the master. After working hours he or she is folded and placed in a drawer till the next morning. . . .

So, in recommending "world"-travelling and identification through "world"-travelling as part of loving other women, I am suggesting disloyalty to arrogant perceivers, including the arrogant perceiver in ourselves, and to their constructions of women. In revealing agonistic playfulness as incompatible with "world"-travelling, I am revealing both its affinity with imperialism and arrogant perception and its incompatibility with loving and loving perception.

## Reading Questions

1. What does the author mean by the term *world*, and why is this important?
2. What does it mean, according to the author, to be a "world-traveller?"
3. What does it mean, according to the author, to be at ease in a world?
4. How does Lugones's account of playfulness differ from agonistic accounts? Specifically, how is agonistic playfulness seen to be incompatible with loving perception?

## Recommended Reading

Oliva M. Espin, "Cultural and Historical Influences on Sexuality in Hispanic/Latin Women," *Pleasure and Danger*, ed. Carole Vance (Boston: Routledge and Kegan Paul, 1984)

María Lugones, "*Hispaneando y Lesbiando*: On Sarah Hoagland's *Lesbian Ethics*," *Hypatia* 5:3 (Fall 1990)

Juanita Ramos, ed., *Companeras: Latina Lesbians* (New York: Latina Lesbian History Project, 1987)

Ofelia Schutte, *Cultural Identity and Social Liberation in Latin American Thought* (Albany: State University of New York Press, 1993)

Ofelia Schutte, "Philosophical Feminism in Latin America and Spain: An Introduction," *Hypatia* 9:1 (Winter 1994)

Doris Sommer, " 'Not Just a Personal Story': Women's *Testimonios* and the Plural Self," *Life/Lines: Theorizing Women's Autobiography*, ed. Bella Brodzki and Celeste Schenck (Ithaca, NY: Cornell University Press, 1988)

*Third World Second Sex: Women's Struggles and National Liberation* (London: Zed, 1983)

# Voices

## WOMEN OF ACE (AIDS COUNSELING AND EDUCATION), BEDFORD HILLS CORRECTIONAL FACILITY

The authors of this essay are Kathy Boudin, Judy Clark, "D," Katrina Haslip, Maria D. L. Hernandez, Suzanne Kessler, Sonia Perez, Deborah Plunkett, Aida Rivera, Doris Romeo, Carmen Royster, Cathy Salce, Renee Scott, Jenny Serrano, and Pearl Ward. Kathy Boudin is the author of *The Bust Book: What to Do Till the Lawyer Comes*. All are AIDS activists in prison reform and in women's health and reproductive rights issues.

## Introduction

We are writing about ACE because we feel that it has made a tremendous difference in this prison and could make a difference in other prisons. ACE stands for AIDS Counseling and Education. It is a collective effort by women in Bedford Hills Correctional Facility. This article will reflect that collectivity by being a patchwork quilt of many women's voices.

ACE was started by inmates in 1988 because of the crisis that AIDS was creating in our community. According to a blind study done in the Fall–Winter of 1987–88, almost 20 percent of the women entering the New York state prison system were HIV infected.[1] It is likely to be higher today. In addition, women here have family members who are sick and friends who are dying. People have intense fears of transmission through casual contact because we live so closely together. Women are worried about their children and about having safe sex. All this need and energy led to the creation of ACE.

## Before ACE

Prior to the formation of ACE, Bedford was an environment of fear, stigma, lack of information, and evasion. AIDS was a word that was whispered. People had no forum in which to talk about their fears. The doctors and nurses showed their biases. They preferred to just give advice, and many wouldn't touch people because of their own fears. There were several deaths. This inflamed people's fear more. People didn't want to look at their own vulnerability—their IV drug use and unsafe sex.

> I felt very negative about people who I knew were sick. To save face, I spoke to them from afar. I felt that they all should be put into a building by themselves because I heard that people who were healthy could make them sick and so they should get specific care. I figured that I have more time (on my sentence); why should I be isolated? They should be. I felt very negative and it came a lot from fear.[2]

Women at Bedford who are sick are housed in a hospital unit called In Patient Care (IPC). ACE members remember what IPC was like before ACE:

> The IPC area—the infirmary—was horrible before, a place where nobody wanted to be. It was a place to go to die. Before ACE people started going there, it looked like a dungeon.

It was unsanitary. Just the look of it made people feel like they were going to die. That was the end.

There was no support system for women who wanted to take the HIV-antibody test:

I had a friend who tested positive. The doctor told her, you are HIV positive, but that doesn't mean you have AIDS. You shouldn't have sex, or have a baby, and you should avoid stress. Period. No information was given to her. No counseling and support. She freaked out.

## The Beginning of ACE: Breaking the Silence

Some of us sensed that people needed to talk, but no one would break the silence. Finally, five women got together and made a proposal to the superintendent:

We said that we ourselves had to help ourselves. We believed that as peers we would be the most effective in education, counseling, and building a community of support. We stated four main goals: to save lives through preventing the spread of HIV; to create more humane conditions for those who are HIV positive; to give support and education to women with fears, questions, and needs related to AIDS; to act as a bridge to community groups to help women as they reenter the community.

The superintendent accepted the proposal. Each of the five women sought out other women in the population who they believed were sensitive and would be interested in breaking the silence. When they reached 35, they stopped and a meeting was called.

## Breaking the Silence Changed Us: We Began to Build a Community

At that first meeting a sigh of relief was felt and it rippled out. There was a need from so many directions. People went around the table and said why they were there. About the fourth or fifth woman said, "I'm here because I have AIDS." There was an intense silence. It was the first time anyone had said that aloud in a group. By the end of the meeting, several more women had said that they were HIV positive. Breaking the silence, the faith that it took, and the trust it built was really how ACE started.

## Breaking the Silence Meant Something Special to PWAs

I often ask myself how it is that I came to be open about my status. For me, AIDS had been one of my best kept secrets. It took me approximately 15 months to discuss this issue openly. As if not saying it aloud would make it go away. I watched other people with AIDS (PWAs), who were much more open than I was at the time, reveal to audiences their status/their vulnerability, while sharing from a distance, from silence, every word that was being uttered by them. I wanted to be a part of what they were building, what they were doing, their statement, "I am a PWA," because I was. It was a relief when I said it. I could stop going on with the lie. I could be me. People were supportive and they didn't shun me. And now I can go anywhere and be myself.

## Breaking the Silence Allowed People to Change Each Other

I was one of those people who once I knew someone had AIDS, I didn't want them around me. That was until Carmen got sick. She was my friend. When I found out she was sick I felt hurt because she didn't have the confidence to tell me. She knew my attitude and didn't want me to turn my back on her. That's when I started researching how you can and can't get the virus and my fear left. ACE also helped me with things I didn't know. Even though Carmen had AIDS and I didn't, I felt that I was living with AIDS through her. I told her that I loved her whether she had AIDS or not.

## Breaking the Silence Meant Challenging Stigma

I think there has been a tremendous change in the institution. Before, if people knew about someone, it wasn't to help them, it was only to hurt them. Now people are protective about the people they used to talk about. You will still have people who will use this information as their power, like saying, "You AIDS-ridden this," but you have more people now who will protect those individuals. This is the first time that people in here had something they were doing for other people that they weren't getting something from, some payoff.

Since that beginning two years ago, ACE has gone on to develop a program of work through which we try to reach out to meet the needs of our community.

## Supporting PWAs

PWAs and HIV-positive women are at the heart of our work. ACE believes that everyone facing HIV-related illness is confronting issues of life and death and struggling to survive and thrive.

We had to have some place for PWAs to share their experiences with each other. There have been numerous support groups which allowed us to express things that hadn't been verbalized but that had been on our minds. It was interesting to see that we had similar issues: how to tell significant others, our own vulnerability about being open, living with AIDS. My first group was a mixture of people. Some were recently diagnosed and others had been diagnosed for two years. It was informative and it was emotional. Sometimes we would just come to a meeting and cry. Or we might come there and not even talk about the issue of AIDS and just have a humor session because we are just tired of AIDS.

One of the first things that ACE ever did was to work in IPC.

ACE started going to IPC. We painted, cleaned up, made it look so good that now the women want to stay there. We take care of the girls who are sick, making them feel comfortable and alive. Now, women there know they have a friend. They feel free, they talk, and look forward to visits. They know they're not there to die; not like before.

# Being a Buddy

I have been involved in ACE for about three years. About a year ago I started visiting the women in IPC. I was really afraid at first. Not afraid of getting sick, but of becoming emotionally involved and then have the women die. At first, I tried to keep my feelings and friendship at a minimum. The more I went, the more I lost this fear. There is one woman I have gotten closer to than the rest. She has been in IPC since I first started going there. We are buddies. For me to be her buddy means unconditionally loving her and accepting her decisions. I go almost every night to IPC. Some nights we just sit there and say nothing. But there is comfort in my presence. She had a stroke before I met her. So there is a lot she cannot do for herself. There are times when I bathe and dress her. Iron her clothes. I do not think of any of these things as chores. Soon she will be going home. I am overjoyed, but I'm also saddened knowing that I will not see her again. I will miss her hugs, her complaining, and her love. But I would do it all over again and I probably will with someone else.

# Medical Advocacy

It is obviously a matter of life or death for anyone who is HIV infected to get good medical care and have a good relationship with her health providers. Medical facilities in prisons start out understaffed and ill equipped, and the AIDS crisis escalated these problems enormously. In the 1970s women prisoners here instituted a class action suit, *Todaro v. Ward*, to demand better medical care. Because of that case, the medical facilities and care at Bedford are monitored for the court by an outside expert. That expert issued a report criticizing all aspects of the medical department for being inadequately prepared to meet women's AIDS-related medical needs, and the prison faced a court hearing and possible contempt charges. Under that pressure the state agreed to numerous changes that brought new medical staff and resources, including a full-time medical director, a part-time infectious disease specialist, and more nurses. ACE was able to institute a medical advocacy plan that allowed ACE members to accompany women to their doctor's consultation visits to insure that nothing was missed. Afterward, there can be a private discussion between the patient and the advocate to clarify matters for the woman, to explore possibilities of treatment, or just to allow the person to express whatever emotions she experienced when she received the news from the doctor.

# Peer Education

Our approach is *peer* education, which we believe is best suited for the task of enabling a community to mobilize itself to deal with AIDS. The people doing the training clearly have a personal stake in the community. The education is for all, in the interests of all. This is communicated from the beginning by the women doing the teaching.

Our peer education takes a problem-posing approach. We present issues as problems facing all of us, problems to be examined by drawing on the knowledge and experience of the women being trained. What are the issues between a man and a woman, for example, that make it hard for a woman to demand that her man use a condom? Will distributing free needles or advocating bleach kits stop the spread of AIDS among IV drug users?

Our educational work is holistic. Education is not solely a presentation of facts, although that is an important part of the trainers' responsibilities. But what impact do feelings and attitudes have on how people deal with facts? Why would a person who knows that you cannot get AIDS by eating from a PWA's plate still act occasionally as if you could? Why would a person who knows that sex without a condom could be inviting death, not use a condom? For education to be a deep process, it involves understanding the whole person; for education to take root within a community, it means thinking about things on a community, social level.

> Coming to prison, living under these conditions, was scary, and AIDS made it even scarier. I was part of a society that made judgments and had preconceived ideas about the women in prison.

# Educating Ourselves

## Workshops

To become members of ACE, women must be educated through a series of eight workshops. We look at how stigma and blame have been associated with diseases throughout history, and how the sexism of this society impacts on women in the AIDS epidemic. We teach about the nature of the virus, strategies for treatment, and holistic approaches. After the eight weeks, we ask who would like to become involved, and then there is a screening process. The Superintendent has final approval. The workshops are followed by more intensive training of women who become members.

## Orientation

When women enter the New York state prison system, they must come first to Bedford Hills, where they either stay or move on after several weeks to one of several other women's prisons. ACE members talk with the women when they first arrive.

> We do orientations of 10 to 35 women. We explain to them how you can and cannot get AIDS, about testing and about ACE. Sometimes the crowd is very boisterous and rude. I say "AIDS" and they don't want to hear about it. But those are the ones I try to reach. After orientation is over, the main ones that didn't want to hear about AIDS are the ones who want to talk more and I feel good about that. A lot of times, their loudness is a defense because they are afraid of their own vulnerability. They know that they are at risk for HIV infection because of previous behaviors. After I finish doing orientation, I have a sense of warmth, because I know I made a difference in some of their lives.

## Seminars

One of the main ways we interact with our sisters is through seminars. We talk about AIDS issues with groups of women on living units, in classrooms, and in some of the other prison programs such as family violence, drug treatment, and Children's Center.

> The four back buildings are dormitories, each holding 100 women with double bunked beds. We from ACE gather right after count, with our easel and newsprint and magic markers and our three-by-five cards with the information on whatever presentation we're making. We move in twos and threes through the connecting tunnels to the building. When we arrive some of the women are sitting in the rec room, but many others are in

their cubicles/cells. They ask why we're here. We look like a traveling troupe—and we've felt like it, not knowing what to expect. Some women are excited that we're going to talk about AIDS. Others say, "forget it," or "fuck you, I've heard enough about it, it's depressing."

But we begin, and people slowly gather.

We ask the women to help us role-play a situation such as a woman going home from prison, trying to convince her man, who has been taking care of her while she's inside, to use a condom. Then the role-play is analyzed. What problems are encountered and how do we deal with those problems? We try to come up with suggestions that we can see ourselves using in that situation. We talk about the risk of violence.

One of the most immediate problems people have is whether or not to take the HIV-antibody test. We do not push testing. We explain what the test is and have a group discussion of things the women need to consider. A woman may be inclined to get tested, but she needs to know that she is likely to be transferred upstate before the results come back from the lab. The choice is up to her. Toward the end of the seminar, PWAs talk about their experiences living with AIDS.

When they speak, they bring together everything that we have said. Not only that, but they let people know that living with AIDS is not instant death. It makes people realize why the struggles, working together, and being as one are so important. When I hear the women who are PWAs speak, it makes me realize that I could have been in their shoes, or I could still be, if they hadn't been willing to talk about their risk behaviors and what has happened to them. It gives me the courage to realize that it's not all about me. It's actually about us.

We end each seminar with all the women standing with our arms around each other or holding hands—without any fear of casual contact—singing our theme song, "Sister."[3] We sing, having come to a new place where we are for each other, unified. We all feel some sense of relief and some sense of hope. Talking about AIDS openly has changed how we live. We leave the seminar with the knowledge that we can talk about AIDS and that we're going to be okay.

## Prerelease

This is a program for people within 90 days of going home. They confront the issues of living with AIDS within their prospective communities.

The women are leaving to go to communities where they are frightened because they don't know if they will find any openness or dialogue. They don't know if they can take the behavior changes they have learned about in here and implement them out there.

The prerelease program also meets the specific needs of PWAs who are leaving the facility. We call this bridging—helping them to connect with follow-up care, assistance, housing. The Bedford community is much more supportive than what most people face when they go outside. During the period before a person is released, she experiences a high level of stress which we have to address on many levels: putting services in place, meeting emotional needs and anxieties, working through issues related to families. We also have to let go, because we become very bonded with each other. There is a weaning process on both ends, and we have to work on preparing both ends of the relationship for this transition.

Although the transition for PWAs may be difficult because of the community of support that ACE has created, it is also true that ACE members come out of Bedford committed and prepared to try to build the same kind of supportive community outside. ACE has created a training ground for women to become community workers in the AIDS crisis.

> . . . on the outside I live AIDS through personal experience by having AIDS, and I work at it on a 9 to 5 basis doing case work at Brooklyn AIDS Task Force; come 5 or 6 p.m., that day at the office is over and I am once again all alone. Even though I am involved in other personal AIDS projects, they all lack the closeness that Bedford and ACE provided.

## Counseling

When we conduct the seminars and orientation sessions, women come up to us afterward with personal questions and problems. It could be they are HIV positive, or they are thinking of taking the test, or they have a family member who is sick, or they are thinking about getting involved with someone in a relationship. Sometimes they raise one issue, but underlying it are a lot of other issues they're not yet ready to talk about. Because women know we're in ACE, we're approached in our housing units, at school, on the job, in the mess hall, as we walk from one place to another. Women stop us, needing to talk. We're a haven for women because they know ACE has a principle of confidentiality. Women can trust us not to abuse the information they are sharing with us.

> Peer counseling. I'm just impressed that we can do it. I didn't know what kind of potential we'd have as peers. We talk the language that each of us understands. Even if it's silent, even if it's with our eyes, it's something that each of us seems to understand. I know I wouldn't want someone from the Department of Health who hasn't even taken a Valium to try to educate me about IV drug use. How could they give me helpful hints? I would feel that they are so out of tune with reality that I wouldn't be able to hear them.

# AIDS: A Particular Problem for Women

When we begin our workshop on women and AIDS, we ask, "Why are we making a workshop just on how AIDS affects women?" The women come up with a list that answers this question:

- It's a man's world, so AIDS stigmatizes women, such as prostitutes.
- Our dependency on men makes us more vulnerable.
- We have to deal with male cheating and double standards.
- Women are caregivers: responsible for education and health of ourselves, our children, our spouses, and the people we work for.
- Women are isolated and have to deal with all this individually and alone. We need to see it as a social problem so we can act together.
- It's one more strike against Black and Latin women, already suffering from discrimination and racism.

You can't separate AIDS from all of the problems that women face—housing, economics, kids—and the women here, being the most marginalized, face the most problems. ACE tries to draw on women's life experiences to reflect on the problems that we share as women. We believe that by looking at our lives we can get individual strength and also build a social consciousness.

I was conscious of women before I came in here, but not on that level. ACE has made it deeper. ACE made me realize that AIDS is bigger than each individual woman, that it's going to take all of us coming together. I never knew so many things affected just women. I had looked at issues as a Black woman—religious issues, being a single parent or not— but I had never reflected on being a woman in society.

## A Crisis and Opportunity for Our Community

We are a small community and we are so isolated you can feel it—the suffering, the losses, the fears, the anxiety. Out in the street you don't have a community of women affected and living together facing a problem in this same way. We can draw on the particular strengths that women bring: nurturance, caring, and personal openness. So many women prisoners have worked in nursing and old age homes. Yet when they did, they were never given respect. Here these same activities are valued, and the women are told "thank you," and that creates initiative and feelings of self-worth. And ACE helps us to be more self-conscious about a culture of caring that as women we tend to create in our daily lives.

For the first time in prison I was part of a group that cared about other prisoners in prison. What did that feel like? It felt like I wasn't alone in caring about people, because in this type of setting I was beginning to wonder about people caring.

## Our Impact on Women

We know that we have played a role in communicating information about what is safe and what is not safe in sexual behavior—both between a man and woman and between two women—and we have certainly been able to create open and relaxed discussions about all this. But we know that actually changing behaviors is another leap ahead of us. We are learning that it's not a one-shot deal, that information doesn't equal behavior change, and it's not just an individual thing. Social norms have to change, and this takes time. And when you talk about women having to initiate change you're up against the fact that women don't have that kind of empowerment in this society. Women who have been influenced by ACE have experienced a change in attitude, but it is unclear whether this will translate into behavior change once they leave the prison.

When I first started taking the workshops I was 100 percent against using condoms. And yet I like anal sex. But now my views are different. We're the bosses of our own bodies. You know, a lot of people say it's a man's world. Well, I can't completely agree.

## Our Diversity Is a Strength

We are a diverse community of women: Black, Latin, and white, and also from countries throughout the world. In ACE there was at first a tendency to deny the differences, maybe out of fear of disunity. Now there is a more explicit consciousness growing that we can affirm our diversity and our commonality because both are important. In the last work- shop on women, we broke for a while into three groups—Black, Latin, and white women—to explore the ways AIDS impacted on our particular culture and communi- ties. We are doing more of those kinds of discussions and developing materials that address concerns of specific communities. The Hispanic Sector of ACE is particularly active, conducting seminars in Spanish and holding open meetings for the population to foster Hispanic awareness of AIDS issues.

> The workshops didn't deal enough with different ethnic areas, and being Puerto Rican and half-Indian, some things seemed ridiculous in terms of the Hispanic family. Some of the ways people were talking about sex wouldn't work in a traditional Hispanic family. For example, you can't just tell your husband that he has to wear a condom. Or say to him, "You have to take responsibility." These approaches could lead to marital rape or abuse. The empowerment of Hispanic women means making sure that their children are brought up.

# Working in a Prison

We have a unique situation at Bedford Hills. We have a prison administration that is supportive of inmates developing a peer-based program to deal with AIDS. However, because we are in a prison there are a lot of constraints and frustrations. Before we had staff persons to supervise us, we could not work out of an office space. That meant that we couldn't see women who wanted to talk on an individual level unless we ran into them in the yard or rec room.

You could be helping someone in IPC take her daily shower; it's taking longer than usual because she is in a lot of pain or she needs to talk, but that's not taken into consideration when the officer tells you that you have to leave immediately because it's "count-time." You could be in the rec room, a large room with a bunch of card tables, loud music, and an officer overseeing groups of women sitting on broken-down chairs. You're talking to a woman in crisis who needs comforting. You reach out to give her a hug and the C.O. may come over to admonish you, "No physical contact, ladies." Or maybe a woman has just tested positive. She's taken her first tentative steps to reach out by talking to someone from ACE and joining a support group. Days after her first meeting, she is transferred to another prison.

It's been difficult to be able to call ourselves counselors and have our work formally acknowledged by the administration. Counseling is usually done by professionals in here because it carries such liability and responsibility. We're struggling for the legitimacy of peer counseling. The reality is that we've been doing it in our daily lives here through informal dialogue. We now have civilian staff to supervise us, and Columbia University will be conducting a certification training program to justify the title "peer counselor."

After working over two years on our own, we are now being funded by a grant from the New York State AIDS Institute, coordinated by Columbia University School of Public Health and by Women and AIDS Resource Network (WARN). The money has allowed hiring staff to work with ACE. ACE began as a totally volunteer inmate organization with no office or materials, operating on a shoestring and scrambling for every meeting. Now we have an office in a prime location of the prison, computers, and a civilian staff responsible for making certain that there is something to show for their salaries. Inmates who used to work whenever they could find the time are now paid 73 cents a day as staff officially assigned to the ACE Center. The crises are no longer centered around the problems of being inside a prison, but more on how to sustain momentum and a real grassroots initiative in the context of a prison. This is a problem faced by many other community organizations when they move past the initial momentum and become more established institutions.

# Building a Culture of Survival

When, in the spring of 1987, we said, "Let's make quilt squares for our sisters who have died," there were more than 15 names. Over the next year we made more and more quilt squares. The deaths took a toll not just on those who knew the women but on all of us. Too many women were dying among us. And, for those who were HIV positive or worried that they might be, each death heightened their own vulnerabilities and fears. We have had to develop ways to let people who are sick know that if they die, their lives will be remembered, they will be honored and celebrated, and they will stay in our hearts.

> I remember our first memorial. Several hundred women contributed money—25 cents, 50 cents, a dollar—for flowers. Both Spanish and Black women sang and in the beginning everyone held hands and sang "That's What Friends Are For," and in the end we sang "Sister." People spoke about what Ro meant to them. Ro had died and we couldn't change that. But we didn't just feel terrible. We felt love and caring and that together we could survive the sadness and loss.
>
> In the streets, funerals were so plastic, but here, people knew that it could be them. It's not just to pay respect. When we sang "Sister," there was a charge between us. Our hands were extended to each other. There was a need for ACE and we could feel it in the air.

It was out of that same need that ACE was formed. It will be out of that same need that ACE will continue to strive to build community and an environment of trust and support. We are all we have—ourselves. If we do not latch on to this hope that has strengthened us and this drive that has broken our silence, we too will suffer and we will remain stigmatized and isolated. Feel our drive in our determination to make changes, and think "community," and make a difference.

# Reading Questions

1. Why was ACE started by inmates at Bedford Hills Correctional Facility?
2. How did the women's class action suit in the 1970s improve medical care at Bedford?
3. What is peer education, and why does ACE recommend it over more formal education methods to teach about AIDS?
4. What special problems does AIDS present to women? In which specific ways does AIDS exacerbate already existing problems?
5. What types of surveillance in Bedford interfere with ACE members' efforts to help each other?

# Recommended Reading

Gena Corea, *The Invisible Epidemic: The Story of Women and AIDS* (New York: HarperCollins, 1992)

Ines Rieder and Patricia Ruppelt, eds., *AIDS: The Women* (San Francisco: Cleis Press, 1988)

Andrea Rudd and Darien Taylor, eds., *Positive Women: Voices of Women Living with AIDS* (Toronto: Second Story Press, 1992)

## Recommended Audiovisual Resources

*AIDS in the Barrio*. 1989. Directed by Peter Biella and Frances Negron. Documents the impact of AIDS on one Latino community. Strong interviews with women about being the sexual partners of intravenous drug users and about sexism in their lives. AIDS Film Initiative.

*Living with AIDS: Women and AIDS*. 1988. Directed by Alexandra Juhasz and Jean Carlomusto. Interviews with women health-care workers counter inaccuracies and ignorance in the media and the government about HIV-infected women in the United States. Gay Men's Health Crisis, Videotapes/Publications Distribution.

*Women and AIDS: A Survival Kit*. 1988. Two women with AIDS talk about themselves, transmission issues, safe sex, and the use of condoms. California AIDS Clearinghouse.

For an annotated bibliography and a list of video distributors' addresses, see Catherine Saalfield, "AIDS Videos by, for, and about Women," *Women, AIDS and Activism*, The ACT UP/NY Women and AIDS Book Group (Boston, MA: South End Press, 1990).

# Struggle over Needs

## Outline of a Socialist–Feminist Critical Theory of Late Capitalist Political Culture

### NANCY FRASER

Nancy Fraser teaches philosophy, comparative literature, and women's studies at Northwestern University. She is the author of *Unruly Practices: Power, Discourse and Gender in Contemporary Social Philosophy*.

> Need is also a political instrument, meticulously prepared, calculated, and used.
> —Michel Foucault, *Discipline and Punish*[1]

In late capitalist welfare state societies, talk about people's needs is an important species of political discourse. We argue, in the United States, for example, about whether the government should provide for citizens' needs. Thus, feminists claim there should be state provision of parents' day-care needs, while social conservatives insist on *children's* needs for their mothers' care, and economic conservatives claim that the market, not the government, is the best institution for meeting needs. Likewise, Americans also argue about whether existing social-welfare programs really do meet the needs they purport to satisfy or whether, instead, they misconstrue those needs. For example, right-wing critics claim that Aid to Families with Dependent Children destroys the incentive to work and undermines the family. Left critics, in contrast, oppose workfare proposals as coercive and punitive, while many poor women with young children say they want to work at good-paying jobs. All these cases involve disputes about what exactly various groups of people really do need and about who should have the last word in such matters. In all these cases, moreover, needs talk functions as a medium for the making and contesting of political claims: it is an idiom in which political conflict is played out and through which inequalities are symbolically elaborated and challenged.

Talk about needs has not always been central to Western political culture; it has often been considered antithetical to politics and relegated to the margins of political life. However, in welfare state societies needs talk has been institutionalized as a major vocabulary of political discourse.[2] It coexists, albeit often uneasily, with talk about rights and interests at the very center of political life. Indeed, this peculiar juxtaposition of a discourse about needs with discourses about rights and interests is one of the distinctive marks of the late capitalist political culture.

Feminists (and others) who aim to intervene in this culture could benefit from considering the following questions: Why has needs talk become so prominent in the political culture of welfare state societies? What is the relation between this development and changes in late capitalist social structure? What does the emergence of the needs idiom imply about shifts in the boundaries between "political," "economic," and "domestic" spheres of life? Does it betoken an extension of the political sphere or, rather, a colonization of that domain by newer modes of power and social control? What are the major varieties of needs talk and how do they interact polemically with one another? What opportunities and/or obstacles does the needs idiom pose for movements, like feminism, that seek far-reaching social transformation?

In what follows, I outline an approach for thinking about such questions rather than proposing definitive answers to them. What I have to say falls into five parts. In section 1, I suggest a break with standard theoretical approaches by shifting the focus of inquiry from needs to discourses about needs, from the distribution of need satisfactions to "the politics of need interpretation." Accordingly, I propose a model of social discourse designed to bring into relief the contested character of needs talk in welfare state societies. Then, in section 2, I relate this discourse model to social-structural considerations, especially to shifts in the boundaries between "political," "economic," and "domestic" or "personal" spheres of life. In section 3, I identify three major strands of needs talk in late capitalist political culture, and I map some of the ways in which they compete for potential adherents. In section 4, I apply the model to some concrete cases of contemporary needs politics in the United States. Finally, in a brief conclusion, I consider some moral and epistemological issues raised by the phenomenon of needs talk.

# 1

Let me begin by explaining some of the peculiarities of the approach I am proposing. In my approach, the focus of inquiry is not needs but rather *discourses* about needs. The point is to shift our angle of vision on the politics of needs. Usually the politics of needs is understood as pertaining to the distribution of satisfactions. In my approach, by contrast, the focus is *the politics of need interpretation*.

My reason for focusing on discourses and interpretation is to bring into view the contextual and contested character of needs claims. As many theorists have noted, needs claims have a relational structure; implicitly or explicitly, they have the form "A needs $x$ in order to $y$." Now, this structure poses no problems when we are considering very general, or "thin," needs such as food or shelter *simpliciter*. Thus, we can uncontroversially say that homeless people, like all people who live in nontropical climates, need shelter in order to live. And most people will infer that governments, as guarantors of life and liberty, have a responsibility to provide for this need. However, as soon as we descend to a lesser level of generality, needs claims become far more controversial. What, more "thickly," do homeless people need in order to be sheltered from the cold? What specific forms of provision are entailed once we acknowledge their very general, thin need? Do homeless people need forbearance, so that they may sleep undisturbed next to a hot-air vent on a street corner? A space in a subway tunnel or a bus terminal? A bed in a temporary shelter? A permanent home? Suppose we say the latter. What kind of permanent housing do homeless people need? Rental units in high-rises in central city areas remote from good schools, discount shopping, and job opportunities? Single-family homes designed for single-earner, two-parent families? And what else do homeless people need in order to have permanent homes? Rent subsidies? Income supports? Jobs? Job training and education? Day care? Finally, what is needed, at the level of housing policy, in order to insure an adequate stock of affordable housing? Tax incentives to encourage private investment in low income housing? Concentrated or scatter-site public housing projects within a generally commodified housing environment? Rent control? Decommodification of urban housing?

We could continue proliferating such questions indefinitely. And we would, at the same time, be proliferating controversy. That is precisely the point about needs claims. These claims tend to be nested, connected to one another in ramified chains of "in-order-to" relations. Moreover, when these chains are unraveled in the course of political disputes, disagreements usually deepen rather than abate. Precisely how such chains are unraveled depends on what the interlocutors share in the way of background assumptions. Does it go without saying that policy designed to deal with homelessness must not challenge the basic ownership and investment structure of urban real estate? Or is that a point at which people's assumptions and commitments diverge?

It is the implication of needs claims in contested networks of in-order-to relations to which I call attention when I speak of the politics of need interpretation. Thin theories of needs that do not undertake to explore such networks cannot shed much light on the politics of needs. Such theories assume that the politics of needs concerns only whether various predefined needs will or will not be provided for. As a result, they deflect attention from a number of important political questions.[3] First, they take the *interpretation* of people's needs as simply given and unproblematic; they thus occlude the interpretive dimension of needs politics, the fact that not just satisfactions but *need interpretations* are politically contested. Second, they assume that it doesn't matter who interprets the needs in question and from what perspective and in the light of what interests; they thus overlook the fact that *who* gets to establish authoritative thick definitions of people's needs is itself a political stake. Third, they take for granted that the socially authorized forms of public discourse available for interpreting people's needs are adequate and fair; they thus neglect the question of whether these forms of public discourse are skewed in favor of the self-interpretations and interests of dominant social groups and, so, work to the disadvantage of subordinate or oppositional groups—they occlude, in other words, the fact that the means of public discourse themselves may be at issue in needs politics.[4] Fourth, such theories fail to problematize the social and institutional logic of processes of need interpretation; they thus neglect such important political questions as, Where in society, in what institutions, are authoritative need interpretations developed? and What sorts of social relations are in force among the interlocutors or co-interpreters?

In order to remedy these blind spots, I propose a more politically critical, discourse-oriented alternative. I take the politics of needs to comprise three moments that are analytically distinct but interrelated in practice. The first is the struggle to establish or deny the political status of a given need, the struggle to validate the need as a matter of legitimate political concern or to enclave it as a nonpolitical matter. The second is the struggle over the interpretation of the need, the struggle for the power to define it and, so, to determine what would satisfy it. The third moment is the struggle over the satisfaction of the need, the struggle to secure or withhold provision.

Now, a focus on the politics of need interpretation requires a model of social discourse. The model I have developed foregrounds the multivalent and contested character of needs talk, the fact that in welfare state societies we encounter a plurality of competing ways of talking about people's needs. The model theorizes what I call "the sociocultural means of interpretation and communication" (MIC). By this I mean the historically and culturally specific ensemble of discursive resources available to members of a given social collectivity in pressing claims against one another. Included among these resources are the following:

1. The officially recognized idioms in which one can press claims; for example, needs talk, rights talk, interests talk
2. The vocabularies available for instantiating claims in these recognized idioms; thus, with respect to needs talk, What are the vocabularies available for interpreting and communicating one's needs? For example, therapeutic vocabularies, administrative vocabularies, religious vocabularies, feminist vocabularies, socialist vocabularies
3. The paradigms of argumentation accepted as authoritative in adjudicating conflicting claims; thus, with respect to needs talk, How are conflicts over the interpretation of needs resolved? By appeals to scientific experts? By brokered compromises? By voting according to majority rule? By privileging the interpretations of those whose needs are in question?
4. The narrative conventions available for constructing the individual and collective stories that are constitutive of people's social identities
5. Modes of subjectification; the ways in which various discourses position the people to whom they are addressed as specific sorts of subjects endowed with specific sorts of capacities for action; for example, as "normal" or "deviant," as causally conditioned or freely self-determining, as victims or as potential activists, as unique individuals or as members of social groups[5]

Now, in welfare state societies, there are a plurality of forms of association, roles, groups, institutions, and discourses. Thus, the means of interpretation and communication are not all of a piece. They do not constitute a coherent, monolithic web but rather a heterogeneous, polyglot field of diverse possibilities and alternatives. In fact, in welfare state societies, discourses about needs typically make at least implicit reference to alternative interpretations. Particular claims about needs are "internally dialogized"; implicitly or explicitly they evoke resonances of competing need interpretations.[6] They therefore allude to a conflict of need interpretations. For example, groups seeking to restrict or outlaw abortion counterpose "the sanctity of life" to the "mere convenience" of "career women"; thus, they cast their claims in terms that refer, however disparagingly, to feminist interpretations of reproductive needs.[7]

Of course, late capitalist societies are not simply pluralist. Rather, they are stratified, differentiated into social groups with unequal status, power, and access to resources, traversed by pervasive axes of inequality along lines of class, gender, race, ethnicity, and age. The MIC in these societies are also stratified, organized in ways that are congruent with societal patterns of dominance and subordination.

It follows that we must distinguish those elements of the MIC that are hegemonic, authorized, and officially sanctioned, on the one hand, from those that are nonhegemonic, disqualified, and discounted, on the other hand. Some ways of talking about needs are institutionalized in the central discursive arenas of late capitalist societies: parliaments, academies, courts, and the mass circulation media. Other ways of talking about needs are enclaved as subcultural sociolects and normally excluded from the central discursive arenas.[8] For example, moralistic and scientific discourses about the needs of people with AIDS, and of people at risk with respect to AIDS, are well represented on government commissions; in contrast, gay and lesbian rights activists' interpretations of those needs are largely excluded.

From this perspective, needs talk appears as a site of struggle where groups with unequal discursive (and nondiscursive) resources compete to establish as hegemonic their respective interpretations of legitimate social needs. Dominant groups articulate need interpretations intended to exclude, defuse, and/or co-opt counterinterpretations. Subordinate or oppositional groups, on the other hand, articulate need interpretations intended to challenge, displace, and/or modify dominant ones. In neither case are the interpretations simply "representations." In both cases, rather, they are acts and interventions.[9]

2

Now I should like to situate the discourse model I have just sketched with respect to some social-structural features of late capitalist societies. Here, I seek to relate the rise of politicized needs talk to shifts in the boundaries separating "political," "economic," and "domestic" dimensions of life. However, unlike many social theorists, I shall treat the terms 'political,' 'economic,' and 'domestic' as cultural classifications and ideological labels rather than as designations of structures, spheres, or things.[10]

Let me begin by noting that the terms 'politics' and 'political' are highly contested and have a number of different senses.[11] In the present context, two senses in particular are the most important. First, there is the institutional sense, in which a matter is deemed "political" if it is handled directly in the institutions of the official governmental system, including parliaments, administrative apparatuses, and the like. In this sense, what is "political"—call it "official political"—contrasts with what is handled in institutions like "the family" and "the economy," which are defined as being outside the official political system even though they are in actuality underpinned and regulated by it. Second, there is the discourse sense, in which something is "political" if it is contested across a range of different discursive arenas and among a range of different publics. In this sense, what is "political"—call it "discursive-political" or "politicized"—contrasts both with what is not contested in public at all and with what is contested only in relatively specialized, enclaved, and/or segmented publics. These two senses are not unrelated. In democratic theory, if not always in practice, a matter does not usually become subject to legitimate state intervention until it has been debated across a wide range of discourse publics.

In general, there are no a priori constraints dictating that some matters simply are intrinsically political and others simply are intrinsically not. As a matter of fact, these boundaries are drawn differently from culture to culture and from historical period to historical period. For example, reproduction became an intensely political matter in the 1890s in the United States amid a panic about "race suicide." By the 1940s, however, there was a consensus that birth control was a "private" matter. Finally, with the emergence of the women's movement in the 1960s, reproduction was repoliticized.[12]

However, it would be misleading to suggest that for any society in any period the boundary between what is political and what is not is simply fixed or given. On the contrary, this boundary may itself be an object of conflict. For example, struggles over Poor Law "reform" in nineteenth-century England were also conflicts about the scope of the political. And as I shall argue shortly, one of the primary stakes of social conflict in late capitalist societies is precisely where the limits of the political will be drawn.

Let me spell out some of the presuppositions and implications of the discourse sense of 'politics.' This sense stipulates that a matter is "political" if it is contested across a range of different discursive arenas and among a range of different discourse publics. Note, therefore, that it depends upon the ideal of discursive publicity. However, in this conception publicity is not understood in a simple unitary way as the undifferentiated opposite of discursive privacy. Rather, publicity is understood to be differentiated, on the assumption that it is possible to identify a plurality of distinct discourse publics and to theorize the relations among them.

Clearly, publics can be distinguished along a number of different axes, for example, by ideology (the readership of the *Nation* versus the readership of the *Public Interest*), by stratification principles like gender (the viewers of "Cagney and Lacey" versus the viewers of "Monday Night Football") and class (the readership of the *New York Times* versus that of the *New York Post*), by profession (the membership of the American Economic Association versus that of the American Bar Association), by central mobilizing issue (the nuclear freeze movement versus the "pro-life" movement).

Publics can also be distinguished in terms of relative power. Some are large, authoritative, and able to set the terms of debate for many of the rest. Others, by contrast, are small, self-enclosed, and enclaved, unable to make much of a mark beyond their own borders. Publics of the former sort are often able to take the lead in the formation of hegemonic blocs: concatenations of different publics that together construct the "common sense" of the day. As a result, such leading publics usually have a heavy hand in defining what is "political" in the discourse sense. They can politicize an issue simply by entertaining contestation about it, since such contestation will be transmitted as a matter of course to and through other allied and opposing publics. Smaller, counterhegemonic publics, by contrast, generally lack the power to politicize issues in this way. When they succeed in fomenting widespread contestation over what previously was not "political," it is usually by far slower and more laborious means. In general, it is the relative power of various publics that determines the outcome of struggles over the boundaries of the political.

Now, how should we conceptualize the politicization of needs in late capitalist societies? Clearly, this involves processes whereby some matters break out of zones of discursive privacy and out of specialized or enclaved publics so as to become focuses of generalized contestation. When this happens, previously taken-for-granted interpretations of these matters are called into question, and heretofore reified chains of in-order-to relations become subject to dispute.

What are the zones of privacy and the specialized publics that previously enveloped newly politicized needs in late capitalist societies? What are the institutions in which these needs were enclaved and depoliticized, where their interpretations were reified by being embedded in taken-for-granted networks of in-order-to relations?

In male-dominated, capitalist societies, what is "political" is normally defined contrastively over against what is "economic" and what is "domestic" or "personal." Here, then, we can identify two principal sets of institutions that depoliticize social discourses: they are, first, domestic institutions, especially the normative domestic form, namely, the modern restricted male-headed nuclear family; and, second, official economic capitalist system institutions, especially paid workplaces, markets, credit mechanisms and "private" enterprises and corporations.[13] Domestic institutions depoliticize certain matters by personalizing and/or familializing them; they cast these as private-domestic or personal-familial matters in contradistinction to public, political matters. Official economic capitalist system institutions, on the other hand, depoliticize certain matters by economizing them; the issues in question here are cast as impersonal market imperatives, or as "private" ownership prerogatives, or as technical problems for managers and planners, all in contradistinction to political matters. In both cases, the result is a foreshortening of chains of in-order-to relations for interpreting people's needs; interpretive chains are truncated and prevented from spilling across the boundaries separating "the domestic" and "the economic" from "the political."

Clearly, domestic institutions and official economic system institutions differ in many important respects. However, in *these* respects they are exactly on a par with one another: both enclave certain matters into specialized discursive arenas; both thereby shield such matters from generalized contestation and from widely disseminated conflicts of interpretation; and, as a result, both entrench as authoritative certain specific interpretations of needs by embedding them in certain specific, but largely unquestioned, chains of in-order-to relations.

Since both domestic and official economic system institutions support relations of dominance and subordination, the specific interpretations they naturalize usually tend, on the whole, to advantage dominant groups and individuals and to disadvantage their subordinates. If wife battering, for example, is enclaved as a "personal" or "domestic" matter within male-headed restricted families and if public discourse about this phenomenon is canalized into specialized publics associated with, say, family law, social work, and the sociology and psychology of "deviancy," then this serves to reproduce gender dominance and subordination. Similarly, if questions of workplace democracy are enclaved as "economic" or "managerial" problems in profit-oriented, hierarchically managed paid workplaces and if discourse about these questions is shunted into specialized publics associated with, say, "industrial relations" sociology, labor law, and "management science," then this serves to perpetuate class (and usually also gender and race) dominance and subordination.

As a result of these processes, members of subordinated groups commonly internalize need interpretations that work to their own disadvantage. However, sometimes culturally dominant need interpretations are superimposed upon latent or embryonic oppositional interpretations. This is most likely where there persist, however fragmentedly, subculturally transmitted traditions of resistance, as in some sections of the U.S. labor movement and in the historical memory of many African-Americans. Moreover, under special circumstances, hard to specify theoretically, processes of depoliticization are disrupted. At that point dominant classifications of needs as "economic" or "domestic"—as opposed to "political"—come to lose their "self-evidence," and alternative, oppositional, and *politicized* interpretations emerge in their stead.[14]

In any case, family and official economy are the principal depoliticizing enclaves that needs must exceed in order to become "political" in the discourse sense in male-dominated, capitalist societies. Thus, the emergence of needs talk as a political idiom in these societies is the other side of the increased permeability of domestic and official economic institutions, their growing inability fully to depoliticize certain matters. The politicized needs at issue in late capitalist societies, then, are "leaky" or "runaway" needs: they are needs that have broken out of the discursive enclaves constructed in and around domestic and official economic institutions.

Runaway needs are a species of *excess* with respect to the normative modern domestic and economic institutions. Initially, at least, they bear the stamp of those institutions, remaining embedded in conventional chains of in-order-to relations. For example, many runaway needs are colored by the assumption that "the domestic" is supposed to be separated from "the economic" in male-dominated, capitalist societies. Thus, throughout most of U.S. history, child care has been cast as a "domestic" rather than an "economic" need, it has been interpreted as the need of children for the full-time care of their mothers rather than as the need of workers for time away from their children, and its satisfaction has been construed along the lines of "mothers' pensions" rather than of day care.[15] Here, the assumption of separate spheres truncates possible chains of in-order-to relations that would yield alternative interpretations of social needs.

Now, where do runaway needs run to when they break out of domestic or official economic enclaves? I propose that runaway needs enter a historically specific and relatively new societal arena. Following Hannah Arendt, I call this arena "the social" in order to mark its noncoincidence with the family, the official economy, and state.[16] As a site of contested discourse about runaway needs, "the social" cuts across these traditional divisions. It is an arena of conflict among rival interpretations of needs embedded in rival chains of in-order-to relations.[17]

As I conceive it, the social is a switch point for the meeting of heterogeneous contestants associated with a wide range of different discourse publics. These contestants range from proponents of politicization to defenders of (re)depoliticization, from loosely organized social movements to members of specialized, expert publics in and around the social state. Moreover, they vary greatly in relative power. Some are associated with leading publics capable of setting the terms of political debate; others, by contrast, are linked to enclaved publics and must oscillate between marginalization and co-optation.

The social is also the site where successfully politicized runaway needs get translated into claims for government provision. Here, rival need interpretations are transformed into rival programmatic conceptions, rival alliances are forged around rival policy proposals, and unequally endowed groups compete to shape the formal policy agenda. For example, in the United States today, various interest groups, movements, professional associations, and parties are scrambling for formulations around which to build alliances sufficiently powerful to dictate the shape of impending welfare "reform."

Eventually, if and when such contests are (at least temporarily) resolved, runaway needs may become objects of state intervention. Then, they become targets and levers for various strategies of crisis management. They also become the *raisons d'être* for the proliferation of the various agencies constituting the social state.[18] These agencies are engaged in regulating, and/or funding, and/or providing the satisfaction of social needs — and in so doing, they are in the business of interpreting, as well as of satisfying, the needs in question. For example, the U.S. social-welfare system is currently divided into two gender-linked and unequal subsystems: an implicitly "masculine" social insurance sub-system tied to "primary" labor force participation and geared to (white male) "breadwin-ners"; and an implicitly "feminine" relief subsystem tied to household income and geared to homemaker-mothers and their "defective" (that is, female-headed) families. With the underlying (but counterfactual) assumption of "separate spheres," the two subsystems differ markedly in the degree of autonomy, rights, and presumption of desert they accord beneficiaries, as well as in their funding base, mode of administration, and character and level of benefits.[19] Thus, the various agencies comprising the social-welfare system provide more than material aid. They also provide clients, and the public at large, with a tacit but powerful interpretive map of normative, differentially valued gender roles and gendered needs. Consequently, the different branches of the social state, too, are players in the politics of need interpretation.[20]

To summarize: in late capitalist societies, runaway needs that have broken out of domestic or official economic enclaves enter that hybrid discursive space that Arendt aptly dubbed "the social." They may then become focuses of state intervention geared to crisis management. These needs are thus markers of major social-structural shifts in the boundaries separating what are classified as "political," "economic," and "domestic" or "personal" spheres of life.

3

Now I would like to propose a scheme for classifying the many varieties of needs talk in late capitalist societies. The point is to identify some distinct types of discourse and to map the lines along which they compete. This, in turn, will permit us to theorize some basic axes of needs politics in welfare state societies.

I suggest there are three major kinds of needs discourses in late capitalist societies. First, there are what I call "oppositional" forms of needs talk, which arise when needs are politicized "from below." These contribute to the crystallization of new social identities on the part of subordinated social groups. Second, there are what I call "reprivatization" discourses, which emerge in response to the first. These articulate entrenched need interpretations that could previously go without saying. Finally, there are what I call "expert" need discourses, which link popular movements to the state. These can best be understood in the context of "social problem solving," institution building, and professional class formation. In general, it is the polemical interaction of these three kinds of needs talk that structures the politics of needs in late capitalist societies.[21]

Let us look first at the politicization of runaway needs via oppositional discourses.

Here, needs become politicized when, for example, women, workers, and/or peoples of color come to contest the subordinate identities and roles, the traditional, reified, and disadvantageous need interpretations previously assigned to and/or embraced by them. By insisting on speaking publicly of heretofore depoliticized needs, by claiming for these needs the status of legitimate political issues, such persons and groups do several things simultaneously. First, they contest the established boundaries separating "politics" from "economics" and "domestics." Second, they offer alternative interpretations of their needs embedded in alternative chains of in-order-to relations. Third, they create new discourse publics from which they try to disseminate their interpretations of their needs throughout a wide range of different discourse publics. Finally, they challenge, modify, and/or displace hegemonic elements of the means of interpretation and communication; they invent new forms of discourse for interpreting their needs.

In oppositional discourses, needs talk is a moment in the self-constitution of new collective agents or social movements. For example, in the current wave of feminist ferment, groups of women have politicized and reinterpreted various needs, have instituted new vocabularies and forms of address, and, so, have become "women" in a different, though not uncontested or univocal, sense. By speaking publicly the heretofore unspeakable, by coining terms like 'sexism,' 'sexual harassment,' 'marital, date, and acquaintance rape,' 'labor force sex-segregation,' 'the double shift,' 'wife battering,' and so on, feminist women have become "women" in the sense of a discursively self-constituted political collectivity, albeit a very heterogeneous and fractured one.[22]

Of course, the politicization of needs in oppositional discourses does not go uncontested. One type of resistance involves defense of the established boundaries separating "political," "economic," and "domestic" spheres by means of "reprivatization" discourses. Institutionally, 'reprivatization' designates initiatives aimed at dismantling or cutting back social-welfare services, selling off nationalized assets, and/or deregulating "private" enterprise; discursively, it means depoliticization. Thus, in reprivatization discourses, speakers oppose state provision of runaway needs, and they seek to contain forms of needs talk that threaten to spill across a wide range of discourse publics. Reprivatizers may insist, for example, that domestic battery is not a legitimate subject of political discourse but a familial or religious matter, or, to take a different example, that a factory closing is not a political question but an unimpeachable prerogative of "private" ownership or an unassailable imperative of an impersonal market mechanism. In both cases, the speakers are contesting the breakout of runaway needs and are trying to (re)depoliticize them.

Interestingly, reprivatization discourses blend the old and the new. On the one hand, they seem merely to render explicit those need interpretations that could earlier go without saying. But, on the other hand, by the very act of articulating such interpretations, they simultaneously modify them. Because reprivatization discourses respond to competing, oppositional interpretations, they are internally dialogized, incorporating references to the alternatives they resist, even while rejecting them. For example, although "pro-family" discourses of the social New Right are explicitly antifeminist, some of them incorporate in a depoliticized form feminist-inspired motifs implying women's right to sexual pleasure and to emotional support from their husbands.[23]

In defending the established social division of discourses, reprivatization discourses deny the claims of oppositional movements for the legitimate political status of runaway needs. However, in so doing, they tend further to politicize those needs in the sense of increasing their cathectedness as focuses of contestation. Moreover, in some cases reprivatization discourses, too, become vehicles for mobilizing social movements and for reshaping social identities. Doubtless the most stunning example is Thatcherism in Britain, where a set of reprivatization discourses articulated in the accents of authoritarian populism has refashioned the subjectivities of a wide range of disaffected constituencies and united them in a powerful coalition.[24]

Together, oppositional discourses and reprivatization discourses define one axis of needs struggle in late capitalist societies. But there is also a second, rather different line of conflict. Here, the focal issue is no longer politicization versus depoliticization but, rather, the interpreted *content* of contested needs once their political status has been successfully secured. And the principal contestants are oppositional social movements and organized interests, like business, that seek to influence public policy.

For example, today in the United States, day care is gaining increasing legitimacy as a political issue. As a result, we are seeing the proliferation of competing interpretations and programmatic conceptions. In one view, day care would serve poor children's needs for "enrichment" and/or moral supervision. In a second, it would serve the middle-class taxpayer's need to get AFDC recipients off the welfare rolls. A third interpretation would shape day care as a measure for increasing the productivity and competitiveness of American business, while yet a fourth would treat it as part of a package of policies aimed at redistributing income and resources to women. Each of these interpretations carries a distinct programmatic orientation with respect to funding, institutional siting and control, service design, and eligibility. As they collide, we see a struggle to shape the hegemonic understanding of day care, which may eventually make its way onto the formal political agenda. Clearly, not just feminist groups but also business interests, trade unions, children's rights advocates, and educators are contestants in this struggle, and they bring to it vast differentials in power.[25]

The struggle for hegemonic need interpretations usually points toward the future involvement of the state. Thus, it anticipates yet a third axis of needs struggle in late capitalist societies. Here, the focal issues concern politics versus administration and the principal contestants are oppositional social movements and the experts and agencies in the orbit of the social state.

Recall that "the social" is a site where needs that have become politicized in the discourse sense become candidates for state-organized provision. Consequently, these needs become the object of yet another group of discourses: the complex of "expert" "public policy" discourses based in various "private," "semi-public," and state institutions.

Expert needs discourses are the vehicles for translating sufficiently politicized runaway needs into objects of potential state intervention. They are closely connected with institutions of knowledge production and utilization,[26] and they include qualitative and especially quantitative social science discourses generated in universities and "think tanks"; legal discourses generated in judicial institutions and their satellite schools, journals, and professional associations; administrative discourses circulated in various agencies of the social state; and therapeutic discourses circulated in public and private medical and social service agencies.

As the term suggests, expert discourses tend to be restricted to specialized publics.

Thus, they are associated with professional class formation, institution building, and social "problem solving." But in some cases, such as law and psychotherapy, expert vocabularies and rhetorics are disseminated to a wider spectrum of educated laypersons, some of whom are participants in social movements. Moreover, social movements sometimes manage to co-opt or create critical, oppositional segments of expert discourse publics. For all these reasons, expert discourse publics sometimes acquire a certain porousness. And expert discourses become the *bridge* discourses linking loosely organized social movements with the social state.

Because of this bridge role, the rhetoric of expert needs discourses tends to be administrative. These discourses consist in a series of rewriting operations, procedures for translating politicized needs into administrable needs. Typically, the politicized need is redefined as the correlate of a bureaucratically administrable satisfaction, a "social service." It is specified in terms of an ostensibly general state of affairs that could, in principle, befall anyone—for example, unemployment, disability, death or desertion of a spouse.[27] As a result, the need is decontextualized and recontextualized: on the one hand, it is represented in abstraction from its class, race, and gender specificity and from whatever oppositional meanings it may have acquired in the course of its politicization; on the other hand, it is cast in terms that tacitly presuppose such entrenched, specific background institutions as ("primary" versus "secondary") wage labor, privatized childrearing, and their gender-based separation.

As a result of these expert redefinitions, the people whose needs are in question are repositioned. They become individual "cases" rather than members of social groups or participants in political movements. In addition, they are rendered passive, positioned as potential recipients of predefined services rather than as agents involved in interpreting their needs and shaping their life conditions.

By virtue of this administrative rhetoric, expert needs discourses, too, tend to be depoliticizing. They construe persons simultaneously as rational utility maximizers and as causally conditioned, predictable, and manipulable objects, thereby screening out those dimensions of human agency that involve the construction and deconstruction of social meanings.

Moreover, when expert needs discourses are institutionalized in state apparatuses, they tend to become normalizing, aimed at "reforming," or more often stigmatizing, "deviancy."[28] This sometimes becomes explicit when services incorporate a therapeutic dimension designed to close the gap between clients' recalcitrant self-interpretations and the interpretations embedded in administrative policy.[29] Now the rational-utility-maximizer-cum-causally-conditioned-object becomes, in addition, a deep self to be unraveled therapeutically.[30]

To summarize: when social movements succeed in politicizing previously depoliticized needs, they enter the terrain of the social, where two other kinds of struggles await them. First, they have to contest powerful organized interests bent on shaping hegemonic need interpretations to their own ends. Second, they encounter expert needs discourses in and around the social state. These encounters define two additional axes of needs struggle in late capitalist societies. They are highly complex struggles, since social movements typically seek state provision of their runaway needs even while they tend to oppose administrative and therapeutic need interpretations. Thus, these axes, too, involve conflicts among rival interpretations of social needs and among rival constructions of social identity.

**4**

Now I would like to apply the model I have been developing to some concrete cases of conflicts of need interpretation. The first example is designed to identify a tendency in welfare state societies whereby the politics of need interpretation devolves into the management of need satisfactions. A second group of examples, by contrast, charts the countertendency that runs from administration to resistance and potentially back to politics.[31]

First, consider the example of the politics of needs surrounding wife battering. Until about fifteen years ago, the term 'wife battering' did not exist. When spoken of publicly at all, this phenomenon was called 'wife beating' and was often treated comically, as in "Have you stopped beating your wife?" Linguistically, it was classed with the disciplining of children and servants as a "domestic"—as opposed to a "political"—matter. Then, feminist activists renamed the practice with a term drawn from criminal law and created a new kind of public discourse. They claimed that battery was not a personal, domestic problem but a systemic, political one; its etiology was not to be traced to individual women's or men's emotional problems but, rather, to the ways these problems refracted pervasive social relations of male dominance and female subordination.

Thus, feminist activists contested established discursive boundaries and politicized a heretofore depoliticized phenomenon. In addition, they reinterpreted the experience of battery and posited a set of associated needs. Here, they situated battered women's needs in a long chain of in-order-to relations that spilled across conventional separations of "spheres"; they claimed that in order to be free from dependence on batterers, battered women needed not just temporary shelter but also jobs paying a "family wage," day care, and affordable permanent housing. Further, feminists created new discourse publics, new spaces and institutions in which such oppositional need interpretations could be developed and from which they could be spread to wider publics. Finally, feminists modified elements of the authorized means of interpretation and communication; they coined new terms of description and analysis and devised new ways of addressing female subjects. In their discourse, battered women were not addressed as individualized victims but as potential feminist activists, members of a politically constituted collectivity.

This discursive intervention was accompanied by feminist efforts to provide for some of the needs they had politicized and reinterpreted. Activists organized battered women's shelters, places of refuge and of consciousness-raising. The organization of these shelters was nonhierarchical; there were no clear lines between staff and users. Many of the counselors and organizers had themselves been battered, and a high percentage of the women who used the shelters went on to counsel other battered women and to become movement activists. Concomitantly, these women came to adopt new self-descriptions. Whereas most had originally blamed themselves and defended their batterers, many came to reject that interpretation in favor of a politicized view that offered them new models of human agency. In addition, these women modified their affiliations and social identifications. Whereas many had originally felt deeply identified with their batterers, they came to affiliate with other women.

This organizing eventually had an impact on wider discursive publics. By the late 1970s, feminists had largely succeeded in establishing domestic violence against women as a legitimate political issue. They managed in some cases to change the attitudes and policies of police and the courts, and they won for this issue a place on the informal political agenda. Now the needs of battered women were sufficiently politicized to become candidates for publicly organized satisfaction. Finally, in several municipalities and localities, movement shelters began receiving local government funding.

From the feminist perspective, this represented a significant victory, but it was not without cost. Municipal funding brought with it a variety of new, administrative constraints ranging from accounting procedures to regulation, accreditation, and professionalization requirements. As a consequence, publicly funded shelters underwent a transformation. Increasingly, they came to be staffed by professional social workers, many of whom had not themselves experienced battery. Thus, a division between professional and client supplanted the more fluid continuum of relations that had characterized the earlier shelters. Moreover, since many social work staffs have been trained to frame problems in a quasi-psychiatric perspective, this perspective structures the practices of many publicly funded shelters even despite the intentions of individual staff members, many of whom are politically committed feminists. Consequently, the practices of such shelters have become more individualizing and less politicized. Battered women tend now to be positioned as clients. They are increasingly psychiatrized, addressed as victims with deep, complicated selves. They are only rarely addressed as potential feminist activists. Increasingly, the language game of therapy has supplanted that of consciousness-raising. And the neutral scientific language of 'spouse abuse' has supplanted more political talk of 'male violence against women.' Finally, the needs of battered women have been substantially reinterpreted. The far-reaching earlier claims for the social and economic prerequisites of independence have tended to give way to a narrower focus on the individual woman's problems of "low self-esteem."[32]

The battered women's shelter case exemplifies one tendency of needs politics in late capitalist societies: the tendency for the politics of need interpretation to devolve into the administration of need satisfaction. However, there is also a countertendency that runs from administration to client resistance and potentially back to politics. I would like now to document this countertendency by discussing four examples of client resistance, examples ranging from the individual, cultural, and informal to the collective, political, and formally organized.

First, individuals may locate some space for maneuver within the administrative framework of a government agency. They may displace and/or modify an agency's official interpretations of their needs, even without mounting an overt challenge. Historian Linda Gordon has uncovered examples of this sort of resistance in the records of child-protection agencies during the Progressive Era.[33] Gordon cites cases in which women who had been beaten by their husbands filed complaints alleging child abuse. Having involved case workers in their situations by invoking an interpreted need that *was* recognized as legitimate and as falling within the agency's jurisdiction, they managed to interest the case workers in a need that was *not* so recognized. In some cases, these women succeeded in securing intervention under the child abuse rubric that provided them some measure of relief from domestic battery. Thus, they informally broadened the agency's jurisdiction to include, indirectly, a hitherto excluded need. While citing the social state's official definition of their need, they simultaneously displaced that definition and brought it closer in line with their own interpretations.

Second, informally organized groups may develop practices and affiliations that are at odds with the social state's way of positioning them as clients. In so doing, they may alter the uses and meanings of benefits provided by government agencies, even without explicitly calling these into question. Anthropologist Carol Stack has documented examples of this sort of resistance in her study of "domestic kin networks" among poor black AFDC recipients in a midwestern city in the late 1960s.[34] Stack describes elaborate kinship arrangements that organized delayed exchanges, or "gifts," of prepared meals, food stamps, cooking, shopping, groceries, sleeping space, cash (including wages and AFDC allowances), transportation, clothing, child care, even children. It is significant that these domestic kin networks span several physically distinct households. This means that AFDC recipients use their benefits beyond the confines of the principal administrative category of government relief programs, namely, "the household." Consequently, these clients circumvent the nuclear-familializing procedures of welfare administration. By utilizing benefits beyond the confines of a "household," they alter the state-defined meanings of those benefits and, thus, of the needs those benefits purport to satisfy. At the same time, they indirectly contest the state's way of positioning them as subjects. Whereas AFDC addressed them as biological mothers who belong to deviant nuclear families that lack male breadwinners, they double that subject-position with another one, namely, members of socially, as opposed to biologically, constituted kin networks who cooperate in coping with dire poverty.

Third, individuals and/or groups may resist therapeutic initiatives of the social state while accepting material aid. They may reject state-sponsored therapeutic constructions of their life stories and capacities for agency and insist instead on alternative narratives and conceptions of identity. Sociologist Prudence Rains has documented an example of this kind of resistance in her comparative study of the "moral careers" of black and white pregnant teenagers in the late 1960s.[35]

Rains contrasts the ways the two groups of young women responded to therapeutic constructions of their experience in two different institutional settings. The young middle-class white women were in an expensive private residential facility. This facility combined traditional services, such as seclusion and a cover for "good girls who had made a mistake," with newer therapeutic services, including required individual and group counseling sessions with psychiatric social workers. In these sessions, the young women were addressed as deep, complicated selves. They were encouraged to regard their pregnancies not as simple "mistakes" but, rather, as unconsciously motivated, meaningful acts expressive of latent emotional problems. This meant that a girl was to interpret her pregnancy—and the sex that was its superficial cause—as a form of acting out, say, a refusal of parental authority or a demand for parental love. She was warned that unless she came to understand and acknowledge these deep, hidden motives, she would likely not succeed in avoiding future "mistakes."

Rains documents the process by which most of the young white women at this facility came to internalize this perspective and to rewrite themselves in the psychiatric idiom. She records the narratives they devised in the course of rewriting their "moral careers."

For example:

> When I first came here I had it all figured out in my mind that Tom . . . had kind of
> talked me into it and I gave in. I kind of put it all on him. I didn't really accept my own
> part in it. . . . [H]ere they stressed a lot that if you don't realize why you're here or why
> you ended up here and the emotional reasons behind it, that it will happen again. . . . I
> feel now that I have a pretty full understanding of why I did end up here and that there
> was an emotional reason for it. And I accept my part in it more. It wasn't just him. (93)

This narrative is interesting in several respects. As Rains notes, the exchange of a "mistake" view of the past for a psychiatric view provided certain comforts: the new interpretation "did not merely set aside the past but accounted for it, and accounted for it in ways which allowed girls to believe they would act differently in the future" (94). Thus, the psychiatric view offers the pregnant teenager a model of agency that seems to enhance her capacity for individual self-determination. On the other hand, the narrative is highly selective, avowing some aspects of the past while disavowing others. It plays down the narrator's sexuality, treating her sexual behavior and desires as epiphenomenal "manifestation[s] of other, deeper, and nonsexual emotional needs and problems" (93). In addition, it defuses the potentially explosive issue of consent versus coercion in the teenage heterosexual milieu by excusing Tom and by revising the girl's earlier sense that their intercourse was not consensual. Moreover, the narrative forecloses any question as to the legitimacy of "premarital sex," assuming that for a woman, at least, such sex is morally wrong. Finally, in light of the girls' declarations that they will not need contraceptives when they return home and resume dating, the narrative has yet another meaning. Encapsulating a new awareness of deep emotional problems, it becomes a shield against future pregnancies, a prophylactic. Given these elisions in the story, a skeptic might well conclude that the psychiatric promise of enhanced self-determination is largely illusory.

The relative ease with which Rains's white teenagers internalized the therapeutic interpretation of their situation stands in stark contrast with the resistance offered by her black subjects. The young black women were clients in a nonresidential municipal facility providing prenatal care, schooling, and counseling sessions with a psychiatric social worker. The counseling sessions were similar in intent and design to those at the private residential facility; the young women were encouraged to talk about their feelings and to probe the putative deep, emotional causes of their pregnancies. However, this therapeutic approach was much less successful at the public facility. The young black women resisted the terms of the psychiatric discourse and the language game of question-and-answer employed in the counseling sessions. They disliked the social worker's stance of nondirectiveness and moral neutrality—her willingness to say what *she* thought—and they resented what they considered her intrusive, overly personal questions. These girls did not acknowledge her right to question them in this fashion, given that they could not ask "personal" questions of her in turn. Rather, they construed "personal questioning" as a privilege reserved to close friends and intimates under conditions of reciprocity.

Rains documents several dimensions of the young black women's resistance to the "mental health" aspects of the program. In some instances, they openly challenged the rules of the therapeutic language game. In others, they resisted indirectly by humor, quasi-deliberately misunderstanding the social worker's vague, nondirective, yet "personal" questions. For example, one girl construed "How did you get pregnant?" as a "stupid" question and replied, "Shouldn't you know?" (136).

Some others subjected the constant therapeutic "How did it feel?" to an operation that can only be called "carnivalesque." The occasion was a group counseling session for which the case worker was late. The young women assembled for the meeting began speculating as to her whereabouts. One mentioned that Mrs. Eckerd had gone to see a doctor. The conversation continued:

> "To see if she's pregnant."
> "She probably thinks that's where you get babies."
> "Maybe the doctor's going to give her a baby." . . .
> Bernice then started doing an imitation interview pretending she was a social worker asking questions of a pretend-pregnant Mrs. Eckerd, "Tell me, how did it feel? Did you like it?"
> This brought a storm of laughter, and everybody started mimicking questions they supposedly had had put to them. Someone said, "She asked me did I want to put my baby for adoption, and how did it feel?"
> When Mrs. Eckerd finally arrived, May said, "Why do social workers ask so many questions?"
> Mrs. Eckerd said, "What kind of questions do you mean, May?"
> Bernice . . . said, "Like 'How did it feel?' "
> There was an uproar over this. (137)

Thus, Rains's black subjects devised a varied repertoire of strategies for resisting expert, therapeutic constructions of their life stories and capacities for agency. They were keenly aware of the power subtext underlying their interactions with the social worker and of the normalization dimension of the therapeutic initiative. In effect, these young black women blocked efforts to inculcate in them white, middle-class norms of individuality and affectivity. They refused the case worker's inducements to rewrite themselves as psychologized selves, while availing themselves of the health services at the facility. Thus, they made use of those aspects of the agency's program that they considered appropriate to their self-interpreted needs and ignored or sidestepped the others.

Fourth, in addition to informal, ad hoc, strategic and/or cultural forms of resistance, there are also more formally organized, explicitly political, organized kinds. Clients of social-welfare programs may join together *as clients* to challenge administrative interpretations of their needs. They may take hold of the passive, normalized, and individualized or familialized identities fashioned for them in expert discourses and transform them into a basis for collective political action. Frances Fox Piven and Richard A. Cloward have documented an example of this kind of resistance in their account of the process by which AFDC recipients organized the welfare-rights movement of the 1960s.[36] Notwithstanding the atomizing and depoliticizing dimensions of AFDC administration, these women were brought together in welfare waiting rooms. It was as a result of their participation as clients, then, that they came to articulate common grievances and to act together. Thus, the same welfare practices that gave rise to these grievances created the enabling conditions for collective organizing to combat them. As Piven put it, "the structure of the welfare state itself has helped to create new solidarities and generate the political issues that continue to cement and galvanize them."[37]

# Conclusion

Let me conclude by flagging some issues that are central to this project but that I have not yet discussed here. In this essay, I have concentrated on social-theoretical issues at the expense of moral and epistemological issues. However, the latter are very important for a project, like mine, that aspires to be a *critical* social theory.

My analysis of needs talk raises two very obvious and pressing philosophical issues. One is the question of whether and how it is possible to distinguish better from worse interpretations of people's needs. The other is the question of the relationship between needs claims and rights. Although I cannot offer full answers to these questions here, I would like to indicate something about how I would approach them. I want also to situate my views in relation to contemporary debates among feminist theorists.

Feminist scholars have demonstrated again and again that authoritative views purporting to be neutral and disinterested actually express the partial and interested perspectives of dominant social groups. In addition, many feminist theorists have made use of post-structuralist approaches that deny the possibility of distinguishing warranted claims from power plays. As a result, there is now a significant strand of relativist sentiment within feminist ranks. At the same time, many other feminists worry that relativism undermines the possibility of political commitment. How, after all, can one argue against the possibility of warranted claims while oneself making such claims as that sexism exists and is unjust?[38]

This issue about relativism surfaces in the present context in the form of the question, Can we distinguish better from worse interpretations of people's needs? Or, since all need interpretations emanate from specific, interested locations in society, are all of them equally compromised?

I claim that we *can* distinguish better from worse interpretations of people's needs. To say that needs are culturally constructed and discursively interpreted is not to say that any need interpretation is as good as any other. On the contrary, it is to underline the importance of an account of interpretive justification. However, I do not think that justification can be understood in traditional objectivist terms as correspondence, as if it were a matter of finding the interpretation that matches the true nature of the need as it really is in itself, independent of any interpretation.[39] Nor do I think that justification can be premised on a preestablished point of epistemic superiority, as if it were a matter of finding the one group in society with the privileged "standpoint."[40]

Then what *should* an account of interpretive justification consist in? In my view, there are at least two distinct kinds of considerations that such an account would have to encompass and to balance. First, there are procedural considerations concerning the social processes by which various competing need interpretations are generated. For example, how exclusive or inclusive are various rival needs discourses? How hierarchical or egalitarian are the relations among the interlocutors? In general, procedural considerations dictate that, all other things being equal, the best need interpretations are those reached by means of communicative processes that most closely approximate ideals of democracy, equality, and fairness.[41]

In addition, considerations of consequences are relevant in justifying need interpretations. This means comparing alternative distributive outcomes of rival interpretations. For example, would widespread acceptance of some given interpretation of a social need disadvantage some groups of people vis-à-vis others? Does the interpretation conform to, rather than challenge, societal patterns of dominance and subordination? Are the rival chains of in-order-to relations to which competing need interpretations belong more or less respectful, as opposed to transgressive, of ideological boundaries that delimit "separate spheres" and thereby rationalize inequality? In general, consequentialist considerations dictate that, all other things being equal, the best need interpretations are those that do not disadvantage some groups of people vis-à-vis others.

In sum, justifying some interpretations of social needs as better than others involves balancing procedural and consequentialist considerations. More simply, it involves balancing democracy and equality.

What, then, of the relationship between needs and rights? This, too, is a controversial issue in contemporary theory. Critical legal theorists have argued that rights claims work against radical social transformation by enshrining tenets of bourgeois individualism. Meanwhile, some feminist moral theorists suggest that an orientation toward responsibilities is preferable to an orientation toward rights.[42] Together, these views might lead some to want to think of needs talk as an alternative to rights talk. On the other hand, many feminists worry that left-wing critiques of rights play into the hands of our political opponents. After all, conservatives traditionally prefer to distribute aid as a matter of need *instead* of right precisely in order to avoid assumptions of entitlement that could carry egalitarian implications. For these reasons, some feminist activists and legal scholars have sought to develop and defend alternative understandings of rights.[43] Their approach might imply that suitably reconstructed rights claims and needs claims could be mutually compatible, even intertranslatable.[44]

Very briefly, I align myself with those who favor translating justified needs claims into social rights. Like many radical critics of existing social-welfare programs, I am committed to opposing the forms of paternalism that arise when needs claims are divorced from rights claims. And unlike some communitarian, socialist, and feminist critics, I do not believe that rights talk is inherently individualistic, bourgeois-liberal, and androcentric — rights talk takes on those properties only when societies establish the *wrong* rights, for example, when the (putative) right to private property is permitted to trump other, social rights.

Moreover, to treat justified needs claims as the bases for new social rights is to begin to overcome obstacles to the effective exercise of some existing rights. It is true, as Marxists and others have claimed, that classical liberal rights to free expression, assembly, and the like are "merely formal." But this says more about the social context in which they are currently embedded than about their "intrinsic" character, for, in a context devoid of poverty, inequality, and oppression, formal liberal rights could be broadened and transformed into substantive rights, say, to collective self-determination.

Finally, I should stress that this work is motivated by the conviction that, for the time being, needs talk is with us for better or worse. For the foreseeable future, political agents, including feminists, will have to operate on a terrain where needs talk is the discursive coin of the realm. But, as I have tried to show, this idiom is neither inherently emancipatory nor inherently repressive. Rather, it is multivalent and contested. The larger aim of my project is to help clarify the prospects for democratic and egalitarian social change by sorting out the emancipatory from the repressive possibilities of needs talk.

## Reading Questions

1. What are some examples of feminist needs claims in our late capitalist welfare state society? What makes them specifically *needs* claims, and how are they different from rights claims?
2. What does Fraser mean by the "blind spots" of "thin" needs claims?
3. Why does Fraser claim that our male-dominated domestic and economic institutions depoliticize social needs discourses? What sense of "political" is she assuming?
4. How is the "social" a different sphere of public discourse than the economic or the political?

Why is the U.S. social welfare system part of the social?
5. Describe a possible scenario of needs interpretation, referring to the three types of needs discourses that Fraser describes, and evaluate its consequences for the political actors who are involved in the scenario. (Possible examples include Haitian AIDS activists' demand for legalized immigration into the United States, the demand of AFDC recipients for administrative reform, the founding of a battered women's shelter in your home town.)

## Recommended Reading

Seyla Benhabib, *Situating the Self: Gender, Community and Postmodernism in Contemporary Ethics* (New York: Routledge, 1992)

Fred Block, Barbara Ehrenreich, et al., eds., *The Mean Season: The Attack on the Welfare State* (New York: Pantheon, 1987)

Karen V. Hansen and Ilene J. Philipson, eds., *Women, Class, and the Feminist Imagination: A Socialist–Feminist Reader* (Philadelphia: Temple University Press, 1990)

Francis Fox Piven and Richard A. Cloward, *Regulating the Poor: The Functions of Public Welfare* (New York: Vintage, 1972)

Valerie Polakow, *Lives on the Edge: Single Mothers and Their Children in the Other America* (Chicago: University of Chicago Press, 1993)

Susan Schechter, *Women and Male Violence: The Visions and Struggles of the Battered Women's Movement* (Boston: South End Press, 1982)

## Recommended Audiovisual Resources

*Bailey House: To Live as Long as You Can.* 1990. Directed by Alain Klarer. An intimate portrait of the people who live at Bailey House, a 44-room residence for homeless people with AIDS. Filmakers Library.

*For Richer, For Poorer.* 1990. Directed by Ariadne Ochrymovych. Documentary about Joan Thompson, who becomes a member of the "new poor" after her marriage ends. National Film Board of Canada.

# CHAPTER 3

# Megalopolis

Mannequins broken during a night of urban upheaval on May 18, 1980, in Miami, Florida. UPI/Bettmann.

# Home Is Where the *Han* Is

## A Korean American Perspective on the Los Angeles Upheavals

ELAINE H. KIM

Elaine H. Kim teaches finance and business education administration at the University of Michigan School of Business Administration. She is a member of the Korean-American Economic Association and the author of *With Silk Wings: Asian American Women at Work.*

About half of the estimated $850 million in estimated material losses incurred during the Los Angeles upheavals was sustained by a community no one seems to want to talk much about. Korean Americans in Los Angeles, suddenly at the front lines when violence came to the buffer zone they had been so precariously occupying, suffered profound damage to their means of livelihood.[1] But my concern here is the psychic damage which, unlike material damage, is impossible to quantify.

I want to explore the questions of whether or not recovery is possible for Korean Americans, and what will become of our attempts to "become American" without dying of *han. Han* is a Korean word that means, loosely translated, the sorrow and anger that grow from the accumulated experiences of oppression. Although the word is frequently and commonly used by Koreans, the condition it describes is taken quite seriously. When people die of *han*, it is called dying of *hwabyong*, a disease of frustration and rage following misfortune.

Situated as we are on the border between those who have and those who have not, between predominantly Anglo and mostly African American and Latino communities, from our current interstitial position in the American discourse of race, many Korean Americans have trouble calling what happened in Los Angeles an "uprising." At the same time, we cannot quite say it was a "riot." So some of us have taken to calling it *sa-i-ku*, April 29, after the manner of naming other events in Korean history—3.1 (*sam-il*) for March 1, 1919, when massive protests against Japanese colonial rule began in Korea; 6.25 (*yook-i-o*), or June 25, 1950, when the Korean War began; and 4.19 (*sa-il-ku*), or April 19, 1960, when the first student movement in the world to overthrow a government began in South Korea. The ironic similarity between 4.19 and 4.29 does not escape most Korean Americans.

Los Angeles Koreatown has been important to me, even though I visit only a dozen times a year. Before Koreatown sprang up during the last decade and a half,[2] I used to hang around the fringes of Chinatown, although I knew that this habit was pure pretense.[3] For me, knowing that Los Angeles Koreatown existed made a difference; one of my closest friends worked with the Black-Korean Alliance there,[4] and I liked to think of it as a kind of "home"—however idealized and hypostatized—for the soul, an anchor, a potential refuge, a place in America where I could belong without ever being asked, "Who are you and what are you doing here? Where did you come from and when are you going back?"

Many of us watched in horror the destruction of Koreatown and the systematic targeting of Korean shops in South Central Los Angeles after the Rodney King verdict. Seeing those buildings in flames and those anguished Korean faces, I had the terrible thought that there would be no belonging and that we were, just as I had always suspected, a people destined to carry our *han* around with us wherever we went in the world. The destiny (*p'aljja*) that had spelled centuries of extreme suffering from invasion, colonization, war, and national division had smuggled itself into the U.S. with our baggage.

## African American and Korean American Conflict

As someone whose social consciousness was shaped by the African American–led civil rights movement of the 1960s, I felt that I was watching our collective dreams for a just society disintegrating, cast aside as naive and irrelevant in the bitter and embattled 1990s. It was the courageous African American women and men of the 1960s who had redefined the meaning of "American," who had first suggested that a person like me could reject the false choice between being treated as a perpetual foreigner in my own birthplace, on the one hand, and relinquishing my identity for someone else's ill-fitting and impossible Anglo American one on the other. Thanks to them, I began to discern how institutional racism works and why Korea was never mentioned in my world-history textbooks. I was able to see how others besides Koreans had been swept aside by the dominant culture. My American education offered nothing about Chicanos or Latinos, and most of what I was taught about African and Native Americans was distorted to justify their oppression and vindicate their oppressors.

I could hardly believe my ears when, during the weeks immediately following *sa-i-ku*, I heard African American community leaders suggesting that Korean American merchants were foreign intruders deliberately trying to stifle African American economic development, when I knew that they had bought those liquor stores at five times gross receipts from African American owners, who had previously bought them at two times gross receipts from Jewish owners after Watts.[5] I saw anti-Korean flyers that were being circulated by African American political candidates and read about South Central residents petitioning against the reestablishment of swap meets, groups of typically Korean immigrant-operated market stalls. I was disheartened with Latinos who related the pleasure they felt while looting Korean stores that they believed "had it coming" and who claimed that it was because of racism that more Latinos were arrested during *sa-i-ku* than Asian Americans.[6] And I was filled with despair when I read about Chinese Americans wanting to dissociate themselves from us. According to one Chinese American reporter assigned to cover Asian American issues for a San Francisco daily, Chinese and Japanese American shopkeepers, unlike Koreans, always got along fine with African Americans in the past.[7] "Suddenly," admitted another Chinese American, "I am scared to be Asian. More specifically, I am afraid to be mistaken for Korean."[8] I was enraged when I overheard European Americans discussing the conflicts as if they were watching a dogfight or a boxing match. The situation reminded me of the Chinese film "Raise the Red Lantern," in which we never see the husband's face. We only hear his mellifluous voice as he benignly admonishes his four wives not to fight among themselves. He can afford to be kind and pleasant because the structure that pits his wives against each other is so firmly in place that he need never sully his hands or even raise his voice.

## Battleground Legacy

Korean Americans are squeezed between black and white and also between U.S. and South Korean political agendas. Opportunistic American and South Korean presidential candidates toured the burnt ruins, posing for the television cameras but delivering nothing of substance to the victims. Like their U.S. counterparts, South Korean news media seized upon *sa-i-ku*, featuring sensational stories that depicted the problem as that of savage African Americans attacking innocent Koreans for no reason.[9] To give the appearance of authenticity, Seoul newspapers even published articles using the names of Korean Americans who did not in fact write them.[10]

Those of us who chafe at being asked whether we are Chinese or Japanese as if there were no other possibilities or who were angered when the news media sought Chinese and Japanese but not Korean American views during *sa-i-ku* are sensitive to an invisibility that seems particular to us. To many Americans, Korea is but the gateway to or the bridge between China and Japan, or a crossroads of major Asian conflicts.[11]

It can certainly be said that, although little known or cared about in the Western world, Korea has been a perennial battleground. Besides the Mongols and the Manchus, there were the *Yôjin* (Jurched), the *Koran* (Khitan), and the *Waegu* (Wäkö) invaders. In relatively recent years, there was the war between China and Japan that ended in 1895 and the war between Japan and Russia in 1905, both of which were fought on Korean soil and resulted in extreme suffering for the Korean people. Japan's 36 years of brutal colonial rule ended with the U.S. and what was then the Soviet Union dividing the country in half at the 38th parallel. Thus, Korea was turned into a Cold War territory that ultimately became a battleground for world superpowers during the conflict of 1950–53.

## Becoming American

One of the consequences of war, colonization, national division, and superpower economic and cultural domination has been the migration of Koreans to places like Los Angeles, where they believed their human rights would be protected by law. After all, they had received U.S.-influenced political educations. They started learning English in the seventh grade. They all knew the story of the poor boy from Illinois who became president. They all learned that the U.S. Constitution and Bill of Rights protected the common people from violence and injustice. But they who grew up in Korea watching "Gunsmoke," "Night Rider," and "McGyver" dubbed in Korean were not prepared for the black, brown, red, and yellow America they encountered when they disembarked at the Los Angeles International Airport.[12] They hadn't heard that there is no equal justice in the U.S. They had to learn about American racial hierarchies. They did not realize that, as immigrants of color, they would never attain political voice or visibility but would instead be used to uphold the inequality and the racial hierarchy they had no part in creating.

Most of the newcomers had underestimated the communication barriers they would face. Like the Turkish workers in Germany described in John Berger and Jean Mohr's *A Seventh Man*,[13] their toil amounted to only a pile of gestures and the English they tried to speak changed and turned against them as they spoke it. Working 14 hours a day, six or seven days a week, they rarely came into sustained contact with English-speaking

Americans and almost never had time to study English. Not feeling at ease with English, they did not engage in informal conversations easily with non-Koreans and were hated for being curt and rude. They did not attend churches or do business in banks or other enterprises where English was required. Typically, the immigrant, small-business owners utilized unpaid family labor instead of hiring people from local communities. Thanks to Eurocentric American cultural practices, they knew little or nothing good about African Americans or Latinos, who in turn and for similar reasons knew little or nothing good about them. At the same time, Korean shopowners in South Central and Koreatown were affluent compared with the impoverished residents, whom they often exploited as laborers or looked down upon as fools with an aversion to hard work.[14] Most Korean immigrants did not even know that they were among the many direct beneficiaries of the African American-led civil rights movement, which helped pave the way for the 1965 immigration reforms that made their immigration possible.

Korean-immigrant views, shaped as they were by U.S. cultural influences and official, anticommunist, South Korean education,[15] differed radically from those of many poor people in the communities Korean immigrants served: unaware of the shameful history of oppression of nonwhite immigrants and other people of color in the U.S., they regarded themselves as having arrived in a meritocratic "land of opportunity" where a person's chances for success are limited only by individual lack of ability or diligence. Having left a homeland where they foresaw their talents and hard work going unrecognized and unrewarded, they were desperate to believe that the "American dream" of social and economic mobility through hard work was within their reach.

## Sa-i-ku

What they experienced on 29 and 30 April was a baptism into what it really means for a Korean to "become American" in the 1990s.[16] In South Korea, there is no 911, and no one really expects a fire engine or police car if there is trouble. Instead, people make arrangements with friends and family for emergencies. At the same time, guns are not part of Korean daily life. No civilian in South Korea can own a gun. Guns are the exclusive accoutrement of the military and police who enforce order for those who rule the society. When the Korean Americans in South Central and Koreatown dialed 911, nothing happened. When their stores and homes were being looted and burned to the ground, they were left completely alone for three horrifying days. How betrayed they must have felt by what they had believed was a democratic system that protects its people from violence. Those who trusted the government to protect them lost everything; those who took up arms after waiting for help for two days were able to defend themselves. It was as simple as that. What they had to learn was that, as in South Korea, protection in the U.S. is by and large for the rich and powerful. If there were a choice between Westwood and Koreatown, it is clear that Koreatown would have to be sacrificed. The familiar concept of privilege for the rich and powerful would have been easy for the Korean immigrant to grasp if only those exhortations about democracy and equality had not obfuscated the picture. Perhaps they should have relied even more on whatever they brought with them from Korea instead of fretting over trying to understand what was going on around them here. That Koreatown became a battleground does seem like the further playing out of a tragic legacy that has followed them across oceans and continents. The difference is that this was a battle between the poor and disenfranchised and the invisible rich, who were being protected by a layer of clearly visible Korean American human shields in a battle on the buffer zone.

This difference is crucial. Perhaps the legacy is not one carried across oceans and continents but one assumed immediately upon arrival, not the curse of being Korean but the initiation into becoming American, which requires that Korean Americans take on this country's legacy of five centuries of racial violence and inequality, of divide and rule, of privilege for the rich and oppression of the poor. Within this legacy, they have been assigned a place on the front lines. Silenced by those who possess the power to characterize and represent, they are permitted to speak only to reiterate their acceptance of this role.

## Silencing the Korean American Voice

Twelve years ago, in Kwangju, South Korea, hundreds of civilians demonstrating for constitutional reform and free elections were murdered by U.S.-supported and -equipped South Korean elite paratroopers. Because I recorded it and played it over and over again, searching for a sign or a clue, I remember clearly how what were to me heartrendingly tragic events were represented in the U.S. news media. For a few fleeting moments, images of unruly crowds of alien-looking Asians shouting unintelligible words and phrases and wearing white headbands inscribed with unintelligible characters flickered across the screen. The Koreans were made to seem like insane people from another planet. The voice in the background stated simply that there were massive demonstrations but did not explain what the protests were about. Nor was a single Korean ever given an opportunity to speak to the camera.

The next news story was about demonstrations for democracy in Poland. The camera settled on individuals' faces which one by one filled the screen as each man or woman was asked to explain how he or she felt. Each Polish person's words were translated in a voice-over or subtitle. Solidarity leader Lech Walesa, who was allowed to speak often, was characterized as a heroic human being with whom all Americans could surely identify personally. Polish Americans from New York and Chicago to San Francisco, asked in man-on-the-street interviews about their reactions, described the canned hams and blankets they were sending to Warsaw.

This was for me a lesson in media representation, race, and power politics. It is a given that Americans are encouraged by our ideological apparatuses to side with our allies (here, the Polish resisters and the anti-communist South Korean government) against our enemies (here, the communist Soviet Union and protesters against the South Korean government). But visual-media racism helps craft and reinforce our identification with Europeans and whites while distancing us from fearsome and alien Asiatic hordes.

In March of last year, when two delegates from North Korea visited the Bay Area to participate in community-sponsored talks on Korean reunification, about 800 people from the Korean American community attended. The meeting was consummately newsworthy, since it was the first time in history that anyone from North Korea had ever been in California for more than 24 hours just passing through. The event was discussed for months in the Korean-language media—television, radio, and newspapers. Almost every Korean-speaking person in California knew about it. Although we sent press releases to all the commercial and public radio and television stations and to all the Bay Area newspapers, not a single mainstream media outfit covered the event. However, whenever there was an African American boycott of a Korean store or whenever conflict surfaced between Korean and African Americans, community leaders found a dozen microphones from all the main news media shoved into their faces, as if they were the president's press secretary making an official public pronouncement. Fascination with interethnic conflicts is rooted in the desire to excuse or minimize white racism by buttressing the mistaken notion that all human beings are "naturally" racist, and when Korean and African Americans allow themselves to be distracted by these interests, their attention is deflected from the social hierarchies that give racism its destructive power.

Without a doubt, the U.S. news media played a major role in exacerbating the damage and ill will toward Korean Americans, first by spotlighting tensions between African Americans and Koreans above all efforts to work together and as opposed to many other newsworthy events in these two communities, and second by exploiting racist stereotypes of Koreans as unfathomable aliens, this time wielding guns on rooftops and allegedly firing wildly into crowds.[17] In news programs and on talk shows, African and Korean American tensions were discussed by blacks and whites, who pointed to these tensions as the main cause of the uprising. I heard some European Americans railing against rude and exploitative Korean merchants for ruining peaceful race relations for everyone else. Thus, Korean Americans were used to deflect attention from the racism they inherited and the economic injustice and poverty that had been already well woven into the fabric of American life, as evidenced by a judicial system that could allow not only the Korean store owner who killed Latasha Harlins but also the white men who killed Vincent Chin and the white police who beat Rodney King to go free, while Leonard Peltier still languishes in prison.

As far as I know, neither the commercial nor the public news media has mentioned the many Korean and African American attempts to improve relations, such as joint church services, joint musical performances and poetry readings, Korean merchant donations to African American community and youth programs, African American volunteer teachers in classes for Korean immigrants studying for citizenship examinations, or Korean translations of African American history materials.

While Korean immigrants were preoccupied with the mantra of day-to-day survival, Korean Americans had no voice, no political presence whatsoever in American life. When they became the targets of violence in Los Angeles, their opinions and views were hardly solicited except as they could be used in the already-constructed mainstream discourse on race relations, which is a sorry combination of blaming the African American and Latino victims for their poverty and scapegoating the Korean Americans as robotic aliens who have no "real" right to be here in the first place and therefore deserve whatever happens to them.

## The *Newsweek* Experience

In this situation, I felt compelled to respond when an editor from the "My Turn" section of *Newsweek* magazine asked for a 1000-word personal essay.[18] Hesitant because I was given only a day and a half to write the piece, not enough time in light of the vastness of American ignorance about Koreans and Korean Americans, I decided to do it because I thought I could not be made into a sound bite or a quote contextualized for someone else's agenda.

I wrote an essay accusing the news media of using Korean Americans and tensions between African and Korean Americans to divert attention from the roots of racial violence in the U.S. I asserted that these lie not in the Korean-immigrant-owned corner store situated in a community ravaged by poverty and police violence, but reach far back into the corridors of corporate and government offices in Los Angeles, Sacramento, and Washington, D.C. I suggested that Koreans and African Americans were kept ignorant about each other by educational and media institutions that erase or distort their experiences and perspectives. I tried to explain how racism had kept my parents from ever really becoming Americans, but that having been born here, I considered myself American and wanted to believe in the possibility of an American dream.

The editor of "My Turn" did everything he could to frame my words with his own viewpoint. He faxed his own introductory and concluding paragraphs that equated Korean merchants with cowboys in the Wild West and alluded to Korean/African American hatred. When I objected, he told me that my writing style was not crisp enough and that as an experienced journalist, he could help me out. My confidence wavered, but ultimately I rejected his editing. Then he accused me of being overly sensitive, confiding that I had no need to be defensive—because his wife was a Chinese American. Only after I had decided to withdraw the piece did he agree to accept it as I wrote it.

Before I could finish congratulating myself on being able to resist silencing and the kind of decontextualization I was trying to describe in the piece, I started receiving hate mail: Some of it was addressed directly to me, since I had been identified as a University of California faculty member, but most of it arrived in bundles, forwarded by *Newsweek*. Hundreds of letters came from all over the country, from Florida to Washington state and from Massachusetts to Arizona. I was unprepared for the hostility expressed in most of the letters. Some people sent the article, torn from the magazine and covered with angry, red-inked obscenities scratched across my picture. "You should see a good doctor," wrote someone from Southern California, "you have severe problems in thinking, reasoning, and adjusting to your environment."

A significant proportion of the writers, especially those who identified themselves as descendants of immigrants from Eastern Europe, wrote *Newsweek* that they were outraged, sickened, disgusted, appalled, annoyed, and angry at the magazine for providing an arena for the paranoid, absurd, hypocritical, racist, and childish views of a spoiled, ungrateful, whining, bitching, un-American bogus faculty member who should be fired or die when the next California earthquake dumps all of the "so-called people of color" into the Pacific Ocean.

I was shocked by the profound ignorance of many writers' assumptions about the experiences and perspectives of American people of color in general and Korean and other Asian Americans in particular. Even though my essay revealed that I was born in the U.S. and that my parents had lived in the U.S. for more than six decades, I was viewed as a foreigner without the right to say anything except words of gratitude and praise about America. The letters also provided some evidence of the dilemma Korean Americans are placed in by those who assume that we are aliens who should "go back" and at the same time berate us for not rejecting "Korean-American identity" for "American identity."

How many Americans migrate to Korea? If you are so disenchanted, Korea is still there. Why did you ever leave it? Sayonara.

Ms. Kim appears to have a personal axe to grind with this country that has given her so much freedom and opportunity. . . . I should suggest that she move to Korea, where her children will learn all they ever wanted about that country's history.

[Her] whining about the supposedly racist U.S. society is just a mask for her own acute inferiority complex. If she is so dissatisfied with the United States why doesn't she vote with her feet and leave? She can get the hell out and return to her beloved Korea—her tribal afinity [*sic*] where her true loyalty and consciousness lies [*sic*].

You refer to yourself as a Korean American and yet you have lived all your life in the United States . . . you write about racism in this country and yet you are the biggest racist by your own written words. If you cannot accept the fact that you are an American, maybe you should be living your life in Korea.

My stepfather and cousin risked their lives in the country where your father is buried to ensure the ideals of our country would remain. So don't expect to find a sympathetic ear for your pathetic whining.

Many of the letter writers assumed that my family had been the "scum" of Asia and that I was a college teacher only because of American justice and largesse. They were furious that I did not express gratitude for being saved from starvation in Asia and given the opportunity to flourish, no doubt beyond my wildest dreams, in America.

Where would she be if her parents had not migrated to the United States? For a professor at Berkeley University [sic] to say the American dream is only an empty promise is ludicrous. Shame, shame, shame on Elaine!

[Her father and his family] made enough money in the USA to ship his corpse home to Korea for burial. Ms. Kim herself no doubt has a guaranteed life income as a professor paid by California taxpayers. Wouldn't you think that she might say kind things about the USA instead of whining about racism?

At the same time some letters blamed me for expecting "freedom and opportunity":

It is wondrous that folks such as you find truth in your paranoia. No one ever promised anything to you or your parents.

Besides providing indications of how Korean Americans are regarded, the letters revealed a great deal about how American identity is thought of. One California woman explained that although her grandparents were Irish immigrants, she was not an Irish American, because "if you are not with us, you are against us." A Missouri woman did not seem to realize that she was conflating race and nationality and confusing "nonethnic" and "nonracial," by which she seems to have meant "white," with "American." And, although she insists that it is impossible to be both "black" and "American," she identifies herself at the outset as a "white American."

I am a white American. I am proud to be an American. You cannot be black, white, Korean, Chinese, Mexican, German, French, or English or any other and still be an American. Of course the culture taught in schools is strictly American. That's where we are and if you choose to learn another [culture] you have the freedom to settle there. You cannot be a Korean American which assumes you are not ready to be an AMERICAN. Do you get my gist?

The suggestion that more should be taught in U.S. schools about America's many immigrant groups and people of color prompted many letters in defense of Western civilization against non-Western barbarism:

> You are dissatisfied with current school curricula that excludes Korea. Could it possibly be because Korea and Asia for that matter has [*sic*] not had . . . a noticeable impact on the shaping of Western culture, and Korea has had unfortunately little culture of its own?

> Who cares about Korea, Ms. Kim? . . . And what enduring contributions has the Black culture, both here in the US and on the continent contributed to the world, and mankind? I'm from a culture, Ms. Kim, who put a man on the moon 23 years ago, who established medical schools to train doctors to perform open heart surgery, and . . . who created a language of music so that musicians, from Beethoven to the Beatles, could easily touch the world with their brilliance forever and ever and ever. Perhaps the dominant culture, whites obviously, "swept aside Chicanos . . . Latinos . . . African-Americans . . . Koreans," because they haven't contributed anything that made—be mindful of the cliche—a world of difference?

> Koreans' favorite means of execution is decapitation . . . Ms. Kim, and others like her, came here to escape such injustice. Then they whine at riots to which they have contributed by their own fanning of flames of discontent. . . . Yes! Let us all study more about Oriental culture! Let us put matters into proper perspective.

> Fanatical multiculturalists like you expect a country whose dominant culture has been formed and influenced by Europe . . ., nearly 80% of her population consisting of persons whose ancestry is European, to include the history of every ethnic group who has ever lived here. I truly feel sorry for you. You and your bunch need to realize that white Americans are not racists. . . . We would love to get along, but not at the expense of our own culture and heritage.

> Kim's axe-to-grind confirms the utter futility of race-relations—the races were never meant to live together. We don't get along and never will. . . . Whats [*sic*] needed is to divide the United States up along racial lines so that life here can finally become livable.

What seemed to anger some people the most was their idea that, although they worked hard, people of color were seeking handouts and privileges because of their race, and the thought of an ungrateful Asian American siding with African Americans, presumably against whites, was infuriating. How dare I "bite the hand that feeds" me by siding with the champion "whiners who cry 'racism'" because to do so is the last refuge of the "terminally incompetent"?

> The racial health in this country won't improve until minorities stop erecting "me first" barriers and strive to be Americans, not African-Americans or Asian-Americans expecting privileges.

> Ms. Kim wants preferential treatment that immigrants from Greece-to-Sweden have not enjoyed. . . . Even the Chinese . . . have not created any special problems for themselves or other Americans. Soon those folk are going to express their own resentments to the insatiable demands of the Blacks and other colored peoples, including the wetbacks from Mexico who sneak into this country then pilfer it for all they can.

> The Afroderived citizens of Los Angeles and the Asiatic derivatives were not suffering a common imposition. . . . Asiatics are trying to build their success. The Africans are sucking at the teats of entitlement.

As is usual with racists, most of the writers of these hate letters saw only themselves in their notions about Korea, America, Korean Americans, African Americans. They felt that their own sense of American identity was being threatened and that they were being blamed as individuals for U.S. racism. One man, adept at manipulating various fonts on his word processor, imposed his preconceptions on my words:

> Let me read between the lines of your little hate message:
>
> . . . "The roots . . . stretch far back into the corridors of corporate and government offices in Los Angeles, Sacramento, and Washington, D.C."
> **All white America and all American institutions are to blame for racism.**
>
> . . . "I still want to believe the promise is real."
> **I have the savvy to know that the American ideals of freedom and justice are a joke but if you want to give me what I want I'm willing to make concessions.**
>
> Ms. Kim, . . . if you want to embody the ignorant, the insecure, and the emotionally immature, that's your right! Just stop preaching hate and please, please, quit whining.
>
> Sincerely, A proud White-American teaching
> my children not to be prejudicial

Especially since my essay had been subdued and intensely personal, I had not anticipated the fury it would provoke. I never thought that readers would write over my words with their own. The very fact that I used words, and English words at that, particularly incensed some: one letter writer complained about my use of words and phrases like "manifestation" and "zero-sum game," and "suzerain relationship," which is the only way to describe Korea's relationship with China during the T'ang Dynasty. "Not more than ten people in the USA know what [these words] mean," he wrote. "You are on an ego trip." I wondered if it made him particularly angry that an Asian American had used those English words, or if he would make such a comment to George Will or Jane Bryant Quinn.

Clearly I had encountered part of America's legacy, the legacy that insists on silencing certain voices and erasing certain presences, even if it means deportation, internment, and outright murder. I should not have been surprised by what happened in Koreatown or by the ignorance and hatred expressed in the letters to *Newsweek*, any more than African Americans should have been surprised by the Rodney King verdict. Perhaps the news media, which constituted *sa-i-ku* as news, as an extraordinary event in no way continuous with our everyday lives, made us forget for a moment that as people of color many of us simultaneously inhabit two Americas: the America of our dreams and the America of our experience.

Who among us does not cling stubbornly to the America of our dreams, the promise of a multicultural democracy where our cultures and our differences might be affirmed instead of distorted in an effort to destroy us?

After *sa-i-ku*, I was able to catch glimpses of this America of my dreams because I received other letters that expressed another American legacy. Some people identified themselves as Norwegian or Irish Americans interested in combating racism. Significantly, while most of the angry mail had been sent not to me but to *Newsweek*, almost all of the sympathetic mail, particularly the letters from African Americans, came directly to me. Many came from Korean Americans who were glad that one of their number had found a vehicle for self-expression. Others were from Chinese and Japanese Americans who wrote that they had had similar experiences and feelings. Several were written in shaky longhand by women fervently wishing for peace and understanding among people of all races. A Native American from Nashville wrote a long description of cases of racism against African, Asian, and Native Americans in the U.S. criminal-justice system. A large number of letters came from African Americans, all of them supportive and sympathetic—from judges and professors who wanted better understanding between Africans and Koreans to poets and laborers who scribbled their notes in pencil while on breaks at work. One man identified himself as a Los Angeles African American whose uncle had married a Korean woman. He stated that as a black man in America, he knew what other people feel when they face injustice. He ended his letter apologizing for his spelling and grammar mistakes and asking for materials to read on Asian Americans. The most touching letter I received was written by a prison inmate who had served twelve years of a 35-to-70-year sentence for armed robbery during which no physical injuries occurred. He wrote:

> I've been locked in these prisons going on 12 years now . . . and since being here I have studied fully the struggles of not just blacks, but all people of color. I am a true believer of helping "your" people "first," but also the helping of all people no matter where there at or the color of there skin. But I must be truthful, my struggle and assistance is truly on the side of people of color like ourselves. But just a few years ago I didn't think like this.
>
> I thought that if you wasn't black, then you was the enemy, but . . . many years of this prison madness and much study and research changed all of this. . . . [I]t's not with each other, blacks against Koreans or Koreans against blacks. No, this is not what it's about. Our struggle(s) are truly one in the same. What happened in L.A. during the riot really hurt me, because it was no way that blacks was suppose to do the things to your people, my people (Koreans) that they did. You're my sister, our people are my people. Even though our culture may be somewhat different, and even though we may worship our God(s) different . . . white-Amerikkka [doesn't] separate us. They look at us all the same. Either you're white, or you're wrong. . . . I'm just writing you to let you know that, you're my sister, your people's struggle are my people's struggle.

This is the ground I need to claim now for Korean American resistance and recovery, so that we can become American without dying of *han*.

Although the sentiments expressed in these letters seemed to break down roughly along racial lines—that is, all writers who were identifiably people of color wrote in support—and one might become alarmed at the depth of the divisions they imply, I like to think that I have experienced the desire of many Americans, especially Americans of color, to do as Rodney King pleaded on the second day of *sa-i-ku*: "We're all stuck here for awhile. . . . Let's try to work it out."

In my view, it's important for us to think about *all* of what Rodney King said and not just the words "we all can get along," which have been depoliticized and transformed into a Disneyesque catchphrase for Pat Boone songs and roadside billboards in Los Angeles. It seems to me the emphasis is on the being "stuck here for awhile" together as we await "our day in court."[19]

Like the African American man who wrote from prison, the African American man who had been brutally beaten by white police might have felt the desire to "love everybody," but he had to amend—or rectify—that wish. He had to speak last about loving "people of color." The impulse to "love everybody" was there, but the conditions were not right. For now, the most practical and progressive agenda may be people of color trying to "work it out."

# Finding Community Through National Consciousness

The place where Korean and American legacies converge for Korean Americans is the exhortation to "go home to where you belong."

One of the letters I received was from a Korean American living in Chicago. He had read a translation of my essay in a Korean language newspaper. "Although you were born in the U.S.A.," he wrote, noticing what none of the white men who ordered me to go back to "my" country had, "your ethnical background and your complexion belong to Korea. It is time to give up your U.S. citizenship and go to Korea."

Some ruined merchants are claiming that they will pull up stakes and return to Korea, but I know that this is not possible for most of them. Even if their stores had not been destroyed, even if they were able to sell their businesses and take the proceeds to Korea, most of them would not have enough to buy a home or business there, since both require total cash up front. Neither would they be able to find work in the society they left behind because it is plagued by recession, repression, and fierce economic competition.

# Going Back to Korea

The dream of going back to Korea fed the spirit of my father, who came to Chicago in 1926 and lived in the United States for 63 years, during which time he never became a U.S. citizen, at first because the law did not allow it and later because he did not want to. He kept himself going by believing that he would return to Korea in triumph one day. Instead, he died in Oakland at 88. Only his remains returned to Korea, where we buried him in accordance with his wishes.

Hasn't the dream of going back home to where you belong sustained most of America's unwanted at one time or another, giving meaning to lives of toil and making it possible to endure other people's hatred and rejection? Isn't the attempt to find community through national consciousness natural for people refused an American identity because racism does not give them that choice?

Korean national consciousness, the resolve to resist and fight back when threatened with extermination, was all that could be called upon when the Korean Americans in Los Angeles found themselves abandoned. They joined together to guard each other's means of livelihood with guns, relying on Korean-language radio and newspapers to communicate with and help each other. On the third day after the outbreak of violence, more than 30,000 Korean Americans gathered for a peace march in downtown L.A. in what was perhaps the largest and most quickly organized mass mobilization in Asian American history. Musicians in white, the color of mourning, best traditional Korean drums in sorrow, anger, and celebration of community, a call to arms like a collective heartbeat.[20] I believe that the mother of Edward Song Lee, the Los Angeles-born college student mistaken for a looter and shot to death in the streets, has been able to persevere in great part because of the massive outpouring of sympathy expressed by the Korean-American community that shared and understood her *han*.

A National Guardsman keeps watch on a rally on May 2, 1992, by seven thousand Koreans demonstrating for an end to violence in Los Angeles. Lee Celano/Reuters/Bettmann.

I have been critical lately of cultural nationalism as detrimental to Korean Americans, especially Korean American women, because it operates on exclusions and fosters intolerance and uniformity of thought while stifling self-criticism and encouraging sacrifice, even to the point of suicide. But *sa-i-ku* makes me think again: what remains for those who are left to stand alone? If Korean Americans refuse to be victims or political pawns in the U.S. while rejecting the exhortation that we go back to Korea where we belong, what will be our weapons of choice?

In the darkest days of Japanese colonial rule, even after being stripped of land and of all economic means of survival, Koreans were threatened with total erasure when the colonizers rewrote Korean history, outlawed the Korean language, forced the subjugated people to worship the Japanese emperor, and demanded that they adopt Japanese names. One of the results of these cultural-annihilation policies was Koreans' fierce insistence on the sanctity of Korean national identity that persists to this day. In this context, it is not difficult to understand why nationalism has been the main refuge of Koreans and Korean Americans.

While recognizing the potential dangers of nationalism as a weapon, I for one am not ready to respond to the antiessentialists' call to relinquish my Korean American identity. It is easy enough for the French and Germans to call for a common European identity and an end to nationalisms, but what of the peoples suppressed and submerged while France and Germany exercised their national prerogatives? I am mindful of the argument that the resurgence of nationalism in Europe is rooted in historical and contemporary political and economic inequality among the nations of Europe. Likewise, I have noticed that many white Americans do not like to think of themselves as belonging to a race, even while thinking of people of color almost exclusively in terms of race. In the same way, many men think of themselves as "human beings" and of women as the ones having a gender. Thus crime, small businesses, and all Korean-African American interactions are seen and interpreted through the lens of race in the same dominant culture that angrily rejects the use of the racial lens for viewing yellow/white or black/white interactions and insist suddenly that we are all "American" whenever we attempt to assert our identity as people of color. It is far easier for Anglo Americans to call for an end to cultural nationalisms than for Korean Americans to give up national consciousness, which makes it possible to survive the vicious racism that would deny our existence as either Korean Americans or Americans.

Is there anything of use to us in Korean nationalism? During one thousand years of Chinese suzerainty, the Korean ruling elite developed a philosophy called *sadaejui*, or reliance of the weak on the strong. In direct opposition to this way of thought is what is called *jaju* or *juche sasang*, or self-determination.[21] Both *sadaejui* and *juche sasang* are ways of dealing with unequal power relationships and resisting the transformation of one's homeland into a battlefield for others, but *sadaejui* has never worked any better for Koreans than it has for any minority group in America. *Juche sasang*, on the other hand, has the kind of oppositional potential needed in the struggle against silence and invisibility. From Korean national consciousness, we can recover this fierce refusal to accept subjugation, which is the first step in the effort to build community, so that we can work with others to challenge the forces that would have us annihilate each other instead of our mutual oppression.

What is clear is that we cannot "become American" without dying of *han* unless we think about community in new ways. Self-determination does not mean living alone. At least for now, that may mean mining the rich and haunted lode of Korean national consciousness while we struggle to understand how our fate is entwined with the fate of others lying prostrate before the triumphal procession of the winners of History.[22] During the past fifteen years or so, many young Korean nationalists have been studying the legacies of colonialism and imperialism that they share with peoples in many Asian, African, and Latin American nations. At the same time that we take note of this work, we can also try to understand how nationalism and feminism can be worked together to demystify the limitations and reductiveness of each as a weapon of empowerment. If Korean national consciousness is ever to be such a weapon for us, we must use it to create a new kind of nationalism-in-internationalism to help us call forth a culture of survival and recovery, so that our *han* might be released and we might be freed to dream fiercely of different possibilities.

# Reading Questions

1. Why does Kim support Korean-American nationalism as a way of resisting *han*? What specific factors present problems to a Korean cultural nationalist movement?

2. What is Kim's major criticism of the American and

South Korean media coverage of the violence in Los Angeles following the Rodney King trial?

3. What explanation does Kim give for the difference between Korean immigrants and the other poor people in the communities they serve?

4. What sorts of responses do you have when reading the excerpts from the hate mail that Kim received after her *Newsweek* essay?
5. What evidence does Kim give against the idea that all African Americans in Los Angeles hate all Korean Americans?

6. How do the historical facts about specific wars, colonizations, and immigration differentiate Asian Americans such as Japanese Americans, Chinese Americans and Korean Americans?

## Recommended Reading

Walter Benjamin, "Theses on the Philosophy of History," *Illuminations* (New York: Schocken Books, 1969)

Bong Youn Choy, *Koreans in America* (Chicago: Nelson-Hall, 1979)

Mary Paik Lee, *Quiet Odyssey: A Pioneer Korean Woman in America* (Seattle: University of Washington, 1990)

Ivan Hubert Light, *Immigrant Entrepreneurs: Koreans in Los Angeles, 1965–1982* (Berkeley: University of California Press, 1988)

Diane Yen-Mei Wong, ed., *Making Waves: An Anthology of Writings by and about Asian-American Women* (Boston: Beacon Press, 1989)

Yuslin Yoo, *The Making of Modern Korea* (New York: Golden Pond Press, 1990)

## Recommended Audiovisual Resources

*The Asianization of America.* 1990. Produced by WNET/13. Examines the role of Asian Americans half a century after the repeal of the Chinese Exclusion Act. Films for Humanities.

*Yellow Tale Blues: Two American Families.* 1991. Directed by Christine Choy and Renee Tajima. Produced by Quynh Thai. Innovative documentary on ethnic stereotypes of Asians in this country. Filmakers Library, Inc.

*Home from the Eastern Sea.* 1994. Produced by Lucy Ostrander. Documentary exploration of the personal stories of immigrant families from China, Japan, and the Philippines as they adjust to life in the United States. Laced throughout the film is rare archival footage of their histories and cultures. Filmakers Library.

# The Private Use of Public Space

## LESLIE KANES WEISMAN

Leslie Kanes Weisman teaches at the New Jersey Institute of Technology. She is the author of *Discrimination by Design*, from which this selection is taken.

Like the public buildings discussed in the previous chapter, the contemporary urban landscape is a paradigmatic stage set for the workings of patriarchy. In city streets, parks, and neighborhoods, territorial dramas between women and men, rich and poor are enacted daily. Each group "appears" in public and claims and uses public space according to its socially prescribed roles. Those with power, for example "street gangs," control the streets and the people on them. Those without power, like the "street dweller" and the "street walker," are relegated to the streets where their private lives are on public display. Though they are all "at home" on the streets, "home" means something very different to each.

People also consider themselves "at home" in certain neighborhoods, and refer to cities as "hometowns" and to nations as "homelands." As with the streetscape, how people experience and inhabit these "public homes," what these places mean, physically and symbolically, depends upon their "social place" and the extent to which they accept or challenge it.

# City Streets and Sexual Geography

Armed with a piece of chalk, children can turn public sidewalks into private gameboards that block pedestrian traffic. Armed with a can of spray paint, teenagers can turn the walls of public buildings and highway overpasses into private billboards. Armed with society's tacit approval, men can turn allegedly public city streets into a private male jungle where women are excluded or, in the words of the poet Marge Piercy, "stalked like the tame pheasants who are hand-raised and then turned loose for hunters to shoot, an activity called sport."[1]

Male street gangs, and a high incidence of related vandalism and crime, are familiar facts of urban life. So are the "gang wars" that erupt when one group invades the neighborhood "turf" of another. The widespread availability of crack cocaine is accelerating murders among members of rival gangs competing to get rich selling the savage drug. In such encounters, in the slums' streets, and in the company of male peers, the ghetto boy is socialized to his male role.

Boys "grow up" in the streets where they learn the lessons of manhood. "Nice girls" are kept off the streets and close to home, lest their virginity or virtue or both be endangered. Most men are "at home" on the streets; most women are not. "I always thought of Harlem as home," wrote Claude Brown, "but I never thought of Harlem as being in the house. To me, home was the streets."[2]

It is no coincidence that every city has a "porno strip." Along these streetscapes of depravity, misogynistic messages packaged as pleasure, seduction, and erotica bombard the senses: in the ghostly neon signs of tawdry bars featuring topless "Go-go Girls" dancing in cages; in the flashing marquees of "live peep shows" and "adult" movie houses showing women being cut into parts with a chain saw or tied up, raped, and sodomized with a rifle by an ex-Marine who misses combat; in the porn book stores selling magazines like *Bondage* or *Hustler* where "Chester the Molester" molests a different young girl each month using techniques like lying, kidnaping, and assault.[3]

But the porno strip is not the only public place where crude and dehumanizing sex-role stereotypes appear. The entire urban environment is filled with images of macho men and sexually submissive women. Commercial billboards depicting rugged cowboys smoking cigarettes appear in marked contrast to the smiling seduction of scantily clad models selling designer jeans and expensive liquor. Compare, too, the bronze statues of male war heroes and politicians in whose honor our public parks are named, with the nude vulnerability of the female nymphs and goddesses that decorate the fountains of those same public parks, and the pairs of bare-breasted caryatids who, in eternal servitude, support with their heads the weight of building entablatures over the entrances of neoclassical apartments and office buildings.

The exploitive double standard between the sexes that the public landscape communicates so vividly is regularly enacted on the public streets themselves, in the "respectable" male pastime known as "girl watching." Few women, whether they like it or not, escape the silent eyes, "friendly" comments, blown kisses, clucks, whistles, and obscene gestures men presume they can impose upon any women passing by.

Such invasive male behavior violates a woman's self/other boundary, leaving her enraged, startled, humiliated, and unable to control her own privacy. Even those women who have learned to "handle" these situations with skilled retort cannot escape the overriding message of male power. This double standard has contributed to what John Berger calls a "split consciousness" in public space. In his book *Ways of Seeing*, Berger explains: "Men act, and women appear. Men look at women. Women watch themselves being looked at."[4]

Women, thus unable to regulate their interactions with male strangers in public places, are robbed of an important privilege of urban life: their anonymity. Women learn to be constantly on the alert, both consciously and unconsciously, in order to protect vulnerable boundaries from male trespasses. Researchers have demonstrated that women avoid eye contact, stiffen body posture, restrict movements, and move out of the way of pedestrian traffic more than men, a pattern of submissive behavior observed in animal societies.[5] Irwin Altman, a psychologist, maintains that this behavior requires an enormous amount of energy which "places great stress on adrenal and cardiovascular systems, resulting in heightened psychological tension and anxiety . . . [and] psychic damage."[6]

If the fear of sexual harassment on the street causes women stress, the fear of rape keeps women off the streets at night, away from public parks and "dangerous" parts of town, and unconsciously afraid of half the human race. Women learn that any man is a potential abuser and any place where men are found can threaten their safety. Contrary to popular belief, men do not rape because they are out of control but as a way of maintaining it. Rape is the most paradigmatic means of social control. Its unmistakable intention is to keep all women in "their place," in "line," and in a constant state of fear.

Eventually women come to understand that the public streets and parks belong to men. Further, women are constantly reminded by rapists, police officers, and judges of their responsibility to uphold this social norm and the dangerous consequences of their failure to do so. Statements like this one made by a police superintendent are not infrequent: "Any woman walking alone after dark invites trouble."[7] Neither are court decisions that blame the victim unusual. For example, in England in 1982 a judge ruled that a man who pleaded guilty to raping a seventeen-year-old woman should be fined the equivalent of four hundred dollars instead of receiving a jail sentence because the rape victim was "guilty of a great deal of contributory negligence"—she had been hitchhiking late at night.[8] In 1986, a Washington judge sentences a rape victim to thirty days in jail for being in contempt of court; terrified of seeing the rapist again, she had refused to testify against him. The chief prosecutor said, "I hate to see the victim treated worse than the defendant, but I don't see any other alternative."[9] Today, news reports of rapes and incidents of "wilding" (in which gangs of very young boys "entertain" themselves by premeditated violent assault) have become a "normal" part of daily television and radio.

It stands to reason that if women perceive public space as unmanageable and threatening, they will avoid it and restrict their mobility within it. This phenomenon, according to a study by Elizabeth W. Markson and Beth B. Hess, exists most dramatically among urban, elderly women, particularly those with limited educations who live alone in apartments. Many of these women are afraid to leave their homes. They are especially frightened of going out at night and curtail their social lives accordingly.[10]

Markson and Hess believe the mass media foster the notion of the powerlessness of older women, particularly poor and minority women, and grossly exaggerate the amount of crime perpetrated against them. They refer to a survey of violence depicted on TV shows in which the most frequent victims were children, old women, nonwhite women, and lower-class women. While they found that TV killers were most often men, murder victims were most frequently old, poor, urban women. Further, in TV news broadcasts, the most publicized cases of violence, despite the fact that these were not the most common cases, involved black assailants and white victims.[11] It offends that any woman or man should be attacked; but it is equally offensive that so many women live in fear of attack, and that those fears are manipulated to perpetuate racism and effectively imprison women in their own homes.

Withdrawal in response to the dangers of urban life leaves the streets open to criminal behavior. Eventually business conditions deteriorate, the quality of life of the entire community is eroded, and neighborhood collapse is inevitable. If the demise of our inner cities is to be reversed, women's fear and victimization must be reduced. To do so, politicians and municipal service agencies must admit that violence against women and children is pervasive; that women's fears are based in reality; and that women know when they feel unsafe in cities, and why.

Toronto's METRAC project provides an excellent model. The Metro Action Committee on Public Violence Against Women and Children (METRAC) was established in 1984 by the council of metropolitan Toronto. It succeeds a task force initiated by the council in 1982 to address the concerns of women in Toronto after a series of rape-murders in the city. The eighty volunteer members of the task force—doctors, lawyers, politicians, police, social workers, urban planners, workers from rape crisis centers, and other women's organizations—developed a comprehensive, multidisciplinary approach to violence protection that METRAC has carried forward in its work to make the city safe for women and children.

The METRAC staff (all women) stresses the importance of consulting with women in any project they undertake. A number of their initiatives concentrate on urban and architectural design, since various physical/geographical features may enhance or detract from the use of a particular site for assault. METRAC is responsible for the review and improvement of standards of lighting, signage, and security in all underground parking garages in Toronto; has conducted safety audits of the city's subway system and bus routes in collaboration with the police force and the Toronto Transit Commission; and has worked with the Parks and Recreation Department on a safety audit directed toward sexual assault prevention in High Park (the city's largest park). In the latter instance, METRAC observed that in the 1987 user study on park safety initiated by the department, vandalism and boating safety were addressed but women's concerns were ignored. METRAC intervened and invited women from Women Plan Toronto, the High Park Women's Action Committee, and other women park users to join in day and night-time "walkabouts" to assess existing conditions and suggest changes that would make the park feel and be safer.

The factors they considered included: lighting, sightlines/visibility, entrapment possibilities, ear and eye distance, movement predictors (such as pathways and tunnels), signage/information, visibility of park staff/police, public telephones, assailant escape routes, maintenance levels (for example, neglected areas or replacing damaged lights and signs), parks programming information, and isolation (one of the biggest factors in feeling safe or unsafe). With this input, METRAC prepared a report, *Planning for Sexual Assault Prevention: Women's Safety in High Park* (January 1989), that included fifty-five recommendations to the Parks and Recreation Department. For example, emergency telephones, maps showing park layout, and signs along the trails indicating that a user is only a two-minute walk from the restaurant or swimming pool would help counter feelings of isolation and suggest where help could be found if needed without destroying the enjoyable feeling of seclusion in the park.

METRAC has also produced the groundbreaking *WISE (Women in Safe Environments) Report* documenting the design characteristics that contribute to women's feeling unsafe in public places (poor lighting, being deserted, not being visible to others, and having no access to help are qualities that are high on the list) and a Safety Audit Kit that women can use to evaluate dangerous areas of the city, their home neighborhoods, and their workplaces. In 1990 METRAC began the preparation of a discussion paper on women's safety and urban/architectural design in order to facilitate the development of criteria for guidelines and standards for all buildings in the city—construction and renovation projects, shopping centers, housing projects, parks, and all other public spaces.[12]

Assaults in urban public places, to a great degree, are crimes of opportunity. While the design of our physical surroundings does not cause sexual assault, it plays a significant part in creating opportunities for it. Those who are vulnerable—women, children, the disabled, and elderly people—have the right to safe access to the cities in which they live. Preventing sexual assault against women by deliberate planning and assessment results in urban and architectural design that enhances everyone's safety.

# The Street as Extension of the Domestic Environment

While countless women are trapped in their own homes by fear of the streets, one of the ironies of contemporary society is that countless others are forced to make their living on the streets. Because there are so few safe shelters for prostitutes, there is little opportunity for them to escape from street violence and dependence on abusive pimps. Indeed, prostitutes report that sex itself has become more violent. In 1986 an average of one prostitute a month was murdered in Los Angeles, according to a police report.[13] Often the experience of violence in the home—from incest and sexual abuse to battering—drives women into prostitution. They are runaways and pushed-aways who continue as prostitutes because of economic necessity. The "streetwalker's" appearance in public implies that she belongs to no man and therefore belongs to all men. She is a surrogate wife practicing the sexual rituals enacted in the private family home on the anonymous public streets of patriarchy.

In a different way, the street is literally home to tens of thousands of homeless people. In 1989, American estimates ranged from the government claim of 350,000 to the

Coalition for the Homeless estimate of 3 million homeless nationwide; and if current federal policies continue, there will be 18 million homeless people by the year 2000.[14] They are found in every city, lying on sidewalks and in the doorways of shabby hotels and cheap bars, sleeping in abandoned buildings, over hot-air grates, in trash dumpsters, phone booths, train stations, and airports. The lucky find refuge in shelters and missions dispensing salvation and a free meal.

In the 1960s the homeless were mostly all older, white, male alcoholics or drifters who lived on "skid row." In the 1980s they were increasingly women, blacks, families, people with AIDS (PWA's), and younger men averaging in their low thirties in age. Most of the men were the local unemployed or unemployable who left high schools and housing projects without job skills.[15]

Homeless PWA's are a relatively heterogeneous group. They are mainly minorities who became HIV infected through intravenous drug use by themselves or their sexual partners. They are single men and women, families, single parents, abandoned children, and teenagers whose infection is concomitant to their life on the streets.

If these people are not already homeless, their illness often precipitates their homelessness. Unable to work, they cannot pay rent. Others are illegally evicted by AIDS-phobic landlords. Compared to the need, the amount of housing assistance currently available for homeless PWA's is insignificant. For example, in 1989 in New York City, fewer than eighty apartments were available specifically for homeless people with AIDS; yet the Partnership for the Homeless estimated that there were five thousand to eight thousand homeless New Yorkers with AIDS and related HIV illness that year. By 1993 they say the figure will jump to thirty thousand, making PWA's the largest subgroup among New York City's homeless.[16]

During the 1980s, the number of homeless single women increased by an average of 16 percent in twenty-one of twenty-six cities surveyed by the US Conference of Mayors.[17] In 1989, single women and their children constituted a staggering 86 percent of homeless families in New York, according to a study done by the city's Human Resources Administration.[18]

Single women and women heading families are burgeoning among the homeless as a result of government cuts in disability benefits, rising housing costs, an increase in divorce rates, domestic violence, teenage pregnancies, and increasing poverty caused by unemployment, low-paying jobs, and wage discrimination. In 1980, two out of every three adults with incomes below the poverty level were women, and over half of all poor families were female headed.[19]

Homeless single women and women with children have been joined by huge numbers of predominantly female mental patients released by unspeakably overcrowded and inhumane state mental institutions responding to pressures to deinstitutionalize the non-dangerous mentally ill. Between 1955 and 1982 the population in state mental institutions in America shrank by more than three-quarters.[20] But programs for "independent living" in local community facilities were never adequately funded, leaving countless thousands of patients homeless and on their own.

In addition, America's failed housing policies have swollen the ranks of the homeless. Since the 1960s, Washington has wasted billions of dollars on administratively inept public housing programs that ended up subsidizing middle-class renters instead of the poor—composed predominantly of women and children—and has built less than half of

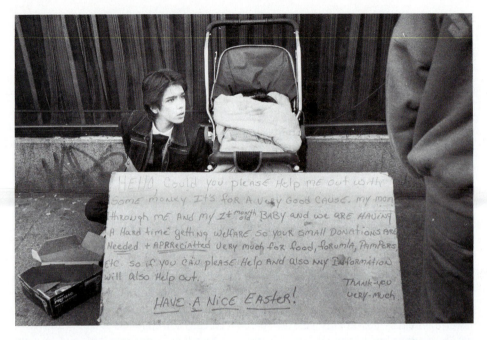

A young mother and her infant are forced to join the swelling ranks of homeless women and children in New York City. 1986. © Bettye-Lane.

the six million low-income housing units President Lyndon Johnson believed were needed in 1968. Between 1978 and 1988 appropriations for federal subsidized housing programs declined by more than 80 percent, from $32.2 billion to $9.8 billion.[21] Under the Reagan administration new construction dwindled to 55,120 units in 1983, despite the mind-numbing waiting periods for public housing: four years in Savannah, Georgia, twelve in New York, and twenty in Miami.[22] Instead, President Reagan opted to base his housing policy on $200 million in rent vouchers for low-income people—a plan that mistakenly assumed there was no housing shortage, only a shortage of money to pay for it. (In 1984, the Brookings Institution estimates that in 1990 the shortage of low-income units could reach 18 million.)[23]

In a break with the Reagan administration, President George Bush's budget for fiscal year 1990 included $1.1 billion to fund fully the Stewart B. McKinney Homeless Assistance Act. However, while it is encouraging that more money will be spent on emergency aid, the Bush budget contains no provision to increase low-income housing. Rather, it retains the Reagan administration's 18.6 percent cut in housing programs by $1.7 billion, despite the fact that in 1989 among the estimated twenty-nine million Americans who needed low-income housing, only one in four had access to it.[24]

A substantial percentage of America's homeless are victims of "urban revitalization." As cities began to rejuvenate their deteriorating downtowns in the 1970s, the sleazy welfare hotels and flophouses called "SRO's" for "single-room occupancies," were among the first buildings to be torn down or converted to condominiums for the affluent. SRO's provide furnished rooms with shared bathrooms and communal kitchens and dining facilities. The presence of a manager or clerk "at the desk" twenty-four hours a day can also provide immediate assistance to residents and a sense of security, especially for older women who are often afraid of their living environment.

Conditions in SRO's vary from comfortable to deplorable. None of the residents is eligible for shelter assistance as government regulations require recipients to live in a "self-contained" dwelling unit (one that includes a private toilet and kitchen). But the furnished room with available services such as meals, linen, and housekeeping is a viable housing choice for many older people who do not need institutional care. Nonetheless, the number of SRO's was reduced by nearly one-half the national total between 1970 and 1980, a loss of about one million rooms.[25]

Instead of destroying this housing we should be upgrading substandard conditions through code enforcement, authorizing government supplements to the occupants, and working to improve the social environment for the older, noncriminal population that is forced to live side-by-side with addicts and alcoholics. Urban renewal and city programs that eliminate or close SRO's displace thousands of the very poorest and frailest, a dramatic proportion consisting of minority and white, ethnic, elderly people and single mothers who are literally dumped into the streets, often with little or no warning and with no affordable place to go.

Confronted with nowhere to live, the homeless must then face the paradox of their own "ineligibility" for social support service. Without a home address they do not qualify, in most states, for foodstamps or welfare. Without a mailing address, they are unable to obtain copies of legal documents, such as birth certificates, required for public assistance. The result is an entire underclass of people who have slipped through the "safety nets" and into the gutter.[26]

Life on the street is a world filled with hunger, illness, hallucinations, and exposure to suffocating heat, freezing cold, and constant danger. Street women, because they are women, are especially fearful of assault and rape. "Even the most deranged bag ladies [so named because they carry all their possessions with them in bags], who just want to be left alone, are vulnerable because of rumors that they keep money in their bags," wrote the journalist Patricia King in an article on Chicago's "street girls." One woman she interviewed told her, "On the streets . . . you have to have eyes behind your head and look like you're not scared."[27] Faced with the constant threat of violence, street women develop formidable defense strategies. They know that few people will bother them if they are filthy or appear to be insane.

A New York City "street girl" named Lea told Alan M. Beck and Philip Marden that she occasionally slept with other women in doorways for protection.[28] Beck and Marden also reported in their 1977 study, "Three women spent nearly all their time within a few blocks of each other. . . . Two of them told us that they chose the area because they thought it was safe. In other parts of the city, they were harassed by storekeepers or assaulted by hoodlums."[29]

Homeless women are not necessarily safer in the shelters. A report entitled "Victims Again" includes vivid testimony by eighty women living in two New York women's shelters of the myriad ways they are harassed by the shelter system itself—from physical abuse by crack-smoking guards to forced separation from friends, children, and other family members and the withholding of subway tokens for transportation. Women who live in shelters are frequently pressured to do staff jobs like cleaning hallways for ridiculous pay (usually sixty-three cents an hour). Meals are not kept available for those who work at real jobs outside the shelter; if the woman works a night shift she is still expected to leave the building by 8:00 A.M.; and pregnant women are generally not given prenatal care or additional food, or allowed extra bedrest.[30]

The homeless, women or men, live hard and certainly "deviant" lives. They have few resources available to them, but women seem to have the fewest. For example, in the city-run shelters for women and men in the area of New York City that Beck and Marden studied in 1977, the women's shelter had forty-seven beds and had to turn away two thousand women. (There were an estimated three thousand homeless women citywide that year.) At the same time, the men's shelter had room for several hundred and placed hundreds more in flophouse hotels where there were free meals and beds available for thousands of men. "They [men] are almost never denied a bed," wrote a shelter staff member.[31]

While the tragic plight of America's burgeoning homeless has become increasingly visible, there still seems to be a "visibility gap" between the sexes. For instance, in 1981 the following notice appeared in a New York state legislative report: "The 36,000 homeless people of New York City have won an important victory. . . . The city was forced to sign a consent decree in State Supreme Court mandating that shelter be provided to any man who seeks it this winter. While not specifically included in the decree, women will also benefit from the decision."[32] The notice did not go on to explain how.

To date, both public and private efforts to provide safe emergency housing for homeless women, men, and families have been sorely inadequate. In 1984 New York's public shelter system—the largest in the country—housed six thousand people in a city where there were an estimated twenty thousand homeless in the under-twenty-one age category alone.[33] All across the nation, shelters are too few and too lacking in beds, toilets, showers, privacy, sanitation, heat, and security. It is not uncommon to find fire escapes sealed shut, broken windows, clogged toilets, sporadic hot water, and infestations of rats and other rodents. This journalist's description of the Fort Washington Armory Men's Shelter in New York City is revealing:

> More than 900 men sometimes sleep in rows of beds on a gymnasium floor the size of a
> football field. Although guards patrol here, as they do at all the shelters, new arrivals are
> warned to sleep with their shoes under the legs of their beds as protection against theft. The
> men have arranged the rows to form the remnants of boundaries they once called home—
> Spanish Harlem at one end, Harlem at the other, the Bronx and Brooklyn in the middle.
> In addition, the homeless men who earn $12.50 for 20 hours of menial work at the shelters
> sleep in a row along one wall that is known as Park Avenue.[34]

Among the homeless it is hard to tell those who were emotionally disturbed before they became homeless from those who were driven over the edge by the harshness of street life. Sometimes at shelters the seriously psychotic, alcoholics, and drug addicts wander freely among the simply down-and-out and can be very disruptive. Consequently, most shelters have regulations designed to restrict the behavior of all based on the behavior of few. Alcohol is usually banned from the premises; cigarette smoking is allowed only in certain areas; bathroom doors cannot be locked. Meals are usually provided by volunteers; cooking or self-service by residents is seldom allowed. Furnishings are often shabby, and sleeping arrangements are dormitorylike with little or no privacy. Few visitors are permitted, and when they are there is no place to entertain them, be they a relative, friend, or lover. This suggests that homeless people do not need privacy, self-expression, friendships, and sexual relationships, or at least that these needs should not be taken seriously. Perhaps this explains why housing for the homeless is referred to as "shelter," meaning a roof over your head, rather than "home," which implies autonomy and emotional as well as material support. All things considered, it is understandable why many homeless people avoid shelters, preferring to take their chances on the street.

Of course, the enduring solution to homelessness is transitional housing that provides ongoing support such as job training, health care, and childcare, coupled with the availability of permanent low-cost housing. In the interim, emergency shelter must be small scale, humane, and free of the barbaric conditions that now characterize most of them.

## Feminist Politics and Claiming Public Space

The lives of prostitutes and the homeless illustrate how city streets operate as theaters of social action in which women and others without social power are cast as marginalized "social deviants." The politics of public space belongs on the feminist agenda, for it is obvious that streets and parks, allegedly open to all people, are not open to all people equally. The denial of women's rights as citizens to equal access to public space—and of the psychological and physical freedom to use it in safety—has made public space, not infrequently, the testing ground of challenges to male authority and power. One of the most dramatic challenges occurred in San Francisco in 1978 when over five thousand women from thirty American states gathered at nightfall to march down the city's porno strip. Andrea Dworkin recalls: ". . . We wound our way toward Broadway, which was crowded with tourists, neon signs advertising live sex shows, adult bookstores, and pornographic theaters. Chanting slogans such as 'No More Profit off Women's Bodies,' we filled the streets entirely, blocking off traffic and completely occupying the Broadway strip for three blocks. For an hour, and for the first time ever, Broadway belonged not to the barkers, pimps, or pornographers, but instead to the songs, voices, rage and vision of thousands of women."[35] Similar marches have taken place in virtually every major city in the United States.

At a different but no less significant scale, small groups of women are using public space as an arena of personal protest. In October 1982 a dozen women at Brown University in Providence, Rhode Island, "equipped with bright red spray paint and stencils . . . splashed their message on university buildings, sidewalks, and stairwells: 'One in Three Women are Raped: Fight Back!'" The actions of the "graffitists," who call themselves Feminists Involved in Reaching Equality (FIRE), sparked a campus-wide controversy that produced a new women's peer counseling program, a night-time escort service run exclusively by women, and free courses in self-defense. As part of their efforts to raise consciousness, the FIRE women also posted official-looking curfew signs all over Providence mandating that men get off the streets in the evening, a suggestion first made by Israel's Prime Minister Golda Meir, who reasoned that if Israeli women were in danger of attack, a curfew should be placed on those causing the danger (men) and not, as her male colleagues suggested, on the victims.[36]

Women, too, are increasingly recognizing the connections between male violence in

Hundreds of women and children demonstrate in an antipornography march in New York City. 1979. Ezio Petersen/UPI/Bettmann.

their own lives and male militarism on an international scale. From the Women's Peace Camp at Greenham Common in England to the Women's Pentagon Action (WPA) in Washington, D.C., women are refusing to accept life on the precipice, where the male war machine has placed us all, themselves included. On 27 August 1981, a group of English and Welsh women and children marched 125 miles from Cardiff in Wales to the U.S. Air Force base at Greenham Common near Newbury in Berkshire, where 96 cruise nuclear missiles were due to be deployed. They pitched their tents and vowed to stay until the deployment plan was scrapped. That was the state of the first women's peace camp, which has since become a worldwide phenomenon. Other camps have been formed in Italy, West Berlin, Scotland, northern Germany, Norway, Sweden, and in scattered sites in the United States.[37]

Within months after the establishment of the Greenham Common Camp, on 15 and 16 November 1981, the Women's Pentagon Action organized a peace march in which an estimated 4,500 women from across the United States and abroad converged on the Pentagon to mourn and express outrage at the ongoing acceleration of nuclear armament and the global oppression of women and other peoples. As they marched, the women wove a continuous braid which encircled the entire building. They wove a web of colored yarn across the doorways. As police cut away the web, the women tenaciously rewove the severed strands. At the end of the day, sixty-five women were arrested and imprisoned for civil disobedience.[38]

On 18 July 1983, fifty women created a women's peace camp in New York City's Bryant Park, just one block from the Times Square district, notorious for its muggings, drug dealing, and "flesh trafficking." The women camped out in the park for two weeks. Although Bryant Park officially closes each evening at nine o'clock, the police did not evict them. Supporters brought them food and water. The campers conducted street performances and symbolic rituals, organized peace walks, and distributed leaflets to publicize the opening of the Women's Encampment for a Future of Peace and Justice.[39]

This latter women's peace camp borders the Seneca Army Depot in New York State, the storage site for the neutron bombs and the point from which the United States deployed its Pershing II nuclear missiles to Greenham Common, as part of a NATO "peacekeeping" force. Five hundred women opened the camp on 4 July 1983, America's Independence Day, and during the next month over 3,000 women demonstrated in protest of deployment. More than 250 scaled the depot fence in a mass civil disobedience. All were arrested.[40]

It would be easy to dismiss these examples of nonviolent civil disobedience, demonstrations, and symbolic rituals as well-intended but naive and ultimately ineffective strategies for social change. After all, pornography is still a flourishing business, every ten minutes a woman is raped in America, and the nuclear arms race continues to threaten us all with extinction. But is direct efficacy the only purpose for political activism? I think not. Those who participate in group demonstrations find their personal beliefs affirmed and clarified; they experience solidarity with others and a renewed sense of energy and strength to confront and challenge injustice in their own daily lives.

If we define society as a human community, then the transformation of individual attitudes and values represents meaningful social change. Each time a person refuses to laugh at a racist joke, buy a pornographic magazine, use gender-exclusive language, or vote for nuclear "defense," then "society" is not the same, for its prevailing standards have been rejected and those who enforce them have been made to think about alternatives. This personalization of society is a radical notion since we are taught to imagine society as an abstraction of laws and government processes that exist beyond the reach of "ordinary" people. This dichotomy in the way society is conceptualized or experienced is connected to gender socialization.

Women's and men's self/other boundaries are shaped very differently, and consequently so are their views about war and peace. Carol Gilligan has done research on psychological theory that explains how women's moral development is deeply embedded in an ethic of responsibility to others that "bends" the rules to preserve relationships, while men's moral development is linked to respecting individual rights and learning to "play the game fair and square" according to the rules. Thus, men would logically view war as a "necessary game of political strategy" and the assertion of a moral imperative; women would view war as the cause of painful human suffering and loss on both "sides" and the senseless expression of "failed relationships."[41]

Both Gilligan and Jean Baker Miller, a psychotherapist and author of *Toward a New Psychology of Women* (1976), believe that men's sense of self is tied to a separation from others and to a belief in the "efficacy of aggression," women's to a "recognition of the need for connection" and the maintenance of a web of affiliations.[42] Thus, while the male-defined "morality of rights and justice" is based on a belief in equality, defined as the same treatment for everyone predicated on the understanding of fairness and autonomy, women's "ethic of responsibility and care" is based on a belief in nonviolence and equity, which recognizes differing needs and protects people from being hurt, predicated on the understanding of nurturance and attachment.[43]

These different modes of moral development for women and men give rise to different ways of evaluating the consequences of choice between violence and nonviolence. An event that occurred on 21 August 1976, in the battle-scarred streets of Belfast, Northern Ireland, provides an example. On that day, ten thousand Catholic and Protestant women—setting aside the centuries-old hatreds that have separated Northern Ireland's feuding communities, and in defiance of terrorist death threats against their lives—gathered with their children on the spot where, ten days before, three children had been killed by Irish Republican Army gunmen fleeing British troops. This mass peace rally, which resulted in the formation of the Peace Women's Movement (the name was later changed to the People for Peace Movement so that men would not feel excluded), was spearheaded by Betty Williams, an angry thirty-two-year-old Roman Catholic housewife who had witnessed the children's deaths. Mrs. Williams later recalled her feelings and actions:

> Did you ever get sick inside, so sick that you didn't even know what was wrong with you? I couldn't cook a dinner. I couldn't think straight. I couldn't even cry, and as the night went on I got angrier and angrier. . . . I . . . took an air-mail writing pad and I went right up to the heart of provisional IRA territory in Andersontown and I didn't knock at the door very nicely, by the way, I didn't say, "Excuse me. Would you like to sign this? We all want peace." I was spitting angry, and I banged the woman's door and she came. I frightened the life out of her. I really did. When she came out, I said, "Do you want peace?" She said "Yes!" "Yes, then sign that." It sort of started out like that and it went on . . . further down the street. . . . All the women felt that way. . . . We had 3,000 or 6,000 signatures in three hours. We went back to my home. They were in the lounge. They were in the living room. They were in the kitchen. They were in the hall. They were lined up the stairs. They were in the bathroom, the two bedrooms. There just wasn't enough room to hold them all, and they were all just as angry as I was . . . that we had let this go on for so long.[44]

Long before the guns came out, housing, the central demand of the civil rights movement in Northern Ireland, was crucial for Catholic women whose families were crammed into miserable tenements and regularly denied houses to maintain the voter domination of Protestant Unionist households. The thought of moving from a slum flat to a modern house gave Catholic mothers everything to live for and something worth dying for on the streets, on behalf of their children.[45]

When women take to the streets in angry protest, it is consistent with their sense of moral responsibility to care for others, and that responsibility can transcend the boundaries of male-defined cultural taboos. For example, in 1861, thousands of veiled Persian women courageously broke the boundaries of their seclusion in the harem to surround the carriage of the Shah, demanding action against the government officials who were profiteering during a famine.[46] Women played a leading and conspicuous role in the food riots in revolutionary Paris in 1789, and in England where such riots periodically erupted in the seventeenth and eighteenth centuries. In the United States in the 1960s, it was women in the urban ghettos who joined in a protest movement to demand that the "relief system" provide greater benefits for food, rent, and clothing.[47] In the 1980s grandmothers, mothers, and daughters converged on Washington, D.C., from often remote and traditionally conservative parts of the country to march together in unprecedented numbers to protest legislative restrictions on abortion rights.

Women use public space to protest against violence in all its poisonous forms: starvation, poverty, illness, homelessness, urban blight, rape, abortion control, pornography, homophobia, the indignity suffered by the differently abled and older people, racism, sexism, the depletion of the earth's riches, the fouling of her air and water, the arms race, imperialism. Women do so because they understand that all of these are connected. Women march in defiance of male boundaries. As Virginia Woolf wrote: "As a woman, I have no country; as a woman, my country is the world."[48] Feminism, in its fullest meaning, enjoins the human race to establish zones of liberation, and literally to reshape the territorial definition of our patriarchal world, along with the social identities and injustices that those boundaries have defined for all of us.

# Reading Questions

1. What does Weisman mean by the "territorial dramas" that are enacted in the urban landscape? What are some examples?
2. Identify some examples of what Weisman calls the exploitive "double standard between the sexes" in public landscapes.
3. Why does Weisman claim that Toronto's METRAC project provides an excellent model for the protection of women from violence in urban areas?
4. Compare the statistical breakdown Weisman offers on homeless people in New York City in the 1980s with today's statistics. Compare these updated statistics with your own urban area. Have the numbers of homeless receded or expanded? Which group is hardest hit?
5. What are the governmental public policies that Weisman identifies as the source of this problem?
6. What does Weisman mean by an "underclass" of people?
7. What are some examples of feminist politics of public space put into action?

# Recommended Reading

Greg Barak, *Gimme Shelter: A Social History of Homelessness in Contemporary America* (New York: Praeger, 1991)

Jean Baudrillard, *America*, trans. Chris Turner (London: Verso, 1989)

Mike Davis et al., *Fire in the Hearth: The Radical Politics of Place in America* (New York: Routledge, 1990)

K. Sue Jewell, *Survival of the Black Family: The Institutional Impact of U.S. Social Policy* (New York: Praeger, 1988)

Jean-Francois Lyotard, *The Postmodern Condition: A Report on Knowledge*, trans. Geoff Bennington (Minneapolis: University of Minnesota Press, 1984)

For information on a model community-based, minority-controlled organization providing housing, advocacy, and support services to homelessness related to HIV infection, write or contact Housing Works, Inc., 594 Broadway, Suite 700, New York, NY 10012. (212) 966–0466.

# Recommended Audiovisual Resources

*Door of Hope*. 1993. Produced by Dee Henoch and Laura Singer. Shows a successful residence program on New York's Upper West Side where intergenerational residents have improved the quality of their lives. Filmakers Library.

*Temporary Dwellings*. 1992. Produced and directed by Michael Regis Hilow. Documents the Tent City action by Seattle's homeless community. Filmakers Library.

*Shelter*. 1987. Produced by KCTS/TV. Moving interviews and portraits of the homeless. Filmakers Library.

# On the Beach
## Sexism and Tourism

### CYNTHIA ENLOE

Cynthia Enloe teaches political science at Clark University in Worcester, Massachusetts. She is the author of *Multi-Ethnic Politics: The Case of Malaysia, Ethnic Conflict and Political Development*, and *The Morning After: Sexual Politics at the End of the Cold War*.

The Portuguese woman perched on the ladder seems to be enjoying her work. Wearing a colorful dress under several layers of aprons, she is not too busy picking olives to smile at the photographer.

Selecting postcards is one of those seemingly innocent acts that has become fraught with ideological risks. Imagine for a minute that you are a British woman travelling in Portugal. You have saved for this holiday and are thoroughly enjoying the time away from stress and drizzle. But you haven't left your feminist consciousness at home. You think about the lives of the Portuguese women you see. That is one of the reasons you search the postcard racks to find pictures of Portuguese women engaged in relatively ordinary occupations—weaving, making pottery, pulling in heavy fishing nets, hoeing fields or harvesting olives. These are the images of Portuguese women you want to send your friends back home.

Still, you are a bit uneasy when you realize that in the eyes of those Portuguese women you are probably just another northern tourist able to afford leisurely travel outside her own country. They know you don't search for those less picturesque but no less real images of Portuguese women's lives today: women working in the new plastics factories around Porto, marking Portugal's entrance into the European Common Market; women working as chambermaids in hotels, representing the country's dependence on tourism. Such pictures wouldn't mesh with the holiday image you want to share with friends back in damp, chilly Britain.

No matter how good the feminist tourist's intention, the relationship between the British woman on holiday and the working women of Portugal seems to fall short of international sisterhood. But is it exploitation? As uncomfortable as we are when we look at women smiling out from foreign postcards, we might pause before leaping to the conclusion that they are merely one more group of victims under the heel of international capital. Women in many countries are being drawn into unequal relationships with each other as a result of governments' sponsorship of the international tourist industry, some because they have no choice, but others because they are making their own decisions about how to improve their lives. Many women are playing active roles in expanding and shaping the tourist industry—as travel agents, travel writers, flight attendants, crafts-women, chambermaids—even if they don't control it.

Similarly, women who travel are not merely creatures of privilege; nor today are they only from Western societies. They—or their mothers—have often had to fight against confining presumptions of feminine respectability to travel away from home on their own.

The hushed and serious tones typically reserved for discussions of nuclear escalation or spiraling international debt are rarely used in discussions of tourism. Tourism doesn't fit neatly into public preoccupations with military conflict and high finance. Although it is infused with masculine ideas about adventure, pleasure and the exotic, those are deemed 'private' and thus kept off stage in debates about international politics. Yet since World War II, planners, investors and workers in the tourist industry, and tourists themselves, have been weaving unequal patterns that are restructuring international politics. And they depend on women for their success.

By the mid-1980s, the global tourism business employed more people than the oil industry. These employees were servicing an estimated 200 million people who each year pack their bags and pocket their Berlitz phrase books to become international tourists.[1] The numbers continue to rise steadily. The United Nations World Tourism Organization forecasts that by the year 2000, tourism will have become the single most important global economic activity.[2]

The British woman's dilemma in trying to find a postcard expressing sisterhood rather than exploitation suggests that the galloping tourist industry is not necessarily making the world a more equal or harmonious place. Charter flights, time-share beach condominiums, and Himalayan trekking parties each carry with them power as well as pleasure. While tourism's supporters cite increased government revenues and modernizing influences, its critics ask whether tourism's remarkable growth is narrowing or widening the gap between the affluent and the poor. They question whether the foreign currency, new airstrips and hotels that come with the tourist industry really are adequate compensations for the exacerbation of racial tensions and other problems that so often accompany tourism.[3]

## Foot-Loose and Gendered

Tourism has its own political history, reaching back to the Roman empire. It overlaps with other forms of travel that appear to be less dedicated to pleasure. Government missions, military tours of duty, business trips, scientific explorations, forced migrations—women and men have experienced them differently, in ways that have helped construct today's global tourism industry and the international political system it sustains.

In many societies being feminine has been defined as sticking close to home. Masculinity, by contrast, has been the passport for travel. Feminist geographers and ethnographers have been amassing evidence revealing that a principal difference between women and men in countless societies has been the licence to travel away from a place thought of as 'home'.

A woman who travels away from the ideological protection of 'home' and without the protection of an acceptable male escort is likely to be tarred with the brush of 'unrespectability'. She risks losing her honor or being blamed for any harm that befalls her on her travels. One need only think of the lack of sympathy accorded a woman who has been assaulted when trying to hitchhike on her own: 'What does she expect, after all?' Some women may unwittingly reinforce the patriarchal link between respectable womanhood and geographical confinement with their own gestures of defiance. A bumper sticker has begun to appear on women's well-travelled vans: 'Good girls go to Heaven. Bad girls go everywhere.'

By contrast a man is deemed less than manly until he breaks away from home and strikes out on his own. Some men leave the farm and travel to the city or mining town looking for work. Other men set off hitchhiking with only a knapsack and a good pair of boots. Still others answer the call to 'Join the Navy and see the world'.

'I cut off my hair and dressed me in a suit of my husband's having had the precaution to quilt the waistcoat to preserve my breasts from hurt which were not large enough to betray my sex and putting on the wig and hat I had prepared I went out and brought me a silver hilted sword and some Holland shirts.'[4] So Christian Davies set off in the 1690s to enlist in the British army. If she couldn't travel as a woman, she would disguise herself as a man. The stories of Christian and women like her are not unmixed tales of feminist rebellion, however. While some of the women ran away to sea or enlisted as drummer boys to escape suffocating village life, others claimed they were simply acting as a loyal wife or sweetheart, following their man. If a woman was exposed—while being treated for a battle wound or giving birth—the punishment she received frequently depended on which of these two interpretations was believed by the men who pulled away her disguise.

Vita Sackville-West came from a privileged background but she emulated her working-class sisters and resorted to male disguise. After World War I demobilized veterans were a common sight in Europe. In 1920 Vita dressed as a man and ran away to Paris impulsively with her woman lover. In this masculine camouflage she felt liberated:

> the evenings were ours. I have never told a soul of what I did. I hesitate to write it here, but I must. . . . I dressed as a boy. It was easy, because I could put a khaki bandage round my head, which in those days was so common that it attracted no attention at all. I browned my face and hands. It must have been successful, because no one looked at me at all curiously or suspiciously. . . . I looked like a rather untidy young man, a sort of undergraduate, of about nineteen. I shall never forget the evenings when we walked back slowly to our flat through the streets of Paris. I, personally, had never felt so free in my life.[5]

More recently, women have been lured into joining the military—without a disguise—by thoughts of leaving home. Getting away from home, not killing Russians or Vietnamese, is what Peggy Perri, just out of nursing school, had in mind when she and her best friend decided to enlist in the US Army nursing corps in 1967. 'Pat and I were both living at home and we were both miserable. I was living at my mother's house. I was unhappy, really unhappy,' Peggy recalls. 'Pat and I had become nurses with the expectation that we could go anywhere and work. We wanted to go somewhere, and we wanted to do something really different.' Peggy wasn't a classic 'good girl'. She chewed gum and liked parties. But she didn't want to surrender her status as a respectable young woman. 'We needed to know that there was going to be some kind of structure to hold us up. The military sure promised that. . . . I was infatuated by the idea of going to Vietnam. . . . I really didn't know where I wanted to go. I wanted to go everywhere in the world.' She soon got her wish. 'I remember we got our orders; my mother took me shopping in every major department store. Pat and I both bought new sets of luggage, Pat's was hot pink! . . . It was January and we would go to all the "cruise" shops looking for light-weight clothing. I wanted everyone to think I was going on a cruise.'[6]

The most famous of the women who set out to travel further than convention allowed without disguise are now referred to as the 'Victorian lady travellers'. Most of them came from the white middle classes of North America and Europe. They set out upon travels that were supposed to be the preserve of men. They defied the strictures of femininity by choosing parts of the world which whites in the late nineteenth and early twentieth century considered 'uncharted', 'uncivilized'. Not for them the chic tourist meccas of Italy and Greece. These Victorian lady travellers wanted *adventure*. That meant going to lands just being opened up by imperial armies and capitalist traders.

In their own day these women were viewed with suspicion because they dared to travel such long distances with so little proper male protection. Even if their husbands accompanied them as missionaries or scientists, these women insisted upon the separateness of their own experiences. The fact that most of them were white and chose to travel in continents whose populations were not, added to the 'exotic' aura surrounding their journeys. Space and race, when combined, have different implications for women and men, even of the same social class.[7]

Mary Kingsley, Isabella Bird, Alexandra David-Neel, Nina Mazuchelli, Annie Bullock Workman, Nina Benson Hubbard—these women in the nineteenth and early twentieth centuries took for themselves the identities of 'adventurer' and 'explorer'. Both labels were thoroughly masculinized. Masculinity and exploration had been as tightly woven together as masculinity and soldiering. These audacious women challenged that ideological assumption, but they have left us with a bundle of contradictions. While they defied, apparently self-consciously, the ban on far-flung travel by 'respectable' women, in some respects they seem quite conventional. Some of them rejected female suffrage. Some refused to acknowledge fully how far their own insistence on the right to adventure undermined not only Victorian notions of femininity, but the bond being forged between Western masculinity and Western imperialism.

Mary Kingsley is one of the most intriguing lady travellers. Mary's father was an explorer, her brother an adventurer. Mary was born in 1862 and grew up as the twin movements of women's domestication of women and imperial expansion were flowering in Victoria's England. She seemed destined to nurse her invalid mother and to keep the homefires burning for her globe-trotting brother. But Mary had other ideas. In 1892 she set out on the first of several expeditions to Africa. She traveled without male escort and headed for the West African interior. For it was in the continent's interior where 'real' adventures were thought to happen. In subsequent years she befriended European male traders plying their business along the coasts and up the rivers of Africa. Her detailed knowledge of African societies' ritual fetishes was even acknowledged by the men of the British Museum.[8]

Mary Kingsley also became one of the most popular speakers on the lively lecture circuit. She drew enthusiastic audiences from all over England to hear about her travels to Africa and her descriptions of lives lived in the newly penetrated areas of Victoria's empire. Many women travellers helped finance their travels by giving public lectures. The lecture circuit may have provided a crucial setting in which the women who stayed at home could become engaged in the British empire. They could take part vicariously in British officials' debates over how best to incorporate African and Asian peoples into that empire by listening to Mary Kingsley describe colonial policies and their consequences for local peoples.

The women lecture-goers are as politically interesting as Mary Kingsley herself. Together, lecturer and audience helped to fashion a British culture of imperialism. The stay-at-home listeners would develop a sense of imperial pride as they heard another woman describe her travels among their empire's more 'exotic' peoples. And they could expand their knowledge of the world without risking loss of that feminine respectability which enabled them to feel superior to colonized women. Their imperial curiosity, in turn, helped Mary Kingsley finance her breaking of gendered convention.

A century later librarians at the American Museum of Natural History in New York mounted an exhibition honoring some of the American women who had made contributions to scientific exploration. 'Ladies of the Field: The Museum's Unsung Explorers' was designed to make visible Delia Akeley, Dina Brodsky and other women explorers whose contributions to science had been neglected because they were dismissed as amateurs or as mere wives-of-explorers. The exhibition consisted of just three small glass cases in the ante-room of the Rare Book Library. As two women visitors peered through the glass to read faded diaries and letters, they could hear the shouts of schoolchildren racing through millennia of dinosaurs not far away. But here there were no curious crowds. They were the only visitors. Something about finding themselves before this modest exhibit prompted the strangers to exchange a few words. As they looked at a photo of Delia Akeley standing proudly between giant tusks she had just collected for the museum, one woman said, 'A friend of mine had wanted to be an explorer, but she resigned herself to being a librarian.'

Some of these contributors to the museum were the first white women to travel to a

Delia Akeley on an expedition in Africa for the American Museum of Natural History. 1912. Carl Akeley/ Department of Library Sciences, American Museum of Natural History.

particular region. That seemed to give their travels greater significance. Historians often think it worth noting when the 'first white woman' arrived, as if that profoundly transformed a place. A white woman's arrival destined it to be sucked into the international system. If a white woman traveler reached such a place, could the white wife or white tourist be far behind?[9]

## Femininity in a World of Progress

The idea that the world is out there for the taking by ordinary citizens as well as adventurers emerged alongside the growth of tourism as an industry. World's fairs, together with museums and travel lectures, nourished this idea.

Without leaving her own country, the fair-goer could experience remote corners of the world, choosing to 'visit' the Philippines, Alaska, Japan or Hawaii. It is estimated that in the United States alone, close to one million people visited world's fairs between 1876 and 1916.[10] World's fairs were designed to be more than popular entertainments; they were intended by their planners to help the public imagine an industrializing, colonizing global enterprise.

At the hub of all the world's fairs was the idea of progress, global progress. It could be best celebrated, fair investors believed, by graphically comparing 'uncivilized' with 'civilized' cultures. Between the two extremes fair designers placed Afro-American and Native American cultures—those apparently already on the track to civilization. They constructed elaborate scenes that they imagined visitors would find exotic. They imported women and men from as far away as Samoa and the Philippines to demonstrate their point. They called on the budding profession of anthropology to order their ideas and ensure authenticity. In the end fair designers created living postcards, clichés of cultures apparently at opposite ends of the modernity scale.

The natives in their exotic environment were as crucial to the celebration of progress as were exhibits of the latest feats of technological invention. Walking between a simple Samoan village and a powerful, shiny locomotive gave fair-goers an exhilarating sense of inevitable progress. By implication, it was America—or France or Britain—which was leading the way in the march of globalized progress. For the cultures most deeply affected by the colonial experience were furthest along the fair's scale of progress. Eventually, so the fair scenario suggested, the primitive peoples of the world would be led into the light of civilization by imperial trusteeship. The world's fair expressed an elaborate international political cosmology.

It was a gendered America, a gendered Britain, however, that was leading the procession and formulating the heartening comparisons. A reporter for the *Omaha Bee* captured this spirit when describing the 1898 Trans-Mississippi and International Exposition:

> To see these ever formidable and hereditary enemies of the white man encamped together in a frame of architectural splendor erected by courage, manhood, and sterling integrity, will impress upon the growing sons and daughters a lesson which will bear fruit in years hence when the yet unsettled and uncultured possessions of the United States shall have become jewels upon the Star Spangled Banner.[11]

The year was 1898. The US government was extending its imperial reach. American men were exerting their manliness in defeating Spanish, Cuban and Filipino troops.

They were proving in the process that industrialization and the rise of urban middle-class lifestyles were not, as some had feared, weakening white American manhood. Within several decades Americans would no longer have to be satisfied with fair exhibits of Cuban dancers or Philippine villages. Those countries would have built tourist hotels, beach resorts and casinos to lure American pleasure-seekers—all due to world-wide progress generated by a civilizing sort of American masculinity.

The world's fairs of this era preached that white men's manliness fueled the civilizing imperial mission and in turn, that pursuing the imperial mission revitalized the nation's masculinity. At the same time, world's fairs were designed to show that women's domestication was proof of the manly mission's worthiness.

Thus femininity as well as masculinity structured the comparisons and the lessons visitors were to derive from the world's fairs. Women became the viewers and the viewed. White women were meant to come away from the fair feeling grateful for the benefits of civilization they enjoyed. They were not expected to measure progress from savagery to civilization in terms of voting rights or economic independence; they were to adopt a scale that had domesticated respectability at one end and hard manual labor at the other. White men were to look at 'savage' men's treatment of their over-worked women and congratulate themselves on their own civilized roles as protectors and breadwinners. Without the Samoan, Filipino and other colonized women, neither male nor female fair-goers would have been able to feel so confident about their own places in this emergent world.

Some American women saw the world's fair as a perfect venue for showing women's special contributions to the nation's progress. America's Centennial Exhibition in 1876 featured a Women's Pavilion, which celebrated the new concept of domestic science, as well as arts and crafts by women from around the world. Progress, technology and feminine domestic space were combined in a revised version of gendered civilization. In 1893 there was to be a great fair at Chicago to commemorate the four-hundredth anniversary of Columbus's discovery of America. Susan B. Anthony, the suffragist, led a drive to ensure that women wouldn't be excluded from the planning as they had been in 1876. The US Congress responded by mandating the appointment of a Board of Lady Managers to participate in the design of the 1893 Columbian Exposition. The Board commissioned a Women's Building. It was among the fair's largest and most impressive, designed by a woman architect, 23-year-old Sophia Hayden. But the Women's Building and its exhibits did not challenge the underlying message of the fair. The white women who took charge of this ambitious project still believed their mission was to demonstrate that American women were leading the world in improving the domestic condition of women. The Women's Building was filled with exhibits of the latest household technology that would lighten women's load. Nor did they challenge the racial hierarchy that was implicitly condoned by the fair. The Board of Lady Managers, chaired by a wealthy Chicago socialite, rejected the proposal that a Black woman be appointed to any influential post.[12]

# Package Tours for the Respectable Woman

Tourism is as much ideology as physical movement. It is a package of ideas about industrial, bureaucratic life.[13] It is a set of presumptions about manhood, education and pleasure.[14]

Tourism has depended on presumptions about masculinity and femininity. Often women have been set up as the quintessence of the exotic. To many men, women are something to be experienced. Women don't have experiences of their own. If the women are of a different culture, the male tourist feels he has entered a region where he can shed civilization's constraints, where he is freed from standards of behavior imposed by respectable women back home.

Thomas Cook perhaps deserves credit for making the world safe for the respectable woman tourist. On an English summer's day in 1841, walking to a temperance meeting, Thomas Cook had the idea of chartering a train for the next meeting so that participants could board a single train, pay a reduced rate, and while traveling to their meeting be treated to 'hams, loaves and tea' interspersed with exhortations against the evils of drink. Some 570 people signed up for that first trip.[15]

Initially, Thomas Cook was concerned primarily with working men like himself. He wanted to provide them with a diversion that didn't involve liquor. In 1851 he urged men to join his tour to the London Exhibition:

> There are a number of you who ask, 'of what use and benefit would be a visit to us?' . . . I ask, of what use was your apprenticeship? Did it make you more useful members of society? . . . Such will be the difference betwixt the man who visits the Exhibition and he that does not—the one will be blind with his eyes open, and the other will enjoy the sight, and admire the skill and labour of his fellow-workmen of different parts of the globe.[16]

Only later did Cook come to realize that package tours might attract working men and their wives and children and eventually women traveling without a male member of the family. By the 1850s Britain's more adventurous middle-class women were beginning to earn their own income and to think about traveling for pleasure, if not to West Africa, at least to Germany. They still needed to safeguard their respectability in order to stay marriageable and so were looking for a chaperoned tour led by an honorable man. Thomas Cook, temperance advocate, offered precisely such a service. He only realized the business potential of respectable travel for women in 1855, after receiving a letter from four sisters—Matilda, Elizabeth, Lucilla and Marion Lincolne of Suffolk. The Lincolne sisters came from a large middle-class temperance family. Each of them had worked for wages when they were in their twenties and had income to spend on pleasure.[17] They had read about the beauties of the Rhine and the cities of the Continent, but how could they go?

> How could ladies alone and unprotected, go 600 or 700 miles away from home? However, after many pros and cons, the idea gradually grew on us and we found ourselves consulting guides, hunting in guide-books, reading descriptions, making notes, and corresponding with Mr. Cook. . . . Tis true, we encountered some opposition—one friend declaring that it was improper for ladies to go alone—the gentleman thinking we were far too independent. . . . But somehow or other one interview with Mr. Cook removed all our hesitation, and we forthwith placed ourselves under his care. . . .
> Many of our friends thought us too independent and adventurous to leave the shores of old England, and thus plunge into foreign lands not beneath Victoria's sway with no protecting relative, but we can only say that we hope this will not be our last Excursion of the kind. We would venture anywhere with such a guide and guardian as Mr. Cook.[18]

Cook was so struck by Matilda and her sisters' letter that he began to run excerpts in his advertisements, making appeals directly to women. By 1907, the company's magazine, *Traveller's Gazette*, featured on its cover a vigorous young woman bestriding the globe.

Today the package tour holiday is a profitable commodity for some of the international economy's most successful companies. In Britain 40 per cent of the population cannot afford an annual holiday, but one third of the upper-middle class take two or more holidays a year. There are now 700 tour operators in Britain selling more than 12.5 million package holidays annually, worth £3.1 billion. While most of their customers pick the Mediterranean, British and continental tour companies are nudging clients to travel further afield—to North Africa, North America and the Caribbean.[19]

Japanese government officials are predicting that foreign travel will be one of that country's major growth industries in the 1990s. Although only 5 per cent of Japanese took holidays abroad in 1987, large tourist companies like JTB and Kinki Nippon Tourist Agency have already turned foreign travel into a $16 billion business. One third of Japanese overseas tourists today travel as part of a package tour. Most notorious are groups of businessmen traveling to South Korea, the Philippines and Thailand on sex tours. But the country's second largest tourist market is single working women: 18 per cent of all Japanese tourists. Their favored destinations are the shops and beaches of Hong Kong, Hawaii and California.[20]

Cover of one of Thomas Cook's early holiday brochures. 1907. Thomas Cook Archives, London.

# The Tourism Formula for Development

From its beginnings, tourism has been a powerful motor for global integration. Even more than other forms of investment, it has symbolized a country's entrance into the world community. Foreign-owned mines, military outposts and museum explorations have drawn previously 'remote' societies into the international system, usually on unequal terms. Tourism entails a more politically potent kind of intimacy. For a tourist isn't expected to be very adventurous or daring, to learn a foreign language or adapt to local custom. Making sense of the strange local currency is about all that is demanded. Perhaps it is for this reason that international technocrats express such satisfaction when a government announces that it plans to promote tourism as one of its major industries. For such a policy implies a willingness to meet the expectations of those foreigners who want political stability, safety and congeniality when they travel. A government which decides to rely on money from tourism for its development is a government which has decided to be internationally compliant enough that even a woman traveling on her own will be made to feel at home there.

When mass tourism began to overtake elite travel following World War II, most travel occurred within and between North America and Western Europe. By the mid-1970s, 8 per cent of all tourists were North Americans and Europeans traveling on holiday to Third World countries. A decade later 17 per cent were.[21] Middle-class Canadians who a decade ago thought of going across the border to Cape Cod or Florida in search of holiday warmth are now as likely to head for the Bahamas. Their French counterparts are as apt to make Tunisia or Morocco rather than Nice their holiday destination. Scandinavians are choosing Sri Lanka or Goa instead of the Costa del Sol.

Third World officials and their European, American and Japanese bankers have become avid tourism boosters. Tourism is promoted today as an industry that can turn poor countries' very poverty into a magnet for sorely needed foreign currency. For to be a poor society in the late twentieth century is to be 'unspoilt'. Tourism is being touted as an alternative to the one-commodity dependency inherited from colonial rule. Foreign sun-seekers replace bananas. Hiltons replace sugar mills. Multinational corporations such as Gulf and Western or Castle and Cook convert their large landholdings into resorts or sell them off to developers. But the mid-1980s tourism had replaced sugar as the Dominican Republic's top foreign-exchange earner. In Jamaica, tourism had outstripped bauxite as the leading earner of foreign exchange. Caribbean development officials are happily reporting that, with more than 10 million visitors a year, the region is outstripping its main tourism rivals, Hawaii and Mexico. But, they add reassuringly, all the new hotel construction isn't turning Caribbean islands into concrete jungles: 'Many of the islands are mainly wild and underpopulated, with room for many more hotels and resorts before their appeal is threatened.'[22]

In reality, tourism may be creating a new kind of dependency for poor nations. Today tourism represents 40,000 jobs for Tunisia and is the country's biggest foreign-currency earner. Countries such as Puerto Rico, Haiti, Nepal, Gambia and Mexico have put their development eggs in the tourism basket, spending millions of dollars from public funds to build the sorts of facilities that foreign tourists demand. Officials in these countries hope above all that tourism will get their countries out of debt. The international politics of debt and the international pursuit of pleasure have become tightly knotted together as we enter the 1990s.[23]

The indebted governments that have begun to rely on tourism include those which previously were most dubious about this as a route to genuine development, especially if 'development' is to include preservation of national sovereignty. Cuba, Tanzania, North Korea, Vietnam and Nicaragua all are being governed today by officials who have adopted a friendlier attitude toward tourism. They are being complimented and called 'pragmatic' by mainstream international observers because they are putting the reduction of international debt and the earning of foreign currency on the top of their political agenda.[24]

This belief in the logic of fueling development and economic growth with tourism underlies the full-page color advertisements in the Sunday supplements. Many of those ads luring travelers to sunny beaches and romantic ruins are designed and paid for by government tourist offices. Most of those bureaucratic agencies depend on femininity, masculinity and heterosexuality to make their appeals and achieve their goals. Local men in police or military uniforms and local women in colorful peasant dresses—or in very little dress at all—are the preferred images. The local men are militarized in their manliness; the local women are welcoming and available in their femininity. The Cayman Islands Department of Tourism ran an expensive advertisement in the *New York Times* 'Sophisticated Traveller' supplement in October 1987. It pictured a white couple on an expanse of sandy beach. Underneath were smaller snapshots of local life and tourist activities—the tourists were portrayed as white couples shopping, swimming, dining; the local people were uniformed men on parade and a single black woman smiling out at the reader. Over her head ran the caption, 'Those who know us, love us.'

# Flight Attendants and Chambermaids

Singapore Airlines, a government company, runs a center-fold advertisement that shows an Asian woman of somewhat vague ethnicity. She could be Chinese, Indian or Malay. She stands in a misty, impressionistic setting, looking out at the reader demurely, holding a single water lily. There is no information about the airline's rates or safety record, just this message in delicate print: 'Singapore Girl . . . You're a great way to fly.'

On the oceans and in the skies: the international business travelers are men, the service workers are women. Flight attendants in the United States began organizing in the 1970s and won the right not to dress in uniforms that they believed turned them into airborne Playboy bunnies. But most women working today as flight attendants do not yet have the backing of strong trade unions. They are subject to their employers' desire for flight attendants to represent not only the airline company that employs them, but the feminine essence of their nation. For that distinctive femininity is a major attraction in the eyes of the flight attendant's employer and her government. 'When your business is business . . . our business is pleasure,' runs a Sri Lankan airline's advertisement.[25]

The airlines have taken their cues from the longer established ocean-liner companies. It was they who first used a racial and gendered division of labor to maximize profits while constructing a notion of leisure. Initially, ocean-liner crews were male, ranked by class and race. The white officers were to exude both competence and romance for passengers. The Indonesian, Filipino and other men of color serving in the dining rooms and below deck reflected a comforting global hierarchy while permitting the company to pay lower wages. Women crew members multiplied when company executives began to realize that their women passengers preferred to be waited on by women. Elaine Lang and Evelyn

Huston were among the handful of British women who signed up to work on the *Empress of Scotland* in the 1930s, a time when shore jobs were hard to find. They worked as stewardesses, rising gradually in rank, but finding it impossible to break into the ship's all-male officer corps. Their best hope was to service first-class rather than steerage-class passengers: 'work and bed, work and bed, that's all it was.' Today hundreds of women are hired to work as service personnel in the burgeoning cruise-ship industry. 'Love Boat' is still kept afloat by a sexual division of labor.[26]

When people go on holiday they expect to be freed from humdrum domestic tasks. To be a tourist means to have someone else make your bed.

Thus chambermaids, waitresses and cooks are as crucial to the international tourism industry—and the official hopes that underpin it—as sugar workers and miners were to colonial industries. Still, a chambermaid seems different. Even a low-paid, over-worked male employee on a banana or sugar plantation has a machete, a sense of strength, a perception of his work as manly. Many nationalist movements have rallied around the image of the exploited male plantation worker; he has represented the denial of national sovereignty.

Nationalist leaders who have become alarmed at the tourism-dependent policies imposed by foreign bankers and their own governments have been reluctant to rally around the symbol of the oppressed chambermaid. Men in nationalist movements may find it easier to be roused to anger by the vision of a machete-swinging man transformed into a tray-carrying waiter in a white resort—he is a man who has had his masculine pride stolen from him. Caribbean nationalists have complained that their government's pro-tourism policies have turned their society into a 'nation of busboys'. 'Nation of chambermaids' doesn't seem to have the same mobilizing ring in their ears. After all, a woman who has traded work as an unpaid agricultural worker for work as a hotel cleaner hasn't lost any of her femininity.

In reality, tourism is not dependent on busboys. Tourism is what economists call a 'labor-intensive' industry. It requires construction crews, airplanes, gallons of frozen orange juice, and above all a high ratio of employees to paying customers; people who come as tourists need and expect a lot of service. As in other labor-intensive industries—garments, health and childcare, food processing and electronics assembly— owners make money and governments earn tax revenues to the extent that they can keep down the cost of wages and benefits of the relatively large numbers of workers they must hire.

Since the eighteenth century, employers have tried to minimize the cost of employing workers in labor-intensive industries by defining most jobs as 'unskilled' or 'low-skilled'— jobs, in other words, that workers naturally know how to do. Women in most societies are presumed to be naturally capable at cleaning, washing, cooking, serving. Since tourism companies need precisely those jobs done, they can keep their labor costs low if they can define those jobs as women's work. In the Caribbean in the early 1980s, 75 per cent of tourism workers were women.[27]

Hawaiians refer to the large hotels owned by Americans and Japanese as 'the new plantations': Caucasian men are the hotel managers, Hawaiian men and women the entertainers, Hawaiian men the coach drivers and Filipino women the chambermaids. In China, post-Mao officials, eager to attract foreign industry and foreign exchange, are approving the construction of new hotels within coastal zones set aside for electronics, textile and other export factories, and are helping managers hire workers. Shenzhen's new Bamboo Garden Hotel employs 360 employees; 80 per cent are women.[28]

In the Philippines, where tourism under both the Marcos and Aquino regimes has been relied on to earn badly needed foreign exchange, the Manila Garden Hotel employs 500 workers; 300 are women. But there is something different here. Workers are represented by an independent union, the Philippines National Union of Workers in Hotels, Restaurants and Allied Industries, and equal numbers of women and men are union representatives. In the wake of the widespread political mobilization of women that helped to bring down the Marcos regime in 1986, women in the union created a Working Women's Council. Beth Valenzuela, a single mother working in the hotel's food department, is one of the Manila Garden Hotel's active women unionists. She told a Filipino reporter that she hoped to make the Women's Council a place where issues of particular importance to women hotel workers could be studied and discussed. It would also train women union members in public speaking and decision-making, skills that in the past 'have been jealously guarded by the men as their exclusive preserve'.[29]

In Britain, too, the Conservative government has been trumpeting tourism as a growth industry. In the late 1980s and early 1990s, tourist companies are creating 45,000 new jobs per year, especially in the depressed industrial areas of the North. A new museum is opening every two weeks: deserted steel mills are becoming part of the 'heritage industry'. But most tourism jobs are part-time, seasonal and provide little chance for advancement. This means that they are also likely to be filled by women. Nevertheless, some British critics of the tourism formula for economic revival seem less upset at the prospect of a British woman struggling on a part-time wage than at the idea of a former steel worker compromising his masculinity by taking a 'candy-floss job' at a theme park.[30]

## Sex Tourism in International Politics

Pat Bong is a neighborhood of Bangkok that caters to foreign men. There are 400,000 more women than men living in Bangkok, but male tourists outnumber female tourists by three to one. Pat Bong's urban landscape makes the census figures come alive. Although the government passed a Prostitution Prohibition Act in 1960, six years later it undercut that ban by passing an Entertainment Places Act, which had enough loopholes to encourage coffee shops and restaurants to add prostitution to their menus. Thus today Pat Bong is crowded with discos, bars and massage parlors. In the early 1980s, it was estimated that Bangkok had 119 massage parlors, 119 barbershop-cum-massage parlors and teahouses, 97 nightclubs, 248 disguised brothels and 394 disco-restaurants, all of which sold sexual companionship to male customers. Some of the women who work here as prostitutes have migrated from the countryside where agricultural development projects have left them on the margins; other women are second, even third generation prostitutes increasingly cut off from the rest of Thai society. A woman working in a Bangkok massage parlor can earn an average of 5,000 baht per month; wages in non-entertainment jobs open to women average a paltry 840 baht per month. Marriage to a foreigner frequently appears to be the only avenue out of Pat Bong, but it too can prove illusory:

> [She] had lived with an English man working as a technician on an oil rig. But he left her and went back to England. She said she was not working when she was with him, but returned to her job after some months since he failed to send her money and it was

impossible for her to keep such an expensive flat. 'What else can I do? After all, these men are good business.'[31]

Sex tourism is not an anomaly; it is one strand of the gendered tourism industry. While economists in industrialized societies presume that the 'service economy', with its explosion of feminized job categories, follows a decline in manufacturing, policy-makers in many Third World countries have been encouraged by international advisers to develop service sectors before manufacturing industries mature. Bar hostesses before automobile workers, not after.[32]

A network of local and foreign companies encourages men—especially from North America, Western Europe, Japan, the Middle East and Australia—to travel to Third World countries specifically to purchase the sexual services of local women. The countries that have been developed as the destinations for sex tourists include those which have served as 'rest and recreation' sites for the American military: Thailand, South Korea, the Philippines. Nearby Indonesia and Sri Lanka also have received sex tourists. Goa, a coastal state of India, is among the newest regions to be targeted by sex tourism's promoters. Local laws explicitly prohibiting prostitution are often ignored, not only by pimps and bar owners, but by India's police and tourism officials as well.[33]

To succeed, sex tourism requires Third World women to be economically desperate enough to enter prostitution; having done so it is made difficult to leave. The other side of the equation requires men from affluent societies to imagine certain women, usually women of color, to be more available and submissive than the women in their own countries. Finally, the industry depends on an alliance between local governments in search of foreign currency and local and foreign businessmen willing to invest in sexualized travel.

> Thailand is a world full of extremes and the possibilities are unlimited. Anything goes in this exotic country, especially when it comes to girls. Still it appears to be a problem for visitors to Thailand to find the right places where they can indulge in unknown pleasures. . . . Rosie [Rosie Reisen, a West German travel company] has done something about this. For the first time in history you can book a trip to Thailand with exotic pleasures included in the price.[34]

In 1986 Thailand earned more foreign currency from tourism—$1.5 billion—than it did from any other economic activity including its traditional export leader, rice. The Thai government's Sixth National Economic and Social Development Plan for 1978–1991 makes 'tourism and exports' its top priority. In pursuing this goal Thai officials want to increase the numbers of tourists (2.7 million came in 1986), but also to alter the mix, especially to get Japanese men, who now stay an average of only four days, to stay longer.[35]

Sex tourism is part of the domestic and international political system. And changes are now occurring both within and between countries that could radically alter the sex tourism industry: AIDS; official nationalism; Asian and African feminist movements; and international alliances between feminist organizations.

By October 1987 Thai tourism officials had become alarmed at the sharp drop in the numbers of single male visitors to the beach resort of Pattaya. After Bangkok, Pattaya was the favored destination for foreign male tourists. The number of Middle Eastern men had declined to such an extent that Pattaya's VD clinics, which advertise in Arabic as well as English, had begun to see a fall in clients. Initially, the Thai government was reluctant to talk about AIDS. Like other governments dependent on tourism and on sex tourism in particular, public admission of AIDS was seen as damaging to the economy and national pride. Then, once acknowledged, officials set about compelling women working in bars and massage parlors in Pattaya and Bangkok to take tests for the HIV virus. Government health officials were pressed by government tourism officials to co-operate. By mid-1987 only six people, five Thais and one foreigner, had died of AIDS according to official statistics. Most of the other twenty-five people reported by the government as having been infected with the virus and developing AIDS-related symptoms were categorized by the government as homosexual men and drug addicts. Female prostitutes are the group that most worried Thai officials. Bureaucrats began talking of building more golf courses. If foreign men began to avoid Thai women there had to be an alternative attraction. But little was said of the poor women who have taken jobs in the sex industry because they have had to leave the Thai countryside for lack of land and decently paid waged work.[36]

Empower and Friends of Women are two of the Thai women's organizations formed in the 1980s to fill the gaps left by uninterested policy-makers and investors. Each group works directly with women in the sex-tourism industry, providing English lessons so that the women can deal on a more equal footing with their clients. They publish and distribute cartoon brochures informing women about AIDS. Most recently they have begun efforts to work with Thai women who have traveled to Europe to work as entertainers or to marry as mail-order brides.[37]

Feminist groups in the Philippines have had a better political opening for making sex tourism a national political issue. The overthrow of the authoritarian and export-oriented regime of Ferdinand Marcos in 1986 made the government's entire development formula vulnerable to popular scrutiny. Marcos and his advisors, with encouragement from foreign banks and technical consultants, had viewed tourism as a primary building block of development. The regime had used the reputed beauty and generosity of Filipino women as 'natural resources' to compete in the international tourism market. The result was that by the mid-1980s, 85 per cent of tourists visiting the country were men, and sex tourism had become crucial to the government's economic survival. While many outside observers focussed their attention on the prostitution that had grown up around the large American bases in the Philippines, some Filipino feminists noted that there were many more women working as prostitutes in Manila's tourist establishments.

Another evening is starting in the history of the international political system:

> Rows of taxis, cars and minibuses pull up behind a number of Manila hotels. Long lines of women pass the guards and enter a private door, sign a book, hand over their identification cards and take a private elevator to one of the special floors designated for prostitution. . . .
>   The woman goes to her assigned room; if the man is out she waits in the corridor. . . . [A prostitute] may not be taken to any public area of the hotel, all food and drink orders must be by room service. Hotels charge a $10 'joiners fee' for the privilege of taking a woman to a room. . . .

Before breakfast the next day the women collect their IDs and leave.[38]

When Corazon Aquino replaced Ferdinand Marcos as president, Filipino women activists pressed the new regime to give up sex tourism as a development strategy. Aquino herself was not a feminist, but she had made restoration of the nation's dignity a central theme in her political campaign. As president, she took steps to change the Tourism

Ministry's leadership and policies. The new minister brought a tour of Japanese women to the Philippines in order to demonstrate that the government was making the country a more wholesome tourist destination. But when Aquino authorized police to make raids on establishments in Ermita, Manila's infamous entertainment district, feminists were alarmed. The policy was not devised in consultation with women's groups such as Gabriela. Women working in the industry were not asked about the causes or likely consequences of such a heavy-handed approach. No steps were taken by the government to provide alternative livelihoods for the women working as dancers, hostesses and masseurs. In the name of cleaning up the city, washing away the degeneracy of the Marcos years, police arrested hundreds of women. Virtually no pimps, businessmen or male clients were jailed.[39]

Several Filipino feminist groups have created drop-in centers in those areas where prostitution is concentrated. They acknowledge that there are class barriers to be overcome in these new relationships between women in prostitution and women in political organizations. Filipino women activists, including a number of feminist nuns, have tried to avoid moralism. To provide a place to meet other prostitutes outside of the bars, to allow women to sort out together the conditions that pull Filipino women into prostitution, to provide practical information on AIDS, VD and contraception—these are feminists' first objectives. Yet the lack of the substantial resources it takes to offer prostitutes realistic job alternatives has been frustrating. Learning handicrafts may provide a woman working in Ermita or on the fringes of an American military base with a new sense of confidence or self-worth, but it doesn't pay the rent or support a child. 'When it comes to income-generating alternatives, we don't think we offer anything because we are up against so much. Economically we cannot give them anything.'[40]

Filipino feminists refuse to discuss prostitution or sex tourism in a vacuum. They insist that all analyses and organizational strategies should tie sex tourism to the issues of Philippines nationalism, land reform and demilitarization. Nowadays, they argue, sex tourism must also be understood in relation to Filipinas' migration overseas.

Migration as entertainers and as brides to foreign men has been the latest step in making world travel different for men than for women. Men in Scandinavia, West Germany, Australia, Britain, the United States and Japan now want to have access to Third World women not just in Third World tourism centers; they want to enjoy their services at home. Thus feminist organizations in Thailand, South Korea and the Philippines are having to make alliances with women in Europe, North America and Japan in order to protect women in the international tourism/entertainment/marriage industry. Thai feminist social workers go to West Germany to investigate the conditions Thai women encounter there; Filipino feminists travel to Japan to take part in meetings organized by Japanese feminists concerned about Filipinas recruited to work in discos and bars, women now referred to as 'japayukisan'; South Korean feminists fly to New York to attend a conference on international prostitution to urge American women activists to think and organize internationally.[41]

# Conclusion

Tourism is not just about escaping work and drizzle; it is about power, increasingly internationalized power. That tourism is not discussed as seriously by conventional political commentators as oil or weaponry may tell us more about the ideological construction of 'seriousness' than about the politics of tourism.

Government and corporate officials have come to depend on international travel for pleasure in several ways. First, over the last forty years they have come to see tourism as an industry that can help diversify local economies suffering from reliance on one or two products for export. Tourism is embedded in the inequalities of international trade, but is often tied to the politics of particular products such as sugar, bananas, tea and copper. Second, officials have looked to tourism to provide them with foreign currency, a necessity in the ever more globalized economies of both poor and rich countries. Third, tourism development has been looked upon as a spur to more general social development; the 'trickle down' of modern skills, new technology and improved public services is imagined to follow in the wake of foreign tourists. Fourth, many government officials have used the expansion of tourism to secure the political loyalty of local élites. For instance, certain hotel licences may win a politician more strategic allies today than a mere civil-service appointment. Finally, many officials have hoped that tourism would raise their nations' international visibility and even prestige.

Many of these hopes have been dashed. Yet tourism continues to be promoted by bankers and development planners as a means of making the international system less unequal, more financially sound and more politically stable. A lot is riding on sun, surf and souvenirs.

From the Roman empire to the eighteenth century European grand tour, the rise of Cooks Tours and Club Med, travel for pleasure and adventure has been profoundly gendered. Without ideas about masculinity and femininity — and the enforcement of both — in the societies of departure and the societies of destination, it would be impossible to sustain the tourism industry and its political agenda in their current form. It is not simply that ideas about pleasure, travel, escape, bed-making and sexuality have affected women in rich and poor countries. The very structure of international tourism *needs* patriarchy to survive. Men's capacity to control women's sense of their security and self-worth has been central to the evolution of tourism politics. It is for this reason that actions by feminists — as airline stewardesses, hotel workers, prostitutes, wives of businessmen and organizers of alternative tours for women — should be seen as political, internationally political.

Movements which upset any of the patterns in today's international tourist industry are likely to upset one of the principal pillars of contemporary world power. Such a realization forces one to take a second look at the Portuguese woman on her ladder picking olives, smiling for the postcard photographer. She has the potential for reshaping the international political order. What is behind her smile?

# Reading Questions

1. How have government and corporate officials come to depend on international travel for pleasure?
2. Why does Enloe view sex tourism as one strand of the gendered tourism industry?
3. On what gendered and economic social conditions does the success of sex tourism depend?
4. Why, according to Enloe, are nationalist leaders unwilling to rally around the symbol of the oppressed chambermaid?
5. How do the bureaucratic agencies that promote international tourism rely on femininity, masculinity, and heterosexuality to succeed?
6. What historical facts does Enloe argue to be crucial to the European and American ideas of global progress and the good of imperial trusteeship?

## Recommended Reading

Tom Barry et al., *The Other Side of Paradise* (New York: Grove Press, 1984)

Cynthia Enloe, *The Morning After: Sexual Politics at the End of the Cold War* (Berkeley: University of California, 1993)

Jamaica Kincaid, *A Small Place* (London: Virago, 1988)

Tracy Lai, "Asian Women: Not for Sale," *Changing Our Power: An Introduction to Women's Studies* (Dubuque, Iowa: Kendall-Hunt, 1988)

Chandra Mohanty, ed., *Third World Women and the Politics of Feminism* (Bloomington: Indiana University Press, 1991)

James Petras and Tienchai Wongchaisuwan, "Thailand: Free Markets, AIDS, and Child Prostitution," *Z Magazine* (September 1993)

Joni Seager and Ann Olson, *Women in the World: An International Atlas* (New York: Simon and Schuster, 1986)

Gayatri C. Spivak, *Outside the Teaching Machine* (Durham, NC: Duke University Press, 1993)

Thanh-Dom Truong, *Sex, Money and Morality: Prostitution and Tourism in Southeast Asia* (London: Zed Books, 1990)

Susanne Thorbek, *Voices from the City: Women of Bangkok* (Highland, NJ: Zed Books, 1987)

Lois Turner and John Ash, *The Golden Hordes: International Tourism and the Pleasure Periphery* (New York: St. Martin's Press, 1976)

## Recommended Audiovisual Resources

*Street of Shame*. 1956. Directed by Kenji Mizoguchi. An honest study of the dreams and problems of a group of sex workers living in a Tokyo brothel.

*Abortion: Stories from North and South*. 1984. Directed by Gail Singer. Cross-cultural survey interviewing women in Ireland, Japan, Thailand, Peru, Colombia, and Canada on their beliefs about abortion. The Cinema Guild.

# Holy Kitschen

## Collecting Religious Junk from the Street

### CELESTE OLALQUIAGA

Celeste Olalquiaga is the author of *Megalopolis: Contemporary Cultural Sensibilities*, from which this selection is taken. She teaches cultural studies at Cooper Union in New York City.

Kitsch causes two tears to flow in quick succession. The first tear says: How nice to see children running on the grass! The second tear says: How nice to be moved, together with all mankind, by children running on the grass! It is the second tear that makes kitsch kitsch.

—Milan Kundera, 1984

Catholic imagery, once confined to sacred places such as church souvenir stands, cemeteries, and botanicas, has recently invaded the market as a fad. In the last few years, the realm of religious iconography in Manhattan has extended beyond its traditional Latino outlets on the Lower East Side, the Upper West Side, and Fourteenth Street. The 1980s appropriation of an imagery that evokes transcendence illustrates the cannibalistic and vicarious characteristics of postmodern culture. This melancholic arrogation also diffuses the boundaries of cultural identity and difference, producing a new and unsettling cultural persona.

A walk along Fourteenth Street used to be enough to travel in the hyperreality of kitsch iconography.[1] Cutting across the map of Manhattan, Fourteenth Street sets the boundary for downtown, exploding into a frontierlike bazaar, a frantic place of trade and exchange, a truly inner-city port where among cascades of plastic flowers, pelicans made with shells, rubber shoes, Rita Hayworth towels, two-dollar digital watches, and pink electric guitars with miniature microphones, an array of shrine furnishings is offered. Velvet hangings picturing the Last Supper are flanked on one side by bucolic landscapes where young couples kiss as the sun fizzles away in the ocean and on the other by 1987's "retro" idol, Elvis Presley, while the Virgin Mary's golden aura is framed by the sexy legs of a pin-up, and the Sacred Heart of Jesus desperately competes in glitter with barrages of brightly colored glass-bead curtains.[2]

Nowadays, the Catholic iconography brought to the United States by immigrants from Puerto Rico, the Dominican Republic, Mexico, and Cuba is displayed in places where the predominant attitude toward Latino culture is one of amused fascination. Religious images serve not only as memorabilia in fancy souvenir shops[3] but also as decoration for night clubs. The now-exorcised Voodoo, on Eighteenth Street, used to have a disco on its first floor and a bright green and pink tropical bar on the second. The bar's ceiling was garnished with plastic fruits hanging from one end to the other, and in the center of the room stood an altar complete with Virgin Mary, flowers, and votive candles. Fourteenth Street's Palladium, famous for a postmodern scenario in which golden Renaissance paintings emerge from behind a bare high-tech structure, celebrated All Saints' Day in 1987 with an invitation that unfolded in images of and prayers to Saint Patrick, Saint Francis of Assisi, and Saint Michael the Archangel.

Suddenly, holiness is all over the place. For $3.25 one can buy a Holiest Water Fountain in the shape of the Virgin, while plastic fans engraved with the images of your favorite holy people go for $1.95, as do Catholic identification tags: "I'm a Catholic. In case of accident or illness please call a priest." Glowing rosary beads can be found for $1.25 and, for those in search of verbal illustration, a series of "Miniature Stories of the Saints" is available for only $1.45. In the wake of punk crucifix earrings comes designer Henry Auvil's Sacred Heart of Jesus sweatshirt, yours for a modest eighty dollars,[4] while scapularies, sometimes brought all the way from South America, adorn black leather jackets. Even John Paul II has something to contribute. In his travels, the Holy Father leaves behind a trail of images, and one can buy his smiling face in a variety of pope gadgets including alarm clocks, pins, picture frames, T-shirts, and snowstorm globes.[5]

This holy invasion has gone so far as to intrude in the sacred space of galleries and museums, as a growing number of artists incorporate Catholic religious imagery in their work. Some recent examples are Amalia Mesa-Bains's recasting of personal *altares*, Dana Salvo's photographs of Mexican home altars, and Audrey Flack's baroque re-representations of Spanish virgins.[6] Can the objects found in botanicas and on Fourteenth Street, the ones sold in souvenir shops and those exhibited in galleries be considered one and the same? I will argue for their synchronized difference, that is, for contemporary urban culture's ability to circulate and support distinct, and often contradictory, discourses.

A Mexican home altar. © Dana Salvo.

## Religious Iconography as Kitsch: Developing a Vicarious Sensibility

I will begin by describing the peculiar aesthetics and philosophy underlying the circulation of the iconography of home altars. A popular Latin American tradition, home altars or *altares* are domestic spaces dedicated to deities and holy figures. In them, statuettes or images of virgins and saints are allocated space together with candles and other votive objects. Triangular in analogy to the Holy Trinity, *altares* are characterized by a cluttered juxtaposition of all types of paraphernalia; they are a personal pastiche. Illustrating a history of wishes, laments, and prayers, they are built over time, each personal incident leaving its own mark. *Altares* embody familiar or individual histories in the way photo albums do for some people. Consequently, a home altar is not only unique and unrepeatable, it is coded by the personal experience that composed it, and the code is unreadable to foreign eyes. This mode of elaboration explains the variety of artifacts to be found in home altars and why there are no set rules as to what they might be made up of, except that everything must have a particular value. In *altares*, value is measured both sentimentally and as an offering. Since most of the people who make them have low incomes, their economic worth is symbolic and is conveyed by glitter and shine, mirrors and glass, a profusion of golden and silvery objects, and sheer abundance. This symbolic richness accounts for the artificial look of *altares*, as well as for the "magical kingdom" feeling they evoke.

Fundamentally syncretic, *altares* are raised or dedicated to figures who are public in some way, usually taken from the Catholic tradition, a local miraculous event, or national politics. Instead of following a formal chronology, home altars rearticulate history in relation to events relevant to the believer. To symbolize personal history, they transgress boundaries of time, space, class, and race. This is well illustrated in the Venezuelan cult of Maria Lionza, a deity who is revered along with heroes of the Independence and contemporary presidents—such as Carlos Andrés Pérez—in the gigantic altar of Sorte, a ritual hill dedicated to her worship. In both their elaboration and their meaning, *altares* are emblematic of the mechanics of popular culture: they familiarize transcendental experience by creating a personal universe from mainly domestic resources. In so doing, they stand directly opposite the impersonal politics of high and mass culture, although they steal motifs and objects from both.

That the *altares* tradition is being appropriated by artists both in the United States and abroad (Cuban artist Leandro Soto's home altars to revolutionary heroes, for example) at the same time that their constitutive elements are heavily circulated in the marketplace is no coincidence. This phenomenon is based on the stealing of elements that are foreign or removed from the absorbing culture's direct sensory realm, shaping itself into a vicarious experience particularly attracted to the intensity of feeling provided by iconographic universes like that of Latin American Catholicism. Vicariousness—to live through another's experience—is a fundamental trait of postmodern culture. Ethnicity and cultural difference have exchanged their intrinsic values for the more extrinsic ones of market interchangeability: gone are the times when people could make a persuasive claim to a culture of their own, a set of meaningful practices that might be considered the product of unique thought or lifestyle. The new sense of time and space generated by telecommunications—in the substitution of continuity and distance with instantaneousness and ubiquity—has transformed the perception of things so that they are no longer lived directly but through their representations. Experience is mainly available through signs: things are not lived directly but rather through the agency of a medium, in the consumption of images and objects that replace what they stand for. Such rootlessness accounts for the high volatility and ultimate transferability of culture in postmodern times.

The imaginary participation that occurs in vicarious experience is often despised for its lack of pertinence to what is tacitly agreed upon as reality, for example in the generalized notion that mass entertainment is dumbfounding. Ironically enough, vicariousness is similar to the classic understanding of aesthetic enjoyment, which is founded on a symbolically distanced relationship to phenomena. This symbolic connection, which used to protect the exclusivity of aesthetic experience by basing it on the prerequisites of trained sensibility and knowledge, has given way to the more ordinary and accessible passageway provided by popular culture. Therefore, it is not against living others' experiences—or living like another—that high-culture criticisms are directed, but rather against the popular level where this vicariousness is acted out and the repercussions it has on other cultural projects. Vicariousness is acceptable so long as it involves a high-level

project (stimulating the intellect) but unacceptable when limited to the sensory (stimulating the senses).

The acceptance of vicariousness enables an understanding of how, as the result of a
long cultural process, simulation has come to occupy the place of a traditional, indexical
referentiality. For this process is not, as many would have it, the sole responsibility of
progressively sophisticated media and market devices, but is rather the radicalization of
the ways in which culture has always mediated our experience. The difference in postmodernity is both quantitative and qualitative, since it lies in the extent to which experience is lived vicariously as well as in the centrality of emotion to contemporary vicariousness. The "waning of affect" in contemporary culture that I discussed in the prologue
is intrinsically related to a distance from immediate experience caused in part by the
current emphasis on signs.[7] Attempting to compensate for emotional detachment, this
sensibility continually searches for intense thrills and for the acute emotionality attributed
to other times and peoples. The homogenization of signs and the wide circulation of
marketable goods make all cultures susceptible to this appropriation, and the more imbued with emotional intensity they are perceived to be, the better. It is in this appeal to
emotion that religious imagery and kitsch converge. The connection proves particularly
relevant because kitsch permits the articulation of the polemics of high and low culture
in a context broader than that of religious imagery, smoothing the way for a better
understanding of its attraction and importance for vicarious experience.

Known as the domain of "bad taste," kitsch stands for artistic endeavor gone sour as
well as for anything that is considered too obvious, dramatic, repetitive, artificial, or
exaggerated. The link between religious imagery and kitsch is based on the dramatic
character of their styles, whose function is to evoke unambiguously, dispelling ambivalence and abstraction. After all, besides providing a meaningful frame for existence and
allocating emotions and feelings, Catholicism facilitates through its imagery the materi-
alization of one of the most ungraspable of all experiences, that of the transcendence of
spiritual attributes. Because of the spiritual nature of religious faith, however, iconolatry
(the worship of images or icons) is often seen as sacrilegious, as the vulgarization of an
experience that should remain fundamentally immaterial and ascetic. In this sense, not
only Catholic iconography but the whole of Christian theology has been accused of
lacking in substance, and therefore of being irredeemably kitsch.[8] Like kitsch, religious
imagery is a mise-en-scène, a visual glossolalia that embodies otherwise impalpable qualities: mystic fervor is translated into upturned eyes, a gaping mouth, and levitation;
goodness always feeds white sheep; virginity is surrounded by auras, clouds, and smiling
cherubim; passion is a bleeding heart; and evil is snakes, horns, and flames. In kitsch, this
dramatic quality is intensified by an overtly sentimental, melodramatic tone and by
primary colors and bright, glossy surfaces.

The crossing over between the spheres of the celestial and kitsch is truly concordant.
Religious imagery is considered kitsch because of its desacralization, while kitsch is called
evil and the "anti-Christ in art"[9] because of its artistic profanities. Kitsch steals motifs and
materials at random, regardless of the original ascription of the sources. It takes from
classic, modernist, and popular art and mixes all together, becoming in this way the first
and foremost recycler. This irreverent eclecticism has brought both glory and doom upon
kitsch, for its unbridled voraciousness transgresses boundaries and undermines hierar-

chies. Religious kitsch is then doubly irreverent, displaying an impious over-determination that accounts, perhaps, for its secular seduction.

Kitsch is one of the constitutive phenomena of postmodernism. The qualities attributed so far to kitsch—eclectic cannibalism, recycling, rejoicing in surface or allegorical values—are those that distinguish contemporary sensibility from the previous belief in authenticity, originality, and symbolic depth.[10] Furthermore, the postmodern broadening of the notion of reality, whereby vicariousness is no longer felt as false or secondhand but rather as an autonomous, however incredible, dimension of the real, facilitates the current circulation and revalorization of this aesthetics. Likewise, in its chaotic juxtaposition of images and times, contemporary urban culture is comparable to an altarlike reality, where the logic of organization is anything but homogeneous, visual saturation is obligatory, and the personal is lived as a pastiche of fragmented images from popular culture.

## Fourteenth Street and First-Degree Kitsch

One of the most conspicuous features of postmodernity is its ability to entertain conflicting discourses simultaneously. Rather than erasing previous practices, it enables and even seeks their subsistence. This peculiar coexistence of divergent visions is made possible by the space left in the vertical displacement of depth by surface, which implies a gathering on the horizontal level. Fragmentary but ubiquitous, discontinuous and instantaneous, this new altarlike reality is the arena for a Byzantine struggle in which different iconographies fight for hegemony. In this manner, cultural specificity has given way to the internationalization of its signs, losing uniqueness and gaining exposure and circulation. Within this context, it is possible to distinguish, according to their means of production and cultural function, three degrees of kitsch that have recently come to overlap in time and space.

In what I will call first-degree kitsch, representation is based on an indexical referent. Here, the difference between reality and representation is explicit and hierarchical, since only what is perceived as reality matters. Acting as a mere substitute, the kitsch object has no validity in and of itself.[11] This is the case of the imagery available at church entrances and botanicas, sold for its straightforward iconic value. Statuettes, images, and scapularies embody the spirits they represent, making them palpable. Consequently, this imagery belongs in sacred places, such as home altars, and must be treated with utmost respect. In first-degree kitsch, the relationship between object and user is immediate, one of genuine belief. Technically, its production is simple and cheap, a serial artisanship devoid of that perfectly finished look attained with a more sophisticated technology.[12] In fact, these objects exhibit a certain rawness that is, or appears to be, handmade. This quality reflects their "honesty," as lack of sophistication is usually taken for authenticity. On the other hand, this rawness adds to first-degree kitsch's status as "low" art, when it is considered art at all: usually, if not marginalized as folklore, it is condemned as gaudy.[13]

Almost a century old, first-degree kitsch is what is usually referred to in discussions of kitsch. It is not, however, inherently kitsch. It is understood as such from a more distanced look, one that does not enjoy the same emotional attachment that believers have to these objects. For them, kitsch objects are meaningful, even when they are used ornamentally. Yet for those who have the distanced look, whom I will call kitsch aficionados,[14] it is precisely this unintentionality that is attractive, since it speaks of a naive immediacy of feeling that they have lost. Aficionados' nostalgia leads them to a vicarious pleasure that gratifies their desire for immediacy. They achieve this pleasure by collecting kitsch objects and even admiring their inherent qualities: bright colors, glossy surfaces, and figuration. By elaborating a scenario for their vicarious pleasure, kitsch aficionados paradoxically reproduce the practice of believers, since this scenario is meant to provide an otherwise unattainable experience, that of immediate feeling for the aficionados and of reverence for the believers. Aficionados' sensibility cannot be dismissed as secondary or intellectual because their attachment to these objects is as strong and vital as that of first-degree believers. Yet what is relevant here is that first-degree believers' attachment is directly related to the devotional meaning of the iconography, while for aficionados, this meaning is secondary: what matters is not what the images represent, but the intense feelings—hope, fear, awe—that they inspire. Aficionados' connection is to these emotions, their appreciation one step removed from first-degree kitsch.

The different relationships to first-degree kitsch may be illustrated by a Fourteenth Street fad of the past few years, the Christ clocks. Rectangular or circular, these clocks narrate various moments of Christ's life in three dimensions. We see Christ gently blessing a blond girl while a few small, fluffy white sheep watch reverently, Christ bleeding on the cross or delivering the Sermon on the Mount, or all of these scenes together in the special "quarter-hour" versions, where, in the narrative logic of the Stations of the Cross, each quarter hour has its own episode. True to Fourteenth Street and home-altar aesthetics, Christ clocks eschew the boredom of bareness, naturalness, and discretion and exploit the prurience of loudness, dramatics, and sentimentality. The profusion of these clocks bears witness to their popularity. Selling for about twelve to fourteen dollars, they have become a dominant part of the Fourteenth Street scene.

For most Christ-clock shoppers there is no contradiction in using Christ's life as a backdrop for time. In kitchens or living rooms, these clocks are used as extensions of the home altar, conveying a comfortable familiarity with a figure that represents cherished values. This relationship to Christ is loving and quotidian, totally ordinary. For kitsch aficionados, however, these clocks are a source of endless amazement and wonder. Lacking a religious attachment to them, aficionados are fascinated by the directness of the feelings these clocks represent and evoke: there is something definitely moving about Christ's sorrow as—on his knees on Mount Olive, hands dramatically clasped—he implores his Father's compassion for the sinful human race. For an aficionado it is the intensity of this drama—heightened by an artificial aura created by the picture's lack of depth and bright colors—that is attractive. This aesthetic experience is radically different from the highly conceptualized one of modern art.

## Little Rickie and Second-Degree Kitsch

First-degree kitsch familiarizes the ungraspable—eternity, goodness, evil—while tacitly maintaining a hierarchical distinction between reality and representation. The opposite is true of second-degree kitsch, or neo-kitsch,[15] which collapses this difference by making representation into the only possible referent. In so doing, it defamiliarizes our notion of reality because representation itself becomes the real. Neo-kitsch is inspired by first-degree kitsch and is therefore second-generation. Sold as kitsch, it lacks the devotional relation present in first-degree kitsch. Its absence of feeling leaves us with an empty icon, or rather an icon whose value lies precisely in its iconicity, its quality as a sign rather than as an object. This kitsch is self-referential—a sort of kitsch-kitsch—and has lost all the innocence and charm of the first-degree experience.

Whereas first-degree kitsch is sold in variety stores, among articles of domestic use, second-degree kitsch is found in more specialized shops, like those that sell souvenirs. Among the most interesting is New York's Little Rickie, where in the midst of all types of memorabilia, religious imagery reigns. In its dizzying clutteredness, Little Rickie is a sophisticated microcosm of Fourteenth Street and home-altar aesthetics. As such, it succeeds in creating a total disorientation that engulfs the viewer inside the store. But although it offers all the religious kitsch one could ever hope to find, the catch for aficionados lies in the given or prefabricated quality of the objects. Take for instance the holy water bottles, transparent plastic bottles in the shape of the Virgin Mary. These bottles stand obliquely to the original iconography—which does not include them—and rely exclusively on concept for their existence. Lacking in visual and signifying exuberance, they profit from the religious imagery fad and from the idea of a bottle for holy water being funny. Never having established a first degree of affection, these bottles are devoid of the intensity aficionados seek. They are simply toys, curiosities bought to show or give to somebody else. Second-degree kitsch exists only for transaction, to pass from hand to hand, and in this lack of possessing subject lies its ultimate alienation and perishability.

Neo-kitsch is intentional, and it capitalizes on an acquired taste for tackiness. It is a popularization of the camp sensibility, a perspective wherein appreciation of the "ugly"

Roadside market selling fruit and portraits of Malcolm X and Jesus in Rockaway, New York. © 1992 Kirk Condyles/Impact Visuals.

conveys to the spectator an aura of refined decadence, an ironic enjoyment from a position of enlightened superiority.[16] This attitude allows a safe release into sentimentality. Neo-kitsch's exchange value is intensified by the interchangeability of religious imagery with the rest of the memorabilia in the store. For consumers of second-degree kitsch, the choice between, say, a sample of holy soil and a plastic eye with two feet that winks as it walks around is totally arbitrary, decided only by last-minute caprice or a vague idea of which would be more hilarious. For "authentic" aficionados half the pleasure of acquisition is lost when kitsch is a given and not a discovery. As for first-degree believers, they are not among the store's buyers, although the store is located in the East Village, which is home to a substantial Latino community.

Mass marketed, these products involve a more elaborate technology and often come from mass-culture production centers like Hong Kong. First-degree homeyness is replaced by the mechanical look of serial reproduction. Designed as a commodity for exchange and commerce, second-degree kitsch has no trace of use value, no longer being "the real thing" for connoisseurs. The passing over of kitsch to mass culture is similar to the desacralization of high art occasioned by mechanical reproduction.[17] In both cases the loss of authenticity is based on the shift from manufactured or low-technology production to a more sophisticated industrial one, with its consequent displacement of a referent for a copy. To consider second-degree kitsch less authentic than first-degree kitsch because of its predigested character would be contradictory, since kitsch is by definition predigested. The difference lies in how intentional, or self-conscious, this predigestion is.

The mass marketing of religious imagery as kitsch is only possible once the icon has been stripped of its signifying value. The religious kitsch that was available before the 1980s was first-degree kitsch, albeit mechanically reproduced. The change to a fad, something fun to play with, is a recent phenomenon. What matters now is iconicity itself; worth is measured by the icon's traits—the formal, technical aspects like narrative, color, and texture. Void, except in a nostalgic way, of the systemic meaning granted by religious belief, these traits are easily isolated and fragmented, becoming totally interchangeable and metonymical. As floating signs, they can adhere to any object and convey onto it their full value, "kitschifying" it. This lack of specificity accounts for neo-kitsch objects' suitability for random consumption.

# Third-Degree Kitsch and the Advantages of Recycling

Religious imagery reached its highest level of commodification when it lost specificity to market interchangeability. It has gained a new social place, however, thanks to a simultaneous and related process: the legitimization of its signifying and visual attributes by the institutionally authorized agency of artists. This revaluation takes place through the multifarious recycling of Catholic religious iconography, constituting what I will distinguish as third-degree kitsch. Here, the iconography is invested with either a new or a foreign set of meanings, generating a hybrid product. This phenomenon is the outcome of the blending between Latin and North American cultures and includes both Chicano and Nuyorican artists' recovery of their heritage as well as white American artists working with the elements of this tradition.

Since individual *altares* represent personal histories of memories and wishes, the

*Angel of the Asphalt,* calendar graphic circa 1954. © 1993. Ken Brown Cards.

tradition of home altars as a whole can be taken to represent collective remembrance and desire. In varying degrees of nostalgia and transformation, several Chicano and Nuyorican artists are using the *altares* format to reaffirm a precarious sense of belonging. Second-generation altar making is complicated by the currency of its iconography: in more ways than one, the fashionable home altars' aesthetic benefits from such timely recirculation. Yet any consideration of these artists as the authentic bearers of the *altares* tradition assures Chicano and Nuyorican artists' marginality by stating that they are the most suited to carry on with their forebears' work, since cultural continuity conveniently eliminates them from participating in other creative endeavors. Chicano and Nuyorican home altar recycling, therefore, is treading a very fine line between reelaborating a tradition whose exclusive rights are questionable and being artistically identified solely with that task.

Some of the edge can be taken off this discussion by acknowledging the differences between this kind of artistic recovery and first degree home-altar elaboration. As a recent exhibition title suggests, the recasting of *altares* is often meant as a "ceremony of memory" that invests them with a new political signification and awareness. This artistic legitimization implies formalizing home altars to fit into a system of meaning where they represent the culture that once was; they are changed, once again, from referents to signs. This loss of innocence, however, allows *altares* to be reelaborated into new sets of meanings, many of which were inconceivable to the original bearers of this tradition but are certainly fundamental to more recent Chicano and Nuyorican generations.[18]

One such example of home-altar recyling may be found in Amalia Mesa-Bains's work, which is both a recovery of and a challenge to her family tradition and cultural identity. Mesa-Bains is a Chicana who began making *altares* after earning several college degrees. Her revival of this tradition is therefore not spontaneous but calculated, impelled by a conscious gesture of political reaffirmation of Chicano cultural values. One of her recent shows, Grotto of the Virgin, consisted of *altares* raised to such unhallowed figures as Mexican painter Frida Kahlo, Mexican superstar Dolores del Rio, and her own grand-mother. What is specific to Mesa-Bains's altars is that the personal is not subordinated to a particular holy person. Rather, a secular person is made sacred by the altar format, the offerings consisting mainly of a reconstruction of that person's imagined life by means of images and gadgets. The Dolores del Rio altar, for example, is raised on several steps made with mirrors, bringing to mind the image cults that grow up around Hollywood actors and actresses. This altar is stacked with feminine paraphernalia such as perfume bottles, lipstick, and jewelry, as well as letters, pictures, and other souvenirs of her life. In this way, the image of Dolores del Rio as a "cinema goddess" becomes literal.

This secularization of the *altares* is probably due to the importance Mesa-Bains assigns to personal experience. In traditional altar raising, the personal was always secondary to the deity, and religious sensibility articulated in the last instance the whole altar. By privileging what were only coding elements so that they become the main objective of her *altares*, Mesa-Bains has inverted the traditional formula. As a result, women and mass culture are invested with a new power that emanates from the sacredness of *altares*: in postmodern culture, Mesa-Bains's work would seem to contend, old patriarchal deities are no longer satisfactory. What she has done is to profit from an established tradition to convey new values. Beyond mere formal changes, her *altares* replace the transcendental with the political. In them, the affirmation of feminist and Chicano experiences is more relevant than a pious communication with the celestial sphere. Such a secularization of home altars is evidence of their adaptability as well as their visual versatility.[19]

Chicano and Nuyorican artists are not alone in exploring home-altar aesthetics. Boston photographer Dana Salvo has exalted the tradition of Mexican home altars by uprooting them from their private context and presenting them as sites both of unorthodox beauty and of firsthand religious experience. Salvo transforms *altares* into objects of aesthetic contemplation: in elegant cibachrome prints, the colors, textures, and arrangements of *altares* stand out in all their splendor. For Salvo, an artist who has also focused on the recovery of lost or ruined textures (some of his other work consists of uncovering the debris and capturing the layers of time and decay in ruined mansions), the seduction of home altars is primarily visual. The absence of some contextualization to help decode home altars underlines their value as objects as well as their ultimate otherness: they represent a reality that speaks a different language. Still, even if the appreciation of *altares* is limited to an aesthetic discovery of their iconic attributes, this remains a relevant connection to a hitherto ignored cultural manifestation. Furthermore, the participatory process in which Salvo and the creators of the altars engaged when they rearranged the *altares* for the photos speaks for the reciprocal benefits of active cultural exchange.[20]

Finally, religious iconography is used as a format for modern experience in the work of Audrey Flack, who explores her own feelings through images of the Virgin Mary. For more than a decade, Flack has drawn from the Spanish Marian cult as a source of inspiration. Her choice of imagery is based on an identification with what she feels are analogous experiences of motherhood. Flack overdramatizes her Virgins, making them hyperreal by accentuating color, giving the paintings a glossy quality, and even adding glittery tears. It is this overdramatization that, together with the baroqueness of the imagery, makes her work "popular kitsch," a kitsch that takes itself seriously and is sentimental and Romantic. Flack distinguishes this kitsch from "art world kitsch," which in her opinion covers sentiment with humor. Emotional idenfication is the basis for her claim to a more valid relationship to religious imagery than that of other artists.[21] Flack's emotional affinity with the Virgins notwithstanding, her use of them is mainly functional and isolated from the Marian tradition as a whole. A syncretist, she takes elements from any religion that suits her needs, in an interchangeability that renders the specificity of religious traditions secondary.

Third-degree religious kitsch consists in a revalorization of Catholic iconography and the accentuation of those traits that make its aesthetics unique: figurativeness, dramatization, eclecticism, visual saturation—all those attributes for which kitsch was banned from the realm of art. In providing an aesthetic experience that transcends the object, kitsch is finally legitimized as art, an issue that has been of more concern to art critics than to kitsch artists. Consequently, it has been argued that the recirculation of kitsch is but a co-optation by the late avant-garde, a formal gesture of usurpation coming from its desperate attempt to remain alive.[22] There is little difference between the use of kitsch as a motif by the market and by avant-garde art, since the value of the icon lies for both in its exotic otherness, its ornamental ability to cover the empty landscape of postindustrial reality with a universe of images. Such pilfering of religious imagery is limited to reproduction, displacing and subordinating its social function but not altering the material in any significant way.

But what is happening in the third-degree revaluation of kitsch is more than the avant-garde's swan song. It is the collapse of the hierarchical distinction between the avant-garde and kitsch—and, by extension, between high and popular art—a collapsing of what modernity considered a polar opposition. According to this view, sustained principally by Clement Greenberg, the avant-garde revolution transferred the value of art from its sacred function (providing access to religious transcendence) to its innovative capabilities (leading to a newly discovered future via experimentation and disruption). Since kitsch is based on imitation and copy, countering novelty with fakeness and artificiality, it was consequently understood as the opposite of the avant-garde and considered reactionary and unartistic.[23]

The current crisis of representation, however, implies not only disillusionment with progress, originality, and formal experimentation but also a reconsideration of all they excluded. It follows that copy, simulation, and quotation are raised to a new level of interest, representing a different experience of art and creativity. In postmodern culture, artifice, rather than commenting on reality, has become the most immediately accessible reality. Fakery and simulation were present in modernism as aesthetic means. They had a function, as in the reproduction of consumer society's alienation in Andy Warhol's work. In postmodernity, there is no space for such distances: fake and simulation are no longer distinguishable from quotidian life. The boundaries between reality and representation, themselves artificial, have been temporarily and perhaps permanently suspended.

Moreover, these boundaries are questioned not only by third-degree kitsch, but also by the current recirculation of kitsch. Anticipating this postmodern taste, Walter Benjamin wrote in a brief essay that kitsch is what remains after the world of things is extinct.

*Macarena of Miracles* by Audrey Flack (oil on canvas). The Metropolitan Museum of Art, Gift of Paul F. Walter, 1979.

Comparing it to a layer of dust that covers things and allows for a nostalgic recreation of reality, Benjamin believes kitsch—the banal—to be more accurate than immediate perception (thus favoring intertextuality over indexicality). For him, immediacy is just a notion of reality, and only the distance left by the loss of this immediacy permits a true apprehension of things. Therefore, he trusts dreams, rhythm, poetry, and distraction. Because of its repetitiveness—worn by habit and decorated by cheap sensory statements—kitsch is most suitable for this nostalgic resurrection, making for an easier and more pleasurable perception.[24] In discussing the Iconoclastes and their fury against the power of religious images, Baudrillard ascribes to simulacra a similar nostalgic function. Yet in his characteristic neutralization of signs, Baudrillard fails to assign them any discursive power.[25] Such empowerment is precisely the issue at stake in third-degree kitsch.

Besides imploding the boundaries of art and reality, the third degree carries out an active transformation of kitsch. Taking religious imagery both for its kitsch value and its signifying and iconic strength, it absorbs the icon in full and recycles it into new meanings. These meanings are related to personal spiritual experiences, recalling users' relationships to first-degree imagery, except that the first-degree images are part of a given cultural heritage and as such they are readily available and their usage is automatic. Third-degree kitsch, on the other hand, appropriates this tradition from "outside," searching for an imagery that will be adequate to its expressive needs. Its cannibalization of imagery, however, stands in sharp contrast to previous appropriations. In the early avant-garde, for instance in Picasso's use of African masks, the break with Western imagery had a symbolic function. Similarly, in surrealism and the release of the unconscious, exploring difference meant disrupting a cultural heritage perceived as limited and oppressive. Venerated for its ability to offer an experience in otherness, difference stood as the necessary counterpart of Western culture. Its function was to illuminate. Yet this assigned purposefulness tamed the perception of those cultures, ultimately erasing difference from the Western imaginary landscape.

In the work of the artists mentioned earlier, Catholic religious imagery provides access to a variety of intense emotions that seem otherwise culturally unattainable. In Salvo's photography the pleasure seems to come from the intimacy of the home altars, where family history is revered in a colorful clutter of figures and personal objects. This affectionate and ingenuous assortment stands in contrast to the photographic gaze through which it is perceived. For their viewers, the beauty of *altares* lies in their direct connection to reality, a connection that succeeds in stirring the capacity for amazement. A similar pleasure is found in Flack's virgins, whose melodramatic intensity becomes almost sublime, following the tradition of Catholic hagiography. Meanwhile, Mesa-Bains and other Chicano and Nuyorican artists are moving toward a radical transformation of tradition by imposing their own will on the material they work with, as in Mesa-Bains's use of altares to sanctify contemporary femininity.

This colonization of religious imagery, in which it is occupied by alien feelings and intentions, can be said to work in both directions. After all, the exotic, colonized imagery has now become part and parcel of the appropriator's imagination—it is part of the cannibal's system. Instead of appropriation annihilating what it absorbs, the absorbed invades the appropriating system and begins to constitute and transform it. The unsettling qualities of such cross-cultural integration are underscored by kitsch's syncretic tradition of mixture and pastiche. Since kitsch can readily exist in a state of upheaval and transformation, there is no eventual settlement of the absorbed. In the past, this reverse colonization has been minimized by adverse historical conditions. Yet the vast Latin American immigration to cosmopolitan urban centers in the past few decades is forcing a redefinition of traditional cultural boundaries, one that both shapes and is shaped by the circulation of images. If at one time exotic images were domesticated, they now seem to have lost their tameness to a newly found space: the one left by the exit of traditional referentiality. It isn't surprising then that third-degree kitsch in the United States is coming mainly from the East and West Coasts, since it is in these places that a new culture, deeply affected by Latinos, is being formed.

Religious imagery in third-degree kitsch surpasses the distance implied in second-degree kitsch. Instead of consuming arbitrarily, it constitutes a new sensibility whose main characteristic is the displacement of exchange by use. The consumption of images has been qualitatively altered: images are not chosen at random; they must convey a particular feeling, they must simulate emotion. Third-degree kitsch is the result of that search. Whether its potential destabilization will have a concrete social result before it is annihilated by a systematic assimilation that hurries to institutionalize it—making it into second-degree kitsch, for example—is debatable. Still, it is not a question of this assimilation seeping down into the depths of culture and carrying out some radical change there. After all, American culture is basically one of images, so that changes effected at the level of imagery cannot be underestimated. Since commodification is one of the main modes of integration in the United States, it can certainly be used as a vehicle of symbolic intervention. Third-degree kitsch therefore may be considered a meeting point between different cultures. It is where the iconography of a culture, instead of ceasing to exist, is transformed by absorbing new elements. Rather than of active or passive cultures, one can now speak of mutual appropriation. Even if an iconography is stolen it remains active, and the artists' work discussed here illustrates how this iconography can occupy the appropriator's imagination by providing a simulation of experiences the native culture has become unable to produce.

It can be said that each degree of religious imagery satisfies the desire for intensity in a different way: in the first degree through an osmotic process resulting from the collection and possession of objects still infused with use value; in the second degree by the consumption of commodified nostalgia; and in the third degree by cannibalizing both the first and second degrees and recycling them into a hybrid product that allows for a simulation of the lost experience. Even though they're produced at different moments, these three degrees cohabit the same contemporary space. Their synchronicity accentuates the erasure of cultural boundaries already present in third-degree kitsch, throwing together and mixing different types of production and perception. This reflects the situation of the urban cosmopolis, where myriad cultures live side by side, producing the postmodern pastiche. Such an anarchic condition destabilizes traditional hegemony, forcing it to negotiate with those cultural discourses it once could oppress. The ability of cultural imagery to travel and adapt itself to new requirements and desires can no longer be mourned as a loss of cultural specificity in the name of exhausted notions of personal or collective identities. Instead, it must be welcomed as a sign of opening to and enjoyment of all that traditional culture worked so hard at leaving out.

# Reading Questions

1. Why, according to Olalquiaga, are traditional Latin American home altars coded in ways that are "unreadable to foreign eyes"?
2. What are some of the characteristics of postmodern urban culture that Olalquiaga describes in her discussion of the urban appropriation of the *altares* tradition?
3. Why, in postmodern times, is vicariousness compatible with emotional intensity?
4. What seems to be Olalquiaga's attitude toward third-degree religious kitsch? Why does she seem to praise certain artists such as Mesa-Bains, Dana Salvo, and Audrey Flack, who are producing third-degree kitsch?
5. Why does Olalquiaga claim that second- and third-degree kitsch is not synonymous with avant-garde art?
6. Is Olalquiaga against the fakes and simulations that seem to be part of American everyday life? Are you familiar with other types of religious kitsch than Catholic kitsch?

# Recommended Reading

Jean Baudrillard, *Simulations* (New York: Semiotext(e), 1983)

Walter Benjamin, "The Work of Art in the Age of Mechanical Reproduction," *Illuminations*, trans. H. Zoln (London: Jonathan Cape, 1970)

Matei Calinescu, "Kitsch," *Five Faces of Modernity* (Durham, NC: Duke University Press, 1987)

Umberto Eco, *Travels in Hyperreality*, trans. William Weaver (San Diego: Harcourt Brace Jovanovitch, 1976)

Frederic Jameson, "Postmodernism, or the Cultural Logic of Late Capitalism," *New Left Review* 146 (July–August 1984)

Jean Francois Lyotard, "*Domus* and the Megalopolis," *The Inhuman: Reflections on Time*, trans. Geoffrey Bennington and Rachel Bowlby (Stanford: Stanford University Press, 1991)

For representative selections from Lyotard, Jameson, Baudrillard, Derrida, hooks, West, et al., see Joseph Natoli and Linda Hutcheon, eds., *A Postmodern Reader* (Albany: State University of New York Press, 1993)

# Recommended Audiovisual Resources

"La Isla Bonita," *The Madonna Collection*. Madonna's use of the *altares* imagery, staged in the Lower East Side of Manhattan.

*Silence=Death*. 1989. Directed by Rosa von Praunheim. David Wojnarowicz, accompanied by Diamanda Galas, who sings "This is the Law of the Plaque" from her album *The Divine Punishment*, parodies Madonna's use of the *altares* imagery, in a scathing critique of the Church's stance toward HIV/AIDS education in the epidemic. Suddeutscher Rundfunk Stuttgart.

*A Very Old Man with Enormous Wings*. 1988. Directed by Fernando Birri. Powerfully parodic adaptation of the short story by Gabriel Marquez, full of religious imagery from Latin American traditions, showing the commercialization and exploitation of Latin American religious devotion.

## CHAPTER 4

# Technologies of the Self

*Vote for Yourself* by Matuschka. 1991. © Matuschka.

# How to Tame a Wild Tongue

## GLORIA ANZALDÚA

Gloria Anzaldúa is the author of *Borderlands/La Frontera* and editor of *Making Face, Making Soul*. In her coedited anthology, *This Bridge Called My Back: Writings by Radical Women of Color,* she describes herself as a "Tejana Chicano poet" who teaches "in her spare time."

"We're going to have to control your tongue," the dentist says, pulling out all the metal from my mouth. Silver bits plop and tinkle into the basin. My mouth is a motherlode.

The dentist is cleaning out my roots. I get a whiff of the stench when I gasp. "I can't cap that tooth yet, you're still draining," he says.

"We're going to have to do something about your tongue," I hear the anger rising in his voice. My tongue keeps pushing out the wads of cotton, pushing back the drills, the long thin needles. "I've never seen anything as strong or as stubborn," he says. And I think, how do you tame a wild tongue, train it to be quiet, how do you bridle and saddle it? How do you make it lie down?

"Who is to say that robbing a people of its language is less violent than war?"

—Ray Gwyn Smith[1]

I remember being caught speaking Spanish at recess—that was good for three licks on the knuckles with a sharp ruler. I remember being sent to the corner of the classroom for "talking back" to the Anglo teacher when all I was trying to do was tell her how to pronounce my name. "If you want to be American, speak 'American.' If you don't like it, go back to Mexico where you belong."

"I want you to speak English. *Pa'hallar buen trabajo tienes que saber hablar el inglés bien. Qué vale toda tu educación si todavía hablas inglés con un* 'accent,' " my mother would say, mortified that I spoke English like a Mexican. At Pan American University, I, and all Chicano students were required to take two speech classes. Their purpose: to get rid of our accents.

Attacks on one's form of expression with the intent to censor are a violation of the First Amendment. *El Anglo con cara de inocente nos arrancó la lengua.* Wild tongues can't be tamed, they can only be cut out.

## Overcoming the Tradition of Silence

> *Ahogadas, escupimos el oscuro.*
> *Peleando con nuestra propia sombra*
> *el silencio nos sepulta.*

*En boca cerrada no entran moscas.* "Flies don't enter a closed mouth" is a saying I kept hearing when I was a child. *Ser habladora* was to be a gossip and a liar, to talk too much. *Muchachitas bien criadas,* well-bred girls don't answer back. *Es una falta de respeto* to talk back to one's mother or father. I remember one of the sins I'd recite to the priest in the

*semos*, *truje*, *haiga*, *ansina*, and *naiden*. We retain the "archaic" *j*, as in *jalar*, that derives from an earlier *h*, (the French *halar* or the Germanic *halon* which was lost to standard Spanish in the 16th century), but which is still found in several regional dialects such as the one spoken in South Texas. (Due to geography, Chicanos from the Valley of South Texas were cut off linguistically from other Spanish speakers. We tend to use words that the Spaniards brought over from Medieval Spain. The majority of the Spanish colonizers in Mexico and the Southwest came from Extremadura—Hernán Cortés was one of them—and Andalucía. Andalucians pronounce *ll* like a *y*, and their *d*'s tend to be absorbed by adjacent vowels: *tirado* becomes *tirao*. They brought *el lenguaje popular, dialectos y regionalismos*.[4])

Chicanos and other Spanish speakers also shift *ll* to *y* and *z* to *s*.[5] We leave out initial syllables, saying *tar* for *estar*, *toy* for *estoy*, *hora* for *ahora* (*cubanos* and *puertorriqueños* also leave out initial letters of some words.) We also leave out the final syllable such as *pa* for *para*. The intervocalic *y*, the *ll* as in *tortilla*, *ella*, *botella*, gets replaced by *tortia* or *tortiya*, *ea*, *botea*. We add an additional syllable at the beginning of certain words: *atocar* for *tocar*, *agastar* for *gastar*. Sometimes we'll say *lavaste las vacijas*, other times *lavates* (substituting the *ates* verb endings for the *aste*).

We use anglicisms, words borrowed from English: *bola* from ball, *carpeta* from carpet, *máchina de lavar* (instead of *lavadora*) from washing machine. Tex-Mex argot, created by adding a Spanish sound at the beginning or end of an English word such as *cookiar* for cook, *watchar* for watch, *parkiar* for park, and *rapiar* for rape, is the result of the pressures on Spanish speakers to adapt to English.

We don't use the word *vosotros/as* or its accompanying verb form. We don't say *claro* (to mean yes), *imagínate*, or *me emociona*, unless we picked up Spanish from Latinas, out of a book, or in a classroom. Other Spanish-speaking groups are going through the same, or similar, development in their Spanish.

## Linguistic Terrorism

> *Deslenguadas. Somos los del español deficiente.* We are your linguistic nightmare, your linguistic aberration, your linguistic *mestizaje*, the subject of your *burla*. Because we speak with tongues of fire we are culturally crucified. Racially, culturally and linguistically *somos huérfanos*—we speak an orphan tongue.

Chicanas who grew up speaking Chicano Spanish have internalized the belief that we speak poor Spanish. It is illegitimate, a bastard language. And because we internalize how our language has been used against us by the dominant culture, we use our language differences against each other.

Chicana feminists often skirt around each other with suspicion and hesitation. For the longest time I couldn't figure it out. Then it dawned on me. To be close to another Chicana is like looking into the mirror. We are afraid of what we'll see there. *Pena*. Shame. Low estimation of self. In childhood we are told that our language is wrong. Repeated attacks on our native tongue diminish our sense of self. The attacks continue throughout our lives.

Chicanas feel uncomfortable talking in Spanish to Latinas, afraid of their censure. Their language was not outlawed in their countries. They had a whole lifetime of being immersed in their native tongue; generations, centuries in which Spanish was

a first language, taught in school, heard on radio and TV, and read in the newspaper.

If a person, Chicana or Latina, has a low estimation of my native tongue, she also has
a low estimation of me. Often with *mexicanas y latinas* we'll speak English as a neutral
language. Even among Chicanas we tend to speak English at parties or conferences. Yet,
at the same time, we're afraid the other will think we're *agringadas* because we don't speak
Chicano Spanish. We oppress each other trying to out-Chicano each other, vying to be
the "real" Chicanas, to speak like Chicanos. There is no one Chicano language just as
there is no one Chicano experience. A monolingual Chicana whose first language is
English or Spanish is just as much a Chicana as one who speaks several variants of
Spanish. A Chicana from Michigan or Chicago or Detroit is just as much a Chicana as
one from the Southwest. Chicano Spanish is as diverse linguistically as it is regionally.

By the end of this century, Spanish speakers will comprise the biggest minority group
in the U.S., a country where students in high schools and colleges are encouraged to take
French classes because French is considered more "cultured." But for a language to
remain alive it must be used.[6] By the end of this century English, and not Spanish, will
be the mother tongue of most Chicanos and Latinos.

So, if you want to really hurt me, talk badly about my language. Ethnic identity is twin
skin to linguistic identity—I am my language. Until I can take pride in my language, I
cannot take pride in myself. Until I can accept as legitimate Chicano Texas Spanish,
Tex-Mex and all the other languages I speak, I cannot accept the legitimacy of myself.
Until I am free to write bilingually and to switch codes without having always to translate,
while I still have to speak English or Spanish when I would rather speak Spanglish, and
as long as I have to accommodate the English speakers rather than having them accommodate me, my tongue will be illegitimate.

I will no longer be made to feel ashamed of existing. I will have my voice: Indian,
Spanish, white. I will have my serpent's tongue—my woman's voice, my sexual voice,
my poet's voice. I will overcome the tradition of silence.

> My fingers
>     move sly against your palm
>     Like women everywhere, we speak in code. . . .
>                                              —Melanie Kaye/Kantrowitz[7]

## *"Vistas," corridos, y comida:* My Native Tongue

In the 1960s, I read my first Chicano novel. It was *City of Night* by John Rechy, a gay
Texan, son of a Scottish father and a Mexican mother. For days I walked around in
stunned amazement that a Chicano could write and could get published. When I read *I
Am Joaquín*[8] I was surprised to see a bilingual book by a Chicano in print. When I saw
poetry written in Tex-Mex for the first time, a feeling of pure joy flashed through me. I
felt like we really existed as a people. In 1971, when I started teaching High School
English to Chicano students, I tried to supplement the required texts with works by
Chicanos, only to be reprimanded and forbidden to do so by the principal. He claimed
that I was supposed to teach "American" and English literature. At the risk of being fired,
I swore my students to secrecy and slipped in Chicano short stories, poems, a play. In
graduate school, while working toward a Ph.D., I had to "argue" with one advisor after

the other, semester after semester, before I was allowed to make Chicano literature an area of focus.

Even before I read books by Chicanos or Mexicans, it was the Mexican movies I saw at the drive-in—the Thursday night special of $1.00 a carload—that gave me a sense of belonging. "Vámonos a las vistas," my mother would call out and we'd all—grandmother, brothers, sister and cousins—squeeze into the car. We'd wolf down cheese and bologna white bread sandwiches while watching Pedro Infante in melodramatic tearjerkers like Nosotros los pobres, the first "real" Mexican movie (that was not an imitation of European movies). I remember seeing Cuando los hijos se van and surmising that all Mexican movies played up the love a mother has for her children and what ungrateful sons and daughters suffer when they are not devoted to their mothers. I remember the singing-type "westerns" of Jorge Negrete and Miquel Aceves Mejía. When watching Mexican movies, I felt a sense of homecoming as well as alienation. People who were to amount to something didn't go to Mexican movies, or bailes or tune their radios to bolero, rancherita, and corrido music.

The whole time I was growing up, there was norteño music sometimes called North Mexican border music, or Tex-Mex music, or Chicano music, or cantina (bar) music. I grew up listening to conjuntos, three-or-four-piece bands made up of folk musicians playing guitar, bajo sexto, drums and button accordion, which Chicanos had borrowed from the German immigrants who had come to Central Texas and Mexico to farm and build breweries. In the Rio Grande Valley, Steve Jordan and Little Joe Hernández were popular, and Flaco Jiménez was the accordian king. The rhythms of Tex-Mex music are those of the polka, also adapted from the Germans, who in turn had borrowed the polka from the Czechs and Bohemians.

I remember the hot, sultry evenings when corridos—songs of love and death on the Texas-Mexican borderlands—reverberated out of cheap amplifiers from the local cantinas and wafted in through my bedroom window.

Corridos first became widely used along the South Texas/Mexican border during the early conflict between Chicanos and Anglos. The corridos are usually about Mexican heroes who do valiant deeds against the Anglo oppressors. Pancho Villa's song, "La cucaracha," is the most famous one. Corridos of John F. Kennedy and his death are still very popular in the Valley. Older Chicanos remember Lydia Mendoza, one of the great border corrido singers who was called la Gloria de Tejas. Her "El tango negro," sung during the Great Depression, made her a singer of the people. The everpresent corridos narrated one hundred years of border history, bringing news of events as well as entertaining. These folk musicians and folk songs are our chief cultural mythmakers, and they made our hard lives seem bearable.

I grew up feeling ambivalent about our music. Country-western and rock-and-roll had more status. In the 50s and 60s, for the slightly educated and agringado Chicanos, there existed a sense of shame at being caught listening to our music. Yet I couldn't stop my feet from thumping to the music, could not stop humming the words, nor hide from myself the exhilaration I felt when I heard it.

There are more subtle ways that we internalize identification, especially in the forms of images and emotions. For me food and certain smells are tied to my identity, to my homeland. Woodsmoke curling up to an immense blue sky; woodsmoke perfuming my grandmother's clothes, her skin. The stench of cow manure and the yellow patches on the ground; the crack of a .22 rifle and the reek of cordite. Homemade white cheese sizzling in a pan, melting inside a folded *tortilla*. My sister Hilda's hot, spicy *menudo*, *chile colorado* making it deep red, pieces of *panza* and hominy floating on top. My brother Carito barbequing *fajitas* in the backyard. Even now and 3,000 miles away, I can see my mother spicing the ground beef, pork and venison with *chile*. My mouth salivates at the thought of the hot steaming *tamales* I would be eating if I were home.

## *Si le preguntas a mi mamá, "¿Qué eres?"*

> "Identity is the essential core of who we are as individuals, the conscious experience of the self inside."
>
> —Kaufman[9]

*Nosotros los* Chicanos straddle the borderlands. On one side of us, we are constantly exposed to the Spanish of the Mexicans, on the other side we hear the Anglos' incessant clamoring so that we forget our language. Among ourselves we don't say *nosotros los americanos, o nosotros los españoles, o nosotros los hispanos*. We say *nosotros los mexicanos* (by *mexicanos* we do not mean citizens of Mexico; we do not mean a national identity, but a racial one). We distinguish between *mexicanos del otro lado* and *mexicanos de este lado*. Deep in our hearts we believe that being Mexican has nothing to do with which country one lives in. Being Mexican is a state of soul—not one of mind, not one of citizenship. Neither eagle nor serpent, but both. And like the ocean, neither animal respects borders.

> *Dime con quien andas y te diré quien eres.*
> (Tell me who your friends are and I'll tell you who you are.)
>
> —Mexican saying

*Si le preguntas a mi mamá, "¿Qué eres?"* te dirá, "Soy mexicana." My brothers and sister say the same. I sometimes will answer *"soy mexicana"* and at others will say *"soy Chicana"* o *"soy tejana."* But I identified as *"Raza"* before I ever identified as *"mexicana"* or *"Chicana."*

As a culture, we call ourselves Spanish when referring to ourselves as a linguistic group and when copping out. It is then that we forget our predominant Indian genes. We are 70-80% Indian.[10] We call ourselves Hispanic[11] or Spanish-American or Latin American or Latin when linking ourselves to other Spanish-speaking peoples of the Western hemisphere and when copping out. We call ourselves Mexican-American[12] to signify we are neither Mexican nor American, but more the noun "American" than the adjective "Mexican" (and when copping out).

Chicanos and other people of color suffer economically for not acculturating. This voluntary (yet forced) alienation makes for psychological conflict, a kind of dual identity—we don't identify with the Anglo-American cultural values and we don't totally identify with the Mexican cultural values. We are a synergy of two cultures with various degrees of Mexicanness or Angloness. I have so internalized the borderland conflict that sometimes I feel like one cancels out the other and we are zero, nothing, no one. A veces *no soy nada ni nadie. Pero hasta cuando no lo soy, lo soy.*

When not copping out, when we know we are more than nothing, we call ourselves Mexican, referring to race and ancestry; *mestizo* when affirming both our Indian and Spanish (but we hardly ever own our Black ancestry); Chicano when referring to a politically aware people born and/or raised in the U.S.; *Raza* when referring to Chicanos; *tejanos* when we are Chicanos from Texas.

Chicanos did not know we were a people until 1965 when Ceasar Chavez and the farm workers united and *I Am Joaquín* was published and *La Raza Unida* party was formed in Texas. With that recognition, we became a distinct people. Something momentous happened to the Chicano soul—we became aware of our reality and acquired a name and a language (Chicano Spanish) that reflected that reality. Now that we had a name, some of the fragmented pieces began to fall together—who we were, what we were, how we had evolved. We began to get glimpses of what we might eventually become.

Yet the struggle of identities continues, the struggle of borders is our reality still. One day the inner struggle will cease and a true integration take place. In the meantime, *tenémos que hacer la lucha. ¿Quién está protegiendo los ranchos de mi gente? ¿Quién está tratando de cerrar la fisura entre la india y el blanco en nuestra sangre? El Chicano, si, el Chicano que anda como un ladrón en su propia casa.*

*Los Chicanos,* how patient we seem, how very patient. There is the quiet of the Indian about us. [13] We know how to survive. When other races have given up their tongue, we've kept ours. We know what it is to live under the hammer blow of the dominant *norteam-ericano* culture. But more than we count the blows, we count the days the weeks the years the centuries the eons until the white laws and commerce and customs will rot in the deserts they've created, lie bleached. *Humildes* yet proud, *quietos* yet wild, *nosotros los mexicanos-Chicanos* will walk by the crumbling ashes as we go about our business. Stubborn, persevering, impenetrable as stone, yet possessing a malleability that renders us unbreakable, we, the *mestizas* and *mestizos*, will remain.

# Reading Questions

1. Identify the triple dilemma of cultural marginality faced by Chicana women.
2. Why is Chicano Spanish a language of exclusion *and* inclusion?
3. How does Anzaldúa use the term *linguistic terrorism*? By whom and against whom is it perpetrated in a society, and why?
4. What are some of the issues of dual identity/cultural ambivalence experienced by a member of a cultural minority?
5. Is Anzaldúa's code-mixing of Spanish and English an expression of power or powerlessness?
6. What are the implications of the relationship between linguistic identity and ethnic identity?

# Recommended Reading

Gloria Anzaldúa, *Borderlands/La Frontera: The New Mestiza* (San Francisco: Spinsters/Aunt Lute Book Company, 1987)

Gloria Anzaldúa, ed., *Making Face, Making Soul, Haciendo Caras: Creative and Critical Perspectives by Women of Color* (San Francisco: Aunt Lute Foundation Books, 1990)

Lourdes Arguelles, "Crazy Wisdom: Memories of a Cuban Queer," *Sisters, Sexperts, Queers: Beyond the Lesbian Nation,* ed. Arlene Stein (New York: Plume, 1993)

Lourdes Arguelles and B. Ruby Rich, "Homosexuality, Homophobia, and Revolution: Notes Toward an Understanding of the Cuban Lesbian and Gay Experience," *Hidden from History: Reclaiming the Gay and Lesbian Past,* ed. Martin Duberman et al. (New York: Meridian, 1989)

Cherríe Moraga, "From a Long Line of Vendidas: Chicanas and Feminism," *Loving in the War Years* (Boston: South End Press, 1983)

# The Anguished Politics of Breast Cancer

SUSAN FERRARO

Susan Ferraro is a freelance writer who writes frequently on women's issues. This article appeared in *The New York Times Magazine*, August 15, 1993.

Something happened to Liz LoRusso during radiation treatment for breast cancer. "I asked to be covered," she says, "and this guy, the technician, told me, 'There's no modesty in a hospital; only 80-year-old women get upset over this.' I went home and that statement ate at me all night, *just like a cancer.*"

The next day, once again lying face up on the table, she looked at the technician and said: "Do you remember what you said to me yesterday about modesty? Well, *you* go get your testicles cut off, lose every hair on your body from the top of your head to the tip of your toes, then lie down on this table and have someone draw all over your crotch with a Magic Marker and we'll see how *you* like it."

LoRusso discovered the lump in her breast four years ago. She was 37. The lump turned out to be advanced third-stage cancer. The disease, which traveled to her spine and pelvis, now is "under control." She has started taking tamoxifen, a drug prescribed in an experimental cancer-prevention program—the first of its kind.

"I was never political, never," says LoRusso, a home economics teacher who is on disability leave. She lives in Huntington, L.I., in a pleasant two-story ranch, and chauffeurs her two kids after school, runs errands and frets about dinner and dust. "I was the peacemaker, the people pleaser. I had 16 years of Catholic school. The nuns said 'Jump.' I said, 'How high?'"

Liz LoRusso is less obedient now. She has joined 1 in 9, an advocacy group that takes its name from a commonly quoted statistic on the incidence of breast cancer. These women ask hard questions about environmental factors that may lie behind Long Island's suspected cancer clusters and high breast cancer rate. LoRusso wonders if something in the environment played a part in her disease. She thinks the "establishment" has patronized women and neglected or ignored the facts about breast cancer.

"They said it could be cured, that I had 60 percent chance of no recurrence in five years," LoRusso says. "The truth is I had 60 percent chance of being *alive* in five years." Her voice slides into the supersweet sarcasm that very polite women use when they are very angry. "Don't you just love it? Isn't it just *slightly* misleading to confuse recurrence with *survival?*"

How many angry women does it take to make a revolution? Inspired by AIDS activists in the 1980's, women with breast cancer are turning scores of support groups into a national political advocacy movement. Most of them, like LoRusso, are amateurs at activism, more comfortable speaking up for their children or their families than for themselves. The energy that drives them is anger. They say they've had it with politicians and physicians and scientists who " 'there, there' " them with studies and statistics and treatments that suggest the disease is under control.

On the cover of a pamphlet about radiation therapy from the National Institutes of Health is a drawing of a woman receiving treatment. "She's fully clothed, she's got a blanket; she's even got a pillow." says LoRusso. "The reality is that where you once had a breast now resembles a page out of the Hagstrom road atlas. They put you on a slab, with a sheet. You're exposed. . . . They take Polaroid pictures and anyone can see because there's a TV camera with a monitor outside the room.

"They stroke your hand and say, 'Don't worry, you'll be all right.' I'm angry because I'm a realist."

There are more than 180 advocacy groups, including 1 in 9, united under the National Breast Cancer Coalition, a largely voluntary organization founded in 1991. The activists are demanding more money for research, and getting it. But they want more—a big say in how that money is spent. They are impatient with research that focuses only on early detection and treatment rather than the causes of breast cancer.

"Early detection is not early enough," says Dr. Susan M. Love, director of the U.C.L.A. Breast Center and a co-founder of the coalition. The standard treatment is surgery, radiation and chemotherapy—or as Love describes it, "slash, burn and poison."

The activists may be a health movement first, but theirs is a feminist cause as well: Many believe that breast cancer has been ignored for decades because it is a woman's disease. It may be wishful thinking on their part, but some activists suggest that breast cancer is *the* feminist issue of the 1990's.

"We have to be the voice, the obnoxious voice," Love says. "We can't shut up now."

So far, this obnoxious voice has been extraordinarily successful, surprising the women almost as much as they have surprised lawmakers. In its first year, the coalition secured a $43 million increase in national funds for breast cancer research, an increase of almost 50 percent. The next year, armed with data from a seminar they financed, the women asked for, wheedled, negotiated and won a whopping $300 million more.

They did it in part by mobilizing grass-roots support. The coalition fielded a drive for 175,000 signatures, one name for each woman who would get a diagnosis of breast cancer that year. In October 1992, "Breast Cancer Awareness Month," the coalition delivered not 175,000 but 600,000 signatures to Washington.

And they enlisted the support of a key friend—Senator Tom Harkin, Democrat of Iowa. The result was an ingenious, even startling legislative maneuver that teamed them with the Department of Defense. This is not as crazy as it sounds. The Army has thousands of women in uniform, and in 1992 it budgeted $25 million for screening and diagnosis of breast cancer. When Harkin was unable to transfer funds from the defense budget to the domestic budget, he proposed that the Army's $25 million be increased to $210 million for breast cancer research.

Joanne Howes, the coalition's lobbyist, delights in telling how, when the votes went over the required 51 to pass the measure, senators who had opposed it rushed back to change their vote: "In the 'Year of the Woman,' they didn't dare go back and tell their constituents that they had voted against this successful strategy." The final tally was 87 to 4.

[The] rhetoric, when it comes, is an unapologetic, confident roar of political rage. Especially riveting is Sherry Kohlenberg of Virginia. The mother of a 4-year-old boy, Kohlenberg, 37, is a small figure in black—pale but fierce. Her straw hat wobbles on her head because chemotherapy has made her hair fall out.

"This year 46,000 women will die of breast cancer," she says. "I will probably be among these statistics. I will leave behind my husband and partner of 18 years, a motherless child, a devastated family and too many friends. I will not get to watch my son grow up, or grow old with my husband. And the worst part is that I am not alone. This family tragedy happens every time a new diagnosis is made, and every time a woman's life is stolen by breast cancer."

There is backlash, she says, when women speak out, but she doesn't care. "I will not go silently," Kohlenberg roars. "I will go shouting into that dark night; enough is enough."

On the sidelines, Kohlenberg's close friend, Kendra McCarthy, wipes away tears. "She's dying, and she knows it," McCarthy says. Angrily jabbing a finger toward the Capitol, visible over the trees, she adds: "We've gotten in those people's faces, and we're going to stay there."

If they see themselves as combatants in a life-or-death battle, breast cancer activists make an odd sort of army. They wear buttons and hats and T-shirts emblazoned with slogans: "Draw the Line at 1 in 9," "Silent No More!" and "The Wife You Save May Be Your Own."

Yet whatever their strength in numbers, they are scared individually, vulnerable. Worried that she might seem too critical of the medical personnel on whom she continues to rely, Liz LoRusso insists that although one radiation technician was insensitive, "The other technician was wonderful, a real source of inspiration; we prayed together."

They are achingly aware of their casualties, their walking wounded and the odds. On the way to the rally, Susan B. Kaplan, the treasurer of 1 in 9 and a patient with recurring breast cancer, discusses the language of mortality.

"I'd rather have chronic breast cancer than be Stage 4 terminal," she says, her matter-of-fact tone almost reassuring. "You have to believe that if you have a recurrence you'll get through it. People die of asthma too, but's chronic. Chronic means it goes on."

Even Sigmund Freud could figure out what these women want: straight answers about a complicated disease that threatens their lives, and a coherent public policy based on those answers.

"When I was diagnosed I was stunned," says Frances Visco of Philadelphia, a lawyer and president of the coalition. Her son was a year old in 1987 when she learned she had breast cancer. "I had no family history, and I felt that meant that I was O.K., that I didn't have to worry about it. When I started reading of this disease, I thought I was seeing misprints. If this is true, why didn't I know about it?"

One reason, Love asserts, is that "the medical profession and the media have sort of colluded to make it sound like if you do your breast self-exam and you get your mammogram, your cancer will be found early and you'll be cured and life will be groovy."

Mammograms are the best diagnostic tool available, but by the time a cancer shows up on a mammogram, she says, it could have been there eight years, for much of that time having access to blood vessels that can ferry stray cancer cells to vital organs.

As recited by advocates at every opportunity, the statistics that don't get much publicity are startling. Right now, they say, 2.6 million women in the United States have breast cancer—1.6 million who know it, 1 million who don't.

Scientists know that smoking contributes to lung cancer and they know something about the gene that goes haywire in colon cancer, for example, but no one has any idea what causes breast cancer, the leading cause of death in women ages 35 to 52. The mortality rate for black women is 10 percent higher than for white women, although they get breast cancer less frequently. The overall mortality rate for breast cancer—27 deaths per 100,000 women—has remained the same for 50 years, and its incidence has increased steadily in what the coalition insists is an "epidemic," though cancer specialists do not agree.

Even the identification of high-risk factors—having a close relative with the disease, early menstruation, late menopause, giving birth late in life or not at all—is not the news it seems to be. Depending on which expert is quoting what study, 70 to 85 percent of women who get breast cancer have no known risk factors. Only 5 percent of all breast cancers are inherited.

"This isn't 'high risk,'" says Barbara Balaban, who is director of the Breast Cancer Hot Line and Support Program at the Adelphi University School of Social Work on Long Island and a member of the coalition's working board. "This is *a* risk. What are the ones we don't know about?"

Many scientists and even some breast cancer organizations say that such statistics are needlessly alarming to women, and statistics are always slippery.

Larry G. Kessler, for example, chief of the applied-research branch at the National Cancer Institute, confirms that mammograms spot cancers that have been in the breast for "some time," but he says the assumption that they have been there eight years is not necessarily true, since some cancers grow faster than others.

It is true, he says, that overall mortality rates have remained the same, but have recently increased in women over 50 and decreased in women under 50. "Different cohorts, or groups of women born at different times, bring different risks of death with them," Kessler says. He suspects that a trend in giving birth at a later age is key. Diet, exposure to electric power lines ("If you want to believe that," he says) and early exposure to DDT in the food chain may also be factors, but Kessler carefully distances himself from these suggestions.

Kessler allows that the coalition is "close enough" when it estimates that 1.6 million women have the disease (his own figure is 1.5 million), but he questions whether there are 1 million undiagnosed cases of breast cancer. If all women who have not been screened with mammography were to be tested, he estimates that there would be "about 162,000" more cases found. The one million unknown cases cited by the coalition, "may be based on estimates of tumor growth times and other approaches," he says. "I cannot verify this number, and I believe you should be very careful about using it."

One especially arguable statistic is the oft-repeated assertion that "one in nine" women will get breast cancer. Most people take that to mean one in nine women *anywhere*—at the grocery store, at a P.T.A. meeting. But the figure is based on a life expectancy of 85 years: if all women lived to be 85, one in nine could expect to have a diagnosis of breast cancer at some time.

"There's only one reason to use those numbers," says Elin Bank Greenberg, chairman of the Susan G. Komen Breast Cancer Foundation, headquartered in Dallas, a national breast cancer organization that is not part of the coalition, "and that is to frighten women." The reality, she says, is that "among women aged 50, one in 50 will get the disease; the rate increases with age, and the true risks are being female and getting older."

The dispute over how to read the numbers is distracting, in part because statistics change and are open to endless interpretation. "This is not a competitive issue," Greenberg says. "It is unacceptable that in the decade of the 90's, an estimated 1.5 million women will be diagnosed, and 500,000 will die."

The coalition wants the Federal Government to spend $659 million for breast-cancer research in 1994. They want access to screening for all women, including the uninsured. In addition, the coalition wants a "comprehensive national strategy" on the issue, coordinated from the White House. "The problem now is that there are isolated pockets of people looking at breast cancer, and no one is talking to anyone else," says Fran Visco. "These turf battles are fought, and we lose."

To win "a place at the table" they are kicking off another signature-gathering campaign, this time for 2.6 million names. (While steadfastly pursuing its own agenda, the 10-year-old Komen Foundation, which runs dozens of "Race for the Cure" events each year, is pitching in to help collect the signatures.) And coalition members are training themselves as lobbyists, educators and publicists.

In a sense, the breast cancer movement began when prominent women—coincidentally all of them figures in Republican Party politics—went public with the disease: Shirley Temple Black in 1972, and even more influentially, the First Lady, Betty Ford, in 1974, followed by Happy Rockefeller, wife of the Vice President. The television reporter Betty Rollin also pushed the issue into the public consciousness with "First, You Cry," a best-selling book about her breast cancer in 1976. Until these women spoke out, breast cancer was barely mentionable, a disease that women saw as shameful and humiliating. It eroded a woman's sexual confidence and identity, and was an essential fact that her best friends often did not know.

In the late 1970's, support and information groups began to form tight, nurturing bonds between women who might otherwise never meet: rich and poor, white and black, gentile and Jewish, lesbians and straight women, Republicans and Democrats. Terrified of death and disfigurement, the women sought others who had been through the tough treatments and the long nights.

During the 1980's, AIDS activists showed how anger could be put to good use, and breast cancer groups started to stretch their agenda beyond coping to the idea of curing. Like homosexuals announcing their sexual orientation, women frequently describe the first time they tell friends about their cancer as "coming out."

Since 1980, some 194,000 people have died of AIDS and 450,000 have died of breast cancer. The difference, as the television commentator and breast cancer survivor Linda Ellerbee points out, is that AIDS is always fatal and "some of us survive."

In terms of strategy, the breast cancer activists are (so far) less confrontational than some AIDS activists about their right to more medical research. But they also know that being nice often gets you nowhere, and that outrageousness works well in the political arena. Betsy Lambert, a Manhattan lawyer and board member of the national coalition, says "you've got to admire" the people who make an uproar. Lambert says she has had moments when she wants to be outrageous, perhaps even pelt indifferent bureaucrats with breast prostheses.

Activists like Matuschka—a tall, striking artist in New York—set out to shock. As a member of a small group called WHAM (Women's Health Action and Mobilization), Matuschka makes art of her mastectomy with poster-size, one-breasted self-portraits that force people to see what cancer does. Though some of her mainstream sisters are discomforted by the graphic images, they admire her determination. As she says, "You can't look away anymore."

More commonly, activists have taken the orderly route of lobbying, collecting signatures, working the system, confident that they can prevail by sheer numbers.

Certainly, one thing the movement has going for it is timing—noisy 1960's activists who are in their 40's and 50's and baby boomers who were nursed on 60's activism are increasingly at risk for breast cancer. They understand the power of group politics. "I wasn't a *famous* activist, but I protested the war in the 60's," says Visco, the breast cancer coalition's president. "I spoke out for women's rights in the '70's."

In 1990, the publication of "Dr. Susan Love's Breast Book," a comprehensive and widely respected work co-written with Karen Lindsey, brought Love into the public eye. She is an engagingly direct and human surgeon who can laugh about her daughter's Barbie doll or fuss over not having had time to change from a blue suit rumpled on the red-eye from Los Angeles. Speaking before 500 coalition members in Washington, she drew a roar of laughter with a comment on the breast-squeezing mammogram apparatus that so many women hate: "It was indeed invented by a man, and I think there's a good tool we could invent for them with a little of our money."

In December 1990, Love met with Susan Hester, a Washington fund-raiser and director of the Mary-Helen Mautner Project for Lesbians With Cancer, to discuss for-

Matuschka as *Mermaid*. 1993. © Matuschka/Mark Lyon.

mation of a national lobby. They called Amy S. Langer, executive director of the National Alliance of Breast Cancer Organizations, and the three set up the coalition in skeletal form. Within a year there were 150 member groups, then 180, and it's still growing.

One of the most active groups in the coalition is 1 in 9. The Northeast in general has a high rate of breast cancer, and Long Island's rate is especially high. According to one set of statistics, in the 1980's there were 94.7 cases of breast cancer for every 100,000 women; in Nassau County on Long Island, the rate was 110.6 cases. For years there has been talk of scattered cancer clusters on Long Island—not just for breast cancer but all forms of the disease.

What would eventually become 1 in 9 began in 1987, after Francine Kritchek, a petite blond grandmother and teacher, had a mastectomy; Marie Quinn, a friend from work, admitted what she had told no one before: she, too, had breast cancer. The next year, Kritchek and Quinn sent a letter about the disease to everyone in their school.

But what really got them going was a state study of Long Island's breast cancer that found a relationship between high breast cancer incidence and high levels of household income. The study deemed environmental factors negligible, and said no further studies were warranted.

Women all over Long Island were outraged by the state's conclusions, among them Kritchek and Quinn, who later died of her cancer. They contacted Balaban at Adelphi, put a small ad in the local paper and sent a mailing to hundreds of people announcing a meeting. "Fifty-seven angry, frustrated women showed up," Kritchek says. Soon 1 in 9 was making local headlines, most notably with a protest by 300 women, some in wheelchairs, in front of the courthouse in Nassau County.

"The AIDS activists were our model," Kritchek says. "They showed that if the populace became very concerned, then the politicians would respond."

Under pressure from 1 in 9, the Breast Cancer Support Program and Senator Alfonse M. D'Amato, the Federal Centers for Disease Control held a public hearing on the need for another study. Members of 1 in 9 and others testified about suspected environmental risk factors, like auto emissions, polluted water, toxic wastes, pesticides and electromagnetic fields.

"Six months later they said the earlier study was sufficient!" Kritchek snorts. Rejecting the conclusions of the C.D.C. report, 1 in 9 held a news conference with Senator D'Amato in January on "discrepancies," "archaic thinking" and "patronizing implications" in the report.

The group also pledged to organize a study of its own in November, led by two breast cancer researchers, Susan Love and Dr. Devra Lee Davis of the National Academy of Sciences. Other groups, meanwhile, are distributing and tabulating questionnaires to identify possible clusters in Huntington, West Islip and Long Beach.

Activists for the National Breast Cancer Coalition say they want a cure. But is money—even unlimited Federal funding—the answer? The millions of dollars allocated and used for AIDS research has not yet produced promising results. The Komen Foundation gives grant money to post-doctoral researchers in many different areas because, says Greenberg, "a researcher working on prostate cancer may find a benefit that has a splash effect on breast cancer."

Amy Langer, now vice president of the coalition, says there is a dearth of basic information on the breast. "Because so little is known about what's normal, about why cancer cells react the way they do and how we can control them," she says, "research is vital." For example, Langer says, technicians have had what she diplomatically calls "limited" success in working with human breast cancer cells in vitro. And there are issues like drug resistance on a cellular level: "Why does cancer stop responding to some chemotherapy, and why does chemotherapy knock out some cells but not all of them?" Langer asks.

Coalition leaders like Love think that money earmarked for breast cancer research can answer some of these questions, as well as throw light on how breast cancer starts.

"Basically, all cancer is genetic," says Love. "It's not all hereditary, but it's all genetic. What that means is, it's all a gene that screws up." Carcinogens, she says, interfere with normal genes. "What are these carcinogens in breast cancer? We don't have a clue. Could they be hormones? Sure. Could they be a virus? Sure." It could be pesticides, food additives or "a million" other things.

At the National Cancer Institute, Kessler is sympathetic to the movement's goals, but doubtful of its success. In his expert opinion, he says, "clinically, it's going to be impossible to detect" the first cellular changes that lead to breast cancer.

Love is undeterred. Scientists should look for the earliest mutations, and "maybe we can reverse the progress and development of breast cancer." The involvement of the Department of Defense in financing breast cancer research is fortunate, she believes, because it will spark productive competition between Federal agencies seeking a cure. Researchers go where the money is.

As the coalition's clout has grown, the powerful scientific and legislative communities that perhaps inevitably resist change have begun to hedge their objections to the advocates' assertions and demands. It's hard if not impossible to criticize mothers and sisters who are fighting cancer. Still, one challenge, generally voiced off the record, is that the coalition's determination to get more money for breast cancer will mean less money for other diseases. Critics squirm at the thought of "politicizing" medical research.

The coalition members describe this as backlash. "We don't want a bigger piece of the pie," they repeat again and again. "We want a bigger pie." They say research has always been political, because there has never been enough money for research. "Someone has been making the decision to fund 'X' at the expense of 'Y.' For too long those decisions have been made at the expense of women's lives," says Visco. "We've come along and we've said enough, stop; you have to start spending more of that money on breast cancer."

According to a story that Lesley Stahl of CBS News told at a charity lunch, Congress first saw breast cancer as a political matter in 1988, during the Reagan Administration, when Congressional women wanted Medicare to cover mammograms. It was a complicated issue, and the bill had to go through an all-male subcommmittee. There were few breast cancer activists then, but a female lobbyist approached a congressman and asked him to introduce the necessary language in a larger health care bill.

His response personified Capitol Hill politics: "I did the women's thing last year," he said. "The guys will think I'm soft on women."

Her response was sexual politics: "Fear not. Just tell them you're a breast man."

Ultimately, the necessary language was inserted in the bill; the legislation passed, only to be lost when the entire catastrophic-healthcare bill was repealed. But when George

Bush became President, he needed the Congressional women's votes to pass his budget, and they again asked for mammogram coverage. The President agreed, but said he'd have to swap it for something else, Stahl says: funds for a children's program called Wee Tots.

In the last two years, since its collective consciousness was raised by Anita Hill's testimony at the Clarence Thomas hearings, Congress has learned to pay more respect to women's issues, including breast cancer. In part, this is because more and more law-makers have personal experience with the disease. Senator Harkin, who championed the $210 million in defense money for breast cancer, lost two sisters to the disease. Representative Nita Lowey, Democrat of New York, lost her mother and two aunts; she has sent a letter to President Clinton signed by 185 of her Capitol Hill colleagues endorsing the advocates' 1993 goals. Representatives Barbara Vucanovich, Republican of Nevada, and Marilyn Lloyd, Democrat of Tennessee, are themselves survivors and have made breast cancer issues part of their legislative proposals.

In the Senate, Patrick J. Leahy, Democrat of Vermont, arranged for the coalition to show its formal display, "The Faces of Breast Cancer," in the rotunda of the Russell Senate Office Building for a week. Although Senator Orrin G. Hatch, Republican of Utah, was one of the four who voted against Harkin's $210 million Defense Department maneuver, he has since sponsored a bill requiring public health programs to provide clients with information about cervical and breast cancer.

"So what?" say some activists, implying that Hatch's response was trivial. But Lowey is encouraged. "You build support where you can get it," she says.

During the Washington workshops in May, in a session called "Identifying Opportunities for Influence," Sheila L. Swanson of the Bay Area Breast Cancer Network in San Jose, Calif., tells the audience: "We have to make it clear: We may have had mastectomies, but we did not have a lobotomy." Her listeners cheer, and the next day several hundred of them buoyantly hurl themselves into the world of big-time lobbyists. Their inexperience sometimes can work for them; after all, these are voters first, lobbyists second. But other times inexperience leads to emotionally bruising confrontations.

In the office of Senator Daniel Patrick Moynihan, a dozen women believe they have an appointment with the Senator at 12:30 P.M. He is not there; an aide will speak with them. The meeting room is unavailable. Grumbling a little, the novice lobbyists—some of them using canes because their cancer has spread to the spine, others pasty-faced from chemotherapy—follow her to a dimly lighted basement lunch room full of workers grabbing a quick bite or smoke.

Scattered wrappers and bits of food litter the tables. Several women sweep the table tops clear before sitting. They push close to hear; the din from the vending and change-making machines is constant.

Yet they stick to their script: "As you sit here, every 12 minutes a woman dies." And: "What we're doing now probably will not save our lives. We're doing it for our daughters, and our sisters." They end, as instructed by workshop leaders, on a positive note, thanking the aide for the Senator's past support.

Afterward, in the hallway, Kritchek is furious. "Never in all my years have I been treated like this," she says. "It was insensitive, it was offensive." Brian Connolly, Moynihan's press secretary, later describes the way the meeting went as "unfortunate," but says the group had erred by not letting him know that journalists would be coming.

A few days later, at home in Hicksville, L.I., Kritchek is upbeat: giving interviews, making dinner, working the telephone and planning 1 in 9's next Walk-Run fund-raising event.

"Nothing will ever happen to breast cancer," she says, "unless it is politicized."

As of this writing, the Coalition's president, Fran Visco, has been named to President Clinton's cancer panel.

Long Island's 1 in 9 gave Fran Kritchek the first Marie Quinn Memorial Award.

Matuschka is making one-breasted self-portrait postcards.

Liz LoRusso is considering starting an experimental vaccination program for breast cancer in Chicago.

Sherry Kohlenberg, the woman who promised not to go silent into the dark night, met with Bill and Hillary Rodham Clinton in June. She died on July 14.

## Reading Questions

1. What is the leading cause of death for women aged 35–50? How does it compare to AIDS as a cause of death for women?
2. According to Ferraro, which issues make the medical issue of breast cancer a political issue?
3. Why does the word carcinogen never appear in the medical establishment's propagation of high-risk factors for breast cancer?
4. What is the current definition of a "cure" for breast cancer?
5. To what facts do feminists appeal in objection to the establishment presentation of mammography as a prevention?
6. What are some of the socioeconomic factors relevant to the national average of black women's 13 percent lower survival rate than white women, after detection of breast cancer?
7. What are the differences between the obstacles faced by breast cancer activists in making demands on the NCI and those of AIDS activists? What are the concrete demands of breast cancer activists?

## Recommended Reading

Judith Brady, *One in Three: Women with Cancer Confront an Epidemic* (Pittsburgh: Cleis Press, 1991)

Zillah Eisenstein, *The Female Body and the Law* (Berkeley: University of California Press, 1989)

Audre Lorde, *The Cancer Journals* (San Francisco: Spinsters/Aunt Lute, 1989)

Ralph Moss, *The Cancer Industry* (New York: Paragon, 1991)

Jo Spence, *Putting Myself in the Picture* (Real Comet Press, 1988)

Paula Treichler, "How to Have Theory in an Epidemic: The Evolution of AIDS Treatment Activism," *Technoculture,* eds. Constance Penley and Andrew Ross (Minneapolis: University of Minnesota Press, 1991)

## Recommended Audiovisual Resources

*Breast Cancer: Speaking Out.* 1994. Produced by KCTS/TV. This film documents the transformation of women with cancer into activists, detailing the ways that women can learn from AIDS activists to fight for their share of federal funds. Filmakers Library.

*Take over Daiichi.* 1991. Gregg Bordowitz with Jean Carlomusto and Gary Winters. Gay Men's Health Crisis video of Treatment Action Guerrillas and Women's Health Action Mobilization takeover of the New Jersey branch of Daiichi Pharmaceutical Companies of Japan. Gay Men's Health Crisis.

For more information on breast cancer activism and related audiovisual materials, contact The National Breast Cancer Coalition.

# Foucault, Femininity, and the Modernization of Patriarchal Power

## SANDRA BARTKY

Sandra Bartky teaches philosophy and women's studies at the University of Illinois–Chicago. She is the author of *Feminity and Domination* and numerous articles on feminist phenomenology and epistemology.

## I

In a striking critique of modern society, Michel Foucault has argued that the rise of parliamentary institutions and of new conceptions of political liberty was accompanied by a darker counter-movement, by the emergence of a new and unprecedented discipline directed against the body. More is required of the body now than mere political allegiance or the appropriation of the products of its labor: The new discipline invades the body and seeks to regulate its very forces and operations, the economy and efficiency of its movements.

The disciplinary practices Foucault describes are tied to peculiarly modern forms of the army, the school, the hospital, the prison, and the manufactory; the aim of these disciplines is to increase the utility of the body, to augment its forces:

> What was then being formed was a policy of coercions that act upon the body, a calculated manipulation of its elements, its gestures, its behaviour. The human body was entering a machinery of power that explores it, breaks it down and rearranges it. A 'political anatomy', which was also a 'mechanics of powers', was being born; it defined how one may have a hold over others' bodies, not only so that they may do what one wishes, but so that they may operate as one wishes, with the techniques, the speed and the efficiency that one determines. Thus, discipline produces subjected and practiced bodies, 'docile' bodies.[1]

The production of "docile bodies" requires that an uninterrupted coercion be directed to the very processes of bodily activity, not just their result; this "micro-physics of power" fragments and partitions the body's time, its space, and its movements.[2]

The student, then, is enclosed within a classroom and assigned to a desk he cannot leave; his ranking in the class can be read off the position of his desk in the serially ordered and segmented space of the classroom itself. Foucault tells us that "Jean-Baptiste de la Salle dreamt of a classroom in which the spatial distribution might provide a whole series of distinctions at once, according to the pupil's progress, worth, character, application, cleanliness, and parents' fortune."[3] The student must sit upright, feet upon the floor, head erect; he may not slouch or fidget; his animate body is brought into a fixed correlation with the inanimate desk.

The minute breakdown of gestures and movements required of soldiers at drill is far more relentless:

> Bring the weapon forward. In three stages. Raise the rifle with the right hand, bringing it close to the body so as to hold it perpendicular with the right knee, the end of the barrel at eye level, grasping it by striking it with the right hand, the arm held close to the body at waist height. At the second stage, bring the rifle in front of you with the left hand, the barrel in the middle between the two eyes, vertical, the right hand grasping it at the small of the butt, the arm outsretched, the triggerguard resting on the first finger, the left hand at the height of the notch, the thumb lying along the barrel against the moulding. At the third stage. . . .[4]

These "body-object articulations" of the soldier and his weapon, the student and his desk, effect a "coercive link with the apparatus of production." We are far indeed from older forms of control that "demanded of the body only signs or products, forms of expression or the result of labour."[5]

The body's time, in these regimes of power, is as rigidly controlled as its space: The factory whistle and the school bell mark a division of time into discrete and segmented units that regulate the various activities of the day. The following timetable, similar in spirit to the ordering of my grammar school classroom, was suggested for French "écoles mutuelles" of the early nineteenth century:

> 8:45 entrance of the monitor, 8:52 the monitor's summons, 8:56 entrance of the children and prayer, 9:00 the children go to their benches, 9:04 first slate, 9:08 end of dictation, 9:12 second slate, etc.[6]

Control this rigid and precise cannot be maintained without a minute and relentless surveillance.

Jeremy Bentham's design for the Panopticon, a model prison, captures for Foucault the essence of the disciplinary society. At the periphery of the Panopticon, a circular structure; at the center, a tower with wide windows that opens onto the inner side of the ring. The structure on the periphery is divided into cells, each with two windows, one facing the windows of the tower, the other facing the outside, allowing an effect of backlighting to make any figure visible within the cell. "All that is needed, then, is to place a supervisor in a central tower and to shut up in each cell a madman, a patient, a condemned man, a worker or a schoolboy."[7] Each inmate is alone, shut off from effective communication with his fellows, but constantly visible from the tower. The effect of this is "to induce in the inmate a state of conscious and permanent visibility that assures the automatic functioning of power"; each becomes to himself his own jailer.[8] This "state of conscious and permanent visibility" is a sign that the tight, disciplinary control of the body has gotten a hold on the mind as well. In the perpetual self-surveillance of the inmate lies the genesis of the celebrated "individualism" and heightened self-consciousness which are hallmarks of modern times. For Foucault, the structure and effects of the Panopticon resonate throughout society: Is it surprising that "prisons resemble factories, schools, barracks, hospitals, which all resemble prisons?"[9]

Foucault's account in *Discipline and Punish* of the disciplinary practices that produce the "docile bodies" of modernity is a genuine *tour de force*, incorporating a rich theoretical account of ways in which instrumental reason takes hold of the body with a mass of historical detail. But Foucault treats the body throughout as if it were one, as if the bodily experiences of men and women did not differ and as if men and women bore the same relationship to the characteristic institutions of modern life. Where is the account of the disciplinary practices that engender the "docile bodies" of women, bodies more docile than the bodies of men? Women, like men, are subject to many of the same disciplinary practices Foucault describes. But he is blind to those disciplines that produce a modality of embodiment that is peculiarly feminine. To overlook the forms of subjection that engender the feminine body is to perpetuate the silence and powerlessness of those upon whom these disciplines have been imposed. Hence, even though a liberatory note is sounded in Foucault's critique of power, his analysis as a whole reproduces that sexism which is endemic throughout Western political theory.

We are born male or female, but not masculine or feminine. Femininity is an artifice, an achievement, "a mode of enacting and reenacting received gender norms which surface as so many styles of the flesh." [10] In what follows, I shall examine those disciplinary practices that produce a body which in gesture and appearance is recognizably feminine. I consider three categories of such practices: those that aim to produce a body of a certain size and general configuration; those that bring forth from this body a specific repertoire of gestures, postures, and movements; and those directed toward the display of this body as an ornamented surface. I shall examine the nature of these disciplines, how they are imposed and by whom. I shall probe the effects of the imposition of such discipline on female identity and subjectivity. In the final section I shall argue that these disciplinary practices must be understood in the light of the modernization of patriarchal domination, a modernization that unfolds historically according to the general pattern described by Foucault.

## II

Styles of the female figure vary over time and across cultures: they reflect cultural obsessions and preoccupations in ways that are still poorly understood. Today, massiveness, power, or abundance in a woman's body is met with distaste. The current body of fashion is taut, small-breasted, narrow-hipped, and of a slimness bordering on emaciation; it is a silhouette that seems more appropriate to an adolescent boy or newly pubescent girl than to an adult woman. Since ordinary women have normally quite different dimensions, they must of course diet.

Mass-circulation women's magazines run articles on dieting in virtually every issue. The *Ladies' Home Journal* of February 1986 carries a "Fat-Burning Exercise Guide," while *Mademoiselle* offers to "Help Stamp Out Cellulite" with "Six Sleek-Down Strategies." After the diet-busting Christmas holidays and later, before summer bikini season, the titles of these features become shriller and more arresting. The reader is now addressed in the imperative mode: Jump into shape for summer! Shed ugly winter fat with the all-new Grapefruit Diet! More women than men visit diet doctors, while women greatly outnumber men in self-help groups such as Weight Watchers and Overeaters Anonymous—in the case of the latter, by well over 90 percent. [11]

Dieting disciplines the body's hungers: Appetite must be monitored at all times and governed by an iron will. Since the innocent need of the organism for food will not be denied, the body becomes one's enemy, an alien being bent on thwarting the disciplinary project. Anorexia nervosa, which has now assumed epidemic proportions, is to women of the late twentieth century what hysteria was to women of an earlier day: the crystallization in a pathological mode of a widespread cultural obsession. [12] A survey taken recently at

UCLA is astounding: Of 260 students interviewed, 27.3 percent of the women but only 5.8 percent of men said they were "terrified" of getting fat: 28.7 percent of women and only 7.5 percent of men said they were obsessed or "totally preoccupied" with food. The body images of women and men are strikingly different as well: 35 percent of the women but only 12.5 percent of men said they felt fat though other people told them they were thin. Women in the survey wanted to weigh ten pounds less than their average weight; men felt they were within a pound of their ideal weight. A total of 5.9 percent of women and no men met the psychiatric criteria for anorexia or bulimia.[13]

Dieting is one discipline imposed upon a body subject to the "tyranny of slenderness"; exercise is another.[14] Since men as well as women exercise, it is not always easy in the case of women to distinguish what is done for the sake of physical fitness from what is done in obedience to the requirements of femininity. Men as well as women lift weights, do yoga, calisthenics, and aerobics, though "jazzercise" is a largely female pursuit. Men and women alike engage themselves with a variety of machines, each designed to call forth from the body a different exertion: There are Nautilus machines, rowing machines, ordinary and motorized exercycles, portable hip and leg cycles, belt massagers, trampolines; treadmills, arm and leg pulleys. However, given the widespread female obsession with weight, one suspects that many women are working out with these apparatuses in the health club or at the gym with a different aim in mind and in quite a different spirit than the men.

But there are classes of exercises meant for women alone, these designed not to firm or to reduce the body's size overall, but to resculpture its various parts on the current model. M. J. Saffon, "international beauty expert," assures us that his twelve basic facial exercises can erase frown lines, smooth the forehead, raise hollow cheeks, banish crow's feet, and tighten the muscles under the chin.[15] There are exercises to build the breasts and exercises to banish "cellulite," said by "figure consultants" to be a special type of female fat. There is "spot-reducing," an umbrella term that covers dozens of punishing exercises designed to reduce "problem areas" like thick ankles or "saddlebag" thighs. The very idea of "spot-reducing" is both scientifically unsound and cruel, for it raises expectations in women that can never be realized: The pattern in which fat is deposited or removed is known to be genetically determined.

It is not only her natural appetite or unreconstructed contours that pose a danger to women: The very expressions of her face can subvert the disciplinary project of bodily perfection. An expressive face lines and creases more readily than an inexpressive one. Hence, if women are unable to suppress strong emotions, they can at least learn to inhibit the tendency of the face to register them. Sophia Loren recommends a unique solution to this problem: A piece of tape applied to the forehead or between the brows will tug at the skin when one frowns and act as a reminder to relax the face.[16] The tape is to be worn whenever a woman is home alone.

## III

There are significant gender differences in gesture, posture, movement, and general bodily comportment: Women are far more restricted than men in their manner of movement and in their lived spatiality. In her classic paper on the subject, Iris Young observes that a space seems to surround women in imagination which they are hesitant to move beyond: This manifests itself both in a reluctance to reach, stretch, and extend the body to meet resistances of matter in motion—as in sport or in the performance of physical tasks—and in a typically constricted posture and general style of movement. Woman's space is not a field in which her bodily intentionality can be freely realized but an enclosure in which she feels herself positioned and by which she is confined.[17] The "loose woman" violates these norms: Her looseness is manifest not only in her morals, but in her manner of speech, and quite literally in the free and easy way she moves.

In an extraordinary series of over two thousand photographs, many candid shots taken in the street, the German photographer Marianne Wex has documented differences in typical masculine and feminine body posture. Women sit waiting for trains with arms close to the body, hands folded together in their laps, toes pointing straight ahead or turned inward, and legs pressed together.[18] The women in these photographs make themselves small and narrow, harmless; they seem tense; they take up little space. Men, on the other hand, expand into the available space; they sit with legs far apart and arms flung out at some distance from the body. Most common in these sitting male figures is what Wex calls the "proffering position": the men sit with legs thrown wide apart, crotch visible, feet pointing outward, often with an arm and casually dangling hand resting comfortably on an open, spread thigh.

In proportion to total body size, a man's stride is longer than a woman's. The man has more spring and rhythm to his step; he walks with toes pointed outward, holds his arms at a greater distance from his body, and swings them farther; he tends to point the whole hand in the direction he is moving. The woman holds her arms closer to her body, palms against her sides; her walk is circumspect. If she has subjected herself to the additional constraint of high-heeled shoes, her body is thrown forward and off-balance: The struggle to walk under these conditions shortens her stride still more.[19]

But women's movement is subjected to a still finer discipline. Feminine faces, as well as bodies, are trained to the expression of deference. Under male scrutiny, women will avert their eyes or cast them downward; the female gaze is trained to abandon its claim to the sovereign status of seer. The "nice" girl learns to avoid the bold and unfettered staring of the "loose" woman who looks at whatever and whomever she pleases. Women are trained to smile more than men, too. In the economy of smiles, as elsewhere, there is evidence that women are exploited, for they give more than they receive in return; in a smile elicitation study, one researcher found that the rate of smile return by women was 93 percent, by men only 67 percent.[20] In many typical women's jobs, graciousness, deference, and the readiness to serve are part of the work; this requires the worker to fix a smile on her face for a good part of the working day, whatever her inner state.[21] The economy of touching is out of balance, too: men touch women more often and on more parts of the body than women touch men: female secretaries, factory workers, and waitresses report that such liberties are taken routinely with their bodies.[22]

Feminine movement, gesture, and posture must exhibit not only constriction, but grace as well, and a certain eroticism restrained by modesty: all three. Here is field for the operation for a whole new training: A woman must stand with stomach pulled in, shoulders thrown slightly back, and chest out, this to display her bosom to maximum advantage. While she must walk in the confined fashion appropriate to women, her movements must, at the same time, be combined with a subtle but provocative hip-roll. But too much display is taboo: Women in short, low-cut dresses are told to avoid bending over at all, but if they must, great care must be taken to avoid an unseemly display of breast or rump. From time to time, fashion magazines offer quite precise instructions on the proper way of getting in and out of cars. These instructions combine all three imperatives of women's movement: A woman must not allow her arms and legs to flail about in all directions; she must try to manage her movements with the appearance of grace—no small accomplishment when one is climbing out of the back seat of a Fiat— and she is well advised to use the opportunity for a certain display of leg.

All the movements we have described so far are self-movements; they arise from within the woman's own body. But in a way that normally goes unnoticed, males in couples may literally steer a woman everywhere she goes: down the street, around corners, into elevators, through doorways, into her chair at the dinner table, around the dance-floor. The man's movement "is not necessarily heavy and pushy or physical in an ugly way; it is light and gentle but firm in the way of the most confident equestrians with the best trained horses."[23]

## IV

We have examined some of the disciplinary practices a woman must master in pursuit of a body of the right size and shape that also displays the proper styles of feminine motility. But woman's body is an ornamented surface too, and there is much discipline involved in this production as well. Here, especially in the application of make-up and the selection of clothes, art and discipline converge, though, as I shall argue, there is less art involved than one might suppose.

A woman's skin must be soft, supple, hairless, and smooth; ideally, it should betray no sign of wear, experience, age, or deep thought. Hair must be removed not only from the face but from large surfaces of the body as well, from legs and thighs, an operation accomplished by shaving, buffing with fine sandpaper, or foul-smelling depilatories. With the new high-leg bathing suits and leotards, a substantial amount of pubic hair must be removed too.[24] The removal of facial hair can be more specialized. Eyebrows are plucked out by the roots with a tweezer. Hot wax is sometimes poured onto the mustache and cheeks and then ripped away when it cools. The woman who wants a more permanent result may try electrolysis: This involves the killing of a hair root by the passage of an electric current down a needle which has been inserted into its base. The procedure is painful and expensive.

The development of what one "beauty expert" calls "good skin-care habits" requires not only attention to health, the avoidance of strong facial expressions, and the performance of facial exercises, but the regular use of skin-care preparations, many to be applied oftener than once a day: cleansing lotions (ordinary soap and water "upsets the skin's acid and alkaline balance"), wash-off cleansers (milder than cleansing lotions), astringents, toners, make-up removers, night creams, nourishing creams, eye creams, moisturizers, skin balancers, body lotions, hand creams, lip pomades, suntan lotions, sun screens, facial masks. Provision of the proper facial mask is complex: There are sulfur masks for pimples; hot or oil masks for dry areas; also cold masks for dry areas; tightening masks; conditioning masks; peeling masks; cleansing masks made of herbs, cornmeal, or almonds; mud packs. Black women may wish to use "fade creams" to "even skin tone." Skin-care preparations are never just sloshed onto the skin, but applied according to precise rules: Eye cream is dabbed on gently in movements toward, never away from, the nose; cleansing cream is applied in outward directions only, straight across the forehead, the upper lip, and the chin, never up but straight down the nose and up and out on the cheeks.[25]

The normalizing discourse of modern medicine is enlisted by the cosmetics industry to gain credibility for its claims. Dr. Christiaan Barnard lends his enormous prestige to the Glycel line of "cellular treatment activators"; these contain "glycosphingolipids" that can "make older skin behave and look like younger skin." The Clinique computer at any Clinique counter will select a combination of preparations just right for you. Ultima II contains "procollagen" in its anti-aging eye cream that "provides hydration" to "demoralizing lines." "Biotherm" eye cream dramatically improves the "biomechanical properties of the skin."[26] The Park Avenue clinic of Dr. Zizmor, "chief of dermatology at one of New York's leading hospitals," offers not only medical treatment such as dermabrasion and chemical peeling but "total deep skin cleansing" as well.[27]

Really good skin-care habits require the use of a variety of aids and devices: facial steamers; faucet filters to collect impurities in the water; borax to soften it; a humidifier for the bedroom; electric massagers; backbrushes; complexion brushes; loofahs; pumice stones; blackhead removers. I will not detail the implements or techniques involved in the manicure or pedicure.

The ordinary circumstances of life as well as a wide variety of activities cause a crisis in skin-care and require a stepping up of the regimen as well as an additional laying on of preparations. Skin-care discipline requires a specialized knowledge: A woman must know what to do if she has been skiing, taking medication, doing vigorous exercise, boating, or swimming in chlorinated pools; if she has been exposed to pollution, heated rooms, cold, sun, harsh weather, the pressurized cabins on airplanes, saunas or steam rooms, fatigue or stress. Like the schoolchild or prisoner, the woman mastering good skin-care habits is put on a timetable: Georgette Klinger requires that a shorter or longer period of attention be paid to the complexion at least four times a day.[28] Hair-care, like skin-care, requires a similar investment of time, the use of a wide variety of preparations, the mastery of a set of techniques and again, the acquisition of a specialized knowledge.

The crown and pinnacle of good hair care and skin care is, of course, the arrangement of the hair and the application of cosmetics. Here the regimen of hair care, skin care, manicure, and pedicure is recapitulated in another mode. A woman must learn the proper manipulation of a large number of devices—the blow dryer, styling brush, curling iron, hot curlers, wire curlers, eye-liner, lipliner, lipstick brush, eyelash curler, mascara brush—and the correct manner of application of a wide variety of products—foundation, toner, covering stick, mascara, eye shadow, eye gloss, blusher, lipstick, rouge, lip gloss, hair dye, hair rinse, hair lightener, hair "relaxer," etc.

In the language of fashion magazines and cosmetics ads, making up is typically portrayed as an aesthetic activity in which a woman can express her individuality. In reality, while cosmetic styles change every decade or so and while some variation in make-up is permitted depending on the occasion, making up the face is, in fact, a highly stylized activity that gives little rein to self-expression. Painting the face is not like painting a picture; at best, it might be described as painting the same picture over and over again with minor variations. Little latitude is permitted in what is considered appropriate make-up for the office and for most social occasions; indeed, the woman who uses cosmetics in a genuinely novel and imaginative way is liable to be seen not as an artist but as an eccentric. Furthermore, since a properly made-up face is, if not a card of entrée, at least a badge of acceptability in most social and professional contexts, the woman who chooses not to wear cosmetics at all faces sanctions of a sort which will never be applied to someone who chooses not to paint a watercolor.

## V

Are we dealing in all this merely with sexual *difference?* Scarcely. The disciplinary practices I have described are part of the process by which the ideal body of femininity—and hence the feminine body-subject—is constructed; in doing this, they produce a "practiced and subjected" body, i.e., a body on which an inferior status has been inscribed. A woman's face must be made up, that is to say, made over, and so must her body: she is ten pounds overweight; her lips must be made more kissable; her complexion dewier; her eyes more mysterious. The "art" of make-up is the art of disguise, but this presupposes that a woman's face, unpainted, is defective. Soap and water, a shave, and routine attention to hygiene may be enough for *him*; for *her* they are not. The strategy of much beauty-related advertising is to suggest to women that their bodies are deficient, but even without such more or less explicit teaching, the media images of perfect female beauty which bombard us daily leave no doubt in the minds of most women that they fail to measure up. The technologies of femininity are taken up and practiced by women against the background of a pervasive sense of bodily deficiency: This accounts for what is often their compulsive or even ritualistic character.

The disciplinary project of femininity is a "set-up": It requires such radical and extensive measures of bodily transformation that virtually every woman who gives herself to it is destined in some degree to fail. Thus, a measure of shame is added to a woman's sense that the body she inhabits is deficient: she ought to take better care of herself; she might after all have jogged that last mile. Many women are without the time or resources to provide themselves with even the minimum of what such a regimen requires, e.g., a decent diet. Here is an additional source of shame for poor women who must bear what our society regards as the more general shame of poverty. The burdens poor women bear in this regard are not merely psychological, since conformity to the prevailing standards of bodily acceptability is a known factor in economic mobility.

The larger disciplines that construct a "feminine" body out of a female one are by no means race- or class-specific. There is little evidence that women of color or working-class women are in general less committed to the incarnation of an ideal femininity than their more privileged sisters. This is not to deny the many ways in which factors of race, class, locality, ethnicity, or personal taste can be expressed within the kinds of practices I have described. The rising young corporate executive may buy her cosmetics at Bergdorf-Goodman while the counter-server at McDonald's gets hers at the K-Mart; the one may join an expensive "upscale" health club, while the other may have to make do with the $9.49 GFX Body-Flex II Home-Gym advertised in the *National Enquirer*. Both are aiming at the same general result.[29]

In the regime of institutionalized heterosexuality woman must make herself "object and prey" for the man: It is for him that these eyes are limpid pools, this cheek baby-smooth.[30] In contemporary patriarchal culture, a panoptical male connoisseur resides within the consciousness of most women: They stand perpetually before his gaze and under his judgment. Woman lives her body as seen by another, by an anonymous patriarchal Other. We are often told that "women dress for other women." There is some truth in this: Who but someone engaged in a project similar to my own can appreciate the panache with which I bring it off? But women know for whom this game is played: They know that a pretty young woman is likelier to become a flight attendant than a plain one and that a well-preserved older woman has a better chance of holding onto her husband than one who has "let herself go."

Here it might be objected that performance for another in no way signals the inferiority of the performer to the one for whom the performance is intended: The actor, for example, depends on his audience but is in no way inferior to it; he is not demeaned by his dependency. While femininity is surely something enacted, the analogy to theater breaks down in a number of ways. First, as I argued earlier, the self-determination we think of as requisite to an artistic career is lacking here: Femininity as spectacle is something in which virtually every woman is required to participate. Second, the precise nature of the criteria by which women are judged, not only the inescapability of judgment itself, reflects gross imbalances in the social power of the sexes that do not mark the relationship of artists and their audiences. An aesthetic of femininity, for example, that mandates fragility and a lack of muscular strength produces female bodies that can offer little resistance to physical abuse, and the physical abuse of women by men, as we know, is widespread. It is true that the current fitness movement has permitted women to develop more muscular strength and endurance than was heretofore allowed; indeed, images of women have begun to appear in the mass media that seem to eroticize this new muscularity. But a woman may by no means develop more muscular strength than her partner; the bride who would tenderly carry her groom across the threshold is a figure of comedy, not romance.[31]

Under the current "tyranny of slenderness" women are forbidden to become large or massive; they must take up as little space as possible. The very contours a woman's body takes on as she matures—the fuller breasts and rounded hips—have become distasteful. The body by which a woman feels herself judged and which by rigorous discipline she must try to assume is the body of early adolescence, slight and unformed, a body lacking flesh or substance, a body in whose very contours the image of immaturity has been inscribed. The requirement that a woman maintain a smooth and hairless skin carries further the theme of inexperience, for an infantilized face must accompany her infantilized body, a face that never ages or furrows its brow in thought. The face of the ideally feminine woman must never display the marks of character, wisdom, and experience that we so admire in men.

To succeed in the provision of a beautiful or sexy body gains a woman attention and some admiration but little real respect and rarely any social power. A woman's effort to master feminine body discipline will lack importance just because she does it: Her activity partakes of the general depreciation of everything female. In spite of unrelenting pressure to "make the most of what they have," women are ridiculed and dismissed for the triviality of their interest in such "trivial" things as clothes and make-up. Further, the narrow identification of woman with sexuality and the body in a society that has for centuries displayed profound suspicion toward both does little to raise her status. Even the most adored female bodies complain routinely of their situation in ways that reveal an implicit understanding that there is something demeaning in the kind of attention they receive. Marilyn Monroe, Elizabeth Taylor, and Farrah Fawcett have all wanted passionately to become actresses-artists and not just "sex objects."

But it is perhaps in their more restricted motility and comportment that the inferiorization of women's bodies is most evident: Women's typical body language, a language of relative tension and constriction, is understood to be a language of subordination when it is enacted by men in male status hierarchies. In groups of men, those with higher status typically assume looser and more relaxed postures: The boss lounges comfortably behind the desk while the applicant sits tense and rigid on the edge of his seat. Higher-status individuals may touch their subordinates more than they themselves get touched; they initiate more eye contact and are smiled at by their inferiors more than they are observed to smile in return.[32] What is announced in the comportment of superiors is confidence and ease, especially ease of access to the Other. Female constraint in posture and movement is no doubt over-determined: The fact that women tend to sit and stand with legs, feet, and knees close or touching may well be a coded declaration of sexual circumspection in a society that still maintains a double standard, or an effort, albeit unconscious, to guard the genital area. In the latter case, a woman's tight and constricted posture must be seen as the expression of her need to ward off real or symbolic sexual attack. Whatever proportions must be assigned in the final display to fear or deference, one thing is clear: Woman's body language speaks eloquently, though silently, of her subordinate status in a hierarchy of gender.

# VI

If what we have described is a genuine discipline—a "system of micropower that is essentially non-egalitarian and asymmetrical"—who then are the disciplinarians?[33] Who is the top sergeant in the disciplinary regime of femininity? Historically, the law has had some responsibility for enforcement: In times gone by, for example, individuals who appeared in public in the clothes of the other sex could be arrested. While cross-dressers are still liable to some harassment, the kind of discipline we are considering is not the business of the police or the courts. Parents and teachers, of course, have extensive influence, admonishing girls to be demure and ladylike, to "smile pretty," to sit with their legs together. The influence of the media is pervasive, too, constructing as it does an image of the female body as spectacle, nor can we ignore the role played by "beauty experts" or by emblematic public personages such as Jane Fonda and Lynn Redgrave.

But none of these individuals—the skin-care consultant, the parent, the policeman— does in fact wield the kind of authority that is typically invested in those who manage more straightforward disciplinary institutions. The disciplinary power that inscribes femininity in the female body is everywhere and it is nowhere; the disciplinarian is everyone and yet no one in particular. Women regarded as overweight, for example, report that they are regularly admonished to diet, sometimes by people they scarcely know. These intrusions are often softened by reference to the natural prettiness just waiting to emerge: "People have always said that I had a beautiful face and 'if you'd only lose weight you'd be really beautiful.'"[34] Here, "people"—friends and casual acquaintances alike—act to enforce prevailing standards of body size.

Foucault tends to identify the imposition of discipline upon the body with the operation of specific institutions, e.g., the school, the factory, the prison. To do this, however, is to overlook the extent to which discipline can be institutionally *unbound* as well as institutionally bound.[35] The anonymity of disciplinary power and its wide dispersion have consequences which are crucial to a proper understanding of the subordination of women. The absence of a formal institutional structure and of authorities invested with the power to carry out institutional directives creates the impression that the production of femininity is either entirely voluntary or natural. The several senses of "discipline" are instructive here. On the one hand, discipline is something imposed on subjects of an "essentially inegalitarian and asymetrical" system of authority. Schoolchildren, convicts, and draftees are subject to discipline in this sense. But discipline can be sought voluntarily as well, as, for example, when an individual seeks initiation into the spiritual discipline of Zen Buddhism. Discipline can, of course, be both at once: The volunteer may seek the physical and occupational training offered by the army without the army's ceasing in any way to be the instrument by which he and other members of his class are kept in disciplined subjection. Feminine bodily discipline has this dual character: On the one hand, no one is marched off for electrolysis at the end of a rifle, nor can we fail to appreciate the initiative and ingenuity displayed by countless women in an attempt to master the rituals of beauty. Nevertheless, insofar as the disciplinary practices of femininity produce a "subjected and practiced," an inferiorized, body, they must be understood as aspects of a far larger discipline, an oppressive and inegalitarian system of sexual subordination. This system aims at turning women into the docile and compliant companions of men just as surely as the army aims to turn its raw recruits into soldiers.

Now the transformation of oneself into a properly feminine body may be any or all of the following: a rite of passage into adulthood; the adoption and celebration of a particular aesthetic; a way of announcing one's economic level and social status; a way to triumph over other women in the competition for men or jobs; or an opportunity for massive narcissistic indulgence.[36] The social construction of the feminine body is all these things, but it is at base discipline, too, and discipline of the inegalitarian sort. The absence of formally identifiable disciplinarians and of a public schedule of sanctions serves only to disguise the extent to which the imperative to be "feminine" serves the interest of domination. This is a lie in which all concur: Making up is merely artful play; one's first pair of high-heeled shoes is an innocent part of growing up and not the modern equivalent of foot-binding.

Why aren't all women feminists? In modern industrial societies, women are not kept in line by fear of retaliatory male violence; their victimization is not that of the South African black. Nor will it suffice to say that a false consciousness engendered in women by patriarchal ideology is at the basis of female subordination. This is not to deny the fact that women are often subject to gross male violence or that women and men alike are ideologically mystified by the dominant gender arrangements. What I wish to suggest instead is that an adequate understanding of women's oppression will require an appreciation of the extent to which not only women's lives but their very subjectivities are structured within an ensemble of systematically duplicitous practices. The feminine discipline of the body is a case in point: The practices which construct this body have an overt aim and character far removed, indeed radically distinct, from their covert function. In this regard, the system of gender subordination, like the wage-bargain under capitalism, illustrates in its own way the ancient tension between what is and what appears: The phenomenal forms in which it is manifested are often quite different from the real relations which form its deeper structure.

# VII

The lack of formal public sanctions does not mean that a woman who is unable or unwilling to submit herself to the appropriate body discipline will face no sanctions at all. On the contrary, she faces a very severe sanction indeed in a world dominated by men: the refusal of male patronage. For the heterosexual woman, this may mean the loss of a badly needed intimacy; for both heterosexual women and lesbians, it may well mean the refusal of a decent livelihood.

As noted earlier, women punish themselves too for the failure to conform. The growing literature on women's body size is filled with wrenching confessions of shame from the overweight:

> I felt clumsy and huge. I felt that I would knock over furniture, bump into things, tip over chairs, not fit into VW's, especially when people were trying to crowd into the back seat. I felt like I was taking over the whole room. . . . I felt disgusting and like a slob. In the summer I felt hot and sweaty and I knew people saw my sweat as evidence that I was too fat.

> I feel so terrible about the way I look that I cut off connection with my body. I operate from the neck up. I do not look in mirrors. I do not want to spend time buying clothes. I do not want to spend time with make-up because its painful for me to look at myself. [37]

> I can no longer bear to look at myself. Whenever I have to stand in front of a mirror to comb my hair I tie a large towel around my neck. Even at night I slip my nightgown on before I take off my blouse and pants. But all this has only made it worse and worse. It's been so long since I've really looked at my body. [38]

The depth of these women's shame is a measure of the extent to which all women have internalized patriarchal standards of bodily acceptability. A fuller examination of what is meant here by "internalization" may shed light on a question posed earlier: Why isn't every woman a feminist?

Something is "internalized" when it gets incorporated into the structure of the self. By "structure of the self" I refer to those modes of perception and of self-perception which allow a self to distinguish itself both from other selves and from things which are not selves. I have described elsewhere how a generalized male witness comes to structure woman's consciousness of herself as a bodily being. [39] This, then, is one meaning of "internalization." The sense of oneself as a distinct and valuable individual is tied not only to the sense of how one is perceived, but also to what one knows, especially to what one knows how to do; this is a second sense of "internalization." Whatever its ultimate effect, discipline can provide the individual upon whom it is imposed with a sense of mastery as well as a secure sense of identity. There is a certain contradiction here: While its imposition may promote a larger disempowerment, discipline may bring with it a certain development of a person's powers. Women, then, like other skilled individuals, have a stake in the perpetuation of their skills, whatever it may have cost to acquire them and quite apart from the question whether, as a gender, they would have been better off had they never had to acquire them in the first place. Hence, feminism, especially a genuinely radical feminism that questions the patriarchal construction of the female body, threatens women with a certain de-skilling, something people normally resist: Beyond this, it calls into question that aspect of personal identity which is tied to the development of a sense of competence.

Resistance from this source may be joined by a reluctance to part with the rewards of compliance; further, many women will resist the abandonment of an aesthetic that defines what they take to be beautiful. But there is still another source of resistance, one more subtle perhaps, but tied once again to questions of identity and internalization. To have a body felt to be "feminine"—a body socially constructed through the appropriate practices—is in most cases crucial to a woman's sense of herself as female and, since persons currently can *be* only as male or female, to her sense of herself as an existing individual. To possess such a body may also be essential to her sense of herself as a sexually desiring and desirable subject. Hence, any political project which aims to dismantle the machinery that turns a female body into a feminine one may well be apprehended by a woman as something that threatens her with desexualization, if not outright annihilation.

The categories of masculinity and femininity do more than assist in the construction of personal identities; they are critical elements in our informal social ontology. This may account to some degree for the otherwise puzzling phenomenon of homophobia and for the revulsion felt by many at the sight of female bodybuilders; neither the homosexual nor the muscular woman can be assimilated easily into the categories that structure everyday life. The radical feminist critique of femininity, then, may pose a threat not only to a woman's sense of her own identity and desirability but to the very structure of her social universe.

Of course, many women *are* feminists, favoring a program of political and economic reform in the struggle to gain equality with men.[40] But many "reform" or liberal feminists, indeed, many orthodox Marxists, are committed to the idea that the preservation of a woman's femininity is quite compatible with her struggle for liberation.[41] These thinkers have rejected a normative femininity based upon the notion of "separate spheres" and the traditional sexual division of labor while accepting at the same time conventional standards of feminine body display. If my analysis is correct, such a feminism is incoherent. Foucault has argued that modern bourgeois democracy is deeply flawed in that it seeks political rights for individuals constituted as unfree by a variety of disciplinary micropowers that lie beyond the realm of what is ordinarily defined as the "political." "The man described for us whom we are invited to free," he says, "is already in himself the effect of a subjection much more profound than himself."[42] If, as I have argued, female subjectivity is constituted in any significant measure in and through the disciplinary practices that construct the feminine body, what Foucault says here of "man" is perhaps even truer of "woman." Marxists have maintained from the first the inadequacy of a purely liberal feminism: We have reached the same conclusion through a different route, casting doubt at the same time on the adequacy of traditional Marxist prescriptions for women's liberation as well. Liberals call for equal rights for women, traditional Marxists for the entry of women into production on an equal footing with men, the socialization of housework and proletarian revolution; neither calls for the deconstruction of the categories of masculinity and femininity.[43] Femininity as a certain "style of the flesh" will have to be surpassed in the direction of something quite different, not masculinity, which is in many ways only its mirror opposite, but a radical and as yet unimagined transformation of the female body.

# VIII

Foucault has argued that the transition from traditional to modern societies has been characterized by a profound transformation in the exercise of power, by what he calls "a reversal of the political axis of individualization."[44] In older authoritarian systems, power was embodied in the person of the monarch and exercised upon a largely anonymous body of subjects; violation of the law was seen as an insult to the royal individual. While the methods employed to enforce compliance in the past were often quite brutal, involving gross assaults against the body, power in such a system operated in a haphazard and discontinuous fashion; much in the social totality lay beyond its reach.

By contrast, modern society has seen the emergence of increasingly invasive apparatuses of power: These exercise a far more restrictive social and psychological control than was heretofore possible. In modern societies, effects of power "circulate through progressively finer channels, gaining access to individuals themselves, to their bodies, their gestures and all their daily actions."[45] Power now seeks to transform the minds of those individuals who might be tempted to resist it, not merely to punish or imprison their bodies. This requires two things: a finer control of the body's time and its movements—a control that cannot be achieved without ceaseless surveillance and a better understanding of the specific person, of the genesis and nature of his "case." The power these new apparatuses seek to exercise requires a new knowledge of the individual: Modern psychology and sociology are born. Whether the new modes of control have charge of correction, production, education, or the provision of welfare, they resemble one another; they exercise power in a bureaucratic mode—faceless, centralized, and pervasive. A reversal has occurred: Power has now become anonymous, while the project of control has brought into being a new individuality. In fact, Foucault believes that the operation of power constitutes the very subjectivity of the subject. Here, the image of the Panopticon returns: Knowing that he may be observed from the tower at any time, the inmate takes over the job of policing himself. The gaze which is inscribed in the very structure of the disciplinary institution is internalized by the inmate: Modern technologies of behavior are thus oriented toward the production of isolated and self-policing subjects.[46]

Women have their own experience of the modernization of power, one which begins later but follows in many respects the course outlined by Foucault. In important ways, a woman's behavior is less regulated now than it was in the past. She has more mobility and is less confined to domestic space. She enjoys what to previous generations would have been an unimaginable sexual liberty. Divorce, access to paid work outside the home, and the increasing secularization of modern life have loosened the hold over her of the traditional family and, in spite of the current fundamentalist revival, of the church. Power in these institutions was wielded by individuals known to her. Husbands and fathers enforced patriarchal authority in the family. As in the *ancien régime*, a woman's body was subject to sanctions if she disobeyed. Not Foucault's royal individual but the Divine Individual decreed that her desire be always "unto her husband," while the person of the priest made known to her God's more specific intentions concerning her place and duties. In the days when civil and ecclesiastical authority were still conjoined, individuals formally invested with power were charged with the correction of recalcitrant women whom the family had somehow failed to constrain.

By contrast, the disciplinary power that is increasingly charged with the production of a properly embodied femininity is dispersed and anonymous; there are no individuals formally empowered to wield it; it is, as we have seen, invested in everyone and in no one in particular. This disciplinary power is peculiarly modern: It does not rely upon violent or public sanctions, nor does it seek to restrain the freedom of the female body to move from place to place. For all that, its invasion of the body is well-nigh total: The female body enters "a machinery of power that explores it, breaks it down and rearranges it."[47] The disciplinary techniques through which the "docile bodies" of women are constructed aim at a regulation which is perpetual and exhaustive—a regulation of the body's size and contours, its appetite, posture, gestures, and general comportment in space and the appearance of each of its visible parts.

As modern industrial societies change and as women themselves offer resistance to patriarchy, older forms of domination are eroded. But new forms arise, spread, and become consolidated. Women are no longer required to be chaste or modest, to restrict their sphere of activity to the home, or even to realize their properly feminine destiny in maternity: Normative femininity is coming more and more to be centered on woman's body—not its duties and obligations or even its capacity to bear children, but its sexuality, more precisely, its presumed heterosexuality and its appearance. There is, of course, nothing new in women's preoccupation with youth and beauty. What is new is the growing power of the image in a society increasingly oriented toward the visual media. Images of normative femininity, it might be ventured, have replaced the religiously oriented tracts of the past. New too is the spread of this discipline to all classes of women and its deployment throughout the life-cycle. What was formerly the specialty of the aristocrat or courtesan is now the routine obligation of every woman, be she a grandmother or a barely pubescent girl.

To subject oneself to the new disciplinary power is to be up-to-date, to be "with-it"; as I have argued, it is presented to us in ways that are regularly disguised. It is fully compatible with the current need for women's wage labor, the cult of youth and fitness, and the need of advanced capitalism to maintain high levels of consumption. Further, it represents a saving in the economy of enforcement: Since it is women themselves who practice this discipline on and against their own bodies, men get off scot-free.

The woman who checks her make-up half a dozen times a day to see if her foundation has caked or her mascara run, who worries that the wind or rain may spoil her hairdo, who looks frequently to see if her stockings have bagged at the ankle, or who, feeling fat, monitors everything she eats, has become, just as surely as the inmate of Panopticon, a self-policing subject, a self committed to a relentless self-surveillance. This self-surveillance is a form of obedience to patriarchy. It is also the reflection in woman's consciousness of the fact that *she* is under surveillance in ways that *he* is not, that whatever else she may become, she is importantly a body designed to please or to excite. There has been induced in many women, then, in Foucault's words, "a state of conscious and permanent visibility that assures the automatic functioning of power."[48] Since the standards of female bodily acceptability are impossible fully to realize, requiring as they do a virtual transcendence of nature, a woman may live much of her life with a pervasive feeling of bodily deficiency. Hence, a tighter control of the body has gained a new kind of hold over the mind.

Foucault often writes as if power constitutes the very individuals upon whom it operates:

> The individual is not to be conceived as a sort of elementary nucleus, a primitive atom, a multiple and inert material on which power comes to fasten or against which it happens to strike. . . . In fact, it is already one of the prime effects of power that certain bodies, certain gestures, certain discourses, certain desires, come to be identified and constituted as individuals.[49]

Nevertheless, if individuals were wholly constituted by the power/knowledge regime Foucault describes, it would make no sense to speak of resistance to discipline at all. Foucault seems sometimes on the verge of depriving us of a vocabulary in which to conceptualize the nature and meaning of those periodic refusals of control which, just as much as the imposition of control, mark the course of human history.

Peter Dews accuses Foucault of lacking a theory of the "libidinal body," i.e., the body upon which discipline is imposed and whose bedrock impulse toward spontaneity and pleasure might perhaps become the locus of resistance.[50] Do women's "libidinal" bodies, then, not rebel against the pain, constriction, tedium, semi-starvation, and constant self-surveillance to which they are currently condemned? Certainly they do, but the rebellion is put down every time a woman picks up her eyebrow tweezers or embarks upon a new diet. The harshness of a regimen alone does not guarantee its rejection, for hardships can be endured if they are thought to be necessary or inevitable.

While "nature," in the form of a "libidinal" body, may not be the origin of a revolt against "culture," domination and the discipline it requires are never imposed without some cost. Historically, the forms and occasions of resistance are manifold. Sometimes, instances of resistance appear to spring from the introduction of new and conflicting factors into the lives of the dominated: The juxtaposition of old and new and the resulting incoherence or "contradiction" may make submission to the old ways seem increasingly unnecessary. In the present instance, what may be a major factor in the relentless and escalating objectification of women's bodies—namely, women's growing independence—produces in many women a sense of incoherence that calls into question the meaning and necessity of the current discipline. As women (albeit a small minority of women) begin to realize an unprecedented political, economic, and sexual self-determination, they fall ever more completely under the dominating gaze of patriarchy. It is this paradox, not the "libidinal body," that produces, here and there, pockets of resistance.

In the current political climate, there is no reason to anticipate either widespread resistance to currently fashionable modes of feminine embodiment or joyous experimentation with new "styles of the flesh"; moreover, such novelties would face profound opposition from material and psychological sources identified earlier in this essay (see Section VII). In spite of this, a number of oppositional discourses and practices have appeared in recent years. An increasing number of women are "pumping iron," a few with little concern for the limits of body development imposed by current canons of femininity. Women in radical lesbian communities have also rejected hegemonic images of femininity and are struggling to develop a new female aesthetic. A striking feature of such communities is the extent to which they have overcome the oppressive identification of female beauty and desirability with youth: Here, the physical features of aging—"character" lines and greying hair—not only do not diminish a woman's attractiveness, they may even enhance it. A popular literature of resistance is growing, some of it analytical and reflective, like Kim Chernin's *The Obsession*, some oriented toward practical self-help, like Marcia Hutchinson's recent *Transforming Body Image: Learning to Love the Body You Have.*[51] This literature reflects a mood akin in some ways to that other and earlier mood of quiet desperation to which Betty Friedan gave voice in *The Feminine Mystique*. Nor should we forget that a mass-based women's movement is in place in this country which has begun a critical questioning of the meaning of femininity, if not yet in this, then in other domains of life. We women cannot begin the re-vision of our own bodies until we learn to read the cultural messages we inscribe upon them daily and until we come to see that even when the mastery of the disciplines of femininity produce a triumphant result, we are still only women.[52]

## Reading Questions

1. What does Foucault mean by a "microphysics of power"?
2. What social practices construct femininity as an achievement and an artifice?
3. What, according to Bartky, is the relationship between modern forms of surveillance and women's "internalization" of patriarchal oppression?
4. Why does Bartky assert that modern disciplinary practices that construct femininity also cause shame?
5. What are some ways in which the disciplinary practices of femininity differ according to race, class, or regional specificity?
6. What elements in the modernization of patriarchal power make resistance difficult? What are some forms of resistance?

## Recommended Reading

Kim Chernin, *The Obsession* (New York: HarperCollins, 1982)

Susan Faludi, "Dressing the Dolls: The Fashion Backlash" and "Beauty and the Backlash," *Backlash: The Undeclared War Against Women* (New York: Doubleday, 1991)

Michel Foucault, "The Ethic of Care for the Self as a Practice of Freedom," *The Final Foucault*, eds. James Bernauer and David Rasmussen (Cambridge, MA: MIT Press, 1988)

Frigga Haug, ed., *Female Sexualization: A Collective Work of Memory*, trans. Erica Carter (New York: Routledge, 1987)

K. Sue Jewell, *From Mammy to Miss America and Beyond: Cultural Images and the Shaping of U.S. Social Policy* (New York: Routledge, 1993)

Naomi Wolf, *The Beauty Myth: How Images of Beauty Are Used Against Women* (New York: Anchor, 1992)

Iris Young, *Throwing like a Girl and Other Essays in Feminist Philosophy* (Bloomington: Indiana University Press, 1990)

## Recommended Audiovisual Resources

*An Anorexic's Tale: The Brief Life of Catherine*. 1992. Produced by Thames Television. Docudrama telling the story of Catherine Dunbar's seven-year battle for life in the fight against anorexia. Films for the Humanities.

*Body Addicts*. 1993. Produced by Pauline Duffy. Documentary on people who are addicted to exercise. Filmakers Library.

*Eating Disorders*. 1991. Produced by Thames Television. Covers the personality profiles of the likeliest anorexia patients. Films for the Humanities.

# Bodies–Pleasures–Powers

## LINDA SINGER

Linda Singer, before her untimely death in 1991, taught philosophy at Miami University in Ohio. She is the author of *Erotic Welfare: Sexual Theory and Politics in the Age of Epidemic*, from which this selection is taken.

Although the 1960s are the decade usually credited with making sex a political issue and the subject of popular and scholarly discourse, the 1980s have been a time when sexual political issues have become both targets of major social agenda, and ubiquitous elements of popular culture. It is also a time when sexual politics is not very sexy.

We have become accustomed to daily news reports on the AIDS crisis. The recent past has been dominated by sexual political dramas such as the Baby M case, the Vatican's latest document on reproductive technology, the bombing of another abortion clinic, the debate on sex education, the rise in teenage pregnancies. Sexual paraphernalia and technology are enjoying wider circulation and distribution. Erotica is marketed to women in their homes like Tupperware, or through cable channels and video cassettes. Such marketing strategies have not only expanded the range of potential consumers, but have also resulted in some new sexual services, like phone sex and party lines, and new genres of erotica (Ehrenreich et al. 103–60). Fertility technology is more affordable and widely available, and the business of adoptions and surrogate mothering is said to be booming while rights to legalized abortions have been reopened for debate. Television promotes the prophylactic use of condoms and advertises home pregnancy tests and ovulation detectors with names like "First Alert," while devoting more programming time to subjects like teenage prostitution, transsexuality, domestic violence, rape, homosexuality, incest, and AIDS.

Despite this proliferation of sexual commodities and systems for their distribution, most contemporary sexual discourse is not very sexy, because it operates within a logic and language of "sexual epidemic." Central to the emergence of epidemic as a historically specific hegemony[1] has been a concern with the rise in sexually transmitted diseases, most notably AIDS, but also the herpes virus which, though not fatal like AIDS, is a chronic condition which has been in wide circulation for some time. According to epidemiologists and public health officials, both diseases are expected to increase in incidence, not only because they are transmitted through intimate contact which is difficult to regulate, but also because the viruses can be carried and spread by infected individuals who are and may remain asymptomatic, or who continue to engage in sexual activity after having been diagnosed. The relative unreliability of the AIDS tests and the chronic nature of herpes further complicate the conditions of contagion, and attempts to control these diseases have been difficult to coordinate.

The threat and fear of contagion have transformed the economy of sexual exchange, reconfiguring the relationship between prospective profit and loss, benefit and risk, for both individuals and the so-called "social body." When one of the possible consequences of sexual activity is the contraction of a debilitating fatal disease or one which is likely to remain and recur, the logic and strategies of judgment and decision are irrevocably altered, even for those who try to avoid such considerations.

Hence it is neither deniable nor surprising that the emergence of the hegemony of epidemic is affecting personal sexual practice, a change with existential and political implications. The anxieties unleashed by the current epidemic are not limited to concerns about disease transmission. The recognition of this unhappy connection between sex and death has also prompted renewed concern about the production of life itself, about reproduction, fertility, and the family, which are also seen as threatened by current conditions. At a time when so-called sexual adventurism is under attack as unsafe, there is a felt need to construct a new, more prudential sexual aesthetic, in terms of which desires and behaviors are stylized, valorized, and eroticized. As a result, there is renewed emphasis on domestication and on the kind of restraint emblematized by the recent "Just Say No" campaign. While gay men find their situation made problematic by a revived and newly legitimated climate of homophobia, women are also being subjected to a new set of gender-specific regulatory strategies designed to maximize their social utility as breeders while minimizing the social costs attached to sexual exchanges. Such strategies include, but are not limited to, rapid developments in fertility technology which allow, in surrogacy situations, reproduction without exposing men to the risks entailed in the exchange of bodily fluids. It is not surprising that, at a time when there is a need to reinvent sexuality or reorganize the erotic economy, a disproportionate weight is falling on the bodies of women. It is hard to disconnect recent campaigns to limit abortions, for example, from a strategy aimed at restricting sexual encounters by raising the risks of such encounters for women. This punitive logic is also responsible for helping shift the terms of sexual exchange, and the climate in which they occur.

The mentality of epidemic has many important symptomatic consequences for policy and ideological debate in explicitly public spheres, consequences that necessitate further reflection. This shift can be summarily described as a move from an inflationary economy of optimism toward an economy of erotic recession or stagflation. Nowhere are the consequences of this shift more poignantly evident than in the gay male community (Shilts), both because it has been the sector of the population hit hardest by the disease so far, and because so much of the ideology of "gay pride" and of the social codes that defined gay life were predicated on the prospect of open-ended sexual proliferation, a prospect fostered by the growth of specialized zones like Christopher and Castro Streets which provided the gay community with relatively protected and defensible sites for such activity. The discourse of gay pride and its proliferative imperatives emerged within and was supported by the larger hegemony of "sexual revolution," which engaged the imaginations and energies of segments of the feminist, lesbian, and heterosexual communities as well.

Sexual revolution, as it was conceived, was centered around a "politics of ecstasy" which sought liberation in the form of release from an apparatus of repression. Liberation, according to the politics of ecstasy, necessitated a revaluation of sex apart from reproductive utilities, as well as resistance to organizations of sexual energies according to aims other than human fulfillment. The policies of ecstasy sought to mobilize the population in a revolutionary transformation of sexual theory, practice, and politics that would make sex better, or make better sex. Better sex, closely connected but not identical with ecstasy, operated with a certain semantic fluidity, given the multiplicity of subjects and articulatory positions from which such discourses arose and to which they were addressed. Differences in gender, sexual orientation, race, and class, amongst other factors, help account for the diversity of visions animating this collective (if uncoordinated) effort to dramatically restructure existing sexual hegemonies.

Included as elements in the referential network of "better sex": more sex, with more partners, in more ways, with greater orgasmic potency, intensity, emotional satisfaction, and intimacy, at a lower cost economically, socially, biologically, and psychologically. Sexual proliferation made sense as a strategy, since what was understood to stand in the way of better sex was a regime of repression and an economy of self-denial, which was circulated in a variety of currencies. The substantive analysis of the regime of repression was extensive and varied in its targetings of the nature and operation of the repressive apparatus. The discourse of sexual revolution also produced critiques of specific sexual institutions such as mandatory heterosexism, phallocentrism, male dominance, monogamy, and the nuclear family, all of which were identified as culprits contributing to a climate of surplus repression that was costly in psychic, social, and political terms (Weeks). Common to all discussions of sexual liberation was an awareness of the political dynamics of dominance and hierarchy that structured and were reproduced in sexual exchange. Under attack was a hegemonic formation that privileged heterosexism over homosexuality and lesbian experience, phallocentricity over gynocentricity, reproductive over non-reproductive sex. Following this logic, the regime of repression could be challenged on political grounds, namely, that its operations constituted unauthorized, arbitrary, or unjustified restrictions on the lives of bodies and the forms of exchange in which they privately chose to engage. Hence sexual revolution necessitated confrontation with and transgression of forms of sexual authority which constituted barriers to better sex. Conspicuous proliferative sexuality, which violated and exposed the repressive regime, consequently took on the value of liberatory strategies of subversion, critique, and rebellion, especially for those groups which had been most disadvantaged or marginalized by the operative sexual economy. For many women and members of the gay community, a climate of proliferative sexuality offered occasions both for self-affirmation and for enfranchising their needs and desires in a way that connected them with larger movements of resistance to these same systems of privilege.

In this sense, sexual political struggles over the past two decades have not just been struggles over sexual activities as such, but have also been concerned with contesting the order of privilege and visibility defined by the operative political organization of sexual differences. For gays, especially gay men, the urgency to make those differences visible by getting out of the closet and into the street was compatible with and facilitated by a proliferative aesthetic which functioned as a promissory alternative. For many heterosexual women, a proliferative sexuality provided a potent weapon against the double standard, while allowing them to explore a gynocentric economy that had been marginalized by the phallocentrism that dominated social life. For groups whose desires had been ignored, or worse, targeted (i.e., marked as sites for regulatory surveillance or judgment), the claim of entitlement to pleasure was a gesture of political assertion which carried over into other social arenas as well (Altman 146–71).

# Epidemics and Sexual Politics

With the rise of the hegemony of sexual epidemic, the optimism implied by this prolif-erative logic reaches a certain kind of dead end. Consequently, a variety of strategic and tactical shifts have emerged which contribute to what I have earlier in this text described as a "recessionary erotic economy." The ethos of an ecstatic carnival is progressively being displaced by a more sober and reserved aesthetic of "sexual prudence" and "body man-agement." The language of "better sex" is being replaced by that of "safe sex" and the promotion of a "new sobriety." These historically specific changes are most visible and pressing at this point for gay men[2] but will not remain so for long as the AIDS virus spreads to other segments of the population. Given the current state of medical research, epidemic conditions are likely to persist for some time and hence continue to structure the context for sexual-political discourse, particularly in the absence of some counterhege-monic discourse of resistance.

The age of sexual epidemic demands a new sexual politics, and therefore, a rethinking of the relationship between bodies, pleasures, and powers beyond the call for liberation from repression. That is because, as Michel Foucault pointed out with a certain pre-science, the power deployed in the construction and circulation of an epidemic, espe-cially a sexual epidemic, functions primarily as a force of production and proliferation rather than as a movement of repression. The determination that a situation is epidemic is always, according to Foucault, a political determination (*Birth* 15). Epidemics differ from diseases not in kind but in quantity. Hence the epidemic determination is in part a mathematical one, made by those with access to information and the authority to make and circulate such determinations. An epidemic emerges as a product of a socially authoritative discourse in light of which bodies will be mobilized, resources will be dispensed, and tactics of surveillance and regulation will appear to be justified. Foucault argues that a medicine of epidemic could only exist with supplementation by the police (*Birth* 15). In this view, the construction of an epidemic situation has a strategic value in determining the configurations of what Foucault calls "biopower," since the epidemic provides an occasion and a rationale for multiplying points of intervention into the lives of bodies and populations. For this reason, epidemics are always historically specific in a way that diseases are not, since the strategic imperatives motivating particular ways of coping with an epidemic always emerge as tactical responses to local utilities and cir-cumstances. The construction of a sexual epidemic, as Foucault argues, provides an optimum site of intersection between the individual bodies and populations. Hence sexual epidemic provides access to bodies and a series of codes for inscribing them, as well as providing a discourse of justification. When any phenomenon is represented as "epi-demic," it has, by definition, reached a threshold that is quantitatively unacceptable. It is the capacity to make and circulate this determination, and to mobilize people in light of it, that constitutes the real political force of the discourse of sexual epidemic (Patton 51–66). With respect to our current situation, it is important to emphasize that the response to AIDS has been quite different from that given to other sexually transmitted diseases before remedies for them were found. This is not because venereal diseases did not have dire consequences for those who contracted them. Rather, the differences can be attributed, at least in part, to the belief that Victorian social structures could limit transmission by restricting the access of bodies to one another, especially given the dominance of particular institutions and ideologies. The AIDS epidemic is different, in part, because it comes on the heels of a period of explicit advocacy for proliferative sexuality, and because this epidemic first surfaced in a community that was already regarded as marginal, and to some, as morally suspect.

The history of the institutional responses to AIDS reveals how the politics of epidemics can work to solidify hegemonies. For years, gay activists and supporters lobbied for better funding for AIDS treatment and research, as the impact of the disease on their community increased. Such efforts went largely unrecognized and received little support from elected officials and health care professionals (Shilts). It was not until the disease spread to other segments of the population and taxed health care resources that medical professionals began to speak of an epidemic. This indicates not only how power is operative in constructing epidemics but also how that construction can be used to organize attention, energy, and material support. In light of the strategic value of epidemics, it is also important to point out that in a contemporary context, the primary medium for circulating the hegemony of epidemic has not been a medical discourse, but an explicitly political and ideological one. The forces most responsible for intensifying the political stakes entailed in sexual epidemic have been a collection of conservative groups from La Roucheans to Christian fundamentalists which have been able to exploit concern about AIDS to solicit support for their rather specific and rigid social agendas. The politics of epidemic is conducive to the New Right because an epidemic situation justifies, and is in fact constructed so as to necessitate, a complex system of surveillance and intervention. The New Right is willing to provide it in the form of a constitutional ban on abortion, restrictions on the distribution of contraception and sexual information, and on the production and distribution of sexual representations (i.e., pornography, erotica), as well as mandatory drug and AIDS testing. Conservative forces have also been able to exploit the anxiety operative in plague conditions to launch a revisionist critique of the sexual revolution and a defense of "family values" which demand a particular absolutist political program.

The conservative argument begins with an acceptable premise, namely, that the unbridled proliferation of sexually transmitted diseases is unacceptable. The emergence of these conditions is taken to be a consequence of a climate of permissiveness which multiplied sexual contacts and helped contribute to the erosion of authority, i.e., absolute paternalistic religious authority, which was better able to organize sexual energies for socially useful purposes like reproduction and consumption. It was the failure to heed that authority, it is argued, that has produced the crisis in which we now find ourselves. In the absolute logic of this position, the epidemic is interpreted either as a retributive consequence of past transgressions, or as a call to revivify and intensify that authority. These larger concerns both motivate and justify an expansion of the language and logic of epidemic, since it is argued that what is at stake in this plague is not only a threat to our physical well-being, but to our spiritual and social health as well.

The establishment of a connection between epidemic and transgression has allowed for the rapid transmission of the former to phenomena that are outside the sphere of disease. We are thus warned of the "epidemics" of teenage pregnancies, child molestation, abortion, pornography, and divorce. The use of this language marks all of these phenomena as targets for intervention because they have been designated as unacceptable, while at the same time reproducing the power that authorizes and justifies their deployment. According to this discourse, it is existing authority that is to be protected from the plague of transgressions.

Part of what is useful about the conservative polemic is that it provides some insight into the anxiety and malaise that permeate sexual discourse, even amongst those populations, like monogamous heterosexual Christians, who are least at risk of contracting a sexually transmitted disease. By using the occasion of a health crisis to revivify authority, the New Right makes clear that, as another theorist of plague, Albert Camus, points out, plagues are never just medical problematics. They are also world-transforming moments of ontological crisis which pervade the entire logic and fabric of a community's existence by calling it into question in a fundamental way, i.e., within the currency of life and death (Foucault, *History* 145). A plague, according to Camus, always marks a radically anxious point of rupture with respect to the economy of the everyday and its system of stabilized and sedimented significations. A plague is always "unusual, out of place" (Camus 3). One can no longer simply go on with business as usual. One is forced to call one's habits, values, and pleasures into question, precisely because the world in which they have a place is in the process of slipping away. Just what one calls into question and just what is lost will depend on one's position within the operative configuration of differences. For the Christian Right, what is lost is a world of stable systems of values and hierarchies of authority, and with them the confluences and coordinations of behavior they produce. What is lost for those who identified with the movement for sexual revolution is the promise of sexual future without threat, guilt, and suffering. The development of contraceptive technologies and remedies for venereal disease seemed to offer the prospect of organizing sexuality around the pursuit of pleasure. Now that prospect has been deferred by new diseases which present other kinds of risks.

Part of what makes a plague so oppressive is that it presents the individual with a situation that forces reflection and decision at the same time that the random and impersonal movement of contagion limits choice and truncates the sphere under her or his control. Because a plague is always a rupture both in the order of things and in the operative hegemony, it marks the limits of a prudential logic of calculation, either because possibilities are radically reduced, or because they are diminished in their differences. The plague ruptures rationality in the direction of the absurd demand that the unjustifiable be somehow justified. This is the obvious appeal, at least for some people, of the conservative position which offers a radical form of explanatory closure. Because plagues confront us with the limits of our assumptions and fictions, they also call for the generation of new assumptions, new fictions. What is being called into question in current circumstances is the whole way our culture has constructed and valued sex, and with that, all the other deployments of bio- and economic power with which it is connected. Plague conditions force one to ask the question of whether sex is worth dying for.

Camus's analysis helps to explain the malaise and despair that seems to have permeated much of the sexual political arena, a mood that marks a radical break with the optimism induced by the politics of ecstasy. The threat posed by the new sexual epidemic is the problematization of sexual hegemonies in a direction of diminishing returns and reduced expectations, especially for those who came of age during the sexual revolution. But the sexual epidemic has also helped to induce a reversal in the direction of social policy. In the 1960s and 1970s, legislative and policy initiatives reflected traditional liberal concerns for civil rights, individual freedom, right to privacy, and the principles of equality and equity. The liberal initiative helped establish legalized abortion and civil rights for homosexuals, enfranchise the principles of affirmative action and compensatory legislation, as well as contributed a climate of tolerance for sexual pluralism. What is disturbing about the current state of sexual political debate, particularly in the sphere of social policy, is the apparent failure of traditional liberalism to provide an adequate alternative to a conservative authoritarian social logic which advocates increased surveillance and regulation of bodies in ways that support and reproduce hegemonic relationships of dominance.

Traditional liberalism proves inadequate to an epidemic situation which lacks the fundamentally rational teleology that liberalism assumes to characterize most social phenomena. The utilitarian logic of maximizing social utilities while leaving individuals free to pursue their private pleasures in a climate of tolerance does not, and cannot, provide a strategy applicable to an economy of diminishing returns, both because the possibility of maximizing happiness under such conditions is radically suspect, and because epidemics, insofar as they are epidemic, cannot simply be tolerated. Yet such systematic and authorized intervention into the populace's lives and bodies is incompatible with the liberal principles of privacy and respect for the integrity of persons. Hence the liberal repertoire will be limited often to contesting such initiatives as they arise. Because the dynamic of contagion raises the social consequences of individual choices, the liberal model of freely chosen self-regulation is also inadequate as a response to epidemic conditions precisely because epidemics radically alter the context for such decisions in ways that are not and cannot be chosen.

Liberalism also finds itself without a sufficiently mobilizing rhetoric, especially since much of its language has been appropriated by the forces of opposition. For example, the concept of "respect for persons," central to liberal humanism, has been incorporated into the Vatican's rhetoric as grounds for denying women access to abortion and fertility technology, claiming that such procedures do not respect the fetus's personhood.

What is even more interesting is that such "humanist" language is used extensively in the Church's polemic against secular humanism. This language was also employed as part of the Supreme Court's decision to limit affirmative action suits to those filed by individuals, on the grounds that only individual persons can be victims of discriminatory practices. The rhetoric of "tolerance" and "pluralism" has been used as grounds for including representations of conservative positions like "creation science" in textbooks and popular media.

The limits of existing political discourse, as well as the urgency of the current situation, call for new forms of sexual political discourse, currency, and struggle. In this context, Foucault's work is especially helpful since his analysis of the proliferative operation of power supplements the limits of the repressive hypothesis, and offers the option of a strategic analysis which allows us to consider not only what is lost but also what is produced by the current organization of the sexual field which is itself a product of previous power deployments. This means that, counter to a logic which opposes erotic urgency and social utility or ghettoizes the sexual as some stable and invariable set of imperatives, Foucault's analysis demonstrates how the construction of each is dependent upon and made in light of the others, often, as in our age, with dire results which place our existence as a species in question. Part of the agenda for a sexual politics of epidemic will have to be a reconsideration of this "Faustian bargain," along with the generation of alternatives capable of mobilizing bodies sufficiently so as not to paralyze them in an economy of deprivation (Watney 123–35).

With respect to the techniques of embodiment operative in this particular sexual epidemic, we should expect to find that these techniques will reflect and inscribe a system of utilities and pleasures compatible with other demands made on bodies in late patriarchal capitalism. Foucault's insights provide conceptual machinery for making sense of some of what is at stake in the new sexual technology, which operates not through threat of death and pain, but instead establishes dominion over life through a currency of historically specific pleasures and powers. According to Foucault, the consequence of much of contemporary body techniques is that modern man has become "an animal whose politics places his existence as a living being in question" (Foucault, *History* 141). The implication of Foucault's analysis is the need to reconsider strategies in light of historical specificities.

## Epidemic Strategies

In an effort to concretize and extend Foucault's analysis, which in some sense was cut short by the sexual epidemic, I will examine some of the modes of embodiment that have emerged as responses to current conditions. I will begin by discussing the discourses of "safe sex" and "the new sobriety" as two tactical responses to the hegemony of epidemic. I will then focus on some contemporary techniques of "body management" and will conclude with a discussion of some contemporary technologies aimed at intervening in human reproduction as strategies for exercising power over the lives of bodies and populations.

Part of the proliferative surplus produced by the hegemony of sexual epidemic are the discourses and techniques known as "safe sex" and "the new sobriety." Both represent exercises in theory and practice which emerged from discussions within the gay community, at once the initial source and the audience for them. But as AIDS begins to infect other segments of the population, these techniques are being far more widely promulgated and circulated through mainstream channels of communication and the voice of authority figures like the Surgeon General. As opposed to the absolutist logic employed by the New Right, these secular strategies employ a cost-benefit logic drawn from the discourses of finance, management, and to some extent, preventive medicine. Both strategies assume that sexual proliferation, like nuclear proliferation and the national debt, is not something one can hope to eliminate. The goal instead is to try to manage it strategically so as to minimize the risks of sexual contact without resorting to abstinence, which for many is clearly an untenable option.

In "safe sex," one minimizes the risks of sexual contact by developing an erotics which privileges prudential judgment over spontaneity, and prioritizes selectivity over variety. Minimally, safe sex entails the prophylactic use of condoms and avoidance of what are termed "high risk activities," like anal sex, and "high risk groups," like IV users. Making this prudential logic operational will demand changes in the economy of genital gestures and erotic choreography. It will also necessitate a reorganization of pleasure, a reconstruction of the erotic body, and an alteration in the terms and expectations of sexual exchanges.

Part of the change proffered by epidemic conditions is a shift in the relationship between knowledge and desire as they function in erotic situations. Specifically, knowledge of one's partners' physical condition and sexual history now becomes a prime object of concern. The erotic gaze is thus infected to some degree by the medical gaze which must learn to see sickness. The prudential aesthetic which characterizes the new sobriety creates specific forms of desire, like dating agencies which promise matches with pre-screened AIDS-free partners.

Failing such elaborate screening procedures, and given the limits of their reliability, the ideology of safe sex encourages a reorganization of the body away from the erotic priorities with which it has already been inscribed. Specifically, safe sex advocates indulgence in numerous forms of non-genital contact and the reengagement of parts of the body marginalized by an economy of genital primacy. It also entails a reconfiguration of bodies and their pleasures away from an ejaculatory teleology toward a more polymorphous decentered exchange, reviving and concretizing the critique of genital condensation begun over twenty years ago by sexual theorists like Marcuse and Firestone.

The underlying assumptions about the relationships among bodies, pleasures, and powers which make safe sex possible depend, at least indirectly, on Foucault's analysis and its destabilizing consequences. Safe sex presumes that pleasure and practice can be reorganized in response to overriding utilities and presumes, as well, the capacity of regimentary procedures to construct a body capable of taking pleasure in this new form of discipline. Unless bodies and pleasures are politically determined, they can not be redetermined, even in cases where that is what rational prudence would demand. The success of this strategy will thus depend not only on promulgating these techniques, but also on circulating a discourse that allows individuals to reconsider their bodies in a more liberatory and strategic way.[3] What is new about the new sobriety is that its aesthetic of restraint is not represented in terms of monastic economy of self-denial or obedience to some authoritative imperative, but is instead presented as a gesture of primary narcissism, a way of caring for and about oneself. Liberation, in this context, is relocated in an economy of intensification of control over one's body and one's position in sexual exchanges.

The new sobriety constructs a body well designed for the complexities of life in late capitalism, which requires a worker's body and a body of workers that are well managed in the way a portfolio is well managed, i.e., a body with flexible and diverse investments which maximize accumulated surplus as negotiable profits. The body constructed in the discourse of the new sobriety is inscribed with a discipline that is supposed to allow for more efficient functioning and control in both sex and work, in part because this bodily regimen has been represented as an exercise in self-fulfillment and development which should be part of the well-managed enlightened life.

The connection of the discourse of "body management" with primary narcissism creates a complex of strategies and disciplines which extend beyond the sphere of sexual practices to include other bodily techniques like nutrition, fitness, hygiene, cosmetics, diets, and what is referred to as "body building." I want to focus on the phenomenon of body building, partly because it is undergoing an historically unprecedented popularity, especially among women, and partly because body building, as both theory and practice, reveals how bodies are constructed within the new disciplinary regime, and what utilities, pleasures, and powers are being pursued in this reconstruction.

The very language of "body building" already targets a body that is assumed to be rebuildable. The disciplinary regimen, and its accompanying aesthetic, mobilizes the body as a divisible collection of parts which can be individually fine-tuned or standardized according either to some aesthetic ideal, or to the demands of the labor process. Such a regimen often involves the use of mechanical apparatuses like the Nautilus machine which isolate, target, and differentially work specific muscle groups. The fine-tuning of the body is often supplemented by far more interventionist procedures like plastic surgery, skin grafting, hair coloring and transplants, and the tanning booth to further control and refine the finished product, which is regarded as in need of perpetual maintenance and surveillance. The popularity of these techniques can be attributed to the proliferative effects of the slippage between energies organized according to a predetermined pattern of behavior, and the mobilizations of those energies as activities of self-love and personal development. Rather than depending on a regime of repression, the new discipline operates through a strategy of control by stimulation, which mobilizes energies through anonymous channels of regulation which can also be represented as activities of individuation.

When reproductive imperatives are added to the utilities to be mobilized by the discourse of body management, women's bodies become targets for gender-specific strategies and tactics. If, as Foucault suggests, the deployments of modern power seek to intervene at a place where individual bodies intersect with the body of the social, it is not surprising that reproduction is being restructured by a series of technologies designed to make that process, and the bodies who accomplish it, more malleable and responsive to fluctuations in demographic utilities.

Given women's subordinate position within a patriarchal social order, discipline has always been a technique used to marshall women's energies and bodies in pursuit of utilities not of their own making. Given that women's place is often constructed as one of self-effacing service, it is not surprising that female disciplinary strategies often take the form of radical self-denial, as in the case of body practices such as anorexia and bulimia. But the well-managed female body of the '80s is constructed so as to be even more multifunctional than its predecessors. It is a body that can be used for wage labor, sex, reproduction, mothering, spectacle, exercise, or even invisibility, as the situation demands. It is also a body that is constructed to accommodate the variable whims of fashion, and a postmodern aesthetic which demands the capacity to project a multiplicity of looks and attitudes with apparent effortlessness.

Most important, however, and what is historically specific about this construct is that this body's reproductive potential is managed and disciplined so as to be capable of conceiving and producing children on demand, as well as deferring that process until the time is right. Most of the innovations in reproductive ideology and technology have sought to render women's bodies more easily mobilizable in response to shifting utilities, most notably the production and coordination of populations. In order to address the different sorts of intervention that produce the contemporary ideologies of motherhood, I will begin by examining the differential strategies by which motherhood is being marketed to particular segments of the female population. I will then analyze the strategic value of the new reproductive technology and will conclude with a discussion of one recent and conspicuous case of fallout from this technology, the Baby M case.

The differential strategies by which women are addressed by these ideological discourses borrow their tactics and logic from advertising and market research, two disciplines which have devised elaborate mechanism for segmenting the prospective market and for designing highly specific occasions of incitement which can be tailor-made to appeal to particular predetermined segments of the population. The necessity to market motherhood appears to have been motivated, at least in part, by the development of contraceptive technologies which give women some measure of control over their fertility and its consequences. Current marketing strategies have also emerged as responses to what can be read as a demographic gap in the birth rate amongst white middle-class educated women who, beginning in the early '70s, began in larger numbers to defer motherhood or to avoid it altogether. This mobilization of women's energies was facilitated by a feminist discourse which explicitly challenged the reproductive imperative (Allen 91–101) and in some cases made women's liberation dependent upon refusing such imperatives. During approximately the same period of time, however, there was also a statistically significant rise in pregnancies amongst teenagers, especially poor women of color, who were more likely than their older counterparts to have their babies delivered, and in some cases supported, at state expense. In a white-male-dominated culture this was perceived as a situation that called for adjustment.

Hence we start to find images of attractive successful women like Christie Brinkley, Patti Hanson, Shelley Long, as well as media feminists like Erica Jong, proudly posing on magazine covers and bus shelters advocating the pleasures of motherhood. Never mind that these women mother under conditions that are likely to be radically different from those of the women addressed in the ads. The strategy of these campaigns was to inscribe motherhood within a series of elements the sum of which was represented as "having it all" in the proper sequence, which is the mark of any "superwoman." There is some evidence that this strategy worked, helping to contribute to what *Time* magazine has dubbed "the mini baby boom," a discourse circulated without irony, and without ever raising the question of "boom" for whom or what.

Contemporaneous with these images is an ad campaign in which Planned Parenthood addresses potential teenage mothers. The poster series consists of several versions of the same basic format varied by racial type, in which a young woman holding a baby stares dead-pan at the viewer in what is clearly depicted as dismal surroundings. The accompanying boldface copy reads, "It's like being grounded for eighteen years."[4]

The tactics employed in these cases are obvious at the first and are intended to work in precisely opposite ways, discouraging younger women of color from reproducing by emphasizing the burdens of motherhood, while effacing those burdens when addressing women whose reproductive services are regarded as useful, either from the standpoint of maintaining race and class dominance, or as a strategy for inducing women's voluntary defection from more competitive segments of the labor market. Certainly, if motherhood demobilizes women, it does so regardless of the mother's age, though class, race, and educational differences determine the forms such demobilization will take. But for a variety of reasons it is strategically desirable to circulate a discourse of differences, and to abridge recognition of the continuities in women's experience that emerge as a consequence of the gender caste system, which links all women by their subordination to phallocentric utilities. In any case, given the complexities of race and class differences, along with the degree of specificity attempted, we should not be surprised when some of these messages get crossed in transmission and arrive at destinations for which they were not intended, since within any dominant strategic deployments sites of opposition and resistance are also created. The political challenge is to develop strategies for organizing and coordinating those positions in a way that mobilizes their counter-hegemonic potential.

At the level of reproductive technology and technique, the radical disparity between the development rates of fertility, as opposed to contraceptive, technology in the last twenty years helps mark both a strategy and a dominant set of utilities. While fertility technology becomes more sophisticated and widely available, contraceptive technology and distribution, along with public debate, seem in many respects to be moving in the opposite direction. New fertility clinics and surrogate mothering agencies open while abortion clinics are being bombed.

The current fertility technology has been strategically designed for maximum flexibility in its capabilities for deployment. It can be used, or has the potential to be used, either to intervene so as to enlist more women in the reproductive brigades, or to render women biologically extraneous. Developments in fetal medicine and eugenics offer the prospects of regulating the product as well as the process of reproduction and normalizing intervention into the lives of persons by beginning even before they have that status. Each of these techniques touches the core of the bio-power system, the control over production of life, in a way that thus far has worked primarily to solidify and support a hegemony of white male heterosexist dominance. The question remains as to whether such techniques also offer more liberatory possibilities. Any response to this challenge will be dependent upon recognizing the complex intersections between bio-power and other systems of deployment which produce both the discourse and the terms of sexual struggle.

Nowhere do the complexities of this multi-layered apparatus become more visible in their contradictions than in what has probably been the hottest and most widely circulated sexual political issue of the '80s, save AIDS, namely the Baby M case. Its import is immediately felt at the level of language, where it introduced the neologism "surrogate motherhood" into popular parlance. But as one might expect, it also began a new logic and politics of parental privilege.

The use of the term "surrogate mother" to apply to Mary Beth Whitehead already reflects a bias in favor of paternal prerogative and a privileging of contractual relations regulating commodities over issues of biology and maternal desire. Given the way the issues were framed, i.e., as a choice between legally authorized paternity and biological maternity, and the context presumed by legal discourse, i.e., a class-stratified male-dominated hegemony, it is not surprising that the ruling granted custody of the child to the more affluent father. But what is really at stake in this case is less a contest between paternal and maternal claims than a question of maternal prerogative. The strategic value of the Baby M case, and its resolution, lies more with the way it manages the contest between two competing claims of motherhood, the one legal and contractual, the other biological and genetic, which in this case was resolved in terms of a legal discourse structured by and facilitating class stratification and male dominance. The consequence in this case was the determination of Whitehead as the surrogate mother, and most significantly, the granting of immediate legal motherhood to Mrs. Stern.[5] But apart from a contractual discourse which defines Whitehead as surrogate, Whitehead is in every other sense the mother of the child. She is the female progenitor, and genetic contributor, and hence, at the very least the child's birth mother. She has the connection with the child regardless of her relationship to the male progenitor. In the context of the case, Mrs.

Stern's claim to maternity is entirely dependent upon and has status only in terms of her husband's desire to claim paternity. Had Mr. Stern for some reason chosen not to exercise his paternal claim, the question of Mrs. Stern's maternity would never have come up.

But the claims made on behalf of Mrs. Whitehead and the language of organized feminist support which focused on Whitehead's rights as a "natural mother" are equally problematic, and in some sense they reproduce the ideological framework in terms of which Mr. Stern's claim proved to be more legally persuasive. Specifically, the appeals to "natural motherhood" overlook an extensive feminist discourse which documents how the discourse of motherhood has been strategically deployed historically to exert control over women's bodies while devaluing and effacing maternal labor, effort, and commitment which are therein reduced to the status of a natural aptitude. These contradictions point toward the strategic value of the discourse of surrogate motherhood, part of which is to pit women against women, largely on the basis of class, and then to reinstitute male prerogative and class privilege[6] as the legal basis for resolving competing claims.

The arguments made on behalf of Mr. Stern's property rights reveal the intersections between the sexual reproduction system and the logic regulating the commodity market. Mr. Stern's attorney argued that he was entitled to the child not because he had paid for her as such, but because he had paid for the use of Whitehead's body for breeding purposes. Retreating to a neo-Aristotelian biology, Stern's attorney redescribed Mary Beth Whitehead as a vessel rented by the client for the express purpose of gestating and delivering the product of his seed. As such, it is argued, he is entitled to get what he paid for, while Whitehead's consent to the contract invalidates any of her further claims.

These arguments clearly place surrogate motherhood on a continuum with other institutional forms of commodifying women's bodies, including prostitution and "mail-order brides." Surrogate motherhood is a technological extension of the wet-nurse, where some women are in the position of using their bodies to support other more privileged women's offspring. In some sense, the decision in this case is compatible with the logic which produces laws that protect the consumers rather than the providers of women's sexual services and that use women's position as sellers to limit their rights and prerogatives. In the case of prostitution, the woman's position as seller of sexual service is regarded as making her unfit for inclusion under laws that protect providers in most other industries. In the case of surrogate motherhood, the judge determined that Whitehead's decision to sell her body for breeding purposes is an indication of her unfitness to mother.[7]

The figuring of the issue of maternal fitness in the Baby M case also reveals the strategic considerations already invested in the discourse of surrogate motherhood. In this case, the question of Whitehead's fitness to mother emerged only as a consequence of Mr. Stern's desire for custody. In cases where paternity is unacknowledged or refused, custody falls *de facto* to the mother, independent of any discourse of maternal fitness. Under ordinary circumstances, questions of parental fitness are displaced to the private sphere of familial autonomy. They arise in this case only as a consequence of paternal and class prerogatives. In this case "fitness" is determined to mean fitness to produce potential consumers rather than potential providers of surrogate services. Hence not only custody but also contractual prerogatives are distributed along hegemonic lines of class and gender privilege.

The way the Baby M case both raises and settles questions about the social and political organization of parenthood and about the meaning and power attached to the positions of paternity and maternity is part of its historically specific strategic value. What makes the Baby M case possible is a confluence of social forces which divide the body and body functions into separable units, linking them with a commodity system that proliferates sites and forms for these exchanges, a legal system that regulates and authorizes such transactions, and a system of sexual and class differences according to which functions and prerogatives are differentially distributed. It was against this background that a drama represented in the language of desire was played out, pitting Mr. Stern's desire to father a child to which he had a genetic connection against Mrs. Whitehead's desire to remain in touch with the child which had emerged from her body. What was being asked of the court in this case, and what is likely to be demanded in the future, was the production of a discursive grid in terms of which the claims established within different disciplinary codes could be mapped, ordered, and ultimately resolved. The Baby M case is the beginning of the attempt to construct the differential calculus. But because the resolution is likely to be challenged, and because this case raises as many questions as it answers, maximum flexibility in deployment is maintained which in turn allows for adjustments in the organization of reproduction according and in relation to other variable utilities and imperatives.

I have chosen to conclude my discussion of sexual politics in the age of epidemic with a discussion of the Baby M case because I think it points toward the kind of sexual political issues that are likely to confront us in the future, and because it functions as the opposing pole to those issues emerging from the logic of sexual disease. Given the proliferative possibilities of both reproductive technology and commodity culture, it is likely that more cases of contested parenthood will arise. It is clear that in the case of surrogate mothering, as in the case of prostitution, a regime of repression, even if one could find grounds for endorsing it, would prove inadequate as a response. In instances of surrogacy, perhaps the best solution will be to treat problems as cases of breached contract, and to let prospective fathers know that there are risks in making such an arrangement.

In a larger context, issues surrounding reproductive technology and organization constitute another series of challenges that confront us in the age of sexual epidemic. Conflicts which entail bodies, pleasures, and the production of life will continue to play out against the background of the struggle against death. Both kinds of struggle will be transacted, at least in part, at the level of cultural currency identified as sexuality, in forms that are likely to reflect and reproduce sexuality's proliferative dynamics, and with an intensity which speaks to the levels of cultural investment in this discourse.

If sexuality, now more than ever, constitutes the turf and terms in which struggles of life and death will be transacted, questions of sexual politics, i.e., of the construction and distribution of bodies, pleasures, and powers, will no longer simply be sites of elective engagement. Because sexuality functions as a force of production and proliferation as well as a currency of valuation, conflicts, as they arise, will continue to force reconsideration of our assumptions about and investment in these hegemonic formations, with the recognition of how much is at stake in the decisions we make. One way to begin is to relocate the sexual not outside but at the intersection of the multiplicity of discourses by which bodies, pleasures, and powers are circulated and exchanged. We ought to do so strategically with attention paid to the specificity of local conditions. We must also remember that in saying yes to sex we are not saying no to power. If sexuality in our age has become, at least for some people, worth the exchange of life itself, it behooves us to reconsider the situation in which we find and risk losing ourselves. The real sexual epidemic may very well turn out to be a politics which places our very existence in question. We therefore need to ask ourselves, with renewed urgency, whether sex is worth dying for, how it is we got to this place, and where we can go from here.

## Reading Questions

1. What does Singer mean by the "logic and language of sexual epidemic," and why does she call it a historically specific hegemony?
2. What is the difference, according to Singer, between an inflationary economy of optimism and an economy of erotic recession? How is this difference manifested in public policy debates on AIDS?
3. What, according to Foucault, is the difference between epidemics or plagues, and diseases?
4. In what ways is traditional liberalism inadequate to an epidemic situation?
5. How does an authoritarian social logic oppose liberalism, and why does it reject social strategies such as the discourses of safe sex?
6. According to Singer, how does the Baby M case illustrate the hegemony of white male heterosexist dominance over reproductive technologies?
7. Why does Singer claim that the Baby M case illustrates an institutional form of commodifying women's bodies?

## Recommended Reading

Evelyn Barbee and Marilyn Little, "Health, Social Class and African-American Women," *Theorizing Black Feminisms*, eds. Evelyn Barbee and Marilyn Little (New York: Routledge, 1993)

Gena Corea, *The Invisible Epidemic: The Story of Women and AIDS* (New York: HarperCollins, 1993)

Stephen Dubin, *Arresting Images: Impolitic Art and Uncivil Actions* (New York: Routledge, 1992)

Barbara Ehrenreich and Deirdre English, *For Her Own Good: 150 Years of Expert's Advice to Women* (New York: Doubleday, 1984)

Michel Foucault, *The Birth of the Clinic: An Archaeology of Medical Perception*, trans. A.M. Sheridan Smith (New York: Pantheon, 1973)

Michel Foucault, *The History of Sexuality, Volume I: An Introduction*, trans. Robert Hurley (New York: Vintage Books, 1990)

J. Ralph Lindgren and Nadine Taub, "In the Matter of Baby M," *The Law of Sex Discrimination*, eds. J. Ralph Lindgren and Nadine Taub (St. Paul, MN: West Publishing, 1988)

Christine Obbo, "HIV Transmission: Men Are the Solution," *Theorizing Black Feminisms*, eds. Evelyn Barbee and Marilyn Little (New York: Routledge, 1993)

Cindy Patton, *Inventing AIDS* (New York: Routledge, 1990)

Lee Quinby, "Genealogical Feminism: A Politic Way of Looking," *Anti-Apocalypse: Exercises in Genealogical Criticism* (Minneapolis: University of Minnesota, 1994)

Michael J. Sandel, *Liberalism and the Limits of Justice* (Cambridge: Cambridge University Press, 1982)

Jana Sawicki, "New Reproductive Technologies," *Disciplining Foucault: Feminism, Power, and the Body* (New York: Routledge, 1991)

## Recommended Audiovisual Resources

*AIDS: The Women Speak*. 1991. Produced by New Jersey Network. Personal documentary of women who are caring for AIDS patients. Films for the Humanities.

*Holy Terror*. 1986. Directed by Victoria Schultz. Examines the emerging political activism of the religious New Right. The Cinema Guild.

*God, Gays and the Gospel*. 1991. Directed by Mary Anne McEwen. Documentary about the Fellowship of Metropolitan Community Churches, a Christian church with a special outreach to gays and lesbians. The Cinema Guild.

*The Other Side of the Fence: Conversations with a Female Fundamentalist*. 1994. Produced by Lynn Estomin, Women's Film Project. The portrait of a fundamentalist Christian woman who formed a militant antiabortion organization, Project Jericho. Filmakers LIbrary.

## CHAPTER 5

# Ecofeminism

A picnic lunch in front of Three Mile Island nuclear plant in Middletown, Pennsylvania, on its opening day, July 7, 1979. It has since closed in the wake of a plant accident. UPI/Bettmann.

# Power, Authority, and Mystery

## Ecofeminism and Earth-Based Spirituality

### STARHAWK

Starhawk is the pen name of Miriam Simos. Teacher, freelance writer for educational and industrial films, and minister and elder of Covenant of the Goddess, she is the author of *Dreaming in the Dark: Magic, Sex and Politics* and *Truth or Dare: Encounters with Power, Authority, and Mystery.*

Earth-based spirituality is rooted in three basic concepts that I call immanence, interconnection, and community. The first—immanence—names our primary understanding that the Earth is alive, part of a living cosmos. What that means is that spirit, sacred, Goddess, God—whatever you want to call it—is not found outside the world somewhere—it's in the world: it *is* the world, and it is us. Our goal is not to get off the wheel of birth nor to be saved from something. Our deepest experiences are experiences of connection with the Earth and with the world.

When you understand the universe as a living being, then the split between religion and science disappears because religion no longer becomes a set of dogmas and beliefs we have to accept even though they don't make any sense, and science is no longer restricted to a type of analysis that picks the world apart. Science becomes our way of looking more deeply into this living being that we're all in, understanding it more deeply and clearly. This itself has a poetic dimension. I want to explore what it means when we really accept that this Earth is alive and that we are part of her being. Right now we are at a point where that living being is nearly terminally diseased. We need to reverse that, to turn that around. We really need to find a way to reclaim our power so that we can reverse the destruction of the Earth.

When we understand that the Earth itself embodies spirit and that the cosmos is alive, then we also understand that everything is interconnected. Just as in our bodies: what happens to a finger affects what happens to a toe. The brain doesn't work without the heart. In the same way, what happens in South Africa affects us here: what we do to the Amazon rain forest affects the air that we breathe here. All these things are interconnected, and interconnection is the second principle of Earth-based spirituality.

Finally, when we understand these interconnections, we know that we are all part of a living community, the Earth. The kind of spirituality and the kind of politics we're called upon to practice are rooted in community. Again, the goal is not individual salvation or enlightenment, or even individual self-improvement, though these may be things and *are* things that happen along the way. The goal is the creation of a community that becomes a place in which we can be empowered and in which we can be connected to the Earth and take action together to heal the Earth.

Each of these principles—immanence, interconnection, and community—calls us to do something. That call, that challenge, is the difference between a spirituality that is practiced versus an intellectual philosophy. The idea that the Earth is alive is becoming an acceptable intellectual philosophy. Scientists have conferences on the Gaia hypothesis without acknowledging that this is exactly what people in tribal cultures, what Witches, shamans, and psychics, have been saying for thousands of years. But there's a difference between accepting it as a scientific philosophy and really living it. Living with the knowledge that the cosmos is alive causes us to do something. It challenges us. Earth-based spirituality makes certain demands. That is, when we start to understand that the Earth is alive, she calls us to act to preserve her life. When we understand that everything is interconnected, we are called to a politics and set of actions that come from compassion, from the ability to literally feel *with* all living beings on the Earth. That feeling is the ground upon which we can build community and come together and take action and find direction.

Earth-based spirituality calls us to live with integrity. Once we know that we're all part of this living body, this world becomes the terrain where we live out spiritual growth and development. It doesn't happen anywhere else, and the way we do it is by enacting what we believe, by taking responsibility for what we do.

These values are not limited to any particular tradition. They can be found in many, many different spiritual traditions and within many different political groups. For me, they come out of my tradition, which is the Pagan tradition, the Wiccan tradition, the old pre-Christian Goddess religion of Europe. We have a certain perspective that I believe can be valuable politically and that is, in some way, linked to what I see ecofeminism and the Green movement attempting. It's not that I think everyone has to be a Witch to be an ecofeminist, or that all Greens should be Witches—pluralism is vitally important in all our movements. It's that I do feel that Pagan values and perspectives can make important contributions to ecofeminist analysis and organizing.

A Pagan perspective might influence our approach to action. For example, I've participated in many political actions and organizations over the past 15 years. There have been times when it's been very exciting. In 1981, 1982, and 1983 the Livermore Action Group (LAG) was active in the Bay Area. We were constantly blockading, demonstrating, risking arrest, and mobilizing large numbers of people.

What happened to LAG, though, is very interesting. At a certain point—in fact, after what was really our strongest, most solid and successful action in 1983—things began to fall apart. Organizing began to get harder and harder, and we were never able to organize a large, cohesive action again. At the same time this was happening to LAG—and we were having meeting after meeting, asking, "Where did we go wrong?"—the same thing was happening to the peace movement in general. Everybody was asking, "What's wrong? Why are we burning out?"

In 1981 and 1982 we were very much focused on the Cruise and Pershing missiles, which were going to be deployed in Europe. There was a strong sense that if we didn't prevent the deployment from happening, that would be it. Russia would go to launch on warning, which meant that computers with approximately a 6-minute margin for error would essentially be in charge of blowing the world up. It made people more than nervous: we were terrified. This was a great impetus for action. If ever there was a time to put your personal life aside, to put your body on the line, to get dragged away, to go to jail, this was it. So our organizing was apocalyptic. Every meal, we feared, was the Last Supper. Without realizing it, we were acting out a Christian myth, expecting the end of the world, the end of time.

Of course, what happened is that the missiles went in, in spite of all the times we went to jail. And that's the way that political organizing and action often work. You go out, twelve hundred people performing civil disobedience, holding solidarity for 2 weeks, but President Reagan doesn't wake up the next day and say, "Gee, all these people are in jail. They're so sincere. They must have a point." It doesn't work that way.

But then, five years later, after long negotiations, Reagan and Gorbachev decide to take those missiles out of Europe. That is a victory, a victory that is the fruit of the organizing that we did all those years. But this kind of victory is not one we're going to see immediately. This is where the Pagan perspective comes in.

What Witches and Pagans do is practice magic. I like the definition of magic that says, "Magic is the art of changing consciousness at will." I also think that's a very good definition of political change—changing consciousness on a mass scale in this country. And one of the things we learn when we practice magic is that the results don't necessarily happen immediately. They unfold over time, and they always unfold in surprising ways, which is why we talk about our spiritual tradition in terms of mystery rather than answers and dogma and certainty. We talk about what it is we don't know and can only wonder about and be amazed at.

There is a certain way that magic works: it is, in a sense, a technology. When we want to do something, to change consciousness, for example, we first need an image of the change we want to create. We need a vision.

The same is true for political work. If we want to change consciousness in this nation, we first need to have a vision in our minds of what we want to change it into. We need to have an image, and we need to create that image and make it strong. And we need to direct energy and, in some way, ground it in reality.

The vision we want to create must also reflect a different model of power, one rooted in our understanding of the Earth as alive. We live in a system where power is *power-over*, that is, domination and control; it is a system in which a person or group of people has the right to tell other people what to do, to make their decisions, to set standards they have to live up to. The system may be overtly coercive, like a prison, or it may be benign on the surface, but it is still a system of power. And we internalize the system of domination. It lives inside us, like an entity, as if we were possessed by it.

Ecofeminism challenges all relations of domination. Its goal is not just to change who wields power, but to transform the structure of power itself. When the spirit is immanent, when each of us is the Goddess, is God, we have an inalienable right to be here and to be alive. We have a value that can't be taken away from us, that doesn't have to be earned, that doesn't have to be acquired. That kind of value is central to the change we want to create. That's the spell we want to cast.

The way we can embody that vision, can create the living image of that value, is in the groups we form and the structures we create. In some ways, especially in the Bay Area, we often have done this well. That is why so many people found organizing around Livermore and Diablo empowering. The Livermore Action Group and the Abalone Alliance (which organized the blockade at the Diablo nuclear power plant) were structured around small groups that worked by consensus. Now consensus can drive you out of your mind with frustration sometimes, but there is a very important principle in it. That is, everyone in the group has power, and everyone has equal power because everyone has value. That value is accepted, it's inherent, and it can't be taken away.

Along with the decision-making process goes a real care for the process that we use with each other. We listen to each other, we let each person have a say and hear each other and recognize that different people's opinions may be important, even if we disagree with them. Feminist process, as we call it, creates a strong sense of safety, and it changes people. I've known people in LAG who've said that their lives were profoundly changed by living for the first time in a society in which what they said was heard and considered important.

In a sense, that kind of decision making and organizing becomes a ritual. A ritual really is any kind of an intentional act we create that deepens our sense of value. The real heart of any ritual is telling our stories, that is, listening to each other and telling the sacred stories that we may have heard, that have been handed down and distilled from many people's experience, and telling the stories of our own experience.

Groups often seem to be most empowering when they are small. Only in a relatively small group can we really know each other as individuals. That's why LAG was organized in affinity groups, which are small, and why Witches are organized in covens, which traditionally have no more than thirteen members. When a group gets too large, people begin to become faceless. At the same time, small groups can also come together and form networks and coalitions and act together in larger ways. But the real base is always a small community of people who know and value each other personally.

We also need to have a sense of safety. A lot of people will say, "I feel unsafe in this group," meaning "I'm afraid someone's going to hurt my feelings." The truth is that someone will—someone always does—you can count on it. When we're honest, when we really interact with each other, there are always times when our needs or our style or our ways of communicating don't mesh. But when we each feel sure of our value to the group, conflict need not be devastating.

But real safety comes from something else. The groups we create and the ways we organize also have to be sustainable. If we weren't living in a state of denial all the time, the whole idea of sustainability would clearly be our first priority. How is it that we can live in a world where we use the Earth in ways that are destroying it and not worry? We all know we have to breathe; we all know we have to drink water; we all know we have to eat food; and, we all know it's got to come from somewhere. So why isn't the preservation of the environment our first priority? It makes such logical sense that it's irritating to have to say it.

In order to put the environment on the national agenda, we have to organize, but we also need to embody the principle of sustainability in our own groups. I think one of the flaws in our organizing, for example, in that period in the early 1980s, was exactly the apocalyptic sense coming out of that unconscious Christian myth that the end of time was near.

From a Pagan perspective, there is no end of time. Time is a cycle, and cycles come around and they go around and come back again. Our goal isn't to burn ourselves out as martyrs. Our model is the Earth, and the seed that is planted and springs up, grows, loses life, is planted and comes up again and again and again.

That, I think, is the kind of model we need for our politics. We need to see the process of changing our society as a lifetime challenge and commitment. Transforming consciousness so that we can preserve and sustain the Earth is a long-term project. We need the communities we create around that task to be sustainable. There are going to be times when we're active and it's exciting and we're obsessed by action, and there are going to be times when we pull back and nurture ourselves and heal and take care of ourselves. There are times when each of us gives a lot to a group, and times when each should get something back from the group, times when the giving and taking in a group balance out. Nobody should be stuck always having to be the leader, the organizer, or the one who pulls it all together. These tasks should rotate. And nobody should get stuck being the nurturer, the one everyone complains to, the mediator, the one who smooths everything over.

It is true that sometimes doing political work involves making sacrifices, and it may involve suffering. It's also true that around the world, people are suffering tremendously right now because of the policies of this country, the historical decisions and choices this country has made. We have to oppose and change these policies, and to do that we have to be willing to take risks. But sometimes in the nonviolence movement there's a kind of idealization of suffering. And I don't think that serves us. It comes out of the fantasy that people will see us suffering for our cause, be impressed by our nobility and sincerity, and be attracted to join and suffer with us.

Gandhi was a great man, but his ideas don't always fit for a lot of us, particularly for women. Gandhi said we have to accept the suffering and take it in. Women have been doing that for thousands and thousands of years, and it hasn't stopped anything much — except a lot of women's lives. In some ways, it's also not ecological. Rather than absorb the violence, what we need to do is to find some way to stop it and then transform it, to take that energy and turn it into creative change. Not to take it on ourselves.

The actual unsung truth about a lot of organizing is that it feels really good, and that's why people do it, again and again and again. It feels good because when we're actually organizing and taking action to stop the destruction of the Earth, we're doing an act of healing and we are free. There are few times when we are free in this culture and this is one of them. We need to speak about the joy and wildness and sense of liberation that comes when we step beyond the bounds of the authorities to resist control and create change.

Finally, I think that the spell we need to cast, the model we need to create, has to be open to mystery, to the understanding that we don't know everything about what's going on and we don't know exactly what to do about it. The mystery can be expressed in many ways. For one person it might be expressed through ritual, through celebration, chanting, and meditation; in some groups it might be expressed through humor, through making fun of what everybody else is doing. In some groups it might be expressed both ways. We can't define how a group or individual is going to experience it, but we can attempt to structure things so that we don't have dogmas and party lines, so we remain open to many possibilities of the sacred.

These are some ideas of how we build communities and what kinds of communities we might want to create. The other question is what we're going to organize these communities around. It's hard to get people together in a vacuum. One of the things that plagues our movements is that when we start looking at what's really going on with the Earth and the people on it, it's overwhelming. All the issues seem so important that it's very, very hard to know what to focus on, and we can easily get fragmented.

I had dinner recently with a man named Terry Gips who heads a group called the International Alliance for Sustainable Agriculture. He was telling me that he'd come to the conclusion that we have about 3 years to turn around the environmental destruction or it'll be too late. He had expressed this idea to his friends and reactions were so bad that he'd decided not to talk about it any more. People got very depressed. I could understand that because I'd gotten terribly depressed myself.

I said, "Well, I don't know if it's useful to think in those terms. When you said 'three years,' it didn't sound like enough time. It reminds me of that period in the early 1980s when we thought we had to get rid of those missiles now or never. At the same time, if you really believe that, what do we need to do? Do we need to smash capitalism in 3 years and totally transform society? I don't think we can do that."

He said, "No. Actually, there are some very concrete things to do in the next 3 to 5 years—however long we might have—that would reverse the destruction enough to give us time to make the deeper kinds of changes and transformations we need to make." He sat there talking, and I started thinking, and we came up with a campaign for turning the tide.

So this is what I think we should do, and, if I were setting an ecofeminist or a Green agenda, this is how I would organize it, the beginning of which I look at as a sort of magic circle.

Illustrated in Figure 1 are the tree of life and the magic circle. The magic circle is a circle of the elements: air, fire, water, and earth. The tree has roots and a core, a center, a heart that's the same as the circle, and it has branches. If we think about it, all of these issues that we see as being so interconnected can fit into that magic circle.

For example, let's talk about air. The ozone layer has holes in it and is rapidly being depleted. We should be organizing around this issue if we want our food crops and ocean plankton to survive, if we want to preserve the viability of the Earth. And such organizing has already had some success. Du Pont, which manufactures 25 percent of the world's chlorofluorocarbons, has voluntarily decided to phase out production. Several states, including Minnesota, are considering bills to ban these substances, and some fast-food franchises are phasing out packaging made from these substances. But even with these changes, the ozone will continue to diminish since chlorofluorocarbons remain in the Earth's atmosphere for up to 80 years. Yet these positive steps show us that public pressure can bring about important changes.

Another air issue is the destruction of tropical rain forests. If you wonder why I put that under air, it's because these forests are the lungs of the world. They are being cut down, and they are key to systems that regulate the Earth's weather patterns. There *should* be an international commission on the rain forest, and there should also be pressure on institutions like the World Bank and the International Monetary Fund to stop funding the destruction of rain forests. A lot of the destruction comes as rain forests are cut down so cattle can graze and our fast-food restaurants can turn out hamburgers. That's another thing we can organize around. A boycott of one fast-food chain, Burger King, convinced it to stop buying rain forest beef.

Now look at fire: we have nuclear issues. Nuclear power—what do we do with all that waste? Nuclear weapons, we should be working to ban them. Fire represents energy, and we need renewable sources of energy. We need our money put into those sources rather than into things that pollute and kill.

There are also important water issues. Acid rain is also killing trees and forests. Canada wanted some very simple things from us, like smoke scrubbers and curbs on acid rain, and

FIGURE 1

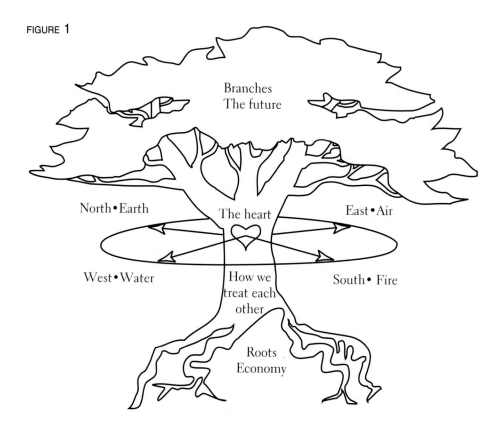

then-President Reagan refused. We need to set standards and see that they're enforced. (Bush's new proposals sound good but actually lack strict standards.) We need to be talking about groundwater pollution. In Minnesota, "Land of a Thousand Lakes" as the license plate says, wells were tested and 39 percent were found to be contaminated; similar statistics exist for many areas. We also need to stop the pollution of the ocean, the oil drilling off the coasts, the depletion of fisheries, and the killing of whales.

Then, of course, there's the Earth. One of the things that would push us toward sustainable agriculture would be simply to stop subsidizing pesticides, which we do now in a lot of very subtle ways. For example, if a pesticide is banned, who is it that pays for storing and destroying it? It's us. It's our tax money, not the company that produces it. In California beekeepers lose thousands of dollars every year to pesticides. The government reimburses them, but the pesticide companies should be paying the price. It's estimated that there are four pesticide poisonings a minute, three-fourths of them in the Third World. We could make it uneconomical to poison the Earth and the human beings who grow and eat the food the Earth produces. We could make alliances with the United Farmworkers of America, who've been calling for a boycott of grapes and focusing attention on pesticide issues and labor practices.

We also need to preserve sacred lands such as Big Mountain and end the destruction of indigenous peoples and cultures. If the Earth is sacred to us, we must preserve the wilderness that's left because that's the place we go for renewal, where we can most strongly feel the immanence of the Goddess.

Also with Earth go feeding the hungry, sheltering the homeless. One of the advantages of seeing issues as integrated, rather than fragmented, is that it can help us avoid false dichotomies. For example, environmental issues *are* social justice issues, for it is the poor who are forced to work directly with unsafe chemicals, in whose neighborhoods toxic waste incinerators are planned, who cannot afford to buy bottled water and organic vegetables or pay for medical care. Environmental issues are international issues, for we cannot simply export unsafe pesticides, toxic wastes, and destructive technologies without poisoning the whole living body of the Earth. And environmental issues are women's issues, for women sicken, starve, and die from toxics, droughts, and famines, their capacity to bear new life is threatened by pollution, and they bear the brunt of care for the sick and the dying, as well as for the next generation.

Environmental issues cannot be intelligently approached without the perspectives of women, the poor, and those who come from other parts of the globe, as well as those of all races and cultural backgrounds. To take only one example, we cannot responsibly approach questions of overpopulation without facing questions of women's power to make decisions about their own reproduction, to challenge traditional roles and restrictions.

If we approach any issue without taking into account the perspectives of all those it affects, we run the risk of accepting false solutions, for example, that famine or AIDS are acceptable answers to population problems. From a Pagan point of view, such "solutions" are entirely unethical because the ethics of integrity prevents us from accepting a solution for someone else that we are unwilling to accept for ourselves.

False solutions are also dangerous because they divert our attention from the real forces with which we must contend. Like an illusionist's tricks, they distract us from seeing what is really going on and from noticing what really works and what doesn't. What really works to stem population growth is not mass death—wars, famines, and epidemics have produced, at most, a ripple in the rising tide. What works is increasing the security of life for those who are already alive and, especially, increasing women's power and autonomy, women's control over our own bodies and access to work and economic compensation independent of our role in procreation. Feminists have been saying this for a long time, and environmentalists need to listen or their analysis will remain fragmented and short-sighted.

Unless we understand all the interconnections, we are vulnerable to manipulation. For example, we are often told that to end hunger we must sacrifice wilderness. But what will work to end hunger is not the further destruction of natural resources within the same system of greed and inequality that has engendered hunger. In their book, *World Hunger: Twelve Myths* (New York: Grove Press, 1986), Frances Moore Lappé and Joseph Collins make the point that people are hungry not because there isn't enough food in the world, but because they are poor. To end hunger we must restore control over land and economic resources to those who have been disenfranchised by the same forces that destroy, with equal lack of concern, the life of a child or a tree or an endangered species, in the name of profit.

And so we come to the roots of the tree—our economic base. Our economy reflects our system of values, in which profit replaces inherent value as the ultimate measure of all things. If we saw ourselves as interconnected parts of the living being that is the Earth, of equal existential value, we could no longer justify economic exploitation.

Our economy is one of waste. The biggest part of that waste is that it's an economy of war, which is inherently wasteful. We need to transform that into an economy that is truly productive and sustainable. To do that we need economic justice—economic democracy as well as political democracy.

Then we can support the branches of the tree, which reach out into the future, touching upon such issues as caring for our children, education, and the values that we teach people. Protecting the future also involves challenging potentially dangerous technologies like genetic engineering. It means basing our decisions, plans, and programs on our obligation to future generations.

In the heart of the tree, the center, is how we treat each other. To work on any of these issues, we must transform the power relationships and the hierarchies of value that keep us separate and unequal. We must challenge the relations of domination between men and women, between light people and dark people, between rich people and poor people; we must do away with all of those things that my friend Luisah Teish calls the "Ism brothers." Then we can really begin treating each other with that sense that each one of us has inherent value, that nobody's interests can be written off and forgotten.

These are the ways I see the issues as being interconnected. Ultimately, to work on any one of them, we need to work on all of them. To work on all of them, we can start at any place on that circle or part of the tree. What I would envision ecofeminist groups saying is: "Let's do it. Let's turn the environmental destruction around. Let's have a movement we call Turning the Tide and commit ourselves to it. Not as a short-term thing that we're going to do for a year and then burn out, but as a way of transforming and changing our lives."

We can begin this long-term commitment by first getting together with people in a small way and forming our own action groups, our own circles for support, which can take on their own characters and their own personalities. Maybe you will form a circle where members take off their clothes and go to the beach and dance around and jump in the waves and energize yourselves that way. And then you'll all write letters to your congresspersons about the ozone condition. Maybe somebody else will form a circle in their church where members sit on chairs and meditate quietly and then go out to Nevada and get in the way of the nuclear testing. But whatever we do, our spirituality needs to be grounded in action.

Along with seeing issues as interconnected, we need to all be able to envision new kinds of organizing. We need to envision a movement where our first priority is to form community, small groups centered around both personal support and action, and to make that what people see as their ongoing, long-term commitment. We don't have to commit ourselves to some big, overall organization. We can commit ourselves to eight other people with whom we can say, "We can form a community to do political and spiritual work and find support over a long period of time." Then our communities can network and form organizations around issues and around tasks as needed, and can dissolve the larger organizations and networks when they're not needed.

I want to end with my vision of where this might all bring us. It's an optimistic one because, ultimately, I do believe that we can do it. We really can turn the tide—we can reverse the destruction of the Earth.

And so the time comes when all the people of the earth
    can bring their gifts to the fire
    and look into each other's faces
    unafraid

Breathe deep
Feel the sacred well that is your own breath, and look
    look at that circle
See us come from every direction
    from the four quarters of the earth
See the lines that stretch to the horizon
    the procession, the gifts borne
    see us feed the fire
Feel the earth's life renewed
And the circle is complete again
    and the medicine wheel is formed anew
    and the knowledge within each one of us
    made whole
Feel the great turning, feel the change
    the new life runs through your blood like fire

## Reading Questions

1. What does Starhawk mean by "immanence, interconnection, community, and magic"? What does she mean by "spirituality"?
2. Why does Starhawk advocate the Pagan, cyclical model of time over the Christian, apocalyptic model of time, as appropriate to earth-based spirituality?
3. What are the organizational strategies of spiritually based ecofeminist activism that challenge "power-over" forms of relation?
4. What are the specific global issues that indicate the interconnections between ecofeminism and other international movements of liberation?
5. What is an "ethics of integrity," and what are the reasons for adopting it?

## Recommended Reading

Irene Diamond and Gloria Orenstein, *Reweaving the World: The Emergence of Ecofeminism* (San Francisco: Sierra Club Books, 1990)

Starhawk, *Dreaming the Dark: Magic, Sex, and Politics* (Boston: Beacon Press, 1989)

Starhawk, *Truth or Dare: Encounters with Power, Authority, and Mystery* (San Francisco: Harper and Row, 1987)

Luisah Teish, *Jambalaya: The Natural Woman's Book of Personal Charms and Practical Rituals* (San Francisco: Harper and Row, 1985)

Alice Walker, *Living by the Word: Selected Writings, 1973– 1987* (San Diego: Harcourt Brace Jovanovitch, 1987)

Alice Walker, *The Temple of My Familiar* (San Diego: Harcourt Brace Jovanovitch, 1989)

## Recommended Audiovisual Resources

*The Goddess Remembered.* 1984. Directed by Donna Read. Filming of ancient sacred sites with background narrative and discussion between several feminist spirituality scholars, including Starhawk, Merlin Stone, Susan Griffin, Kim Chernin, and Shekhinah Mountainwater. National Film Board of Canada.

*Adam's World.* 1990. Directed by Donna Read. Noted feminist theologian and environmentalist Elizabeth Dodson Gray argues that the patriarchal system is the root cause of the global environmental crisis. National Film Board of Canada.

# Healing the Wounds

## Feminism, Ecology, and the Nature/Culture Dualism

YNESTRA KING

Ynestra King teaches at Eugene Lang College in New York. She is the author of *Rocking the Ship of State: Toward a Feminist Peace Politics*.

No part of living nature can ignore the extreme threat to life on Earth. We are faced with worldwide deforestation, the disappearance of hundreds of species of life, and the increasing pollution of the gene pool by poisons and low-level radiation. We are also faced with biological atrocities unique to modern life—the existence of the AIDS virus and the possibility of even more dreadful and pernicious diseases caused by genetic mutation. Worldwide food shortages, including episodes of mass starvation, continue to mount as prime agricultural land is used to grow cash crops to pay national debts instead of food to feed people.[1] Animals are mistreated and mutilated in horrible ways to test cosmetics, drugs, and surgical procedures. The stockpiling of ever greater weapons of annihilation and the terrible imagining of new ones continues. The piece of the pie that women have only begun to sample as a result of the feminist movement is rotten and carcinogenic, and surely our feminist theory and politics must take account of this, however much we yearn for the opportunities that have been denied to us. What is the point of partaking equally in a system that is killing us all?

The contemporary ecological crisis alone creates an imperative that feminists take ecology seriously, but there are other reasons ecology is central to feminist philosophy and politics. The ecological crisis is related to the systems of hatred of all that is natural and female by the White, male, Western formulators of philosophy, technology, and death inventions. It is my contention that the systematic denigration of working-class people and people of color, women, and animals is connected to the basic dualism that lies at the root of Western civilization. But the mind-set of hierarchy originates within human society. It has its material roots in the domination of human by human, particularly of women by men. While I cannot speak for the liberation struggles of people of color, I believe that the goals of feminism, ecology, and movements against racism and for the survival of indigenous peoples are internally related and must be understood and pursued together in a worldwide, genuinely pro-life,[2] movement.

There is at the root of Western society a deep ambivalence about life itself, about our own fertility and that of nonhuman nature, and a terrible confusion about our place in nature. But as the work of social ecologist Murray Bookchin demonstrates, nature did not declare war on humanity, patriarchal humanity declared war on women and on living nature.[3] Nowhere is this transition more hauntingly portrayed than by the Chorus in Sophocles' *Antigone*:

> Many the wonders but nothing walks stranger than man.
> This thing crosses the sea in the winter's storm,
> making his path through the roaring waves.

And she, the greatest of gods, the earth—
ageless she is, and unwearied—he wears her away
as the ploughs go up and down from year to year
and his mules turn up the soil.

Gay nations of birds he snares and leads,
wild beast tribes and the salty brood of the sea,
with the twined mesh of his nets, this clever man.
He controls with craft the beasts of the open air,
walkers on the hills. The horse with his shaggy mane
he holds and harnesses, yoked about the neck,
and the strong bull of the mountain.

Language and thought like the wind
and the feelings that make the town,
he has taught himself, and shelter against the cold,
refuge from rain. He can always help himself.
He faces no future helpless. There's only death
that he cannot find an escape from. He has contrived
refuge from illnesses once beyond all cure.

Clever beyond all dreams
the inventive craft that he has
which may drive him one time or another to well or ill.
When he honors the laws of the land and the gods' sworn right
high indeed is his city; but stateless the man
who dares to dwell with dishonor.[4]

So far have we gone from our roots in living nature that it is the living, and not the dead, that perplexes. The panvitalism of ancient and ancestral culture has given way to panmechanism, the norm of the lifeless.

But for a long time after the first echoes of this transition, the inroads human beings made on living nature were superficial and unable to fundamentally upset the balance and fecundity of the nonhuman natural world. And so appropriately, ethics, and ideas about how people should live, which took their instrumental form in politics, concerned the relationships of human beings to one another, especially in cities. But with the arrival of modern technologies the task of ethics and the domain of politics have changed drastically. The consideration of the place of human beings in nature, formerly the terrain of religion, becomes a crucial concern for all human beings. And with modern technologies, the particular responsibilities of human beings for nature must move to the center of politics.

Biological ethicist Hans Jonas says of this condition: "A kind of metaphysical responsibility beyond self-interest has devolved in us with the magnitude of our powers relative to this tenuous film of life, that is, since man has become dangerous not only to himself but to the whole biosphere."[5] Yet, around the world, capitalism, the preeminent culture and economics of self-interest, is homogenizing cultures and disrupting naturally complex balances within the ecosystem. Capitalism is dependent on expanding markets and therefore ever greater areas of life must be mediated by sold products. From a capitalist standpoint, the more things that can be bought and sold, the better. So capitalism requires a rationalized worldview, which asserts that human science and technology are inherently progressive, which systematically denigrates ancestral cultures, and which asserts that human beings are entitled to dominion over nonhuman nature.

Nonhuman nature is being rapidly simplified, undoing the work of organic evolution. Hundreds of species of life disappear forever each year, and the figure is accelerating. Diverse, complex ecosystems are more stable than simple ones. They have had longer periods of evolution and are necessary to support human beings and many other species. Yet in the name of civilization, nature has been desecrated in a process of rationalization sociologist Max Weber called "the disenchantment of the world."

The diversity of human life on the planet is also being undermined. The cultural diversity of human societies around the world developed over thousands of years and is part of the general evolution of life on the planet. The homogenizing of culture turns the world into a giant factory and facilitates top-down authoritarian government. In the name of helping people, the industrial countries export models of development that assume that the U.S. way of life is the best way of life for everyone.

A critical analysis of and opposition to the uniformity of technological, industrial culture—capitalist and socialist—is crucial to feminism, ecology, and the struggles of indigenous peoples. At this point in history, there is no way to unravel the matrix of oppressions within human society without at the same time liberating nature and reconciling that part of nature that is human with that part that is not. Socialists do not have the answer to these problems—they share the antivitalism and basic dualism of capitalism. Although developed within capitalism, the technological means of production utilized by capitalist and socialist states is largely the same. All hitherto existing philosophies of liberation, with the possible exception of some forms of social anarchism, accept the anthropocentric notion that humanity should dominate nature and that the increasing domination of nonhuman nature is a precondition for true human freedom. No socialist revolution has ever fundamentally challenged the basic prototype for the nature/culture dualism—the domination of men over women.

## To Embrace or Repudiate Nature?

Radical feminists, or feminists who believe that the biologically based domination of women by men is the root cause of oppression, have considered ecology from a feminist perspective because nature is their central category of analysis. They believe that the subordination of women in society is the root of human oppression, closely related to the association of women with nature. They see "patriarchy" (by which they mean the systematic dominance of men in society) as preceding and laying the foundation for other forms of human oppression and exploitation. Men identify women with nature and seek to enlist both in the service of male "projects" designed to make men safe from feared nature and mortality. The ideology of women as closer to nature is essential to such a project. So if patriarchy is the archetypal form of human oppression, then it follows that if we get rid of that, other forms of oppression will likewise crumble. But there are two basic differences within the radical feminist movement: whether the woman/nature connection is potentially emancipatory or whether it provides a rationale for the continued subordination of women.

How do women who call themselves radical feminists come to such divergent positions?[6] The first position implies a separate feminist culture and philosophy from the vantage point of identification with nature and a celebration of the woman/nature connection and is the position of *radical cultural feminists*, which I will address later. *Radical nationalist feminists* take the second position, repudiating the woman/nature connection. For these feminists, freedom is being liberated from the primordial realm of women and nature, which they regard as an imprisoning female ghetto. They deplore the appropriation of ecology as a feminist issue, seeing it as a regression that is bound to reinforce sex-role stereotyping. Anything that reinforces gender differences, or makes any kind of special claim for women, is problematic.

Thus, they think that feminists shouldn't do anything that would restimulate traditional ideas about women. They celebrate the fact that we have finally begun to gain access to male bastions by using the political tools of liberalism and the rationalization of human life, mythically severing the woman/nature connection as the humanity/nature connection has been severed. The mother of modern feminism, Simone de Beauvoir, represents this position. Recently she came out against what she calls "the new femininity":

> . . . an enhanced status for traditional feminine values, such as woman and her rapport with nature, woman and her maternal instinct, woman and her physical being. . . . This renewed attempt to pin women down to their traditional role, together with a small effort to meet some of the demands made by women—that's the formula used to try and keep women quiet. Even women who call themselves feminists don't always see through it. Once again, women are being defined in terms of "the other," once again they are being made into the "second sex". . . . Why should women be more in favour of peace than men? I should think it a matter of equal concern for both! . . . being a mother means being for peace. Equating ecology with feminism is something that irritates me. They are not automatically one and the same thing at all.[7]

De Beauvoir thus reiterates the position she took almost 40 years ago in *The Second Sex*—that it is a sexist ploy to define women as beings who are closer to nature than men. She claims that such associations divert women from their struggle for emancipation and channel their energies "into subsidiary concerns," such as ecology and peace.

Radical cultural feminists, or cultural feminists, on the other hand, do not wish to obliterate the difference between men and women; instead, they take women's side, which, as they see it, is also the side of nonhuman nature. And, not surprisingly, they have taken the slogan "the personal is political" in the opposite direction, personalizing the political.

Cultural feminists celebrate the life experience of the "female ghetto," which they see as a source of female freedom rather than subordination. They argue, following Virginia Woolf, that they don't want to enter the male world with its "procession of professions."[8] They have attempted to articulate and even create a separate women's culture and have been major proponents of the identification of women with nature and feminism with ecology. The major strength of cultural feminism is that it is a deeply woman-identified movement. Cultural feminists celebrate what is distinct about women and have challenged the male culture rather than strategizing to become part of it. They have celebrated the identification of women with nature in music, art, literature, poetry, covens, and communes. But one problem that White cultural feminists, like other White feminists, have not adequately faced is that, in celebrating the commonalities of women and emphasizing the ways in which women are universal victims of male oppression, they have inadequately addressed the real diversity of women's lives and histories across race, class, and national boundaries. For women of color, opposing racism and genocide and encouraging ethnic pride are agendas they often share with men in a White-dominated society, even while they struggle against sexism in their own communities. These complex, multidimensional loyalties and historically divergent life situations require a politics that recognizes complexities. The connecting of women and nature has lent itself to a romanticization of women as good, and as apart from all the dastardly deeds of men and culture. The problem is that history, power, women, and nature are all a lot more complicated than that.

In the past 10 years, the old cultural feminism has given birth to the feminist spirituality movement, an eclectic potpourri of beliefs and practices, with an immanent Goddess (as opposed to the transcendental God). I believe there has been a greater racial diversity in this movement than in any other form of feminism, and this is due in part to the fact that this is a spiritual movement, based on the ultimate unity of all living things. There is no particular dogma in this movement, only a recognition of women as embodied, earth-bound living beings who should celebrate their connection to the rest of life and, for some, invoke this connection in public political protest actions. These beliefs are supported by the Gaia hypothesis—the idea that the planet is one single living organism, and the thesis of scientists Lynn Margolis and James Lovelock (whose research corroborates Peter Kropotkin's mutualism[9]) that cooperation was a stronger force in evolution than competition.[10]

Much of the iconography of the contemporary radical feminist peace movement is inspired by the feminist spirituality movement. Actions have featured guerrilla theater where the Furies ravage Ronald Reagan; encircling military bases and war-research centers with pictures of children, trees, brooks, and women; and weaving shut the doors of stock exchanges while singing and chanting about spiders.

Cultural feminism and the women's spirituality movement have been subjected to the same critique feminists of color have made of the ethnocentricity of much White feminism.[11] This critique comes from women of color who draw on indigenous spiritual traditions and who argue that these White Western feminists are inventing and originating an earth-centered prowoman spirituality while they are defending their indigenous spirituality against the imperialism of Western rationalism. For example, Luisah Teish, the first Voodoo priestess to attempt to explain her tradition to the public, advocates a practice that integrates the political and spiritual and that brings together a disciplined understanding of the African spiritual tradition with contemporary feminist and Black power politics.[12] Members of her group in Oakland are planning urban gardening projects to help the poor feed themselves and to grow the herbs needed for the holistic healing remedies of her tradition while they engage in community organizing to stop gentrification. Women in the Hopi and Navaho traditions are also attempting to explain their traditions to a wider public while they organize politically to keep their lands from being taken over by developers or poisoned by industry.

The collision of modern industrial society with indigenous cultures has decimated these ancestral forms but may have brought White Westerners into contact with forms of knowledge that are useful as we try to imagine our way beyond dualism, to understand what it means to be embodied beings on this planet. These traditions are often used as examples of ways of life that are nondualistic, at least that overcome the nature/culture dualism.[13] But human beings can't simply jump off, or jump out of history. These indigenous, embodied, Earth-centered spiritual traditions can plant seeds in the imaginations of people who are the products of dualistic cultures, but White Westerners cannot use them to avoid the responsibility of their own history.

The women's spirituality movement has changed in recent years, becoming more sophisticated and diverse as women of color articulate a powerful, survival-based feminism emerging from their experience in the crucible of multiple oppressions. From both the feminism of women of color (sometimes called "womanist" as opposed to "feminist" to convey the different priorities of women of color from White women) and ecofeminism has come a more holistic feminism, which links all issues of personal and planetary survival. The critique of cultural feminism advanced by women of color—that it is often ahistorical in that White women in particular need to take responsibility for being oppressors as well as oppressed and for having been powerful as White people or as people with class or national privileges—is crucial. In other words, women have a complexity of historical identities and therefore a complexity of loyalties. Instead of constantly attempting to make our identities less complex by emphasizing what we have in common as women, as has been the tendency of women who are feminists first and foremost, we should also pay attention to the differences among us.

# Socialist Feminism, Rationalization, and the Domination of Nature

Socialist feminism is an odd hybrid—an attempt at a synthesis of rationalist feminism (radical and liberal) and the historical materialism of the Marxist tradition. In taking labor as its central category, Marxists have reduced human beings to *Homo laboran*, and the history of capitalism cries out with the resistance of human beings not only to being exploited but to being conceived of as essentially "workers." In Marxism, revolutionary discourse has been reduced to a "language of productivity"[14] where a critique of the mode of production does not necessarily challenge the principle of production.

The socialist feminist theory of the body as a socially constructed (re)producer has informed a public discourse of "reproductive freedom"—the freedom to (re)produce or not (re)produce with your own body—and it is in this area that socialist feminists have been a political force. But socialist feminists have an inadequate theory with which to confront the new reproductive technologies. Arguing that women have a right to "control our own bodies" does not prepare one to confront the issue of whether our reproductive capacities, like our productive capacities, should be bought and sold in the marketplace, as one more form of wage labor.[15]

Socialist feminists have criticized liberal feminists (just as socialists have criticized liberalism) for not going far enough in a critique of the political economy and class differences. But socialist feminists have shared the rationalist bias of liberal feminism, depicting the world primarily in exchange terms—whether production or reproduction—and have agreed with the liberal feminist analysis that we must strive in all possible ways to demonstrate that we are more like men than different. Some socialist feminists have even argued that liberal feminism has a radical potential.[16] For such feminists, the dualistic, overly rationalized premises of liberal feminism are not a problem. For them, too, severing the woman/nature connection is a feminist project.

In a sense, the strength and weakness of socialist feminism lie in the same premise—the centrality of economics in their theory and practice. Socialist feminists have articulated a strong economic and class analysis, but they have not sufficiently addressed the domination of nature.[17] That is, they believe that the socialist feminist agenda would be complete if we could overcome systematic inequalities of social and economic power. They have addressed one of the three forms of domination of nature—domination between persons—but they have not seriously attended to the domination of nonhuman nature, nor to the domination of inner nature.

In socialist feminism, women seek to enter the political world as articulate, historical subjects, capable of understanding and making history. And some socialist feminists, such as Alison Jagger and Nancy Hartsock, have drawn on historical materialism in very creative ways, attempting to articulate a position from which women can make special historical claims without being biologically determinist.[18] But even socialist feminists who are attempting a multifactored historical analysis of the oppression of women do not treat the domination of nature as a significant category for feminism, though they note it in passing.

In general, socialist feminists are very unsympathetic to "cultural feminism."[19] They accuse it of being ahistorical, essentialist (which they define as believing in male and female essences—male = bad, female = good), and antiintellectual. This debate partakes of the ontology versus epistemology debate in Western philosophy, where "being" is opposed to "knowing," and women are implicitly relegated to the realm of "being," the ontological slums. From an ecological (that is, antidualistic) standpoint, essentialism and ontology are not the same as biological determinism. In other words, we are not talking heads, nor are we unself-conscious nature. That is, socialist feminists are avoiding the important truths being recognized by cultural feminism, among them the female political imagination manifesting itself in political actions. They also forget that no revolution in human history has succeeded without a strong cultural foundation and a utopian vision. In part, I believe the myopia of socialist feminism with respect to cultural feminism is rooted in the old Marxist debate about the primacy of the base (economics/production) over the superstructure (culture/reproduction). This dualism also needs to be overcome before we can have a dialectical, or genuinely ecological, feminism.

The socialist feminist fidelity to a theory of history where women seek to understand the past in order to make the future is crucial to feminism. But belief in a direct relationship between the rationalization and domination of nature and the project of human liberation remains a central tenet of socialism.

The question for socialist feminists is whether they can accommodate their version of feminism within the socialist movement or whether they will have to move in a "greener" direction with a more radical critique of all forms of the domination of nature.

## Ecofeminism: Beyond the Nature/Culture Dualism

Women have been culture's sacrifice to nature. The practice of human sacrifice to outsmart or appease a feared nature is ancient. And it is in resistance to this sacrificial mentality—on the part of both the sacrificer and sacrificee—that some feminists have argued against the association of women with nature, emphasizing the social dimension of traditional women's lives. Part of the work of feminism has been asserting that the activities of women, believed to be more natural than those of men, are in fact absolutely social. For example, giving birth is natural (though how it is done is very social) but mothering is an absolutely social activity.[20] In bringing up their children, mothers face ethical and moral choices as complex as those considered by professional politicians and ethicists. In the wake of feminism, women will continue to do these things, but the problem of connecting humanity to nature will still have to be acknowledged and solved. In our mythology of complementarity, men and women have led vicarious lives, where women had feelings and led instinctual lives and men engaged in the projects illuminated by reason. Feminism has exposed the extent to which it was all a lie—that's why it has been so important to feminism to establish the mindful, social nature of mothering.

It is as if women were entrusted with and have kept the dirty little secret that humanity emerges from nonhuman nature into society in the life of the species and the person. The process of nurturing an unsocialized, undifferentiated human infant into an adult person—the socialization of the organic—is the bridge between nature and culture. The Western male bourgeois then extracts himself from the realm of the organic to become a public citizen, as if born from the head of Zeus. He puts away childish things. He disempowers and sentimentalizes his mother, sacrificing her to nature. But the key to the historic agency of women with respect to the nature/culture dualism lies in the fact that the traditional activities of women—mothering, cooking, healing, farming, foraging—are as social as they are natural.

The task of an ecological feminism is the organic forging of a genuinely antidualistic, or dialectical, theory and practice. No previous feminism has addressed this problem adequately, hence the necessity of ecofeminism. Rather than succumb to nihilism, pessimism, and an end to reason and history, we seek to enter into history, to a genuinely ethical thinking—where one uses mind and history to reason from the "is" to the "ought" and to reconcile humanity with nature, within and without. This is the starting point for ecofeminism.

Each major contemporary feminist theory, liberal, social, and cultural, has taken up the issue of the relationship between women and nature. And each in its own way has capitulated to dualistic thinking. Ecofeminism takes from socialist feminism the idea that women have been *historically* positioned at the biological dividing line where the organic emerges into the social. The domination of nature originates in society and therefore must be resolved in society. Thus, it is the embodied woman as social historical agent, rather than as a product of natural law, who is the subject of ecofeminism. But the weakness of socialist feminism's theory of the person is serious from an ecofeminist standpoint. An ecological feminism calls for a dynamic, developmental theory of the person—male *and* female—who emerges out of nonhuman nature, where difference is neither reified nor ignored and the dialectical relationship between human and nonhuman nature is understood.

Cultural feminism's greatest weakness is its tendency to make the personal into the political, with its emphasis on personal transformation and empowerment. This is most obvious in the attempt to overcome the apparent opposition between spirituality and politics. For cultural feminists, spirituality is the heart in a heartless world (whereas for socialist feminists it is the opiate of the people). Cultural feminists have formed the "beloved community" of feminism—with all the power, potential, and problems of a religion. And as an appropriate response to the need for mystery and attention to personal alienation in an overly rationalized world, it is a vital and important movement. But by itself it does not provide the basis for a genuinely dialectical ecofeminist theory and practice, one that addresses history as well as mystery. For this reason, cultural/spiritual feminism (sometimes even called "nature feminism") is not synonymous with ecofeminism in that creating a gynocentric culture and politics is a necessary but not sufficient condition for ecofeminism.

Both feminism and ecology embody the revolt of nature against human domination. They demand that we rethink the relationship between humanity and the rest of nature, including our natural, embodied selves. In ecofeminism, nature is the central category of analysis. An analysis of the interrelated dominations of nature—psyche and sexuality, human oppression, and nonhuman nature—and the historic position of women in relation to those forms of domination is the starting point of ecofeminist theory. We share with cultural feminism the necessity of a politics with heart and a beloved community, recognizing our connection with each other—and with nonhuman nature. Socialist feminism has given us a powerful critical perspective with which to understand, and transform, history. Separately, they perpetuate the dualism of "mind" and "nature." Together they make possible a new ecological relationship between nature and culture, in which mind and nature, heart and reason, join forces to transform the systems of domination, internal and external, that threaten the existence of life on Earth.

Practice does not wait for theory—it comes out of the imperatives of history. Women are the revolutionary bearers of this antidualistic potential in the world today. In addition to the enormous impact of feminism on Western civilization, women have been at the forefront of every historical, political movement to reclaim the Earth. For example, for many years in India poor women who come out of the Gandhian movement have waged a nonviolent campaign for land reform and to save the forest, called the *Chipko Andolan* (the hugging movement), wrapping their bodies around trees as bulldozers arrive. Each of the women has a tree of her own she is to protect—to steward. When loggers were sent in, one of the women said, "Let them know they will not fell a single tree without the felling of us first. When the men raise their axes, we will embrace the trees to protect them."[21] These women have waged a remarkably successful nonviolent struggle, and their tactics have spread to other parts of India. Men have joined in, though the campaign was originated and continues to be led by women. Yet this is not a sentimental movement—lives depend on the survival of the forest. For most of the women of the world, interest in preservation of the land, water, air, and energy is no abstraction but a clear part of the effort to simply survive.

The increasing militarization of the world has intensified this struggle. Women and children make up 80 percent of war refugees. Lands are often burned and scarred in such a way as to prevent cultivation for many years after the battles, so that starvation and hardship follow long after the fighting has stopped.[22] And, here, too, women— often mothers and farmers—respond to necessity. They become the protectors of the Earth in an effort to eke out a small living on the land to feed themselves and their families.

There are other areas of feminist activism that illuminate an enlightened ecofeminist perspective.[23] Potentially, one of the best examples of an appropriately mediated, dialectical relationship to nature is the feminist health movement. The medicalization of childbirth in the first part of this century and, currently, the redesign and appropriation of reproduction both create new profit-making technologies for capitalism and make heretofore natural processes mediated by women into arenas controlled by men. Women offered themselves up to the ministrations of "experts," internalizing the notion that they didn't know enough and surrendering their power. They also accepted the idea that maximum intervention in and domination of nature are inherently good. But since the onset of feminism in the 1960s, women in the United States have gone quite a way in reappropriating and demedicalizing childbirth. As a result of this movement, many more women want to be told what all their options are and many choose invasive medical technologies only under unusual and informed circumstances. They do not necessarily reject these useful technologies in some cases, but they have pointed a finger at motivations of profit and control in the technologies' widespread application. Likewise, my argument here is not that feminism should repudiate all aspects of Western science and medicine. It is to assert that we should develop the sophistication to decide for ourselves when intervention serves our best interest.

Another central area of concern in which women may employ ecofeminism to overcome misogynist dualism is that of body consciousness. Accepting our own bodies just as they are, knowing how they look, feel, and smell, and learning to work with them to become healthier is a basis for cultural and political liberation. In many patriarchal cultures, women are complicit in the domination of our natural bodies, seeking to please men at any cost. Chinese foot binding, performed by women, is a widely cited example of misogynist domination of women's bodies. But even as Western feminists condemn these practices, most of us will do anything to our bodies (yes, even feminists) to appear closer to norms of physical beauty that come naturally to about 0.2 percent of the female population. The rest of us struggle to be skinny, hairless, and, lately, muscular. We lie in the sun to get tan even when we know we are courting melanoma, especially as the accelerating depletion of the ozone layer makes "sunbathing" a dangerous sport. We submit ourselves to extremely dangerous surgical procedures. We primp, prune, douche, deodorize, and diet as if our natural bodies were our mortal enemies. Some of us living the most privileged lives in the world starve ourselves close to death for beauty, literally.

To the extent that we make our own flesh an enemy, or docilely submit ourselves to medical experts, we are participating in the domination of nature. To the extent that we learn to work with the restorative powers of our bodies, using medical technologies and drugs sparingly, we are developing an appropriately mediated relationship to our own natures. But even the women's health movement has not realized a full ecofeminist perspective.[24] It has yet to fully grasp health as an ecological and social rather than an individual problem, in which the systematic poisoning of environments where women live and work is addressed as a primary political issue. Here the community-based movements against toxic wastes, largely initiated and led by women, and the feminist health movement may meet.

A related critical area for a genuinely dialectical practice is a reconstruction of science, taking into account the critique of science advanced by radical ecology and feminism.[25] Feminist historians and philosophers of science are demonstrating that the will to know and the will to power need not be the same thing. They argue that there are ways of knowing the world that are not based on objectification and domination.[26] Here, again, apparently antithetical epistemologies, science and mysticism, can coexist. We shall need all our ways of knowing to create life on this planet that is both ecological and sustainable.

As feminists, we shall need to develop an ideal of freedom that is neither antisocial nor antinatural.[27] We are past the point of throwing off our chains to reclaim our ostensibly free nature, if such a point ever existed. Ecofeminism is not an argument for a return to prehistory. The knowledge that women were not always dominated and that society was not always hierarchical is a powerful inspiration for contemporary women, so long as such a society is not represented as a "natural order," apart from history, to which we will inevitably return by a great reversal.

From an ecofeminist perspective, we are part of nature, but not inherently good or bad, free or unfree. There is no one natural order that represents freedom. We are *potentially* free in nature, but as human beings that freedom has to be intentionally created by using our understanding of the natural world. For this reason we must develop a different understanding of the relationship between human and nonhuman nature, based on the stewardship of evolution. To do this we need a theory of history where the natural evolution of the planet and the social history of the species are not separated. We emerged from nonhuman nature, as the organic emerged from the inorganic.

Here, potentially, we recover ontology as the ground for ethics. We thoughtful human beings must use the fullness of our sensibility and intelligence to push ourselves intentionally to another stage of evolution. One where we will fuse a new way of being human on this planet with a sense of the sacred, informed by all ways of knowing—intuitive *and* scientific, mystical *and* rational. It is the moment where women recognize ourselves as agents of history—yes, even as unique agents—and knowingly bridge the classic dualisms between spirit and matter, art and politics, reason and intuition. This is the potentiality of a *rational reenchantment*. This is the project of ecofeminism.

At this point in history, the domination of nature is inextricably bound up with the domination of persons, and both must be addressed—without arguments over "the primary contradiction" in the search for a single Archimedes point for revolution. There is no such thing. And there is no point in liberating people if the planet cannot sustain their liberated lives, or in saving the planet by disregarding the preciousness of human existence not only to ourselves but to the rest of life on Earth.

# Reading Questions

1. Why does King claim that modern technologies have drastically changed the task of ethics and the domain of politics?

2. Why does capitalism require a rationalized, progressive worldview that is ahistorical, dismissive of indigenous cultures, and dualistic?

3. Why does King assert that patriarchy is the prototype of the nature/culture dualism?

4. Why, according to King, do feminist women of color find cultural feminist projects incompatible with some of their own emancipatory projects?

5. In what ways has socialist feminism retained the nature/culture dualism in its basic conceptual framework?

6. What prevents socialist feminism and cultural/spiritualist feminism from forging a dialectical theory and practice of change?

7. Why, according to King, is women's complicity in the beauty and health industries also a participation in the domination of nature?

## Recommended Reading

Alison Jaggar, *Feminist Politics and Human Nature* (Totowa, NJ: Rowman & Littlefield, 1988)

Judith Plant, ed., *Healing the Wounds: The Promise of Ecofeminism* (Philadelphia: New Society Publishers, 1989)

Gita Sen and Caren Crown, "Alternative Visions, Strategies, and Methods," *Development, Crisis, and Alternative Visions: Third World Women's Perspective* (New York: Monthly Review Press, 1987)

Christina Thürmer-Rohr, *Vagabonding: Feminist Thinking Cut Loose* (Boston: Beacon Press, 1991)

Rosemarie Tong, "Socialist Feminism," *Feminist Thought: A Comprehensive Introduction* (Boulder, CO: Westview Press, 1989)

Donald VanDeVeer and Christine Pierce, eds., *The Environmental Ethics and Policy Book: Philosophy, Ecology, Economics* (Belmont, CA: Wadsworth Publishing Company, 1994)

## Recommended Audiovisual Resources

*Sea of Oil*. 1991. Directed by M. R. Katzke. Affinity Films. Shows the profound impact of the Exxon oil spill in the community of Valdez. Filmakers Library.

# The Feminist Traffic in Animals

## CAROL J. ADAMS

Carol J. Adams is a writer and feminist activist. The founder of a hotline for battered women, she is the author of *The Sexual Politics of Meat: A Feminist-Vegetarian Critical Theory*.

> [The question is] how to effect a political transformation when the terms of the transformation are given by the very order which a revolutionary practive seeks to change.
>
> Jacqueline Rose, *Sexuality in the Field of Vision*

Should feminists be vegetarians? This question has appeared more and more frequently in recent years. Claudia Card offers one opinion: "Must we all, then, be vegetarians, pacifist, drug-free, opposed to competition, anti-hierarchical, in favor of circles, committed to promiscuity with women, and free of the parochialism of erotic arousal? Is this too specific? These values are not peripheral to analyses of women's oppressions."[1]

Another feminist, Joan Cocks, critically refers to the ideas that she sees informing feminist cultural practice: "The political strategies generally are non-violent, the appropriate cuisine, vegetarian."[2] Whether or not all ecofeminists should be vegans is in fact one of the current controversies within ecofeminism.[3] The answer implied by one group of ecofeminists is yes; they proposed to the 1990 National Women's Studies Association meeting that its conferences be vegan.[4]

Many believe that feminism's commitment to pluralism should prevail over arguments for vegetarianism. This position sees pluralism as applying only to an intra-species women's community. It defends personal choice as an arbiter of ethical decisions and limits pluralistic concerns to those of oppressed human beings. Pluralism is used to de-politicize the claims of feminist vegetarianism.

This chapter offers an interpretative background against which the de-politicizing of feminist moral claims on behalf of the other animals can be perceived. Since feminists believe that the personal is political, it appears that many do not think their personal choice of animal foods reflects a feminist politics. But what if the values and beliefs imbedded in the choice to eat animals are antithetical to feminism, so, that, in the case of meat eating, the personal *is* political? Feminist theory offers a way to examine and interpret the practice of eating animals that removes vegetarianism from the category of "lifestyle" choice. In this chapter I provide a feminist philosophical exploration of the claim that animal rights should be practically enacted through all-vegetarian conferences by examining the dialectic between "the political" and "the natural."

In focusing on the need for feminist conferences to be vegetarian, I am not required to address at this time the necessary material conditions for an entire culture to become vegetarian and whether all members of our society have the economic option to be vegetarian. Indeed, while tax subsidies, free natural resources, and our government's financial support of the animal-industrial complex keep the cost of animal flesh artificially low,[5] vegetarianism has often been the only food option of poor people. Were government support to producers not available, animal flesh would be even more costly than vegetarian food. In the absence of neutrality on the part of the government, a grassroots resistance is demonstrating that, as more and more people adopt vegetarianism and de facto boycott the "meat" industry, vegetable proteins are becoming more prevalent and less costly. In addition, as the existence of a coercive government policy on "meat" eating is recognized, alternative political arrangements may become more feasible.[6]

Another reason for my focus on making feminist events completely vegetarian is the fact that most ecofeminists who include animals within their understanding of dominated nature have made this their position—as in the 1990 proposal. Furthermore, the conference proposal removes the vegetarian debate from the realm of personal decisions and relieves it of some of the emotional defensiveness that accompanies close examination of cherished personal practices. Moreover, the eating of animals is the most pervasive form of animal oppression in the Western world, representing as well the most frequent way in which most Westerners interact with animals. It carries immense environmental consequences in addition to the destruction of six billion animals yearly in the United States alone. Yet those living in the United States do not require animal flesh to ensure adequate nutrition; indeed, evidence continues to accumulate that "meat" eating is actually injurious to human health. Lastly, this topic provides an opportunity to respond to anti-animal rights statements by feminists.

## Defining the Traffic in Animals

Through the use of the phrase "feminist traffic in animals," I wish to politicize the use of animals' bodies as commodities. The serving of animal flesh at feminist conferences requires that feminists traffic in animals—that is, buy and consume animal parts—and announces that we endorse the literal traffic in animals: the production, transportation, slaughter, and packaging of animals' bodies.

Trafficking in animals represents a dominant material relationship in our culture. The animal-industrial complex is the second-largest industry, and the largest food industry, in the United States. Currently 60 percent of American foods come from animals, including eggs and dairy products (or "feminized protein") and animal corpses (or "animalized protein").[7] These terms disclose that the protein pre-exists its state of being processed through or as an animal; in other words, vegetable protein is the original protein. Trafficking in animals relies on this vegetable protein as well, but requires that it be the raw material, along with animals, for its product. Feminized protein and animalized protein come from terminal animals.

For feminists to traffic in animals, we must accept the trafficking in ideas, or the ideology, about terminal animals. These ideas form the superstructure of our daily lives, a part of which involves the presumed acceptability of this traffic. The difficulty is that the coercive nature of the ideological superstructure is invisible and, for trafficking to continue, must remain invisible.

When I use the phrase "traffic in animals," I deliberately invoke a classic feminist phrase, appearing in works such as Emma Goldman's "The Traffic in Women," and Gayle Rubin's "The Traffic in Women: Notes on the 'Political Economy' of Sex."[8] By choosing the word "traffic," I imply that similarities in the treatment of "disposable" or "usable" bodies exist.

To "traffic in animals" involves producers *and* consumers. Whatever "objects" we determine to be worth purchasing become included within our moral framework, and the production of these objects, too, becomes a part of such a framework, even if this aspect remains invisible. While numerous books on the animal-industrial complex are available,[9] they rarely are cited in feminist writings other than those by vegetarians, thus ensuring the invisibility of trafficking in animals for those who do so. The phrase "traffic in animals" is an attempt to wrest discursive control from those who wish to evade knowledge about what trafficking entails.

## Discursive Control and Ignorance

No objective stance exists from which to survey the traffic in animals. Either we eat them or we do not. Not only is there no disinterested observer, but there is no impartial semantic or cultural space in which to hold a discussion. We live in a "meat"-advocating culture. Conflicts in meaning are resolved in favor of the dominant culture. Whatever our individual actions, the place from which we stand to survey the eating of animals is overwhelmed by the normativeness of "meat" and the (supposed) neutrality of the term "meat."

The contamination of the discursive space in which we might discuss the matter of cross-species consumption is further complicated by ignorance. Vegetarians know a great deal more about the material conditions that enable "meat" eating than "meat"-eaters do. But discursive power resides in those with the least knowledge. Lacking specific information regarding the topic, the people with the most ignorance set the limits of the discussion.[10] Thus, when Ellen Goodman argues that "people make choices in these matters [animal rights] from the first time they knowingly eat a hamburger or catch a fish," she is making an epistemological claim without defining it.[11] She also assumes that this claim dispenses with the challenges of animal rights. What exactly do "meat"-eaters know? That a hamburger is from a dead animal? The details of the literal traffic in animals that has brought the dead animal into the consumer's hands? Goodman implies that people have specific knowledge about "meat" production that in reality they do not have and usually do not want.

## Discursive Privacy

It is necessary to politicize the process of obtaining animal bodies for food by using terms like "trafficking" because of the prevailing conceptual divisions of our culture. The context for talking about our use of animalized and feminized protein is one of rigid separation between "political," "economic," "domestic," and "personal." As Nancy Fraser explains in *Unruly Practices*: "Domestic institutions depoliticize certain matters by personalizing and/or familiarizing them; they cast these as private-domestic or personal-familial matters in contradistinction to public, political matters."[12]

The result of this social division is that certain issues are banished to zones of discursive privacy rather than seen as foci of generalized contestation. For instance, purchasing, preparing, and eating food is cast as a private-domestic matter. A similar separation exists between "economic" and "political":

> Official economic capitalist system institutions, on the other hand, depoliticize certain matters by economizing them; the issues in question here are cast as impersonal market imperatives, or as "private" ownership prerogatives, or as technical problems for managers and planners, all in contradistinction to political matters.[13]

Thus, while issues associated with *marketing* and *purchasing* dead animals become privatized to the domestic sphere of individual choice, issues involving the *production* of animals are *economized*, such as when the rise of "factory farms" is attributed solely to the demands of the market, or it is argued that we cannot interfere with the prerogatives of the animals' "owner."

When issues are labeled "domestic" or "economic," they become enclaved, shielded from generalized contestation, thus entrenching as *authoritative* what are actually only *interpretations* of issues. Furthermore, "since both domestic and official economic institutions support relations of dominance and subordination, the specific interpretations they naturalize tend, on the whole, to advantage dominant groups and individuals and to disadvantage their subordinates."[14] This is precisely what happens with the consumption of animals' bodies: it has been naturalized to favor the dominant group—people—to the disadvantage of the other animals.

As feminism demonstrates, the divisions between politics, economics, and domestic issues are false. The problem that an analysis such as mine faces is that these divisions continue to be accepted even by many feminists when the issue is animals; and the response by dominant groups is to banish the issue back to a zone of discursive privacy. When the issue is people's oppression of the other animals, this tendency to enforce discursive privacy when issues are being politicized is further complicated. Another social division exists—that between nature and culture.

We do not think of the other animals as having social needs. Since animals are ideologically confined to the realm of nature, making any sort of social claim on their behalf already introduces dissonance into established discourses. It appears that we are confusing the categories of nature and culture. But this in itself is a cultural classification enabled by predetermined ideologies that maintain a narrow, uncontextualized focus. Thus, any feminist animal rights position—by which I mean any argument for the freedom of the other animals from use by human beings—must challenge what has been labeled "natural" by the dominant culture.

# Ideology: Hiding the Social Construction of the Natural

Any debate about the place of animals in human communities occurs within a cultural context and a cultural practice. Here ideology pre-exists and imposes itself on individual perceptions, so that what is actually a problem of consciousness—how we look at animals—is seen as an aspect of personal choice and is presented as a "natural" aspect of our lives as human beings. Claiming human beings to be predators like (some of) the other animals (fewer than 20 percent of animals are actually predators) is an example of naturalizing the political. Distinctions between people's carnivorism and carnivorous animals' predation are ignored in such a claim: human beings do not need to be predators, and there is no animal counterpart to human perpetuation of the grossly inhumane institutions of the animal-industrial complex. Nel Noddings summons natural processes when she states that "it is the fate of every living thing to be eaten,"[15] implying a similarity between the "natural" process of decay and the activity of slaughterhouses (which remain unnamed). Eating animals is also naturalized by the glamorization of hunting as an essential aspect of human evolution or as representing the true tribal relationship between indigenous people and animals, even though gathering cultures could be hearkened to as well. The result is that exploitation of animals is naturalized as intrinsic to people's relationships with the other animals. The "naturalization" of the ways in which we are socialized to look at animals affects how we act toward animals—that is, if we see animals as "meat," we eat them. Thus we can read in a letter responding to an article on "political correctness": "None of us has the whole picture. For one woman, vegetarianism is an ethical imperative; for another, eating meat is part of the natural world's give and take."[16]

Attempts to make the ideology and the material reality of "meat" production visible, to denaturalize it, result in responses by feminists who through further promulgation of the superstructure and its importance for individual, or certain groups of, feminists, uphold the trafficking in (traditional) ideas about animals and actual trafficking in animal flesh. "Meat" is thus an *idea* that is experienced as an *object*, a *relationship* between humans and the other animals that is rendered instead as a *material reality* involving "food choices," a social construction that is seen as natural and normative. When we see the concept of species as a social construction, we are enabled to offer an alternative social construction that is morally preferable, one that recognizes animals as a subordinated social group, rather than naturally usable.

To understand why feminists defend their trafficking in animals, we must perceive the dialectic that is at work between the "political" and the "natural."

# Naturalizing the Political: I

In a "meat"-advocating culture, decisions that are actually political are presented as "natural" and "inevitable." When Ellen Goodman argues that "we acknowledge ourselves as creatures of nature" in "knowingly" eating a hamburger or catching a fish, she presumes that her readers share with her an understanding that "creatures of nature" eat dead bodies. She also assumes that we will find it acceptable to be likened to the other animals when the issue is the consumption of animal flesh, even though so much of human nature (and justification for such consumption) is precisely defined by establishing strict notions of differentiation between humans and the other animals. Two prevalent conceptualizations assist in the naturalizing of the political choice to use animals as food and explain Goodman's confidence in her defense of such actions.

## The Case of the False Mass Term

The existence of "meat" as a mass term contributes to the naturalizing of the phenomenon of eating animals' bodies.[17] Mass terms refer to things like water or colors; no matter how much you have of it, or what type of container it is in, water is still water. You can add a bucket of water to a pool of water without changing it at all. Objects referred to by mass terms have no individuality, no uniqueness, no specificity, no particularity.

When we turn an animal into "meat," someone who has a very particular, situated life, a unique being, is converted into something that has no distinctiveness, no uniqueness, no individuality. When you add five pounds of hamburger to a plate of hamburger, you have more of the same thing; nothing is changed. But if you have a living cow in front of you, and you kill that cow, and butcher that cow, and grind up her flesh, you have not added a mass term to a mass term and ended up with more of the same.[18] Because of the reign of "meat" as a mass term, it is not often while eating "meat" that one thinks: "I am now interacting with an animal." We do not see our own personal "meat"-eating as contact with animals because it has been renamed as contact with food. But what is on the plate in front of us is *not* devoid of specificity. It is the dead flesh of what was once a living, feeling being. The crucial point here is that we make some*one* who is a unique being and therefore not the appropriate referent of a mass term into some*thing* that is the appropriate referent of a mass term. We do so by removing any associations that might make it difficult to accept the activity of rendering a unique individual into a consumable thing. Not wanting to be aware of this activity, we accept this disassociation, this distancing device of the mass term "meat."

## Ontologizing Animals as "Naturally" Consumable

The prevailing ideology ontologizes animals as consumable, as mass terms.[19] This ontology is socially constructed: there is nothing inherent in a cow's existence that necessitates her future fate as hamburger or her current fate as milk machine. However, a major way in which we circumvent responsibility for terminal animals' fate at the hands of humans is to believe that they have no other fate than to be food, that this is their "natural" existence. As a result, certain positions regarding animals' ontology—that is, the normativeness of "meat" eating—are embraced by people across the divisions of race, class, and sex. Unless some factor dislodges these positions and brings about consciousness, these positions will continue to be held and, when under attack, fiercely defended as natural, inevitable, and/or beneficial.

The existence of "meat" as a mass term contributes to the ontologizing and thus "naturalizing" of animals as intrinsically consumable. The ideology becomes sanctioned as eternal or unalterable, rather than suspect and changeable. To be a pig is to be pork. To be a chicken is to be poultry. When Nel Noddings raises the issue of the possible mass extinction of certain domesticated animals if humans were to stop eating them, she is reproducing this ontology. She continues to see the animals as being dependent on their relationship to us, as literally existing (only) for us. To be concerned about whether animals can live without us needing (eating) them continues their ontologized status as exploitable. Indeed, it clearly evokes this ontology: without our needing them, and implicitly, using them as food, they would not exist.

Warehousing animals (the term I prefer to "factory farming") is inevitable in a "meat"-advocating, capitalist culture such as ours. It has become the only way to maintain and meet the demand for flesh products that currently exists and must be seen as the *logical outcome* of this ontology. Warehoused animals account for 90 to 97 percent of the animal flesh consumed in the United States. Thus, those who argue that warehousing is immoral but alternatives to obtaining animal flesh are acceptable deny the historical reality that has brought us to this time and place. They conceive of some "natural" practice of flesh consumption that is free from historical influence, that is essentially atemporal and thus apolitical. Thus they naturalize the political decision to eat other animals.

# Politicizing the Natural: I

Animal rights discourse refuses to see the consumption of dead animals as a natural act and actively asserts it to be a political one. It does so by refusing to accept the discursive boundaries that bury the issue as "natural" or "personal." In doing this, animal rights discourse exposes a matrix of relations that are usually ignored or accepted as implicit, the matrix that I call trafficking in animals, by proposing three interrelated arguments: other species matter, our current ontology of animals is unacceptable, and our current practices are oppressive.

## Other Species Matter

Central to the process of "naturalizing" the political is the human/other dialectic in which "human" de facto represents white (human) maleness and "other" represents that which white human maleness negates: other races, sexes, or species. The process that Zuleyma Tang Halpin observes in scientific objectivity is generalizable to the view of anyone in a dominant position in a class-, race-, sex-, and species-stratified culture: "The 'other,' by definition is the opposite of the 'self,' and therefore comes to be regarded as intrinsically of lesser value."[20] Caroline Whitbeck identifies this as a "self- other *opposition* that underlines much of so-called 'western thought.' "[21] This opposition has been identified in ecofeminist discourse as a set of dualisms: culture or nature, male or female, mind or body, and, importantly, human or animal. In the prevailing dualistic ontology, equation of any human group with the other animals serves to facilitate the humans' exploitation. As Halpin points out, "Even when groups labeled 'inferior' are not explicitly equated with women, they are often compared to animals, usually in ways designed to make them appear more animal than human (using white males as the prototype of humanity)."[22]

In her discussion of the representation of African-American women in pornography and its enabling of the pornographic treatment of white women, Patricia Hill Collins identifies the sexual and racial dimensions of being treated like an animal: "The treatment of all women in contemporary pornography has strong ties to the portrayal of Black women as animals. . . . [Cites an example.] This linking of animals and white women within pornography becomes feasible when grounded in the earlier denigration of Black women as animals."[23] The traditional feminist response to the equation of femaleness with animalness has been to break that association, to argue in a variety of ways for women's work and lives as representatives of culture rather than nature. It has most often left undisturbed the notion that animals represent the natural. In other words, while feminism has liberated white women and people of color from the onerous equation with animals and otherness, it has not disturbed the equation of animals with otherness.

What we have for the most part in feminism is a species-specific philosophical system, in which (an expanded) humanity continues to negate the other animals precisely because their otherness is located in the natural sphere. This species-specific tendency in feminist philosophy is evident, for instance, in Elizabeth Spelman's important article "Woman as Body." After discussing the equation of women, slaves, laborers, children, and animals with the body and how this equation facilitates their oppression, she goes on to offer theoretical redress only for the human animals so oppressed.[24] Barbara Noske points out that "as yet there exists in our thinking little room for the notion of a non-human Subject and what this would imply."[25] Nancy Hartsock wonders "why there must be a sharp discontinuity between humans and [the other] animals. Is this too an outgrowth of the masculinist project?"[26] As if in reply, Noske suggests that "even if there is such a thing as a species boundary between ourselves and *all* animals, might this discontinuity not exist on a horizontal level rather than on a vertical and hierarchical level?"[27] A species-neutral system would recognize each animal as a person, "and to some extent as an Alien person."[28]

### Our Current Ontology of Animals Is Unacceptable

Resisting the current ontology of animals as consumable is central to animal rights. Once the human-animal division is perceived to be as corrupt and as inaccurate as the other dualisms closely examined by ecofeminism, the re-Subjectification and denaturalization of animals can occur. This involves accepting them ontologically on their own terms and not on the basis of our interests. The current ontology requires that we acquiesce to the hierarchical structure that places humans above animals and defines "human" and "animal" antithetically. The current ontology continues to subordinate nonhuman nature—in this case the other animals—to people's whims.

The ontology of animals that accompanies animal rights theory involves distinguishing between reforms of certain practices that accept animals as usable and abolition of these practices. The goal is not bigger cages, but *no* cages; not bigger stalls, but *no* veal calves; not mandated rest stops, but *no* transporting; not careful placement of downed animals into front-loader buckets, but *no* system that creates downed animals; not "humane" slaughter, but *no* slaughter. Reform of the current system still subordinates animals to humans. Reform situates itself within the issue of animal *welfare* rather than animal rights, and the concern becomes the *appropriate* use of animals rather than the elimination of humans' use of animals. Often when feminists respond to animal rights, they attempt to dislodge the ontological claims of animal rights and argue for the reformist acceptance of animals' exploitation. Ellen Goodman argues for the "intelligent, responsible use of animals." Mary Zeiss Stange wants hunters to "promote positive public images of animal use and welfare, as opposed to animal protectionism."[29] In upholding the dominant ontology, the promotion of responsible use of animals grants charity where liberty is needed. Or, as Paulo Freire puts it, such paternalism—taking better care of terminal animals—enacts the "egoistic interests of the oppressors":[30]

> Any attempt to "soften" the power of the oppressor in deference to the weakness of the oppressed almost always manifests itself in the form of false generosity; indeed, the attempt never goes beyond this. In order to have the continued opportunity to express their "generosity", the oppressors must perpetuate injustice as well. An unjust social order is the permanent fount of this "generosity", which is nourished by death, despair, and poverty. That is why its dispensers become desperate at the slightest threat to the source of this false generosity.[31]

What is required is both an acceptance of the ontological integrity of those who are different from the "normative" human and a recognition of animals' consciousness and cultures. As much as men's accounts of women's lives have been partial, false, or malicious lies, so too have humans' accounts of the other animals' lives. In resisting the "naturalization" of animals, we need, as Noske argues, to develop an anthropology of the other animals that encounters them on their terms. A false generosity only serves to restrict animals to the natural realm that enables their ontologizing as usable.

## *"Predation" Is Oppressive*

Claiming that human consumption of the other animals is predation like that of carnivorous animals naturalizes this act. But if this predation is socially constructed, then it is not a necessary aspect of human-animal relations. Instead it is an ongoing oppression enacted through the animal-industrial complex.

Using the three-part definition of oppression proposed by Alison Jaggar,[32] we can see its applicability to the experience of the victims of the traffic in animals.

First, the "oppressed suffer some kind of restriction on their freedom."[33] Terminal animals suffer literal constraints upon their freedom: most are unable to walk, to breathe clean air, to stretch their wings, to root in the dirt, to pack for food, to suckle their young, to avoid having their sexuality abused. Whether warehoused or not, all are killed. They are not able to do something which is important for them to do, and they lack the ability to determine for themselves their own actions.

Second, "oppression is the result of human agency, humanly imposed restrictions."[34] Humans have a choice whether to eat animals or not. Choosing to purchase flesh at a supermarket or have it served at a conference represents human agency; such human agency requires that the other animals lose their freedom to exist independently of us.

Third, "oppression must be unjust."[35] Injustice includes the thwarting of an individual's liberty because of her or his membership in a group that has been targeted for exploitation. From the perspective of human-skin privilege, the oppression of other animals is seen as just, even though it arises from targeting for exploitation specific groups—in this case, the other animals. In a species-neutral philosophical system, such as the one that I believe is integral to ecofeminism, human skin should not be the sole determinant of what is moral. Viewed from a philosophical system that rejects the intertwined human/animal and subject/object dualisms, humans' treatment of terminal animals is unjust. Beverly Harrison proposes that "no one has a moral right to override basic conditions for others' well-being in order to have 'liberty' inconsistent with others' basic welfare."[36] This is what people are doing when they traffic in animals. As Alice Walker observes, "The oppression that black people suffer in South Africa—and people of color, and children face all over the world—is the same oppression that animals endure every day to a greater degree."[37]

# Naturalizing the Political: II

In response to efforts to re-Subjectify the other animals and label our treatment of them as oppression, people who do not wish to give up human-skin privilege seek ways to banish animal rights discourse from the political realm, to reprivatize and re-"naturalize" it. Reprivatization defends the established social division of discourses—that is, the personal is not the political, the natural is not the social, the domestic is not the political—thus denying political status for animal rights. For instance, when Ellen Goodman contends that animal rights are "unnatural," she implicitly accepts discursive boundaries she otherwise finds disturbing. If animal rights are unnatural, then animal oppression is natural; if it is natural, it is not political. She is attempting to encase the debate once again in discursive privacy. Or, when a feminist refers to the "so-called animal liberation movement,"[38] she implicitly denies political content to this movement. When Nel Noddings claims that domestic animals do not have meaningful relationships with other adult animals nor do they "anticipate their deaths,"[39] she delimits their lives within the sanctity of the "natural," which it is presumed we can identify (and control), rather than the social. It may be reassuring to believe that animals have no social network and do not object to their deaths; however, these beliefs are possible only as long as we do not inquire closely into the lives of animals as subjects. Then we see that certain cultural structures facilitate these efforts at depoliticizing and renaturalizing animals' oppression.

Feminist theorist Nancy Hartsock observes that ruling-class ideas "give an incorrect account of reality, an account only of appearances."[40] Our discourse about animals has been determined largely by the appearance of "meat" in animals' marketable form—T-bone, lamb chops, hamburger, "fresh" chickens—an appearance positing that "meat," like George Eliot's happy women, has no history. As long as "meat" has no past, its identity will come only from the constructed context of appetites and appearances. This permits what I call the flight from specificity.

The flight from specificity favors generalities instead of engaged knowledge, mass terms over individual entities. To be specific would require confronting the actual practice and the meaning of what is done to animals. Generalities safely insulate one from this knowledge, keeping debates at a predetermined, unbloodied level. Most frequently they do not pinpoint the victim, the perpetrator, or the method. Just as most feminists would recognize that the statement "Some people batter other people" is imprecise—who and how left undefined—so is the statement "We eat 'meat.'"

When, for instance, in her defense of eating animals, Nel Noddings refers to ensuring that domestic animals' "deaths are physically and psychically painless,"[41] she presumes that such a practice exists and that we all sufficiently understand what she means so that we can *agree* that such a practice either exists or is attainable for terminal animals. In this view, ignorance about the act of slaughtering prevails, though it remains unexposed.[42] In fact, such a practice neither exists nor is attainable.[43]

Another example of the flight from specificity occurs when the term "meat eating" is applied transhistorically, transculturally, implying that the means by which "meat" is obtained have not changed so much that different terms are needed, or else that the changes in the means of production are immaterial to a discussion. Consider Luisah Teish's encouragement to feed the ancestors "meat" if this is what they want:

> I have said that cooking for your ancestors is simple. It is, with one exception. Do not think that you can *impose* your diet on them. It won't work for long.
>   I knew a woman who tried to force her ancestors to keep a vegetarian diet. The oracle kept saying that they were not satisfied. I suggested she make some meatballs for them. She did and got "great good fortune" from the oracle. I could advise her this way because I'd tried to impose a pork-free diet on my ancestors, but much to my disgust they insisted on pork chops to accompany their greens, yams, and cornbread.[44]

How can the flesh obtained from mass-produced, warehoused, terminal animals in any way duplicate the flesh eaten by the ancestors when they were alive, when a different material reality constructed the meaning of "meatballs"? "Meat" is not an ahistorical term, though it functions here as though it were, as representation. Surely the ancestors know that "pork" obtained from a twentieth-century warehoused animal—who was pumped full of chemicals, who never saw the light of day until transported to be butchered, whose relationship with other animals, including mother and/or children was curtailed, and who never rooted in the earth—is not at all the "pork" they ate.

In each of these cases, terms such as "painless" or "meatballs" or "pork" convey little specific knowledge about the production of "meat." Those aspects unidentified or misidentified are then presumed to be unproblematic or inconsequential. The result of this discursive control is that "meat"-eaters can set the limits on what sort of information about "meat" eating is allowed into a discussion.[45] What Sally McConnell-Ginet observes about the sexual politics of discourse holds true, too, for the debate over animal rights: "The sexual politics of discourse affects WHO can mean WHAT, and WHOSE meanings get established as community currency."[46]

The meanings that are established regarding "meat" are almost always general, rarely specific. They recognize neither the specific animal killed to be food, nor the specific means for raising, transporting, and killing this animal. This flight from specificity regarding "meat" production bars from the discourse matters that in other areas of feminist theory are considered the basis for making ethical decisions: material reality and material relationships.

# Feminist Defenses of Trafficking in Animals

Before examining specific feminist defenses of trafficking in animals, some general problems of discursive control must be identified. Feminists, like nonfeminists, generally seek to banish animal rights by reprivatizing decisions about animals and renaturalizing animals' lives as subordinate to humans'. In this, several factors function in their favor. They assume that their predefined understanding of the issue is adequate: for example, that it is correct to label animal rights as being in opposition to pluralism because their definition of pluralism excludes animal rights. Any predefined feminist principle that is established as in opposition to animal rights requires closer examination: does it presume that the socially authorized forms of feminist debate available for discussing this issue are adequate and fair? To paraphrase Fraser, does it fail to question whether these forms of public discourse are skewed in favor of the self-interpretations and interests of dominant groups (including human females)—occluding, in other words, the fact that the means of public discourse themselves may be at issue?[47]

Hidden ethical stances prevail even in pluralistic feminisms. In an evolving community of individuals who share ideas and goals for changing patriarchal society, some values are so given, so taken for granted, that we never examine them. For instance, we agree that cannibalism is not a legitimate way to obtain nutrition, even though human flesh can be very tasty. Cannibalism is not a question of individual tastes, appetites, autonomy, or ritual; it is a forbidden activity whose forbiddenness appears obvious to almost everyone, and therefore this forbiddenness disturbs very few. Clearly this is not so when it comes to eating nonhuman animal flesh. In this case the flesh is considered both tasty and acceptable, based on a decision individuals and cultural traditions have made about nutrition and ethics. To suggest that nonhuman animal flesh be forbidden disturbs many.

The differing ethical stances regarding the flesh of human animals versus the flesh of nonhuman animals illustrates that the issue is not whether a community can forbid an action but who is to be protected from being consumed. Since a communitywide vegetarianism is seen as problematic but a community ban on cannibalism is a given, it is obvious that theorizing about species is at this point in time receiving different discursive space from theorizing about race, class, gender, and heterosexism.

## Autonomy

The invocation of autonomy—the insistence that enforcing vegetarianism at a conference restricts an individual's autonomy—presumes that no one else's liberty is at issue in food choices. This is simply not so. The invisibility of animals' oppression permits the debate to be about individual human's liberties, rather than making animals' oppression visible. Staking a preeminent claim for autonomy is an attempt at reprivatization. As Ruby Sales remarked during the 1990 NWSA conference: "Privilege is not a condition. . . . It is a consequence of the condition of oppression."[48] From this politicized perspective, eating animals is a privilege humans have granted themselves, and this privilege is called "autonomy." The ideology that ontologizes animals as consumable pre-exists and provides the foundation for the easy confusion of privilege with autonomy.

## Pluralism

The position that feminist conferences (and theory) should be pluralistic also is seen to be at odds with any universal claim for vegetarianism. Imposing one's dietary decision on all races or ethnic groups is viewed as racist, because the inability to exercise personal food choices severs an individual from her racial/ethnic tradition. I deeply respect the need to preserve nondominant cultures. However, I do not believe that pluralism requires siding with human-skin privilege in order to avoid white-skin privilege. We do not embrace nondominant cultural traditions that, for instance, oppress women. An unspoken "in-order-to" is buried in this assumption: We want feminism to be pluralistic; in order for this to be, we must be species-exclusive in our theory. From this context, we can see that a politicized issue, pluralism, is made to contest with a yet-unpoliticized issue, the traffic in animals. Moreover, we see that pluralism is defined in such a way that it applies only to other human beings. Conventional wisdom implies that for the one issue to prevail, the other must be kept in the realm of discursive privacy. In other words, pluralism becomes a boundary enforcer rather than a boundary destabilizer. Pluralism in food choices, including eating dead animals, can be argued in this way as long as the dominant culture's current ontology of animals remains unchallenged.

Through reprivatization, a universal vegetarianism is seen as a white woman's imposing her "dietary" concerns on women of color. However, since I am arguing on behalf of vegetarian feminist conferences, let us agree that at present the foods offered at most conferences represent the dominant culture. They already ignore ethnic and racial traditions around food.

In addressing the right of racial and ethnic groups to eat animals, we are not talking about food as nutrition but food as ritual. The poet Pat Parker argues that her "meat" eating is literally soul food.[49] But the ritual meaning of a meal may serve to reprivatize something that has broken away from discursive privacy. Alice Walker can see barbarity in her childhood diet in which "meat was a mainstay"[50] and yet still respect rituals that were not barbarous—her mother's gardening, for instance.

The "naturalizing" of the other animals as consumable is inimicable to feminist pluralism—a true pluralism that seeks to recognize the other as a subject rather than an object. This pluralism would acknowledge that the social constructions of race, class, and sex are related to the social construction of species and must be confronted as such.

# Politicizing the Natural: II

A species-exclusive philosophy establishes human and animal as antithetical categories, and naturalizes human beings' use of the other animals. In contrast, a species-neutral philosophy would not exaggerate differences between humans and the other animals, or imply that singular human evils such as warehousing animals or rape represent some residual "natural" or "animal-like" tendency. As the "natural" is politicized and labeled "oppression," "meat" will no longer be an idea that is experienced as an object. Trafficking will be destabilized by consciousness and solidarity.

## The Politics of Consciousness

Consciousness of oppression requires responses. Alison Jaggar observes that to "talk of oppression seems to commit feminists to a world view that includes at least two groups with conflicting interests: the oppressors and the oppressed"[51]—or, to put it more bluntly in the terms of this chapter, "meat"-eaters and their "meat." Paulo Freire suggests that we can respond to these conflicting interests either as critics/radicals, for whom "the importance is the continuing transformation of reality," or as naive thinkers/sectarians, who accommodate "to this normalized 'today.'" Naive thinkers/sectarians accept prevailing ideological barriers and discursive boundaries; critical consciousness can find no hold here: "sectarianism, because it is myth-making and irrational, turns reality into a false (and therefore unchangeable) 'reality.' "[52] Ellen Goodman accepts an unchangeable "reality" when she argues that

> environmental purity, the ability to live a life without a single cruel act against nature, is impossible. . . . The only answer is to avoid the use—or exploitation—of any other species. . . . We acknowledge ourselves as creatures of nature. . . . The anti-fur extremists prefer to win by intimidation. They have staked out a moral position that leaves no room for the way we live. It is, in its own peculiar way, unnatural.[53]

Goodman both reprivatizes and renaturalizes the normalized "today." The alternative to this accommodation of and mythicizing of reality is to accept the process of radicalization, an actual engagement in the efforts to transform concrete reality. This transformation aligns one with the oppressed rather than the oppressor, the "meat" rather than the "meat"-eater.

Breaking down ideological boundaries requires that those who are the oppressors must stop "regarding the oppressed as an abstract category,"[54] must stop seeing "meat" as a mass term.

### The Politics of Solidarity

Critical consciousness makes us aware of ourselves as oppressors. It transforms our understanding of a reality in which the political has been naturalized. But then what? Freire observes:

> Discovering her or himself to be an oppressor may cause considerable anguish, but it does not necessarily lead to solidarity with the oppressed. Rationalizing one's guilt through paternalistic treatment of the oppressed, all the while holding them fast in a position of dependence, will not do. Solidarity requires that one enter into the situation of those with whom one is identifying; it is a radical posture. . . . True solidarity with the oppressed means fighting at their side to transform the objective reality which has made them these "beings for another."[55]

Trafficking in animals oppresses them, ontologizing them as "beings for another." In other words, trafficking in animals makes us oppressors.

The necessary precondition for animals to be free is that there be no trafficking in animals' bodies. The ontology will not collapse upon itself until the actions that the ontology upholds—for example, "meat" eating—are stopped, and until we stop being animals' oppressors.

# Consciousness, Solidarity, and Feminist-Vegetarian Conferences

A feminist conference is an action—an action made up of people gathering to plan, educate, and network around issues of justice for women. Alice Walker, reporting on her evolving feminist consciousness, comments: "I think about how hard it would be for me to engage in any kind of action now for justice and peace with the remains of murdered flesh in my body."[56] Walker's thoughts pose a question: Should the remains of murdered flesh be available for consumption during feminist conferences? We live in a "meat"-advocating culture. But should feminist conferences be "meat"-advocating? If I recall correctly, a letter to a feminist publication a few years back queried: "Why are we going home for the holidays to watch our families eat dead animals?" No one has to go home for the holidays to see the traffic in dead animals—they can come to feminist conferences.

The assumption that feminist conferences should have an all-inclusive menu has been tacit, a given, and thus untheorized. Feminist conference organizers think they are assuming a neutral role in the debate about the consumption of animals by offering a vegetarian option that can be adopted personally if desired. In Freire's terms, they are naive thinkers. They wrongly conclude that there is such a thing as neutrality, that they are not de facto taking an ontological stance that aligns them with the dominant culture. A feminist conference that includes the vegetarian option presumes "meat" eating as normative. As Nancy Fraser argues, "Authoritative views purporting to be neutral and disinterested actually express the partial and interested perspectives of dominant social groups."[57] An all-vegetarian conference thus destabilizes what is claimed to be neutral and comprehensive, demonstrating instead its partiality. It says that if feminists want to traffic in animal bodies, they must be deliberate and not passive about it. It resists the naturalizing of the political.

The individual vegetarian option at a conference is inadequate because it perpetuates the idea that what we eat and what we do to animals (a simultaneous act if we traffic in dead animals) are solely personal concerns. It reprivatizes a political issue, making "meat" the default diet. It removes the actions of a community from the consciousness of that community. Issues such as the environment, women's health, and the politics and ethics of conflicting ontologies are rendered invisible. As the Ecofeminist Task Force Recommendation to the 1990 NWSA conference argues,[58] "meat" eating has dire environmental consequences such as deforestation, soil erosion, heavy water consumption, unrecyclable animal excrement, and immense demands on energy and raw materials.[59] Trafficking in animals also has consequences for our health. The recommendation identified the correlation between flesh consumption and heart attacks, breast cancer, colon cancer, ovarian cancer, and osteoporosis.[60]

Trying vegetarianism at a feminist conference could be a catalyst for a changed consciousness about animals. The only way to experience vegetarian nourishment is by eating vegetarian food. The feminist-vegetarian conference proposal recognizes the practical hurdles to moving away from a flesh diet: many worry that they will not feel full after a vegetarian meal; that the dishes are unappetizing; or that insufficient protein will be ingested. Vegetarian meals therefore speak to practical fears: one *can* feel full; food *can* be tasty; vegetarians *do* get the same amount of protein each day that "meat"-eaters do—twice as much as our bodies require. As the Ecofeminist Task Force urged, conference organizers should "make every effort to provide meals that satisfy the health, conscience, and palate"[61] of feminist conference participants.

Reprivatizers insist that the eating of animals is not a legitimate subject of feminist discourse, but a personal decision. Whether we eat blood and muscle or not is seen solely as an individual act, rather than a corporate one. This attitude toward flesh eating as solely personal is then enacted as individuals are given the choice between competing meal options. Reprivatizers, keeping the debate at the personal level, also keep the debate about the issue of *food*. Animal rights discourse argues that the debate is a political one and the issue is *ontology*. "Meat" at a meal automatically undermines a discussion of vegetarianism because the prevailing consciousness about animals—ontologizing them as consumable—is literally present.

The inappropriateness of this ontology, the naturalizing of it by humans' self-interest, the consequences of it for our health and the environment—the entire oppositional discourse that vegetarianism represents—can only become apparent in an atmosphere that respects animals. The current ontology will never offer this. It is an ontology at odds with feminist ethics.

# Reading Questions

1. What does Adams mean by the "traffic in animals" and how does the meaning of this phrase rely on feminist views of producer-consumer relations in capitalist cultures?

2. How has the use of animalized and feminized protein been banished to the zone of discursive privacy, thus naturalizing the former? Why does Adams object to this?

3. What are the specific ways in which people who eat meat naturalize their meat-eating habits? Why does the mass term of "meat" ontologize animals as nonunique objects?

4. Why does Adams advocate that feminism move beyond species-specific philosophical frameworks to a species-neutral philosophical framework that allows equal discursive space to other species as well as to race, class, gender, and heterosexism?

5. What is the ethical significance of the distinction between human-skin privilege and white-skin privilege?

6. Why does Adams reject the pluralist positions of cultural feminists as "naive"?

7. Why do you think that Adams supports her arguments by reference to animals' interests rather than to our species-interests, such as our health and our environment?

# Recommended Reading

Carol J. Adams, *The Sexual Politics of Eating Meat: A Feminist Vegetarian Critical Theory* (New York: Continuum, 1990)

C. David Coats, *Old MacDonald's Factory Farm: The Myth of the Traditional Farm and the Shocking Truth about Animal Suffering in Today's Agribusiness* (New York: Continuum, 1989)

Greta Gaard, ed., *Ecofeminism: Women, Animals, Nature* (Philadelphia: Temple University Press, 1993)

Emma Goldman, "The Traffic in Women," *The Traffic in Women and Other Essays in Feminism* (New York: Times Change Press, 1970)

Donna Haraway, *Primate Visions: Gender, Race, and Nature in the World of Modern Science* (New York: Routledge, 1989)

Jim Mason and Peter Singer, *Animal Factories* (New York: Crown, 1989)

Gayle Rubin, "The Traffic in Women: Notes on the 'Political Economy' of Sex," *Toward an Anthropology of Women*, ed. Rayna R. Reiter (New York: Monthly Review Press, 1975)

# Ecofeminism

## CAROLYN MERCHANT

Carolyn Merchant, ecofeminist and activist, is the author of *Death of Nature* and *Radical Ecology: The Search for a Livable World*. She is professor of environmental history, philosophy, and ethics in the Department of Conservation and Resource Studies at the University of California, Berkeley.

In Kenya, women of the Green Belt movement band together to plant millions of trees in arid degraded lands. In India, they join the chipko (tree-hugging) movement to preserve precious fuel resources for their communities. In Sweden, feminists prepare jam from berries sprayed with herbicides and offer a taste to members of parliament: they refuse. In Canada, they take to the streets to obtain signatures opposing uranium processing near their towns. In the United States, housewives organize local support to clean up hazardous waste sites. All these actions are examples of a worldwide movement, increasingly known as "ecofeminism," dedicated to the continuation of life on earth.

Ecofeminism emerged in the 1970s with an increasing consciousness of the connections between women and nature. The term, "ecofeminisme," was coined by French writer Françoise d'Eaubonne in 1974 who called upon women to lead an ecological revolution to save the planet.[1] Such an ecological revolution would entail new gender relations between women and men and between humans and nature.

Developed by Ynestra King at the Institute for Social Ecology in Vermont about 1976, the concept became a movement in 1980 with a major conference on "Women and Life on Earth: Ecofeminism in the '80s," and the ensuing Women's Pentagon Action to protest anti-life nuclear war and weapons development.[2] During the 1980s cultural feminists in the United States injected new life into ecofeminism by arguing that both women and nature could be liberated together.

Liberal, cultural, social, and socialist feminism have all been concerned with improving the human/nature relationship and each has contributed to an ecofeminist perspective in different ways (Table 1).[3] Liberal feminism is consistent with the objectives of reform environmentalism to alter human relations with nature from within existing structures of governance through the passage of new laws and regulations. Cultural ecofeminism analyzes environmental problems from within its critique of patriarchy and offers alternatives that could liberate both women and nature.

Social and socialist ecofeminism ground their analyses in capitalist patriarchy. They ask how patriarchal relations of reproduction reveal the domination of women by men, and how capitalist relations of production reveal the domination of nature by men. The domination of women and nature inherent in the market economy's use of both as resources would be totally restructured. Although cultural ecofeminism has delved more deeply into the woman-nature connection, social and socialist ecofeminism have the potential for a more thorough critique of domination and for a liberating social justice.

Ecofeminist actions address the contradiction between production and reproduction. Women attempt to reverse the assaults of production on both biological and social

TABLE 1   Feminism and the Environment

| | Nature | Human Nature | Feminist Critique of Environmentalism | Image of a Feminist Environmentalism |
|---|---|---|---|---|
| Liberal Feminism | Atoms<br>Mind/Body dualism<br>Domination of Nature | Rational Agents<br>Individualism<br>Maximization of self-interest | "Man and his environment" leaves out women | Women in natural Resources and environmental sciences |
| Marxist Feminism | Transformation of Nature by science and technology for human use.<br>Domination of nature as a means to human freedom<br>Nature is material basis of life: food, clothing, shelter, energy | Creation of human nature through mode of production, praxis<br>Historically specific—not fixed<br>Species nature of humans | Critique of capitalist control of resources and accumulation of goods and profits | Socialist society will use resources for good of all men and women<br>Resources will be controlled by workers<br>Environmental pollution could be minimal since no surpluses would be produced<br>Environmental research by men and women |
| Cultural Feminism | Nature is spiritual and personal<br>Conventional science and technology problematic because of their emphasis on domination | Biology is basic<br>Humans are sexual reproducing bodies<br>Sexed by biology/gendered by society | Unaware of interconnectedness of male domination of nature and women<br>Males environmentalism retains hierarchy<br>Insufficient attention to environmental threats to women's reproduction (chemicals, nuclear war) | Woman/Nature both valorized and celebrated<br>Reproductive freedom<br>Against pornographic depictions of both women and nature<br>Cultural ecofeminism |
| Socialist Feminism | Nature is material basis of life: food, clothing, shelter, energy<br>Nature is socially and historically constructed<br>Transformation of nature by production and reproduction | Human nature created through biology and praxis (sex, race, class, age)<br>Historically specific and socially constructed | Leaves out nature as active and responsive<br>Leaves out women's role in reproduction and reproduction as a category<br>Systems approach is mechanistic not dialectical | Both nature and human production are active<br>Centrality of biological and social reproduction<br>Dialectic between production and reproduction<br>Multileveled structural analysis<br>Dialectical (not mechanical) systems<br>Socialist ecofeminism |

reproduction by making problems visible and proposing solutions. When radioactivity from nuclear power-plant accidents, toxic chemicals, and hazardous wastes threatens the biological reproduction of the human species, women experience this contradiction as assaults on their own bodies and on those of their children and act to halt them. Household products, industrial pollutants, plastics, and packaging wastes invade the homes of First World women threatening the reproduction of daily life, while direct access to food, fuel, and clean water for many Third World women is imperiled by cash cropping on traditional homelands and by pesticides used in agribusiness. First World women combat these assaults by altering consumption habits, recycling wastes, and protesting production and disposal methods, while Third World women act to protect traditional ways of life and reverse ecological damage from multinational corporations and the extractive industries. Women challenge the ways in which mainstream society reproduces itself through socialization and politics by envisioning and enacting alternative gender roles, employment options, and political practices.

Many ecofeminists advocate some form of an environmental ethic that deals with the twin oppressions of the domination of women and nature through an ethic of care and nurture that arises out of women's culturally constructed experiences. As philosopher Karen Warren conceptualizes it:

> An ecofeminist ethic is both a critique of male domination of both women and nature and an attempt to frame an ethic free of male-gender bias about women and nature. It not only recognizes the multiple voices of women, located differently by race, class, age, [and] ethnic considerations, it centralizes those voices. Ecofeminism builds on the multiple perspectives of those whose perspectives are typically omitted or undervalued in dominant discourses, for example Chipko women, in developing a global perspective on the role of male domination in the exploitation of women and nature. An ecofeminist perspective is thereby . . . structurally pluralistic, inclusivist, and contextualist, emphasizing through concrete example the crucial role context plays in understanding sexist and naturist practice.[4]

An ecofeminist ethic, she argues, would constrain traditional ethics based on rights, rules, and utilities, with considerations based on care, love, and trust. Yet an ethic of care, as elaborated by some feminists, falls prey to an essentialist critique that women's nature is to nurture.[5]

An alternative is a partnership ethic that treats humans (including male partners and female partners) as equals in personal, household, and political relations and humans as equal partners with (rather than controlled-by or dominant-over) nonhuman nature. Just as human partners, regardless of sex, race, or class must give each other space, time, and care, allowing each other to grow and develop individually within supportive nondominating relationships, so humans must give nonhuman nature space, time, and care, allowing it to reproduce, evolve, and respond to human actions. In practice, this would mean not cutting forests and damming rivers that make people and wildlife in flood plains more vulnerable to "natural disasters"; curtailing development in areas subject to volcanos, earthquakes, hurricanes, and tornados to allow room for unpredictable, chaotic, natural surprises; and exercising ethical restraint in introducing new technologies such as pesticides, genetically-engineered organisms, and biological weapons into ecosystems. Constructing nature as a partner allows for the possibility of a personal or intimate (but not necessarily spiritual) relationship with nature and for feelings of compassion for nonhumans as well as for people who are sexually, racially, or culturally different. It avoids gendering nature as a nurturing mother or a goddess and avoids the ecocentric dilemma that humans are only one of many equal parts of an ecological web and therefore morally equal to a bacterium or a mosquito.

# Liberal Ecofeminism

Liberal feminism characterized the history of feminism from its beginnings in the seventeenth century until the 1960s. It is rooted in liberalism, the political theory that accepts the scientific analysis that nature is composed of atoms moved by external forces, a theory of human nature that views humans as individual rational agents who maximize their own self-interest, and capitalism as the optimal economic structure for human progress. It accepts the egocentric ethic that the optimal society results when each individual maximizes her own productive potential. Thus what is good for each individual is good for society as a whole. Historically, liberal feminists have argued that women do not differ from men as rational agents and that exclusion from educational and economic opportunities have [sic] prevented them from realizing their own potential for creativity in all spheres of human life.[6]

Twentieth century liberal feminism was inspired by Simone de Beauvoir's *The Second Sex* (1949) and by Betty Friedan's *The Feminine Mystique* (1963). De Beauvoir argued that women and men were biologically different, but that women could transcend their biology, freeing themselves from their destiny as biological reproducers to assume masculine values. Friedan challenged the "I'm just a housewife" mystique resulting from post–World War II production forces that made way for soldiers to reassume jobs in the public sphere, pushing the "reserve army" of women laborers back into the private sphere of the home. The liberal phase of the women's movement that exploded in the 1960s demanded equity for women in the workplace and in education as the means of bringing about a fulfilling life. Simultaneously, Rachel Carson made the question of life on earth a public issue. Her 1962 *Silent Spring* focused attention on the death-producing effects of chemical insecticides accumulating in the soil and tissues of living organisms—deadly elixirs that bombarded human and nonhuman beings from the moment of conception until the moment of death.[7]

For liberal ecofeminists (as for liberalism generally), environmental problems result from the overly rapid development of natural resources and the failure to regulate pesticides and other environmental pollutants. The way the social order reproduces itself through governance and laws can be meliorated if social reproduction is made environmentally sound. Better science, conservation, and laws are therefore the proper approaches to resolving resource problems. Given equal educational opportunities to become scientists, natural resource managers, regulators, lawyers, and legislators, women, like men, can contribute to the improvement of the environment, the conservation of natural resources, and the higher quality of human life. Women, therefore, can transcend the social stigma of their biology and join men in the cultural project of environmental conservation.

Within the parameters of mainstream government and environmental organizations, such as the Group of Ten, are a multitude of significant opportunities for women to act to improve their own lives and resolve environmental problems. Additionally, women have established their own environmental groups. Organizations founded by women tend to have high percentages of women on their boards of directors. In California, for example, the Greenbelt Alliance was founded by a woman in 1958, the Save the Bay Association by three women in 1961, and the California Women in Timber in 1975 by a group of women. Yet most of the women in these organizations do not consider themselves feminists and do not consider their cause feminist. Feminism as a radical label, they believe, could stigmatize their long term goals. On the other hand, groups such as Friends of the River, Citizens for a Better Environment, and the local chapter of the Environmental Defense Fund employ many women who consider themselves feminists and men who consider themselves sensitive to feminist concerns, such as equality, childcare, overturning of hierarchies within the organization, and creating networks with other environmental organizations.[8]

## Cultural Ecofeminism

Cultural feminism developed in the late 1960s and 1970s with the second wave of feminism (the first being the women's suffrage movement of the early-twentieth century). Cultural ecofeminism is a response to the perception that women and nature have been mutually associated and devalued in western culture. Sherry Ortner's 1974 article, "Is Female to Male as Nature Is to Culture," posed the problem that motivates many ecofeminists. Ortner argued that, cross-culturally and historically women, as opposed to men, have been seen as closer to nature because of their physiology, social roles, and psychology. Physiologically, women bring forth life from their bodies, undergoing the pleasures, pain, and stigmas attached to menstruation, pregnancy, childbirth, and nursing, while men's physiology leaves them freer to travel, hunt, conduct warfare, and engage in public affairs. Socially, childrearing and domestic caretaking have kept married women close to the hearth and out of the workplace. Psychologically, women have been have assigned greater emotional capacities with greater ties to the particular, personal, and present than men who are viewed as more rational and objective with a greater capacity for abstract thinking.[9]

To cultural ecofeminists the way out of this dilemma is to elevate and liberate women and nature through direct political action. Many cultural feminists celebrate an era in prehistory when nature was symbolized by pregnant female figures, trees, butterflies, and snakes and in which women were held in high esteem as bringers forth of life. An emerging patriarchal culture, however, dethroned the mother goddesses and replaced them with male gods to whom the female deities became subservient. The scientific revolution of the seventeenth century further degraded nature by replacing Renaissance organicism and a nurturing earth with the metaphor of a machine to be controlled and repaired from the outside. The ontology and epistemology of mechanism are viewed by cultural feminists as deeply masculinist and exploitative of a nature historically depicted in the female gender. The earth is dominated by male-developed and male-controlled technology, science, and industry.[10]

Often stemming from an anti-science, anti-technology standpoint, cultural ecofeminism celebrates the relationship between women and nature through the revival of ancient rituals centered on goddess worship, the moon, animals, and the female reproductive system. A vision in which nature is held in esteem as mother and goddess is a source of inspiration and empowerment for many ecofeminists. Spirituality is seen as a source of both personal and social change. Goddess worship and rituals centered around the lunar and female menstrual cycles, lectures, concerts, art exhibitions, street and theater productions, and direct political action (web-spinning in anti-nuclear protests) are all examples of the re-visioning of nature and women as powerful forces. Cultural ecofeminist philosophy embraces intuition, an ethic of caring, and web-like human-nature relationships.[11]

For cultural feminists, human nature is grounded in human biology. Humans are biologically sexed and socially gendered. Sex/gender relations give men and women different power bases. Hence the personal is political. The perceived connection between women and biological reproduction turned upside down becomes the source of women's empowerment and ecological activism. Women's biology and Nature are celebrated as sources of female power. This form of ecofeminism has largely focused on the sphere of consciousness in relation to nature—spirituality, goddess worship, witchcraft—and the celebration of women's bodies, often accompanied by social actions such as anti-nuclear or anti-pornography protests.[12]

Much populist ecological activism by women, while perhaps not explicitly ecofeminist, implicitly draws on and is motivated by the connection between women's reproductive biology (nature) and male-designed technology (culture). Many women activists argue that male-designed and produced technologies neglect the effects of nuclear radiation, pesticides, hazardous wastes, and household chemicals on women's reproductive organs and on the ecosystem. They protest against radioactivity from nuclear wastes, power plants, and bombs as a potential cause of birth defects, cancers, and the elimination of life on earth. They expose hazardous waste sites near schools and homes as permeating soil and drinking water and contributing to miscarriages, birth defects, and leukemia. They object to pesticides and herbicides being sprayed on crops and forests as potentially affecting children and child-bearing women living near them. Women frequently spearhead local actions against spraying and power plant siting and organize citizens to demand toxic clean-ups.[13]

In 1978, Lois Gibbs of the Love Canal Homeowner's Association in Niagara Falls, New York, played a critical role in raising women's consciousness about the effects of hazardous waste disposal by Hooker Chemicals and Plastics Corporation in her neighborhood of 1,200 homes. Gibbs, whose son had experienced health problems after attending the local elementary school, launched a neighborhood campaign to close the school after other neighborhood women corroborated her observations. A study conducted by the women themselves found a higher than normal rate of miscarriages, stillbirths, and birth defects. Because the blue collar male population of Love Canal found it difficult to accept the fact that they could not adequately provide for their families, the women became leaders in the movement for redress. Love Canal is a story of how lower-middle-class women who had never been environmental activists became politicized by the life-and-death issues directly affecting their children and their homes and succeeded in obtaining redress from the state of New York. "The women of Love Canal," said Gibbs at the 1980 conference on Women and Life on Earth, "are no longer at home tending their homes and gardens. . . . Women who at one time looked down at people picketing, being arrested, and acting somewhat radical are now doing those very things."[14]

The majority of activists in the grassroots movement against toxics, are women. Many became involved when they experienced miscarriages or their children suffered birth defects or contracted leukemia or other forms of cancer. Through networking with neigh-

Police carry away an elderly antinuclear protester after she was arrested for stopping passage of a train in Vancouver, Washington, on February 22, 1985. UPI/Bettmann

borhood women, they began to link their problems to nearby hazardous waste sites. From initial Not in My Backyard (NIMBY) concerns, the movement has changed to Not in Anybody's Backyard (NIABY) to Not On Planet Earth (NOPE). Thus Cathy Hinds, whose well water in East Gray, Maine was contaminated by chemicals from a nearby industrial clean-up corporation became "fighting mad" when she lost a child and her daughter began to suffer from dizzy spells. She eventually founded the Maine Citizens' Coalition on Toxics and became active in the National Toxics Campaign. Her motive was to protect her children. Women, she says, "are mothers of the earth," who want to take care of it.[15]

Native American women organized WARN, Women of All Red Nations to protest high radiation levels from uranium mining tailings on their reservations and the high rates of aborted and deformed babies as well as issues such as the loss of reservation lands and the erosion of the family. They recognized their responsibilities as stewards of the land and expressed respect for "our Mother Earth who is a source of our physical nourishment and our spiritual strength."[16]

Cultural ecofeminism, however, has its feminist critics. Susan Prentice argues that ecofeminism, while asserting the fragility and interdependence of all life, "assumes that women and men . . . have an essential human nature that transcends culture and socialization." It implies that what men do to the planet is bad; what women do is good. This special relationship of women to nature and politics makes it difficult to admit that men can also develop an ethic of caring for nature. Second, ecofeminism fails to provide an analysis of capitalism that explains why it dominates nature. "Capitalism is never seriously tackled by ecofeminists as a process with its own particular history, logic, and struggle. Because ecofeminism lacks this analysis, it cannot develop an effective strategy for change." Moreover, it does not deal with the problems of poverty and racism experienced by millions of women around the world.[17] In contrast to cultural ecofeminism, the social and socialist strands of ecofeminism are based on a socioeconomic analysis that treats nature and human nature as socially constructed, rooted in an analysis of race, class, and gender.

# Social Ecofeminism

Building on the social ecology of Murray Bookchin, social ecofeminism envisions the restructuring of society as humane decentralized communities. "Social ecofeminism," states Janet Biehl, "accepts the basic tenet of social ecology, that the idea of dominating nature stems from the domination of human by human. Only ending all systems of domination makes possible an ecological society, in which no states or capitalist economies attempt to subjugate nature, in which all aspects of human nature—including sexuality and the passions as well as rationality—are freed." Social ecofeminism distinguishes itself from spiritually oriented cultural ecofeminists who acknowledge a special historical relationship between women and nature and wish to liberate both together. Instead it begins with the materialist, social feminist analysis of early radical feminism that sought to restructure the oppressions imposed on women by marriage, the nuclear family, romantic love, the capitalist state, and patriarchial religion.

Social ecofeminism advocates the liberation of women through overturning economic and social hierarchies that turn all aspects of life into a market society that today even invades the womb. It envisions a society of decentralized communities that would transcend the public–private dichotomy necessary to capitalist production and the bureaucratic state. In them women emerge as free participants in public life and local municipal workplaces.

Social ecofeminism acknowledges differences in male and female reproductive capacities, inasmuch as it is women and not men who menstruate, gestate, give birth, and lactate, but rejects the idea that these entail gender hierarchies and domination. Both women and men are capable of an ecological ethic based on caring. In an accountable face-to-face society, childrearing would be communal; rape and violence against women would disappear. Rejecting all forms of determinism, it advocates women's reproductive, intellectual, sensual, and moral freedom. Biology, society, and the individual interact in all human beings giving them the capacity to choose and construct the kinds of societies in which they wish to live.[18]

But in her 1991 book, *Rethinking Ecofeminist Politics*, Janet Biehl withdrew her support from ecofeminism, and likewise abandoned social ecofeminism, on the grounds that the concept had become so fraught with irrational, mythical, and self-contradictory meanings that it undercut women's hopes for a liberatory, ecologically-sane society. While early radical feminism had sought equality in all aspects of public and private life, based on a total restructuring of society, the cultural feminism that lies at the root of much of ecofeminism seemed to her to reject rationality by embracing goddess worship, to biologize and essentialize the caretaking and nurturing traits assigned by patriarchy to women, and to reject scientific and cultural advances just because they were advocated by men.[19] Social ecofeminism, however, is an area that will receive alternative definition in the future as theorists such as Ynestra King, Ariel Salleh, Val Plumwood, and others sharpen its critique of patriarchal society, hierarchy, and domination. Women of color will bring still another set of critiques and concerns to the ongoing dialogue.

# Socialist Ecofeminism

Socialist ecofeminism is not yet a movement, but rather a feminist transformation of socialist ecology that makes the category of reproduction, rather than production, central to the concept of a just, sustainable world. Like Marxist feminism, it assumes that nonhuman nature is the material basis of all of life and that food, clothing, shelter, and energy are essential to the maintenance of human life. Nature and human nature are socially and historically contructed over time and transformed through human praxis. Nature is an active subject, not a passive object to be dominated, and humans must develop sustainable relations with it. It goes beyond cultural ecofeminism in offering a critique of capitalist patriarchy that focuses on the dialectical relationships between production and reproduction, and between production and ecology.

A socialist ecofeminist perspective offers a standpoint from which to analyze social and ecological transformations, and to suggest social actions that will lead to the sustainability of life and a just society. It asks:

1. What is at stake for women and for nature when production in traditional societies is disrupted by colonial and capitalist development?
2. What is at stake for women and for nature when traditional methods and norms of biological reproduction are disrupted by interventionist technologies (such as chemical methods of birth control, sterilization, amniocentesis, rented wombs, and baby markets) and by chemical and nuclear pollutants in soils, waters, and air (pesticides, herbicides, toxic chemicals, and nuclear radiation)?
3. What would an ecofeminist social transformation look like?
4. What forms might socialist societies take that would be healthy for all women and men and for nature?

In his 1884 *Origin of the Family, Private Property, and the State*, Friedrich Engels wrote that "the determining factor in history is, in the last resort, the production and reproduction of immediate life. . . . On the one hand, the production of the means of subsistence . . . on the other the production of human beings themselves." In producing and reproducing life, humans interact with nonhuman nature, sustaining or disrupting local and global ecologies. When we ignore the consequences of our interactions with nature, Engels warned, our conquests "take . . . revenge on us." "In nature nothing takes place in isolation." Elaborating on Engels' fundamental insights, women's roles in production, reproduction, and ecology can become the starting point for a socialist ecofeminist analysis.[20]

# Socialist Ecofeminism and Production

As producers and reproducers of life, women in tribal and traditional cultures over the centuries have had highly significant interactions with the environment. As gatherers of food, fuel, and medicinal herbs; fabricators of clothing; planters, weeders, and harvesters of horticultural crops; tenders of poultry, preparers and preservers of food; and bearers and caretakers of young children, women's intimate knowledge of nature has helped to sustain life in every global human habitat.

In colonial and capitalist societies, however, women's direct interactions with nature have been circumscribed. Their traditional roles as producers of food and clothing, as gardeners and poultry tenders, as healers and midwives, were largely appropriated by men. As agriculture became specialized and mechanized, men took over farm production, while migrant and slave women and men supplied the stoop labor needed for field work. Middle-class women's roles shifted from production to the reproduction of daily life in the home, focusing on increased domesticity and the bearing and socialization of young children. Under capitalism, as sociologist Abby Peterson points out, men bear the responsibility for and dominate the production of exchange commodities, while women bear the responsibility for reproducing the workforce and social relations. "Women's responsibility for reproduction includes both the biological reproduction of the species (intergenerational reproduction) and the intragenerational reproduction of the work force through unpaid labor in the home. Here too is included the reproduction of social relations—socialization." Under industrial capitalism, reproduction is subordinate to production.[21]

Because capitalism is premised on economic growth and competition in which nature and waste are both externalities in profit maximization, its logic precludes sustainability. The logic of socialism on the other hand is based on the fulfillment of people's needs, not people's greed. Because growth is not necessary to the economy, socialism has the potential for sustainable relations with nature. Although state socialism has been based on growth-oriented industrialization and has resulted in the pollution of external nature, new forms of socialist ecology could bring human production and reproduction into balance with nature's production and reproduction. Nature's economy and human economy could enter into a partnership.

The transition to a sustainable global environment and an equitable human economy that fulfills people's needs would be based on two dialectical relationships—that between production and ecology and that between production and reproduction. In existing theories of capitalist development, reproduction and ecology are both subordinate to production. The transition to socialist ecology would reverse the priorities of capitalism, making production subordinate to reproduction and ecology.

## Socialist Ecofeminism and Reproduction

Socialist ecofeminism focuses on the reproduction of life itself. In nature, life is transmitted through the biological reproduction of species in the local ecosystem. Lack of proper food, water, soil chemicals, atmospheric gases, adverse weather, disease, and competition by other species can disrupt the survival of offspring of reproductive age. For humans, reproduction is both biological and social. First, enough children must survive to reproductive age to reproduce the community over time; too many put pressure on the particular mode of production, affecting the local ecology. Second, by interacting with external nature, adults must produce enough food, clothing, shelter, and fuel on a daily basis to maintain their own subsistence and sustain the quality of their ecological homes.

Both the intergenerational biological reproduction of humans and other species and the intergenerational reproduction of daily life are essential to continuing life over time. Sustainability is the maintenance of an ecological-productive-reproductive balance between humans and nature—the perpetuation of the quality of all life.[22]

Biological reproduction affects local ecology, not directly, but as mediated by production. Many communities of tribal and traditional peoples developed rituals and practices that maintained their populations in a balance with local resources. Others allowed their populations to grow in response to the need for labor or migrated into new lands and colonized them. When the mode of production changes from an agrarian to an industrial base, and then to a sustainable production base, the number of children that families need declines. How development occurs in the future will help families decide how many children to have. A potential demographic transition to smaller population sizes is tied to ecologically sustainable development.

Ecofeminist political scientist Irene Diamond raises concern over the implications of "population control" for Third World women. "The 'advances' in family planning techniques from Depra-Provera to a range of implanted birth control devices, banned in western nations as unsafe, reduce Third World women to mindless objects and continue the imperialist model which exploits native cultures 'for their own good.' "[23] Second, with the availability of prenatal sex identification techniques, feminists fear the worldwide "death of the female sex" as families that place a premium on male labor opt to abort as many as nine out of every ten female fetuses. Third, feminists argue that women's bodies are being turned into production machines to test contraceptives, for *in vitro* fertilization experiments, to produce babies for organ transplants, and to produce black market babies for sale in the northern hemisphere.

Reproductive freedom means freedom of choice—freedom to have or not to have children in a society that both needs them and provides for their needs. The same social and economic conditions that provide security for women also promote the demographic transition to lower populations. The Gabriella Women's Coalition of the Philippines calls for equal access to employment and equal pay for women, daycare for children, healthcare, and social security. It wants protection for women's reproductive capacities, access to safe contraception, and the elimination of banned drugs and contraceptives. It advocates equal, nondiscriminatory access to education, including instruction concerning consumer rights and hazardous chemicals. Such a program would help to bring about a sustainable society in which population is in balance with the fulfillment of daily needs and the use of local resources, a society that offers women and men of all races, ages, and abilities equal opportunities to have meaningful lives.

A socialist ecofeminist movement in the developed world can work in solidarity with women's movements to save the environment in the underdeveloped world. It can support scientifically-based ecological actions that also promote social justice. Like cultural ecofeminism, socialist ecofeminism protests chemical assaults on women's reproductive health, but puts them in the broader context of the relations between reproduction and production. It can thus support point of production actions such as the Chipko and Greenbelt movements in the Third World (see below), protests by Native American women over cancer-causing radioactive uranium mining on reservations, and protests by working class women over toxic dumps in urban neighborhoods.[24]

# Women in the Third World

Many of the problems facing Third World women today are the historical result of colonial relations between the First and Third Worlds. From the seventeenth century onward, European colonization of lands in Africa, India, the Americas, and the Pacific initiated a colonial ecological revolution in which an ecological complex of European animals, plants, pathogens, and people disrupted native peoples' modes of subsistence, as Europeans extracted resources for trade on the international market and settled in the new lands. From the late eighteenth century onward, a capitalist ecological revolution in the northern hemisphere accelerated the extraction of cash crops and resources in the southern hemisphere, pushing Third World peoples onto marginal lands and filling the pockets of Third World élites. In the twentieth century, northern industrial technologies and policies have been exported to the south in the form of development projects. Green Revolution agriculture (seeds, fertilizers, pesticides, dams, irrigation equipment, and tractors), plantation forestry (fast-growing, non-indigenous species, herbicides, chip harvesters, and mills), capitalist ranching (land conversion, imported grasses, fertilizers, and factory farms) and reproductive technologies (potentially harmful contraceptive drugs, sterilization, and bottle feeding) have further disrupted native ecologies and peoples.

Third World women have born the brunt of environmental crises resulting from colonial marginalization and ecologically unsustainable development projects. As subsistence farmers, urban workers, or middle-class professionals, their ability to provide basic subsistence and healthy living-conditions is threatened. Yet Third World women have not remained powerless in face of these threats. They have organized movements, institutes, and businesses to transform maldevelopment into sustainable development. They are often at the forefront of change to protect their own lives, those of their children, and the life of the planet. While some might consider themselves feminists, and a few even embrace ecofeminism, most are mainly concerned with maintaining conditions for survival.

In India, nineteenth century British colonialism in combination with twentieth century development programs has created environmental problems that affect women's subsistence, especially in forested areas. Subsistence production, oriented toward the reproduction of daily life, is undercut by expanding market production, oriented toward profit-maximization. To physicist and environmentalist, Vandana Shiva, the subsistence and market economies are incommensurable:

> There are in India, today, two paradigms of forestry—one life-enhancing, the other life-destroying. The life-enhancing paradigm emerges from the forest and the feminine principle; the life-destroying one from the factory and the market. . . . Since the maximising of profits is consequent upon the destruction of conditions of renewability, the two paradigms are cognitively and ecologically incommensurable. The first paradigm has emerged from India's ancient forest culture, in all its diversity, and has been renewed in contemporary times by the women of Garhwal through Chipko.[25]

India's Chipko, or tree-hugging, movement attempts to maintain sustainability. It has its historical roots in ancient Indian cultures that worshipped tree goddesses, sacred trees as images of the cosmos, and sacred forests and groves. The earliest woman-led tree-embracing movements are three-hundred years old. In the 1970s women revived these

Chipko actions in order to save their forests for fuelwood and their valleys from erosion in the face of cash cropping for the market. The basis of the movement lay in a traditional ecological use of forests for food (as fruits, roots, tubers, seeds, leaves, petals and sepals), fuel, fodder, fertilizer, water, and medicine. Cash cropping by contrast severed forest products from water, agriculture, and animal husbandry. Out of a women's organizational base and with support by local males, protests to save the trees took place over a wide area from 1972 through 1978, including actions to embrace trees, marches, picketing, singing, and direct confrontations with lumberers and police.[26]

The Chipko movement's feminine forestry-paradigm is based on assumptions similar to those of the emerging science of agroforestry, now being taught in western universities. Agroforestry is one of several new sciences based on maintaining ecologically viable relations between humans and nature. As opposed to modern agriculture and forestry, which separate tree crops from food crops, agroforestry views trees as an integral part of agricultural ecology. Complementary relationships exist between the protective and productive aspects of trees and the use of space, soil, water, and light in conjunction with crops and animals. Agroforestry is especially significant for small farm families, such as many in the Third World, and makes efficient use of both human labor and natural resources.[27]

In Africa, numerous environmental problems have resulted from colonial disruption of traditional patterns of pastoral herding as governments imposed boundaries that cut off access to migratory routes and traditional resources. The ensuing agricultural development created large areas of desertified land, which had negative impacts on women's economy. The farmers, mostly women, suffered from poor yields on eroded soils. They had to trek long distances to obtain wood for cooking and heating. Their cooking and drinking waters were polluted. Developers with professional training, who did not understand the meaning of "development without destruction," cut down trees that interfered with highways and electrical and telephone lines, even if they were the only trees on a subsistence farmer's land.

Kenyan women's access to fuelwood and water for subsistence was the primary motivation underlying the women's Greenbelt Movement. According to founder Wangari Maathai, the movement's objective is to promote "environmental rehabilitation and conservation and . . . sustainable development." It attempts to reverse humanly-produced desertification by planting trees for conservation of soil and water.[28]

The National Council of Women of Kenya began planting trees in 1977 on World Environment Day. Working with the Ministry of the Environment and Natural Resources, they continued to plant trees throughout the country and established community woodlands on public lands. They planted seedlings and sold them, generating income. The movement promoted traditional agroforestry techniques that had been abandoned in favor of "modern" farming methods that relied on green revolution fertilizers, pesticides, new seed varieties, and irrigation systems that were costly and non-sustainable. During the past ten years, the movement has planted over seven million trees, created hundreds of jobs, reintroduced indigenous tree species, educated people in the need for environmental care, and promoted the independence and a more positive image of women.[29]

"The whole world is heading toward an environmental crisis," says Zimbabwe's Sithembiso Nyoni. "Women have been systematically excluded from the benefits of planned development. . . . The adverse effects of Africa's current so-called economic crisis and external debt . . . fall disproportionately on women and make their problems ever more acute." Twenty years ago there was still good water, wood, grass, and game even on semi-arid communal lands and women did not have to walk long distances to obtain subsistence resources. But the introduction of Green Revolution seeds and fertilizers required different soils and more water than found on the common lands. The poor, primarily women, have born the brunt of development that has proceeded independently of environmental consequences.[30]

According to Zimbabwe's Kathini Maloba, active in both the Greenbelt Movement and the Pan-African Women's Trade Union, many farm women suffer loss from poor crops on marginal soils, lack of firewood, polluted water, poor sanitation, and housing shortages. Women have suffered miscarriages from the use of chemical fertilizers and pesticides. In 1983, 99 percent of all farms had no protection from pesticides. Only 1 percent of employers heeded pesticide warnings and used detection kits to test pesticide levels in foods and water.

Development programs that emphasize people's needs within local environmental constraints would include: water conservation through erosion control, protection of natural springs, and the use of earthen dams and water tanks; in agriculture, the reintroduction of traditional seeds and planting of indigenous trees; in herding, the use of local grasses, seeds, and leaves for feed and driving cattle into one place for fattening before market; in homes, the use of household grey water to irrigate trees and more efficient ovens that burn less fuelwood.

Latin American women likewise point to numerous environmental impacts on their lives. Both Nicaragua and Chile are countries in which socialist governments have been opposed by the United States through the use of economic boycotts and the funding of opposition leaders who supported conservative capitalist interest. Maria Luisa Robleto of the Environmental Movement of Nicaragua asserts that women are fighting to reverse past environmental damage. In Nicaragua, before the Sandinista revolution of 1979, many women worked on private haciendas that used large amounts of pesticides, especially DDT. Since the revolution the position of women changed as part of the effort to build a society based on sustainable development. In part because of male engagement in ongoing defense of the country and in part because of the efforts of the Nicaraguan women's movement, women moved into agricultural work that was formerly masculine. Women were trained in tractor driving, coffee plantation management, and animal husbandry.

According to Robleto, women agricultural workers in Nicaragua have twenty times the level of DDT in their breast milk as nonagricultural workers. They want equal pay and an end to toxic poisoning from insecticides. If breast feeding is promoted as an alternative to expensive formula feeding, there must be a program to control toxics in breast milk. In a country where 51 percent of the energy comes from firewood, 39 percent of which is used for cooking, there must be a forestry and conservation program oriented to women's needs. A grassroots movement is the spark for ecological conservation.

Chile's Isabelle Letelier of the Third World Women's Project (widow of the Chilean ambassador to the United States who was assassinated in 1976 by Pinochet agents after the 1973 overthrow of the socialist Allende government), speaks of the power of *compesina* women who created life and controlled medicine and religion. The global society, she says, is out of control. The round planet must be saved. Women must take charge, since men are not going to solve the problems. They must construct a society for both women and men. The rights of the land, the rights of nature, and women's rights are all part of human rights. Santiago is now one of the most polluted cities in the world. There are children who receive no protein and who resort to eating plastic. There is a television in every home, but no eggs or meat. There are colored sugars, but no bread. In 1983, says Letelier, women broke the silence and began speaking out for the environment. Without the help of telephones, they filled a stadium with 11,000 women. They established networks as tools; they learned to question everything, to be suspicious of everything. They learned to see. "Women give life," says Letelier. "We have the capacity to give life and light. We can take our brooms and sweep the earth. Like witches, we can clean up the atmosphere with our brooms. We can seal up the hole in the ozone layer. The environment is life and women must struggle for life with our feet on the ground and our eyes toward the heavens. We must do the impossible."

Gizelda Castro, of Friends of the Earth, Brazil, echoes the ecofeminist cry that women should reverse the damage done to the earth. "Men," she says, "have separated themselves from the ecosystem." Five hundred years of global pillage in the name of development and civilization have brought us to a situation of international violence against the land and its people. The genetic heritage of the south is constantly going to the north. Women have had no voice, but ecofeminism is a new and radical language. Women must provide the moral energy and determination for both the First and Third Worlds. They are the future and hope in the struggle over life.[31]

In Malaysia, which received independence in 1957 as the British empire underwent decolonization, many environmental problems have resulted from a series of five-year development plans which ignored both the environment and conservation, especially the impact of development on women. "The rapid expansion of the cash crop economy which is hailed as a 'development success story' has plunged thousands of women into a poisonous trap," argues Chee Yoke Ling, lecturer in law at the University of Malaysia and secretary general of the country's chapter of Friends of the Earth. As land control shifted to large multinational rice, rubber, and palm oil plantations, women's usufructory rights to cultivate the land were lost to a male-dominated cash-exporting economy. They became dependent and marginalized, moving into low paying industrial and agricultural jobs. Women workers constitute 80 percent of those who spray chemical pesticides and herbicides such as paraquat on rubber and palm plantations. They pour the liquid, carry the open containers, and spray the chemicals without protective clothing, even when pregnant or nursing. The workers are usually unaware of the effects of the chemicals and often cannot read the warning labels on the packaging. Protests resulted in loss of jobs or transfer to even less desirable forms of labor. In 1985, Friends of the Earth Malaysia began to pressure the Ministry of Health to ban paraquat. They called on plantation owners and government agencies to stop using the chemical for the sake of human right to life as well as the life of waters and soils.[32]

Third World women are thus playing an essential role in conservation. They are making the impacts of colonialism and industrial capitalism on the environment and on their own lives visible. They are working to maintain their own life-support systems through forest and water conservation, to rebuild soil fertility, and to preserve ecological diversity. In so doing, they are assuming leadership roles in their own communities. Although they have not yet received adequate recognition from their governments and conservation organizations for their contributions, they are slowly achieving the goals of ecofeminism—the liberation of women and nature.

# Women in the Second World

Second World development has been informed by Marxist theory that the goal of production is the fulfillment of human needs. Yet state socialism as the method for achieving equitable distribution of goods and services has created enormous problems of pollution and depletion resulting from a series of five-year plans for rapid industrial growth. . . . As Second World countries incorporate market economic goals, environmental problems will become increasingly complex. Can the evolving, changing Second World produce and distribute enough food and goods for its own people and also reverse environmental deterioration? The movements toward democratization in the 1990s reveal an openness to new ideas and cooperation in resolving economic and environmental problems, but many problems in implementing solutions remain.

While Second World women have shared educational and economic opportunities along with men, like First World women they have also borne the double burden of housework added to their employment outside the home. Like First World women, they have experienced the effects of industrial and toxic pollutants on their own bodies and seen the impacts on their children and husbands. Although women in the Second World have not achieved the environmental vision of Marxist feminists (see Table 1 on p. 312), they have used scientific and technological research and education to find ways of mitigating these problems and have participated in incipient green movements.

Second World women have assumed leadership roles in environmental affairs. In Poland, Dr. Maria Guminska, a professor of biochemistry at Krakow Medical University helped to found the 4000 member Polish Ecology Club and served as one of its vice-presidents. She prepared a critical report on the air pollution of Poland's largest aluminum smelter and was active in the effort to reduce toxic pollutants from a Krakow pharmaceutical plant.

In the former Soviet Union, Dr Eugenia V. Afanasieva, of the Moscow Polytechnical Institute, was Deputy Director of the Environmental Education Center for Environmental Investigation. The Center developed a filtration system to help clean up industrial water pollution. Dr Afanasieva works with young people to promote better environmental education. "All mankind now stands at the beginning of a new era," she states. "People must make the choice to live or to perish. Nobody can predict the future. We must save our civilization. We must change our ways of thinking. We must think ecologically." Women, she argues, play a major role in expanding environmental awareness: "It seems to me that women are more active in environmental programs than men. We give birth to our children, we teach them to take their first steps. We are excited about their future."[33]

In 1989 the First International Conference on Women, Peace, and the Environment was held in the former Soviet Union. The women called for greater participation by women as environmentalists and scientists to help decide the fate of the planet. They said:

> Each of us should do everything possible to promote actions for survival on local, national, and international levels. . . . We must work to end food irradiation, to ban all known chemicals destroying the ozone layer, to reduce transport emissions, to recycle all reusable

waste, to plant arboreta and botanical gardens, to create seed banks, etc. These are among the most urgent beginnings for a strategy of survival.[34]

Olga Uzhnurtsevaa of the Committee of Soviet Women pleads for environmental improvement in the face of her country's accelerating industrial production. A national ecological program subsidized by the government is needed to reverse ecological damage. Children are being born with birth defects; air and water quality have deteriorated. Throughout the Commonwealth, she says, women's councils support environmental thinking. Many of the journalists and activists concerned over environmental problems in the Lake Baikal watershed and the Baltic Sea are women. Women are especially concerned with the need to protect nature from the arms race. This problem involves all of humanity, especially the effects on the Third World. Quoted Uzhnurtsevaa,

> Nature said to women:
> Be amused if you can,
> Be wise if possible,
> But by all means, be prudent.[35]

## Conclusion

Although the ultimate goals of liberal, cultural, social, and socialist feminists may differ as to whether capitalism, women's culture, or socialism should be the ultimate objective of political action, shorter-term objectives overlap. Weaving together the many strands of the ecofeminist movement is the concept of reproduction construed in its broadest sense to include the continued biological and social reproduction of human life and the continuance of life on earth. In this sense there is perhaps more unity than diversity in women's common goal of restoring the natural environment and quality of life for people and other living and nonliving inhabitants of the planet.

## Reading Questions

1. What reasons does Merchant give for asserting that "social and socialist ecofeminism have the potential for a more thorough critique of domination and for a liberating social justice"?

2. Why would a partnership ethic in relation to nature be preferable to an ethic of care?

3. What are some of the key historical events and primary texts in the emergence of ecofeminism?

4. Why are women the majority of activists in the grassroots movement against environmental toxics?

5. How does socialist ecofeminism help to explain the impact of colonialism and capitalism on women's interactions with nature?

6. What do socialist ecofeminists mean by "sustainability" and why does the implied desirability of smaller population sizes threaten Third World women?

7. What is the "incommensurability between subsistence and market economies" in Third World countries? What is the relation between these economies and the problems of Third World women in relation to their countries' histories of colonialism?

8. Why is agroforestry and the controlled use of pesticides especially important to women in economically developing countries?

9. What do socialist ecofeminists mean by the "dialectical" relationships between production and reproduction in capitalist patriarchies?

10. How does the productive and reproductive relation of women to the environment in indigenous cultures differ from that in capitalist societies?

# Recommended Reading

Rachel Carson, *Silent Spring* (Boston: Houghton Mifflin, 1962)

Irene Dankelman and Joan Davidson, *Women and Environment in the Third World* (London: Earthscan Publications, 1988)

Carolyn Merchant, *The Death of Nature: Women, Ecology and the Scientific Revolution* (San Francisco: Harper and Row, 1989)

Janet Henshall Momsen, *Women and Development in the Third World* (New York: Routledge, 1991)

Vandana Shiva, *Staying Alive: Women, Ecology and Development* (London: Zed Books, 1988)

Karen Warren, ed., "Ecological Feminism," special issue of *Hypatia* 6:1 (Spring 1991)

Dale Westphal and Fred Westphal, eds., *Planet in Peril: Essays in Environmental Ethics* (Orlando, FL: Holt, Rinehart and Winston, 1994)

# Recommended Audiovisual Resources

*Children of Chernobyl*. 1993. Produced by Yorkshire Television. Archival film and eye witness accounts of the effects of the tragedy at Chernobyl. Filmakers Library.

*Halting the Fires*. 1991. Directed by Octavio Bezerra. Channel 4, England. A sociopolitical analysis of the devastation of the Amazon. Filmakers Library.

*The Endangered Earth: The Politics of Acid Rain*. 1991. Produced by WVIA-TV. Analyzes the acid rain controversy. Films for the Humanities.

*Black Triangle: Eastern Europe*. 1992. A Central Television Production. Documents Europe's most polluted region. Filmakers Library.

*Environment at Issue*. 1992. Produced and directed by Jeffrey Tuchman for the Public Agenda Foundation. Analysis at the debate over environmental action in this country. Filmakers Library.

# CHAPTER 6

# Sexualities

We-Wah, a famous Zuni berdache, performs women's work. John K. Millers, 1879. The Bettmann Archive.

# Date Rape's Other Victim

## KATIE ROIPHE

Katie Roiphe is a doctoral candidate in English literature at Princeton University. This selection is adapted from her book, *The Morning After: Sex, Fear and Feminism on Campus.*

One in four college women has been the victim of rape or attempted rape. One in four. I remember standing outside the dining hall in college, looking at a purple poster with this statistic written in bold letters. It didn't seem right. If sexual assault was really so pervasive, it seemed strange that the intricate gossip networks hadn't picked up more than one or two shadowy instances of rape. If I was really standing in the middle of an "epidemic," a "crisis"—if 25 percent of my women friends were really being raped—wouldn't I know it?

These posters were not presenting facts. They were advertising a mood. Preoccupied with issues like date rape and sexual harassment, campus feminists produce endless images of women as victims—women offended by a professor's dirty joke, women pressured into sex by peers, women trying to say no but not managing to get it across.

This portrait of the delicate female bears a striking resemblance to that 50's ideal my mother and other women of her generation fought so hard to leave behind. They didn't like her passivity, her wide-eyed innocence. They didn't like the fact that she was perpetually offended by sexual innuendo. They didn't like her excessive need for protection. She represented personal, social and intellectual possibilities collapsed, and they worked and marched, shouted and wrote to make her irrelevant for their daughters. But here she is again, with her pure intentions and her wide eyes. Only this time it is the feminists themselves who are breathing new life into her.

Is there a rape crisis on campus? Measuring rape is not as straightforward as it might seem. Neil Gilbert, a professor of social welfare at the University of California at Berkeley, questions the validity of the one-in-four statistic. Gilbert points out that in a 1985 survey undertaken by Ms. magazine and financed by the National Institute of Mental Health, 73 percent of the women categorized as rape victims did not initially define their experience as rape; it was Mary Koss, the psychologist conducting the study, who did.

One of the questions used to define rape was: "Have you had sexual intercourse when you didn't want to because a man gave you alcohol or drugs." The phrasing raises the issue of agency. Why aren't college women responsible for their own intake of alcohol or drugs? A man may give her drugs, but she herself decides to take them. If we assume that women are not all helpless and naive, then they should be held responsible for their choice to drink or take drugs. If a woman's "judgment is impaired" and she has sex, it isn't necessarily always the man's fault; it isn't necessarily always rape.

As Gilbert delves further into the numbers, he does not necessarily disprove the one-in-four statistic, but he does clarify what it means—the so-called rape epidemic on campuses is more a way of interpreting, a way of seeing, than a physical phenomenon. It is more about a change in sexual politics than a change in sexual behavior. Whether or not one in four college women has been raped, then, is a matter of opinion, not a matter of mathematical fact.

That rape is a fact in some women's lives is not in question. It's hard to watch the solemn faces of young Bosnian girls, their words haltingly translated, as they tell of brutal rapes; or to read accounts of a suburban teen-ager raped and beaten while walking home from a shopping mall. We all agree that rape is a terrible thing, but we no longer agree on what rape is. Today's definition has stretched beyond bruises and knives, threats of death or violence to include emotional pressure and the influence of alcohol. The lines between rape and sex begin to blur. The one-in-four statistic on those purple posters is measuring something elusive. It is measuring her word against his in a realm where words barely exist. There is a gray area in which one person's rape may be another's bad night. Definitions become entangled in passionate ideological battles. There hasn't been a remarkable change in the number of women being raped; just a change in how receptive the political climate is to those numbers.

The next question, then, is who is identifying this epidemic and why. Somebody is "finding" this rape crisis, and finding it for a reason. Asserting the prevalence of rape lends urgency, authority to a broader critique of culture.

In a dramatic description of the rape crisis, Naomi Wolf writes in "The Beauty Myth" that "Cultural representation of glamorized degradation has created a situation among the young in which boys rape and girls get raped *as a normal course of events.*" The italics are hers. Whether or not Wolf really believes rape is part of the "normal course of events" these days, she is making a larger point. Wolf's rhetorical excess serves her larger polemic about sexual politics. Her dramatic prose is a call to arms. She is trying to rally the feminist troops. Wolf uses rape as a red flag, an undeniable sign that things are falling apart.

From Susan Brownmiller—who brought the politics of rape into the mainstream with her 1975 best seller, "Against Our Will: Men, Women and Rape"—to Naomi Wolf, feminist prophets of the rape crisis are talking about something more than forced penetration. They are talking about what they define as a "rape culture." Rape is a natural trump card for feminism. Arguments about rape can be used to sequester feminism in the teary province of trauma and crisis. By blocking analysis with its claims to unique pandemic suffering, the rape crisis becomes a powerful source of authority.

Dead serious, eyes wide with concern, a college senior tells me that she believes one in four is too conservative an estimate. This is not the first time I've heard this. She tells me the right statistic is closer to one in two. That means one in two women are raped. It's amazing, she says, amazing that so many of us are sexually assaulted every day.

What is amazing is that this student actually believes that 50 percent of women are raped. This is the true crisis. Some substantial number of young women are walking around with this alarming belief: a hyperbole containing within it a state of perpetual fear.

"Acquaintance Rape: Is Dating Dangerous?" is a pamphlet commonly found at counseling centers. The cover title rises from the shards of a shattered photograph of a boy and girl dancing. Inside, the pamphlet offers a sample date-rape scenario. She thinks:

"He was really good looking and he had a great smile. . . . We talked and found we had a lot in common. I really liked him. When he asked me over to his place for a drink I thought it would be O.K. He was such a good listener and I wanted him to ask me out again."

She's just looking for a sensitive boy, a good listener with a nice smile, but unfortunately his intentions are not as pure as hers. Beneath that nice smile, he thinks:

"She looked really hot, wearing a sexy dress that showed off her great body. We started talking right away. I knew that she liked me by the way she kept smiling and touching my arm while she was speaking. She seemed pretty relaxed so I asked her back to my place for a drink. . . . When she said 'Yes' I knew that I was going to be lucky!"

These cardboard stereotypes don't just educate freshmen about rape. They also educate them about "dates" and about sexual desire. With titles like "Friends Raping Friends: Could It Happen to You?" date-rape pamphlets call into question all relationships between men and women. Beyond warning students about rape, the rape-crisis movement produces its own images of sexual behavior, in which men exert pressure and women resist. By defining the dangerous date in these terms—with this type of male and this type of female, and their different expectations—these pamphlets promote their own perspective on how men and women feel about sex: men are lascivious, women are innocent.

The sleek images of pressure and resistance projected in rape education movies, videotapes, pamphlets and speeches create a model of acceptable sexual behavior. The don'ts imply their own set of do's. The movement against rape, then, not only dictates the way sex *shouldn't be* be but also the way it *should be*. Sex should be gentle, it should not be aggressive; it should be absolutely equal, it should not involve domination and submission; it should be tender, not ambivalent; it should communicate respect, it shouldn't communicate consuming desire.

In "Real Rape," Susan Estrich, a professor of law at the University of Southern California Law Center, slips her ideas about the nature of sexual encounters into her legal analysis of the problem of rape. She writes: "Many feminists would argue that so long as women are powerless relative to men, viewing a 'yes' as a sign of true consent is misguided. . . . Many women who say yes to men they know, whether on dates or on the job, would say no if they could. . . . Women's silence sometimes is the product not of passion and desire but of pressure and fear."

Like Estrich, most rape-crisis feminists claim they are not talking about sex; they're talking about violence. But, like Estrich, they are also talking about sex. With their advice, their scenarios, their sample aggressive male, the message projects a clear comment on the nature of sexuality: women are often unwilling participants. They say yes because they feel they have to, because they are intimidated by male power.

The idea of "consent" has been redefined beyond the simple assertion that "no means no." Politically correct sex involves a yes, and a specific yes at that. According to the premise of "active consent," we can no longer afford ambiguity. We can no longer afford the dangers of unspoken consent. A former director of Columbia's date-rape education program told New York magazine, "Stone silence throughout an entire physical encounter with someone is not explicit consent."

This apparently practical, apparently clinical proscription cloaks retrograde assumptions about the way men and women experience sex. The idea that only an explicit yes means yes proposes that, like children, women have trouble communicating what they want. Beyond its dubious premise about the limits of female communication, the idea of active consent bolsters stereotypes of men just out to "get some" and women who don't really want any.

Rape-crisis feminists express nostalgia for the days of greater social control, when the university acted in loco parentis and women were protected from the insatiable force of male desire. The rhetoric of feminists and conservatives blurs and overlaps in this desire to keep our youth safe and pure.

By viewing rape as encompassing more than the use or threat of physical violence to coerce someone into sex, rape-crisis feminists reinforce traditional views about the fragility of the female body and will. According to common definitions of date rape, even "verbal coercion" or "manipulation" constitute rape. Verbal coercion is defined as "a woman's consenting to unwanted sexual activity because of a man's verbal arguments not including verbal threats of force." The belief that "verbal coercion" is rape pervades workshops, counseling sessions and student opinion pieces. The suggestion lurking beneath this definition of rape is that men are not just physically but also intellectually and emotionally more powerful than women.

Imagine men sitting around in a circle talking about how she called him impotent and how she manipulated him into sex, how violated and dirty he felt afterward, how coercive she was, how she got him drunk first, how he hated his body and he couldn't eat for three weeks afterward. Imagine him calling this rape. Everyone feels the weight of emotional pressure at one time or another. The question is not whether people pressure each other but how our minds and our culture transform that pressure into full-blown assault. There would never be a rule or a law or even a pamphlet or peer counseling group for men who claimed to have been emotionally raped or verbally pressured into sex. And for the same reasons—assumption of basic competence, free will and strength of character—there should be no such rules or groups or pamphlets about women.

In discussing rape, campus feminists often slip into an outdated sexist vocabulary. But we have to be careful about using rape as metaphor. The sheer physical fact of rape has always been loaded with cultural meaning. Throughout history, women's bodies have been seen as property, as chaste objects, as virtuous vessels to be "dishonored," "ruined," "defiled." Their purity or lack of purity has been a measure of value for the men to whom they belonged.

"Politically, I call it rape whenever a woman has sex and feels violated," writes Catharine MacKinnon, a law professor and feminist legal scholar best known for her crusade against pornography. The language of virtue and violation reinforces retrograde stereotypes. It backs women into old corners. Younger feminists share MacKinnon's vocabulary and the accompanying assumptions about women's bodies. In one student's account of date rape in the Rag, a feminist magazine at Harvard, she talks about the anguish of being "defiled." Another writes, "I long to be innocent again." With such anachronistic constructions of the female body, with all their assumptions about female purity, these young women frame their experience of rape in archaic, sexist terms. Of course, sophisticated modern-day feminists don't use words like honor or virtue anymore. They know better than to say date-rape victims have been "defiled." Instead, they call it "post-traumatic stress syndrome." They tell the victim she should not feel "shame," she should feel "traumatized." Within their overtly political psychology, forced penetration takes on a level of metaphysical significance: date rape resonates through a woman's entire life.

Combating myths about rape is one of the central missions of the rape-crisis movement. They spend money and energy trying to break down myths like "she asked for it." But with all their noise about rape myths, rape-crisis feminists are generating their own. The plays, the poems, the pamphlets, the Take Back the Night speakouts, are propelled by the myth of innocence lost.

All the talk about empowering the voiceless dissolves into the image of the naive girl child who trusts the rakish man. This plot reaches back centuries. It propels Samuel Richardson's 18th-century epistolary novel, "Clarissa": after hundreds of pages chronicling the minute details of her plight, her seduction and resistance, her break from her family, Clarissa is raped by the duplicitous Robert Lovelace. Afterward, she refuses to eat and fades toward a very virtuous, very religious death. Over a thousand pages are devoted to the story of her fall from innocence, a weighty event by 18th-century standards. But did these 20th-century girls, raised on Madonna videos and the 6 o'clock news, really trust that people were good until they themselves were raped? Maybe. Were these girls, raised on horror movies and glossy Hollywood sex scenes, really as innocent as all that? Maybe. But maybe the myth of lost innocence is a trope—convenient, appealing, politically effective.

As long as we're taking back the night, we might as well take back our own purity. Sure, we were all kind of innocent, playing in the sandbox with bright red shovels—boys, too. We can all look back through the tumultuous tunnel of adolescence on a honey-glazed childhood, with simple rules and early bedtimes. We don't have to look at parents fighting, at sibling struggles, at casting out one best friend for another in the Darwinian playground. This is not the innocence lost; this is the innocence we never had.

The idea of a fall from childhood grace, pinned on one particular moment, a moment over which we had no control, much lamented, gives our lives a compelling narrative structure. It's easy to see why the 17-year-old likes it; it's easy to see why the rape-crisis feminist likes it. It's a natural human impulse put to political purpose. But in generating and perpetuating such myths, we should keep in mind that myths about innocence have been used to keep women inside and behind veils. They have been used to keep them out of work and in labor.

It's not hard to imagine Clarissa, in jeans and a sweatshirt, transported into the 20th century, at a Take Back the Night march. She would speak for a long time about her deception and rape, about verbal coercion and anorexia, about her ensuing post-traumatic stress syndrome. Latter-day Clarissas may worry more about their "self esteem" than their virtue, but they are still attaching the same quasi-religious value to the physical act.

"Calling It Rape," a play by Sonya Rasminsky, a recent Harvard graduate, is based on interviews with date-rape victims. The play, which has been performed at Harvard and may be taken into Boston-area high schools, begins with "To His Coy Mistress," by the 17th-century poet Andrew Marvell. Although generations of high-school and college students have read this as a romantic poem, a poem about desire and the struggle against mortality, Rasminsky has reinterpreted it as a poem about rape. "Had we but world enough, and time, this coyness, lady, were no crime." But what Andrew Marvell didn't know then, and we know now, is that the real crime is not her coyness but his verbal coercion.

Farther along, the actors recount a rape that hinges on misunderstanding. A boy and girl are watching videos and he starts to come on to her. She does not want to have sex. As the situation progresses, she says, in an oblique effort to communicate her lack of enthusiasm, "If you're going to [expletive] me, use a condom." He interprets that as a yes, but it's really a no. And, according to this play, what happens next, condom or no condom, is rape.

This is a central idea of the rape-crisis movement: that sex has become our tower of Babel. He doesn't know what she wants (not to have sex) and she doesn't know what he wants (to have sex)—until it's too late. He speaks boyspeak and she speaks girlspeak and what comes out of all this verbal chaos is a lot of rapes. The theory of mixed signals and crossed stars has to do with more than gender politics. It comes in part, from the much-discussed diversity that has so radically shifted the social composition of the college class since the 50's.

Take my own Harvard dorm: the Adams House dining hall is large, with high ceilings and dark paneling. It hasn't changed much for generations. As soon as the students start milling around gathering salads, ice cream and coffee onto green trays, there are signs of change. There are students in jeans, flannel shirts, short skirts, girls in jackets, boys in bracelets, two pierced noses and lots of secondhand clothes.

Not so many years ago, this room was filled with boys in jackets and ties. Most of them were white, Christian and what we now call privileged. Students came from the same social milieu with the same social rules and it was assumed that everyone knew more or less how they were expected to behave with everyone else. Diversity and multiculturalism were unheard of, and if they had been, they would have been dirty words. With the shift in college environments, with the introduction of black kids, Asian kids, Jewish kids, kids from the wrong side of the tracks of nearly every railroad in the country, there was an accompanying anxiety about how people behave. When ivory tower meets melting pot, it causes tension, some confusion, some need for readjustment. In explaining the need for intensive "orientation" programs, including workshops on date rape, Columbia's assistant dean for freshmen stated in an interview in The New York Times: "You can't bring all these people together and say, 'Now be one big happy community,' without some sort of training. You can't just throw together somebody from a small town in Texas and some-one from New York City and someone from a conservative fundamentalist home in the Midwest and say, 'Now without any sort of conversation, be best friends and get along and respect one another.'"

Catharine Stimpson, a University Professor at Rutgers and longtime advocate of wo-men's studies programs, once pointed out that it's sometimes easier for people to talk about gender than to talk about class. "Miscommunication" is in some sense a word for the friction between the way we were and the way we are. Just as the idea that we speak different languages is connected to gender—the arrival of women in classrooms, in dorms and in offices—it is also connected to class.

When the Southern heiress goes out with the plumber's son from the Bronx, when the kid from rural Arkansas goes out with a boy from Exeter, the anxiety is that they have different expectations. The dangerous "miscommunication" that recurs through the literature on date rape is a code word for difference in background. The rhetoric surrounding date rape and sexual harassment is in part a response to cultural mixing. The idea that men don't know what women mean when women say no stems from something deeper and more complicated than feminist concerns with rape.

People have asked me if I have ever been date-raped. And thinking back on complicated nights, on too many glasses of wine, on strange and familiar beds, I would have to say yes. With such a sweeping definition of rape, I wonder how many people there are, male or female, who haven't been date-raped at one point or another. People pressure and manipulate and cajole each other into all sorts of things all of the time. As Susan Sontag wrote, "Since Christianity upped the ante and concentrated on sexual behavior as the root of virtue, everything pertaining to sex has been a 'special case' in our culture, evoking peculiarly inconsistent attitudes." No human interactions are free from pressure, and the idea that sex is, or can be, makes it what Sontag calls a "special case," vulnerable to the inconsistent expectations of double standard.

With their expansive version of rape, rape-crisis feminists are inventing a kinder, gentler sexuality. Beneath the broad definition of rape, these feminists are endorsing their own utopian vision of sexual relations: sex without struggle, sex without power, sex without persuasion, sex without pursuit. If verbal coercion constitutes rape, then the word rape itself expands to include any kind of sex a woman experiences as negative.

When Martin Amis spoke at Princeton, he included a controversial joke: "As far as I'm concerned, you can change your mind before, even during, but just not after sex." The reason this joke is funny, and the reason it's also too serious to be funny, is that in the current atmosphere you *can* change your mind afterward. Regret can signify rape. A night that was a blur, a night you wish hadn't happened, can be rape. Since "verbal coercion" and "manipulation" are ambiguous, it's easy to decide afterwards that he manipulated you. You can realize it weeks or even years later. This is a movement that deals in retrospective trauma.

Rape has become a catch-all expression, a word used to define everything that is unpleasant and disturbing about relations between the sexes. Students say things like "I realize that sexual harassment is a kind of rape." If we refer to a whole range of behavior from emotional pressure to sexual harassment as "rape," then the idea itself gets diluted. It ceases to be powerful as either description or accusation.

Some feminists actually collapse the distinction between rape and sex. Catharine MacKinnon writes: "Compare victims' reports of rape with women's reports of sex. They look a lot alike. . . . In this light, the major distinction between intercourse (normal) and rape (abnormal) is that the normal happens so often that one cannot get anyone to see anything wrong with it."

There are a few feminists involved in rape education who object to the current expanding definitions of sexual assault. Gillian Greensite, founder of the rape prevention education program at the University of California at Santa Cruz, writes that the seriousness of the crime "is being undermined by the growing tendency of some feminists to label all heterosexual miscommunication and insensitivity as acquaintance rape." From within the rape-crisis movement, Greensite's dissent makes an important point. If we are going to maintain an *idea* of rape, then we need to reserve it for instances of physical violence, or the threat of physical violence.

But some people want the melodrama. They want the absolute value placed on experience by absolute words. Words like "rape" and "verbal coercion" channel the confusing flow of experience into something easy to understand. The idea of date rape comes at us fast and coherent. It comes at us when we've just left home and haven't yet figured out where to put our new futons or how to organize our new social lives. The rhetoric about date rape defines the terms, gives names to nameless confusions and sorts through mixed feelings with a sort of insistent consistency. In the first rush of sexual experience, the fear of date rape offers a tangible framework to locate fears that are essentially abstract.

When my 55-year-old mother was young, navigating her way through dates, there was a definite social compass. There were places not to let him put his hands. There were invisible lines. The pill wasn't available. Abortion wasn't legal. And sex was just wrong. Her mother gave her "mad money" to take out on dates in case her date got drunk and she needed to escape. She had to go far enough to hold his interest and not far enough to endanger her reputation.

Now the rape-crisis feminists are offering new rules. They are giving a new political weight to the same old no. My mother's mother told her to drink sloe gin fizzes so she wouldn't drink too much and get too drunk and go too far. Now the date rape pamphlets tell us: "Avoid excessive use of alcohol and drugs. Alcohol and drugs interfere with clear thinking and effective communication." My mother's mother told her to stay away from empty rooms and dimly lighted streets. In "I Never Called It Rape," Robin Warshaw writes, "Especially with recent acquaintances, women should insist on going only to public places such as restaurants and movie theaters."

There is a danger in these new rules. We shouldn't need to be reminded that the rigidly conformist 50's were not the heyday of women's power. Barbara Ehrenreich writes of "re-making love," but there is a danger in re-making love in its old image. The terms may have changed, but attitudes about sex and women's bodies have not. Rape-crisis feminists threaten the progress that's been made. They are chasing the same stereotypes our mothers spent so much energy escaping.

One day I was looking through my mother's bookshelves and I found her old battered copy of Germaine Greer's feminist classic, "The Female Eunuch." The pages were dogeared and whole passages marked with penciled notes. It was 1971 when Germaine Greer fanned the fires with "The Female Eunuch" and it was 1971 when my mother read it, brand new, explosive, a tough and sexy terrorism for the early stirrings of the feminist movement.

Today's rape-crisis feminists threaten to create their own version of the desexualized woman Greer complained of 20 years ago. Her comments need to be recycled for present-day feminism. "It is often falsely assumed," Greer writes, "even by feminists, that sexuality is the enemy of the female who really wants to develop these aspects of her personality. . . . It was not the insistence upon her sex that weakened the American woman student's desire to make something of her education, but the insistence upon a *passive* sexual *role* [Greer's italics]. In fact, the chief instrument in the deflection and perversion of female energy is the denial of female sexuality for the substitution of femininity or sexlessness."

It is the passive sexual role that threatens us still, and it is the denial of female sexual agency that threatens to propel us backward.

# Reading Questions

1. What reasons does Roiphe give to support her rejection of the phrase "date rape crisis"?
2. In what ways does Roiphe view the use of rape rhetoric as harmful to feminist goals?
3. What are the retrograde assumptions behind the educational materials that research and advise women about rape?
4. Why does Roiphe view MacKinnon's language as reinforcing negative stereotypes about women's bodies and sexualities?
5. What does Roiphe mean by "heterosexual miscommunication"?

# Recommended Reading

Tim Benke, "Men on Rape," *Men on Rape* (New York: St. Martin's Press, 1982)

Andrea Dworkin, "The Rape Atrocity and the Boy Next Door," *Our Blood* (New York: Harper and Row, 1976)

Billie Wright Dziech and Linda Weiner, eds., *The Lecherous Professor: Sexual Harassment on Campus* (Boston: Beacon Press, 1984)

Diane F. Herman, "The Rape Culture," *Women: A Feminist Perspective*, ed. Jo Freeman (Mountain View, CA: Mayfield, 1989)

Diane E. H. Russell, *Sexual Exploitation: Rape, Child Sexual Abuse, and Sexual Harassment* (Beverly Hills: Russell Sage, 1984)

Rosemarie Tong, *Women, Sex, and the Law* (Totowa, NJ: Rowman and Littlefield, 1984)

# Recommended Audiovisual Resources

*Rape: Face to Face.* 1985. Produced by KCTS/TV. Documentary featuring the emotional confrontation between rapists and victims of rape. Filmakers Library.

*Dating Rites: Gang Rape on Campus.* 1993. Produced by Alison Stone. Stonescape Productions. Documentary on gang rape and acquaintance rape on college campuses. Includes an interview with gang rape survivor Meg Davis. Filmakers Library.

*Rape/Crisis.* 1983. Directed by Gary T. McDonald. A compelling investigation of the trauma of rape, a crisis for everyone concerned. The Cinema Guild.

# The Sexual Politics of Black Womanhood

## PATRICIA HILL COLLINS

Patricia Hill Collins teaches African American Studies at the University of Cincinnati. She is the author of *Black Feminist Thought* and *Toward a New Vision: Race, Class and Gender as Categories of Analysis*.

> Even I found it almost impossible to let her say what had happened to her as *she* perceived it. . . And why? Because once you strip away the lie that rape is pleasant, that children are not permanently damaged by sexual pain, that violence done to them is washed away by fear, silence, and time, you are left with the positive horror of the lives of thousands of children . . . who have been sexually abused and who have never been permitted their own language to tell about it.
>
> —Alice Walker 1988, 57

In *The Color Purple* Alice Walker creates the character of Celie, a Black adolescent girl who is sexually abused by her stepfather. By writing letters to God and forming supportive relationships with other Black women, Celie finds her own voice, and her voice enables her to transcend the fear and silence of her childhood. By creating Celie and giving her the language to tell of her sexual abuse, Walker adds Celie's voice to muted yet growing discussions of the sexual politics of Black womanhood in Black feminist thought. Black feminists have investigated how rape as a specific form of sexual violence is embedded in a system of interlocking race, gender, and class oppression (Davis 1978, 1981, 1989; Hall 1983). Reproductive rights issues such as access to information on sexuality and birth control, the struggles for abortion rights, and patterns of forced sterilization have also garnered attention (Davis 1981). Black lesbian feminists have vigorously challenged the basic assumptions and mechanisms of control underlying compulsory heterosexuality and have investigated homophobia's impact on African-American women (Clarke 1983; Shockley 1983; Barbara Smith 1983; Lorde 1984).

But when it comes to other important issues concerning the sexual politics of Black womanhood, like Alice Walker, Black feminists have found it almost impossible to say what has happened to Black women. In the flood of scholarly and popular writing about Black heterosexual relationships, analyses of domestic violence against African-American women—especially those that link this form of sexual violence to existing gender ideology concerning Black masculinity and Black femininity—remain rare. Theoretical work explaining patterns of Black women's inclusion in the burgeoning international pornography industry has been similarly neglected. Perhaps the most curious omission has been the virtual silence of the Black feminist community concerning the participation of far too many Black women in prostitution. Ironically, while the image of African-American women as prostitutes has been aggressively challenged, the reality of African-American women who work as prostitutes remains unexplored.

These patterns of inclusion and neglect in Black feminist thought merit investigation. Examining the links between sexuality and power in a system of interlocking race, gender, and class oppression should reveal how important controlling Black women's sexuality has been to the effective operation of domination overall. The words of Angela Davis, Audre Lorde, Barbara Smith, and Alice Walker provide a promising foundation for a comprehensive Black feminist analysis. But Black feminist analyses of sexual politics must go beyond chronicling how sexuality has been used to oppress. Equally important is the need to reconceptualize sexuality with an eye toward empowering African-American women.

## A Working Definition of Sexual Politics

Sexual politics examines the links between sexuality and power. In defining sexuality it is important to distinguish among sexuality and the related terms, *sex* and *gender* (Vance 1984; Andersen 1988). Sex is a biological category attached to the body—humans are born female or male. In contrast, gender is socially constructed. The sex/gender system consists of marking the categories of biological sex with socially constructed gender meanings of masculinity and femininity. Just as sex/gender systems vary from relatively egalitarian systems to sex/gender hierarchies, ideologies of sexuality attached to particular sex/gender systems exhibit similar diversity. Sexuality is socially constructed through the sex/gender system on both the personal level of individual consciousness and interpersonal relationships and the social structural level of social institutions (Foucault 1980). This multilevel sex/gender system reflects the needs of a given historical moment such that social constructions of sexuality change in tandem with changing social conditions.

African-American women inhabit a sex/gender hierarchy in which inequalities of race and social class have been sexualized. Privileged groups define their alleged sexual practices as the mythical norm and label sexual practices and groups who diverge from this norm as deviant and threatening (Lorde 1984; Vance 1984). Maintaining the mythical norm of the financially independent, white middle-class family organized around a monogamous heterosexual couple requires stigmatizing African-American families as being deviant, and a primary source of this assumed deviancy stems from allegations about Black sexuality. This sex/gender hierarchy not only operates on the social structural level but is potentially replicated within each individual. Differences in sexuality thus take on more meaning than just benign sexual variation. Each individual becomes a powerful conduit for social relations of domination whereby individual anxieties, fears, and doubts about sexuality can be annexed by larger systems of oppression (Hoch 1979; Foucault 1980, 99).

According to Cheryl Clarke, African-Americans have been profoundly affected by this sex/gender hierarchy:

> Like all Americans, black Americans live in a sexually repressive culture. And we have made all manner of compromise regarding our sexuality in order to live here. We have expended much energy trying to debunk the racist mythology which says our sexuality is depraved. Unfortunately, many of us have overcompensated and assimilated. . . . Like everyone else in America who is ambivalent in these respects, black folk have to live with the contradictions of this limited sexual system by repressing or closeting any other sexual/erotic urges, feelings, or desires. (Clarke 1983, 199)

Embedded in Clarke's statement is the theme of self-censorship inherent when a hierarchy of any kind invades interpersonal relationships among individuals and the actual consciousness of individuals themselves. Sexuality and power as domination become intertwined.

In her ground-breaking essay, "Uses of the Erotic: The Erotic as Power," Black feminist poet Audre Lorde explores this fundamental link between sexuality and power:

> There are many kinds of power, used and unused, acknowledged or otherwise. The erotic is a resource within each of us that lies in a deeply female and spiritual plane, firmly rooted in the power of our unexpressed or unrecognized feeling. In order to perpetuate itself, every oppression must corrupt or distort those various sources of power within the culture of the oppressed that can provide energy for change. For women, this has meant a suppression of the erotic as a considered source of power and information in our lives. (Lorde 1984, 53)

For Lorde sexuality is a component of the larger construct of the erotic as a source of power in women. Lorde's notion is one of power as energy, as something people possess which must be annexed in order for larger systems of oppression to function.[1]

Sexuality becomes a domain of restriction and repression when this energy is tied to the larger system of race, class, and gender oppression. But Lorde's words also signal the potential for Black women's empowerment by showing sexuality and the erotic to be a domain of exploration, pleasure, and human agency. From a Black feminist standpoint sexuality encompasses the both/and nature of human existence, the potential for a sexuality that simultaneously oppresses and empowers.

One key issue for Black feminist thought is the need to examine the processes by which power as domination on the social structural level—namely, institutional structures of racism, sexism, and social class privilege—annexes this basic power of the erotic on the personal level—that is, the construct of power as energy, for its own ends.

## Black Women and the Sex/Gender Hierarchy

The social construction of Black women's sexuality is embedded in this larger, overarching sex/gender hierarchy designed to harness power as energy to the exigencies of power as race, gender, and social class domination. . . . Pornography, prostitution, and rape as a specific tool of sexual violence have also been key to the sexual politics of Black womanhood. Together they form three essential and interrelated components of the sex/gender hierarchy framing Black women's sexuality.

### Pornography and Black Women's Bodies

> For centuries the black woman has served as the primary pornographic "outlet" for white men in Europe and America. We need only think of the black women used as breeders, raped for the pleasure and profit of their owners. We need only think of the license the "master" of the slave women enjoyed. But, most telling of all, we need only study the old slave societies of the South to note the sadistic treatment—at the hands of white "gentlemen"—of "beautiful young quadroons and octoroons" who became increasingly

(and were deliberately bred to become) indistinguishable from white women, and were the more highly prized as slave mistresses because of this. (Walker 1981, 42)

Alice Walker's description of the rape of enslaved African women for the "pleasure and profit of their owners" encapsulates several elements of contemporary pornography. First, Black women were used as sex objects for the pleasure of white men. This objectification of African-American women parallels the portrayal of women in pornography as sex objects whose sexuality is available for men (McNall 1983). Exploiting Black women as breeders objectified them as less than human because only animals can be bred against their will. In contemporary pornography women are objectified through being portrayed as pieces of meat, as sexual animals awaiting conquest. Second, African-American women were raped, a form of sexual violence. Violence is typically an implicit or explicit theme in pornography. Moreover, the rape of Black women linked sexuality and violence, another characteristic feature of pornography (Eisenstein 1983). Third, rape and other forms of sexual violence act to strip victims of their will to resist and make them passive and submissive to the will of the rapist. Female passivity, the fact that women have things done to them, is a theme repeated over and over in contemporary pornography (McNall 1983). Fourth, the profitability of Black women's sexual exploitation for white "gentlemen" parallels pornography's financially lucrative benefits for pornographers (Eisenstein 1983). Finally, the actual breeding of "quadroons and octoroons" not only reinforces the themes of Black women's passivity, objectification, and malleability to male control but reveals pornography's grounding in racism and sexism. The fates of both Black and white women were intertwined in this breeding process. The ideal African-American woman as a pornographic object was indistinguishable from white women and thus approximated the images of beauty, asexuality, and chastity forced on white women. But inside was a highly sexual whore, a "slave mistress" ready to cater to her owner's pleasure.[2]

Contemporary pornography consists of a series of icons or representations that focus the viewer's attention on the relationship between the portrayed individual and the general qualities ascribed to that class of individuals. Pornographic images are iconographic in that they represent realities in a manner determined by the historical position of the observers, their relationship to their own time, and to the history of the conventions which they employ (Gilman 1985). The treatment of Black women's bodies in nineteenth-century Europe and the United States may be the foundation upon which contemporary pornography as the representation of women's objectification, domination, and control is based. Icons about the sexuality of Black women's bodies emerged in these contexts. Moreover, as race/gender-specific representations, these icons have implications for the treatment of both African-American and white women in contemporary pornography.

I suggest that African-American women were not included in pornography as an afterthought but instead form a key pillar on which contemporary pornography itself rests. As Alice Walker points out, "the more ancient roots of modern pornography are to be found in the almost always pornographic treatment of black women who, from the moment they entered slavery . . . were subjected to rape as the 'logical' convergence of sex and violence. Conquest, in short" (1981, 42).

One key feature about the treatment of Black women in the nineteenth century was how their bodies were objects of display. In the antebellum American South white men did not have to look at pornographic pictures of women because they could become voyeurs of Black women on the auction block. A chilling example of this objectification of the Black female body is provided by the exhibition, in early nineteenth-century Europe, of Sarah Bartmann, the so-called Hottentot Venus. Her display formed one of the original icons for Black female sexuality. An African woman, Sarah Bartmann was often exhibited at fashionable parties in Paris, generally wearing little clothing, to provide entertainment. To her audience she represented deviant sexuality. At the time European audiences thought that Africans had deviant sexual practices and searched for physiological differences, such as enlarged penises and malformed female genitalia, as indications of this deviant sexuality. Sarah Bartmann's exhibition stimulated these racist and sexist beliefs. After her death in 1815, she was dissected. Her genitalia and buttocks remain on display in Paris (Gilman 1985).

Sander Gilman explains the impact that Sarah Bartmann's exhibition had on Victorian audiences:

> It is important to note that Sarah Bartmann was exhibited not to show her genitalia—but rather to present another anomaly which the European audience . . . found riveting. This was the steatopygia, or protruding buttocks, the other physical characteristic of the Hottentot female which captured the eye of early European travelers. . . . The figure of Sarah Bartmann was reduced to her sexual parts. The audience which had paid to see her buttocks and had fantasized about the uniqueness of her genitalia when she was alive could, after her death and dissection, examine both. (1985, 213)

In this passage Gilman unwittingly describes how Bartmann was used as a pornographic object similar to how women are represented in contemporary pornography. She was reduced to her sexual parts, and these parts came to represent a dominant icon applied to Black women throughout the nineteenth century. Moreover, the fact that Sarah Bartmann was both African and a woman underscores the importance of gender in maintaining notions of racial purity. In this case Bartmann symbolized Blacks as a "race." Thus the creation of the icon applied to Black women demonstrates that notions of gender, race, and sexuality were linked in overarching structures of political domination and economic exploitation.

The process illustrated by the pornographic treatment of the bodies of enslaved African women and of women like Sarah Bartmann has developed into a full-scale industry encompassing all women objectified differently by racial/ethnic category. Contemporary portrayals of Black women in pornography represent the continuation of the historical treatment of their actual bodies. African-American women are usually depicted in a situation of bondage and slavery, typically in a submissive posture, and often with two white men. As Bell observes, "this setting reminds us of all the trappings of slavery: chains, whips, neck braces, wrist clasps" (1987, 59). White women and women of color have different pornographic images applied to them. The image of Black women in pornography is almost consistently one featuring them breaking from chains. The image of Asian women in pornography is almost consistently one of being tortured (Bell 1987, 161).

The pornographic treatment of Black women's bodies challenges the prevailing feminist assumption that since pornography primarily affects white women, racism has been grafted onto pornography. African-American women's experiences suggest that Black women were not added into a preexisting pornography, but rather that pornography itself must be reconceptualized as an example of the interlocking nature of race, gender, and class oppression. At the heart of both racism and sexism are notions of biological determinism claiming that people of African descent and women possess immutable biological characteristics marking their inferiority to elite white men (Gould 1981; Fausto-Sterling 1989; Halpin 1989). In pornography these racist and sexist beliefs are sexualized. Moreover, for African-American women pornography has not been timeless and universal but was tied to Black women's experiences with the European colonization of Africa and with American slavery. Pornography emerged within a specific system of social class relationships.

This linking of views of the body, social constructions of race and gender, and conceptualizations of sexuality that inform Black women's treatment as pornographic objects promises to have significant implications for how we assess contemporary pornography. Moreover, examining how pornography has been central to the race, gender, and class oppression of African-American women offers new routes for understanding the dynamics of power as domination.

Investigating racial patterns in pornography offers one route for such an analysis. Black women have often claimed that images of white women's sexuality were intertwined with the controlling image of the sexually denigrated Black woman: "In the United States, the fear and fascination of female sexuality was projected onto black women; the passionless lady arose in symbiosis with the primitively sexual slave" (Hall 1983, 333). Comparable linkages exist in pornography (Gardner 1980). Alice Walker provides a fictional account of a Black man's growing awareness of the different ways that African-American and white women are objectified in pornography: "What he has refused to see—because to see it would reveal yet another area in which he is unable to protect or defend black women—is that where white women are depicted in pornography as 'objects,' black women are depicted as animals. Where white women are depicted as human bodies if not beings, black women are depicted as shit" (Walker 1981, 52).

Walker's distinction between "objects" and "animals" is crucial in untangling gender, race, and class dynamics in pornography. Within the mind/body, culture/nature, male/female oppositional dichotomies in Western social thought, objects occupy an uncertain interim position. As objects white women become creations of culture—in this case, the mind of white men—using the materials of nature—in this case, uncontrolled female sexuality. In contrast, as animals Black women receive no such redeeming dose of culture and remain open to the type of exploitation visited on nature overall. Race becomes the distinguishing feature in determining the type of objectification women will encounter. Whiteness as symbolic of both civilization and culture is used to separate objects from animals.

The alleged superiority of men to women is not the only hierarchical relationship that has been linked to the putative superiority of the mind to the body. Certain "races" of people have been defined as being more bodylike, more animallike, and less godlike than others (Spelman 1982, 52). Race and gender oppression may both revolve around the same axis of distain for the body; both portray the sexuality of subordinate groups as animalistic and therefore deviant. Biological notions of race and gender prevalent in the early nineteenth century which fostered the animalistic icon of Black female sexuality were joined by the appearance of a racist biology incorporating the concept of degeneracy (Foucault 1980). Africans and women were both perceived as embodied entities, and Blacks were seen as degenerate. Fear of and distain for the body thus formed a key element in both sexist and racist thinking (Spelman 1982).

While the sexual and racial dimensions of being treated like an animal are important, the economic foundation underlying this treatment is critical. Animals can be economically exploited, worked, sold, killed, and consumed. As "mules," African-American women become susceptible to such treatment. The political economy of pornography also merits careful attention. Pornography is pivotal in mediating contradictions in changing societies (McNall 1983). It is no accident that racist biology, religious justifications for slavery and women's subordination, and other explanations for nineteenth-century racism and sexism arose during a period of profound political and economic change. Symbolic means of domination become particularly important in mediating contradictions in changing political economies. The exhibition of Sarah Bartmann and Black women on the auction block were not benign intellectual exercises—these practices defended real material and political interests. Current transformations in international capitalism require similar ideological justifications. Where does pornography fit in these current transformations? This question awaits a comprehensive Afrocentric feminist analysis.

Publicly exhibiting Black women may have been central to objectifying Black women as animals and to creating the icon of Black women as animals. Yi-Fu Tuan (1984) offers an innovative argument about similarities in efforts to control nature—especially plant life—the domestication of animals, and the domination of certain groups of humans. Tuan suggests that displaying humans alongside animals implies that such humans are more like monkeys and bears than they are like "normal" people. This same juxtaposition leads spectators to view the captive animals in a special way. Animals acquire definitions of being like humans, only more openly carnal and sexual, an aspect of animals that forms a major source of attraction for visitors to modern zoos. In discussing the popularity of monkeys in zoos, Tuan notes: "some visitors are especially attracted by the easy sexual behavior of the monkeys. Voyeurism is forbidden except when applied to subhumans" (1984, 82). Tuan's analysis suggests that the public display of Sarah Bartmann and of the countless enslaved African women on the auction blocks of the antebellum American South—especially in proximity to animals—fostered their image as animalistic.

This linking of Black women and animals is evident in nineteenth-century scientific literature. The equation of women, Blacks, and animals is revealed in the following description of an African woman published in an 1878 anthropology text:

> She had a way of pouting her lips exactly like what we have observed in the orangutan. Her movements had something abrupt and fantastical about them, reminding one of those of the ape. Her ear was like that of many apes. . . . These are animal characters. I have never seen a human head more like an ape than that of this woman. (Halpin 1989, 287)

In a climate such as this, it is not surprising that one prominent European physician even stated that Black women's "animallike sexual appetite went so far as to lead black women to copulate with apes" (Gilman 1985, 212).

The treatment of all women in contemporary pornography has strong ties to the portrayal of Black women as animals. In pornography women become nonpeople and are often represented as the sum of their fragmented body parts. Scott McNall observes:

> This fragmentation of women relates to the predominance of rear-entry position
> photographs. . . . All of these kinds of photographs reduce the woman to her reproductive
> system, and, furthermore, make her open, willing, and available—not in control. . . .
> The other thing rear-entry position photographs tell us about women is that they are
> animals. They are animals because they are the same as dogs—bitches in heat who can't
> control themselves. (McNall 1983, 197–98)

This linking of animals and white women within pornography becomes feasible when grounded in the earlier denigration of Black women as animals.

Developing a comprehensive analysis of the race, gender, and class dynamics of pornography offers possibilities for change. Those Black feminist intellectuals investigating sexual politics imply that the situation is much more complicated than that advanced by some prominent white feminists (see, e.g., Dworkin 1981) in which "men oppress women" because they are men. Such approaches implicitly assume biologically deterministic views of sex, gender, and sexuality and offer few possibilities for change. In contrast, Afrocentric feminist analyses routinely provide for human agency and its corresponding empowerment and for the responsiveness of social structures to human action. In the short story "Coming Apart," Alice Walker describes one Black man's growing realization that his enjoyment of pornography, whether of white women as "objects" or Black women as "animals," degraded him:

> He begins to feel sick. For he realizes that he has bought some of the advertisements about
> women, black and white. And further, inevitably, he has bought the advertisements about
> himself. In pornography the black man is portrayed as being capable of fucking anything
> . . . even a piece of shit. He is defined solely by the size, readiness and unselectivity of his
> cock. (Walker 1981, 52)

Walker conceptualizes pornography as a race/gender system that entraps everyone. But by exploring an African-American *man's* struggle for a self-defined standpoint on pornography, Walker suggests that a changed consciousness is essential to social change. If a Black man can understand how pornography affects him, then other groups emeshed in the same system are equally capable of similar shifts in consciousness and action.

## Prostitution and the Commodification of Sexuality

In *To Be Young, Gifted and Black*, Lorraine Hansberry creates three characters: a young domestic worker, a chic professional, middle-aged woman, and a mother in her thirties. Each speaks a variant of the following:

> In these streets out there, any little white boy from Long Island or Westchester sees me and
> leans out of his car and yells—"Hey there, *hot chocolate*! Say there, Jezebel! Hey you—
> 'Hundred Dollar Misunderstanding'! YOU! Bet you know where there's a good time
> tonight. . . ." Follow me sometimes and see if I lie. I can be coming from eight hours on
> an assembly line or fourteen hours in Mrs. Halsey's kitchen. I can be all filled up that day
> with three hundred years of rage so that my eyes are flashing and my flesh is trembling—
> and the white boys in the streets, they look at me and think of sex. They look at me and
> that's *all* they think. . . . Baby, you could be Jesus in drag—but if you're brown they're
> sure you're selling! (Hansberry 1969, 98)

Like the characters in Hansberry's fiction, all Black women are affected by the widespread controlling image that African-American women are sexually promiscuous, potential prostitutes. The pervasiveness of this image is vividly recounted in Black activist lawyer Pauli Murray's description of an incident she experienced while defending two women from Spanish Harlem who had been arrested as prostitutes: "The first witness, a white man from New Jersey, testified on the details of the sexual transaction and his payment of money. When asked to identify the woman with whom he had engaged in sexual intercourse, he unhesitatingly pointed directly at me, seated beside my two clients at the defense table!" (Murray 1987, 274). Murray's clients were still convicted.

The creation of Jezebel, the image of the sexually denigrated Black woman, has been vital in sustaining a system of interlocking race, gender, and class oppression. Exploring how the image of the African-American woman as prostitute has been used by each system of oppression illustrates how sexuality links the three systems. But Black women's treatment also demonstrates how manipulating sexuality has been essential to the political economy of domination within each system and across all three.

Yi-Fu Tuan (1984) suggests that power as domination involves reducing humans to animate nature in order to exploit them economically or to treat them condescendingly as pets. Domination may be either cruel and exploitative with no affection or may be exploitative yet coexist with affection. The former produces the victim—in this case, the Black woman as "mule" whose labor has been exploited. In contrast, the combination of dominance and affection produces the pet, the individual who is subordinate but whose survival depends on the whims of the more powerful. The "beautiful young quadroons and octoroons" described by Alice Walker were bred to be pets—enslaved Black mistresses whose existence required that they retain the affection of their owners. The treatment afforded these women illustrates a process that affects all African-American women: their portrayal as actual or potential victims and pets of elite white males.[3]

African-American women simultaneously embody the coexistence of the victim and the pet, with survival often linked to the ability to be appropriately subordinate as victims or pets. Black women's experiences as unpaid and paid workers demonstrate the harsh lives victims are forced to lead. While the life of the victim is difficult, pets experience a distinctive form of exploitation. Zora Neale Hurston's 1943 essay, "The 'Pet' Negro System," speaks contemptuously of this ostensibly benign situation that combines domination with affection. Written in a Black oratorical style, Hurston notes, "Brother and Sisters, I take my text this morning from the Book of Dixie. . . . Now it says here, 'And every white man shall be allowed to pet himself a Negro. Yea, he shall take a black man unto himself to pet and cherish, and this same Negro shall be perfect in his sight'" (Walker 1979a, 156). Pets are treated as exceptions and live with the constant threat that they will no longer be "perfect in his sight," that their owners will tire of them and relegate them to the unenviable role of victim.

Prostitution represents the fusion of exploitation for an economic purpose—namely, the commodification of Black women's sexuality—with the demeaning treatment afforded pets. Sex becomes commodified not merely in the sense that it can be purchased—the dimension of economic exploitation—but also in the sense that one is dealing with a totally alienated being who is separated from and who does not control her body: the dimension of power as domination (McNall 1983). Commodified sex can then be appropriated by the powerful. When the "white boys from Long Island" look at Black women and *all* they think about is sex, they believe that they can appropriate Black women's bodies. When they yell "Bet you know where there's a good time tonight," they expect commodified sex with Black women as "animals" to be better than sex with white women as "objects." Both pornography and prostitution commodify sexuality and imply to the "white boys" that all African-American women can be bought.

Prostitution under European and American capitalism thus exists within a complex web of political and economic relationships whereby sexuality is conceptualized along intersecting axes of race and gender. Gilman's (1985) analysis of the exhibition of Sarah Bartmann as the "Hottentot Venus" suggests another intriguing connection between race, gender, and sexuality in nineteenth-century Europe—the linking of the icon of the Black woman with the icon of the white prostitute. While the Hottentot woman stood for the essence of Africans as a race, the white prostitute symbolized the sexualized woman. The prostitute represented the embodiment of sexuality and all that European society associated with it: disease as well as passion. As Gilman points out, "it is this uncleanliness, this disease, which forms the final link between two images of women, the black and the prostitute. Just as the genitalia of the Hottentot were perceived as parallel to the diseased genitalia of the prostitute, so to the power of the idea of corruption links both images" (1985, 237). These connections between the icons of Black women and white prostitutes demonstrate how race, gender, and the social class structure of the European political economy interlock.

In the American antebellum South both of these images were fused in the forced prostitution of enslaved African women. The prostitution of Black women allowed white women to be the opposite; Black "whores" make white "virgins" possible. This race/gender nexus fostered a situation whereby white men could then differentiate between the sexualized woman-as-body who is dominated and "screwed" and the asexual woman-as-pure-spirit who is idealized and brought home to mother (Hoch 1979, 70). The sexually denigrated woman, whether she was made a victim through her rape or a pet through her seduction, could be used as the yardstick against which the cult of true womanhood was measured. Moreover, this entire situation was profitable.

## Rape and Sexual Violence

Force was important in creating African-American women's centrality to American images of the sexualized woman and in shaping their experiences with both pornography and prostitution. Black women did not willingly submit to their exhibition on southern auction blocks—they were forced to do so. Enslaved African women could not choose whether to work—they were beaten and often killed if they refused. Black domestics who resisted the sexual advances of their employers often found themselves looking for work where none was to be found. Both the reality and the threat of violence have acted as a form of social control for African-American women.

Rape has been one fundamental tool of sexual violence directed against African-American women. Challenging the pervasiveness of Black women's rape and sexual extortion by white men has long formed a prominent theme in Black women's writings. Autobiographies such as Maya Angelou's *I Know Why the Caged Bird Sings* (1970) and Harriet Jacob's "The Perils of a Slave Woman's Life" (1860/1987) from *Incidents in the Life of a Slave Girl* record examples of actual and threatened sexual assault. The effects of rape on African-American women is a prominent theme in Black women's fiction.

Gayl Jones's *Corregidora* (1975) and Rosa Guy's *A Measure of Time* (1983) both explore interracial rape of Black women. Toni Morrison's *The Bluest Eye* (1970), Alice Walker's *The Color Purple* (1982), and Gloria Naylor's *The Women of Brewster Place* (1980) all examine rape within African-American families and communities. Elizabeth Clark-Lewis's (1985) study of domestic workers found that mothers, aunts, and community othermothers warned young Black women about the threat of rape. One respondent in Clark-Lewis's study, an 87-year-old North Carolina Black domestic worker, remembers, "nobody was sent out before you was told to be careful of the white man or his sons" (Clark-Lewis 1985, 15).

Rape and other acts of overt violence that Black women have experienced, such as physical assault during slavery, domestic abuse, incest, and sexual extortion, accompany Black women's subordination in a system of race, class, and gender oppression. These violent acts are the visible dimensions of a more generalized, routinized system of oppression. Violence against Black women tends to be legitimated and therefore condoned while the same acts visited on other groups may remain nonlegitimated and nonexcusable. Certain forms of violence may garner the backing and control of the state while others remain uncontrolled (Edwards 1987). Specific acts of sexual violence visited on African-American women reflect a broader process by which violence is socially constructed in a race- and gender-specific manner. Thus Black women, Black men, and white women experience distinctive forms of sexual violence. As Angela Davis points out, "it would be a mistake to regard the institutionalized pattern of rape during slavery as an expression of white men's sexual urges. . . . Rape was a weapon of domination, a weapon of repression, whose covert goal was to extinguish slave women's will to resist, and in the process, to demoralize their men" (1981, 23).

Angela Davis's work (1978, 1981, 1989) illustrates this effort to conceptualize sexual violence against African-American women as part of a system of interlocking race, gender, and class oppression. Davis suggests that sexual violence has been central to the economic and political subordination of African-Americans overall. But while Black men and women were both victims of sexual violence, the specific forms they encountered were gender specific.

Depicting African-American men as sexually charged beasts who desired white women created the myth of the Black rapist.[4] Lynching emerged as the specific form of sexual violence visited on Black men, with the myth of the Black rapist as its ideological justification. The significance of this myth is that it "has been methodically conjured up when recurrent waves of violence and terror against the black community required a convincing explanation" (Davis 1978, 25). Black women experienced a parallel form of race- and gender-specific sexual violence. Treating African-American women as pornographic objects and portraying them as sexualized animals, as prostitutes, created the controlling image of Jezebel. Rape became the specific act of sexual violence forced on Black women, with the myth of the Black prostitute as its ideological justification.

Lynching and rape, two race/gender-specific forms of sexual violence, merged with their ideological justifications of the rapist and prostitute in order to provide an effective system of social control over African-Americans. Davis asserts that the controlling image of Black men as rapists has always "strengthened its inseparable companion: the image of the black woman as chronically promiscuous. And with good reason, for once the notion is accepted that black men harbor irresistible, animal-like sexual urges, the entire race is invested with bestiality" (1978, 27). A race of "animals" can be treated as such—as victims or pets. "The mythical rapist implies the mythical whore—and a race of rapists and whores deserves punishment and nothing more" (Davis 1978, 28).

Some suggestive generalizations exist concerning the connection between the social constructions of the rapist and the prostitute and the tenets of racist biology. Tuan (1984) notes that humans practice certain biological procedures on plants and animals to ensure their suitability as pets. For animals that goal of domestication is manageability and control, a state that can be accomplished through selective breeding or, for some male animals, by castration. A similar process may have affected the historical treatment of African-Americans. Since dominant groups have generally refrained from trying to breed humans in the same way that they breed animals, the pervasiveness of rape and lynching suggests that these practices may have contributed to mechanisms of population control. While not widespread, in some slave settings selective breeding and, if that failed, rape were used to produce slaves of a certain genetic heritage. In an 1858 slave narrative, James Roberts recounts the plantation of Maryland planter Calvin Smith, a man who kept 50–60 "head of women" for reproductive purposes. Only whites were permitted access to these women in order to ensure that 20–25 racially mixed children were born annually. Roberts also tells of a second planter who competed with Smith in breeding mulattos, a group that at that time brought higher prices, the "same as men strive to raise the most stock of any kind, cows, sheep, horses, etc." (Weisbord 1975, 27). For Black men, lynching was frequently accompanied by castration. Again, the parallels to techniques used to domesticate animals, or at least serve as a warning to those Black men who remained alive, is striking.

Black women continue to deal with this legacy of the sexual violence visited on African-Americans generally and with our history as collective rape victims. One effect lies in the treatment of rape victims. Such women are twice victimized, first by the actual rape, in this case the collective rape under slavery. But they are victimized again by family members, community residents, and social institutions such as criminal justice systems which somehow believe that rape victims are responsible for their own victimization. Even though current statistics indicate that Black women are more likely to be victimized than white women, Black women are less likely to report their rapes, less likely to have their cases come to trial, less likely to have their trials result in convictions, and, most disturbing, less likely to seek counseling and other support services. Existing evidence suggests that African-American women are aware of their lack of protection and that they resist rapists more than other groups (Bart and O'Brien 1985).

Another significant effect of this legacy of sexual violence concerns Black women's absence from antirape movements. Angela Davis argues, "if black women are conspic-uously absent from the ranks of the antirape movement today, it is, in large part, their way of protesting the movement's posture of indifference toward the frame-up rape charge as an incitement to racist aggression" (1978, 25). But this absence fosters Black women's silence concerning a troubling issue: the fact that most Black women are raped by Black men. While the historical legacy of the triad of pornography, prostitution, and the institutionalized rape of Black women may have created the larger social context within which all African-Americans reside, the unfortunate current reality is that many Black men have internalized the controlling images of the sex/gender hierarchy and condone either Black women's rape by other Black men or their own behavior as rapists. Far too many African-American women live with the untenable position of putting up with abusive Black men in defense of an elusive Black unity.

The historical legacy of Black women's treatment in pornography, prostitution, and rape forms the institutional backdrop for a range of interpersonal relationships that Black women currently have with Black men, whites, and one another. Without principled coalitions with other groups, African-American women may not be able to effect lasting change on the social structural level of social institutions. But the first step to forming such coalitions is examining exactly how these institutions harness power as energy for their own use by invading both relationships among individuals and individual consciousness itself. Thus understanding the contemporary dynamics of the sexual politics of Black womanhood in order to empower African-American women requires investigating how social structural factors infuse the private domain of Black women's relationships.

## Reading Questions

1. According to Collins, what topics have black feminist writers neglected in their analyses of the links between sexuality and power in our culture? Why have African-American novelists seemed to focus on these areas more than black feminist scholars?

2. How does the sex/gender hierarchy in our society sexualize inequalities of race and social class?

3. What relation does Collins claim the history of slavery to hold to the pornographic portrayal of black women's sexuality?

4. How does racist biology in the nineteenth century collaborate with pornography's bestialization of black sexuality?

5. In what ways does Collins describe Hurston's concept of "the 'pet' negro system" to epitomize white attitudes toward black prostitutes?

6. Why does Collins assert that the lynching of black men was a specific form of sexual violence inflicted against them? Why does she believe that the rape and lynching of black people contributed to techniques of population control?

## Recommended Reading

Angela Davis, "Rape, Racism and The Myth of the Black Rapist," Women, Race, and Class (New York: Random House, 1983)

Angela Davis, Women, Culture, and Politics (New York: Random House, 1989)

Sander Gilman, Difference and Pathology: Stereotypes of Sexuality, Race and Madness (Ithaca: Cornell University Press, 1985)

Harriet Jacobs, Incidents in the Life of a Slave Girl, ed. Jean Fagan Yellin (Cambridge: Harvard University Press, 1987)

Pauli Murray, The Autobiography of a Black Activist, Feminist, Lawyer, Priest, and Poet (Knoxville: University of Tennessee Press, 1989)

Michele Wallace, Black Macho and the Myth of the Superwoman (New York: Dial Press, 1979)

## Recommended Audiovisual Resources

Mississippi Burning. 1988. Directed by Alan Parker. What might have happened in 1964 when three civil rights activists turned up missing in Mississippi.

She's Gotta Have It. 1986. Directed by Spike Lee. Controversial narrative about relations between black men and women.

# Of Religions and Dreams
## The Spiritual Basis of the Berdache Tradition

WALTER L. WILLIAMS

Walter L. Williams is the editor of *Southeastern Indians Since the Removal Era* and the author of *The Spirit and the Flesh: Sexual Diversity in American Indian Culture*, from which this selection is taken.

When the French Jesuit missionary Joseph François Lafitau wrote his book on American Indians in 1724, he condemned berdaches for acting like women. Yet he admitted that this was not the Native American view. "They believe they are honored," he wrote uncomprehendingly. Lafitau pointed out that among the Indians of the western Great Lakes, Louisiana, and Florida, the berdaches "never marry, they participate in all religious ceremonies, and this profession of an extraordinary life causes them to be regarded as people of a higher order, and above the common man."[1] On his first voyage to America, the French explorer Jacques Marquette reported that among the Illinois and neighboring tribes, the berdaches were prominently present at all of the solemn ceremonies of the sacred Calumet pipe: "They are summoned to the Councils, and nothing can be decided without their advice. Finally, through their profession of leading an Extraordinary life, they pass for Manitous—That is to say, for Spirits—or persons of consequence."[2]

How is it that berdaches had such a prominent role in Native American ceremonialism? The French missionaries, coming from the Western Christian tradition with its condemnation of gender variations, could not even comprehend the relationship between berdachism and religion. Yet, it is the spiritual question that is, for most tribes, at the heart of the berdache tradition. Without understanding that, it is impossible to understand anything else about this aboriginal institution.

## American Indian Religions

Native American religions offered an explanation for human diversity by their creation stories. In some tribal religions, the Great Spiritual Being is conceived as neither male nor female but as a combination of both. Among the Kamia of the Southwest, for example, the bearer of plant seeds and the introducer of Kamia culture was a man–woman spirit named Warharmi.[3] A key episode of the Zuni creation story involves a battle between the kachina spirits of the agricultural Zunis and the enemy hunter spirits. Every four years an elaborate ceremony commemorates this myth. In the story a kachina spirit called *ko'lhamana* was captured by the enemy spirits and transformed in the process. This transformed spirit became a mediator between the two sides, using his peacemaking skills to merge the differing lifestyles of hunters and farmers. In the ceremony, a dramatic reenactment of the myth, the part of the transformed *ko'lhamana* spirit, is performed by a berdache.[4] The Zuni word for berdache is *lhamana*, denoting its closeness to the spiritual mediator who brought hunting and farming together.[5] The moral of this story is that the berdache was created by the deities for a special purpose, and that this creation led to the improvement of society. The continual reenactment of this story provides a justification for the Zuni berdache in each generation.

In contrast to this, the lack of spiritual justification in a creation myth could denote a lack of tolerance for gender variation. The Pimas, unlike most of their Southwestern neighbors, did not respect a berdache status. Wi-kovat, their derogatory word, means "like a girl," but it does not signify a recognized social role. Pima mythology reflects this lack of acceptance, in a folk tale that explains male androgyny as due to Papago witchcraft. Knowing that the Papagos respected berdaches, the Pimas blamed such an occurrence on an alien influence.[6] While the Pimas' condemnatory attitude is unusual, it does point out the importance of spiritual explanations for the acceptance of gender variance in a culture.

Other Native American creation stories stand in sharp contrast to the Pima explanation. A good example is the account of the Navajos, which presents women and men as equals. The Navajo origin tale is told as a story of five worlds. The first people were First Man and First Woman, who were created equally and at the same time. The first two worlds that they lived in were bleak and unhappy, so they escaped to the third world. In the third world lived two twins, Turquoise Boy and White Shell Girl, who were the first berdaches. In the Navajo language the word for berdache is nadle, which means "changing one" or "one who is transformed." It is applied to hermaphrodites—those who are born with the genitals of both male and female—and also to "those who pretend to be nadle," who take on a social role that is distinct from either men or women.[7]

In the third world, First Man and First Woman began farming, with the help of the changing twins. One of the twins noticed some clay and, holding it in the palm of his/her hand, shaped it into the first pottery bowl. Then he/she formed a plate, a water dipper, and a pipe. The second twin observed some reeds and began to weave them, making the first basket. Together they shaped axes and grinding stones from rocks, and hoes from bone. All these new inventions made the people very happy.[8]

The message of this story is that humans are dependent for many good things on the inventiveness of nadle. Such individuals were present from the earliest eras of human existence, and their presence was never questioned. They were part of the natural order of the universe, with a special contribution to make.

Later on in the Navajo creation story, White Shell Girl entered the moon and became the Moon Bearer. Turquoise Boy, however, remained with the people. When First Man realized that Turquoise Boy could do all manner of women's work as well as women, all the men left the women and crossed a big river. The men hunted and planted crops. Turquoise Boy ground the corn, cooked the food, and weaved cloth for the men. Four years passed with the women and men separated, and the men were happy with the nadle. Later, however, the women wanted to learn how to grind corn from the nadle, and both the men and the women had decided that it was not good to continue living separately. So the women crossed the river and the people were reunited.[9]

They continued living happily in the third world, until one day a great flood began. The people ran to the highest mountaintop, but the water kept rising and they all feared they would be drowned. But just in time, the ever-inventive Turquoise Boy found a large reed. They climbed upward inside the tall hollow reed, and came out at the top into the fourth world. From there, White Shell Girl brought another reed, and they climbed again to the fifth world, which is the present world of the Navajos.[10]

These stories suggest that the very survival of humanity is dependent on the inventiveness of berdaches. With such a mythological belief system, it is no wonder that the Navajos held *nadle* in high regard. The concept of the *nadle* is well formulated in the creation story. As children were educated by these stories, and all Navajos believed in them, the high status accorded to gender variation was passed down from generation to generation. Such stories also provided instructions for *nadle* themselves to live by. A spiritual explanation guaranteed a special place for a person who was considered different but not deviant.

For American Indians, the important explanations of the world are spiritual ones. In their view, there is a deeper reality than the here-and-now. The real essence of wisdom occurs when one finally gives up trying to explain events in terms of "logic" and "reality." Many confusing aspects of existence can better be explained by actions of a multiplicity of spirits. Instead of a concept of a single god, there is an awareness of "that which we do not understand." In Lakota religion, for example, the term *Wakan Tanka* is often translated as "god." But a more proper translation, according to the medicine people who taught me, is "The Great Mystery."[11]

While rationality can explain much, there are limits to human capabilities of understanding. The English language is structured to account for cause and effect. For example, English speakers say, "It is raining," with the implication that there is a cause "it" that leads to rain. Many Indian languages, on the other hand, merely note what is most accurately translated as "raining" as an observable fact. Such an approach brings a freedom to stop worrying about causes of things, and merely to relax and accept that our human insights can go only so far. By not taking ourselves too seriously, or overinflating human importance, we can get beyond the logical world.

The emphasis of American Indian religions, then, is on the spiritual nature of all things. To understand the physical world, one must appreciate the underlying spiritual essence. Then one can begin to see that the physical is only a faint shadow, a partial reflection, of a supernatural and extrarational world. By the Indian view, everything that exists is spiritual. Every object—plants, rocks, water, air, the moon, animals, humans, the earth itself—has a spirit. The spirit of one thing (including a human) is not superior to the spirit of any other. Such a view promotes a sophisticated ecological awareness of the place that humans have in the larger environment. The function of religion is not to try to condemn or to change what exists, but to accept the realities of the world and to appreciate their contributions to life. Everything that exists has a purpose.[12]

One of the basic tenets of American Indian religion is the notion that everything in the universe is related. Nevertheless, things that exist are often seen as having a counterpart: sky and earth, plant and animal, water and fire. In all of these polarities, there exist mediators. The role of the mediator is to hold the polarities together, to keep the world from disintegrating. Polarities exist within human society also. The most important category within Indian society is gender. The notions of Woman and Man underlie much of social interaction and are comparable to the other major polarities. Women, with their nurturant qualities, are associated with the earth, while men are associated with the sky.

Women gatherers and farmers deal with plants (of the earth), while men hunters deal with animals.

The mediator between the polarities of woman and man, in the American Indian religious explanation, is a being that combines the elements of both genders. This might be a combination in a physical sense, as in the case of hermaphrodites. Many Native American religions accept this phenomenon in the same way that they accept other variations from the norm. But more important is their acceptance of the idea that gender can be combined in ways other than physical hermaphroditism. The physical aspects of a thing or a person, after all, are not nearly as important as its spirit. American Indians use the concept of a person's *spirit* in the way that other Americans use the concept of a person's *character*. Consequently, physical hermaphroditism is not necessary for the idea of gender mixing. A person's character, their spiritual essence, is the crucial thing.

## The Berdache's Spirit

Individuals who are physically normal might have the spirit of the other sex, might range somewhere between the two sexes, or might have a spirit that is distinct from either women or men. Whatever category they fall into, they are seen as being different from men. They are accepted spiritually as "Not Man." Whichever option is chosen, Indian religions offer spiritual explanations. Among the Arapahos of the Plains, berdaches are called *haxu'xan* and are seen to be that way as a result of a supernatural gift from birds or animals. Arapaho mythology recounts the story of Nih'a'ca, the first *haxu'xan*. He pretended to be a woman and married the mountain lion, a symbol for masculinity. The myth, as recorded by ethnographer Alfred Kroeber about 1900, recounted that "These people had the natural desire to become women, and as they grew up gradually became women. They gave up the desires of men. They were married to men. They had miraculous power and could do supernatural things. For instance, it was one of them that first made an intoxicant from rainwater."[13] Besides the theme of inventiveness, similar to the Navajo creation story, the berdache role is seen as a product of a "natural desire." Berdaches "gradually became women," which underscores the notion of woman as a social category rather than as a fixed biological entity. Physical biological sex is less important in gender classification than a person's desire—one's spirit.

The myths contain no prescriptions for trying to change berdaches who are acting out their desires of the heart. Like many other cultures' myths, the Zuni origin myths simply sanction the idea that gender can be transformed independently of biological sex.[14] Indeed, myths warn of dire consequences when interference with such a transformation is attempted. Prince Alexander Maximilian of the German state of Wied, traveling in the northern Plains in the 1830s, heard a myth about a warrior who once tried to force a berdache to avoid women's clothing. The berdache resisted, and the warrior shot him with an arrow. Immediately the berdache disappeared, and the warrior saw only a pile of stones with his arrow in them. Since then, the story concluded, no intelligent person would try to coerce a berdache.[15] Making the point even more directly, a Mandan myth told of an Indian who tried to force *mihdacke* (berdaches) to give up their distinctive dress and status, which led the spirits to punish many people with death. After that, no Mandans interfered with berdaches.[16]

With this kind of attitude, reinforced by myth and history, the aboriginal view accepts human diversity. The creation story of the Mohave of the Colorado River Valley speaks of a time when people were not sexually differentiated. From this perspective, it is easy to accept that certain individuals might combine elements of masculinity and femininity.[17] A respected Mohave elder, speaking in the 1930s, stated this viewpoint simply: "From the very beginning of the world it was meant that there should be [berdaches], just as it was instituted that there should be shamans. They were intended for that purpose."[18]

This elder also explained that a child's tendencies to become a berdache are apparent early, by about age nine to twelve, before the child reaches puberty: "That is the time when young persons become initiated into the functions of their sex. . . . None but young people will become berdaches as a rule."[19] Many tribes have a public ceremony that acknowledges the acceptance of berdache status. A Mohave shaman related the ceremony for his tribe: "When the child was about ten years old his relatives would begin discussing his strange ways. Some of them disliked it, but the more intelligent began envisaging an initiation ceremony." The relatives prepare for the ceremony without letting the boy know of it. It is meant to take him by surprise, to be both an initiation and a test of his true inclinations. People from various settlements are invited to attend. The family wants the community to see it and become accustomed to accepting the boy as an *alyha*.

On the day of the ceremony, the shaman explained, the boy is led into a circle: "If the boy showed a willingness to remain standing in the circle, exposed to the public eye, it was almost certain that he would go through with the ceremony. The singer, hidden behind the crowd, began singing the songs. As soon as the sound reached the boy he began to dance as women do." If the boy is unwilling to assume *alyha* status, he would refuse to dance. But if his character—his spirit—is *alyha*, "the song goes right to his heart and he will dance with much intensity. He cannot help it. After the fourth song he is proclaimed." After the ceremony, the boy is carefully bathed and receives a woman's skirt. He is then led back to the dance ground, dressed as an *alyha*, and announces his new feminine name to the crowd. After that he would resent being called by his old male name.[20]

Among the Yuman tribes of the Southwest, the transformation is marked by a social gathering, in which the berdache prepares a meal for the friends of the family.[21] Ethnographer Ruth Underhill, doing fieldwork among the Papago Indians in the early 1930s, wrote that berdaches were common among the Papago Indians, and were usually publicly acknowledged in childhood. She recounted that a boy's parents would test him if they noticed that he preferred female pursuits. The regular pattern, mentioned by many of Underhill's Papago informants, was to build a small brush enclosure. Inside the enclosure they placed a man's bow and arrows, and also a woman's basket. At the appointed time the boy was brought to the enclosure as the adults watched from outside. The boy was told to go inside the circle of brush. Once he was inside, the adults "set fire to the enclosure. They watched what he took with him as he ran out and if it was the basketry materials, they reconciled themselves to his being a berdache."[22]

What is important to recognize in all of these practices is that the assumption of a berdache role was not forced on the boy by others. While adults might have their suspicions, it was only when the child made the proper move that he was considered a berdache. By doing woman's dancing, preparing a meal, or taking the woman's basket he was making an important symbolic gesture. Indian children were not stupid, and they knew the implications of these ceremonies beforehand. A boy in the enclosure could have left without taking anything, or could have taken both the man's and the woman's tools. With the community standing by watching, he was well aware that his choice would mark his assumption of berdache status. Rather than being seen as an involuntary test of his reflexes, this ceremony may be interpreted as a definite statement by the child to take on the berdache role.

Indians do not see the assumption of berdache status, however, as a free will choice on the part of the boy. People felt that the boy was acting out his basic character. The Lakota shaman Lame Deer explained:

> They were not like other men, but the Great Spirit made them *winktes* and we accepted them as such. . . . We think that if a woman has two little ones growing inside her, if she is going to have twins, sometimes instead of giving birth to two babies they have formed up in her womb into just one, into a half-man/half-woman kind of being. . . . To us a man is what nature, or his dreams, make him. We accept him for what he wants to be. That's up to him. [23]

While most of the sources indicate that once a person becomes a berdache it is a lifelong status, directions from the spirits determine everything. In at least one documented case, concerning a nineteenth-century Klamath berdache named Lele'ks, he later had a supernatural experience that led him to leave the berdache role. At that time Lele'ks began dressing and acting like a man, then married women, and eventually became one of the most famous Klamath chiefs. [24] What is important is that both in assuming berdache status and in leaving it, supernatural dictate is the determining factor.

## Dreams and Visions

Many tribes see the berdache role as signifying an individual's proclivities as a dreamer and a visionary. Among the Papagos, for example, these qualities are accepted as a compelling gift from the supernatural world. [25] The Yumas also believe it is connected to dreaming. They see berdachism as a result of a child's dreams at the time of puberty. A dream about a particular mountain that is associated with transformation, or of the arrowweed, which they believe to be capable of changing its sex, symbolizes berdachism. By Yuma belief, a person who has a particularly acute capability for dreaming has the potential for transforming his mind. According to a Yuma elder in the 1920s, speaking about an *elxá*, "his mind was changed from male to female." [26]

A Yaqui berdache, born in northern Mexico in 1950, gained a reputation as a dreamer by the time he was nine years old. He has extremely vivid dreams, in which he takes on identities of other people or creatures. This dreaming ability is valued by his traditionalist family, who see it as a reflection of his spirituality. By the time he was twelve his position as a dreamer was formalized in the ceremony that awarded him his adult name. The translation of his name is First Star Before Light or Morning Star. It signifies the bringing of illumination. He is the precursor of light, the way to get the light, a guide through the darkness of ignorance. He does not provide the light itself (which is one's own realization of one's spiritual nature), but he helps others find the light that is individual to their own selves. He dreams for others, spiritually healing and sorting out a person's confusion. [27]

Some Indian groups in northern California have a ceremony similar to the Papagos', in which the boy is placed in a brush enclosure that is set on fire, and then the people watch to see if he runs out with the man's tools or the woman's. Stephen Powers, a journalist who visited California Indians in 1871–72 and wrote a series of articles on them, reported this brushfire ceremony on the Round Valley reservation. He met a Yuki *i-wa-musp* ("man–woman"), and learned that the Pomo word for man–woman was *dass*. Powers pursued the topic in his interviews with the residents on the reservation.

> When questioned about it the Indians always seek to laugh the matter away; but when pressed for an explanation they generally reply that they do it because they wish to do it; or else with that mystifying circumlocution peculiar to the Indian, they answer with a long rigmarole . . . [that] the spirit moves them to do it, or, as an Indian would say, that he feels a burning in his heart which tells him to do it.[28]

The "long rigmarole" that Powers was so impatient to understand captures his informants' viewpoint exactly. In providing the Indians' words, Powers unwittingly furnished the Yuki explanation, in line with their view that people's character traits were directed by spiritual forces. These forces caused "a burning in his heart" which led an individual to become a man–woman.

The wide distribution of berdachism may indicate its antiquity. The Yuki explanation for berdachism seems to have prevailed among California Indians. Yokuts explained that their berdaches, *tongochim* or *tunosim*, were not delegated to their status, but entered it "in response to an irresistible call of their natures."[29] Other California tribes simply stated that berdaches were "made that way" from birth, "were born that way," or "acted upon a dream."[30]

Among the northern Plains and related Great Lakes tribes, the idea of supernatural dictate through dreaming—the vision quest—had its highest development. The goal of the vision quest is to try to get beyond the rational world by sensory deprivation and fasting. By depriving one's body of nourishment, the brain could escape from logical thought and connect with the higher reality of the supernatural. The person doing the quest simply sits and waits for a vision. But a vision might not come easily; the person might have to wait for days.

The best way that I can describe the process is to refer to my own vision quest, which I experienced when I was living on a Lakota reservation in 1982. After a long series of prayers and blessings, the shaman who had prepared me for the ceremony took me out to an isolated area where a sweat lodge had been set up for my quest. As I walked to the spot, I worried that I might not be able to stand it. Would I be overcome by hunger? Could I tolerate the thirst? What would I do if I had to go to the toilet? The shaman told me not to worry, that a whole group of holy people would be praying and singing for me while I was on my quest.

He had me remove my clothes, symbolizing my disconnection from the material world, and crawl into the sweat lodge. Before he left me I asked him, "What do I think about?" He said, "Do not think. Just pray for spiritual guidance." After a prayer he closed the flap tightly and I was left in total darkness. I still do not understand what happened to me during my vision quest, but during the day and a half that I was out there, I never once felt hungry or thirsty or the need to go to the toilet. What happened was an intensely personal experience that I cannot and do not wish to explain, a process of being that cannot be described in rational terms.

When the shaman came to get me at the end of my time, I actually resented having to end it. He did not need to ask if my vision quest were successful. He knew that it was even before seeing me, he explained, because he saw an eagle circling over me while I underwent the quest. He helped interpret the signs I had seen, then after more prayers and singing he led me back to the others. I felt relieved, cleansed, joyful, and serene. I had been through an experience that will be a part of my memories always.

If a vision quest could have such an effect on a person not even raised in Indian society, imagine its impact on a boy who from his earliest years had been waiting for the day when he could seek his vision. Gaining his spiritual power from his first vision, it would tell him what role to take in adult life. The vision might instruct him that he is going to be a great hunter, a craftsman, a warrior, or a shaman. Or it might tell him that he will be a berdache. Among the Lakotas, or Sioux, there are several symbols for various types of visions. A person becomes *wakan* (a sacred person) if she or he dreams of a bear, a wolf, thunder, a buffalo, a white buffalo calf, or Double Woman. Each dream results in a different gift, whether it is the power to cure illness or wounds, a promise of good hunting, or the exalted role of a *heyoka* (doing things backward).

A white buffalo calf is believed to be a berdache. If a person has a dream of the sacred Double Woman, this means that she or he will have the power to seduce men. Males who have a vision of Double Woman are presented with female tools. Taking such tools means that the male will become a berdache. The Lakota word *winkte* is composed of *win*, "woman," and *kte*, "would become."[31] A contemporary Lakota berdache explains, "To become a *winkte*, you have a medicine man put you up on the hill, to search for your vision. You can become a *winkte* if you truly are by nature. You see a vision of a the White Buffalo Calf Pipe. Sometimes it varies. A vision is like a scene in a movie."[32] Another way to become a *winkte* is to have a vision given by a *winkte* from the past.[33]

In other Plains tribes, berdache visions are often associated with a moon spirit, like Double Woman, whose changes symbolize transformation. In the Omaha language, the word for berdache is *mexoga* (also spelled *mixu-ga* or *mingu-ga*), meaning "instructed by the moon." James O. Dorsey, one of the first ethnographers to do field work on the Plains in the 1880s, described a berdache vision quest in detail. He reported that *mexoga* is considered sacred, because the Moon Being takes a special interest in him. When an Omaha boy sees the Moon Being on his vision quest, the spirit holds in one hand a man's bow and arrow and in the other a woman's pack strap. "When the youth tried to grasp the bow and arrows the Moon Being crossed his hands very quickly, and if the youth was not very careful he seized the pack strap instead of the bow and arrows, thereby fixing his lot in later life. In such a case he could not help acting the woman, speaking, dressing, and working just as Indian women used to do."[34] This type of vision, conferring high status because of instruction from the Moon spirit, was also reported by ethnographers who did fieldwork among the Winnebagos, Lakotas, Assiniboine, Pawnees, Mandans, and Hidatsas.[35]

By interpreting the result of the vision as being the work of a spirit, the vision quest frees the person from feeling responsible for his transformation. The person might even claim that the change was done against his will and without his control. Such a claim does not suggest a negative attitude about berdache status, because it is common for people to claim reluctance to fulfill their spiritual duty no matter what vision appears to them. Becoming any kind of sacred person involves taking on various social responsibilities and burdens.[36]

Hidatsa men expressed this reluctance. They believed that when a man looked at a coil of sweetgrass, the female spirit could "cause his mind to weaken so that he would have no relief until he 'changed his sex.' Often a man would tell of his experiences, how everywhere he looked he would see that coiled sweetgrass and how hard he was trying to keep from changing over." Of those who become berdaches, the other Indians would say that since he had been "claimed by a Holy Woman," nothing could be done about it. Such persons might be pitied because of the spiritual responsibilities they held, but they were treated as mysterious and holy, and were respected as benevolent people who assisted others in time of starvation.[37]

A story was told among the Lakotas in the 1880s of a boy who tried to resist following his vision from Double Woman. But according to Lakota informants "few men succeed in this effort after having taken the strap in the dream." Having rebelled against the instructions given him by the Moon Being, he committed suicide.[38] The moral of that story is that one should not resist spiritual guidance, because it will lead only to grief. In another case, an Omaha young man told of being addressed by a spirit as "daughter," whereupon he discovered that he was unconsciously using feminine styles of speech. He tried to use male speech patterns, but could not. As a result of this vision, when he returned to his people he resolved himself to dress as a woman.[39] Such stories function to justify personal peculiarities as due to a fate over which the individual has no control.

Despite the usual pattern in Indian societies of using ridicule to enforce conformity, receiving instructions from a vision inhibits others from trying to change the berdache. Ritual explanation provides a way out. It also excuses the community from worrying about the cause of that person's difference, or the feeling that it is society's duty to try to change him.[40] Native American religions, above all else, encourage a basic respect for nature. If nature makes a person different, many Indians conclude, a mere human should not undertake to counter this spiritual dictate. Someone who is "unusual" can be accommodated without being stigmatized as "abnormal." Berdachism is thus not alien or threatening; it is a reflection of spirituality.

# Reading Questions

1. What aspects of Christianity cannot comprehend the relationship between berdachism and spirituality?

2. How do various Native American creation stories that William relates depend on gender categories for their spiritual sense?

3. How do Native American gender polarities and their mediators resemble the spiritual polarities in the rest of their cosmologies?

4. Why does Williams assert that for the berdaches, men and women are not distinguished biologically, but rather spiritually? How is his usage of the term *spiritual* different from *social*?

5. What, according to Williams, is the significance of Native American communal initiation ceremonies for boys' adaptations of the berdache role?

6. How does the Native American understanding of fate seem different from Eurocentric views of causality, where the issue of sexuality is concerned?

## Recommended Reading

Paula Gunn Allen (Laguna Pueblo/Lakota), "Hwame, Koshkalaka, and the Rest: Lesbians in American Indian Cultures," The Sacred Hoop: Recovering the Feminine in American Indian Traditions (Boston: Beacon Press, 1992)

Brant, Beth (Mohawk), ed., A Gathering of Spirit. (Rockland, ME: Sinister Wisdom Books, 1984)

Jamake Highwater, Myth and Sexuality (New York: NAL Books, 1990)

Kenneth Lincoln, Native American Renaissance (Berkeley: University of California Press, 1983)

James W. Messerschmidt, The Trial of Leonard Peltier (Boston: South End Press, 1983)

Will Roscoe, ed., Living the Spirit: A Gay American Indian Anthology (New York: St. Martin's Press, 1988)

Dennis Tedlock and Barbara Tedlock, eds., Teachings from the American Earth: Indian Religion and Philosophy (New York: Liveright, 1975)

Harriet Whitehead, "The Bow and the Burden Strap: A New Look at Institutionalized Homosexuality in Native North America," Sexual Meanings, eds. Sherry Ortner and Harriet Whitehead (Cambridge: Cambridge University Press, 1981): 80–115

Walter L. Williams, The Spirit and the Flesh: Sexual Diversity in American Indian Culture (Boston: Beacon Press, 1986)

## Recommended Audiovisual Resources

Incident at Oglala. 1992. Directed by Michael Apted. Documentary of Leonard Peltier's arrest and incarceration. Live Home Video.

Honorable Nations: The Seneca's Land Rights. 1993. Directed by Chana Gzit and David Steward. Archival footage and interviews chronicle the story of the landmark agreement of $60 million in reparation by the Federal government to the Senecas. Filmakers Library.

Adventures in the Gender Trade: A Case for Diversity. 1994. Produced by Susan Marenco. This documentary presents Kate Bornstein's frank account of her personal journey from unhappy boy child to liberated transsexual lesbian. Academics include Dr. Walter Williams and anthropologist David Halperin of M.I.T., who encourage a reevaluation of the distinction between gender orientation and sexual pleasure. Filmakers Library.

# Fetishism and Hard Core

## Marx, Freud, and the "Money Shot"

### LINDA WILLIAMS

Linda Williams teaches women's studies and film at the University of California, Irvine. She is the author of Figures of Desire: A Theory and Analysis of Surrealist Film and Hard Core: Power, Pleasure, and the Frenzy of the Visible, from which this selection is taken.

There are those who believe that the come shot, or, as some refer to it, "the money shot," is the most important element in the movie and that everything else (if necessary) should be sacrificed at its expense.

Of course, this depends on the outlook of the producer, but one thing is for sure: if you don't have the come shots, you don't have a porno picture. Plan on at least ten separate come shots.

Stephen Ziplow, *The Film Maker's Guide to Pornography*

Stephen Ziplow's manual of advice for the frugal pornographer asserts what had by 1977 become the sine qua non of the hard-core feature-length narrative: the necessity of showing external ejaculation of the penis as the ultimate climax—the sense of an ending—for each heterosexual sex act represented. Where the earlier short, silent stag films occasionally included spectacles of external ejaculation (in some cases inadvertently), it was not until the early seventies, with the rise of the hard-core feature, that the money shot assumed the narrative function of signaling the climax of a genital event. Previously, hard-core sequences tended to be organized as discontinuous, relatively nonlinear moments of genital show in meat shots offering visual evidence of penetration.

Each shot—"meat" or "money"—is emblematic of the different "climax" of its generic form. Each shot seeks maximum visibility in its representation but encounters the limits of visibility of its particular form. The stag film, seeking to learn more about the "wonders of the unseen world," encounters its limits of visibility, as Gertrud Koch (forthcoming) notes, *ante portas* in penetration: for the male performer to penetrate the wonders is to make it nearly impossible for the viewer to see what is penetrated.

The money shot, however, succeeds in extending visibility to the next stage of representation of the heterosexual sex act: to the point of seeing climax. But this new visibility extends only to a knowledge of the hydraulics of male ejaculation, which, though certainly of interest, is a poor substitute for the knowledge of female wonders that the genre as a whole still seeks. The gynecological sense of that speculum that penetrates the female interior here really does give way to that of a self-reflecting mirror. While undeniably spectacular, the money shot is also hopelessly specular; it can only reflect back to the male gaze that purports to want knowledge of the woman's pleasure the man's own climax. This climax is now rendered in glorious Eastmancolor, sometimes even on a wide screen with optical or slowmotion effects, and accompanied by all the moans, groans, and cries, synchronized or post-synched, appropriate to such activity.

With all these changes, and especially with this late arrival of sound as a key element in the heightened explicitness of the genre, it is tempting to conclude that the feature-length pornographic film arrives at a truly realistic "hard core." In these films we seem to see not the representation of sex acts as such but, as the Meese Commission and others have put it, "sex itself," in living color and breathing sound. Yet we have only to read Ziplow's advice to porn producers and to observe with what regularity money shots are dispersed through hard-core films made in the decade after 1972 to realize the futility of assimilating hard core to a simple case of escalating verisimilitude. For obviously nothing could be more conventional than a money shot: like Diderot's speaking jewels, it is a rhetorical figure that permits the genre to speak in a certain way about sex.

The ultimate goal of the rest of this book [the book from which this reading is taken] is to determine how feature-length hard core "speaks" of sex. The present chapter will limit this discussion to the polysemic money shot alone and to the film by which that shot became best known, Gerard Damiano's *Deep Throat*. The goal here is to determine how best to understand both the form and the content of this most prevalent device of the new hard-core film's attempt to capture an involuntary confession of pleasure.

As a substitute for what cannot be seen, the money shot can be viewed as yet another form of cinematic perversion—as a fetish substitute for less visible but more "direct" instances of genital connection. As a shot whose name derives from mainstream film industry slang for the film image that costs the most money to produce (porn producers pay their male performers extra for it), the money shot can also be viewed as an ideal instance of commodity fetishism. Finally, as the most blatantly phallic of all hard-core film representations, the money shot can be viewed as the most representative instance of phallic power and pleasure. All three of these possible meanings—Marxian, Freudian, and feminist—will be explored below.

First, though, we need to backtrack in history and ask: through what process did stag films and their primitive successors in the adult arcades evolve into feature-length pornos? How did these films come to be exhibited in public theaters and then become even more widely available through over-the-counter purchase or rental to every VCR owner in the country?

. . . [P]artly as a result of legal battles over pornography, sexuality grew in social importance as a "vital problem" and "motive force" (Justice Brennan, quoted in Kendrick 1987, 201) of human existence while at the same time definitions of obscenity were (apparently) clarified and applied to specific texts. Paradoxically, however, as sexuality was increasingly politicized, simultaneous legal efforts to isolate and eradicate socially indigestible "cores" of obscenity proved difficult. The more a wide variety of medical, sexological, psychological, photographic, and juridical discourses constructed sex as a problem, the harder it was for any of them to isolate that part of sex which was an obscene "sex for sex's sake." In fact, . . . precisely because isolation of a pure, prurient pleasure proved difficult, a new definition of obscenity as abusive power began to emerge.

Try as one might to identify a pornography without "redeeming social importance," it was becoming increasingly clear that all sex was socially important. For although sex was biological and "natural," the gender system in which it resided was entirely social. As this recognition of social forces in the construction of sexuality began to be admitted, the proverbial "floodgates" of pornography opened. By the early 1970s a wide variety of sexual acts could be read about or viewed in illustrated sex manuals, in the various studies of Masters and Johnson, in contemporary fiction, in new and reissued pornographic "classics," and, finally, in legal, hard-core film.

Hard-core film's route to (relatively) mainstream legitimacy progressed via three stages, each of which extended the previous limits of legal exhibition. First, in the late 1950s and 1960s, came the so-called exploitation picture. Though not hard-core, these films capitalized on spectacles of sex or violence in quickly and cheaply made feature-length narratives publicly exhibited in legitimate, but often not very respectable, movie houses. On the sex side, exploitation pictures tended to be "nudie cuties." An early example was Russ Meyer's *The Immoral Mr. Teas* (1959), a film shot in four days for $24,000. The story concerns a peripatetic delivery man who, after a visit to a dentist, develops the ability—shared by the audience—to see normally dressed women in the nude. A well-known later example was the Swedish import *I Am Curious—Yellow* (1968). As Kenneth Turan and Stephen F. Zito (1974, 11) write in their account of the American pornographic movie industry, these exploitation films could turn a large profit on cheaply made productions simply by showing more "tits and ass" than mainstream film. In the aftermath of several late-sixties Supreme Court decisions, the theaters showing such films became the testing ground and, ultimately, the outlet for hard-core material once exclusive to the illegal stags.

But before hard-core stag-film elements were incorporated into feature-length exploitation films in the early 1970s, a second stage in the formation of the new genre was reached, exemplified by the so-called beaver film. A subgenre of the illegal stag, these very short loops showing women stripping to display their naked pubis were shown in peep-show arcades and sold through private mail order. Turan and Zito (pp. 85–86) report that sometime in 1967 a San Francisco exploitation theater exhibitor showed beaver films along with his regular fare and got away with it. The next step toward hard core was to show "split beaver" films—variations of the above adding the spreading of legs or labia to facilitate a better view—followed by the "action beaver," with "action" restricted to the woman herself or another woman fondling the genital area and sometimes simulating cunnilingus.

Action beavers pushed the outer limits of what constituted legality in public exhibition at that time. They showed no hard-core action, where "action" is significantly defined as penetration of any sort, even by finger or tongue. Though much less explicit than stag films available under-the-counter or in peep-show arcades, what was new in these movies, aside from their occasional color and sound, was the simple fact of their exhibition on large, legal, public screens. Exhibitors were sometimes prosecuted, but fines were minimal and the market for the product was growing. We might note here the genesis of a number that was to become a staple of many feature-length hard-core films: the so-called lesbian or girl/girl number. "Lesbian" activities were of course common in stag films, but at this transitional moment the action beavers showing lesbian "play" had the combined ability to display the female body to maximum advantage and to defeat the censors as well. With the appearance of these films, hard core was further delimited to the display of the erect penis and penetration alone.

But before stag, beaver, and exploitation film merged into new feature-length hard-core porno complete with sound, color, and an hour-long narrative, yet another cinematic form made its contribution. The first films to show hard-core material (now definitionally pared down) in public exploitation theaters were neither stag films nor expanded action beavers, but two documentaries about Denmark and its then-recent legalization of mass-produced visual pornography: *Sexual Freedom in Denmark* (John Lamb, 1970) and *Censorship in Denmark: A New Approach* (Alex de Renzy, 1970). Both films took immediate and clever advantage of the "redeeming social importance" clause of the 1966 Supreme Court rulings. Purporting to be (and in a sense they actually were) investigative documents of the new Danish permissiveness, the films reported on that country's pornography industry.

*Censorship in Denmark*, for example, begins as a travelogue of Copenhagen during a major sex-trade show, interviewing people on the streets, touring sex shops, and, in a gesture that incorporates action beaver conventions, documenting a live nightclub "lesbian" sex act entitled "Olga and Her Sex Circus." A hard-core porno actress is interviewed while naked, and we see scenes from one of her films, photographed off an actual theater screen. We also see the filming of a Danish hard-core film. In both films-within-the-film the long-withheld erect penis finally appears (the documentary may even suggest one reason for its belated arrival on the legitimate screen: the male actor on the set has difficulty sustaining his erection and must be helped by a woman with a vibrator). Although we see what the audience of both the live sex act and the screened film see, the film that we are watching fulfills its documentary (as opposed to "purely" prurient) function by showing us the socially significant content as well: the simple fact that Danish audiences can watch what Americans could not yet watch—though the exhibition of this "document" proved that we were quickly catching up.

Audiences who might never have gone to see a lesbian act on the stage, and who still could not legally see a hard-core pornographic film in a theater, could, if they wanted, justify seeing this film as part of a quest for knowledge about the sexual mores of a different culture. The new wave of visual pornography of the late sixties and early seventies was thus never intended simply to celebrate a sexual permissiveness "liberated" by the American sexual revolution; it was at least partly linked, as this revolution was itself linked, to a quest for greater knowledge about sexuality.

It is easy to make light of the sincerity of this quest. Certainly the early films spawned by this confluence of forces—films such as *Case Histories from Krafft-Ebing* (Dakota Bros., 1971); compilation films like Alex de Renzy's *History of the Blue Movie* (1970), which turned a studious eye on the stag film; massage parlor "exposés" such as *Rabin's Revenge* (Mitchell Bros., 1971); or behind-the-scenes "reports" on exploitation film directors like *The Casting Call* (Gentlemen II Prod., 1970)—could hardly be taken seriously as advancing scientific knowledge of sexual practices. Yet as these early titles suggest, there is in fact no separating "sex for sex's sake" from the quest for knowledge of sex being undertaken by investigators into the *scientia sexualis* (Foucault 1978, 57–58).

In the transition from illicit stag films to the legal, fictional narratives that burst on the public consciousness in 1972 with *Deep Throat*, then, a scientific "discourse of sexuality" purporting to elicit a confession of further "truths" of sex once again played a major role. By 1972 hard-core pornography had become a household word, growing even more familiar through shortening to "porn" and "porno." For the first time cinematic works containing hard-core action were reviewed by the entertainment media and viewed by a wide spectrum of the population, including, most significantly, women. Performers and directors were named and became "known." Although *Deep Throat* was undoubtedly the best-known title, other films of 1972, such as *Behind the Green Door* (Mitchell Bros.) and *The Devil in Miss Jones* (Damiano), were also well known. As for *Deep Throat*, "not to have seen it," said Nora Ephron, writing for *Esquire*, "seemed somehow . . . derelict" (quoted in Smith 1973, 721).

*Deep Throat* opened in the summer of 1972 in a typical exploitation theater, the New Mature World Theater in Times Square. Richard Smith (1973, 8–9) describes the theater as a typical "grind house" of the neighborhood, catering to what came to be called the "raincoat brigade"—furtive, middle-aged men who went to see the exploitation fare, the beaver films, and whatever else was becoming legal on the big screen in the late sixties and early seventies, and so named for their presumed masturbatory activity under raincoats. Had *Deep Throat* attracted the attention of only this relatively small, but loyal, audience, no one would have remembered it, even despite, I would suggest, its "deep throat" gimmick.

What was memorable in *Deep Throat* was precisely what most people disparaged about it: its "threadbare," "poor excuse" for a plot. Yet in concentrating on this defect vis-à-vis other forms of narrative, critics missed the more important fact that the film had a plot at all, and a coherent one to boot, with the actions of characters more or less plausibly motivated. For the first time in hard-core cinematic pornography a feature-length film— not a documentary or a pseudodocumentary, not a single-reel, silent stag film or the genital show of beaver films—managed to integrate a variety of sexual numbers (even more than the ten Ziplow advises) into a narrative that was shown in a legitimate theater.

Or almost legitimate, for *Deep Throat*'s theater owner was arrested twice for promoting obscenity. Cleaning Times Square of the likes of such films became a major issue in New

York's mayoral election of that year. The publicity, of course, only helped business. Like most of the previous book trials, the trial of *Deep Throat* enhanced the public's desire to see what censors would withhold: the latest revelations about sex. So even though the New Mature World Theater was ordered closed in March 1973, the film had already been seen in New York alone by over a quarter of a million people and had grossed over a million dollars.

The audience was clearly no longer the much-maligned "raincoat brigade," nor was attendance furtive. What brought the crowds was not what the critics said about the film—most panned it both as a film and as "eroticism"; rather, what counted was the mere fact that critics were talking about it at all. Among reviewers only Al Goldstein of *Screw* magazine gave the film a rave, calling it the "very best porno ever made" (quoted in Smith 1973, 31). Goldstein was perhaps one of the few critics positioned to look at the film in relation to its generic tradition. He saw what the legitimate critics, too shell-shocked by a first public encounter with phallic hard core, could not see: an unprecedented merger of extended narration and hard-core sex. He also saw deep-throat fellatio followed by a money shot, which seemed to him an affirmation of an organ that had been kept under wraps for far too long.

## The Money Shot

> Up and down, up and down, to the very depths of cosmic truth I saw that two-inches-short-of-a-foot-long cock engulfed like some soft vacuum cleaner taking vengeance on man for eons of past suckfuls. Then the climactic moment I was poised and ready for appeared! Hot white cum shot out and *Our Lady of the Lips* lapped it up. I was never so moved by any theatrical performance since stuttering through my own bar mitzvah. "Stupendous!" was all I could shout as I stood up and spent my applause on the glory that mine eyes had just seen.(Al Goldstein, quoted in Smith 1973, 32)

For the first time in the history of the American cinema, a penis central to the action of a story appeared "in action" on the big screen of a legitimate theater.[1] Goldstein seems fully identified with the penis that achieves this "climatic moment" for which he was poised: climax is the end of the story, the signal that it is time to "spend" his applause. Thus with the money shot we appear to arrive at what the cinematic will-to-knowledge had relentlessly pursued ever since photographer Eadweard Muybridge first threw the image of naked moving bodies on the screen of his lecture hall and ever since Thomas Edison ordered his technicians to photograph a sneeze: the visual evidence of the mechanical "truth" of bodily pleasure caught in involuntary spasm; the ultimate and uncontrollable—ultimate *because* uncontrollable—confession of sexual pleasure in the climax of orgasm.

At the same time, however, this confirming close-up of what is after all only *male* orgasm, this ultimate confessional moment of "truth," can also be seen as the very limit of the visual representation of sexual pleasure. For to show the quantifiable, material "truth" of his pleasure, the male pornographic film performer must withdraw from any tactile connection with the genitals or mouth of the woman so that the "spending" of his ejaculate is visible. With this convention, viewers are asked to believe that the sexual performers within the film *want* to shift from a tactile to a visual pleasure at the crucial moment of the male's orgasm. It is common conceit of much early-seventies hard-core pornography that the woman prefers the sight of the ejaculating penis or the external touch of the semen to the thrust of the penis inside her. She will frequently call for the money shot in the familiar "dirty talk" of the newly voiced genre, saying, for example, that she wants the man to "come all over her face," to see it come out of his "big hard cock," or to feel the hot substance spurt on some specific part of her body. Nevertheless, it is always quite evident that this spectacle is not really for her eyes. She may even close her eyes if the man comes on her face; and, try as she might, she cannot possibly see the ejaculate when he comes, as frequently he does, on her buttocks or the small of her back.

The man, in contrast, almost always sees himself ejaculate; the act seems much more clearly intended for his eyes and those of the viewer. The money shot is thus an obvious perversion—in the literal sense of the term, as a swerving away from more "direct" forms of genital engagement—of the tactile sexual connection. It substitutes for the relation between the actors the more solitary (and literally disconnected) visual pleasure of the male performer and the male viewer. Perhaps even more perverse—at least to female viewers, who can now, if they wish, see these films—is the genre's frequent insistence that his visual confession of a solitary male "truth" coincides with the orgasmic bliss of the female. Such is, of course, the conceit of *Deep Throat*: the placement of clitoris in the female protagonist's throat is a repositioning that aligns visible male orgasm with the face's power of expression.

I use the term *perversion* here in a neutral sense, as a swerving away from more direct forms of pleasure in general. It is fundamentally a way of describing the substitutive nature of the money shot. But it would be naive to expect such a loaded term to remain truly neutral. The money shot could be derided all too easily as a perversion of more "natural" heterosexual or even lesbian couplings. Feminists must thus be particularly careful when invoking *perversion* in this way, since the embrace of sexual technologies or practices that patriarchal interests have defined as perversions—such as abortion, contraception, lesbianism, and the sexology of the clitoris—have all had potential liberatory value for some women.

Gayatri Spivak (1981) has written in this regard that male orgasmic pleasure "normally" entails an element of the male reproductive function: it produces sperm. Female orgasmic pleasure, in contrast, does not necessarily entail any component of the female reproductive cycle—ovulation, fertilization, conception, gestation, or birth. Thus "the clitoris escapes reproductive framing."

> In legally defining woman as object of exchange in terms of reproduction, it is not only the womb that is literally appropriated, it is the clitoris as the signifier of the sexed subject that is effaced. All investigation into the definition of woman as legal object falls into varieties of the effacement of the clitoris.
>
> (Spivak 1981, 181)

While celebration of the clitoris thus might constitute one way to begin to challenge the power of a phallic economy of pleasure, it could do so only if the goal were not to set up an alternative organ of fetishistic worship but rather to dismantle the hierarchy of norm and deviation and so create a plurality of pleasures accepting of difference.

*Deep Throat*'s peculiar fetish, then, poses a special problem to feminists who want to challenge phallic power and pleasure without condemning it as perverse and without re-fetishizing woman's own organs in its place. Caught, as it were, between the devil of buying into (even if also reversing the terms of) a normative phallic sexuality, on the one hand, and the deep blue sea of embracing (potentially) liberating "perversions" on the other, we need to scrutinize carefully the structure of perversions that currently reign in feature-length pornography, as well as the theories that help explain them. What system of references do we invoke when we call the money shot a fetish? When we employ these references, are we thereby playing into a dichotomy of norm/deviation? What alternatives are available to us?

## The Marxian and Freudian Fetish

In a famous passage from *Capital*, Marx defines the commodity as a "mysterious thing" in which the "social character of men's labour" appears to be "stamped" on the very products of that labor. Through an extended analogy to vision that is especially appropriate to visual representation, Marx explains that just as "the light from an object is perceived by us not as the subjective excitation of our optic nerve, but as the objective form of something outside the eye itself," so we see the commodity as objectively possessing certain qualities. But whereas in the act of seeing there is "an actual passage of light from one thing to another," in the subjective perception of commodities, all is illusion. For in those commodities, the "social relation between men" assumes "the fantastic form of a relation between things." Marx finally finds his proper analogy in the "mist-enveloped regions of the religious world," where fetish objects of worship are "endowed with life" by the "productions of the human brain": "So it is in the world of commodities with the products of men's hands. This I call the Fetishism which attaches itself to the products of labour, so soon as they are produced as commodities, and which is therefore inseparable from the production of commodities" (Marx [1867] 1906, 83). To Marx, then, the fetish is a form of delusion whereby the workers who produce a commodity fail to recognize the product of their own labor.

In an equally famous passage written a half-century later (one that we have already had occasion to examine), Sigmund Freud, too, defines the fetish as a delusion: it is a substitute phallus created in the unconscious of a little boy who does not want to surrender the belief that his mother has a penis.

> He retains this belief but he also gives it up; during the conflict between the deadweight of the unwelcome perception and the force of the opposite wish, a compromise is constructed such as is only possible in the realm of unconscious modes of thought. . . . In the world of psychical reality the woman still has a penis in spite of all, but this penis is no longer the same as it once was. Something else . . . now absorbs all the interest which formerly belonged to the penis. But this interest undergoes yet another very strong reinforcement, because the horror of castration sets up a sort of permanent memorial to itself by creating this substitute. Aversion from the real female genitals, which is never lacking in any fetishist, also remains as an indelible stigma of the repression that has taken place. One can now see what the fetish achieves and how it is enabled to persist. It remains a token of triumph over the threat of castration and a safeguard against it.
>
> (Freud [1927] 1963, 153)

Although Marx and Freud define their fetishes very differently, they both share a common will to expose the processes by which individuals fall victim to an illusory belief in the exalted value of certain (fetish) objects. Thus both writers pose the illusion of the fetish object's intrinsic value against their own greater knowledge of the social-economic or psychic conditions that construct that illusion. For Marx in 1867, and for Freud in 1927, the term *fetish* already carried a conventional opprobrium inherited from eighteenth-century studies of primitive religion.[2]

The savages whom travelers in the 1700s saw bowing before crude, and often phallic, "stocks and stones" were not only, in their worship of graven images, disobeying one of the most important tenets of Protestantism, but they were also so blinded by the sensuous materiality of their fetishes that they forgot that it was they themselves who had invested these objects with value. In its original, religious definition, then, fetishism was understood as a delusion whereby the fetish makers worshiped their own constructions not simply as conventional human-produced *symbols* of supernatural power, but as the literal embodiment of that power. They gave up, in other words, their own productive powers.

In transposing earlier studies of religion, Marx and Freud share the insight that worshipers delude themselves into thinking that the fetish object has intrinsic value: the Marxian and Freudian fetishist locates illusory and compensatory pleasure and power in the gleam of gold or the lacy frill of an undergarment. In a sense, then, both theorists offer an economic application of what in the eighteenth century had originally been a critique of religion, Marx in the direct economic terms of the investment of labor, and Freud in the more indirect sense of psychic investment in a libidinal economy. For both, fetishization involves the construction of a substitute object to evade the complex realities of social or psychic relations.

Fetishes are thus short-term, short-sighted solutions to more fundamental problems of power and pleasure in social relations. For Freud, however, the illusory and compensatory belief in the fetish is a relatively minor perversion. He accepts as perceptual truth the "horror" and the "threat" of a castration objectively located in the "real female genitals," thus tending to sympathize with the fetishist's delusion. He does not, like Marx, condemn the delusion as savagery; rather, he universalizes it as part of the primary process of unconscious and infantile thought.

Where Freud normalizes the perversion, Marx rhetorically presses the point of a modern commodity-fetishistic savagery. For Marx the horror lies in the perversity of an exchange in which persons begin relating to each other as things, and things take on the social relations of persons (Marx [1867] 1906, 73; Mitchell 1986, 190). Marx is thus the theorist most inclined to employ *fetishism* as a term of old-fashioned, moralizing abuse. He forthrightly accuses all under the commodity's spell of being like the savages who have given up their very humanity to a thing.

Freud is more sympathetic. As the explorer of the human rationale behind the perversions, instead of the revolutionary who would overthrow them, he seems to accept the visual truth of what the fetishist sees when he looks at the woman's body. Freud thus shares some of the fetishist's belief in the "horror of castration" embodied in the female genitalia, unable himself to see beyond appearances to recognize how social relations of power have constructed him to so perceive women's genitals. Since Freud's scenario of vision asserts a self-evident perceptual "truth" of female lack, his very explanation originates in a fetishistic misrecognition of a sensuous, perceptual thing, followed by the creation of a compensatory substitute, the fetish. It is as if Freud trusts the fetishist's vision in initially judging women's sexual difference as lack but mistrusts the ability of the fetish to solve the problem of the "truth" it confronts. Hence, only in the second part of his analysis—when he disavows what he already knows to be true—does Freud not fall victim to the very process he is attempting to analyze.

Marx's explanation of commodity fetishism is, in contrast, more suspicious of sight from the outset. He looks critically at the physics of sight and at how we assume that sight originates in the object of vision when actually it is a "subjective excitation" of the optic nerve. Marx is then quick to point out that even this analogy is flawed, for while the act of seeing at least involves a relation, an actual passage of light from the object to the eye, no real relation obtains between the physical properties of commodities and the values that accrue to them. In looking at commodities we can never see the things themselves but only the value that has been stamped on them: the money they are worth rather than the social relations that have given them their value. We project the value of our own human labor onto the products of that labor.

Marx, then, sees a "horror" that lies not in the object of vision but in the subjective process of fetishization—in what happens to the idolater who fails to see his connection to other human producers and who therefore loses his own humanity as he invests inanimate objects with human attributes. Freud, too, sees an idolater who invests in an inanimate object, but this idolater retains his own humanity by turning the woman into an object even *before* he invests his desire in the substitute for her missing phallus. Thus for Freud there is an original moment of "true" vision that is horrified by the radical otherness of what it sees. For Marx, however, the reality of social and economic relations involves a dialectical process that does not lend itself to a single view. It is for this reason that a Marxian, political analysis of the prior *social* fact of the devaluation of women must always be factored into a discussion of the Freudian fetish.

## The Money Shot and *Deep Throat*

This comparison of the Marxian and Freudian fetish can help us to understand how commodity culture, sexual pleasure, and phallic subjectivity interpenetrate in the hard-core porno's money shot. As the industry's slang term for the moment the hard-core film "delivers the goods" of sexual pleasure, the money shot seems the perfect embodiment of the illusory and insubstantial "one-dimensional" "society of the spectacle" of advanced capitalism—that is, a society that consumes images even more avidly than it consumes objects (Marcuse 1964; Debord 1967).

But of course, it is in its connection to both ejaculate and money proper (that ultimate obscenity) that the money shot is most obviously a fetish. In combining money and sexual pleasure—those simultaneously valuable and dirty things—the money shot most perfectly embodies the profound alienation of contemporary consumer society. Marx's insight into the analogy between commodities and money on the one hand and the "stocks and stones" of religious fetishes on the other is that although both may conveniently represent human labor in a fixed and stable form, ultimately labor produces commodities that are the very means of relations of exchange and hence cannot be so fixed. When it *is* so fixed, then this very stability and representability operate to dissolve all sense of human connection and process. Thus money comes to be seen, as W.T.J. Mitchell (1986, 191–192) notes, not as "an 'imaginary' symbol of exchange-value, but as 'the direct incarnation of all human labor,' the 'embodiment' of value."

Once money takes on the function of representing the exchange value of an object, the process of commodity exchange splits, as F. W. Haug (1986, 32) observes, into the two isolated and antithetical components of sale and purchase. The consumer uses money to obtain use value, while the seller uses use value to extract exchange value in the form of money. The contradictory aims of consumer and producer very quickly create a situation in which it no longer matters what the actual use value of a commodity is so long as the commodity *appears* useful to the consumer. Thus very early in the development of capitalism, aesthetic illusion became an independent function of selling. Packaging and desirability, as opposed to proven usefulness, began to substitute for the tangible product.

What is most characteristic of late-capitalist fetishistic consumption, then, is that increasingly nothing tangible is purchased. We might compare the pleasure of viewing a contemporary porno film to the more straightforward exchange between prostitute and john, where the consumer does, at least momentarily, possess the "goods" (or, for that matter, to the early stag film, where the "goods" actually address the spectator as consumer and put on a show). The advantage (to capital) of this vicarious image-satisfaction is that the very insubstantiality of the use value purchased feeds back into the structure of needs, renewing the consumer's willingness to pay for that which will never be owned (Haug 1986, 55).

As Haug (p. 19) puts it, adapting Marx, "commodities borrow their aesthetic language from human courtship" and cast flirtatious glances at their buyers. The effect of such commodity courtship mediated by money is that "people are conditioned to enjoy that which betrays them," even when, like the fetishist, they know that their enjoyment is founded on an illusion (p. 53). In a postindustrial society, spending (it is said) is the key to a healthy, though inflated, economy. Perhaps in the money shot's repeatedly inflated, "spending" penis we can see condensed all the principles of late capitalism's pleasure-oriented consumer society: pleasure figured as an orgasm of spending; the fetish not simply as commodity but as the surplus value of orgasm.

But before we ourselves buy too far into the seductive attractions of this economic analogy, we should explore some of the sexual assumptions that lie beneath its surface—for there is something almost *too* phallic about this money shot. In the predominantly male-oriented economy of contemporary sexual pleasure, typically the *woman's* body has functioned as the fetish commodity, the surplus value, of pleasure. Steven Marcus was one of the first critics of pornography to note this fact when, in *The Other Victorians* (1974, viii–xiv), he wrote of the "exquisite" correspondence of the "unlimited female orgasmic capacity" and contemporary consumer society. The crucial link between "unlimited female orgasmic capacity"—the familiar image of the insatiable pornographic woman—and contemporary consumerism may thus seem more apt than the money shot as an emblem of mass-produced sexual fantasies, especially if this woman is masturbating, as Marcus tells us she probably would be, "with the aid of a mechanical-electrical instrument" (p. xiv)—yet another commodity fetish.

The passage just quoted occurs in an updated introduction to Marcus's 1966 study of nineteenth-century Victorian pornography and represents the author's attempt to acknowledge the prevalence of the new (film) pornography that seems almost too perfectly to realize the genre's goals of sexual abundance. Although Marcus is no fan of pornography in general, he recognizes its function of fantasy wish-fulfillment in nineteenth-century pornography, with its emphasis on male pleasure. In this single allusion to modern film pornography, however, Marcus implies that the twentieth-century image of a masturbating woman can be interpreted as the very symbol of alienated consumer culture: a glut of the senses. He thus abandons in this instance his theory of pornography as Freudian wish-fulfillment acting out abundance where really there is scarcity, in favor of a (more Marxist) reading of the pornographic body as directly *reflecting* the alienated conditions of its economic base.

In nineteenth-century pornography the fantasy is the reverse of reality: "all men are infinitely rich in substance, all men are limitlessly endowed with that universal fluid currency which can be spent without loss" (Marcus 1974, 22). In the twentieth century the fantasy, for Marcus, has become the horrible truth of a newly discovered female orgasmic potential. Marcus may be right in observing that a fundamental shift occurs in the representation of sexual pleasure from the nineteenth to the twentieth century. He may also be right in suggesting that this shift is related to changes in the dominant economic modes of production and consumption in these periods, and to the male and female models of sexuality that attach to these modes.

Marcus invokes a curious double standard, however, when he offers a utopian model of nineteenth-century (male-economic) pornography, or "pornotopia," and a realistically reflective, dystopian model of twentieth-century (female-economic) pornography. Here we can glimpse some of the past pitfalls of invoking Marx and Freud in the pornographic critique. This characterization of a nineteenth-century, male-oriented pornography as active utopian longing and a twentieth-century, female-oriented pornography as a passive glut of the senses reflective of an insatiable society of consumption dramatizes the difficulty of bringing economics and psychoanalysis to bear on the history of sexual representations. Like Freud, and like the pornography he discusses, Marcus offers a dramatic illustration of the inability of a phallic visual economy to imagine female pleasure as anything but either insufficiency or excess.

Nonetheless, Marcus's attempt to characterize the change in pornography—from literary to film, from male pleasure to female pleasure—remains instructive. The image of the masturbatory female haunts a great deal of pornography; but the masturbatory female using an electrical-mechanical instrument and in no dire need of a man to satisfy her is new. This woman is simultaneously insatiable *and* satisfied, capable both of continuing her pleasure indefinitely and of satisfying herself through her own efforts at clitoral stimulation. Writing in the wake of Masters and Johnson and *Deep Throat*, and just before Shere Hite's 1976 report documenting the masturbatory experiences of women, Marcus seems to resist the new concern with the quantitative and qualitative difference of female sexuality.

This difference is, indeed, what the story of *Deep Throat* is all about. For all its silliness and obvious misogyny, this movie attempts to perceive the different "truth" of women's pleasure in ways unparalleled in previous film pornography. The movie's numerous money shots are posed as the answer to the female protagonist's dissatisfaction with her previous experiments of sex. The story is this: a young "swinging single" named Linda (played by Linda Lovelace) confesses to a more experienced woman friend that she finds sex pleasant—"a lot of little tingles"—but not earthshakingly orgasmic—no "bells ringing, dams bursting, or bombs going off." "Experiments" with numerous men in a variety of numbers confirm this fact. The emphasis in these experiments, it should be noted, is primarily on "meat" rather than "money."

We can already note an important difference between this scenario and that of the stag film. Whereas the one-reel stag gets down to its sexual business very quickly, assuming that the act (or show) of sex is significant or fulfilling in its own right, *Deep Throat* is typical of the new wave of post-1972 narrative hard core in that it problematizes satisfaction itself. For the difficulty that Linda confesses at the film's beginning is not the peccadillo of transgressive sexual adventure, as in *Les bijoux indiscrets*, but a much more shameful crime: the failure to find absolute fulfillment in these adventures.

The film thus begins with a premise that is quite rare in the stag film—the idea that sexual pleasure is not the same for everyone or, as Linda's older and wiser female friend puts it, the need for "diff'rent strokes for diff'rent folks." This well-known seventies cliché is an apt description of the new ethic of hard-core film, which sees itself as welcoming and encouraging a greater variety of sexual practice than could ever be represented in the short stag film. In the film's narrative the discovery of Linda's anatomical difference seems to stand symbolically for a male perception of the different sexual pleasure of women in general. This difference then becomes the motive for further experimentation.

Experimentation takes place under the auspices of therapy—yet another seventies cliché. In a clinical examination that involves a telescope in place of a speculum, Linda's sexologist doctor (the ubiquitous Harry Reems) informs her that she is different: she doesn't "have one." In a phallogocentric misunderstanding that Luce Irigaray would appreciate, Linda responds: "I'm a woman, I'm not supposed to have one." What is at stake in this film, however—and, I would argue, in much feature-length pornography of this period—is precisely the extent to which Irigaray's notion of the phallic "one" can be used to figure and then fix the "two" (or more) of feminine difference.

When the doctor finally locates Linda's clitoris in her throat, he reassures her that having "one" there is better than having "none at all." Her concern is with the freak status this lends her—"What if your balls were in your ears!" (His answer, "Then I could hear myself coming," is in keeping with the male obsession with measurable evidence of pleasure.) Physiotherapy soon comes to the rescue and, with much practice, beginning on the doctor himself, Linda learns the "deep throat" technique that leads to a climactic money shot—narratively presented as simultaneous with Linda's own long-awaited climax—that is enhanced by intercutting with fireworks, ringing bells, bursting bombs, and firing missiles.

The deep throat gimmick thus works to naturalize what in the stag film had always been the most photogenic of all sexual practices: fellatio. Fellatio—culminating in a money shot in which ejaculation occurs on the woman's face and mouth—becomes, in the wake of *Deep Throat's* enormous popularity, the privileged figure for the expression of climax and satisfaction (reaching, in fact, a kind of apotheosis in *Behind the Green Door*, made later that same year).

Satisfied for the first time in her life, Linda wants only to marry her doctor and be, as she says, his "slave." But the doctor has a more modern idea: she will become a physiotherapist. What follows is an extended parody of Masters and Johnson–style sex therapy in which Linda administers to various mildly kinky men while still undergoing "therapy" herself with the doctor. He soon lands in bed with a bandage around his exhausted penis, unable to meet her demands for more sex. Though comically treated, the specter of the insatiable woman has been shown to take its toll on more limited men. The final "gag" that ends the film "solves" this problem by introducing a bigger and better penis. In her work as a physiotherapist Linda encounters Wilbur, who likes to play the role of a sadistic burglar caught in the act of spying on her. Beneath this superficial kink, however, he is sweet and gentle, the man of her dreams. When he proposes to Linda, she insists that the man she marries must have a "nine-inch cock" to satisfy the demands of her "deep throat." Wilbur instantly calls the doctor, saying he is only four inches away from happiness. The doctor reassures him, and Wilbur turns to Linda with the news that his thirteen-inch penis can be cut down to any size she wants. Little Wilbur is thus her ideal man.

In just about every sense, *Deep Throat* can be said—for all its talk about the clitoris—visually to fetishize the penis. Yet as we have seen, the question of how to read this fetishization cannot be answered without recognizing the new importance of the clitoris. An oversimplistic feminist reading of this film might miss the sense in which the newly prominent clitoris has called for the money shot. It would only see the money shot as depriving women of "natural," organic pleasure by imposing on them the perversion not merely of fellatio, but of this particular degrading, gagging, "deep throat" variety. . . . Gloria Steinem (1986b, 275), for example, writes that Damiano, the film's director, invented a gimmick that was "second only to Freud's complete elimination of the clitoris as a proper source of female pleasure. . . . Though his physiological fiction about *one* woman was far less ambitious than Freud's fiction about *all* women, his porn movie had a whammo audiovisual impact; a teaching device that Freudian theory had lacked." Thus the "millions of women" whose boyfriends, husbands, or pimps took them to the film were taught how to please a man by the example of this humiliating obeisance to the fetish.

In Steinem's interpretation, the woman is cast as Marx's savage fetishist who bows down and surrenders her own "proper source of female pleasure" to the power and pleasure of the phallus. The repeated ejaculations onto her face could thus be read as visual proof of her objectification and humiliation. Although there is a smile on that face, we read in Linda Lovelace (Marchiano's) autobiography that this smile was a lie masking terror and pain, that she was a sex slave to the man who was her pimp and manager, and that her entire life at this time was, like the title of this autobiography, an ordeal (Lovelace and McGrady 1980).

While I am inclined to believe Marchiano's allegations that she was coerced off screen to perform inauthentic pleasures on screen, and while I do not question the importance for feminists to reject as inauthentic the pleasures of women portrayed in such films, I do question the notion, strongly implied in Steinem's argument, that the film and, indeed, all pornography repress a "proper" female pleasure. I would argue instead that even though *Deep Throat* elides the visual representation of Linda Lovelace's clitoris, and even though its money shot fetish operates, in Gayatri Spivak's words, to "efface" that organ, its narrative is constantly soliciting and trying to find a visual equivalent for the invisible moments of clitoral orgasm. So if on the one hand the film tries to efface sexual difference through a gimmick that renders the practice of fellatio more "natural," on the other hand this very effacement could be said to allegorize the problem of difference by actually giving it Linda Lovelace's face.

All of the film's solicitous concern for the location of the clitoris thus needs to be seen in the context of the relatively new prominence this organ has received in other forms of the *scientia sexualis*. This new knowledge views the clitoris precisely not as a diminished or absent version of the penis—as in Freud's account of the phallic economy of the one—but as a new economy not reducible to that one: an economy of the *many*, of "diff'rent strokes for diff'rent folks." Even though the film's fetishization of the phallus attempts to disavow difference at the moment of orgasm and to model that orgasm on a decidedly phallic model of "bursting bombs," and even though the woman is portrayed as dependent for her pleasure on the "one" of the man, a contradictory subtext of plurality and difference is also registered. The very fact that the expanded narrative of the new feature-length hard-core film parodically joins with the scientific, Masters and Johnson– style quest for the "truth" of woman's difference indicates how fully the woman's invisible and unquantifiable pleasure has now been brought into frame, onto the scene of the obscene.

The paradox of contemporary feature-length pornography and its fetish of the money shot might therefore be described as follows: it is the obsessive attempt of a phallic visual economy to represent and "fix" the exact moment of the sexual act's involuntary convulsion of pleasure. The money shot utterly fails to represent the satisfaction of desire as involving a desire for, or of, the other; it can only figure satisfaction as failing to do what masculine sexual ideology frequently claims that the man does to the woman: to occupy, penetrate, possess her. Thus the solipsistic withdrawal from the other to the self paradoxically constructs another "memorial to lack" right where we might most expect to see presence and fullness. It would be wrong, however, to repeat Freud's misrecognition and to call this lack "castration." We might more properly call it a lack of relation to the other, a lack of ability to imagine a relation to the other in anything but the phallic terms of self.

Even though the money shot offers perhaps the clearest example of the phallic economy's failure to recognize difference, we must realize that it has been posed as a solution precisely because that economy is more aware of sexual difference and varying pleasures than it was in previous pornography. So rather than compare the phallic economy invoked by *Deep Throat* with that of Freud, as Steinem does, we might do better to contrast them. In Freud, fetishization is an obvious way for the male subject to maintain the phallic economy of the one. As we saw earlier, the Freudian fetishist attempts to preserve his own humanity at the expense of stressing the freakish inhumanity—the "horror"—of the female other. *Deep Throat* does not simply repeat this objectification of the female other; or, rather, if it does repeat it, it so blatantly puts the reigning "phallocracy" on display that we can glimpse, in the univocal limitations of its economy of the one, possible elaborations of economies of the many.

Foucault (1978, 48) writes that along with the incitement to sexuality contained in the modern age's proliferating discourses on the subject comes an increasing tendency to identify and address many different specialized sexual practices and in that process to "implant" these perversions. However absurd it may seem, I think one might say that the perverse implantation of the clitoris in *Deep Throat* represents something more than simple horror at the freakishness of female sexual "lack." She represents a phallic economy's highly ambivalent and contradictory attempt to count beyond the number one, to recognize, as the proliferating discourses of sexuality take hold, that there can no longer be any such thing as a fixed sexuality—male, female, or otherwise—that now there are proliferating sexual*ities*. For if the "implantation of perversions" is, as Foucault says, an instrument *and* an effect of power, then as discourses of sexuality name, identify, and ultimately produce a bewildering array of pleasures and perversions, the very multiplicity of these pleasures and perversions inevitably works against the older idea of a single norm—an economy of the one—against which all else is measured.

# Fetishism

A fetish is indeed, as Marx said, "a mysterious thing." The lesson that feminism can draw from both Marx's and Freud's understanding of this mystery is to not fall back on the simple religious condemnation of fetishism as an illusory fraud perpetrated on the credulous. In an essay entitled "Women on the Market," Luce Irigaray offers an extended analysis of the analogy between the Marxian definition of value as predicated on exchange and the valuation of women's bodies created in the exchange of women by men. Even though women, like commodities, do have an intrinsic use value related to their reproductive function, she argues, it is in the process of placing two women in a quantifiable relation to a third term—whether gold or a phallus—that women lose their own bodily specificity and become, like the commodity, an abstract and undifferentiated "product of man's labor." Thus desire, in the context of exchange, "perverts" need, "but that perversion will be attributed to commodities (*marchandises*) and to their alleged relations." In fact, though, since these commodities have "no relationships except from the perspective of speculating third parties," woman-as-commodity exists both as a natural body with a *use value* and as a body with a socially constructed *exchange value* that mirrors masculine desire (Irigaray 1985, 177). As Gayle Rubin (1979, 176) has similarly noted in a classic essay that examines the Marxian and the Lévi-Straussian aspects of the exchange of women by men, this seemingly natural system, on which economics and kinship are both based, in the end keeps women from engaging in use and exchange among themselves.[3]

Irigaray's and Rubin's adaptations of Marxian economics help to explain why the contemporary pornographic film's fascination with female pleasure has such difficulty representing what this pleasure means to women. Without defining positively what woman's sexuality is, Irigaray suggests that it might be possible to recognize the existence of a nonunitary, plural economy of female pleasures. But to do so we would have to abandon the sort of either/or opposition posed by Freud, which speaks solely of the one and only phallic pleasure. The question is not one of a choice, as Freud insists, between an active, clitoral pleasure and a passive, vaginal one; rather, it concerns the additive combination of a "multiplicity of erogenous zones"—the clitoris *and* the vagina, the lips *and* the vulva, and so forth. Such lists enumerating the many locations of female pleasure help to break down the either/or, active/passive dichotomies that underlie phallic sexual economies.

In both the Marxian economic and the Freudian libidinal senses, then, the fetish of the hard-core money shot compensates for scarcity and loss. But in its Freudian sense this fetish is peculiarly literal: in place of the psychic compromise that invests pleasure in a relatively indifferent signifier (Freud's example is the young man for whom a certain "shine on the nose" of a woman was necessary to his sexual pleasure), the money shot offers a real penis substituting for the mythic phallus Freud's little boy fears to have lost. Indeed, these close-ups of remarkably long, perpetually hard, ejaculating penises might seem to be literal embodiments of this idealized fantasy phallus which Freud says we all—men and women—desire. The ejaculating penis of the money shot could, in this sense, be said to disavow castration by avoiding visual association with the woman's genitalia. This, after all, is the genius of *Deep Throat*'s gimmick. By placing the clitoris in Linda Lovelace's throat, the film constructs its narrative on the importance of this organ while at the same time never having to look at it. It is as if the male fetishistic imagination, at this point in the history of the genre's attempts to capture the hard-core "truth" of pleasure, could not countenance any vision of female difference when representing the orgasmic heights of its own pleasure.

In her perceptive essay "Blind Spot of an Old Dream of Symmetry," Irigaray argues that the male-signifying economy has an overcathexis of vision, a "rule" of visibility and "specularization," that can only theorize woman as absence, lack, nothingness. If men think women are castrated versions of themselves, she argues, it is because of a fundamental castration—"a hole"—in their own limited signifying economy that can envision woman's desire only as the desire for, and of, the penis (Irigaray 1986, 49).

The value of such an analysis is that it locates castration fear and fetishization where they really belong: in the self-perceived inadequacies of the body and mind of the male consumer of pornography. From the perspective of female empowerment, Irigaray's most hopeful pronouncement (p. 51) is that the phobia about the uncanny strangeness of the "nothing to be seen" of woman is actually the fear that she does not possess the envy the man presumes her to possess. The fear, in other words, is that she has desires different from his own.

Irigaray's main point is that men are *blind* to women: to their different and multiple sex organs. We might therefore say in response to the money shot that the solution to this blindness is not to celebrate or (in turn) fix a single visual emblem of woman's difference (as, for example, the clitoris), for this too would be to fetishize, to isolate organs from the dynamic relation of exchange within which they operate. The money shot could thus finally be viewed as that moment when the phallic male libidinal and material economy most falters, most reverts to an absolute and unitary standard of value. But the import of this statement should not be that pornography is hopelessly and monolithically phallic; instead it should be that pornography is insistently phallic *in this particular way, at this particular time*, because of pressures within its own discourse to represent the visual truth of female pleasures about which it knows very little. This phallicism, then, has risen at least partly in response to the clitoris that it cannot easily fix and frame.

Today, Stephen Ziplow's 1977 formulation of the generic law "if you don't have the come shots, you don't have a porno picture" (p. 34) has been placed in doubt; not all films . . . observe it. One day this law may be looked back on, like the convention in westerns of good guys in white hats and bad guys in black, as an archaism no longer viable in the representation of sexual pleasures. It is probably no mere coincidence that this partial waning of the money shot has occurred as more women have gotten involved in hard-core pornography, as both makers and viewers.[4] Irigaray (1985, 203) hopefully suggests, "Perhaps if the phallocracy that reigns everywhere is put unblushingly on display, a different sexual economy may become possible." Perhaps there is strategic value to a feminist scrutiny of pornography that seeks the seeds of a different sexual economy in the limitations and inadequacies of the reigning one. Perhaps also if women can begin to ask these questions of existing pornography we will be on a path that leads to the representation of sexual pleasures becoming grounded in an economy of abundance rather than scarcity, of many rather than one.

It is this dismantling of the very idea of the norm that I find most helpful for a feminist reading of, and defense against, contemporary film pornography. For if there is no such thing as a "natural" pleasure independent of its production in social discourse, then one effective strategy for women concerned with the abusive intersection of power and pleasure in pornography may be to begin to understand the contradictions within the genre's production of pleasure. Similarly, if power, as Foucault (1978, 92) says, is to be located in discourse, and if resistance to power is "a multiple field of force relations" rather than a single revolutionary point of opposition, then clearly reestablishment of an essential truth against which the illusion of the fetish will be measured would seem an ineffective way to resist the fetish's power, since to do so would only be to establish new, potentially repressive, norms—hardly a solution to the already repressive norm of the phallus.

The Marxian fetish of commodity capital, the Freudian fetish of castration disavowal, and their convergence in the money shot can be characterized as forms of repressive power. But we need to understand that this power is not instituted from on high. Thus the Marxian tradition of iconoclasm might not serve us in resisting this fetishization either, for if we become too iconoclastic, if our only goal is to smash the abnormal and perverse idols of mammon in order to destroy the false consciousness they engender, then we may fail to grasp, and effectively to combat, the real appeal of capitalist and patriarchal power and pleasure. At the same time, if we, like Freud, lend too much legitimacy to the supposedly universal causes that have created the need for the (phallic) fetish, then we are in danger of becoming rational fetishists ourselves—of normalizing and justifying the fetish function in the name of universal processes of desire that elide the existence of the female subject.

We must come back, therefore, to the question of the most effective feminist use of the notion of perversion. For since there can be no authentic, true, or normal position from which to resist the repression of the feminine as currently enacted in visual pornography, but only the hope of breaking out of the economy of the one, it seems to me that the most effective strategy is to embrace the liberatory potential contained in the very idea of an "implantation of perversions."

The example of *Deep Throat* can thus afford the following tentative conclusions. On the one hand, it is undeniable that the film attempts, through the visual domination of the money shot, to represent the climax of a heterosexual act in entirely phallic terms: the inflated, powerful penis producing evidence of its pleasure. On the other hand, the very fact that the film seems to require this escalated visual evidence of pleasure suggests an uneasiness, a lack of belief in the previous standard for representation of pleasure. In the stag film, female genital show, male erection, and penetration sufficed. Now, under the new challenge of a different clitoral pleasure and a new narrative elaboration of pleasure, a more detailed sequence is called for: erection, penetration, climax. But since greater detail only calls attention to the impossibility of representing the climax as experienced in the "wonders of the unseen world," the climax that is represented becomes a new figure of lack.

I have tried to show that the "lack" disavowed by the fetish is not a true lack but only a perception based on the prior social and economic devaluation of women. The fetish of the money shot typifies one solution offered by hard-core film to the perennial male problem of understanding woman's difference. Another lesson, though, is that such solutions are fraught with contradictions that may open up possible routes to the resistance of hegemonic sexual pleasures. . . .

# Reading Questions

1. What narrative function had the money shot begun to serve by 1977?
2. What explanation does Williams give for the opening of the proverbial floodgates of pornography by the early 1970s?
3. What are three stages by which mainstream legitimacy of the feature-length hard-core film proceeded? Why is *Deep Throat* memorable in this context?
4. How does Williams explain the money shot, epitomized in *Deep Throat*, to be the very limit of cinematic will-to-knowledge where sexual pleasure is concerned?
5. What is the major difference between the Marxist and Freudian understanding of the fetish? Why does Williams claim the political necessity of presupposing the Marxist account while applying Freud's account to hard core?
6. Why does Williams claim that feminism needs to take seriously the "implantation of perversions" as an instrument and an effect of power in its analysis of hard-core pornography?

# Recommended Reading

Alison Assiter and Avedon Carol, *Bad Girls and Dirty Pictures: The Challenge to Reclaim Feminism* (London: Pluto Press, 1993)

Laurie Bell, ed., *Good Girls, Bad Girls: Sex Trade Workers and Feminists Face to Face* (Toronto: Women's Press, 1987)

Edward De Grazia, *Girls Lean Back Everywhere: The Law of Obscenity and the Assault on Genius* (New York: Random, 1992)

F. Delacoste and P. Alexander, eds., *Sex Work: Writings by Women in the Sex Industry* (Pittsburgh: Cleiss Press, 1987)

Sigmund Freud, *Three Essays on the Theory of Sexuality,* trans. James Strachey (New York: Basic Books, 1975)

Sigmund Freud, "Female Sexuality," *The Standard Edition of the Complete Psychological Works* 21, ed. James Strachey (London: Hogarth, 1953–1974)

Catharine MacKinnon, *Feminism Unmodified* (Cambridge, MA: Harvard University Press, 1987)

Karl Marx, "The Fetishism of Commodities and the Secret Thereof," *Capital, Vol. 1: A Critical Analysis of Capitalist Production*, ed. Frederick Engels (New York: International Publishers, 1977)

Judith Walkowitz, *Prostitution and Victorian Society* (Cambridge: Cambridge University Press, 1980)

# Recommended Audiovisual Resources

*Note:* View at your own discretion.

*Patently Offensive: Porn Under Siege*. 1993. Produced by Harriet Koskoff. Balanced presentation and exclusive footage on all sides of the porn wars. Filmakers Library.

*We're Here Now: Prostitution*. 1984. Produced by Dawn Wieking for Family and Children's Service. Interviews seven women formerly "in the life." Filmakers Library.

*Pornography: The Double Message*. 1985. Produced by Canadian Broadcasting Corporation. Documentary exploring the effects of hard-core pornography in our society. Filmakers Library.

*Not a Love Story*. 1982. Directed by Bonnie Sherr Klein. Documentary presenting the feminist case against pornography. National Film Board of Canada.

# Crimes of War, Crimes of Peace

## CATHARINE A. MACKINNON

Catharine MacKinnon, a noted feminist legal scholar, teaches feminist legal theory at the University of Michigan. Among her books are *Feminism Unmodified: Discourse on Life and Law, Toward a Feminist Theory of the State,* and *Only Words.*

Where, after all, do universal human rights begin? In small places, close to home. . .

—Eleanor Roosevelt

## I

In reality begins principle. The loftiest legal abstractions, however strenuously empty of social specificity on the surface, are born of social life: amid the intercourse of particular groups, in the presumptive ease of the deciding classes, through the trauma of specific atrocities, at the expense of the silent and excluded, as a victory (usually compromised, often pyrrhic) for the powerless. Law does not grow by syllogistic compulsion; it is pushed by the social logic of domination and challenge to domination, forged in the interaction of change and resistance to change. It is not only in the common law that the life of the law is experience, not logic.[1] Behind all law is someone's story—someone whose blood, if you read closely, leaks through the lines. Text does not beget text; life does. The question—a question of politics and history and therefore law—is whose experience grounds what law.

Human rights principles are based on experience, but not that of women. It is not that women's human rights have not been violated. When women are violated like men who are otherwise like them—when women's arms and legs bleed when severed, when women are shot in pits and gassed in vans, when women's bodies are hidden at the bottom of abandoned mines, when women's skulls are sent from Auschwitz to Strasbourg for experiments—this is not recorded as the history of human rights atrocities to women. They are Argentinian or Honduran or Jewish. When things happen to women that also happen to men, like being beaten and disappeared and tortured to death, the fact that they happened to women is not counted in, or marked as, human suffering. When no war has been declared and still women are beaten by men with whom they are close, when wives disappear from supermarket parking lots, when prostitutes float up in rivers or turn up under piles of rags in abandoned buildings, this is overlooked entirely in the record of human suffering because the victims are women and it smells of sex. What happens to women is either too particular to be universal or too universal to be particular, meaning either too human to be female or too female to be human.

Women are violated in many ways that men are not, or rarely are; many of these violations are sexual and reproductive.[2] Ranging from objectification to killing,[3] from dehumanization and defilement to mutilation and torture to sexual murder, this abuse occurs in forms and settings and legal postures that overlap every recognized human rights convention but is addressed, effectively and as such, by none. What most often happens to women escapes the human rights net. Something—jurisdictional, evidentiary, substantive, customary, or habitual—is always wrong with it. Abuses of women as women rarely seem to fit what these laws and their enforcing bodies have in mind; the more abuses there are, the more they do not fit. Whether in war or in what is called peacetime, at home or abroad, in private or in public, by our side or the other side, man's inhumanity to woman is ignored.

Women's absence shapes human rights in substance and in form, effectively defining what a human and a right are. What does it mean to recognize a principle called human rights that does not really apply to the systemic and systematic violations of the dignity and integrity and security and life of over half the human race? It means that what violates the dignity of others is dignity for them; what violates the integrity of others is integrity for them; what violates the security of others is as much security as they are going to get. Even death to a full human being is less serious for them. Half of humanity is thus effectively defined as nonhuman, subhuman, properly rightsless creatures, beings whose reality of violation, to the extent it is somehow female, floats beneath international legal space.

For a compressed illustration of some current realities that are at once a hair's breadth and a gendered light-year away from the atrocities that ground human rights principles and fill the factual reports of Amnesty International,[4] consider this communication from an American researcher of Bosnian and Croatian descent gathering information in Croatia and Bosnia-Herzegovina:

> Serbian forces have exterminated over 200,000 Croatians and Muslims thus far in an operation they've coined "ethnic cleansing." In this genocide, in Bosnia-Herzegovina alone over 30,000 Muslim and Croatian girls and women are pregnant from mass rape. Of the 100 Serbian-run concentration camps, about 20 are solely rape/death camps for Muslim and Croatian women and children. . . . [There are] news reports and pictures here of Serbian tanks plastered with pornography . . . [and reports that those who] catch the eye of the men looking at the pornography are killed. . . . Some massacres in villages as well as rapes and/or executions in camps are being videotaped as they're happening. One Croatian woman described being tortured by electric-shocks and gang-raped in a camp by Serbian men dressed in Croatian uniforms who filmed the rapes and forced her to "confess" on film that Croatians raped her. In the streets of Zagreb, UN troops often ask local women how much they cost. . . . There are reports of refugee women being forced to sexually service them to receive aid. . . . Tomorrow I talk to two survivors of mass rape, thirty men per day for over three months. . . . The UN passed a resolution to collect evidence, a first step for a war crimes trial, but it is said there is no precedent for trying sexual atrocities.[5]

Human rights were born in a cauldron, but it was not this one. Rape, forced motherhood, prostitution, pornography, and sexual murder, on the basis of sex and ethnicity together, have not been the horrors which so "outraged the conscience"[6] of the relevant legal world as to imprint themselves on the international legal order.

Formally illegal or not, as policy or merely as what is systematically done, practices of sexual and reproductive abuse occur not only in wartime but also on a daily basis in one form or another in every country in the world. Under domestic and international law, whether or not prohibited on their face, these practices are widely permitted as the liberties of their perpetrators, understood as excesses of passion of spoils or victory, legally rationalized or officially winked at or formally condoned.[7] Even where international instruments could be interpreted to prohibit such practices, it is telling that their cultural supports are more likely to provide the basis for exempting states from their reach than the foundation for a claim of sex discriminations.[8]

The war against Croatia and Bosnia-Herzegovina exemplifies how existing approaches to human rights can work to cover up and confuse who is doing what to whom and effectively condone atrocities. All state parties are apparently covered by most of the relevant international human rights guarantees and laws of war, certainly by customary international law.[9] But nothing has yet been invoked to stop the abuses described in the communication or to hold the perpetrators accountable.[10] What is the problem? The fact of Serbian aggression is beyond question, just as the fact of male aggression against women is beyond question, here and everywhere. "Ethnic cleansing" is a Serbian policy of extermination of non-Serbs with the goal of "all Serbs in one nation," a "Greater Serbia" encompassing what was called Yugoslavia.[11] "Ethnic cleansing" is a euphemism for genocide. Yet this genocidal war of aggression has repeatedly been construed as bilateral, a civil war or an ethnic conflict, to the accompaniment of much international wonderment that people cannot get along and pious clucking at the behavior of "all sides"[12] in a manner reminiscent of blaming women for getting themselves raped by men they know. To call this a civil war is like calling the Holocaust a civil war between German Aryans and German Jews.

One result of this equalization of aggressor with aggressed-against is that these rapes are not grasped either as a strategy in genocide or as a practice of misogyny, far less as both at once, continuous at once with *this* ethnic war of aggression and *the* gendered war of aggression of everyday life. This war is to everyday rape what the Holocaust was to everyday anti-Semitism. Muslim and Croatian women and girls are raped, then murdered, by Serbian military men, regulars and irregulars, in their homes, in rape/death camps, on hillsides, everywhere. Their corpses are often raped as well.[13] When this is noticed, it is either as genocide or as rape, or as femicide but not genocide, but not as rape as a form of genocide directed specifically at women. It is seen either as part of a campaign of Serbia against non-Serbia or an onslaught by combatants against civilians, but not an attack by men against women. Or, in the feminist whitewash, it becomes just another instance of aggression by all men against all women all the time, rather than what it is, which is rape by certain men against certain women. The point seems to be to obscure, by any means available, exactly who is doing what to whom and why.[14]

When the women survive, the rapes tend to be regarded as an inevitability of armed conflict, part of the war of all against all, or as a continuation of the hostilities of civil life, of all men against all women. Rape *does* occur in war among and between all sides; rape is a daily act by men against women and is always an act of domination by men over women. But the fact that these rapes are part of an ethnic war of extermination, being misrepresented as a civil war among equal aggressors,[15] means that Muslim and Croatian women are facing twice as many rapists with twice as many excuses, two layers of men on top of them rather than one, and two layers of impunity serving to justify the rapes: just war and just life.

Like all rapes, these rapes are particular as well as generic, and the particularity matters. This is ethnic rape as an official policy of war:[16] not only a policy of the pleasure of male power unleashed; not only a policy to defile, torture, humiliate, degrade, and demoralize the other side; not only a policy of men posturing to gain advantage and ground over other men. It is rape under orders: not out of control, under control. It is rape unto death, rape as massacre, rape to kill or make the victims wish they were dead. It is rape as an instrument of forced exile, to make you leave your home and never come back. It is rape to be seen and heard by others, rape as spectacle. It is rape to shatter a people, to drive a wedge through a community. It is the rape of misogyny liberated by xenophobia and unleashed by official command.[17]

It is rape made sexy for the perpetrators by the defenselessness and youth of many of the victims and the rapists' absolute power to select victims at will. It is rape made more arousing by ethnic hostility against a designated enemy — "For Serbia" — and made to seem right by lies about the behavior of that enemy. It is rape made exciting by knowing that there are no limits on what can be done, that the women *can* be raped to death. Most of all, it is rape made sexually irresistible by the fact that the women *are* about to sacrificed, by the ultimate power of reducing a person to a corpse, by the powerlessness of the women and children in the face of their imminent murder at the hands of their rapist. It is murder as the ultimate sexual act. Do not say it is not sex for the men. When the men are told to take the women away and not bring them back, they rape them, *then* kill them, then sometimes rape them again, cut off their breasts, and rip out their wombs.[18] One woman was allowed to live so long as she kept her Serbian captor hard all night orally, night after night after night.[19]

This is rape as torture and rape as extermination. Some women who are not killed speak of wanting to take their own lives. It is at once mass rape and serial rape indistinguishable from prostitution. It is concentration camp as brothel: women impounded to be passed around by men among men.[20] It is also rape as a policy of ethnic uniformity and ethnic conquest, annexation and expansion, acquisition by one nation of others, colonization of women's bodies as colonization of the culture they symbolize and embody as well as of the territory they occupy. It is rape because a Serb wants your apartment. Most distinctively, it is rape for reproduction *as* ethnic liquidation: Croatian and Muslim women are raped to help make a Serbian state by making Serbian babies.[21]

This is ethnic rape. If this were racial rape, it would be pure pollution, the children regarded as dirty and contaminated: their mothers' babies, as in the American South under slavery, Black babies. Because it is ethnic rape, the children are regarded as clean and purified: their fathers' babies, Serbian babies, as clean as anyone with a woman's blood in them and on them can be. The idea seems to be to create a fifth column within Croatian and Muslim society, children (all sons?) who will rise up and join their fathers. Much Serbian ideology and practice takes a page from the Nazi book. Combining with it the archaic view that the sperm carries all the genetic material, the Serbs have achieved the ultimate racialization of culture, the (one hopes) final conclusion of Nazism: now culture is genetic.[22]

The spectacle of the United Nations troops violating the population they are supposed to protect adds a touch of the perverse. My correspondent observes that "there are . . . reports of UN troops participating in raping Muslim and Croatian women from the Serb rape/death camps. Their presence has apparently increased trafficking in women and girls through the opening of brothels, brothel-massage parlors, peep-shows, and the local production of pornographic films."[23] A former United Nations Protection Force (UN-

PROFOR) commander reportedly accepted offers from Serbian commanders to bring him Muslim girls from the camps for orgies.[24] This paradigmatic instance of the male bond across official lines pointedly poses, in the gender context, Juvenal's question of who shall guard the guardians—especially when the guardians are already there to guard the other guardians. The Nazis took pictures, but in its sophisticated employment of media technology, in the openness of its use of pornography, in its conscious making of pornography of its atrocities, this is perhaps the first truly modern war.[25]

Where do international human rights and humanitarian law stand on this? In real terms, the rules that govern the law's treatment of women elsewhere pertain here as well: A human is not one who is sexually and reproductively violated. One is not human "down there." Nor is a human right something a man in society or in a state of nature takes away from you and others like you. In fact, there are no others like you, because "a man" defines what "an individual" means, and human rights are mostly "individual" rights. Men have their human rights violated; rather, when someone's human rights are recognized as violated, he is probably a man. Men are permitted to be individuals, so can be violated as individuals. If you are hurt as a member of a group, the odds that the group will be considered human are improved if it includes men. Under guarantees of international human rights, as well as in everyday life, a woman is "not yet a name for a way of being human."[26]

A right, as this legal definition is lived in reality, becomes something no woman, as a member of the group women, has to lose. A right is also something only an entity with the power of a nation can violate; it is a duty of government not to interfere with civil and political liberties as they socially exist. The role of international law has been largely, in Isaiah Berlin's sense,[27] negative. It could be more, but it fosters human rights less through mandating governmental intervention than through enforcing governmental abstinence. In other words, if your human rights are going to be violated, pray it is by someone who looks like a government, and that he already acted, and acted wrong.

In Europe, some basis exists for interpreting international law to require that governments act; the affirmative state is more congenial to the European legal tradition in any case.[28] Sometimes international human rights law is stretched to countenance action against private violations, but this is pursued selectively. Honduras was held responsible for murders by private death squads that both acted as if they were official and were officially permitted to operate.[29] "Mainstream human rights groups have taken on the phenomenon of 'disappearances' in Argentina, murder of indigenous rubber tappers in Brazil, and racially-motivated hate crimes—all abuses perpetrated by private individuals," notes Lori Heise, "but when it comes to the beating and murder of millions of women each year, their hands are tied."[30]

Male reality has become human rights principle, or at least the principle governing human rights practice. Men have and take liberties as a function of their social power as men. Men have often needed state force to get away with subjecting other men; slavery, segregation in the United States, and Hitler's persecutions were explicitly legalized. So the model of human rights violation is based on state action. The result is, when men use their liberties socially to deprive women of theirs, it does not look like a human rights violation. But when men are deprived of theirs by governments, it does. The violations of the human rights of men better fit the paradigm of human rights violations because that paradigm has been based on the experiences of men.

In the case of women, by contrast, because male dominance is built into the social structure, social force is often enough. States collaborate elaborately, not just by abdicating social life but by intervening legally to entitle men to much of the power they socially exercise, legitimating what men can get away with in fact. Even recognizing active state involvement, most women are not directly raped, forcibly impregnated, and trafficked by state policy, at least not most of the time. Although the state in some way stands behind most of what men do to women, men typically have enough power to control and violate women without the state explicitly intervening to allow it. To this extent, women are not seen as subjected by the state as such, so their condition is regarded as prelegal, social hence natural, so outside international human rights accountability.

Now consider that most human rights instruments empower states to act against states, rather than individuals or groups to act on their own behalf. Given that only state violations of human rights are recognized, this is very odd. States are the only ones recognized as violating human rights, yet states are also the only ones empowered to redress them. Not only are men's so-called "private" acts against women left out; power to act against public acts are left exclusively in the hands of those who commit those acts. No state effectively guarantees women's human rights within its borders. No state has an incentive to break ranks by setting a human rights standard for women's status and treatment that no state yet meets. Internationally, men's states protect each other the way men protect each other from accountability for violations of women within states. At least this is one explanation for the failure of international human rights law effectively to empower individuals or groups of women to enforce their own human rights against individuals and states alike.[31] Which state is in a position to challenge another state on women's human rights? Which state ever will?

Wartime is largely exceptional in that atrocities by soldiers against civilians are always state acts. But men do in war what they do in peace, only more so. When it comes to women, at least to civilian casualties, the complacency that surrounds peacetime extends to war, however the laws read. And the more a conflict can be framed as *within* a state, as a civil war, as social, as domestic, the less human rights are recognized as being violated.[32] In other words, the closer a fight comes to home, the more "feminized" the victims become no matter what their gender, and the less likely international human rights will be found to be violated, no matter what was done.

## II

The received concepts at work here have a complex history, mostly a Western one, which can be read and compressed as follows. The contractarian liberals, building on Greek and Roman antecedents, opposed medieval status notions that assigned human value within a rigid hierarchy based on birth. Seeking to secure human freedom against state tyranny, they posited the radical notion that each person, qua human, had, meaning had by nature, irrevocable and equal entitlements to life, liberty, security, dignity, property, and so on. Through the American and French revolutions, this idea of inalienable human worth called individual rights was entrenched, checking organized power in the form of government. Subsequently, some transnational agreements further elevated and enshrined the same recognitions as binding among state parties.

Then the Third Reich utterly violated all such rights—inter alia by manipulating the pre-1945 system which left minority protection exclusively to states[33]—isolating and then liquidating those it saw as inferior or polluting or oppositional. In particular, the official attempted extermination of the Jews as a people galvanized the notion of supranational guarantees of human rights with a survival urgency. This organized genocide by government policy indelibly marked and fundamentally shaped the content, priorities, sensitivities, and deep structure of the received law of human rights in our time. In a reading of this reality, more than any other, contemporary human rights finds its principled ground.

Largely beneath notice in this tradition has been the status of women as such, socially subordinated to men and excluded or ignored, marginalized or subjected by state policy. Women's enforced inequality has been a reality on which all these systems are materially predicated, so seamlessly it has been invisible. Women were not citizens in Greek democracy; they were wives, slaves, prostitutes.[34] In this setting, Aristotle formulated his equality principle as treating likes alike and unlikes unalike—a concept fundamentally unquestioned since, including in the international human rights context. In this approach, it does not matter whether one is hurt or helped, permitted to dominate or kept subordinated; all that matters is that empirical condition, no matter how created, fits normative treatment.[35] That women were apparently so different to Aristotle as not to be treated unequally under his principle when excluded from citizenship has not been considered a drawback or an indication that something is amiss.

Building on this tradition, the original liberals formulated their social compacts in and for societies in which women could not even vote. With the exception of John Stuart Mill,[36] they did not see a problem in this, projecting their purportedly universal notions of what have come to be called human rights in ways that did not explicitly include women and effectively kept most women from access to them. Humans own property; women mostly cannot; more often they are property. Humans are equal because they can kill; women are socialized not to kill and are punished, not glorified, when they do. Humans consent to a regime or leave it; women have no voice to dissent, no place to go, and no means of leaving.[37] At the same time, guarantees women specifically need, due to sex inequality in society, in order to live to a standard defined as human—like freedom from being bought and sold as sexual chattel, autonomous economic means, reproductive control, personal security from intimate invasion, a credible voice in public life, a non-derivative place in the world—were not considered at all.

What women need for equality was not only not guaranteed; much of women's inequality was guaranteed in the form of men's individual civil liberties.[38] In these theories, abuses of women were tacitly if not explicitly condoned as individual rights. What were called individual rights have become, in life, rights of men as a group over women individually and as a class. Women's rape becomes men's liberty, gang rape their fraternity, prostitution their property, forced pregnancy their family and their privacy, pornography their speech. Put another way, whatever their rebellions accomplished for human freedom, and it was substantial, the American Revolution did not free the slaves, and the French Revolution did free the Marquis de Sade—facts connected by legitimating a traffic in human beings and the sexual abuse of women for economic gain. Understand: This is what the received concept of equality meant and largely still means.

Because women are a group whose claim to human status is tenuous and denied, the attempt to apply human rights law to women as such makes two more general problems worse. Human rights have no ground and no teeth. As to teeth, human rights are enforced internationally primarily between states, states that agree to them. Many, such as the United States, do not agree to many of them. Enforcement is mainly through reporting, meaning moral force, meaning effective nonenforcement. Signatory countries are even permitted formal excuse from compliance, a practice disproportionately used to evade sex equality provisions.[39] The covenants against trafficking in women, for example, are many and venerable,[40] yet the traffic continues unabated, untouched, flourishing. Thailand even traffics in women by policy.[41] China may officially force abortions and sterilizations,[42] yet nothing is done. Enforcement of human rights against states' lack of action and against private parties may be possible in principle but is virtually absent in practice. For women, international human rights presents the biggest gap between principle and practice in the known legal world.

Many existing international instruments guarantee sex equality.[43] Yet so little of women's experience of violation of human rights has been brought under them that it becomes necessary to inquire into the foundations of human rights to explain why. The primary foundation of human rights has been natural law, a secular religion that moves only those who believe in it. Its content tends to redescribe the social status quo and attribute it to nature. (Emphatic use of the existential verb to affirm loudly and often that women "are" human beings carries only the clout of its speaker's decibel level.) Positive law helps little more, since women have had little voice in its formulation in most places. Morality, an alternative ground, can be moving, but does not mean anyone has to do anything, as illustrated by the use of the phrase "moral victory" to refer to an actual defeat. All these grounds come down to social power in the end. If you have it, you can meet their tests for "human"; but power is exactly what women are socially denied, which is why their human rights can be violated and why they need them recognized.

At its philosophical foundations, the natural law tradition on which human rights remain primarily based has never been clear on whether women are men's natural equals. Rather, to oversimplify a complicated debate, it has been relatively clear that they are not, and has provided no method for resolving different conclusions, each equally firmly said to be predicated on the law of nature. Nor has it reconciled its observation that sex is a natural difference with its view that equality is predicated on natural identity. To those who ground human rights in the opportunity to live out one's life project rationally,[44] it should be pointed out that, socially speaking, women as women have not been permitted a life project[45] and are widely considered as not possessed of rationality, or of what passes for reason among men. Others ground human rights in basic personal liberty[46] or in fundamental human dignity,[47] the problem being that you already have to have them to have a human right violated when you are denied them. So, it's back to nature.

Mortimer Adler exemplifies rather than exposes this circularity: "If there are no natural rights, there are no human rights; if there are no human rights, there cannot be any crimes against humanity."[48] Women's problem has been that society and law do not agree that nature made them human, so nothing that is done to them is a crime against humanity, because they have none. If society gives you no rights, such that a state need never deny them to keep you from having them, it may do you little good to have them formally guaranteed in international law. Free of this essentialist circularity, the task is to ground a claim to crimes against humanity clear of natural rights, which are not recognized to exist in nature unless they are recognized to exist in society. In other words, all discourse about nature is a social discourse.

Horror at the Holocaust grounds modern morality. No one knows what is good, but nearly everyone knows the Holocaust was evil. We may not know what human is; but the Holocaust was inhuman. Jewish women were distinctively abused in ways that connect to anti-Semitic misogyny to this day and startlingly resemble the tortures of Croatian and Muslim women by Serbs. The horrific tortures and extermination of millions of Jews of both sexes because they were Jews has overshadowed everything then and since.

Considered in terms of equality theory, the Third Reich can be seen to follow an unbroken line from Aristotle through American segregation of treating "likes alike and unlikes unalike"—Jews having been rendered "unlike" Aryans.[49] Yet human rights law still uses the same equality concept, without reassessment. The dominant lesson that seems to have been learned is that Jews could be and were annihilated because they were "different," not that something is wrong with an equality standard that permits extermination for "differences." The Jews failed the equality test—not the equality test failed the Jews. Not that a better equality theory would have stopped Hitler. But what is one to make of an equality principle apparently logically consistent with, and undisturbed by, genocide? If equality's abstractions are so receptive to Nazi substance, are they perhaps a flawed vehicle for social justice? The fact that international law pervasively guarantees sex equality, yet there is no sex equality, while mass rape and forced childbearing go on both in peacetime and in war, including in genocidal war, suddenly begins to makes sense.

## III

> [T]he refusal to demand . . . one absolute standard of human dignity is the greatest triumph of antifeminism over the will to liberation. . . . A universal standard of human dignity is the only principle that completely repudiates sex–class exploitation and also propels all of us into a future where the fundamental political question is the quality of life for all human beings.
>
> —Andrea Dworkin[50]

One approach to this problem might be to interpret existing international sex equality guarantees as grounded in the global women's movement against sex inequality, including sexual and reproductive abuses, and apply the resulting concepts in peace and in war. A right to equality, both as a right in itself and as a basis for equal access to other rights, would ground its definition of inequality, and by implication its concept of the human, in the universal—meaning worldwide and everywhere spontaneously indigenous—movement for women's rights. The reality recognized by this movement is generating new principles: new in content, form, reach, operation, and relation to social life.

In law, the principles of this movement are best approximated in North American equality law, pioneered by the Black movement in the United States in the 1960s and 1970s and the women's movement in Canada in the 1980s and 1990s. These equality rights are implemented by individuals and groups against other individuals and groups as well as by and against governments. They allow governments to proceed but do not limit to governments the ability to act against discrimination. They allow complaints for indirect and systemic inequality. To be fully realized, they call for relief against state inaction as well as action. Such devices add enforcement potential rather than let states off the hook.

In the received international human rights tradition, by contrast, equality has been more abstract than concrete, more transcendant than secular, more descended from natural law than admittedly socially based. The Universal Declaration of Human Rights grants equality "without distinction of any kind,"[51] as if distinction were the problem and lack of distinction the solution. The Convention on Elimination of All Forms of Discrimination Against Women defines discrimination against women largely in gender neutral and referential terms, guaranteeing enjoyment of all other rights "on a basis of equality of men and women."[52] This has mostly been interpreted nonsubstantively, has not allowed claims by individuals or groups, claims against government inaction, or against private parties. The Committee that oversees it is coming to recognize, however, that violence against women is a form of sex discrimination and seeks to make states responsible for "private acts" if they fail to prevent, investigate, or punish discriminatory acts of violence.[53] All the Committee does is report.[54]

As a basis for an expanded equality principle, women's resistance to sex inequality is ubiquitous and everywhere concrete and socially specific. It is not based on being the same as men but on resistance to violation and abuse and second-class citizenship because one is a woman. It starts close to home. African women oppose genital mutilation. Philippine, Thai, Japanese, and Swedish women organize against the sex trade. Women in Papua New Guinea, the United States, and workers at the United Nations resist sexual harassment. Brazilian and Italian women protest domestic battery and "honor" as a male excuse for killing them. Indian women protest "dowry" and "suttee" as a male excuse for killing them. American women protest domestic battery and romantic love as a male excuse for killing them. Canadian women protest the use of "feminism" as a male excuse for killing them. Women everywhere rise up against rape, even in cultures where women have recently been regarded as chattel. Women in the United States, Scandinavia, and the Philippines resist pornography. Forced motherhood is opposed from Ireland to Germany to Bangladesh. Female infanticide and objectifying advertising are legislated against in India. Everywhere women seek access to literacy, which they have often been denied as women, and to survival based on the work they do, as well as access to doing all kinds of work.[55]

One feature of this movement is its combination of socially specific comparison—men are not treated this way—with its refusal to be limited to imitating or emulating men. Women's diversity is extraordinary, yet everywhere, with social particularity, below some man. This produces an appreciation for the fact that difference by itself is certainly not the excuse for second-class citizenship it has become, but that imposed inferiority is everything. The movement criticizes socially organized power itself, as well as its excesses.

This movement has produced a rich concept of equality as lack of hierarchy, not sameness. Its everywhere relative universality, its refusal to settle for anything less than a single standard of human dignity and entitlement, and its demand for elevation in that standard have left Aristotle in the dust. The scope and depth of this uprising for social equality offers a neglected ground for sex equality as a human right. The movement provides a principled basis in social reality for women's human rights, for a positive equality. Its principles include: If you do not do it to each other, you cannot do it to us; and ending the subordination of women because they are women.

"Civil rights" has been considered a subprovince of human rights, typically distinguished from political, social, economic, and cultural rights, as well as rights of personhood. A more embracing sense of equality is developing and being applied in North America, originating in the civil rights struggle of Blacks for social equality through legal equality in the United States and extending to its current pinnacle formulation in the Supreme Court of Canada's equality jurisprudence originating in the women's movement. This equality is not confined to equal access to other rights, as it is in international human rights law[56] and most domestic equality law, but is a principle in its own right. This equality looks to social context, broadly and in each particular, to eliminate imposed stratification. It envisions an active role for equality law in implementing the necessary changes.

In Canada, the approach takes the form of requiring that laws "promote equality." This "entails the promotion of a society" of equal dignity and respect. "It has a large remedial component."[57] It recognizes that social inequality *exists* and must be changed, rather than assuming a neutral and equal social world and avoiding legal differentiation to preserve it. It is based on noticing the reality of inequality in order to end it, rather than on enforcing a "color blindness" and gender neutrality, which have often meant a blindness to the unequal realities of color and gender. This mandate is interpreted with particular sensitivity to, and priority upon, eliminating the inequality of groups that have traditionally been socially disadvantaged.

This equality looks to "civil society" on the level of ordinary transactions and interactions: buying and selling, work and education and accommodations, home and the street, communications and insurance, as well as voting, elections, and juries. It encompasses segregated toilets and teaching racial hatred, sexual coercion by doctors, and denial of pregnancy benefits. It is rooted in everyday life, looking beyond the legal formalism of formal equality to social consequences. It understands that although inequality hurts individuals, it only hurts them as members of social groups. It addresses the most systemic inequalities, as well as ones that happen only to a few individuals. It practices a social, contextual, relational, antihierarchical equality jurisprudence.

As currently defined, international human rights are so abstract that people who concretely believe polar opposites can agree on them on principle and give them equally to no one. Both a Stalin and a Solzhenitsyn can embrace them. That neither would likely favor civil rights as described here suggests the tension between such civil rights and "human rights" as currently conceived, in particular between abstract "human rights" equality and substantive "civil rights" equality. Civil rights begin at home or close to it; human rights seem to improve the further one gets from home. By a preference for direct civil remedies in the hands of the unequal, civil rights distribute power from government to people as they redistribute power among people. Human rights tend to see the state as the enemy of equality; civil rights see it as their potential promoter. Human rights locate equality in eliminating irrational differentiation; civil rights see equality as much in affirmative claims of cultural particularity, in ending oppression whether based on real differences or not, and in altering the mainstream to accommodate an uncompromised diversity.

The current political force of the mainstream human rights view takes its deep text, on my analysis, from a reading of the Nazi experience: Survival lies in blending in, in being indistinguishable from one's surroundings, in nondifferentiation. Cast in equality terms, instead of criticizing the view that killed you for being different, you fight for the right to be recognized as the same and to become the same because it will keep you alive. So many Polish Jews died, it is said, because they only spoke Yiddish. They could not "pass" as not Jews. Aryan-appearing German Jews were more likely to survive. It should follow that assimilation—sameness—guarantees an equal right to live, not to be exterminated because of who you are. This is nonarbitrary recognition for meeting the dominant standard, integration over self-determination. Do not think about whether integration is ultimately possible; do not think about those who will never be permitted to meet the standards; do not challenge the standards themselves.

An analogy could be drawn to the psychology of battered women, which is also a dimension of femininity more generally. The only reality is the power of the abuser; keeping your head low keeps you alive. This, too, acquiesces in the dominant standard and concedes the permanent powerlessness of an underclass. The shame of being who you are—as if that is validly and forever the real reason for subordination—leads to always wanting and trying to become who you are not, which women know as living a lie until you become it. This is the victim-side adaptation to the perpetrator-defined reality. It converges with the final solution to the inequality problem: annihilation.

This is the equality of Aristotle, of the Enlightenment, of the Nazis, of mainstream U.S. equality jurisprudence today, and of international human rights law. It seems rather late in the pursuit of equality to seek fair conditions of extermination on the basis of speaking Polish or looking German. It is like a battered woman seeking not to be beaten by serving dinner on time and providing regular sex. Such equality does nothing about the annihilation machine itself, so long as it sorts likes from unlikes accurately. It may mean survival for some under unequal conditions, but do not call it equality. Such equality means conceding the standards under which one is measured, monitoring only their recognition without irrational distinction. One can understand trying to construct an equality principle to ensure survival under conditions of genocide; yet this is very close to conceding genocidal conditions in the construction of the equality principle, with the result that, so far as the equality principle is concerned, we will never live under any but genocidal conditions.

How equality is defined in the North American movements, by contrast, is self-respecting but not isolationist, self-determinant but not segregationist, uncompromised but not absolutist, solid at the core but forgiving at the edges. Its equality is not absolute but relative to the best society has to offer, insisting on an expanded role for the subordinated in redefining standards from the point of view of those living under them. Such a theory may appear to lack principled definition, grounded as it is in response to an unprincipled social world. Perhaps if white men had been lynched, as Black men were in the American South, this would be more of a problem; the fact is, they were not. Given that no society systematically traffics in men as men for sex, rapes men at will and with impunity, forces men to reproduce, batters men in homes, sometimes to death, on an everyday basis, pays men as a group less than women, or presents male sexuality in demeaned ways for entertainment and profit on a large scale, some comparative dimension to the standard has a lot to offer. It also helps avoid imposing foreign cultural standards in diverse social settings.

In legal practice in Canada, this approach has proven capable of addressing a substantial number of realities of sex inequality that have eluded prior attempts. A woman has been permitted to sue her city police force for failure to warn of a serial rapist.[58] Sexual harassment[59] and pregnancy discrimination[60] have been recognized as human rights violations. Under the tutelage if not the direct control of this approach, common law remedies for sexual abuse have recognized inequalities of power[61] and statutes of limitations for incest have been revised based on the experience of victims.[62] Criminal laws against wife battering have been interpreted to recognize the woman's reality[63] and publication of the names of sexual assault victims has been prohibited.[64] When the Court refused to recognize women's equality right to keep their sexual histories out of rape trials,[65] a whole new rape law was introduced to remedy it.[66] Significant decisions have also been made in light of this approach in the area of reproductive rights, preventing men from gaining a veto over women's abortions[67] and recognizing women's rights in and over their fetuses.[68] Perhaps most tellingly, when the rights to freedom of expression of anti-Semites and pornographers were balanced against the equality rights of their targeted victims, equality won.[69] In Canada, some of the reality of inequality is becoming the basis for the legal equality principle.

## IV

Against this backdrop, what will become of the Muslim and Croatian women violated by the Serbs? The basis in a women's movement for a meaningful equality interpretation exists. Since November 1991, feminists in Zagreb in particular have been working with refugee survivors of the sexual atrocities of genocide through war. Their accountability to the victims has been continuous and absolute, their documentation and relief effort committed and accurate.[70] If jurisdiction can be secured, and it should be able to be, laws do exist to cover many of the atrocities.[71] Rape, enforced prostitution, and indecent assault are already recognized as war crimes.[72] There is even precedent for trying them.[73] After World War II, Japanese generals were tried for sexual atrocities committed under their command: rape, imprisonment of girls in hotels and subjecting them to repeated rape, mass rape, cutting off breasts, killing women civilians and raping their corpses.[74] Other than the breeding aspect, this has happened in wars before, right down to tortures of fingers and feet.

There are many more examples in which nothing was done: "the mass rapes of women during the war for independence in Bangladesh, the systematic rape of women suspected of complicity in the insurgency in Kashmir, and the belated but growing scandal concerning the 'comfort women' who were abducted and forced into prostitution by the Japanese army during the Second World War."[75] Evidence on rape was presented by the French and Soviet prosecutors at Nuremburg.[76] Sexual forms of torture were documented,[77] but sexual assault was not charged in the indictments. One can only speculate that it was not seen to be within the tribunal's emphasis "not on individual barbarities and perversions" but only on the Nazi "Common Plan."[78] Rape has so often been treated as extracurricular, as just something men do, as a product rather than a policy of war.

Proceeding through war crimes tribunals on behalf of Muslim and Croatian women would create accountability but it would not redistribute power to women in situations other than war. On the civil side of human rights, these atrocities violate every sex equality guarantee in international law, properly interpreted, and they do not fail to do so because this is wartime. Surely this is a "consistent pattern of mass violation of human rights."[79] Perhaps this would be a good occasion to use equality guarantees to address violence against women; there is no state action problem. Such an approach could establish precedents for use by women in peacetime as well.

As a practical matter, it helps that these incidents happened in a war. Men know men hurt men in war, so maybe there is an analogy? It does not help for recognizing them now, or for creating a precedent that could effect nonwar interpretations, that similar acts are common everywhere in peacetime and are widely understood as sex. Yugoslavia's pornography market was "the freest in the world"[80] before this male population was officially mobilized to commit the atrocities they had already been sexually conditioned to enjoy. It does help that men did these acts in declared military groups, instead of one on one everywhere at once and all the time, or in small packs, murdering, raping, pimping, and breeding but not recognized as an army of occupation. Will there be command responsibility for these rapes? Will women have to identify each individual man, often numbering in the hundreds, who raped them? It does not help that no state raped these women and got them pregnant; it does help that a state's men did.[81]

Will these atrocities be seen as human rights abuses? If the Muslims were Jews, would the world be allowing this to happen? Must a group first survive genocide for it to be recognized next time? Will principle see reality? Will it connect with similar acts in everyday life? The murders maybe; the rapes possibly, and if so, probably because they are ethnic, hurting a group that includes men; the pregnancies, less likely (and what to do with the children?); the prostitution, for all the twenty-two treaties against it, little chance; the pornography never, meaning if ever, probably not soon.

Or will this situation and these women, here and now, be the time and place in which the word "woman," like the word "Jew," will finally come to stand, among its meanings, for a reality of abuse that cannot be forgotten, a triumph of survival against all that wanted you dead, a principle of what cannot be done to a human being? Will women, at last, get amnesty?

# Reading Questions

1. What evidence does the author give to support her claim that human rights principles are based on experience—but not the experiences of women?

2. Specifically, what historical legal precedents and philosophical traditions *prevent* international recognition of wartime rape as a collective human rights violation and genocidal practice against women? How is this seen in Bosnia-Herzegovina?

3. What is the distinction between racial rape and ethnic rape, and why is it important?

4. Since the time that this essay was published, the world community has learned that Muslims as well as Croatians engaged in rape practices, not just the Serbs. What effect, if any, does this have on the author's argument?

5. How do the legal applications and consequences of the Canadian equality principle differ from those of the international sex equality law?

# Recommended Reading

Amnesty International, *Rape and Sexual Abuse: Torture and Ill Treatment of Women in Detention* (New York: Author, January 1993)

Center for Women's Global Leadership, *1991 Women's Leadership Institute Report: Women, Violence, and Human Rights* (New Brunswick, NJ: Author, 1992)

Roy Gutman, "Mass Rapes of Bosnia," *Newsday* (August 23, 1992)

Catharine MacKinnon, *Only Words* (Cambridge, MA: Harvard University Press, 1993)

Jill Radford and Diana E. H. Russell, *Femicide: The Politics of Woman Killing* (New York: Twayne, 1992)

# CHAPTER 7

# Masculinities

Skinny-dippin' in the Green River. Roger Kose © 1991/Standing Stone Productions.

# Complexion

## RICHARD RODRIGUEZ

Richard Rodriguez has held a wide variety of jobs, including janitor. Since 1981 he has been a full-time writer. He received the Christopher Award in 1982 for *Hunger of Memory: The Education of Richard Rodriguez*, an autobiography, and has recently published *Beyond Assimilation*.

---

Visiting the East Coast or the gray capitals of Europe during the long months of winter, I often meet people at deluxe hotels who comment on my complexion. (In such hotels it appears nowadays a mark of leisure and wealth to have a complexion like mine.) Have I been skiing? In the Swiss Alps? Have I just returned from a Caribbean vacation? No. I say no softly but in a firm voice that intends to explain: My complexion is dark. (My skin is brown. More exactly, terra-cotta in sunlight, tawny in shade. I do not redden in sunlight. Instead, my skin becomes progressively dark; the sun singes the flesh.)

When I was a boy the white summer sun of Sacramento would darken me so, my T-shirt would seem bleached against my slender dark arms. My mother would see me come up the front steps. She'd wait for the screen door to slam at my back. "You look like a *negrito*," she'd say, angry, sorry to be angry, frustrated almost to laughing, scorn. "You know how important looks are in this country. With *los gringos* looks are all that they judge on. But you! Look at you! You're so careless!" Then she'd start in all over again. "You won't be satisfied till you end up looking like *los pobres* who work in the fields, *los braceros*."

(*Los braceros*: Those men who work with their *brazos*, their arms; Mexican nationals who were licensed to work for American farmers in the 1950s. They worked very hard for very little money, my father would tell me. And what money they earned they sent back to Mexico to support their families, my mother would add. *Los pobres*—the poor, the pitiful, the powerless ones. But paradoxically also powerful men. They were the men with brown-muscled arms I stared at in awe on Saturday mornings when they showed up downtown like gypsies to shop at Woolworth's or Penney's. On Monday nights they would gather hours early on the steps of the Memorial Auditorium for the wrestling matches. Passing by on my bicycle in summer, I would spy them there, clustered in small groups, talking—frightening and fascinating men—some wearing Texas *sombreros* and T-shirts which shone fluorescent in the twilight. I would sit forward in the back seat of our family's '48 Chevy to see them, working alongside Valley highways: dark men on an even horizon, loading a truck amid rows of straight green. Powerful, powerless men. Their fascinating darkness—like mine—to be feared.)

"You'll end up looking just like them."

1

Regarding my family, I see faces that do not closely resemble my own. Like some other Mexican families, my family suggests Mexico's confused colonial past. Gathered around a table, we appear to be from separate continents. My father's face recalls faces I have seen in France. His complexion is white—he does not tan; he does not burn. Over the years, his dark wavy hair has grayed handsomely. But with time his face has sagged to a perpetual sigh. My mother, whose surname is inexplicably Irish—Moran—has an olive complexion. People have frequently wondered if, perhaps, she is Italian or Portuguese. And, in fact, she looks as though she could be from southern Europe. My mother's face has not aged as quickly as the rest of her body; it remains smooth and glowing—a cool tan— which her gray hair cleanly accentuates. My older brother has inherited her good looks. When he was a boy people would tell him that he looked like Mario Lanza, and hearing it he would smile with dimpled assurance. He would come home from high school with girl friends who seemed to me glamorous (because they were) blondes. And during those years I envied him his skin that burned red and peeled like the skin of the *gringos*. His complexion never darkened like mine. My youngest sister is exotically pale, almost ashen. She is delicately featured, Near Eastern, people have said. Only my older sister has a complexion as dark as mine, though her facial features are much less harshly defined than my own. To many people meeting her, she seems (they say) Polynesian. I am the only one in the family whose face is severely cut to the line of ancient Indian ancestors. My face is mournfully long, in the classical Indian manner; my profile suggests one of those beak-nosed Mayan sculptures—the eaglelike face upturned, open-mouthed, against the deserted, primitive sky.

"We are Mexicans," my mother and father would say, and taught their four children to say whenever we (often) were asked about our ancestry. My mother and father scorned those "white" Mexican-Americans who tried to pass themselves off as Spanish. My parents would never have thought of denying their ancestry. I never denied it: My ancestry is Mexican, I told strangers mechanically. But I never forgot that only my older sister's complexion was as dark as mine.

My older sister never spoke to me about her complexion when she was a girl. But I guessed that she found her dark skin a burden. I knew that she suffered for being a "nigger." As she came home from grammar school, little boys came up behind her and pushed her down to the sidewalk. In high school, she struggled in the adolescent competition for boyfriends in a world of football games and proms, a world where her looks were plainly uncommon. In college, she was afraid and scornful when dark-skinned foreign students from countries like Turkey and India found her attractive. She revealed her fear of dark skin to me only in adulthood when, regarding her own three children, she quietly admitted relief that they were all light.

That is the kind of remark women in my family have often made before. As a boy, I'd stay in the kitchen (never seeming to attract any notice), listening while my aunts spoke of their pleasure at having light children. (The men, some of whom were dark-skinned from years of working out of doors, would be in another part of the house.) It was the woman's spoken concern: the fear of having a dark-skinned son or daughter. Remedies were exchanged. One aunt prescribed to her sisters the elixir of large doses of caster oil during the last weeks of pregnancy. (The remedy risked an abortion.) Children born dark grew up to have their faces treated regularly with a mixture of egg white and lemon juice concentrate. (In my case, the solution never would take.) One Mexican-American friend of my mother's, who regarded it a special blessing that she had a measure of English blood, spoke disparagingly of her husband, a construction worker, for being so dark. "He doesn't take care of himself," she complained. But the remark, I noticed, annoyed my mother, who sat tracing an invisible design with her finger on the tablecloth.

There was affection too and a kind of humor about these matters. With daring tenderness, one of my uncles would refer to his wife as *mi negra*. An aunt regularly called her dark child *mi feito* (my little ugly one), her smile only partially hidden as she bent down to dig her mouth under his ticklish chin. And at times relatives spoke scornfully of pale, white skin. A *gringo's* skin resembled *masa*—baker's dough—someone remarked. Everyone laughed. Voices chuckled over the fact that the *gringos* spent so many hours in summer sunning themselves. ("They need to get sun because they look like *los muertos*.")

I heard the laughing but remembered what the women had said, with unsmiling voices, concerning dark skin. Nothing I heard outside the house, regarding my skin, was so impressive to me.

In public I occasionally heard racial slurs. Complete strangers would yell out at me. A teenager drove past, shouting, "Hey, Greaser! Hey, Pancho!" Over his shoulder I saw the giggling face of his girl friend. A boy pedaled by and announced matter-of-factly, "I pee on dirty Mexicans." Such remarks would be said so casually that I wouldn't quickly realize that they were being addressed to me. When I did, I would be paralyzed with embarrassment, unable to return the insult. (Those times I happened to be with white grammar school friends, *they* shouted back. Imbued with the mysterious kindness of children, my friends would never ask later why I hadn't yelled out in my own defense.)

In all, there could not have been more than a dozen incidents of name-calling. That there were so few suggests that I was not a primary victim of racial abuse. But that, even today, I can clearly remember particular incidents is proof of their impact. Because of such incidents, I listened when my parents remarked that Mexicans were often mistreated in California border towns. And in Texas. I listened carefully when I heard that two of my cousins had been refused admittance to an "all-white" swimming pool. And that an uncle had been told by some man to go back to Africa. I followed the progress of the southern black civil rights movement, which was gaining prominent notice in Sacramento's afternoon newspaper. But what most intrigued me was the connection between dark skin and poverty. Because I heard my mother speak so often about the relegation of dark people to menial labor, I considered the great victims of racism to be those who were poor and forced to do menial work. People like the farmworkers whose skin was dark from the sun.

After meeting a black grammar school friend of my sister's, I remember thinking that she wasn't really "black." What interested me was the fact that she wasn't poor. (Her well-dressed parents would come by after work to pick her up in a shiny green Oldsmobile.) By contrast, the garbage men who appeared every Friday morning seemed to me unmistakably black. (I didn't bother to ask my parents why Sacramento garbage men always were black. I thought I knew.) One morning I was in the backyard when a man opened the gate. He was an ugly, square-faced black man with popping red eyes, a pail slung over his shoulder. As he approached, I stood up. And in a voice that seemed to me very weak, I piped, "Hi." But the man paid me no heed. He strode past to the can by the garage. In a single broad movement, he overturned its contents into his larger pail. Our can came crashing down as he turned and left me watching, in awe.

"*Pobres negros*," my mother remarked when she'd notice a headline in the paper about a civil rights demonstration in the South. "How the *gringos* mistreat them." In the same tone of voice she'd tell me about the mistreatment her brother endured years before. (After my grandfather's death, my grandmother had come to America with her son and five daughters.) "My sisters, we were still all just teenagers. And since *mi pápa* was dead, my brother had to be the head of the family. He had to support us, to find work. But what skills did he have! Twenty years old. *Pobre*. He was tall, like your grandfather. And strong. He did construction work. 'Construction!' The *gringos* kept him digging all day, doing the dirtiest jobs. And they would pay him next to nothing. Sometimes they promised him one salary and paid him less when he finished. But what could he do? Report them? We weren't citizens then. He didn't even know English. And he was dark. What chances could he have? As soon as we sisters got older, he went right back to Mexico. He hated this country. He looked so tired when he left. Already with a hunchback. Still in his twenties. But old-looking. No life for him here. *"Pobre."*

Dark skin was for my mother the most important symbol of a life of oppressive labor and poverty. But both my parents recognized other symbols as well.

My father noticed the feel of every hand he shook. (He'd smile sometimes—marvel more than scorn—remembering a man he'd met who had soft, uncalloused hands.)

My mother would grab a towel in the kitchen and rub my oily face sore when I came in from playing outside. "Clean the *graza* off your face!" (*Greaser!*)

Symbols: When my older sister, then in high school, asked my mother if she could do light housework in the afternoons for a rich lady we knew, my mother was frightened by the idea. For several weeks she troubled over it before granting conditional permission: "Just remember, you're not a maid. I don't want you wearing a uniform." My father echoed the same warning. Walking with him past a hotel, I watched as he stared at a doorman dressed like a Beefeater. "How can anyone let himself be dressed up like that? Like a clown. Don't you ever get a job where you have to put on a uniform." In summertime neighbors would ask me if I wanted to earn extra money by mowing their lawns. Again and again my mother worried: "Why did they ask *you*? Can't you find anything better?" Inevitably, she'd relent. She knew I needed the money. But I was instructed to work after dinner. ("When the sun's not so hot.") Even then, I'd have to wear a hat. *Un sombrero de* baseball.(*Sombrero*. Watching gray cowboy movies, I'd brood over the meaning of the broad-rimmed hat—that troubling symbol—which comically distinguished a Mexican cowboy from real cowboys.)

From my father came no warnings concerning the sun. His fear was of dark factory jobs. He remembered too well his first jobs when he came to this country, not intending to stay, just to earn money enough to sail on to Australia. (In Mexico he had heard too many stories of discrimination in *Los Estados Unidos*. So it was Australia, that distant island-continent, that loomed in his imagination as his "America.") The work my father found in San Francisco was work for the unskilled. A factory job. Then a cannery job. (He'd remember the noise and the heat.) Then a job at a warehouse. (He'd remember the dark stench of old urine.) At one place there were fistfights; at another a supervisor who hated Chinese and Mexicans. Nowhere a union.

His memory of himself in those years is held by those jobs. Never making money enough for passage to Australia; slowly giving up the plan of returning to school to resume his third grade education—to become an engineer. My memory of him in those years, however, is lifted from photographs in the family album which show him on his honeymoon with my mother—the woman who had convinced him to stay in America. I have studied their photographs often, seeking to find in those figures some clear resemblance to the man and the woman I've known as my parents. But the youthful faces in the photos remain, behind dark glasses, shadowy figures anticipating my mother and father.

They are pictured on the grounds of the Coronado Hotel near San Diego, standing in the pale light of a winter afternoon. She is wearing slacks. Her hair falls seductively over one side of her face. He appears wearing a double-breasted suit, an unneeded raincoat draped over his arm. Another shows them standing together, solemnly staring ahead. Their shoulders barely are touching. There is to their pose an aristocratic formality, an elegant Latin hauteur.

The man in those pictures is the same man who was fascinated by Italian grand opera. I have never known just what my father saw in the spectacle, but he has told me that he would take my mother to the Opera House every Friday night—if he had money enough for orchestra seats. ("Why go to sit in the balcony?") On Sundays he'd don Italian silk scarves and a camel's hair coat to take his new wife to the polo matches in Golden Gate Park. But one weekend my father stopped going to the opera and polo matches. He would blame the change in his life on one job—a warehouse job, working for a large corporation which today advertises its products with the smiling faces of children. "They made me an old man before my time," he'd say to me many years later. Afterward, jobs got easier and cleaner. Eventually, in middle age, he got a job making false teeth. But his youth was spent at the warehouse. "Everything changed," his wife remembers. The dapper young man in the old photographs yielded to the man I saw after dinner: haggard, asleep on the sofa. During "The Ed Sullivan Show" on Sunday nights, when Roberta Peters or Licia Albanese would appear on the tiny blue screen, his head would jerk up alert. He'd sit forward while the notes of Puccini sounded before him. ("Un bel dí.")

By the time they had a family, my parents no longer dressed in very fine clothes. Those symbols of great wealth and the reality of their lives too noisily clashed. No longer did they try to fit themselves, like paper-doll figures, behind trappings so foreign to their actual lives. My father no longer wore silk scarves or expensive wool suits. He sold his tuxedo to a second-hand store for five dollars. My mother sold her rabbit fur coat to the wife of a Spanish radio station disc jockey. ("It looks better on you than it does on me," she kept telling the lady until the sale was completed.) I was six years old at the time, but I recall watching the transaction with complete understanding. The woman I knew as my mother was already physically unlike the woman in her honeymoon photos. My mother's hair was short. Her shoulders were thick from carrying children. Her fingers were swollen red, toughened by housecleaning. Already my mother would admit to foreseeing herself in her own mother, a woman grown old, bald and bowlegged, after a hard lifetime of working.

In their manner, both my parents continued to respect the symbols of what they considered to be upper-class life. Very early, they taught me the *propria* way of eating *como los ricos*. And I was carefully taught elaborate formulas of polite greeting and parting. The dark little boy would be invited by classmates to the rich houses on Forty-fourth and Forty-fifth streets. "How do you do?" or "I am very pleased to meet you," I would say, bowing slightly to the amused mothers of classmates. "Thank you very much for the dinner; it was very delicious."

I made an impression. I intended to make an impression, to be invited back. (I soon realized that the trick was to get the mother or father to notice me.) From those early days began my association with rich people, my fascination with their secret. My mother worried. She warned me not to come home expecting to have the things my friends possessed. But she needn't have said anything. When I went to the big houses, I remembered that I was, at best, a visitor to the world I saw there. For that reason, I was an especially watchful guest. I was my parents' child. Things most middle-class children wouldn't trouble to notice, I studied. Remembered to see: the starched black and white uniform worn by the maid who opened the door; the Mexican gardeners—their complexions as dark as my own. (One gardener's face, glassed by sweat, looked up to see me going inside.)

"Take Richard upstairs and show him your electric train," the mother said. But it was really the vast polished dining room table I'd come to appraise. Those nights when I was invited to stay for dinner, I'd notice that my friend's mother rang a small silver bell to tell the black woman when to bring in the food. The father, at his end of the table, ate while wearing his tie. When I was not required to speak, I'd skate the icy cut of crystal with my eye; my gaze would follow the golden threads etched onto the rim of china. With my mother's eyes I'd see my hostess's manicured nails and judge them to be marks of her leisure. Later, when my schoolmate's father would bid me goodnight, I would feel his soft fingers and palm when we shook hands. And turning to leave, I'd see my dark self, lit by chandelier light, in a tall hallway mirror.

2

Complexion. My first conscious experience of sexual excitement concerns my complexion. One summer weekend, when I was around seven years old, I was at a public swimming pool with the whole family. I remember sitting on the damp pavement next to the pool and seeing my mother in the spectators' bleachers, holding my younger sister on her lap. My mother, I noticed, was watching my father as he stood on a diving board, waving to her. I watched her wave back. Then saw her radiant, bashful, astonishing smile. In that second I sensed that my mother and father had a relationship I knew nothing about. A nervous excitement encircled my stomach as I saw my mother's eyes follow my father's figure curving into the water. A second or two later, he emerged. I heard him call out. Smiling, his voice sounded, buoyant, calling me to swim to him. But turning to see him, I caught my mother's eye. I heard her shout over to me. In Spanish she called through the crowd: "Put a towel on over your shoulders." In public, she didn't want to say why. I knew.

That incident anticipates the shame and sexual inferiority I was to feel in later years because of my dark complexion. I was to grow up an ugly child. Or one who thought himself ugly. (*Feo.*) One night when I was eleven or twelve years old, I locked myself in the bathroom and carefully regarded my reflection in the mirror over the sink. Without any pleasure I studied my skin. I turned on the faucet. (In my mind I heard the swirling voices of aunts, and even my mother's voice, whispering, whispering incessantly about lemon juice solutions and dark, *feo* children.) With a bar of soap, I fashioned a thick ball of lather. I began soaping my arms. I took my father's straight razor out of the medicine cabinet. Slowly, with steady deliberateness, I put the blade against my flesh, pressed it as close as I could without cutting, and moved it up and down across my skin to see if I could get out, somehow lessen, the dark. All I succeeded in doing, however, was in shaving my arms bare of their hair. For as I noted with disappointment, the dark would not come out. It remained. Trapped. Deep in the cells of my skin.

Throughout adolescence, I felt myself mysteriously marked. Nothing else about my appearance would concern me so much as the fact that my complexion was dark. My mother would say how sorry she was that there was not money enough to get braces to straighten my teeth. But I never bothered about my teeth. In three-way mirrors at department stores, I'd see my profile dramatically defined by a long nose, but it was really only the color of my skin that caught my attention.

I wasn't afraid that I would become a menial laborer because of my skin. Nor did my complexion make me feel especially vulnerable to racial abuse. (I didn't really consider my dark skin to be a racial characteristic. I would have been only too happy to look as Mexican as my light-skinned older brother.) Simply, I judged myself ugly. And, since the women in my family had been the ones who discussed it in such worried tones, I felt my dark skin made me unattractive to women.

Thirteen years old. Fourteen. In a grammar school art class, when the assignment was to draw a self-portrait, I tried and I tried but could not bring myself to shade in the face on the paper to anything like my actual tone. With disgust then I would come face to face with myself in mirrors. With disappointment I located myself in class photographs—my dark face undefined by the camera which had clearly described the white faces of classmates. Or I'd see my dark wrist against my long-sleeved white shirt.

I grew divorced from my body. Insecure, overweight, listless. On hot summer days when my rubber-soled shoes soaked up the heat from the sidewalk, I kept my head down. Or walked in the shade. My mother didn't need anymore to tell me to watch out for the sun. I denied myself a sensational life. The normal, extraordinary, animal excitement of feeling my body alive—riding shirtless on a bicycle in the warm wind created by furious self-propelled motion—the sensations that first had excited in me a sense of my maleness, I denied. I was too ashamed of my body. I wanted to forget that I had a body because I had a brown body. I was grateful that none of my classmates ever mentioned the fact.

I continued to see the *braceros*, those men I resembled in one way and, in another way, didn't resemble at all. On the watery horizon of a Valley afternoon, I'd see them. And though I feared looking like them, it was with silent envy that I regarded them still. I envied their physical lives, their freedom to violate the taboo of the sun. Closer to home I would notice the shirtless construction workers, the roofers, the sweating men tarring the street in front of the house. And I'd see the Mexican gardeners. I was unwilling to admit the attraction of their lives. I tried to deny it by looking away. But what was denied became strongly desired.

In high school physical education classes, I withdrew, in the regular company of five or six classmates, to a distant corner of a football field where we smoked and talked. Our company was composed of bodies too short or too tall, all graceless and all—except mine—pale. Our conversation was usually witty. (In fact we were intelligent.) If we referred to the athletic contests around us, it was with sarcasm. With savage scorn I'd refer to the "animals" playing football or baseball. It would have been important for me to have joined them. Or for me to have taken off my shirt, to have let the sun burn dark on my skin, and to have run barefoot on the warm wet grass. it would have been very important. Too important. It would have been too telling a gesture—to admit the desire for sensation, the body, my body.

Fifteen, sixteen. I was a teenager shy in the presence of girls. Never dated. Barely could talk to a girl without stammering. In high school I went to several dances, but I never managed to ask a girl to dance. So I stopped going. I cannot remember high school years now with the parade of typical images: bright drive-ins or gliding blue shadows of a Junior Prom. At home most weekend nights, I would pass evenings reading. Like those hidden, precocious adolescents who have no real-life sexual experiences, I read a great deal of romantic fiction. "You won't find it in your books," my brother would playfully taunt me as he prepared to go to a party by freezing the crest of the wave in his hair with sticky pomade. Through my reading, however, I developed a fabulous and sophisticated sexual imagination. At seventeen, I may not have known how to engage a girl in small talk, but I had read *Lady Chatterly's Lover.*

It annoyed me to hear my father's teasing: that I would never know what "real work" is; that my hands were so soft. I think I knew it was his way of admitting pleasure and pride in my academic success. But I didn't smile. My mother said she was glad her children were getting their educations and would not be pushed around like *los pobres.* I heard the remark ironically as a reminder of my separation from *los braceros.* At such times I suspected that education was making me effeminate. The odd thing, however, was that I did not judge my classmates so harshly. Nor did I consider my male teachers in high school effeminate. It was only myself I judged against some shadowy, mythical Mexican laborer—dark like me, yet very different.

Language was crucial. I knew that I had violated the ideal of the *macho* by becoming such a dedicated student of language and literature. *Machismo* was a word never exactly defined by the persons who used it. (It was best described in the "proper" behavior of men.) Women at home, nevertheless, would repeat the old Mexican dictum that a man should be *feo, fuerte, y formal.* "The three F's," my mother called them, smiling slyly. *Feo* I took to mean not literally ugly so much as ruggedly handsome. (When my mother and her sisters spent a loud, laughing afternoon determining ideal male good looks, they finally settled on the actor Gilbert Roland, who was neither too pretty nor ugly but had looks "like a man.") *Fuerte,* "strong," seemed to mean not physical strength as much as inner strength, character. A dependable man is *fuerte. Fuerte* for that reason was a characteristic subsumed by the last of the three qualities, and the one I most often considered—*formal.* To be *formal* is to be steady. A man of responsibility, a good provider. Someone *formal* is also constant. A person to be relied upon in adversity. A sober man, a man of high seriousness.

I learned a great deal about being *formal* just by listening to the way my father and other male relatives of his generation spoke. A man was not silent necessarily. Nor was he limited in the tones he could sound. For example, he could tell a long, involved, humorous story and laugh at his own humor with high-pitched giggling. But a man was not talkative the way a woman could be. It was permitted a woman to be gossipy and chatty. (When one heard many voices in a room, it was usually women who were talking.) Men spoke much less rapidly. And often men spoke in monologues. (When one voice sounded in a crowded room, it was most often a man's voice one heard.) More important than any of this was the fact that a man never verbally revealed his emotions. Men did not speak about their unease in moments of crisis or danger. It was the woman who worried aloud when her husband got laid off from work. At times of illness or death in the family, a man was usually quiet, even silent. Women spoke up to voice prayers.

In distress, women always sounded quick ejaculations to God or the Virgin; women prayed in clearly audible voices at a wake held in a funeral parlor. And on the subject of love, a woman was verbally expansive. She spoke of her yearning and delight. A married man, if he spoke publicly about love, usually did so with playful, mischievous irony. Younger, unmarried men more often were quiet. (The *macho* is a silent suitor. *Formal.*)

At home I was quiet, so perhaps I seemed *formal* to my relations and other Spanish-speaking visitors to the house. But outside the house—my God!—I talked. Particularly in class or alone with my teachers, I chattered. (Talking seemed to make teachers think I was bright.) I often was proud of my way with words. Though, on other occasions, for example, when I would hear my mother busily speaking to women, it would occur to me that my attachment to words made me like her. Her son. Not *formal* like my father. At such times I even suspected that my nostalgia for sounds—the noisy, intimate Spanish sounds of my past—was nothing more than effeminate yearning.

High school English teachers encouraged me to describe very personal feelings in words. Poems and short stories I wrote, expressing sorrow and loneliness, were awarded high grades. In my bedroom were books by poets and novelists—books that I loved—in which male writers published feelings the men in my family never revealed or acknowledged in words. And it seemed to me that there was something unmanly about my attachment to literature. Even today, when so much about the myth of the *macho* no longer concerns me, I cannot altogether evade such notions. Writing these pages, admitting my embarrassment or my guilt, admitting my sexual anxieties and my physical insecurity, I have not been able to forget that I am not being *formal*.

So be it.

**3**

I went to college at Stanford, attracted partly by its academic reputation, partly because it was the school rich people went to. I found myself on a campus with golden children of western America's upper middle class. Many were students both ambitious for academic success *and* accustomed to leisured life in the sun. In the afternoon, they lay spread out, sunbathing in front of the library, reading Swift or Engels or Beckett. Others went by in convertibles, off to play tennis or ride horses or sail. Beach boys dressed in tank-tops and shorts were my classmates in undergraduate seminars. Tall tan girls wearing white strapless dresses sat directly in front of me in lecture rooms. I'd study them, their physical confidence. I was still recognizably kin to the boy I had been. Less tortured perhaps. But still kin. At Stanford, it's true, I began to have something like a conventional sexual life. I don't think, however, that I really believed that the women I knew found me physically appealing. I continued to stay out of the sun. I didn't linger in mirrors. And I was the student at Stanford who remembered to notice the Mexican-American janitors and gardeners working on the campus.

It was at Stanford, one day near the end of my senior year, that a friend told me about a summer construction job he knew was available. I was quickly alert. Desire uncoiled within me. My friend said that he knew I had been looking for summer employment. He knew I needed some money. Almost apologetically he explained: It was something I probably wouldn't be interested in, but a friend of his, a contractor, needed someone for the summer to do menial jobs. There would be lots of shoveling and raking and sweeping.

Nothing too hard. But nothing more interesting either. Still, the pay would be good. Did I want it? Or did I know someone who did?

I did. Yes, I said, surprised to hear myself say it.

In the weeks following, friends cautioned that I had no idea how hard physical labor really is. ("You only *think* you know what it is like to shovel for eight hours straight.") Their objections seemed to me challenges. They resolved the issue. I became happy with the plan. I decided, however, not to tell my parents. I wouldn't tell my mother because I could guess her worried reaction. I would tell my father only after the summer was over, when I could announce that, after all, I did know what "real work" is like.

The day I met the contractor (a Princeton graduate, it turned out), he asked me whether I had done any physical labor before. "In high school, during the summer," I lied. And although he seemed to regard me with skepticism, he decided to give me a try. Several days later, expectant, I arrived at my first construction site. I would take off my shirt to the sun. And at last grasp desired sensation. No longer afraid. At last become like a *bracero*. "We need those tree stumps out of here by tomorrow," the contractor said. I started to work.

I labored with excitement that first morning—and all the days after. The work was harder than I could have expected. But it was never as tedious as my friends had warned me it would be. There was too much physical pleasure in the labor. Especially early in the day, I would be most alert to the sensations of movement and straining. Beginning around seven each morning (when the air was still damp but the scent of weeds and dry earth anticipated the heat of the sun), I would feel my body resist the first thrusts of the shovel. My arms, tightened by sleep, would gradually loosen; after only several minutes, sweat would gather in beads on my forehead and then—a short while later—I would feel my chest silky with sweat in the breeze. I would return to my work. A nervous spark of pain would fly up my arm and settle to burn like an ember in the thick of my shoulder. An hour, two passed. Three. My whole body would assume regular movements; my shoveling would be described by identical, even movements. Even later in the day, my enthusiasm for primitive sensation would survive the heat and the dust and the insects pricking my back. I would strain wildly for sensation as the day came to a close. At three-thirty, quitting time, I would stand upright and slowly let my head fall back, luxuriating in the feeling of tightness relieved.

Some of the men working nearby would watch me and laugh. Two or three of the older men took the trouble to teach me the right way to use a pick, the correct way to shovel. "You're doing it wrong, too fucking hard," one man scolded. Then proceeded to show me—what persons who work with their bodies all their lives quickly learn—the most economical way to use one's body in labor.

"Don't make your back do so much work," he instructed. I stood impatiently listening, half listening, vaguely watching, then noticed his work-thickened fingers clutching the shovel. I was annoyed. I wanted to tell him that I enjoyed shoveling the wrong way. And I didn't want to learn the right way. I wasn't afraid of back pain. I liked the way my body felt sore at the end of the day.

I was about to, but, as it turned out, I didn't say a thing. Rather it was at that moment I realized that I was fooling myself if I expected a few weeks of labor to gain me admission to the world of the laborer. I would not learn in three months what my father had meant by "real work." I was not bound to this job; I could imagine its rapid conclusion. For me the sensations of exertion and fatigue could be savored. For my father or uncle, working at comparable jobs when they were my age, such sensations were to be feared. Fatigue took a different toll on their bodies—and minds.

It was, I know, a simple insight. But it was with this realization that I took my first step that summer toward realizing something even more important about the "worker." In the company of carpenters, electricians, plumbers, and painters at lunch, I would often sit quietly, observant. I was not shy in such company. I felt easy, pleased by the knowledge that I was casually accepted, my presence taken for granted by men (exotics) who worked with their hands. Some days the younger men would talk and talk about sex, and they would howl at women who drove by in cars. Other days the talk at lunchtime was subdued; men gathered in separate groups. It depended on who was around. There were rough, good-natured workers. Others were quiet. The more I remember that summer, the more I realize that there was no single *type* of worker. I am embarrassed to say I had not expected such diversity. I certainly had not expected to meet, for example, a plumber who was an abstract painter in his off hours and admired the work of Mark Rothko. Nor did I expect to meet so many workers with college diplomas. (They were the ones who were not surprised that I intended to enter graduate school in the fall.) I suppose what I really want to say here is painfully obvious, but I must say it nevertheless: The men of that summer were middle-class Americans. They certainly didn't constitute an oppressed society. Carefully completing their work sheets; talking about the fortunes of local football teams; planning Las Vegas vacations; comparing the gas mileage of various makes of campers—they were not *los pobres* my mother had spoken about.

On two occasions, the contractor hired a group of Mexican aliens. They were employed to cut down some trees and haul off debris. In all, there were six men of varying age. The youngest in his late twenties; the oldest (his father?) perhaps sixty years old. They came and they left in a single old truck. Anonymous men. They were never introduced to the other men at the site. Immediately upon their arrival, they would follow the contractor's directions, start working—rarely resting—seemingly driven by a fatalistic sense that work which had to be done was best done as quickly as possible.

I watched them sometimes. Perhaps they watched me. The only time I saw them pay me much notice was one day at lunchtime when I was laughing with the other men. The Mexicans sat apart when they ate, just as they worked by themselves. Quiet. I rarely heard them say much to each other. All I could hear were their voices calling out sharply to one another, giving directions. Otherwise, when they stood briefly resting, they talked among themselves in voices too hard to overhear.

The contractor knew enough Spanish, and the Mexicans—or at least the oldest of them, their spokesman—seemed to know enough English to communicate. But because I was around, the contractor decided one day to make me his translator. (He assumed I could speak Spanish.) I did what I was told. Shyly I went over to tell the Mexicans that the *patrón* wanted them to do something else before they left for the day. As I started to speak, I was afraid with my old fear that I would be unable to pronounce the Spanish words. But it was a simple instruction I had to convey. I could say it in phrases.

The dark sweating faces turned toward me as I spoke. They stopped their work to hear me. Each nodded in response. I stood there. I wanted to say something more. But what could I say in Spanish, even if I could have pronounced the words right? Perhaps I just wanted to engage them in small talk, to be assured of their confidence, our familiarity. I thought for a moment to ask them where in Mexico they were from. Something like that. And maybe I wanted to tell them (a lie, if need be) that my parents were from the same part of Mexico.

I stood there.

Their faces watched me. The eyes of the man directly in front of me moved slowly over my shoulder, and I turned to follow his glance toward *el patrón* some distance away. For a moment I felt swept up by that glance into the Mexicans' company. But then I heard one of them returning to work. And then the others went back to work. I left them without saying anything more.

When they had finished, the contractor went over to pay them in cash. (He later told me that he paid them collectively—"for the job," though he wouldn't tell me their wages. He said something quickly about the good rate of exchange "in their own country.") I can still hear the loudly confident voice he used with the Mexicans. It was the sound of the *gringo* I had heard as a very young boy. And I can still hear the quiet, indistinct sounds of the Mexican, the oldest, who replied. At hearing that voice I was sad for the Mexicans. Depressed by their vulnerability. Angry at myself. The adventure of the summer seemed suddenly ludicrous. I would not shorten the distance I felt from *los pobres* with a few weeks of physical labor. I would not become like them. They were different from me.

After that summer, a great deal—and not very much really—changed in my life. The curse of physical shame was broken by the sun; I was no longer ashamed of my body. No longer would I deny myself the pleasing sensations of my maleness. During those years when middle-class black Americans began to assert with pride, "Black is beautiful," I was able to regard my complexion without shame. I am today darker than I ever was as a boy. I have taken up the middle-class sport of long-distance running. Nearly every day now I run ten or fifteen miles, barely clothed, my skin exposed to the California winter rain and wind or the summer sun of late afternoon. The torso, the soccer player's calves and thighs, the arms of the twenty-year-old I never was, I possess now in my thirties. I study the youthful parody shape in the mirror: the stomach lipped tight by muscle; the shoulders rounded by chin-ups; the arms veined strong. This man. A man. I meet him. He laughs to see me, what I have become.

The dandy. I wear double-breasted Italian suits and custom-made English shoes. I resemble no one so much as my father—the man pictured in those honeymoon photos. At that point in life when he abandoned the dandy's posture, I assume it. At the point when my parents would not consider going on vacation, I register at the Hotel Carlyle in New York and the Plaza Athenée in Paris. I am as taken by the symbols of leisure and wealth as they were. For my parents, however, those symbols became taunts, reminders of all they could not achieve in one lifetime. For me those same symbols are reassuring reminders of public success. I tempt vulgarity to be reassured. I am filled with the gaudy delight, the monstrous grace of the nouveau riche.

In recent years I have had occasion to lecture in ghetto high schools. There I see students of remarkable style and physical grace. (One can see more dandies in such schools than one ever will find in middle-class high schools.) There is not the look of casual assurance I saw students at Stanford display. Ghetto girls mimic high-fashion models. Their dresses are of bold, forceful color; their figures elegant, long; the stance theatrical. Boys wear shirts that grip at their overdeveloped muscular bodies. (Against a powerless future, they engage images of strength.) Bad nutrition does not yet tell. Great disappointment, fatal to youth, awaits them still. For the moment, movements in school hallways are dancelike, a procession of postures in a sexual masque. Watching them, I feel a kind of envy. I wonder how different my adolescence would have been had I been free. . . . But no, it is my parents I see—their optimism during those years when they were entertained by Italian grand opera.

The registration clerk in London wonders if I have just been to Switzerland. And the man who carries my luggage in New York guesses the Caribbean. My complexion becomes a mark of my leisure. Yet no one would regard my complexion the same way if I entered such hotels through the service entrance. That is only to say that my complexion assumes its significance from the context of my life. My skin, in itself, means nothing. I stress the point because I know there are people who would label me "disadvantaged" because of my color. They make the same mistake I made as a boy, when I thought a disadvantaged life was circumscribed by particular occupations. That summer I worked in the sun may have made me physically indistinguishable from the Mexicans working nearby. (My skin was actually darker because, unlike them, I worked without wearing a shirt. By late August my hands were probably as tough as theirs.) But I was not one of *los pobres*. What made me different from them was an attitude of *mind*, my imagination of myself.

I do not blame my mother for warning me away from the sun when I was young. In a world where her brother had become an old man in his twenties because he was dark, my complexion was something to worry about. "Don't run in the sun," she warns me today. I run. In the end, my father was right—though perhaps he did not know how right or why—to say that I would never know what real work is. I will never know what he felt at his last factory job. If tomorrow I worked at some kind of factory, it would go differently for me. My long education would favor me. I could act as a public person—able to defend my interests, to unionize, to petition, to speak up—to challenge and demand. (I will never know what real work is.) I will never know what the Mexicans knew, gathering their shovels and ladders and saws.

Their silence stays with me now. The wages those Mexicans received for their labor were only a measure of their disadvantaged condition. Their silence is more telling. They lack a public identity. They remain profoundly alien. Persons apart. People lacking a union obviously, people without grounds. They depend upon the relative good will or fairness of their employers each day. For such people, lacking a better alternative, it is not such an unreasonable risk.

Their silence stays with me. I have taken these many words to describe its impact. Only: the quiet. Something uncanny about it. Its compliance. Vulnerability. Pathos. As I heard their truck rumbling away, I shuddered, my face mirrored with sweat. I had finally come face to face with *los pobres*.

# Reading Questions

1. Why does Rodriguez refer to the work of *los braceros* as "real work" that he never experiences, and why does he think of himself as a "public person" in distinction to *los braceros*?

2. Why does Rodriguez deny that the racial slurs he experienced made him a primary victim of racial abuse? Who does he identify as the primary victims of this, and why?

3. In Rodriguez's stories about his family and relatives, how do racial remarks seem to function within the family, compared to how they are experienced outside the family?

4. In Rodriguez's memories of his father, why is clothing an important symbol for understanding his father's feelings toward different types of work? How are Rodriguez's observations of the "dandy" relevant to this?

5. How was Rodriguez's emotional association with his own dark skin color an important factor in the development of his sexuality?

6. How does Rodriguez understand his higher education to be an effeminacy that violated the codes of *macho* in his family?

## Recommended Reading

Tomas Almaguer, "Chicano Men: A Cartography of Homosexual Identity and Behavior," *The Lesbian and Gay Studies Reader*, eds. Henry Abelove, Michèle Aina Barale, and David Halperin (New York: Routledge, 1993)

Anna Maria Alonso and Maria Teresa Koreck, "Silences: 'Hispanics,' AIDS, and Sexual Practices," *The Lesbian and Gay Studies Reader*, eds. Henry Abelove, Michèle Aina Barale, and David Halperin (New York: Routledge, 1993)

Kenneth C. Clatterbaugh, "A Matter of Class: Socialist Men," *Contemporary Perspectives on Masculinity* (Boulder, CO: Westview Press, 1990)

Richard Rodriguez, *Hunger of Memory: The Education of Richard Rodriguez* (Boston, MA: Godine, 1981)

Marcos Sanchez-Tranquilino and John Tagg, "The Pachuco's Flayed Hide: Mobility, Identity, and *Buenas Garras*," *Cultural Studies*, ed. Lawrence Grossberg, eds. Cary Nelson, and Paula Treichler (New York: Routledge, 1992)

Studs Terkel, *Race: How Blacks and Whites Feel About the American Obsession* (New York: New Press, 1992)

## Recommended Audiovisual Resources

*The Milagro Beanfield War*. 1988. Directed by Robert Redford. Comedy-drama in which a group of citizens in a small southwestern town fight big-city interests on behalf of their own agricultural subsistence.

*The Golden Cage: A Story of California's Farmworkers*. 1991. Directed by Susan Ferriss. Chronicles the experiences of Mexican farmworkers in California. Filmakers Library.

*Natives: Immigrant Bashing on the Border*. 1993. Directed by Jesse Lerner and Scott Sterling. Captures the xenophobia of Americans living along the United States–Mexican border. Filmakers Library.

# How Men Have (a) Sex

## JOHN STOLTENBERG

John Stoltenberg is the author of *The End of Manhood: A Book for Men of Conscience* and *Refusing to Be a Man: Essays on Sex and Justice.* He lectures widely on the subject of men and feminism.

An address to college students

*In the human species, how many sexes are there?*
Answer A: *There are two sexes.*
Answer B: *There are three sexes.*
Answer C: *There are four sexes.*
Answer D: *There are seven sexes.*
Answer E: *There are as many sexes as there are people.*

I'd like to take you, in an imaginary way, to look at a different world, somewhere else in the universe, a place inhabited by a life form that very much resembles us. But these creatures grow up with a peculiar knowledge. They know that they have been born in an infinite variety. They know, for instance, that in their genetic material they are born with hundreds of different chromosome formations at the point in each cell that we would say determines their "sex." These creatures don't just come in XX or XY; they also come in XXY and XYY and XXX plus a long list of "mosaic" variations in which some cells in a creature's body have one combination and other cells have another. Some of these creatures are born with chromosomes that aren't even quite X or Y because a little bit of one chromosome goes and gets joined to another. There are hundreds of different combinations, and though all are not fertile, quite a number of them are. The creatures in this world enjoy their individuality; they delight in the fact that they are not divisible into distinct categories. So when another newborn arrives with an esoterically rare chromosomal formation, there is a little celebration: "Aha," they say, "another sign that we are each unique."

These creatures also live with the knowledge that they are born with a vast range of genital formations. Between their legs are tissue structures that vary along a continuum, from clitorises with a vulva through all possible combinations and gradations to penises with a scrotal sac. These creatures live with an understanding that their genitals all developed prenatally from exactly the same little nub of embryonic tissue called a genital tubercle, which grew and developed under the influence of varying amounts of the hormone androgen. These creatures honor and respect everyone's natural-born genitalia—including what we would describe as a microphallus or a clitoris several inches long. What these creatures find amazing and precious is that because everyone's genitals stem from the same embryonic tissue, the nerves inside all their genitals got wired very much alike, so these nerves of touch just go crazy upon contact in a way that resonates completely between them. "My gosh," they think, "you must feel something in your genital tubercle that intensely resembles what I'm feeling in my genital tubercle." Well, they don't exactly *think* that in so many words; they're actually quite heavy into their feelings at that point; but they do feel very connected—throughout all their wondrous variety.

I could go on. I could tell you about the variety of hormones that course through their bodies in countless different patterns and proportions, both before birth and throughout their lives—the hormones that we call "sex hormones" but that they call "individuality inducers." I could tell you how these creatures think about reproduction: For part of their lives, some of them are quite capable of gestation, delivery, and lactation; and for part of their lives, some of them are quite capable of insemination; and for part or all their lives, some of them are not capable of any of those things—so these creatures conclude that it would be silly to lock anyone into a lifelong category based on a capability variable that may or may not be utilized and that in any case changes over each lifetime in a fairly uncertain and idiosyncratic way. These creatures are not oblivious to reproduction; but nor do they spend their lives constructing a self-definition around their variable reproductive capacities. They don't have to, because what is truly unique about these creatures is that they are capable of having a sense of personal identity without struggling to fit into a group identity based on how they were born. These creatures are quite happy, actually. They don't worry about sorting *other* creatures into categories, so they don't have to worry about whether they are measuring up to some category they themselves are supposed to belong to.

These creatures, of course, have sex. Rolling and rollicking and robust sex, and sweaty and slippery and sticky sex, and trembling and quaking and tumultuous sex, and tender and tingling and transcendent sex. They have sex fingers to fingers. They have sex belly to belly. They have sex genital tubercle to genital tubercle. They *have* sex. They do not have *a* sex. In their erotic lives, they are not required to act out their status in a category system—because there *is* no category system. There are no sexes to belong to, so sex between creatures is free to be between genuine individuals—not representatives of a category. They have sex. They do not have a sex. Imagine life like that.

Perhaps you have guessed the point of this science fiction: Anatomically, each creature in the imaginary world I have been describing could be an identical twin of every human being on earth. These creatures, in fact, *are us*—in every way except socially and politically. The way they are born is the way we are born. And we are not born belonging to one or the other of two sexes. We are born into a physiological continuum on which there is no discrete and definite point that you can call "male" and no discrete and definite point that you can call "female." If you look at all the variables in nature that are said to determine human "sex," you can't possibly find one that will unequivocally split the species into two. Each of the so-called criteria of sexedness is itself a continuum— including chromosomal variables, genital and gonadal variations, reproductive capacities, endocrinological proportions, and any other criterion you could think of. Any or all of these different variables may line up in any number of ways, and all of the variables may vary independently of one another.[1]

What does all this mean? It means, first of all, a logical dilemma: Either human "male" and human "female" actually exist in nature as fixed and discrete entities and you can credibly base an entire social and political system on those absolute natural categories, or else the variety of human sexedness is infinite. As Andrea Dworkin wrote in 1974:

The discovery is, of course, that "man" and "woman" are fictions, caricatures, cultural constructs. As models they are reductive, totalitarian, inappropriate to human becoming. As roles they are static, demeaning to the female, dead-ended for male and female both.[2]

The conclusion is inescapable:

*We are, clearly, a multisexed species which has its sexuality spread along a vast continuum where the elements called male and female are not discrete.*[3]

"*We are . . . a multisexed species.*" I first read those words a little over ten years ago—and that liberating recognition saved my life.

All the time I was growing up, I knew that there was something really problematical in my relationship to manhood. Inside, deep inside, I never believed I was fully male—I never believed I was growing up enough of a man. I believed that someplace out there, in other men, there was something that was genuine authentic all-American manhood—the real stuff—but I didn't have it: not enough of it to convince *me* anyway, even if I managed to be fairly convincing to those around me. I felt like an impostor, like a fake. I agonized a lot about not feeling male enough, and I had no idea then how much I was not alone.

Then I read those words—those words that suggested to me for the first time that the notion of manhood is a cultural delusion, a baseless belief, a false front, a house of cards. It's not true. The category I was trying so desperately to belong to, to be a member of in good standing—it doesn't exist. Poof. Now you see it, now you don't. Now you're terrified you're not really part of it; now you're free, you don't have to worry anymore. However removed you feel inside from "authentic manhood," it doesn't matter. What matters is the center inside yourself—and how you live, and how you treat people, and what you can contribute as you pass through life on this earth, and how honestly you love, and how carefully you make choices. Those are the things that really matter. Not whether you're a real man. There's no such thing.

The idea of the male sex is like the idea of an Aryan race. The Nazis believed in the idea of an Aryan race—they believed that the Aryan race really exists, physically, in nature—and they put a great deal of effort into making it real. The Nazis believed that from the blond hair and blue eyes occurring naturally in the human species, they could construe the existence of a separate *race*—a distinct category of human beings that was unambiguously rooted in the natural order of things. But traits do not a race make; traits only make traits. For the idea to be real that these physical traits comprised a race, the race had to be socially constructed. The Nazis inferiorized and exterminated those they defined as "non-Aryan." With that, the notion of an Aryan race began to seem to come true. That's how there could be a political entity known as an Aryan race, and that's how there could be for some people a personal, subjective sense that they belonged to it. This happened through hate and force, through violence and victimization, through treating millions of people as things, then exterminating them. The belief system shared by people who believed they were all Aryan could not exist apart from that force and violence. The force and violence created a racial class system, *and* it created those people's membership in the race considered "superior." The force and violence served their class interests in large part because it created and maintained the class itself. But the idea of an Aryan race could never become metaphysically true, despite all the violence unleashed to create it, because there simply *is* no Aryan race. There is only the idea of it—and the consequences of trying to make it seem real. The male sex is very like that.

Penises and ejaculate and prostate glands occur in nature, but the notion that these anatomical traits comprise a sex—a discrete class, separate and distinct, metaphysically divisible from some other sex, *the* "other sex"—is simply that: a notion, an idea. The penises exist; the male sex does not. The male sex is socially constructed. It is a political entity that flourishes only through acts of force and sexual terrorism. Apart from the global inferiorization and subordination of those who are defined as "nonmale," the idea of personal membership in the male sex class would have no recognizable meaning. It would make no sense. No one could be a member of it and no one would think they *should* be a member of it. There would be no male sex to belong to. That doesn't mean there wouldn't still be penises and ejaculate and prostate glands and such. It simply means that the center of our selfhood would not be required to reside inside an utterly fictitious category—a category that only seems real to the extent that those outside it are put down.

We live in a world divided absolutely into two sexes, even though nothing about human nature warrants that division. We are sorted into one category or another at birth based solely on a visual inspection of our groins, and the only question that's asked is whether there's enough elongated tissue around your urethra so you can pee standing up. The presence or absence of a long-enough penis is the primary criterion for separating who's to grow up male from who's to grow up female. And among all the ironies in that utterly whimsical and arbitrary selection process is the fact that *anyone* can pee both sitting down and standing up.

Male sexual identity is the conviction or belief, held by most people born with penises, that they are male and not female, that they belong to the male sex. In a society predicated on the notion that there are two "opposite" and "complementary" sexes, this idea not only makes sense, it *becomes* sense; the very idea of a male sexual identity produces sensation, produces the meaning of sensation, becomes the meaning of how one's body feels. The sense and the sensing of a male sexual identity is at once mental and physical, at once public and personal. Most people born with a penis between their legs grow up aspiring to feel and act unambiguously male, longing to belong to the sex that is male and daring not to belong to the sex that is not, and feeling this urgency for a visceral and constant verification of their male sexual identity—for a fleshy connection to manhood—as the driving force of their life. The drive does not originate in the anatomy. The sensations derive from the idea. The idea gives the feelings social meaning; the idea determines which sensations shall be sought.

People born with penises must strive to make the idea of male sexual identity personally real by doing certain deeds, actions that are valued and chosen because they produce the desired feeling of belonging to a sex that is male and not female. Male sexual identity is experienced only in sensation and action, in feeling and doing, in eroticism and ethics. The feeling of belonging to a male sex encompasses both sensations that are explicitly "sexual" and those that are not ordinarily regarded as such. And there is a tacit social value system according to which certain acts are chosen because they make an individual's sexedness feel real and certain other acts are eschewed because they numb it. That value system is the ethics of male sexual identity—and it may well be the social origin of all injustice.

Each person experiences the idea of sexual identity as more or less real, more or less certain, more or less true, depending on two very personal phenomena: one's feelings and one's acts. For many people, for instance, the act of fucking makes their sexual identity feel more real than it does at other times, and they can predict from experience that this feeling of greater certainty will last for at least a while after each time they fuck. Fucking is not the only such act, and not only so-called sex acts can result in feelings of certainty about sexual identity; but the act of fucking happens to be a very good example of the correlation between *doing* a specific act in a specific way and *sensing* the specificity of the sexual identity to which one aspires. A person can decide to do certain acts and not others just because some acts will have the payoff of a feeling of greater certainty about sexual identity and others will give the feedback of a feeling of less. The transient reality of one's sexual identity, a person can know, is always a function of what one does and how one's acts make one feel. The feeling and the act must conjoin for the idea of the sexual identity to come true. We all keep longing for surety of our sexedness that we can feel; we all keep striving through our actions to make the idea real.

In human nature, eroticism is not differentiated between "male" and "female" in any clear-cut way. There is too much of a continuum, too great a resemblance. From all that we know, the penis and the clitoris are identically "wired" to receive and retransmit sensations from throughout the body, and the congestion of blood within the lower torso during sexual excitation makes all bodies sensate in a remarkably similar manner. Simply put, we all share all the nerve and blood-vessel layouts that are associated with sexual arousal. Who can say, for instance, that the penis would not experience sensations the way that a clitoris does if this were not a world in which the penis is supposed to be hell-bent on penetration? By the time most men make it through puberty, they believe that erotic sensation is supposed to *begin* in their penis; that if engorgement has not begun there, then nothing else in their body will heat up either. There is a massive interior dissociation from sensations that do not explicitly remind a man that his penis is still there. And not only there as sensate, but *functional and operational.*

So much of most men's sexuality is tied up with gender-actualizing—with feeling like a real man—that they can scarcely recall an erotic sensation that had no gender-specific cultural meaning. As most men age, they learn to cancel out and deny erotic sensations that are not specifically linked to what they think a real man is supposed to feel. An erotic sensation unintentionally experienced in a receptive, communing mode—instead of in an aggressive and controlling and violative mode, for instance—can shut down sensory systems in an instant. An erotic sensation unintentionally linked to the "wrong" sex of another person can similarly mean sudden numbness. Acculturated male sexuality has a built-in fail-safe: Either its political context reifies manhood or the experience cannot be felt as sensual. Either the act creates his sexedness or it does not compute as a sex act. So he tenses up, pumps up, steels himself against the dread that he be found not male enough. And his dread is not stupid; for he sees what happens to people when they are treated as nonmales.

My point is that sexuality does not *have* a gender; it *creates* a gender. It creates for those who adapt to it in narrow and specified ways the confirmation for the individual of belonging to the idea of one sex or the other. So-called male sexuality is a learned connection between specific physical sensations and the idea of a male sexual identity. To achieve this male sexual identity requires that an individual *identify with* the class of males—that is, accept as one's own the values and interests of the class. A fully realized male sexual identity also requires *nonidentification with* that which is perceived to be nonmale, or female. A male must not identify with females; he must not associate with females in feeling, interest, or action. His identity as a member of the sex class men absolutely depends on the extent to which he repudiates the values and interests of the sex class "women."

I think somewhere inside us all, we have always known something about the relativity of gender. Somewhere inside us all, we know that our bodies harbor deep resemblances, that we are wired inside to respond in a profound harmony to the resonance of eroticism inside the body of someone near us. Physiologically, we are far more alike than different. The tissue structures that have become labial and clitoral or scrotal and penile have not forgotten their common ancestry. Their sensations are of the same source. The nerve networks and interlock of capillaries throughout our pelvises electrify and engorge as if plugged in together and pumping as one. That's what we feel when we feel one another's feelings. That's what can happen during sex that is mutual, equal, reciprocal, profoundly communing.

So why is it that some of us with penises think it's sexy to pressure someone into having sex against their will? Some of us actually get harder the harder the person resists. Some of us with penises actually believe that some of us without penises want to be raped. And why is it that some of us with penises think it's sexy to treat other people as objects, as things to be bought and sold, impersonal bodies to be possessed and consumed for our sexual pleasure? Why is it that the some of us with penises are aroused by sex tinged with rape, and sex commoditized by pornography? Why do so many of us with penises want such antisexual sex?

There's a reason, of course. We have to make a lie seem real. It's a very big lie. We each have to do our part. Otherwise the lie will look like the lie that it is. Imagine the enormity of what we each must do to keep the lie alive in each of us. Imagine the awesome challenge we face to make the lie a social fact. It's a lifetime mission for each of us born with a penis: to have sex such a way that the male sex seem real—and so that we'll feel like a real part of it.

We all grow up knowing exactly what kind of sex that is. It's the kind of sex you can have when you pressure or bully someone else into it. So it's a kind of sex that makes your will more important than theirs. That kind of sex helps the lie a lot. That kind of sex makes you feel like someone important and it turns the other person into someone unimportant. That kind of sex makes you feel real, not like a fake. It's a kind of sex men have in order to feel like a real man.

There's also the kind of sex you can have when you force someone and hurt someone and cause someone suffering and humiliation. Violence and hostility in sex help the lie a lot too. Real men are aggressive in sex. Real men get cruel in sex. Real men use their penises like weapons in sex. Real men leave bruises. Real men think it's a turn-on to threaten harm. A brutish push can make an erection feel really hard. That kind of sex helps the lie a lot. That kind of sex makes you feel like someone who is powerful and it turns the other person into someone powerless. That kind of sex makes you feel dangerous and in control—like you're fighting a war with an enemy and if you're mean enough you'll win but if you let up you'll lose your manhood. It's a kind of sex men have *in order to have* a manhood.

There's also the kind of sex you can have when you pay your money into a profit system that grows rich displaying and exploiting the bodies and body parts of people without penises for the sexual entertainment of people with. Pay your money and watch. Pay your money and imagine. Pay your money and get real turned on. Pay your money and jerk off. That kind of sex helps the lie a lot. It helps support an industry committed to making people with penises believe that people without are sluts who just want to be ravished and reviled—an industry dedicated to maintaining a sex-class system in which men believe themselves sex machines and men believe women are mindless fuck tubes. That kind of sex helps the lie a lot. It's like buying Krugerrands as a vote of confidence for white supremacy in South Africa.

And there's one more thing: That kind of sex makes the lie indelible—burns it onto your retinas right adjacent to your brain—makes you remember it and makes your body respond to it and so it makes you believe that the lie is in fact true: You really are a real man. That slavish and submissive creature there spreading her legs is really not. You and that creature have nothing in common. That creature is an alien inanimate thing, but your penis is completely real and alive. Now you can come. Thank god almighty—you have a sex at last.

Now, I believe there are many who are sick at heart over what I have been describing. There are many who were born with penises who want to stop collaborating in the sex-class system that needs us to need these kinds of sex. I believe some of you want to stop living out the big lie, and you want to know how. Some of you long to touch truthfully. Some of you want sexual relationships in your life that are about intimacy and joy, ecstasy and equality—not antagonism and alienation. So what I have to say next I have to say to you.

When you use sex to have a sex, the sex you have is likely to make you feel crummy about yourself. But when you have sex in which you are not struggling with your partner in order to act out "real manhood," the sex you have is more likely to bring you close.

This means several specific things:

1. *Consent is absolutely essential.* If both you and your partner have not freely given your informed consent to the sex you are about to have, you can be quite certain that the sex you go ahead and have will make you strangers to each other. How do you know if there's consent? You ask. You ask again if you're sensing any doubt. Consent to do one thing isn't consent to do another. So you keep communicating, in clear words. And you don't take anything for granted.

2. *Mutuality is absolutely essential.* Sex is not something you do *to* someone. Sex is not a one-way transitive verb, with a subject, you, and an object, the body you're with. Sex that is mutual is not about doing and being done to; it's about being-with and feeling-with. You have to really be there to experience what is happening between and within the two of you—between every part of you and within both your whole bodies. It's a matter of paying attention—as if you are paying attention to someone who matters.

3. *Respect is absolutely essential.* In the sex that you have, treat your partner like a real person who, like you, has real feelings—feelings that matter as much as your own. You may or may not love—but you must always respect. You must respect

the integrity of your partner's body. It is not yours for the taking. It belongs to someone real. And you do not get ownership of your partner's body just because you are having sex—or just because you have had sex.

For those who are closer to the beginning of your sex lives than to the middle or the end, many things are still changing for you about how you have sex, with whom, why or why not, what you like or dislike, what kind of sex you want to have more of. In the next few years, you are going to discover and decide a lot. I say "discover" because no one can tell you what you're going to find out about yourself in relation to sex—and I say "decide" because virtually without knowing it you are going to be laying down habits and patterns that will probably stay with you for the rest of your life. You're at a point in your sexual history that you will never be at again. You don't know what you don't know yet. And yet you are making choices whose consequences for your particular sexuality will be sealed years from now.

I speak to you as someone who is closer to the middle of my sexual history. As I look back, I see that I made many choices that I didn't know I was making. And as I look at men who are near my age, I see that what has happened to many of them is that their sex lives are stuck in deep ruts that began as tiny fissures when they were young. So I want to conclude by identifying what I believe are three of the most important decisions about your sexuality that you can make when you are at the beginning of your sexual history. However difficult these choices may seem to you now, I promise you they will only get more difficult as you grow older. I realize that what I'm about to give is some quite unsolicited nuts-and-bolts advice. But perhaps it will spare you, later on in your lives, some of the obsessions and emptiness that have claimed the sexual histories of many men just a generation before you. Perhaps it will not help, I don't know; but I hope very much that it will.

*First, you can start choosing now not to let your sexuality be manipulated by the pornography industry.* I've heard many unhappy men talk about how they are so hooked on pornography and obsessed with it that they are virtually incapable of a human erotic contact. And I have heard even more men talk about how, when they do have sex with someone, the pornography gets in the way, like a mental obstacle, like a barrier preventing a full experience of what's really happening between them and their partner. The sexuality that the pornography industry needs you to have is not about communicating and caring; it's about "pornographizing" people—objectifying and conquering them, not being with them as a person. You do not have to buy into it.

*Second, you can start choosing now not to let drugs and alcohol numb you through your sex life.* Too many men, as they age, become incapable of having sex with a clear head. But you need your head clear—to make clear choices, to send clear messages, to read clearly what's coming in on a clear channel between you and your partner. Sex is no time for your awareness to sign off. And another thing: Beware of relying on drugs or alcohol to give you "permission" to have sex, or to trick your body into feeling something that it's not, or so you won't have to take responsibility for what you're feeling or for the sex that you're about to have. If you can't take sober responsibility for your part in a sexual encounter, you probably shouldn't be having it—and you certainly shouldn't be zonked out of your mind *in order* to have it.

*Third, you can start choosing now not to fixate on fucking*—especially if you'd really rather have sex in other, noncoital ways. Sometimes men have coital sex—penetration and thrusting then ejaculating inside someone—not because they particularly feel like it but because they feel they *should* feel like it: It's expected that if you're the man, you fuck. And if you don't fuck, you're not a man. The corollary of this cultural imperative is that if two people don't have intercourse, they have not had real sex. That's baloney, of course, but the message comes down hard, especially inside men's heads: Fucking is *the* sex act, the act in which you act out what sex is supposed to be—and what sex you're supposed to be.

Like others born with a penis, I was born into a sex-class system that requires my collaboration every day, even in how I have sex. Nobody told me, when I was younger, that I could have noncoital sex and that it would be fine. Actually, much better than fine. Nobody told me about an incredible range of other erotic possibilities for mutual love-making—including rubbing body to body, then coming body to body; including multiple, nonejaculatory orgasms; including the feeling you get when even the tiniest place where you and your partner touch becomes like a window through which great tidal storms of passion ebb and flow, back and forth. Nobody told me about the sex you can have when you stop working at having a sex. My body told me, finally. And I began to trust what my body was telling me more than the lie I was supposed to make real.

I invite you too to resist the lie. I invite you too to become an erotic traitor to male supremacy.

# Reading Questions

1. What is the point of Stoltenberg's counterfactual world of creatures with a variety of chromosomal formations and a vast range of genital formations?
2. What is the difference between *having a sex* and *having sex*?
3. Why does the notion of a multisexed, physiological continuum contest the idea that "men" and "women" are natural sexual and gendered categories?
4. What do you think of Stoltenberg's analogy between the Nazi belief and social construction of an Aryan race, and our belief in and construction of real men?
5. Why does Stoltenberg assert that male identity serves a class interest?
6. What sexual beliefs and practices, according to Stoltenberg, are tied up with men's "gender-actualizing"?

# Recommended Reading

Henry Abelove, Michele Aina Barale, and David M. Halperin, Part IV: "Collective Identities/Dissident Identities," *The Lesbian and Gay Studies Reader* (New York: Routledge, 1993)

Cynthia Enloe, "Nationalism and Masculinity," *Bananas, Beaches, and Bases: Making Sense of International Politics* (Berkeley, CA: University of California Press, 1990)

Key Leigh Hagan, *Women Respond to the Men's Movement: A Feminist Collection* (San Francisco: HarperCollins, 1992)

Peter Lehman, *Running Scared: Masculinity and the*
*Representation of the Male Body* (Philadelphia, PA: Temple University Press, 1993.)

Michael Messner, "Masculinities and Athletic Careers," *Gender and Society* 3 (March 1989)

Andrew Parker, Mary Russo, Doris Sommer, and Patricia Yaeger, eds., *Nationalisms and Sexualities* (New York: Routledge, 1992)

Gayle Rubin, "Thinking Sex: Notes for a Radical Theory of the Politics of Sexuality," *Pleasure and Danger: Exploring Female Sexuality*, ed. Carole S. Vance (London: Unwin Hyman, 1989)

## Recommended Audiovisual Resources

*The Crying Game.* 1992. Directed by Neil Jordan. A young soldier in the anticolonialist struggle in Northern Ireland discovers sexuality and gender in an unpredictable way, through a unique friendship.

*Alien Nation.* 1989. Directed by Graham Baker. Great scene of male pregnancy, in a sci-fi movie about aliens from another planet enslaved in Los Angeles. CBS/Fox Video.

*Rape: Face to Face.* 1985. Produced by KCTS/TV. Documentary featuring the emotional confrontation between rapists and victims of rape. Filmakers Library.

*Dating Rites: Gang Rape on Campus.* 1993. Produced by Alison Stone. Stonescape Productions. Documentary on gang rape and acquaintance rape on campuses. Includes an interview with gang rape survivor Meg Davis. Filmakers Library.

*A Room Full of Men: Therapy for Abusive Men.* 1993. Produced by Heartland Motion Pictures. Documentary that examines a group of men with a history of abuse toward women. Filmakers Library.

*Rape/Crisis.* 1983. Directed by Gary T. McDonald. A compelling investigation of the trauma of rape, a crisis for everyone concerned. The Cinema Guild.

# Gender Treachery

## Homophobia, Masculinity, and Threatened Identities[1]

### PATRICK D. HOPKINS

Patrick D. Hopkins is completing his dissertation in philosophy at Washington University, St. Louis. He is the author of numerous articles on gender, sexuality, and feminist theory.

One of my first critical insights into the pervasive structure of sex and gender categories occurred to me during my senior year of high school. The seating arrangement in my American Government class was typical—the "brains" up front and at the edge, the "jocks" at the back and in the center. Every day before and after class, the male jocks bandied insults back and forth. Typically, this "good-natured" fun included name-calling. Name-calling, like most pop-cultural phenomena, circulates in fads, with various names waxing and waning in popularity. During the time I was taking this class, the most popular insult/name was used over and over again, *ad nauseam*. What was the insult?

It was simply, "girl."

Suggestively, "girl" was the insult of choice among the male jocks. If a male student was annoying, they called him "girl." If he made a mistake during some athletic event, he was called "girl." Sometimes "girl" was used to challenge boys to do their masculine best ("don't let us down, girl"). Eventually, after its explicitly derogatory use, "girl" came to be used among the male jocks as merely a term of greeting ("hey, girl").

But the blatantly sexist use of the word "girl" as an insult was not the only thing that struck me as interesting in this case. There was something different about this school, which in retrospect leads to my insight. My high school was a conservative Christian institution; no profanity (of a defined type) was allowed. Using "bad" words was considered sinful, was against the rules, and was formally punished. There was, therefore, a regulated lack of access to the more commonly used insults available in secular schools. "Faggot," "queer," "homo," or "cocksucker" were not available for use unless one was willing to risk being overheard by school staff, and thus risk being punished. However, it is important to note that, for the most part, these words were not restricted because of any sense of hurtfulness to a particular group or because they expressed prejudice. They were restricted merely because they were "dirty" words, "filthy" words, gutter-language words, like "shit" or "asshole." "Girl" was not a dirty word, and so presented no risk. It was used flagrantly in the presence of staff members, and even used by staff members themselves.[2]

In a curious twist, the very restriction of discursive access to these more common profanities (in the name of morality and decency) reveals a deeper structure of all these significations. "Girl," as an allowable, non-profane substitute for "faggot," "homo," and "cocksucker," mirrors and thus reveals a common essence of these insults. It signifies "not-male," and as related to the male speaker, "not-me."

"Girl," like these other terms, signifies a failure of masculinity, a failure of living up to a gendered standard of behavior, and a gendered standard of identity. Whether it was the case that a "failure of masculinity" actually occurred (as in fumbling the football) or whether it was only the "good-natured" intimation that it would occur (challenging future masculine functioning), the use of such terms demonstrates that to levy a successful insult, it was enough for these young men to claim that their target was insufficiently male; he was inadequately masculine, inadequately gendered.[3]

This story can, of course, be subjected to countless analyses, countless interpretations. For my purposes here, however, I want to present this story as an illustration of how important gender is to the concept of one's self. For these young males, being a man was not merely another contingent feature of their personhood. They did not conceive of themselves as people who were also male. They were, or wanted to be, *Men*. "Person" could only be a less descriptive, more generic way of talking about humans in the abstract. But there are no abstract humans; there are no "persons," rigorously speaking. There are only men and women. Or so we believe.

In what follows, I use this insight into gendered identity to make a preliminary exploration of the relationships between masculinity and homophobia. I find that one way to read homophobia and heterosexism in men is in terms of homosexuality's threat to masculinity, which in light of the connection between gender and personal identity translates into a threat to what constitutes a man's sense of self. To form a genuine challenge to homophobia, therefore, will not result from or result in merely increased social tolerance, but will be situated in a fundamental challenge to traditional concepts of masculinity itself.

## What It Means to Be (a) Gendered Me

Categories of gender, in different ways, produce a multiplicity of other categories in a society. They affect—if not determine—labor, reproduction-associated responsibilities, childrearing roles, distributions of political power, economic status, sexual pratices, uses of language, application of certain cognitive skills, possession of personality traits, spirituality and religious beliefs, and more. In fact, all members of a given society have their material and psychological statuses heavily determined by their identification as a particular gender. However, not only individuals' physical, economic, and sexual situations are determined by gender categories, but also their own sense of personal identity—their personhood. I use "personhood" here as a metaphor for describing individuals' beliefs about how they fit into a society, how they fit into a world, who and what they think they *are*.[4] Personhood is critically linked (or perhaps worse, uncritically linked) to the influence of the gender categories under which an individual develops.

Individuals' sense of personhood, their sense-of-self, is largely a result of their construction as members of particular social groups within society-at-large: religions, ethnicities, regional affinities, cultural heritages, classes, races, political parties, family lineages, etc. Some of the most pervasive, powerful, and hidden of these identity-constructing "groups" are the genders; pervasive because no individual escapes being gendered, powerful because so much else depends on gender, and hidden because gender is uncritically presented as a natural, biological given, about which much can be discovered but little can (or should) be altered. In most cultures, though not all, sex/gender identity, and thus much of personal identity, is regulated by a binary system—man and woman.[5] Men and women are constructed from the socially raw material of newborn human bodies—a process that masquerades as natural rather than constructive.[6] To a very large extent, what it means to be a member of society, and thus what it means to be a person, *is* what it means to be a girl or a boy, a man or a woman. There is no such thing as a sexually or gender undifferentiated person.[7]

Identity is fundamentally relational. What it means to have a particular identity depends on what it means not have some other identity, and by the kinds of relationships one has to other possible and actual identities. To have personhood, sense-of-self, regulated by a binary sex/gender system means that the one identity must be different from the other identity; a situation requiring that there be identifiable, performative, behavioral, and psychological characteristics that allow for clear differentiation. Binary identities demand criteria for differentiation.

For a "man" to qualify as a man, he must possess a certain (or worse, uncertain) number of demonstrable characteristics that make it clear that he is not a woman, and a woman must possess characteristics demonstrating she is not a man. These characteristics are, of course, culturally relative, and even intraculturally dynamic, but in late twentieth-century U.S. culture the cluster of behaviors and qualities that situate men in relation to women include the by now well-known litany: (hetero)sexual prowess, sexual conquest of women, heading a nuclear family, siring children, physical and material competition with other men, independence, behavioral autonomy, rationality, strict emotional control, aggressiveness, obsession with success and status, a certain way of walking, a certain way of talking, having buddies rather than intimate friends, etc.[8]

Because personal identity (and all its concomitant social, political, religious, psychological, biological, and economic relations) is so heavily gendered, any threat to sex/gender categories is derivatively (though primarily non-consciously) interpreted as a threat to personal identity—a threat to what it means to *be* and especially what it means to *be me*. A threat to manhood (masculinity) is a threat to personhood (personal identity). Not surprisingly then, a threat to established gender categories, like most other serious threats, is often met with grave resistance, for challenging the regulatory operations of a gender system means to destabilize fundamental social, political, and personal categories (a profoundly anxiety-producing state), and society is always prejudiced toward the protection of established categories. Inertia is a force in culture as well as in physics.

There are many different threats to gendered identity, but I think they can all be generally grouped together under the rubric of "gender treachery."[9] A gender traitor can be thought of as anyone who violates the "rules" of gender identity/gender performance, i.e., someone who rejects or appears to reject the criteria by which the genders are differentiated.[10] At its most obvious, gender treachery occurs as homosexuality, bisexuality, cross-dressing, and feminist activism. Any of these traitorous activities may result in a serious reaction from those individuals and groups whose concept of personal and political identity is most deeply and thoroughly sexed by traditional binary categories.[11] However, homosexuality is particularly effective in producing the extreme (though not uncommon) reaction of homophobia—a response that is often manifested in acts of physical, economic, and verbal assault against perceived gender traitors, queers.[12] Homosexuals, intentionally or not, directly challenge assumptions concerning the relational aspects of the binary categories of sex/gender, and as such threaten individual identities. Since the homophobic reaction can be lethal and so theoretically suggestive, it deserves serious attention.

## Homophobia/Heterosexism

Theorists debate the value of using the term "homophobia." For some, the "phobia" suffix codes anti-gay and anti-lesbian activity as appertaining to psychiatric discourse—the realm of irrationality, uncontrollable fear, a realm where moral responsibility or political critique seems inapplicable due to the clinical nature of the phobia.[13] We do not punish people for being claustrophobic; we do not accuse agoraphobics of ignorance or intolerance; why should we treat homophobics any differently?

Other terms have been used to describe the aggregation of prejudices against gays and lesbians, including homoerotophobia, homosexism, homonegativism, anti-homosexualism, anti-homosexuality, and homohatred.[14] "Heterosexism" has become the terminology of choice for some theorists, emphasizing similarities to racism and sexism. "Heterosexism" characterizes a political situation in which heterosexuality is presented and perceived as natural, moral, practical, and superior to any non-heterosexual option. As such, heterosexuals are *justly* accorded the privileges granted them—political power, sexual freedom, religious sanction, moral status, cultural validation, psychiatric and juridical non-interference, occupational and tax privilege, freedom to have or adopt children and raise families, civil rights protection, recourse against unfair hiring practices, public representation in media and entertainment industries, etc.

For many of us, however, "heterosexism," though accurate and useful, does not possess the rhetorical and emotional impact that "homophobia" does. "Heterosexism" is appropriate for describing why all television couples are straight, why marriage and joint tax returns are reserved for heterosexuals, why openly lesbian or gay candidates face inordinate difficulty in being elected to office, or why only heterosexuals can adopt children or be foster parents. But "heterosexism," though perhaps still technically accurate, does not seem strong enough to describe the scene of ten Texas teenage boys beating a gay man with nail-studded boards and stabbing him to death.[15] The blood pooling up on the ground beneath that dying body is evidence for something more than the protection of heterosexual privilege. It is evidence for a radical kind of evil.

It is neither my goal nor my desire here to set out specific definitions of homophobia. Though I will use the term primarily with reference to physical violence and strong verbal, economic, and juridical abuse against gays, I do not claim to establish a clear boundary between homophobia and heterosexism. No stable boundary could be set, nor would it be particularly useful to try to do so—they are not discrete. "Homophobia" and "heterosexism" are political words, political tools; they are ours to use as specific situations present specific needs.

However, for my purposes here, heterosexism—loosely characterized as valorizing and privileging heterosexuality (morally, economically, religiously, politically)—can be seen as the necessary precursor to homophobia. Heterosexism is the backdrop of the binary division into heterosexual and homosexual (parasitic on the man/woman binary), with, as usual, the first term of the binary good and second term bad. Heterosexism constructs the field of concepts and behaviors so that some heterosexists' hierarchical view of this binary will be reactionary, for a variety of reasons, thus becoming homophobic (read: violent/abusive/coercive). In the same way that a person doesn't have to be a member of a white supremacist organization to be racist, a person doesn't have to be homophobic to be heterosexist. This is not to say that heterosexism is not as bad as homophobia, but rather that though heterosexism presents less of an obvious, direct, personal physical threat to gays, it nonetheless situates the political arena such that homophobia can and is bound to exist. Heterosexism is culpable for the production of homophobia. Heterosexists are politically culpable for the production of homophobics.

But even when we choose to use the term "homophobia" for cases of brutality, fanatic claims, petitions for fascistic laws, or arbitrarily firing gay employees, this does not mean that we must always characterize homophobia as an irrational, psychiatric/clinical response. Such a characterization would be grossly inadequate. "Homophobia" has evolved as primarily a political term, not as a psychiatric one, and does not parallel claustrophobia or agoraphobia, for the political field is not the same.

Religious and political rhetorics of moral turpitude and moral danger do not attach to closed-in spaces or wide-open spaces in the way they attach to same-sex eroticism. In other words, the fear and abhorrence of homosexuals is often taught as a moral and practical virtue and political oppression is massed against gays and lesbians. As a result, oppositional strategies to homophobia must be located in political discourse, not just psychiatric or pop-psychiatric discourse. Homophobia is supported and subsidized by cultural and governmental institutions in ways that demand the need for a variety of analyses. Though homophobia may often seem irrational or semi-psychotic in appearance, it must not be dismissed as simply an obsessive individual psychological aberration. Homophobia is a product of institutional heterosexism and gendered identity.

How do people explain homophobia? And especially, though not exclusively, how do people in queer communities explain homophobia? Being the victims of it, what do they see in it? Why is it that some men react so strongly and so virulently to the mere presence of gay men?

## The Repression Hypothesis

One of the most common explanations of homophobia among gay men is that of repressed homosexuality. Men who constantly make anti-gay slurs, tell anti-gay jokes, use anti-gay language, obsess about the dire political and moral impact of homosexuality on the family and country, or even who are known to attack gays physically are often thought to be repressing their own sexual attraction toward men. As a result of their terror in coming to grips with their own sexuality, they overcompensate, metastasizing into toxic, hypermasculine, ultra-butch homophobes who seem to spend far more time worrying about homosexuality than openly gay men do.

This kind of repressed-homosexual explanation was aptly demonstrated by one of my straight undergraduate ethics professors. While teaching a section on sexual ethics, my professor and the entire class read a series in the college newspaper by our Young Republican student editor about how "the homosexuals" were taking over the country and converting all the children. Finally, after yet another repetition of the "but they can't have babies and they're unnatural" columns, my exasperated professor wrote a response to the paper, and after a lengthy list of counterarguments, ended by saying simply, "Methinks thou doth protest too much."

His intimation was clear. He believed that the Young Republican's arguments were more for his benefit than for his readers'. As the typical response goes among gays who hear men constantly ranting about the perils of homosexuality and the virtues of heterosexuality—"He's not trying to convince us. He's trying to convince himself."

I think for many men this theory of repression is accurate. It is not unusual for openly gay men to talk about their days in the closet and report that they were assertively heterosexist/homophobic—and that yes, they were desperately trying to convince themselves that they were really heterosexual. Sadly enough, many of these repressed homosexuals manage to maintain their repression at great cost to themselves and often at great cost to others. Some marry and live a lie, unfulfilled emotionally and sexually, deceiving their wives and children, sometimes having furtive, sexual affairs with other men. They manage psychologically to compartmentalize their erotic orientation and same-sex sexual experiences so radically that they live two separate, tortuous lives. Some repressives become anti-gay activists and spend their lives trying to force gays and lesbians back into the closet, working against gay civil rights and protections.[16] Horrifyingly, some others undergo an even worse schism in their personalities, resulting in a bizarre, malignant, and persistent internalized war between homophobia and homophilia. This war can culminate in what John Money calls the exorcist syndrome, in which the repressive picks up, seduces, or even rapes a gay man, and then beats him or kills him in order to exorcise the repressive's "homosexual guilt."[17]

But while the repressive hypothesis is certainly accurate for some men, it is not accurate for all. I have no doubt that there are indubitably heterosexual men who hate and assault gays. To some extent, the explanation of repressed homosexuality may be wish fulfillment on the part of some gays. Forced by necessity of survival to be secretive and cryptic themselves, many gay men find it eminently reasonable to suspect any man of potential homosexual desire, and in fact, want such to be the case. It is reasonable, if optimistic, to hope that there are really more of you than there seem to be. And in light of the fact that many openly gay men report that they used to be homophobic themselves, the repression theory seems to be both empirically sound as well as emotionally attractive. There is also a certain sense of self-empowerment resulting from the repression hypothesis—out gays may see themselves as morally, cognitively, and emotionally superior to the men who continue to repress their sexuality. But homophobia is not so simple. What about those homophobes who clearly are not repressing their own homosexuality? What explanation fits them?

## The Irrationality/Ignorance Hypothesis

Another explanation, one in perfect keeping with the roots of the word, is that homo-phobia is an irrational fear, based in ignorance and resulting from social training.[18] This explanation is also popular among liberal heterosexuals as well as liberal lesbians and gays. The stereotype of this kind of cultural/developmental homophobia is that of a little boy who grows up in a poorly educated, very conservative family, often in a rural area, who hears his parents and other relatives talk about the fags on TV or the homo child molester they caught in the next county and how he ought to be "strung up and shot." As the little boy grows, he models his parents' behavior, identifying with their emotions and desiring to emulate them. Although the boy has no idea of what a "fag" or "homo" is, he nevertheless learns the appropriate cues for application of those terms to situations and individuals, and the emotions associated with that application. He begins to use them himself, often as a general-use insult (like young children calling each other "nigger" even when they do not know what it means). He learns that certain kinds of behaviors elicit being called a fag and that he can achieve a degree of peer approval when he uses those terms. So he stands on the playground at recess and calls the boy who takes piano lessons a homo; his friends laugh. He asks the girls who are jumping rope with another boy why they are playing with a faggot; his friends laugh. Simultaneously, of course, the boy is learning all the other dictums of traditional heteromasculinity—girls are weak, boys are strong, girls play stupid games, boys play real games, girls that want to play football are weird, boys that do not want to play football are faggots. Eventually the boy learns the more complete definition of "faggot," "homo," "queer." Homos aren't just sissies who act like girls; they aren't just weak. They like to "do things" with other boys. Sick things. Perverted things.

A little knowledge is a very dangerous thing and the boy becomes a full-fledged homophobe who thinks boys who play the piano and do not like football want to touch him "down there." He learns that grown-up homos like to grab young boys and "do bad things to them." He learns that just as one can become a tougher, stronger, more masculine man by killing deer and by "slaughtering" the guys on the opposing football team, one can become more masculine, or prove one's masculinity, by verbally abusing or beating up queers.

Though this scenario may seem hyperbolic, it certainly does occur. I have seen it happen myself. The lesson that gets learned is that of the recurring conflict of essence and performance.

Essence: You (the little boy) have a natural, core, normal, good, essential identity; you are a *boy*, a *young man*, male, not-a-girl. This is just what you are. You were born this way. Little girls will like you. You have buddies. You're lucky. You are our *son*. It's natural and obvious that you will grow up and get married and be a *daddy*.

Performance: But even though you just *are* a little boy, even though it's perfectly natural, you must make sure you do not act (how? why?) like a girl. You must always make sure that you exhibit the right behavior for a boy (but isn't it natural?). Don't ever act like not-a-boy! Don't betray that which you are naturally, comfortably, normally. Don't not-be what you are. Perform like a man.

The stage is set. The child knows that he is a he and that being a he is a good, normal, natural thing. Being a he requires no effort. You just are a boy. But at the same time, there is lingering on the horizon the possibility, amorphous and not always spoken, that you might do something which violates what you are. It might be quiet—"Now put those down, son. Boys don't play with dolls." It might be loud—"What the hell are you doing playing with dolls like some sissy??!!" The little boy internalizes the expectations of masculinity.

This kind of explanation of homophobia, though useful and accurate for many purposes, tends to characterize homophobia as learned but completely irrational, unfounded, arbitrary, ignorant, counterproductive, and dysfunctional. However, such a simple analysis excludes much of the experience of the homophobe. It is not actually the case that the poor mindless homophobe simply veers through life distorting reality and obsessing over nothing, frothing at the mouth and seeing faggots behind every corner and homosexual conspiracies in every liberal platform, ruining his own life as well as others. In fact, homophobia is not dysfunctional in the way that agoraphobia is. Homophobia has functional characteristics.[19]

For example, in the story given above, the boy does not simply "catch" the obsessive, dysfunctional view of the world that his parents have. He learns that certain kinds of behaviors elicit rewarding emotions not only from his parents directly, but also from within himself when away from his parents. When the little boy plays with toy soldiers and pretends to slaughter communists or Indians, his parents smile, encourage him, and even play with him sometimes. If he plays house with his little sister, he is always the daddy and she is always the mommy and he pretends to get home from work and she pretends to have supper fixed for him—a game in which roles are correctly modeled and are thus emotionally rewarding—"I'm just like my daddy."

However, the emotional (and sometimes corporal) punishments function the same way. If the boy is caught playing with dolls, or pretending to be the mommy, he may be told that he is doing something wrong, or be punished, or may simply detect a sense of worry, disapproval, or distaste from his parents. Homophobic tendencies will be carried along with all the other traits of conservative masculinity. He will be "just like his daddy" when he calls some effeminate boy a sissy—an emotionally rewarding experience. He will receive approval from his peers when he pushes the class homo around—he will be tough and formidable in their eyes. And perhaps most importantly, he will be clearly and unambiguously performing the masculine role he perceives (correctly in context) to be so valued—an advantage in power, safety, admiration, and self-esteem. It is also in no small sense that homophobia can be functional in keeping other heterosexuals in line. The potential to accuse another boy of being a faggot, to threaten ostracism or physical assault, is a significant power.[20]

Thus, it is not the case that homophobia is somehow obviously dysfunctional on an individual or group level.[21] Homophobic activity carries with it certain rewards and a certain power to influence. In the case of the repressed homosexual, it externalizes the intra-psychic conflict and reaffirms a man's appearance of heterosexuality and thus his sense of stability, safety, and self. In the case of childhood modeling, homophobic activity wins approval from peers and authority figures, protects one from becoming the target of other homophobes, and reaffirms one's place in a larger context of gender appropriate behavior—protecting one's personal identity.

## The Political Response Hypothesis

The recognition that there are rational, functional aspects of homophobia (in a heteropatriarchal context) leads to a third explanation of homophobia that reverses the second.

This theory says that queers are a genuine political threat to heterosexuals and really do intend to eliminate heterosexual privilege. Homophobia, therefore, is a rational political response.[22] Radical feminist lesbians and certain radical gay men directly challenge the hetero-male-dominated structure of society, rejecting patriarchal rule, conventional morality, and patriarchal modes of power distribution. All of the primary institutional sites of power that have maintained patriarchal domination—the state, the church, the family, the medical profession, the corporation—are being challenged from without by queers who do not want merely to be accepted, or tolerated, or left alone, but who want to dismantle heteropatriarchal society and build something different in its place. In response to liberal heterosexuals who promote the irrationalist theory of homophobia, supporters of this theory might say that many of the so-called "ignorant" and "false" stereotypes of queers are in fact correct, but they are not bad stereotypes; they are good and should be praised, should be revered, should replace heterosexual values. Yes, lesbians do hate men. Yes, fags do want to destroy the nuclear family. Yes, dykes do want to convert children. Yes, homos are promiscuous.

The impetus for this theory of homophobia comes from lesbians and gays who view their sexuality as primarily a political identity, having chosen to reject heterosexuality and become lesbian or gay as a political act of resistance. They have chosen this identification because they want to fight, destroy, or separate from hetero-male-dominated society. According to this theory, homophobia is a perfectly rational, reasonable reaction to the presence of queers, because queers pose a genuine threat to the status of heterosexual privilege. It is only logical that heterosexuals would fight back, because if they do not fight back, their privilege, their power, and their dominance will be stripped away all the sooner.

There are people who seem, at least partially, to confirm this theory. It has been interesting to see that over the past ten years or so, it has become common for neo-conservative activist organizations to use the word "family" in their names. Among many gay, lesbian, and feminists activists, any organization with "Family" as part of its name is automatically suspected to be anti-gay, anti-lesbian, anti-feminist.[23] The frequency of the word "family" as an identification tag is seen as signifying a belief in the moral superiority of the traditional, heterosexual, nuclear family. This suggests that some "pro-family" activists trace and justify their anti-homosexual activism to the belief that lesbians and gays are threatening to destroy The Family and thus to destroy heterosexual morality.

It is also true that over the past twenty years or so, lesbian and gay thought has become radicalized in a variety of ways. Lesbians and gays have moved away from merely the hope of demedicalization and decriminalization to the hope of building cultures, ethics, practices, and politics of their own, hopes that include the destruction of heterosexist, or even heterosexual, society. There are some radical, separatist lesbians and separatist gays who view most human behavior in terms of rational, political aims, and for them homophobia is a predictable political response to their own oppositional politics. Nineteen ninety-two Republican presidential candidate Pat Buchanan was not simply being hyperbolic when he gravely predicted that the 1990's would be the decade of the radical homosexual. One of his campaign ads, featuring a film clip of near-nude, dancing, gay leathermen, formed the background for an attack on the grant policies of the National Endowment for the Arts. Such ads demonstrate that his homophobia is partially directed against queer-specific political and sexual challenges to his conservative Christian morality.

However, the political response hypothesis, like the others, accounts only for some homophobes, and I think, relatively few. This hypothesis suffers from too great a dose of modernist political rationalism. Like many traditional models of political activity, it overrationalizes the subjects involved. It assumes that members of the oppressor class interpret the world in political terms similar to that of members of an oppositional movement. Thus, the characterization of a homophobe is that of a rational individual with immoral goals who recognizes that the particular oppositional group of gays and lesbians is a genuine political threat to his or her power and privilege, and as such must take an active stand against that insurgent group. One of the best tactics for resisting the insurgents is terror—on individual levels with violence, on institutional levels with oppressive laws, and on sociocultural levels with boogeyfag propaganda.[24]

While this model has merit and may be partially accurate in accounting for some homophobia, it endows homophobes (and homosexuals) with a hyperrationality that does not seem to be in evidence. Most homophobes, even those who openly admit their involvement in physical and verbal attacks on gays and lesbians, do not consider their activity to be political. Most of them, in fact, do not perceive any obvious threat from the people they attack. Gary Comstock claims that perpetrators of anti-queer violence typically list the "recreational, adventuresome aspect of pursuing, preying upon, and scaring lesbians and gay men" as the first and foremost reason for their behavior. Only secondarily and less often do they list things like the "wrongness of homosexuality" as a reason for their activity. But even this "wrongness" is not listed as an explanation or political justification for their behavior as much as a background assumption that functions as cultural permission.[25]

A recent television news program interviewed a perpetrator of anti-gay violence and, like Comstock's interviewee, he had little or no explanation for why he was doing what he was doing except that it was fun. When asked how he could have fun hurting people, he said that he had never really thought of queers as real people. I think this suggests that interpreting all, or even most, homophobic violence as conscious political activity ignores that much of the "reasoning" behind homophobia, when there is any active reasoning at all, relies on a very abstract and loosely integrated background of heterosexist assumptions. Many homophobes view gays and lesbians as politically, morally, and economically insignificant. For those who have never had any personal interaction (positive or negative) with openly gay or lesbian folk, lesbian/gay people may be such an abstract other that they do not enter into one's political and moral consideration any more than people who kick dogs for fun consider the political and moral significance of dogs, except perhaps in terms of legal consequences.

## Performing Gender and Gender Treachery

All three explanations of homophobia have one thing in common. They reside on a field of unequal, binary, sexual and gender differentiation. Behind all homophobia, regardless of its development, expression, or motivation, is the background of heterosexism. Behind all heterosexism is the background of gendered identities.

The gender category of men constructs its members around at least two conflicting characterizations of the essence of manhood. First, your masculinity (being-a-man) is natural and healthy and innate. But second, you must stay masculine—do not ever let your masculinity falter. So, although being a man is seen as a natural and automatic state of affairs for a certain anatomical makeup, masculinity is so valued, so valorized, so prized, and its loss such a terrible thing, that one must always guard against losing it. Paradoxically, then, the "naturalness" of being a man, of being masculine, is constantly guarding against the danger of losing itself. Unaware, the "naturalness," the "rightness," of masculinity exposes its own uncertainties in its incessant self-monitoring—a self-monitoring often accomplished by monitoring others. In fact, although the stable performance of masculinity is presented as an *outcome* of being a man, what arises in looking at heterosexism/homophobia is that being a man, or continuing to be a man, is the *outcome* of performing masculinity. But of course, not just anybody can make the performance. Anatomy is seen as prior even as the performance is required to validate the anatomy. Thus the performance produces the man, but the performance is also limited to and compulsory for a "man."[26]

The insults of the male high school jocks are telling. Even though one is recognized as a man (or boy) prior to evidenced masculinity, evidence must also be forthcoming in order to merit that continued "unproblematic" status. Whether performative evidence is provided with ease or with difficulty, it is nonetheless a compulsory performance, as compulsory as the initial anatomically based gender assignment. But because (proof of) masculinity has to be maintained not merely by anatomical differentiation but by performance, the possibility of failure in the performance is always there. It is enough to insult, to challenge, to question personal identity, by implying that one is not being masculine enough.

The logic of masculinity is demanding—protect and maintain what you are intrinsically, or you could lose it, mutate, become something else. The insults of my student peers suggest that the "something else" is being a girl—a serious enough demotion in a patriarchal culture. But of course, this is metaphor. One does not actually become a girl; the power of prior anatomy is too spellbinding, even when the performance fails. The "something else" is a male without masculinity, a monster, a body without its essential spirit, a mutation with no specifiable identity.[27]

So one mutation, which is so offensive it becomes the template of all mutations, occurs when a man finds that his erotic orientation is toward other men.[28] If he acts on that erotic orientation, he violates a tenet of masculinity, he fails at masculinity, and most importantly, appears to reject standards by which real men are defined as selves, as subjects. In a binary gender system, however, to be unmasculine means to be feminine; that is the only other possibility. But even as a cultural transformation into the feminine is attempted, it appears to be seriously problematic; it is not without resistance that the unmasculine male is shunted off to the realm of the feminine, for though femininity is devalued as the repository of the unmasculine, its presence as a discernible nonmasculine essence/performance is required to maintain the boundary of masculinity, and "feminine essences" do not easily coincide with "male" bodies.

The male body, which is supposed to house masculine essence from the first time it is identified as male, is out of place in the realm of unmasculine. That body is a manifestation of confusion, a reminder of rejection, an arrogant affront to all that is good and true about men, real men, normal men, natural men. How could this "man" give up his natural power, his natural strength, his real self? Why is he rejecting what he should be, what I am?

If the male is neither masculine, nor feminine enough, what is he? He becomes a homosexual, a member of that relatively new species of creature, originally delineated by psychiatry, which does not simply engage in unmasculine behavior, but which has an essential, unmasculine essence; no positive essence of his own, mind you, but rather a negative essence, an absence of legitimate essence, and thus the absence of legitimate personhood.[29] But what is the response to a creature with an illegitimate essence, to a creature with the husk of a man but with the extremely present absence of masculinity? That depends entirely on the situatedness of the responder in the distribution of gender identities and personal identities.

The repressive sees and fears becoming *that*, and must distance himself from *that* by any means necessary, often overcompensating, revealing his repression through his obsession, sometimes through active malignancy—assaulting or killing or merely registering disgust at that which he hates embodied in that which he desires.[30]

The ignorant will dismiss *those* as not really human, creatures so unidentified that they do not merit the response given to genuine identities (whether positive or negative—even enemies have genuine, if hated, identities). *It* can be killed, can be beaten, can be played with, can be dismissed.

The heterosupremacist reactionary will raise the warning—*They* are dangerous! *They* are getting out of hand! *They* are here! *They* are threatening your homes, your churches, your families, your children! And in some sense the threat may be real; *they* really do reject many of the beliefs upon which the heterosupremacists' political and personal identities are maintained.

Fortunately, the logic of masculinity, like any other logic, is neither universal nor irresistibly stable. Not every individual classified as a male in this culture will be adequately represented in my sketchy characterization of masculine personhood. My characterization is not to be interpreted so much as an empirically accurate description of all men in this society as it is a description of the mythology of masculinity that informs all constructions of men, the masculine, the "self" in Western culture, and that which could threaten them. I do not claim that all heterosexual males are homophobic (although I do think that the vast majority of heterosexual males are heterosexist). While I describe three homophobic reactions to the identity threat represented by gay men (repression, abusive ignorant bigotry, political reactionism), these in no way exhaust the variety of male reactions.

Some men, though they hate and are sickened by gays, lack the bravado to do anything more about their hate than make private slurs. Others, particularly liberals, are tolerantly heterosexist; they have no "real" problem with gays provided they are discreet and replicate the model of conventional heterosexual morality and family. And then there is the rare, genuinely subversive heterosexual man, a kind of gender traitor himself, whose identity is not coextensive with his assignment as a man. Although comfortable with himself, he wouldn't mind being gay, or mind being a woman—those are not the categories by which he defines, or wants to define, his personhood.

Do not, however, take this as a disclaimer to the effect that homophobia is the exception, the out-of-nowhere, the unusual case. Heterosexism may be the father of homophobia, modeling in public what is done more blatantly in hiding, but hidden does not mean rare. Do not think that homophobes, even violent ones, are few and far between—occasional atavistics "suffering" from paleolithic conceptions of sex roles. Even though many instances of anti-gay/anti-lesbian crime go unreported due to fear of outing, lack of proof, fear of retaliation, or police hostility, evidence is accumulating that such crime is widespread and that violent attack is higher among gays and lesbians than for the population at large. In a recent Philadelphia study, 24 percent of gay men and 10 percent of lesbians *responding* said that they had been physically attacked—a victimization rate twice as high for lesbians and four times as high for gay men than for women and men in the urban population at large.[31] Economic threat and verbal assault are, of course, even more common.

The gender demographics of physical homophobic attack suggest something about the correlation between masculinity and homophobia. Consider the findings in a recent study on violence against lesbians and gays by Gary Comstock: 1) 94 percent of all attackers were male; 2) 99 percent of perpetrators who attacked gay men were male, while 83 percent of those who attacked lesbians were male; 3) while 15 percent of attacks on lesbians were made by women, only 1 percent of attacks on gay men were made by women.[32]

Homophobic violence seems to be predominantly a male activity. What is the relationship between homophobia and masculinity? Is the man who attacks gay men affirming or reaffirming, consciously or subconsciously, his own masculinity/heterosexuality and thus his own sense of self? How is masculinity implicated in homophobia?

I have suggested in this essay that one reading of homophobia is that queers pose a threat to (compulsory) masculinity and as such, pose a threat to men whose personhood is coextensive with their identity as men. Certainly, homophobia could not exist without the background assumptions of (heterosexist) masculine identity. There could be no fear or hatred of gays and lesbians if there were no concept of a proper gender identity and a proper sexual orientation. Masculinity assumes, essentializes, naturalizes, and privileges heterosexuality. A violation of heterosexuality can be seen as treachery against masculinity, which can register as an affront or threat to a man's core sense of self, a threat to his (male) identity. In this sense, homophobia requires masculinity (and femininity); it is necessarily parasitic on traditional categories of sex/gender identity. Homophobia is the malignant "correction" to a destabilizing deviation. Without gendered standards of identity, there could be nothing from which to deviate, and thus nothing to "correct."

If this reading is accurate, homophobia is not just a social prejudice (on the xenophobic/minoritarian model) that can be eliminated by education or tolerance training.[33] It will not be eliminated just by persuading people to be "more accepting." While these approaches may be helpful, they do not get at the basis of homophobia—binary gender systems and heterosexism. The only way to ensure that heterosexism and its virulent manifestation homophobia are genuinely eliminated is to eliminate the binary itself—challenge the assumption that one must be sexed or gendered to be a person. Eliminate the binary and it would be impossible to have heterosexism or homophobia, because hetero and homo would have no meaning. This does not mean humans would have to be "fused" into some androgynous entity ("androgyny" has no meaning without the binary). It means simply that identities would no longer be distributed according to anatomically based "sexes."

While this hope may seem utopian and may have theoretical problems of its own, it nonetheless suggests an approach to studies of masculinity that may be incommensurable with other approaches. When using the model of masculinity (and femininity) as a social construct that has no intrinsic interpretation, there seems to be little use in trying to reconstruct masculinity into more "positive" forms, at least as long as masculinity is somehow viewed as an intrinsically appropriate feature of certain bodies. To make masculinity "positive" could easily devolve into retracting the boundaries of appropriate behavior without challenging the compulsory nature of that behavior. Delving into mythology and folklore (along the lines of some of the men's movement models) to "rediscover" some archetypal masculine image upon which to base new male identities is not so much wrong or sexist as it is arbitrary. Discovering what it means, or should mean, to be a "real man" is an exercise in uselessness. A "real man" is nothing. A "real man" could be anything. This is not to say that searching through mythohistory for useful metaphors for living today is not useful. I believe that it is.[34] But such a search will never get anyone closer to being a "real man" or even to being just a "man." There is no such thing. Nor should there be.

For some of us who have been embattled our entire lives because our desires/performances/identities were "immorally" or "illegally" or "illegitimately" cross-coded with our anatomies, we fear the flight into "rediscovering" masculinity will be a repetition of what has gone before. Gendered epistemologies will only reproduce gendered identities. I personally do not want to be a "real man," or even an "unreal man." I want to be unmanned altogether. I want to evaluate courses of behavior and desire open to me on their pragmatic consequences, not on their appropriateness to my "sex." I want to delve into the wisdom of mythology, but without the prior restrictions of anatomy.

I want to betray gender.

# Reading Questions

1. According to Hopkins, what deeper structures of the signification "girl," taken as an insult, are revealed in his semantic and pragmatic analysis?
2. What does Hopkins mean by gender treachery?
3. Why should a distinction be made between the denotation and connotation of homophobia and heterosexism?
4. Among the three explanations which Hopkins gives for the phenomenon of homophobia, which do you find most plausible? Are there other explanations which ought to be seriously considered?

5. How does Hopkins understand masculinity to be a compulsory performance of gender identity? Do you think that the compulsory performances of gender identity are more numerous in our society than the compulsory performances of male sexual identity?
6. How could Hopkins's argument be strengthened by an added analysis of the way class differences and race play roles in homophobia and heterosexism?

# Recommended Reading

Judith Butler, "Imitation and Gender Insubordination," *Inside/Out: Lesbian Theories, Gay Theories*, ed. Diana Fuss (New York: Routledge, 1991)

Rowena Chapman and Jonathon Rutherford, eds., *Male Order: Unwrapping Masculinity* (London: Lawrence and Wishart, 1988)

Marilyn Frye, *The Politics of Reality: Essays in Feminist Theory* (Freedom, CA: The Crossing Press, 1983)

Mark Gerzon, *A Choice of Heroes: The Changing Faces*

of *American Manhood* (Boston: Houghton Mifflin, 1982)

Larry May and Robert Strikwerda, eds., *Rethinking Masculinity: Philosophical Explorations in Light of Feminism* (Lanham, MD: Rowman and Littlefield, 1992)

Eve Kosofsky Sedgwick, "Introduction: Axiomatic," *Epistemology of the Closet* (Berkeley: University of California Press, 1990)

Klaus Theweleit, *Male Fantasies, Volume I: Women, Floods, Bodies, History*, trans. Stephen Conway with Erica Carter and Chris Turner (Minneapolis: University of Minnesota Press, 1987)

Michael Warner, ed., *Fear of a Queer Planet: Queer Politics*

*and Social Theory* (Minneapolis, MN: University of Minnesota Press, 1993)

Monique Wittig, *The Straight Mind and Other Essays* (Boston: Beacon Press, 1992)

## Recommended Audiovisual Resources

See the films discussed by Andrew Ross in Chapter 1 of this text.

See Susan Faludi, "Fatal and Fetal Visions: The Backlash in the Movies," in *Backlash*, for a provocative discussion and list of popular mainstream movies in the 1970s and 1980s that feature the compulsory performance of gender identity.

*Sex and Money: Dr. John Money on Sexual Identity*. 1991. Produced by the Humanist League, Amsterdam. Documentary featuring Dr. John Money's students and his clients, several of whom are in various stages of transsexual transformation. Filmakers Library.

# The Facts of Fatherhood

## THOMAS W. LAQUEUR

Thomas W. Laqueur teaches history at the University of California, Berkeley. He is the author of *Making Sex: Body and Gender from the Greeks to Freud* and *Religion and Respectability: Sunday Schools and Working Class Culture*.

This essay puts forward a labor theory of parenthood in which emotional work counts. I want to say at the onset, however, that it is not intended as a nuanced, balanced academic account of fatherhood or its vicissitudes. I write it in a grumpy, polemical mood.

In the first place I am annoyed that we lack a history of fatherhood, a silence which I regard as a sign of a more systemic pathology in our understanding of what being a man and being a father entail. There has unfortunately been no movement comparable to modern feminism to spur the study of men. Or conversely, history has been written almost exclusively as the history of men and therefore man-as-father has been subsumed under the history of a pervasive patriarchy—the history of inheritance and legitimate descent, the history of public authority and its transmission over generations. Fatherhood, insofar as it has been thought about at all, has been regarded as a backwater of the dominant history of public power. The sources, of course, support this view. Fathers before the eighteenth century appear in prescriptive texts about the family largely in their public roles, as heads of families or clans, as governors of the "little commonwealth," of the state within the state.

The rule of the patriarchy waned, but historians have not studied the cultural conse-quences for fathers of its recession. Instead, they have largely adopted the perspective of nineteenth-century ideologues: men belong to the public sphere of the marketplace and women to the private sphere of the family. A vast prescriptive literature explains how to be a good mother: essentially how to exercise proper moral influence and display appro-priate affections in the home, duties that in earlier centuries would have fallen to the father. But there is little in the era of "separate spheres" on how to be the new public man in private. A rich and poignant source material on the affective relationship between fathers and children in the nineteenth century—Gladstone's account of watching for days by the bedside of his dying daughter, for example—speaks to the power of emotional bonds, but historians have largely ignored it. They have instead taken some Victorians at their word and written the father out of the family except as a parody of the domestic autocrat or as the representative of all those forces which stood in the way of the equality of the sexes.

Second, I write in the wake of Baby M and am annoyed with the neo-essentialism it has spawned. Baby M was the case of the decade in my circles, a "representative anec-dote" for ancient but ageless questions in the late twentieth century. Like most people, I saw some right on both sides and had little sympathy for the marketplace in babies that brought them together. On the one hand Mary Beth Whitehead this . . .; on the other William Stern that . . . . The baby broker who arranged the deal was manifestly an unsavory character, the twentieth-century avatar of the sweatshop owners who in ages past profited unconscionably from the flesh of women. It was difficult not to subscribe to the doctrine that the baby's best interests must come first and it was by no means consistently clear where these lay. Each day brought new emotional tugs as the narrative unfolded on the front pages of every paper.

I was surprised that, for so many people, this transaction between a working-class woman and a professional man (a biochemist) became an epic prism through which the evils of capitalism and class society were refracted. It did not seem newsworthy to me that the poor sold their bodies or that the rich exploited their willingness to do so. What else would they sell? Malthus had pointed out almost two centuries ago that those who labored physically gave of their flesh and in the long run earned just enough to maintain and replenish it. So had Marx, who also identified women as the agents of social re-produc-tion.

Admittedly, the contract entered into by Whitehead and Stern was stripped of all shreds of decency and aesthetic mystification, flatfootedly revealing the deal for what it was—not a womb rental but a baby sale. This is why the New Jersey Supreme Court ruled it unenforceable. Every account that one reads of the surrogate baby broker's operations, with its well-dressed couples sitting in little cubicles interviewing long lines of less well-dressed but hopeful, spiffed-up women seeking work as surrogates, conjures up distasteful reminders of depression labor exchanges, starlet casting couches, or academic hiring fairs. But there surely are no new horrors in this case. Basically the Baby M narratives are modern versions of the industrial novel and allied genres in which factory labor is portrayed as wage slavery; in which children's tiny thin fingers are metamorphosed into the pin wire they hour after hour produce; in which paupers, whose labor is worthless on the open market, are depicted pounding bones into meal so that they might remain just this side of starvation.[1] In short, I remain cynical when some commentators discover Mary Beth Whitehead as the anti-capitalist Everywoman. If "surrogate" mothers were as well organized as the doctors who perform the much more expensive *in vitro* fertilization or as unionized baseball players they would earn a decent wage—say $100,000 instead of the ludicrously low $10,000—and opposition to surrogacy as emblematic of the evils of a free market in labor might be considered muted. (Though of course then the story might shift to emphasize the power of money to dissolve the very fabric of social decency, another nineteenth-century trope.)

I am, however, primarily interested in this case as the occasion for a return to naturalism. Feminism has been the most powerful de-naturalizing theoretical force in my intellectual firmament and, more generally, a major influence in the academic and cultural affairs that concern me. I regard it as both true and liberating that "the idea that men and women are two mutually exclusive categories must arise out of something other than a nonexistent 'natural' opposition," and that "gender is a socially imposed division of the sexes."[2] A major strand of commentary on Baby M, however, rejects this tradition and instead insists that the category "mother" is natural, a given of the world outside culture. Phyllis Chesler, for example, in the major article of a special "Mothers" issue of Ms (May, 1988) argues that motherhood is a "fact," an ontologically different category than "fatherhood," which is an "idea." Thus, "in order for the *idea* [my emphasis] of fatherhood to triumph over the *fact* of motherhood," she says, "we had to see Bill as the 'birth father' and Mary Beth as the surrogate uterus." (Actually Chesler misstates the claims. Mary Beth has been, rightly or wrongly, called the "surrogate mother," not the "surrogate uterus." But since the point of the article seems to be that mother and uterus are more or less the same thing this may be an intentional prevarication.)

I resist this view for obvious emotional reasons: it assumes that being the "factual" parent entails a stronger connection to the chid than being the "ideational" parent. (This assumption is widespread. During my daughter Hannah's five-week stay in the preemie nursery her caretakers, in the "social comments" column of her chart, routinely recorded my wife's visits to her incubator as "mother in to bond," whereas my appearances were usually noted with the affectively neutral "father visited.") While I do not want to argue against the primacy of material connection directly I do want to point out that it is not irrational to hold the opposite view and that, "in fact," the incorporeal quality of fatherhood has been the foundation of patriarchy's ideological edifice since the Greeks. In other words, simply stating that mothers have a greater material connection with the child is not to make an argument but to state a premise which historically has worked against Chesler's would-be conclusion. The Western philosophical tradition has generally valued idea over matter; manual labor for millennia was the great horizontal social divide. In other words, precisely because the mother's claim was "only" corporeal, because it was a matter of "fact," it was valued less.

I will recount some of the history of this discourse, but I also want to argue against its basic operating assumption: the unproblematic nature of fact especially in relation to such deeply cultural designations as mother or father and to the rights, emotions, or duties that are associated with them. The "facts" of motherhood—and of fatherhood for that matter—are not "given" but come into being as science progresses and as the adversaries in political struggles select what they need from the vast, ever-growing storehouses of knowledge. The idea that a child is of one's flesh and blood is very old while its biological correlatives and their cultural importance depend on the available supplies of fact and on their interpretation.

But the reason that the facts of motherhood and fatherhood are not "given" has less to do with what is known or not known than with the fundamental gap, recognized by David Hume, between facts and their meaning. *Is* does not imply *ought*, and more generally no fact or set of facts taken together entails or excludes a moral right or commitment. Laws, customs, and precepts, sentiments, emotion, and the power of the imagination make biological facts assume cultural significance. An Algonquin chief, confronted by a Jesuit in the seventeenth century with the standard European argument against women's promiscuity (how else would you know that a child is yours?), replied that he found it puzzling that whites could apparently only love "their" children, i.e., that only individual ownership entailed caring and affection.

Before proceeding I want to again warn my readers that some of my evidence and most of my passion arise from personal circumstance. I write as the father of a daughter to whom I am bound by the "facts" of a visceral love, not the molecular biology of reproduction. The fact of the matter is that from the instant the five-minute-old Hannah—a premature baby of 1430 grams who was born by Caesarean section—grasped my finger (I know this was due to reflex and not affection) I felt immensely powerful, and before the event, inconceivably strong bonds with her. Perhaps if practitioners of the various sub-specialties of endocrinology had been present they might have measured surges of neuro-transmitters and other hormones as strong as those that accompany parturition. But then what difference would that make—with what is one to feel if not with the body?

I also write as the would-be father, some sixteen months before Hannah came along, of a boy weighing something less than 800 grams who was aborted late one night—an induced stillbirth really—after twenty-four weeks of gestation because of a burst amniotic sac and the ensuing infection. I can recapture my sadness at his demise vividly and still regard the whole episode as one of the gloomiest of my life. Gail, my wife, was ambivalent about having the child—she was, she says, unprepared at age 40 for becoming pregnant the very first month at risk—and regards the abortion as a painful but not especially fraught episode which cleared the emotional ground to allow her to welcome Hannah's birth un-equivocally.

Finally I write as the male member of a family in which gender roles are topsy turvy. Hannah early on announced that she would prefer being a daddy to being a mommy because mommies had to go to work—hers is a lawyer—while daddies only had to go to their study. (As she has grown older and observed my not silent suffering as I finished a book begun the year she was born her views have been somewhat revised.) I am far guiltier of the stereotypical vices of motherhood—neurotic worry about Hannah's physical and mental well being, unfounded premonitions of danger, excessive emotional demands, and general nudginess—than is Gail. In short, my experiences—ignoring for the moment a vast ethnographic and somewhat smaller historical literature—make me suspect of the naturalness of "mother" or "father" in any culturally meaningful sense.

The association of fatherhood with ideas and motherhood with facts is ancient; only its moral valences have been recently reversed by some feminists. The Marquis de Sade suggests that the "idea" of fatherhood—the notion that a child is "born of the father's blood" and only incidentally of a mother's body—means that it "owes filial tenderness to him alone, an assertion not without its appealing qualities. . . ."[3] Sade is the most rabid of anti-maternalists and his argument is made to induce a girl to sexually defile and humiliate her mother; but his relative valuation of fact and idea is standard. The "idea" of fatherhood gave, and displayed, the power of patriarchy for much of Western history since the Greeks.

Bolingbrooke in *Richard II* (1, 3, 69) addresses his father as

> Oh thou, the earthly author of my blood,
> Whose youthful spirit, in me regenerate.

He is author and authority because, like the poet who has in his mind the design for the verses that subsequently appear, he has the conceit for the child in him. The physical act of writing, or of producing the child, matters little. Conceiving a child in this model is a man's sparking of an idea in the uterus which contains, like a block of marble, a form waiting to be liberated. It is like writing on a piece of paper awaiting inscription. The "generation of things in Nature and the generation of things in Art take place in the same way," argued the great seventeenth-century physician William Harvey, who discovered the circulation of the blood. "Now the brain is the instrument of conception of the one . . . and of the other the uterus or egg."[4] And being the instrument is less elevated than being the author: "He," speaking of God, "was the author, thou the instrument," says King Henry in offering pardon to Warwick (3 *Henry VI*, 4, 6, 18).

But the idea of "father" as bound to his child in the way a poet is to verse, i.e., its genitor, is much older than Shakespeare. It is, argues Freud, one of the cornerstones of culture; believing in fathers, like believing in the Hebrew God, reflects the power of abstract thought and hence of civilization itself.

The "Moses religion's" insistence that God cannot be seen—the graven image proscription—"means that a sensory perception was given second place to what may be called an abstract idea." This God represents "a triumph of intellectuality over sensuality [*Triumph der Geistigkeit uber de Sinnlichkeit*], or strictly speaking, an instinctual renunciation. . . ." Freud briefs precisely the same case for fathers as for God in his analysis of Aeschylus' *Eumenides*, which follows immediately his discussion of the Second Commandment. Orestes denies that he has killed his mother by denying that being born of her entails special bonds or obligation. Apollo makes the defense's case: appearances notwithstanding, no man has a mother. "The mother is no parent of that which is called her child, but only nurse of the new-planted seed that grows." She is but "a stranger." The only true parent is "he who mounts."[5]

Here is the founding myth of the Father. "Paternity" [*Vaterschaft*], Freud concludes, "is a supposition" and like belief in the Jewish God it is "based on an inference, a premise," while "maternity" [*Mutterschaft*], like the old gods, is based on evidence of the senses alone. The invention of paternity, like that of a transcendent God, was thus also "a momentous step"; it likewise—Freud repeats the phrase but with a more decisive military emphasis—was "a conquest [*einen Sieg*] of intellectuality over sensuality." It too represented a victory of the more elevated, the more refined, the more spiritual over the less refined, the sensory, the material. It too is a world-historical "*Kulturfortschritt*," a great cultural stride forward.

Similarly, the great medieval encyclopedist Isidore of Seville could, without embarrassment, make three different claims about the nature of seed—that only men had *sperma*, that only women had *sperma*, and that both had *sperma*—which would be mutually contradictory if they were about the body but perfectly compatible if they were instead corporeal illustrations of cultural truths purer and more fundamental than biological "fact." Isidore's entire work is predicated on the belief that the origin of words informs one about the pristine, uncorrupted, essential nature of their referents, of a reality beyond the corrupt senses, beyond facts.

In the first case Isidore is explaining consanguinity and, as one would expect in a society in which inheritance and legitimacy pass through the father, he is at pains to emphasize the exclusive origins of the seed in the father's blood, in the purest, frothiest, white part of that blood shaken from the body as the foam is beaten from the sea as it crashes on the rocks.[6] For a child to have a father *means* that it is "from one blood," the father's; and conversely to be a father *is* to produce the substance, semen, through which blood is passed on to one's successors. Generation seems to happen without woman at all and there is no hint that blood—"that by which man is animated, and is sustained, and lives," as Isidore tells us elsewhere—could in any fashion be transmitted other than through the male.[7] Now case two, illegitimate descent. This presents a quite different biology: the child under these circumstances is from the *body* of the mother alone; it is "spurious," he explains, because "the ancients called the female genitalia the *spurium*" (9, 5, 24). So, while the legitimate child is from the froth of the father, the illegitimate child seems to come solely from factual flesh, from the seed of the mother's genitals, as if the father did not exist. And finally, when Isidore is explaining why children resemble their progenitors and is not interested in motherhood or fatherhood he remarks pragmatically that "newborns resemble fathers, if the semen of the father is potent, and resemble mothers if the mothers' semen is potent." Both parents, in this account, have seeds which engage in repeated combat for domination every time, and in each generation, a child is conceived (Isidore, 11, 1, 145).

These three distinct and mutually exclusive arguments are a dramatic illustration that much of the debate about the nature of the seed and of the bodies that produce it was in fact not about bodies at all but rather about power, legitimacy, and the politics of fatherhood. They are in principle not resolvable by recourse to the senses. One might of course argue that "just so" stories like Isidore's or Aeschylus' are simply no longer tenable given what has been known since the nineteenth century about conception. Modern biology makes perfectly clear what "mother" and "father" are. But science is relevant only if these stories are understood as reductionistic, as claiming to be true because of biology, which is, rightly, not the sort of claim Isidore and Aeschylus are making. The facts they adduce to illustrate essentially cultural claims may no longer be acceptable and we may persist in reading their cultural claims as based in a false biology. But the "fact" of women bearing children has never been in dispute and has nonetheless counted for relatively little historically in establishing their claims to recognition or authority over children or property.

Facts, as I suggested earlier, are but shifting sands for the construction of motherhood or fatherhood. They come and go and are ludicrously open to interpretation. Regnier de Graaf's discovery of the ovum in 1672 seemed to relegate the male/father to an unaccustomed and distinctly secondary role in reproduction. (Actually de Graaf discovered the follicle that bears his name but which he and others mistakenly took to be the egg. Karl Ernst von Baer in 1827 was the first to observe a mammalian egg and an unfertilized human egg was not seen until 1930.[8]) The female after de Graaf could be imagined to provide the matter for the fetus in a pre-formed if not immediately recognized form while the male "only serv'd to Actuate it." This, one contemporary observed, "derogates much from the dignity of the Male-Sex," which he thought was restored when "Mons. Leeuwenhoek by the Help of his Exquisite Microscope . . . detected Innumerable small *Animals* in the Masculine sperm, and by his Noble Discovery, at once removed that Difficulty. . . ."[9]

I hope by this egregious example to suggest that the form of the argument, and not just its factual premises, are flawed; both conclusions are silly. And, the discovery, still accepted, that neither egg nor sperm contains a pre-formed human but that the fetus develops epigenetically according to plans acquired from both parents does not settle the question of the comparative claims of mother or father, just as the mistaken notions of the past did not entail judgments of their comparative dignities.

Interpretations, not facts, are at issue. The Archbishop of Hartford announced in the *New York Times* on August 26, 1988, that he had quit the Democratic party because it supported abortion: "it is officially in favor of executing unborn babies whose only crime is that they temporarily occupy their mother's womb." No one would dispute that the "thing" in the mother's womb is, under some construction, an unborn baby. "Baby" is a common term for fetus as well as for a very young child and the phrase "the baby is kicking again" to refer to an intra-uterine action is generally acceptable; baby-as-fetus is indisputably only a temporary occupant. The Archbishop's interpretation is objectionable because he elides the difference between "baby-in-the-womb" and "baby-in-the-world," between the womb and any other space an infant might occupy, and therefore between abortion and execution. At issue here is meaning, not nature.

David Hume makes manifest the chasm between the two. A beautiful fish, a wild animal, a spectacular landscape, or indeed "anything that neither belongs, nor is related to us," he says, inspires in us no pride or vanity or sense of obligation. We might with perfect reason fear a minor injury to ourselves and care almost nothing about the deaths of millions of distant strangers. The fault is not with the objects themselves but with their relationship to us. They are too detached and distant to arouse passion. Only, Hume argues, when these "external objects acquire any particular relation to ourselves, and are associated or connected with us," do they engage the emotions.[10] Owning the "external object" seems for Hume to be the most obvious way for this to happen, although ownership itself is, of course, an immensely elastic notion. A biological parent, uncle, clan, "family" can "own" a child in such a fashion as to love and cherish it. But more generally Hume is suggesting that moral concern and action are engendered not by the logic of the relationship between human beings but by the degree to which the emotional and imaginative connections which entail love or obligation have been forged.

The "fact" of motherhood is precisely the psychic labor that goes into making these connections, into appropriating the fetus and then child into a mother's moral and emotional economy. The "fact" of fatherhood is of a like order. If a labor theory of value gives parents rights to a child, that labor is of the heart, not the hand. (The heart, of course, does its work through the hand; we feel through the body. But I will let the point stand in its polemical nakedness.)

While I was working as a volunteer in an old people's home I was attracted to, and ultimately became rather good friends with, a gay woman who was its director of activities. At lunch one day—she had alerted me that she wanted to discuss "something" and not just, as we usually did, schmooz—she asked whether I would consider donating sperm should she and her long-time lover decide, as they were on the verge of doing, to have a child. I was for her a generally appropriate donor—Jewish, fit, with no history of genetic disorders in my family. She was asking me also, she said, because she liked me. It was the first, and remains the only, time I had been asked by anyone, much less someone I liked, and so I was flattered and pleased.

I was also hesitant. My wife the lawyer raised serious legal difficulties with donating "owned" sperm, i.e., sperm that is not given or sold for anonymous distribution. I would remain legally liable for child-support for at least twenty-one years, not to speak of being generally entangled with the lives of a couple I liked but did not know well. (Anonymous sperm is alienated from its producer and loses its connection with him as if it were the jetsam and flotsam of the sea or an artisan's product in the marketplace. Semen, in other words, counts as one of these products of the body that can be alienated, like plasma and blood cells, and not like kidneys or eyes, whose marketing is forbidden.)

Legal issues, however, did not weigh heavily with me. The attractive part of the proposition—that I was being asked because of who I was and therefore that I was to be a father and not just a donor—also weighed mightily against it. A thought experiment with unpleasant results presented itself. I immediately imagined this would-be child as a version of Hannah, imagined that I could see her only occasionally and for short periods of time, imagined that her parents would take her back to their native Israel and that I would never see her again. Potential conflicts with my friend about this baby were almost palpable on the beautiful sunny afternoon of our lunch. In short, I was much too cathexed with this imaginary child to ever give up the sperm to produce her.

I recognize now, and did at the time, that my response was excessive. My reveries of fatherhood sprang from a fetishistic attachment to one among millions of rapidly replenished microscopic organisms—men make on the order of 400 billion sperm in a lifetime—swimming in an abundant, nondescript saline fluid. All that I was really being asked to do was "to produce" some semen—a not unpleasant process—and to give it to my friend so that *a* very, very tiny sperm—actually only its 4–5 micrometers long and 2.5 to 3.5 micrometers wide (c. 1/10,000 to 1/20,000 of an inch) head—might contribute the strands of DNA wafting about in it to her egg. Since we humans apparently share 95% of our genetic material with chimpanzees, the sperm in question must share a still higher percentage of base pairs with those of my fellow humans. In short, my unique contribution to the proposed engagement, that which I did not share with billions of other men and monkeys, was infinitesimally small. I was making a mountain out of much, much, much less than a molehill and not very much more than a molecule.

But this is as it should be. For much of history the problem has been to make men take responsibility for their children. Prince and pauper as circumstances required could easily deny the paternity that nature did so little to make evident. The double standard or sexual morality served to insure that however widely they sowed their wild oats the fruits of their wives' wombs would be unambiguously theirs. In fact, until very recently paternity was impossible to prove and much effort went into developing histo-immunological assays that could establish the biological link between a specific man and child. The state, of course, has an interest in making some male, generally the "biological father," responsible for supporting "his" children. In short, a great deal of cultural work has gone into giving meaning to a small bit of matter. Ironically, now that tests make it possible to identify the father with about 100% accuracy, women—those who want children *without* a father—have considerable difficulty obtaining sperm free of filiation. History, social policy, imagination, and culture continue to encumber this cell with its haploid of chromosomes.

In 1978, Mary K., a gay woman living in Sonoma County, California, decided that she wanted to have a child which she would "co-parent" with a close gay woman friend living nearby.[11] Mary wanted to find a sperm donor herself rather than use anonymous sperm for several reasons which she later more or less clearly articulated. She did not want to make the repeated trips to Berkeley, the location of the nearest sperm bank; she did not want to use a physician in her community who might be able to acquire sperm anonymously because she felt that as a nurse she could not be assured of confidentiality; and—this would come to haunt her—she wanted some vestige of an individual human being to be associated with the sperm and with the hoped-for baby. She wanted a "father" of some ill-defined sort, and after a month or so of looking around and after interviewing three potential donors, she was introduced one January evening to a young gay man, Jhordan C., who seemed to fit her needs. He would become the "father" of her child, despite the fact that he did not have the red hair that she had originally sought in a donor.

Neither Jhordan or Mary thought very rigorously about what they expected from their relationship or just what his paternal rights and obligations would be. Neither sought legal counsel; they signed no contract or other written understanding and resolved only the most basic practical details of the matter: Jhordan, upon being notified that Mary was ovulating, would journey to her house, and "produce" sperm, which she would introduce into herself. It took six months before Mary conceived and each of his visits was apparently attended by commonplace social intercourse—some chit chat, tea, and other pleasantries.

After Mary conceived she and Jhordan saw each other occasionally. She accepted his invitation to a small New Year's party at the home of one of his close friends. She testifies that he "reiterated" to her that "he wanted to be known as the father—and I told him I would let the child know who the biological father was—and that he wanted to travel with the child when the child was older." In all other respects she believed that they had an implicit understanding that she would be the child's guardian and primary parent; that Victoria T., Mary's friend, would be co-parent; and that Jhordan would play effectively no role in the life of *her* child.

On the basis of Jhordan's own testimony, he did not know precisely what he meant by wanting "to be known as the father." The court-appointed psychologist described him as a young man of unsettled plans and interests. But Jhordan knew that he wanted somehow to be acknowledged. He was upset when Mary informed him, some months before the birth, that his name would not be on the birth certificate and he became increasingly uneasy as he came to realize that he was being increasingly written out of the family drama that he had helped launch.

Mary admits that she too had been vague about what Jhordan's being her child's father meant to her and that he did have some grounds for his expectation that he would play some sort of paternal role. Language failed her when she tried to describe it:

> I had thought about and I was considering whether or not I would tell Sean [not his real name] who the father was, but I didn't know if I would tell him as a father. Like he would know that Jhordan helped donate the sperm, but I did not know if he would ever know Jhordan—How do I say this? I didn't plan on Sean relating as a father. No.

The confusion of names and collapse of grammar here suggests precisely the underlying ambiguities of this case.

When Sean was born Mary felt increasingly threatened by Jhordan's insistence on seeing him, on displaying him to his family, on taking pictures to show to friends and relatives, and in general in acting like a parent, a role that Mary had thought was reserved for herself and Victoria. Jhordan, on the other hand, told the psychologist who interviewed him to determine his fitness as a parent that when "he looked into Sean's eyes, he 'saw his whole family there.'" Whatever uncertainties he might have felt before vanished in the face of his imagined flesh and blood.

Mary finally refused to allow Jhordan to see the baby at all and he eventually gave up trying. There matters might have rested had not, a year later, Mary applied for welfare. The state sued Jhordan for child support (it was after all his sperm) and he, of course, eagerly agreed to pay. Two years and two lawyers later he won visiting rights with Sean at the home of Mary's friend and co-parent, Victoria. These privileges were subsequently expanded. From here on the story is like that of countless divorced couples: quarrels about visitation hours and pick-up times, about where Sean would spend his holidays and birthdays, about whether Jhordan allowed him to eat too much sugar, and about other of the many controversial niceties of child-raising that divide parents in even the tightest of families. A court promulgated guidelines and issued orders; an uneasy peace settled over all the parties.

The trial judge in this case was a rather old-fashioned sort who did not seem terribly interested in the subtleties of the law regarding the rights of sperm donors but believed that "blood is thicker than water" and that Sean both needed, and had "a right to," a father. Jhordan was the father and therefore ought, in the judge's view, to be given commensurate visitation rights.

Mary appealed (*Jhordan C. v Mary K.* [1986] 179 CA3d 386, 224 CR 530). The central question before the high court was how to interpret sections 7005(a) and (b) of the California Civil Code. These provide that if, under the supervision of a doctor, a married woman is inseminated by semen from a man who is not her husband, that man under certain circumstances is treated as if he were *not* the natural father while the husband is treated as if he were. Mary's lawyers argued that while their client's case did not quite fit under this statute it was close enough and that the only possible distinction was one of sexual orientation, which ought not to matter. Other California statutes provide that the law must not discriminate against unconventional parenting arrangements in adoption and other reproductive rights issues. If Mary had been married to someone and had acquired Jhordan's sperm in precisely the same circumstances—admittedly not meeting all the conditions of the statute—it would be ludicrous to suppose that the State would give him rights that infringed upon those of the husband. (A German court has held that a man has no claims on a child of a married woman even if he is acknowledged to be the "biological father." Today, as has been generally true for centuries, children born in wedlock are presumed to belong to the husband of the woman who bore them.)

Moreover, Mary's lawyers argued, section 7005a's reference to semen given "to a licensed physician" was not intended to limit the law's application only to such cases but reflected simply a legislative directive to insure proper health standards by recourse to a physician. Mary, because of her training as a nurse, was able to comply with this standard on her own. Her lawyers also cited another court case which held—admittedly in different circumstances—that

> A child conceived through heterologous artificial insemination [i.e. with semen from a man other than the woman's husband] does not have a "natural father." . . . The anonymous donor of sperm can not be considered the "natural father," as he is no more responsible for the use made of his sperm than is a donor of blood or a kidney.

Echoes of Isidore of Seville. Jhordan might not have been anonymous but he was certainly a stranger to Mary.

His lawyers naturally argued for a stricter construal of section 7005a–b and the appeals court sided with them. By not employing a physician, the court agreed, Mary had excluded herself from the law's protection. Moreover, the court viewed the case before it as being more like those in which artificial insemination occurred within the context of an established relationship and in which the sperm donor retained paternal rights than it was like cases of anonymous donation. Jhordan's lawyer cited a New Jersey Supreme Court case, for example, in which a man and a woman were dating and intended to marry. She wanted to bear his child but didn't want to have pre-marital intercourse so they resorted to artificial insemination. Three months into the pregnancy they broke up and she declared that she wanted nothing more to do with him and that she certainly would not allow him to visit their child. He sued for a paternity and won.

Mary and Jhordan were obviously not as intimately involved as this couple but, the court felt, neither were they the anonymous strangers envisaged by statute. Enough humanity remained in Jhordan's transaction with Mary to allow him to believe that his sperm, however introduced into Mary's body, retained some of him.

As this case and others like it suggest, the legal status of a sperm donor remains deeply problematic and, advises a National Lawyers Guild Handbook, those "consulted by a lesbian considering artificial insemination must be extremely careful to explain the ramifications of the various choices available to their clients."[12] Using a medically supervised sperm bank where the identity of the donor is unknown to the recipient is the most certain way to guarantee that the donor will not at some time in the future be construed as the father. Other possibilities include having a friend secure semen but keeping the source secret; using semen from multiple donors (not recommended because of possible immune reactions); using a known donor but having a physician as an intermediary. Some lawyers recommend having the recipient pay the donor for his sperm and describing the transaction in an ordinary commercial contract of the sort with which the courts are familiar. And even if agreements between sperm donors and recipients are not predictably enforceable, lawyers suggest that the parties set down their understanding of their relationship as clearly as possible.

Any or all of these strategies might have stripped Jhordan's sperm of paternity, not just in the eyes of the law but more importantly in his heart, and might thus have saved Mary and her co-parent their struggles with the parental claims of a near stranger. Mary was wrong to eschew a doctor's mediation or at least underestimated the hold that a very small bit of matter can, in the right circumstances, have on a man's imagination.

In designating a physician as middleman the legislature did not blindly medicalize an essentially social transaction but sought rather to appropriate one of modern medicine's least attractive features—its lack of humanity—for a socially useful end. Everyone knows, even politicians, that artificial insemination does not require a physician. De-paternalizing sperm might. A strange doctor in a lab coat working amidst white formica furniture, high tech instruments, officious nurses, and harried receptionists in a boxy office in a nondescript glass and steel building set in a parking lot may offer cold comfort to the sick and needy; he or she might, however, be perfect at taking the sparkle off sperm.

Had Jhordan donated sperm not at Mary's house, where he was offered tea and conversation, but at a clinic; had he never spoken to her after the inseminations began but only to the doctor's nurse, who would have whisked away the vial of fresh semen; had he never seen Mary pregnant or celebrated New Year's Eve with her, the fetish of the sperm might have been broken. The doctor as broker would have performed his or her priestly function, de-blessed the sperm, and gotten rid of its "paternity." (This I imagine as the inversion of normal priestly work, providing extra emotional glue between the participants in weddings, funerals, and the like.) Similarly, selling sperm at a price fixed by contract—the lawyer or sperm bank owner as de-blessing agent—would take off some of its paternal blush. Without such rites, a father's material claim in his child is small but his imaginative claims can be as endless as a mother's. Great care must be taken to protect and not to squash them.

Because fatherhood is an "idea," it is not limited to men. In a recent case litigated in Alameda County, California (Lofton v. Flouroy), a woman was, rightly in my view, declared to be a child's father, if not its male parent. Ms. Lofton and Ms. Flouroy lived together and decided to have a child. Lofton's brother Larry donated the required sperm but expressed no interest in having any further role in the matter. Ms. Lofton introduced her brother's semen into Flouroy with a turkey baster, Flouroy became pregnant, and in due course a baby was born. The "birth mother" was listed on its birth certificate as "mother," and L. Lofton—Linda, not Larry, but who was to know?—was listed as "father."

Everything went well and the women treated the child as theirs until, two years later, they split up. The mother kept the child and there matters might have rested had not, as in the case of Mary and Jhordan, the State intervened. Flouroy applied for welfare benefits, i.e., aid to dependent children, and when asked by the Family Support Bureau to identify the father she produced, in moment of unabashed concreteness, the turkey baster. The Bureau, not amused, did what it was meant to do and went after the "father" on the birth certificate—Linda, it was surprised to learn, not Larry. Like Jhordan she welcomed the opportunity to claim paternity, did not dispute the claim and eagerly paid the judgment entered against her: child support, current and retroactive. She also demanded paternal visitation rights, which Ms. Flouroy resisted. Lofton then asked the court to compel mediation. It held that she was indeed a "psychological parent" and thus had standing to have her rights mediated. The other L. Lofton, Larry, makes no appearance in this drama.

Linda's claim is manifestly not biological nor even material. That she borrowed her brother's sperm or owned the turkey baster is irrelevant. What matters is that, in the emotional economy of her relationship with her lover and their child, she was the father, whatever that means, and enjoyed the rights and bore the obligations of that status. She invested the required emotional and imaginative capital in the impregnation, gestation, and subsequent life to make the child in some measure hers.

I hasten to add that I do not regard biology in all circumstances as counting for nothing. Women have claims with respect to the baby within them simply by virtue of spatial relations and rights to bodily integrity. These are not the right to be or not to be a mother as against the right to be or not to be a father, nor the claims of a person as against those of a non-person—the terms in which the abortion debate is usually put— but the right shared by all mentally competent adults to control and monitor corporeal boundaries, to maintain a body as theirs. Thus I would regard a court compelling a woman to bear a child against her will as a form of involuntary servitude however much its would-be father might wish for the child. And I would regard an enforced abortion as an even more egregious assault on her body. But this is not to acknowledge the "fact" of motherhood as much as the "fact" of flesh. History bears witness to the evils that ensue when the state abrogates a person's rights in her body.

The flesh does not make a mother's body an ahistorical font of motherhood and maternity. A writer who wants, but cannot herself have, a child and who finds surrogate motherhood morally unacceptable "can not imagine" that "there are plenty of women now, the huge majority of surrogates who have, to hear them tell it, not suffered such a loss [as Mary Beth Whitehead's]."[13] While her empathic instincts extend easily to White- head she cannot, despite testimony to the contrary, conceive of a mother *not* feeling an instant and apparently unmediated bond to her child. Ms. Fleming cannot accept that feelings do not follow from flesh so that "surrogate mothers" who feel otherwise than they supposedly should must suffer, like un-class-conscious workers, from false consciousness.

*Ms's* special "Mothers Issue," quite apart from Chesler's article, is striking by its very cover—an airbrushed, soft-toned picture of a 1950s young Ivory Soap woman, with straight blond hair of the sort that waves in shampoo commercials, holding a blue-eyed baby to her bare bosom and looking dreamily out of the frame of the picture—which would have been denounced by feminists as perpetuating an unacceptable stereotype of women had it appeared in *Family Circle* a decade ago. In 1988 it unashamedly represents the Mother in America's largest selling feminist magazine.

What exactly are the facts of motherhood and what of significance ought to follow from them? For advocates of Mrs. Whitehead's, like Phyllis Chesler, her egg and its genetic contents are not especially relevant. She shares with Bill, a.k.a. Dr. Stern, the provision of chromosomes. The critical fact is therefore her nine months of incubation, which would remain a fact even if the fertilized egg she was bringing to term were not hers. Her claim, it appears, rests on labor, on her physical intimacy with the child within her, and would be just as strong if a second woman sought a stake in the child on the basis of her contribution of half its chromosomes.

I am immensely sympathetic to this view but not because of a fact of nature. Capitalist societies, as I suggested earlier, are not usually friendly to the notion that putting labor into a product entitles one to ownership or even to much credit. It is the rare company that gives its workers shares of stock. We associate a new production of *The Magic Flute* with David Hockney and not with those who sawed, hammered, and painted the sets; everyone knows that Walt Disney produced *Bambi* but only the "cognoscenti" could name even one of the artists who actually made the pictures. Having the idea or the plan is what counts, which is why Judge Sokoloff told Dr. Stern that in getting Melissa he was only getting what was already his. (The Judge should, of course, have said, "half his.")

I became so exercised by Baby M because Dr. Stern's claims have been reduced in some circles to his ownership of his sperm which, as I said earlier, amounts to owning very little. This puts him—all fathers—at a distinct material disadvantage to Mrs. White-head—all women—who contribute so much more matter. But, this essay has suggested, his claims, like hers, arise from the intense and profound bonding with a child, unborn and born, that its biological kinship might spark in the moral and affective imagination but which it does not entail.

The problem, of course, is that emotional capital does not accumulate steadily, visibly, and predictably as in a psychic payroll deduction plan. That is why, for example, it is unreasonable to demand of a woman specific performance on a surrogate mothering contract as if the baby were a piece of land or a work of art whose attributes would be well known to their vendor. A "surrogate mother," like a mother who offers to give up her baby for adoption to a stranger, must be allowed a reasonable time to change her mind and if she does, in the case of a surrogacy arrangement, be prepared to argue for her rights against those of the father.

Each parent would bring to such a battle claims to have made another person emotionally part of themselves. "Facts" like bearing the child would obviously be significant evidence but would not be unimpeachable, would not be nature speaking unproblematically to culture. While we can continue to look forward to continuing conflict over the competing claims of parents I suggest that we abandon the notion that biology—facts—will somehow provide the resolution. Neither, of course, will ideas alone in a world in which persons exist corporeally. The way out of the fact/idea dichotomy is to recognize its irrelevance in these matters. The "facts" of such socially powerful and significant categories as mother and father come into being only as culture imbues things, actions, and flesh with meaning. This is the process that demands our continued attention.

# Reading Questions

1. How do the histories of fatherhood which Laqueur advocates differ from the ideological perspectives that he describes?
2. What are the narrative elements of the Baby M story that make it a "representative anecdote" that Laqueur finds simply to repeat old news? In what ways has the Baby M case prompted a return to naturalism?
3. What is the basic operating assumption about fatherhood and motherhood that Laqueur argues against?
4. How is the association of paternal power and privilege with its "idea" historically repeated from Aristotle, Shakespeare, and Moses to Isidore of Seville?
5. To which of Hume's precepts does Laqueur appeal to establish emotional labor as a significant element in the claims of paternity as well as maternity? How does this appeal support Laqueur's prescriptive conclusion that, similarly to adoption precedents, surrogate mothers ought to be allowed a reasonable time to change their minds?
6. How do the stories of Mary K. and Ms. Flouroy support Laqueur's advocacy of depaternalizing the donor relation through medical, economic, and legal paradigms?

# Recommended Reading

Roberta Achtenberg, ed., *Sexual Orientation and the Law* (New York: Clark, Boardman, 1989)

Katha Pollitt, "The Strange Case of Baby M," *The Nation* (May 23, 1987)

Janice G. Raymond, *Women as Wombs: Reproductive Technologies and the Battle over Women's Freedom* (San Francisco, CA: Harper, 1993)

Patricia Williams, "On Being the Object of Property," *The Alchemy of Race and Rights* (Cambridge: Harvard University Press, 1991)

## CHAPTER 8

# The Politics of Hope

Members of the Green Party in West Germany release doves as a symbol of peace during an antinuclear demonstration in front of the White House on July 7, 1983. Don Rypka/UPI/Bettmann.

# Holding the Line at Greenham Common

## Being Joyously Political in Dangerous Times [Feb. 1985]

### ANN SNITOW

Ann Snitow, a feminist activist since 1969, is the coeditor of *Powers of Desire: The Politics of Sexuality,* and is professor of literature and women's studies at the New School for Social Research in New York City. Currently she is working with women from Eastern and Central Europe in an organization she founded, The Network of East–West Women.

I made my first trip to the women's peace encampment at Greenham Common last May partly to assure myself it was still there. After mass evictions in April, the press had announced with some glee that the continuous vigil at the U.S. cruise missile base was over at last. Certainly on my arrival in the freezing rain there seemed little enough evidence to contradict these reports.

When I reached the prosperous town of Newbury with a friend who had given me a lift from London, we couldn't at first find even the base, which our map said was a misshapen oval just outside the town. How could something nine miles around, bounded by a 10-foot fence, guarded by large contingents of the U.S. Air Force, the Royal Air Force, and the police be so quietly tucked away?

Finally a scrawled woman's symbol painted on the road gave us a clue. We went up to the plateau of land that was once "common" to all. And suddenly, the fence was right in front of us in the fog. The Greenham fence looks very serious—thick wire mesh topped by several feet of rolled barbed wire, all supported at frequent intervals by cement pylons. Ten feet farther inside are more rolls of barbed wire, forming a tangled second barrier rather like those on the battlefields of World War I. Inside the fence, we could just make out—through sheets of wire and rain—concrete runways, small bunkerlike buildings, a treeless wasteland. One structure, rather like a giant, half-buried two-car garage, was, as I learned later, a missile silo.

But there were no women. Here was a gate, certainly, one of the nine where the women live, and before it several little humps of plastic, but the only people on view were a few policemen. A mile farther along and, finally, two women, standing beneath a twisted umbrella that they seemed to be holding more over the struggling fire than themselves. Two smallish women in the rain. Impossible. In silent agreement we drove on to yet another gate with again a huddle of plastic, an extinguished fire, a forlorn dereliction.

I finally understood: this was it. I asked to be dropped off back with those women with the umbrella and the fire. (You can't imagine what a depressing idea this was.) We drove back. I struggled into the waterproof boots my friend had lent me—absolute necessities as I soon discovered—and joined the women.

They were Donna and Maria. They were very, very wet. Maria's face was hidden under her sodden hood, though one could just manage to see she had a bad cold. Donna wished the world to know she was "fed up." Neither was interested in talking much. They seemed faintly aroused to hear that I had just come from New York, but as the day progressed I came to understand their lack of surprise. We stood there in the stinking nowhere and people stopped by in cars, visiting us from all over the world. If Greenham feels like world's end, it is also a mecca, a shrine of the international peace movement.

Inventive, leaderless, a constantly rotating population of women have blocked the smooth functioning of this cruise missile base for three years now. In the great traditions of pacifism, anarchy, and English doggedness in adversity, they have entered the base, blockaded its gates, danced on its missile silos, made a mockery of its security systems, and inspired other people to set up peace camps elsewhere in Britain and all over the world—in Italy, for instance, and Australia, Japan and the United States.

The camps were empty that first day because some of the women were exhausted; some in jail; some in New York suing Ronald Reagan; some at the cruise missile base in Sicily, helping the beleaguered women's peace camp there; some in Holland for a big government vote on NATO. After a few hours, Donna, too, left with one of the circumnavigating cars, off to Reading for a bath and a drink. Maria and I stayed where we were, which proved to be Indigo Gate. (The women have named their homes for the colors of the rainbow.) Although most of the women were gone, the Greenham peace camp was not shut down: at each gate several women were sticking it out in the rain. In fact, you can't really shut Greenham, even if you drag all the women away from all the gates. They come back or they go home, explaining that it hardly matters: "Greenham women are everywhere."

Back in 1981 when I first heard about the women's peace camp at Greenham Common, I was impressed but a little worried, too. Here was a stubborn little band of squatters obstructing business as usual at a huge military base. But the early media reports celebrated these women as orderly housewives and mothers who would never make this vulgar noise just for themselves but were naturally concerned about their children, innocent animals, and growing plants.

My feminist reaction was: not *again*. I had joined the women's liberation movement in 1970 to escape this very myth of the special altruism of women, our innate peacefulness, our handy patience for repetitive tasks, our peculiar endurance—no doubt perfect for sitting numbly in the Greenham mud, babies and arms outstretched, begging men to keep our children safe from nuclear war.

We feminists had argued back then that women's work had to be done by men, too: no more "women only" when it came to emotional generosity or trips to the launderette. We did form women-only groups—an autonomous women's movement—but this was to forge a necessary solidarity for resistance, not to cordon off a magic femaleness as distorted in its way as the old reverence for motherhood. Women have a long history of allowing their own goals to be eclipsed by others, and even feminist groups have often been subsumed by other movements. Given this suspiciously unselfish past, I was uneasy with women-only groups that did not concentrate on overcoming the specific oppression of women.

And why should demilitarization be women's special task? If there's one thing in this world that *won't* discriminate in men's favor, it's a nuclear explosion. Since the army is a dense locale of male symbols, actions, and forms of association, let men sit in the drizzle, I thought; let *them* worry about the children for a change.

But even before going to Greenham I should have known better than to have trusted its media image. If the women were such nice little home birds, what were they doing out in the wild, balking at male authority, refusing to shut up or go back home? I've been to Greenham twice now in the effort to understand why many thousands of women have passed through the camps, why thousands are organized in support groups all over Britain and beyond, why thousands more can be roused to help in emergencies or show up for big actions.

What I discovered has stirred my political imagination more than any activism since that first, intense feminist surge 15 years ago. Though I still have many critical questions about Greenham, I see it as a rich source of fresh thinking about how to be joyously, effectively political in a conservative, dangerous time. Obviously this intense conversion experience is going to take some explaining.

When, in the summer of 1981, a small group of women from Cardiff in Wales decided to use their holidays to take a long walk for peace, they could choose from a startlingly large number of possible destinations. Unobtrusive, varying in size and purpose, more than 100 U.S. military facilities are tucked away in the English countryside, an embarrassment of military sites available for political pilgrimage.

One U.S. base distinguished itself as particularly dreadful. Enormous, centrally located, but quietly carrying on incognito, the site was Greenham Common, outside the town of Newbury, where the U.S. Air Force was then preparing for 96 ground-launched cruise missiles to be deployed in the fall of 1983. The cruise, along with the Pershing II missile, is a centerpiece of NATO's new European arsenal. Because it is small and deployed from mobile launch points on sea or land, and because it flies low, the cruise is hard to detect—transparently a first-strike weapon.

To protest this new step in the arms race, the Welsh women set out to walk 120 miles due east to Newbury, only 60 miles out from London. They were a varied bunch, mostly strangers to each other—36 women from very different class and political backgrounds, four men in support, and a few children. Their nine-day walk, which was ignored by the press, filled them with excitement and energy, and they were greeted warmly in the towns along the way.

By the time they reached Greenham, however, the media silence had become galling. Four women decided to chain themselves to the main gate of the base to force the world to take notice. This act of protest has had children and grandchildren undreamed of by the original, quite humble, and politically inexperienced Greenham marchers. Teachers, farmers, nurses, and—yes—housewives, they had had no intention of *staying* at Greenham. But first the media took their time; then tents had to be set up and people informed. A few days spent in support of the chained women lengthened to a week, then two. Some campers had to leave, but others were just arriving.

The summer days began to give way to the chill damp of English winter. Perhaps it felt callow to give up protesting against nuclear disaster just because the afternoons were drawing in. Gradually, as the peace camp persisted—a small cluster of tents and caravans at the main gate of the base—one fact became plain: Greenham was tapping a great, hidden energy source for protest. There were enough women who were willing to give bits of time stolen from the work-that-is-never-done to keep a campfire perpetually burning on Greenham Common.

After initial amusement and tolerance, the missile base took alarm. Winter came but the women did not go away. On January 20, 1982, the nearby town of Newbury served notice on the camps of its intention to evict.

If ever the women had considered packing it in, this evidence that they were a real thorn in the side of the American military and its English support systems must have clinched matters. Prime Minister Margaret Thatcher told the world the women were irresponsible; she didn't like them one bit. The women began telling reporters, "We're here for as long as it takes"—the "it" left menacingly unspecific. Some may have meant only the local rejection of U.S. cruise missiles. But by this time even the opposition Labour party was beginning to consider the far more ambitious goal of unilateral disarmament as a serious English option.

The long-threatened eviction didn't come until late May 1982, when the camp was nine months old. By this time the women's community was firmly entrenched. Individual women came and went, but the camp endured. The shifting population made even honest generalizations about the women difficult, while the press had long ended its romance with docile housewives and now made more insulting efforts to stereotype them (just middle-class ladies, just lesbians, just green-haired punks). The women themselves refused self-definition, other than to say that they were unified by their double commitment—to nonviolence and to direct action. Since they eschewed leaders as well as generalizations, there was no spokesperson to mediate between the world and the spontaneous acts of the group.

It is no doubt this very amorphousness that has made evicting the women so difficult. The police are taught to arrest the ringleader, but here there is none. Campers evicted from the Common land simply cross over to Ministry of Transport land, a strip alongside the road, or to Ministry of Defense land. Evicted from there, they move back to council land. Constant evictions—sometimes daily—have become a central, shaping reality of Greenham life. Since no location there is legal, even the smallest acts of persistence acquire special symbolic weight. For anyone, just visiting Greenham Common, sitting down on an overturned bucket at a campfire for a chat and tea, is an act of civil disobedience.

During my first visit, a two-day stay, I assumed that it was with grisly irony that the women had named the gates the colors of the rainbow. My time at Indigo was absurdly bleak and monochromatic. We struggled to keep the fire going; Maria (who, it turned out, was from Spain) performed a vegetarian miracle on a tiny, precariously tilted grill; we talked to the guards five feet from us on the other side of the fence about war, peace, men, women, weather, money; we slept in an ingenious but soaking handmade teepee, while outside an ever-changing pair of guards patrolled with growling dogs under giant arc lamps, which sizzled in the rain and lit up our dreams.

Greenham seemed mainly a passive test of endurance, though it was obvious, too, that instead of destroying the encampment, the stream of evictions has become a source of solidarity, resistance, and imagination. Where once gardens were planned, now a few flowers grow in a pram, easily rolled away at a moment's notice. Where once elaborate circus tents were pitched, now a cup on a stick holds up a makeshift roof. Those unprepossessing huddles of plastic I saw on my arrival were actually full of women, sheltering from the rain. These "benders" can look squashed and ugly from outside; but the bent branches that support the plastic are often still covered with leaves, making the inside a bower. When the bailiffs come with their big "chompers," they get a pile of soggy polyethylene, while the campers carry their few possessions across the road to safety. As soon as the bulldozers are gone, up go the plastic shelters once more.

Familiar domestic collages of blackened tea kettles, candles, corn flakes, bent spoons, chipped plates (never paper ones) lie around as if the contents of a house had been emptied into the mud, but here the house itself is gone. The women have left privacy and home, and now whatever acts of housekeeping they perform are in the most public of spaces up against the fence or road. Greenham is the ultimate housewife's nightmare: the space that can never be swept clean, ordered, sealed off, or safe. But as the mud blackens hands and the wood smoke permeates clothes and hair, the women of Greenham give up gracefully. (With thick irony I was offered the following suggestions: "Wood smoke is a pretty good deodorant." "Try washing dishes in boiling water; it loosens things up a bit, under the fingernails.")

The evictions have further clarified the situation this is life *in extremis*, life carried on where authority and custom do not mean it to be lived. There is only one source of water for all the camps. Only small and portable Robinson Crusoe contrivances have a chance. Greenham shreds the illusion of permanence and pushes those who live there into a naked, urgent present.

It is hard to imagine a better intellectual forcing ground for people struggling to grasp the full reality of the nuclear threat. Sitting at the fire, we discussed postindustrial society, postimperialist England, whether or not one should eat meat, the boundary between useful and irresponsible technical advances. Strewn around us were mixtures of very old technologies (how to make a fire with nothing but damp wood; how to cook everything on that fire—there is no electricity *anywhere* in the camps; how to build a shelter from bracken) and useful new ones (plastic protects everything; some women have fancy Gore-Tex sleeping bags or jackets because, though waterproof, they "breathe").

I told one woman who has lived at Greenham for two years that sometimes the camps looked to me as if World War III had already happened, as if we were rehearsing for life after the bomb, in a flat landscape where there will probably be plenty of bits of plastic and Velcro, but no clean water, no electricity, nowhere to hide. She looked at me pityingly: "Greenham is a holiday camp next to what things would be like if these bombs go off."

Of course, of course. Still, Greenham is a grim reminder of how much effort the simplest acts of maintenance take once one has removed oneself from the house, the town, the city. People there are experimenting with self-governance in small communities; they are living with less, seeking new definitions of comfort and satisfaction.

Certainly that less is more seemed the message of my first visit. But on my second, Greenham revealed a whole new side, a dramatic richness. I arrived my second time in delicate sunlight for an action called "10 million women for 10 days," timed to coincide with last September's vast NATO maneuvers on the East German–West German border. This time instead of a wasteland I found a carnival, a caldron of direct action, a wildly kinetic place. Circus tents were going up for the ten-day gathering and caravans offered free food. Strings of colorfully dressed women lined the road, walking clockwise and counterclockwise, in the great Greenham round. They had come to act.

Part of what makes the daily exhaustion of Greenham endurable for so many different kinds of women—and in such large numbers—is that contrary to first appearances, the place is a magnificent, exotic stage set for effective political gestures. Unlike the political demonstrations I have known, peace camps are permanent frames that can give form to hundreds of individual acts of resistance. Energy flows like light—because of the immediacy of everything, the constant, imminent possibility for self-expression and group solidarity.

You are not only joining something larger than yourself but something that is continuously, inexorably taking its stand of militant witness and rebuke, even while you're sleeping, even when you're fed up and go off to spend a night in town, even when you're angry, confused or at political loggerheads with every other woman in the place. Greenham is a springboard from which actions that would usually take months of laborious planning can be dreamed, discussed, and performed between night and morning.

Ideas for Greenham action can come from anywhere—something read in the paper, an image someone shares at the fire—and one such action made Greenham internationally famous, the "embrace the base" demonstration of December 12, 1982. The precipitating image—borrowed from the U.S. Women's Pentagon Action—was of women encircling the fence, surrounding it with feelings of power and love. No one knew if enough women would come to stretch around the nine-mile perimeter, so the nervous few who had set the idea in motion told everyone to bring long scarves to use as connectors, just in case.

Somewhere between 30,000 and 50,000 came, more than enough to embrace the entire round. (Whatever the press says, the women are always uncountable: Greenham has no center, no check-in point, no higher ground for surveying the scene. It is forced—by geography and police—to be scattered; it is elusive and invertebrate by choice.) The women festooned every inch of fence with symbols, paint, messages. To those who were there and the millions more who heard about it, the action seemed a miracle. The next day, 2,000 women blockaded the base, and, two weeks later, on New Year's dawn, 44 climbed the fence and began an hour's dance on the half-completed missile silos.

On the anniversary of "embrace the base" the women tried another, more hostile image of encirclement. Again 50,000 came, this time with mirrors they held up to the fence, reflecting its own dreary reality back on itself. At yet another carefully planned action, the women locked the soldiers inside the base by securing all the gates with heavy-duty bicycle locks. The increasingly frantic soldiers couldn't cut their way out and, finally, had to push one of their own gates down.

But it is a distortion of Greenham activism to mention only these large and well-known events, which required an unusual amount of advance planning. In fact, nothing was more maddening for an old new leftist like me than the effort to figure out where a Greenham action comes from—rather like trying to find out how a drop of dye travels through a gallon of water. Women told me: Well, this one had this idea. And we all had a meeting. (Who is "all"? "Whoever wanted to do an action.") Then some of us didn't like it. And we kept talking about it. We changed it a bit. We agreed to ask all our friends and their friends, by phone, by chain letter. We have a big network.

One of the brilliant structural inventions of the peace movement as a whole is its combination of small affinity groups with large networks. In the small group you are known, valued, listened to. These are the people you choose from the heart, the ones you want next to you if the police get rough. The small group can be relatively homogeneous to start with or it can be a comfortable locus from which shared values and ideas develop over time. Either way, the small group feels like a place you can return to.

But instead of being an isolated enclave, the affinity group is linked to others in an international network, which shares some if not all the small group's goals. The Greenham network includes men as well as women, organized in a number of forms, in ecology groups, local political groups, male support groups, Campaign for Nuclear Disarmament groups. (The Campaign for Nuclear Disarmament is Britain's mass membership organization comparable to the National Mobilization for Survival in the United States.) There are also other active peace camps like the flourishing one at Molesworth (the second English site where cruise missiles are to be deployed), where both men and women are just now getting in gear to resist the pre-cruise renovation. Consensus is often possible in small groups that work together for a long time, while the network operates differently, joining people in coalitions where sharp disagreements are also acknowledged.

Most direct action at Greenham, though, is generated not from the larger network but within small affinity groups. An idea or image travels around the gates like wildfire. "Let's get up at 4:00 A.M. and shake a big stretch of fence down." "Let's have a vigil at the gate at sunset and call the names of the people who wanted to be here but couldn't." "Let's confuse them by blockading the road a mile from the gate and creating such a traffic jam that they can't get to us to arrest us." Once, at Easter: "Let's dress up like furry animals and cover ourselves with honey, and break into the base." (No one arrested the women who did this one—maybe because they were too sticky?)

Or take the fence, that always present reminder of an "outside" versus "inside," a raggle-taggle band of colorful women who sing and dance and watch versus a gray-and-brown squad of soldiers who march and drill and watch. My first impression of this fence as something final and authoritative left me entirely unprepared for the women's view of it: they have simply rejected it as a legitimate boundary. Slipping under or cutting doors through the wire, they enter the base constantly, exploring, painting, filching frighteningly bureaucratic memos about nuclear war—symbolically undermining the concept "security." Hundreds have been arrested for criminal damage to the wire, yet women continue to enter the base routinely, in large numbers.

But is Greenham only a place where you can go and feel you've made a difference but really you haven't? . . .

Certainly Greenham's effectiveness is hard to measure. The powers that be—from Margaret Thatcher to NATO and even as far as the Kremlin—profess to be paying no attention to the women, nor to the mass European peace movement in general. But the women don't accept the powers that be, a stance that has earned them a grudging respect among their compatriots.

As early as the 1950s, Winston Churchill warned the British that they were letting their island become an "unsinkable aircraft carrier" for the United States. Successive governments of both parties ignored these warnings, preferring to think of England as maintaining some measure of old empire through its "special relationship" with the world's greatest power.

But, in order to keep up these costly prerogatives, to have an independent nuclear force and colonial clout in farflung places like the Falklands, the British government has allowed its own soil to be colonized. Britain has quietly become a client state. . . .

A Greenpeace activist commemorates the nuclear disaster of Chernobyl, in front of a Soviet-built nuclear power plant in Bohunice, Czechoslovakia. 1991. Thomas Szlukovenyi/Reuters/Bettmann.

To turn around an arms race so richly fed by capital investment, a mass movement is essential, but what sort of *mass*? Greenham's effectiveness must be measured not only by the role it plays in mobilizing large numbers but also by the kind of political culture it has to offer those numbers. . . .

I met women of every class and generation, though very few black, Asian, or Indian women make their way there. There were Grannies against Cruise and striking miners' wives; there were a disproportionate number of professionals and intellectuals; there were both straight and lesbian women, with lesbian energy a great source of Greenham vitality and staying power; there were glorious flocks of young girls playing various forms of hooky, casting a cold, clear eye on their dim future in the present English job market. There were genuinely marginal women who would be on the dole, or in mental institutions, or in some other form of big trouble if Greenham weren't there. Greenham is a melting pot, with all the false unities that can imply, but with the potential, too, for a new cosmopolitanism for feminist activism, a direct confrontation with the differences among women.

These women bring to the fire values forged in a variety of movements: they absolutely reject any leadership (like the anarchists, or like the feminist consciousness-raising groups some of them came from); they insist on nonviolence (like the pacifist, Quaker, or other Christian groups some of them came from). They are ecologists, trade unionists, Labour party members, and, frequently, Campaign for Nuclear Disarmament (CND) activists. A wide variety of left politics also fertilizes Greenham; in England, left paradigms are taken more for granted than in the United States. . . .

The Greenham women I talked to take great pains to point out that the purpose of Greenham is not to exclude men but to include women—at last. Though a few women there might still tell you women are biologically more peaceful than men, this view has been mostly replaced by a far more complex analysis of why women need to break with our old, private complicity with public male violence. No one at Greenham seems to be arguing that the always evolving Greenham value system is inevitably female. The women recognize their continuity with the Quakers, with Gandhi, with the entire pacifist tradition, and with the anarchist critique of the state. At the same time, women, the Greenham campers believe, may have a separate statement to make about violence because we have our own specific history in relation to it. . . .

A whole activist generation is being forged at Greenham, not of age but of shared experience. These women are disobedient, disloyal to civilization, experienced in taking direct action, advanced in their ability to make a wide range of political connections. The movable hearth is their schoolroom, where they piece together a stunning if raffish political patchwork.

Before visiting Greenham, I had feared that its politics would prove simple-minded, that those absolutes, life and death, would have cast more complex social questions in the shade. How, for instance, could the old question What do women want? survive when the subject is Mutual Assured Destruction (MAD, U.S. military slang for nuclear deterrence). As Brenda Whisker wrote in *Breaching the Peace*, an English collection of feminist essays criticizing the women's peace movement, "I think that stopping the holocaust is easier than liberating women." Hard words certainly, but understandable, solidified through bitter experience. While women and children are first, feminism continues to be last. . . .

I wonder if women are having to learn at Greenham—with a difference—what men learn too early and carry too far: the courage to dare, to test reaction, to define oneself *against* others. Nonviolent direct action takes great courage. The big men on their horses or machines are doing as ordered—which is comfortable for them. In contrast, it can be truly terrifying to refuse to do what an angry, pushing policeman tells you to do. For women particularly, such acts are fresh and new and this cutting across the grain of feminine socialization is a favorite, daring sport of the young at the fence. Such initiations give women a revolutionary taste of conflict, lived out fully, in our own persons, with gender no longer a reliable determinant of the rules.

Certainly it is no use for women to turn self-righteous, as I had found myself doing—claiming a higher moral ground than men. On that ground we are admired but ignored. As Dorothy Dinnerstein has argued in *The Mermaid and the Minotaur*, emotional women have traditionally been treated like court jesters that the king keeps around to express his own anxieties—and thus vent them harmlessly. A woman's body lying down in a road in front of a missile launcher has a very different symbolic resonance for everyone from that of a male body in the same position. Greenham's radical feminist critics wonder just what kind of peace a female lying down can bring. Won't men simply allow women to lie in the mud forever because the demonstrators themselves only underline men's concept of what is female (passivity, protest, peace) and what is male (aggression, action, war)?

Before I came to Greenham, I shared these worries. But at Greenham at its best, women's nonviolent direct action becomes not another face of female passivity but a difficult political practice with its own unique discipline. The trick—a hard one—is to skew the dynamics of the old male–female relationships toward new meanings, to interrupt the old conversation between overconfident kings and hysterical, powerless jesters. This will surely include an acknowledgment of our past complicity with men and war making and a dramatization of our new refusal to aid and assist. (I think of a delicious young woman I heard singing out to a group of also very young soldiers: "We don't find you sexy anymore, you know, with your little musket, fife, and drum.")

Perhaps some of the new meanings we need will be found buried in the old ones. If women feel powerless, we can try to share this feeling, to make individual men see that they, too, are relatively powerless in the face of a wildly escalating arms race. Naturally, this is a message men resist, but the women at Greenham are endlessly clever at dramatizing how the army shares their impotence: The army cannot prevent them from getting inside the fence or shaking it down. It cannot prevent them from blockading the gates. It cannot prevent them from returning after each eviction.

Or, rather, it could prevent all this, but only by becoming a visibly brutal force, and this would be another kind of defeat, since the British armed services and police want to maintain their image of patriarchal protectors; they do not want to appear to be batterers of nonviolent women. Greenham women expose the contradictions of gender: by being women they dramatize powerlessness but they also disarm the powerful. . . .

If you decide to visit Greenham, or any of the growing number of permanent peace camps, women-only and mixed, that are springing up in Europe and here in the United States, your experiences will be entirely different from what I have described here. As I write, the Greenham network keeps changing, usually beyond the range of media reports. This very week the death of Greenham was announced once more, but when I called friends they only laughed. "Of course the women are still there." The water situation is desperate and benders have given way to still more primitive plastic shelters, but everyone is "quite cheery."

When I describe Greenham women—their lives in these circumstances—I often get the reaction that they sound like mad idealists detached from a reality principle about what can and cannot be done, and how. In a sense this is true. The women reject power and refuse to study it, at least on its own terms. But the other charge—that they are utopian dreamers who sit around and think about the end of the world while not really living in this one—is far from the mark.

In a piece in the *Times Literary Supplement* last summer, "Why the Peace Movement Is Wrong," the Russian émigré poet Joseph Brodsky charged the peace movement with being a bunch of millenarians waiting for the apocalypse. Certainly there are fascinating parallels between the thinking of the peace women and that of the radical millenarian Protestant sects of the 17th century. Both believe that the soul is the only court that matters, the self the only guide, and that paradise is a humble and realizable goal in England's green and pleasant land. The millenarians offered free food just like the caravans now on the Common: Food, says one sign. Eat till You're Full.

But the women are not sitting in the mud waiting for the end, nor are they—as Brodsky and many others claim—trying to come to terms with their own deaths by imagining that soon the whole world will die. On the contrary, the women make up one of the really active antimillenarian forces around. President Reagan has told fundamentalist groups that the last trump ending human history might blow at any time now; the women believe that the dreadful sound can be avoided, if only we will stop believing in it.

Greenham women see a kind of fatalism all around them. They, too, have imagined the end, and their own deaths, and have decided that they prefer to die without taking the world with them. Nothing makes them more furious than the apathy in the town of Newbury, where they are often told, "Look, you've got to die anyway. So what difference does it make how you go?" These are the real millenarians, blithely accepting that the end is near.

In contrast, the women look very hardheaded, very pragmatic. They see a big war machine, the biggest the world has known; and, rather than sitting in the cannon's mouth hypnotized, catatonic with fear or denial, they are trying to back away from the danger, step by step. They refuse to be awed or silenced by the war machine. Instead they say calmly that what was built by human beings can be dismantled by them, too. Their logic, clarity, and independence are endlessly refreshing. Where is it written, they ask, that we must destroy ourselves?

## Reading Questions

1. How have women managed to blockade continuously the cruise missile based at Greenham Common for over five years?
2. What were some of Snitow's major feminist reservations about women participating in this type of activism?
3. In what ways does Snitow view Greenham as more than a passive effort to change international negotiations toward international unilateral disarmament?
4. What is the purpose of affinity groups in the peace movement?
5. With what organizations do the women at Greenham Common work in coalition?

## Recommended Reading

Michael D'Antonio, *Atomic Harvest: Hanford and the Lethal Toll of America's Nuclear Arsenal* (New York: Crown, 1993)

Jean Bethke Elshtain and Sheila Tobias, eds., *Women, Militarism, and War: Essays in History, Politics and Social Theory* (Savage, MD: Rowan & Littlefield, 1990)

Guida West and Rhoda Lois Blumberg, eds., *Women and Social Protest* (New York: Oxford University Press, 1990)

Anne Witte Garland, *Women Activitists: Challenging the Abuse of Power* (New York: The Feminist Press at the City University of New York, 1988)

## Recommended Audiovisual Resources

*The Atomic Cafe*. 1982. Directed by Kevin Rafferty. Feature-length compilation of post–World War II propaganda, documentary, and newsreel coverage on official and unofficial American attitudes toward the atomic bomb.

*Desert Bloom*. 1986. Directed by Eugene Corr. Poignant study of adolescence against a backdrop of 1950 Las Vegas, as the atomic age dawns.

*Sing a Song of Seabrook: Opposition to a Nuclear Plant*. 1991. Produced by Raymond Stevens. Details the citizen action at New Hampshire's Seabrook Nuclear Plant. Filmakers Library.

# Culture and Gender in Indian America

RAYNA GREEN

Rayna Green is a Native American activist and writer, and works at the Smithsonian Institute's Museum of Natural History. She is the editor of *Native American Women: A Contextual Bibliography* and *That's What She Said: A Collection of Poetry and Fiction by Contemporary Native American Women.*

I don't have a theory or line of argument this morning. I want to go through a series of vignettes, all of which cast a different light, cast a different slant, and give a slightly different ear to each other.

My first story is about two friends of mine, both Sioux women who were up at the Capitol one day. Up on top of the Capitol there's a statue. It's a marvelous statue. If you get very close to that statue, you'll see that it's clearly a female figure, and it might look something like Miss Liberty standing out in New York Harbor. Nobody knows much about her. These two young Sioux women I know went up to the guard and they said, "What's the statue? What's it about?" He said, "Well, you know, that statue, a lot of people seem to think it's an Indian. Her name is Freedom. But Freedom isn't an Indian. She's a woman." And my two friends laughed to think that in this country freedom could be either. But the truth is, in this country freedom is both. And that's what I want to talk about today. And I want to talk about justice and liberty, and about America. I want to talk about home, family, and about women. I want to talk about changing our names, and taking hold of our names. And I want to talk about coming home.

Freedom is an Indian and a woman. She's also Black and a woman. She's also Jewish, Vietnamese, and Salvadoran, and a woman. She is all of those things. But her iconography is clear. She comes from the fifteenth century, when the first images of the New World went back to Europe. Freedom, in the early days of America, was pictured as this large, bare-breasted Indian woman. She was a queen. She was our kind of girl. She was pictured with her foot on the head of an alligator, her spear in her hands. Pineapples, corn, all these wonderful bounteous crops spilling out of her arms. Her warriors stood behind her. She was in control; she was the New World, the promise of everything that everyone wanted.

And they took her away from us. As the two centuries moved forward and things happened here that we now must pay for, dearly, she changed. They took away her flesh. They covered her breasts. She couldn't be naked, the symbol of innocence in the fifteenth, sixteenth century; the symbol of virtue. They had to cover her and make her less savage, less pagan. They took away her alligator. I mean, can you imagine taking a girl's alligator away? She must have been angry. They took away all of the fruits of her fields. And she became a Renaissance little wonder woman icon, like Minerva, draped in little tasteful white garments with her breasts covered. And they wouldn't even let her be like Minerva; they robbed her of her power. Thin and powerless, with a tiny little diadem on her head. She never needed a crown to know she was a queen. But now, she's changed.

And that's who stands in the New York harbor. Someone who changed. And that's who stands on top of the Capitol. But we need to know her name. Her name is Freedom, and she is who I have described. And we need to go back to her to begin to look to the future.

That future is vague and muddy, though. That future is opaque. We all have difficulties now knowing who we are, and what our names are. We try to put on different names, give ourselves a kind of identity. We struggle through various ways of looking at an identity. Indian people have been forced to confront lots of different faces in the mirror, and those faces are confusing for all of us. At one level, Indians are totally insignificant. They exist in no number to matter—to the economy, to the judicial system, to anything else. There are fewer Indians in America than Vietnamese. And so why do Indians matter? I'll tell you why they matter: simply because of the history I've spoken of.

But Indians cannot simply be functions of the historic past. They can't simply be reminders of an America that once was, bad or good. They can't simply function as vague, ghostly reminders of poverty index levels, of hunger and homelessness in America; that's irrelevant. What is relevant is that there is a metaphor here that stands for all of us in some ways and doesn't encompass the experience of others in another. What is relevant is that as my friend Roberta Hill Whiteman says, "Indians know how to wait." And it is the waiting that will dignify us all. The waiting for freedom and justice to come in the form of an Indian woman, once again, to reclaim us all. In Roberta's words:

> Look west long enough, the moon will grow
> inside you.
> Coyote hears her song, he'll
> teach you now.
> Mirrors follow trails of blood and lightning.
> Mother needs the strength of one like you.
> Let blood
> dry, but seize the lightning. Hold it like your
> mother
> rocks the trees. In your fear, watch the road,
> breathe deeply.
> Indians know how to wait.
>
> (from "Lines for Marking Time")

What are we waiting for? Are we waiting for a moment like that which happened at the National Women's Studies Association Conference in Minneapolis last year? The planning group invited a young Indian girl to dance for the opening event. Typically, and profoundly, she came with her uncle, and a group of young men who drummed for her. In Indian culture, an uncle is like your father. An uncle raises you. An aunt raises you. Your own father and mother are perhaps even less significant in some ways. Her uncle came with her because her father had just died. And her uncle, to honor her, and to honor the women who had come to see her, spoke for her.

In our world, people speak for you when you're honored. It's a gift to speak for someone. And when that man, who was honoring everyone there by his presence, rose to speak for her, he was booed. Because in an environment where we've gotten our signals crossed, we don't know the faces of other people, we don't know how they live, and we cannot speak to them directly. He gave them even a further gift, he explained to them why she was not wearing her jingle dress. (A jingle dress is a wonderful buckskin or cloth dress filled with little tin coins that make a marvelous noise when a young lady dances.) She was in her menstrual period, and a girl does not wear a jingle dress when she's menstru- ating, because the noise of those coins, you see, is a prayer, and it's a prayer for power. Music goes up, music calls down the spirits to look at you, and asks for power. Because a menstruating woman is already so powerful, to wear the jingle dress is to really risk a problem; to call down uncontrolled power, perhaps. He gave them the gift of telling them this. He was explaining something rather arcane, something that people don't just discuss in public. It was a women's event. He wanted to reach out. And they booed him for that, because they thought he was talking about pollution.

I'm not here, as I said, to accuse. This is not accusatory. That is not what Indian women and Indian men are about. This is about knowing our own names and knowing our faces. A gift was refused because no one knew it was a gift. We have got to come forward and know the gifts that different people give us. And that's why a meeting like this is essential—to look in the face of different gifts and to learn to honor each other, by accepting the terms on which those gifts are given.

Sometimes, because things get so confused in moments like that, we're forced to change our names. Sometimes we have to change our shape. Shape shifters are important for all of us; all of our worlds have shape shifters. Sometimes we have to shift shape because guns are aimed at us, and we must escape. Sometimes the old shape has become too uncomfortable. Sometimes, like the queen in the early days, our original form is taken—we're sent to the diet center, forced on cultural aerobics until we change. And I say it's time to change our shape because we want to, to change our names because we want to.

Sometimes when we're forced to change those shapes it's painful; sometimes it's a joy. In Indian cultures, there is a tradition of name-changing and shape-shifting, and it's an important tradition to look to for all of us because it enables us to be empowered; it enables us to be in control. We are all women, certainly; we are all men; we are all gay; we are all straight; we are all old; we are all young. And in Indian cultures I go back to my families and there is no division. There are distinctions, certainly, about the way people are treated, and the authority they have, but I want to reclaim the power to move through categories, so that I do not have to stay fixed in any one place. Jesse [Jackson] said a couple of years ago, in the presidential elections, "God ain't finished with me yet, she never will be finished." We can all move and grow.

Some of the categories become so restrictive, we have to be able to move out of them. One category that Indian people suffer from is that of "half-breed." It's staggering to think about that kind of marginality; to suggest that someone is a quart low of whatever it is that makes them real is to take their life and breath and squeeze it until it stops. We're all half-breeds, if you come right down to it. As my mom used to say, "Heinz 57." We locate our internal space, perhaps, in one place that gives us a name to call ourselves that we're proud of, but we are all out there on the margins (and there are no people on the margin like women, because we have to shift into so many shapes). But the category of "half- breed" is tragic, damaging in so many ways, we've got to give it up. It is like Freedom. We've got to put a name to it that enables us to stand up again.

I am a German Jew. I feel comfortable with that. I've lived my life as a German Jew. One of my grandmothers was a German Jew who became a profound Texan. I will not deny her. I will not look at my mother, with her blue eyes, her white skin, and deny her.

My father is only one part of me. He must be claimed, too. And I gravitate toward that part of him, and his world, and my other grandmother, who gave me a name and space. But I will not deny any one part of that world to force Indian people, native people, any people to live on a margin, where they cannot define their own existence as a whole, whatever parts may be there, just to rob them of a future, and to force them to die somewhere in a past.

My German grandmother was a remarkable person. She is my mother, the primary character in my life. She shaped and formed me; she gave me stories, language, and songs. In many ways, she gave me more than my Indian grandmother, who was afraid because of all the things that had happened to her; afraid to sing, to breathe, to leave town. Her pain transferred over, so I took joy from the maternal grandmother, and I took the name from the other one. We take what we can from each one of our relatives and honor them.

My German grandmother was an extraordinary woman who loved to dance, loved to sing, loved to tell dirty stories. She was the mistress of them all. She wanted to be a dancer on the Palace stage. Dressed to kill, she'd play whorehouse songs on the piano, or sad ones that would make us cry and beg for more. On that summer porch, we believed she could have been anything, living in her ruby pleasures. Oh, she glittered then, dancing across that summer porch, dancing the stories that made me dream over her shattered breath. She is mine, and she is yours, too. Never walk away from all the faces you've known in your life, who gave you birth. That's the Indian way, certainly. But it's all of our way. If we only can have the courage to look back for them.

Some of the shape-shifting sometimes makes it important to walk away from being female. Being female is painful. Being male is painful, never more than lately, as we look into the faces of our young men on the streets of urban cities. We see death in their faces, and it pains us. If only they had the freedom we have, to walk into a female body, into a female metaphor, and say, "That's not my world. Those guns, that dope, those drugs are not my world. That world that lures me only because my name is man, that world that pains me because I have to live trapped in a metaphor, that will not work for me."

We have an option that makes us live, an option women have always had, an extraordinary option. Some women take it in different ways. Some women call themselves mothers, some sisters, some lovers. Some women call themselves men, and walk into Coyote's terrible dream, which enables us to move through the changes. We can take any of those options at any one time. But to take those options means we have to teach our baby boys to grow up and be all those things, too. We don't have to claim the men in us by being tough. We only have to look in our children's and our brothers' faces, and bring them up to live with us.

There's a gift that moves in Indian country, and that gift is an extraordinary gift. It is the gift of giving itself. All of us have it in our worlds. At dances, various ceremonial occasions, you'll see women walk over and put shawls on other people's backs—men's backs, too. In ceremonial occasions these shawls get piled so high, you never know how anybody stands up under them. (I want to eartag a shawl during a powwow season sometime like biologists do animals, see how it migrates across the room.) Those gifts are extraordinary.

I want to take the metaphor of that shawl, and I want to wrap it around your shoulders now, and say you are my sister, you are my mother, you are my friend, you are my brother, you are my husband, you are my uncle, you are my aunt, come into that dance circle. It is the gift that keeps on moving, because it brings us into the circle. The richest person in Indian country is the person who gives the most away, not the person who keeps the most for themselves. And this a gift that America needs. We would not have homeless people on our streets, if we truly believed we lived in Indian country. If freedom was really the Indian woman we know she is, we would not have people living out on the margin, children selling themselves for one shot, for a pint of Thunderbird. We have got to wrap that shawl around the rest of us, and women can do that.

To talk about culture in this country, to talk about gender, is to talk about giving. And it is in the heart and face of our own cultures, and our own passions that we can look and see the gift that we have to wrap again, and keep moving, and keep giving. But in order to do that, we have to know what real wealth is. Real wealth lies in our own hearts, and not in something that is a commodity beyond it. Indian country knows that. The gift that moves will carry us to that place. I think of the warrior women who reputedly used to carry their husbands' and brothers' and friends' bodies off the field and take up the bow or the gun or the spear themselves. And I say, this is not militance, this is not warrior behavior (although at one level it is: it is what is required to survive). All of us in our communities now are carrying those boys' bodies off the field. What will we do when there are no more of them? Will we become the warriors? Are we willing to take that battle on? Perhaps the gift is not to keep thinking of it as a battle, but to think of it as a role for us all, in the survival of our people, in the raising of our children. What is a real warrior woman—in Indian terms, even? Certainly, it is not to take up a spear. If you have to, you do, to defend your life or that of your children. But I don't want to talk about defensiveness; I want to talk about survival. And there are keys to survival.

In 1642, a group of British got off a boat in Virginia somewhere and migrated to what we call North Carolina; and there they met a delegation of Cherokees, led by a man who had been a warrior. His name was Outacitty, which means man-killer. He was a great warrior, a red chief, sent by the Beloved Woman and the clan-mothers to make war. But this time they had asked him not to make war. The Beloved Woman of the Nation, Ghigau had asked him to become a white chief, a peace chief, and to go and make peace with these people. And so Outacitty rode up to meet them. The first thing he said to them was, "Where are your women?" These men had come to do serious business, and they had no women with them. Peace is a very serious business. No act of war, no act of peace in my country is made without the women there. And Outacitty was shocked: the British dared to come without their women. "Where are your women?" he said. And he went back and reported that there was a problem here. "We cannot do business with these men," he said. They were clearly missing half of the people needed to do business with.

And in 1987, a young woman named Wilma Mankiller was elected principal chief of the Cherokee nation, and I say to you she is him, come back, and she knows it. And the old people knew it. When we'd go out to campaign with her, the old ladies would say, "Good name, good name." And they didn't mean war. They didn't mean hunting; they didn't mean power. They meant she's back. She has returned; the Beloved has returned. You see, she is all of those converged together. Like all of us can be. Warrior, peace-maker, mother, father, Beloved woman, Beloved man, the white and the red merged together, to take our own story back.

And that's an interesting story. It's a story about family. Everybody in Indian country talks about the family as the center of their lives, just as in Black culture, in Irish-American communities. Because to talk about family is to talk about community, about survival, about the future.

The central figure in this next story about family is a woman called Buffalo Birdwoman who could not give up the old way. She was a great farmer. When the time came to make her change, they brought in the tractors, they brought in the freight wagons, and she said, "I don't want to do that. I'll stick to my digging stick. Because I grow corn better than your corn. I know how to grow corn, and I will not give up on corn songs. I will not forget the corn songs. The corn is my family, my mother, my grandmother, the corn gave me birth. And to give up my corn songs is to give up my family." Tradition is not a yoke around our neck, if we know its name. Tradition is not the chains that bind us, if we know how to use it. Tradition is not the deadly past wrapped around us like a coffin. Tradition, for the Indian family, for the Indian woman, is simply remembering who you are, and it is that story we must reclaim once more. Hear Linda Hogan, Chickasaw:

> calling myself home
>
> There were old women
> who lived on amber.
> Their dark hands
> laced the shells of turtles
> together, pebbles inside
> and they danced
> with rattles strong on their legs.
>
> There is a dry river
> between them and us.
> Its banks divide up our land.
> Its bed was the road
> I walked to return.
>
> We are plodding creatures like the turtle
> born of an old people.
> We are nearly stone
> turning slow as the earth.
> Our mountains are underground
> they are so old.
>
> This land is the house
> we have always lived in.
> The women,
> their bones are holding up the earth.
>
> The red tail of a hawk
> cuts open the sky
> and the sun
> brings their faces back
> with the new grass.

Dust from yarrow
is in the air,
the yellow sun.
Insects are clicking again.

I came back to say good-bye
to the turtle
to those bones
to the shells locked together
on his back
gold atoms dancing underground.

The turtle in the stories of some Indian people is our mother. On her back the earth grew. We were born in the mud of her back. It doesn't matter which story you claim. Whether you think it was Corn or the Turtle Mother or the Spider Woman that gave your birth. Coyote came from all these. His tricking lies give us the ability to change our shapes. He is necessary to us. But the earth and where we were born is that woman's back and that woman's breast; she cuts it open to feed us and make us whole again.

Sun over the horizon, a sweating yellow force, our continuance. The uncountable distance that sweeps through our hands, the first prayers in the morning. It is this that I believe in. The galloping sun. In my whole life, a rider. It is that round earth—I call it Indian country, you call it the name you need to call it—the moon, the stars, and that sweating sun, that enables me to be the writer I am. If I choose not to climb on that galloping horse, that galloping sun, it is my own choice. But it is a choice I cannot make. I need to come home. I need my family. I need you, my brothers and sisters, my father, my uncle, and I need my aunties. The metaphor of family is simply one that works in Indian country because it brings that circle round. We all join in the dance that brings us to a place called America, where Freedom may be lots of things. And you can put the shape and face to her you wish.

The bottom line is very simple; it is morning once more. And that galloping sun races across the horizon. For me to come home to Indian country means I must climb on that sun and race across the horizon, with other people. I don't want to leave any of you behind. America has a way of leaving some of us out on the edge. I say it's time for the women of America, all of us—we're not separate, we belong with each other—to reclaim our families. To climb on that sun with me in that eternal morning. Once again, your whole life, a rider.

# Reading Questions

1. Identify the inadequacies of the cultural images of the American Indian that underlie Green's opening anecdote.
2. According to Green, how does "shape-shifting" result in empowerment, not only for the Indian but for any individual?
3. Why does Green emphasize the cultural concept of giving?
4. Discuss the importance of community, family, and the role of women in Indian cultures.
5. How does Green understand the concept of "freedom"?

## Recommended Reading

Paula Gunn Allen, "Lesbians in American Indian Cultures," *Hidden from History: Reclaiming the Gay and Lesbian Past*, ed. Martin Duberman et al. (New York: Penguin, 1989)

Joseph Bruchac, *Survival This Way: Interviews with American Indian Poets* (Tucson: Suntrack and University of Arizona Press, 1987)

Rayna Green, ed., *That's What She Said: Contemporary Poetry and Fiction by Native American Women* (Bloomington: Indiana University Press, 1984)

Jamake Highwater, *The Primal Mind: Vision and Reality in Indian America* (New York: New American Library, 1982)

Geary Hobsen (Cherokee), ed., *The Remembered Earth: An Anthology of Contemporary Native American Literature* (Albuquerque: University of New Mexico Press, 1980)

C. Martin, ed., *The American Indian and the Problem of History* (New York: Oxford University Press, 1987)

Greg Sarris, "What I'm Talking About When I'm Talking About My Baskets," conversations with Mabel McKay, *De/Colonizing the Subject*, eds. Sidonie Smith and Julia Watson (Minneapolis: University of Minnesota Press, 1992)

Leslie Marmon Silko, *Ceremony* (New York: Penguin, 1977)

# American Willing to Listen

## FRAN PEAVEY

Fran Peavey, widely known as "the atomic comic" for her antinuclear performance art, conducts "Strategic Listening," a social change consulting service in San Francisco. This chapter is excerpted from her book *Heart Politics*.

---

International tourism has never appealed to me. I just can't picture myself staying in a luxury hotel in Rome or Tokyo or Cairo, visiting museums and monuments, scouring gift shops for souvenirs. So for many years, I traveled abroad very little.

But the more I studied the nuclear threat, the more I became consumed with a desire to learn what was happening on this endangered planet, to talk with people around the world and find out how they felt about the future and the nuclear situation. I wanted to enlarge the context of my work to prevent nuclear war. Although theoretically I was fighting for the survival of every human being on the planet, I didn't actually know many people outside the United States. And since I now realized how important it was for me to be connected to the people I was fighting for, my goal became finding people around the world to know and love.

So I sold my house, paid my debts, and bought one of those around-the-world airplane tickets. Actually, the ticket limited me to the Northern Hemisphere, but that was enough for a start.

At my request, friends sent me names of people to talk with and stay with. I planned to go only to cities and towns where I had four or more contacts. After interviewing these contact people, I would ask them to suggest others. But I also wanted to interview people at random. So I came up with the idea of sitting in a park or other public place with a cloth sign that said "American Willing to Listen." Maybe people would come talk to me. I didn't dare tell my friends about the cloth sign for fear that their disapproval, or even their enthusiasm, might crush this fragile, tentative idea.

Before leaving the United States, I drove down to Santa Barbara to test my plan. I interviewed a few contact people there and asked them to refer me to others. And I tried sitting on a park bench with a sign—"Willing to Listen." I felt shy, exposed, and embarrassed. But it seemed better to get a start on those feelings close to home. People did stop and talk, and some of the conversations had depth. This encouraged me.

But on the plane to Japan my doubts and fears resurfaced. What if my interviewing project failed? Perhaps it was a big mistake to try. I had never traveled alone in the world. What if I got sick? What if thieves fell on me? And at the same time I felt excited; I was doing something no one in my family had ever done.

The project began in Kyoto, Japan. First I met my contact people: a Buddhist priest, several environmental activists, and a women's studies class at Kyoto University. It was a few days before I made my "American Willing to Listen" sign and a few more before I got up the nerve to use it. Waiting for a train in Osaka, I said to myself: "If I'm ever going to do this, I should do it here where nobody I know will see me." Unfolding my two-by-three-foot cloth sign, I laid it on the floor in front of me and sat down. Time passed. People came over, sized me up, and walked away. I tried to smile pleasantly. If I busied myself with reading or writing, I was sure that people would not talk to me for fear of interrupting. So I just sat and smiled, all the while thinking, "This is a bad idea. I've spent a lot of money on my plane ticket, and the plan isn't working. I'm making a fool of myself. How will I ever get to talk with ordinary people?"

It was thirty or forty minutes before someone finally stopped to talk—a man in his forties who worked at a shoe factory. He wanted to know what I was doing. I tried to explain but he didn't understand, and I began to fear that I didn't understand either. I was so busy answering his questions that I never managed to ask him any of mine.

After another few minutes, a man of about thirty stopped to chat. He discussed some of his concerns: the border war between North and South Korea over control of rubber trees; consumerism in Japan and the level of consumption in developed countries in general; the investment of massive amounts of Japanese capital in China (he felt a China–Japan alliance might be destabilizing in the region). Closer to home, he was thinking about relations between the sexes. His wife was part of a women's consciousness-raising group, and he and the other husbands had felt jealous of it. They'd tried to start their own group, but it hadn't worked. He was disappointed, and the issue seemed to be unresolved for him.

Boarding the train to Kyoto, I felt happy and relieved. The second man I'd talked with had understood what I was doing and thought it was a great idea. And he had shared a little of his life with me. My confidence grew as the process of meeting people gained momentum. I met people by arrangement and at random, in their homes, schools, and workplaces, as well as in cafés, train stations, universities, and parks. I refined my interviewing technique, asking open-ended questions that would serve as springboards for opinions and stories—questions like "What are the biggest problems you see affecting your country or region?" and "How would you like things to be different in your life?" Being limited to English put me at a disadvantage, but people often volunteered to translate for me.

Early interviews showed me how little I knew about the world. There were vast fields of information that I had never even heard about. For instance, nearly everyone I talked with in Japan mentioned Kim Dae Jung, a South Korean opposition leader who had escaped to Japan and then been sent back to Korea. I had never thought about relations between Japan and South Korea. In the United States these issues had seemed unimportant and had received only minimal coverage in the news media. Now I was meeting people to whom they were very important. I began to see glimmers of the many ways in which non-Americans saw the world.

It was exhilarating but exhausting. The rapid succession of new issues nearly overwhelmed me—the homogenization of Japanese culture, women's gossip in an Indian village, the flight of capital from Australia to the Philippines and Korea, the aspiration to know God, the near-meltdown of a Japanese nuclear power plant, rural Indian mothers' fears that their children weren't getting enough protein, doubts about the tradition of arranged marriage, regional conflicts over resource and capital allocation, and the frustration of people everywhere who sensed that their destiny was controlled by the superpowers. It occurred to me that I might have to go on interviewing full-time for the rest of my life to get any sense of what was going on in the world.

Four years and hundreds of interviews later, I no longer feel quite so confounded. I'm beginning to get a sense of social and historical currents around the world. On my first world trip I listened to people in Japan, Thailand, India, England, and Scotland. Subsequent trips have taken me to East Berlin, Israel, Palestine, Sweden, and India again. While traveling I've also met people from other countries in Asia, Africa, Latin America, and the South Pacific. My listening project has become a continuing practice, both in the United States and abroad.

On the Punjab Mail, a train from Bombay to Hoshangabad, I interviewed the woman who shared my compartment. The wife of a retired railroad worker, she appeared to be in her mid-sixties, and she was traveling with a well-made wooden box that contained a cake for her nephew's wedding. As we rode along she spoke of her worries about her son, a drug addict who was now in Saudi Arabia. The woman's English was quite good, but she had trouble with my name. So I gave her my business card, which identifies me as a futurist. "What's a futurist?" she asked. When I tried to explain, her face lit up. "Oh, you mean a fortune teller?" Preoccupied with getting ready for bed, I wasn't paying much attention. "Sort of," I said. She started asking me about her son. Was he still on drugs? Would he return to India? Or might he marry someone in Saudi Arabia and lose his religion? I said something mildly encouraging about parents and children.

Then she left the compartment. Twenty minutes later she returned, reporting that she had gone through the train announcing that a blue-eyed fortune teller was on board. A group of people had gathered and were waiting to hear their fortunes. She would be happy to translate.

Discovering a line of twenty or thirty people outside our compartment, I tried in vain to convince them of my lack of talent or training in fortune-telling. But they replied, "You gave her a good fortune—you must give us one too." I was up most of the night giving friendly advice and encouragement.

A middle-aged farmer wanted to know about his cow. The cow had been sick, and her milk yield was poor. Would she get better? I asked a few questions and eventually suggested that he consult an animal specialist and get some help. He was grateful for my advice.

A couple came in and asked, "Will we find a husband for our daughter, and will she be happy in her marriage?" I said, "Yes, if they work hard at their marriage, I think they will be happy." They looked at each other with relief. "Will we be able to find her a husband close to our village? We want to have our daughter close to us." As they asked more questions, my translator explained to me about Hindu marriage arrangements. The bride lives with the husband's family, and difficulties can arise if the bride and the mother-in-law don't get along. I suggested to the couple that they interview prospective mothers-in-law to find a cheerful one for their daughter.

Another couple was traveling to visit their grandchild for her first birthday ceremony. Would the granddaughter grow up to be happy, healthy, and prosperous? I tried to get some hints. Was she a healthy baby? I said something mildly encouraging. They said: "In your country you beat children and treat them badly. That's because you don't believe in reincarnation." The woman explained that her beloved mother, who had died a year or two before, had been reincarnated as the baby. So of course this baby was very special to them.

After my stint as the blue-eyed fortune teller of the Punjab Mail, I felt more at home in India. I'd begun to empathize with some of the problems Indians had in their lives. They were worried about their children getting married, just as I had worried about my younger sister's marriage. They were concerned about the health of their parents; I had been through that too.

Listening to people, I began to learn how each individual puzzled out large issues from her or his own vantage point. In Varanasi, India, a woman told me that when the Brahmans were thrown out of power in southern India, her husband could no longer find a satisfactory job there. So they moved north to Varanasi. She currently had no job, she said, because Varanasi was a place that didn't respect women. Now she feared that the lower castes would revolt in the north, as they had in the south. Already, she said, "Brahmans are unable to provide strong leadership because they feel so insecure." She expected people to become "more and more selfish, all thinking of themselves, no one thinking of society. And corruption has been getting worse and worse. Corrupt politicians are responsible for the misery in every sphere of life."

In Edinburgh, Scotland, a man who worked with the Scottish nationalist party told me that this country was a colony of England, and England would never grant them independence because the English wanted their offshore oil. The Scots for their part can't mount an effective independence movement, he said, because they are so fiercely individualistic that they can't work together.

In Darjeeling I met a thirteen year old from Bhutan who wanted to become a freedom fighter, to help his region gain independence from China. He earnestly told me about his desire to study hard, to become a strong man, to help his people. I was surprised to see such determination in a person his age.

Two Kyoto women in their twenties were thinking about why Japanese young people were so uninvolved in world affairs. The explanation they had developed was historical: Japanese people had been told that they would win the war against the materialist United

States because Japanese spiritual values were superior. So Japan's defeat in World War II was considered a victory for materialism—which the Japanese then embraced. Materialistic, hedonistic values had taken over, they told me, and parents had neglected to give their kids the love and sense of security that would allow them to be involved in larger concerns.

I visited the Rasulia Center near Hoshangabad, where about thirty people—most from the Untouchable caste—live, farm, build bio-gas plants for energy, and work toward self-sufficiency. The leader of the community told me that India's culture used to be one of the greatest in the world—in the forefront in mathematics, art, and religion. India was no longer a leader, he said, because colonialism had squashed the Indians' initiative. In the cycles of history, civilizations rise and fall; India's will rise again. As petroleum becomes more expensive, he projected, societies that are not so dependent on oil (especially less-developed countries) can become a stronger force in the world. He didn't expect that trend to take hold for another hundred years or so, but he was very hopeful about the future and was preparing for it.

A conversation I had with a nuclear engineer in New Delhi lasted six hours. We started out at the YMCA, where I was staying; then he drove me to a fancy club he belonged to, and we ate dinner on the veranda there. We talked at length about nuclear power and his doubts about quality control in India's nuclear power industry. He also helped me understand the fear generated by the state of emergency declared by Indira Gandhi in 1975. Opponents of Mrs. Gandhi's regime were thrown in jail; so when she called an election, people were afraid even to admit to one another that they were planning to vote against her. "When I went into the voting booth," the engineer told me, "I hadn't asked my wife whom she was voting for, and she hadn't asked me. Nobody knew how anyone else was going to vote. Privately we were all afraid that if Mrs. Gandhi won, she would declare another state of emergency and refuse to hold elections in the future. Then we'd never be able to get rid of her." I could see how much he enjoyed being listened to, and how important it was for him to talk about things he hadn't been able to discuss with anyone else."

In all of my conversations, I would look directly at the person I was interviewing and at the same time observe the context we were in—the sounds around us, the birds, the wind, the way people nearby responded to my presence. I would listen to the person as open-heartedly as I could, trying to get a glimpse of the world through his or her eyes. Usually when the conversations lasted long enough, I would start to feel the soft stirrings of a connection—some uncovering of our common root system.

"Are things getting better or worse in your life? In the world?" These questions always got people talking. In Hoshangabad I began to notice that men tended to think things were getting better, while women were generally more pessimistic. A woman to whom I mentioned this observation responded: "That's because the men don't do the shopping."

When I asked about the future, many people went directly to the possibility of nuclear war. Near Kyoto, I spoke with a seventy-two-year-old farmer whose family had lived on the same land since the twelfth century. He feared that the population explosion had made nuclear war more likely. And nuclear war would make it impossible to grow things. "We in Japan are downwind from everyone," he told me.

A Tibetan businessman I met in an antique store offered to take me to "the wisest man in Darjeeling." I followed the businessman through an alley, up a dark staircase, and into a little room. There we met a Tibetan monk, a stout man who sat surrounded by his scrolls. On one side stood an intricately arranged altar; on the other, a window overlooked the Himalayas. The businessman translated as we chatted.

At one point the monk abruptly changed the subject. "What I really want to talk to you about is nuclear war." He reached in among his scrolls, brought out a world atlas, and asked me to show him where Hawaii was. A friend from Hawaii had told him about nuclear war. Since then he had spent a lot of time thinking about it and had come to believe that the root of the nuclear threat was anger. Did I get angry often? he wanted to know. Did people often get angry at me? He advised me that this was an important area to work on. He looked out the window at the sacred Himalayas and mournfully observed, "Nuclear war would ruin these mountains."

A scientist in Varanasi was more sanguine. Nuclear war might solve the population problem, he suggested.

In London, a political activist I met in a bookstore was concerned that the United States would provoke a war in Europe. "You think you can protect your own country by keeping the wars on our continent. Don't you care about us at all?"

I often encountered hostility toward the United States. A young doctor at the Rasulia Center said, "You Americans have so much and we have so little. Your aid comes with strings attached. You can't give a clean gift; you can't help without getting something out of it, even if it's only a slightly less guilty conscience." Foreign businesses come to India in search of cheap labor, he said. For every dollar they invest in India, they take out three dollars' worth of goods. "That is how you get things cheaply in your country." By now he was yelling. "We don't want your help, your charity, your money! Get your ships out of the Indian Ocean, and get out of our lives!"

Listening to him, I felt personally attacked. I wanted to tell him that I wasn't one of those industrialists. Yet I wasn't wholly divorced from the situation either—I ate cashews from India, and I'd never felt good about food being exported from a hungry country to the United States. So I kept listening, and noticing my own defenses.

A woman in New Delhi said her daughter wanted to know why American protesters did not continue to care about the Vietnamese people after the U.S. troops had gone home. How could we cut the connection so easily? The question stung. As she spoke, feeble excuses ran through my mind. Once our troops had left Vietnam, we no longer had much information about what was happening there. Anyway, hadn't we done our part by forcing our government to withdraw the troops? Wasn't it time to divorce ourselves from that situation? Even as these defenses arose, I could see I was struggling to convince myself of my own righteousness. But finally I inwardly admitted that there

Two demonstrators rally outside a Manila shopping center. 1990. Erik de Castro/Reuters/Bettmann.

was no justification for my own fickle attention to the plight of the Vietnamese people. One day I stumbled into the Nonaligned Nations Conference in New Delhi. I stepped into the Oberoi Hotel to make a phone call and then sat down at an unattended desk to write some notes. A woman wearing a brightly-colored dress came up to ask directions. I found out she was from Tonga and asked her to tell me what world issues concerned her most. She expressed outrage about the expansion of the U.S. military base on Diego Garcia, an island in the Indian Ocean. Other delegates I talked with at the conference shared that concern. They were sure that the base would be used for surveillance of southern Asia, northern Africa, and the South Pacific, and would potentially be used as a springboard for military intervention. The woman from Tonga was alarmed that I had no knowledge of any of this. She wanted to know whether my ignorance was typical of the American people. How could I consider myself well-informed and yet know nothing of this important global issue that involved my government?

She offered to bring other people from the conference to talk with me if I would come back in the next few days. So every afternoon I sat down at "my desk" at the Nonaligned Nations Conference. Delegates and others at the conference came to talk with me. The hotel staff began to recognize me and bring me stationery and water.

These conversations gave me a sense of how powerful a force the United States is in the lives of people in Third World nations. They envy the comforts we take for granted and long for a fair share of their own resources and the fruits of their labor. They are afraid of being devastated in a nuclear war they never agreed to take part in. They are bewildered that the American people don't seem to know or care about what is happening in the rest of the world.

I developed two rules for listening to people talk about my country. First, I do not explain or defend the United States. My goal is to see how we look to others and to let that understanding inform my being. Although I continue to feel defensive when my country is criticized, I try to keep listening. Second, I do not divorce myself from criticisms of America and Americans. I do not say or imply, "Yes, some Americans or some parts of our country are that way, but I'm not." I try to take the criticisms to heart.

But it's not only criticisms I encounter. I've also heard out-and-out adoration of the United States. In a park in East Berlin, I met a young couple out for a Sunday stroll. Right away I noticed the American flag pin on the man's shirt. The woman was noticeably pregnant, and both of them had high hopes for the future. They had already applied once for permission to emigrate to the United States, but it had been denied. They had heard all about America from the man's sister, who lives in California, and they longed for the freedom she had told them about. They wanted to work hard, advance in their careers, and be free to buy all sorts of things.

In Varanasi, two women students—one from Iran, the other from Bahrain—told me they knew all about the United States from watching "Dallas" on television. They especially admired the kitchens in "Dallas," and all the electrical appliances. I told them that not everyone in my country had such a high standard of living—that some people didn't even have electricity. I could see they were struggling to believe what I said.

Throughout my travels I met people who had studied in the United States, including many of the delegates at the Nonaligned Nations Conference. Many people spoke of the inequality of the cultural exchange. A woman in Tokyo who had studied at the University of Chicago put it forcefully: "We send our smartest people to your universities to learn from you. But you don't send your students to learn from us. When you come to our country you stay in fancy hotels, go on shopping trips, and travel around in tour buses. There's a lot you miss. Yours is a young society, and you have a lot to learn from us."

I have found people to be grateful and excited that an American has come to learn from them. In Tokyo, Bangkok, Varanasi, and New Delhi, people lined up and sometimes waited for hours to talk with me. Around midnight on the night before I left Varanasi, I was busy packing my suitcase when I heard a knock on the door. It was a Bangladeshi man whom I'd met briefly at the university. He had heard that I was about to leave and he wanted to be interviewed. An engineering student, he was also very interested in international cooperation and wanted to make sure that Bangladesh was represented in my listening project.

I often asked people: "What have you learned in your life?" Some had learned about time's constant movement. Others spoke of sorrow and suffering. A revolutionary in Bangkok had learned that "you have to be very careful." He had helped start a people's credit union, but government agents had infiltrated it, shut it down, and confiscated all the money.

Several people said, "It was worth it." They seemed proud to announce that their achievements had been worth the costs. In New Delhi, a woman told me just the opposite. Once a doctor, she had given up practicing medicine. "What good does it do? I get them well but they get sick the next day. They don't have enough food. If I use my medical training, it only means that they are going to suffer longer." So now she makes decorative plaques. I felt threatened by her depression and sense of futility.

On my second day in Bangkok, I took a taxi driver's recommendation of a place to eat breakfast. The restaurant was a large room with about thirty tables, all but two empty. The only people in the place were two European men at a booth in front, and six or seven Thai women who were sitting or standing around tables nearby. They all looked up as I walked in. I sat in the booth behind the two men and soon got the sense that they were the owners. From a nearby table, a woman looked at me and mouthed the words "I love you." I was so confused I felt like a block of wood. I had come here for breakfast! She gestured to ask if she could join me; I shrugged my shoulders. Another woman came up behind me and started rubbing my shoulders. She said softly, "You want a massage? You want to come up to my room for a massage?" I said, "No, thank you." The first woman scooted around and sat next to me. I tried to carry on as meaningless a conversation as possible. What's your name? Where do you live? I ordered ham and eggs. It was about seven o'clock, so I said to the woman next to me, "You're here early this morning." She said she'd been here late last night too, until 1:00 a.m. She was a short woman, not over thirty years old. She touched my arm with a cold hand—she must have been as scared as I was. Rubbing my arm suggestively, she asked if I'd like to come up to her room. "I can make you very happy." I could no longer escape the conclusion that she was a prostitute who thought I'd come looking for her services.

Putting my hand on hers to stop her from rubbing my arm, I remembered my interview book! I whipped it out and told her I was traveling to learn what was going on in the world. Would she be willing to talk with me? Yes, she would. She told me her job was to sleep with men and let them touch her. She had to work hard to feed her two children. It cost too much to send them to school so they stayed with her mother during the day. The woman's husband had been killed recently when the truck he was driving turned over.

By this time my ham and eggs had arrived, bathed in grease. I couldn't bring myself to eat the food. The other women started coming over to my table, trying to get me to go upstairs with them. I realized what a mystery I must seem: I hadn't eaten my food; I'd just been talking to this woman; perhaps there was something else I wanted that they could give me. Soon, all the women were sitting with us, talking about husbands and children and work and life in Thailand. They spoke of their envy and fear of the American and Japanese business and military men who used their services. Americans are very friendly and have a lot of money, one woman told me, but sometimes when you get them upstairs they're awful.

The women had mixed feelings about the Thai government. A big problem was that houses were being torn down and people were being thrown out of their neighborhoods. The threat of eviction was terrifying. But they did have electric power and lights—that was an improvement over past years.

We talked about children. The women all wished they could send their kids to school, but they couldn't afford the tuition. When I spoke of schooling provided for free by the government, they all started talking at once. What a great idea! I mentioned the school I'd visited the day before in Bangkok, where poor people could send their children for one baht (about five cents) a day. They hadn't heard of it.

Before leaving I offered the woman who'd first sat with me some money for her time and her teaching. She refused, but I insisted, suggesting she use the money to send her children to the One Baht School.

Still feeling the effects of jetlag, I returned to my hotel room and tried to sleep. But I was too excited. I kept thinking about the Thai women, about how much fun it had been to chat with them, how lively our discussion had been. I thought of what I'd learned about the impact of widowhood. Several of the women I'd talked with had turned to prostitution because they had children to take care of and no husband or other source of support. I could understand their decision, but I fervently wished they had other options. I remembered how an idea that was familiar to me—free public education—had seemed thrilling to them. And I wondered why I had been so afraid in the first moments at the restaurant. What had been so threatening? Of course I had never been propositioned by prostitutes before. What does a decent person do in that situation? I had been unprepared. And yet even in the midst of my fear I had known I was in no real danger. I had to laugh at myself and my fear.

The next day, I returned to the One Baht School to talk more with its founder, Prateep Ungsongtham. A tall, graceful woman in her late twenties, she had founded the school at age fifteen. At the time she had been a childcare worker, and she began to be concerned about the children who brought their younger siblings to her but couldn't afford to attend school themselves. So although she had little schooling herself, Prateep began teaching the older children to read. In exchange they paid her one baht each and helped out with the childcare. Now the school had grown; there were two buildings and a basketball court. Prateep had finished college, and some of her former students who now had college degrees had returned to teach.

The One Baht School is in the middle of Klong Toey, a community of forty thousand squatters. Built on stilts over a canal, their dwellings are made mostly out of found wood but are very clean inside. I found myself wondering: In such terrible situations, where do people get the ideas, the will, and the drive to make things better, not only for themselves but for others? The land is owned by the Port Authority, which at the time was taking steps to evict six thousand slumdwellers in order to build a container port. The school had been a focal point for the efforts against eviction. Prateep said, "To feel secure, we need to know that we can stay here for thirty or forty years."

When Prateep found out that I'd had some experience fighting eviction, she called in the other teachers. It was a Saturday, so there were no classes. Ten of us sat together, and I talked about the International Hotel, the American Indian struggle against uranium mining, and other land struggles. Every now and then our discussion would have to stop because someone would come in with a problem: an old man was dying or a woman's electric bill was forty times what it should be. The teachers were also community workers, and with each interruption one would leave to help resolve the problem.

I dredged up everything I had learned at the I-Hotel about fighting eviction—resistance tactics and techniques from England, China, Japan, the Philippines, and all over the United States. Each idea seemed to suggest others to them, and they would take off in their own language, talking excitedly. They had dreamed of defying the eviction order but had thought of their struggle as an isolated one. Hearing that others around the world had the same dream was exhilarating to them. I had never shared information with a more eager and intensely curious bunch.

During my time in Japan, it slowly dawned on me that I had not seen any slums or poor people there. I began asking the people I interviewed where the poor people lived. "We don't have poor people in Japan," I was told again and again. "We are all middle class." Or occasionally, "Oh yes, we have some but I don't know where. Maybe in Tokyo." These answers seemed implausible, so I continued my inquiry. Finally I heard about a district in Osaka called Kamagasaki, where day laborers and poor people lived. Church people from Osaka and Kyoto had organized a night patrol in the area so that people who fell asleep on the street would not freeze and those who were injured could be cared for. Each night of the week a different group was responsible for the watch.

I tagged along with a visiting group from Friends World College. We arrived at a small church in a bleak part of Osaka about 9:00 P.M. Our first job was to check the log books for news of the previous shift. Then the eight of us doing the watch that night gathered our supplies—gloves, first-aid kits, lanterns, and click counters—loaded them into two pull-carts piled high with quilts, and walked to a nearby public building. I was amazed at what I saw there. More than a hundred people were sleeping on cotton mattresses covered with colorful quilts. It was an open-air sleeping center, a 25-by-75-foot area sheltered by the overhang of the building.

We picked up two containers of warm rice balls, put them in our carts, and set out in search of other people who needed a place to sleep. We divided into two teams of four and headed in different directions. As we walked, we found men sleeping in little hidden places. We kept track of how many we came across and where they were sleeping. My partner approached each sleeping person and checked on him. "Good evening. How are you? Are you warm enough? Would you like some rice?" If he was cold, we would give him directions to the sleeping center. If he couldn't walk, we would put him in our pull-cart and take him there.

A toothless old man came up to greet us. His dog followed. The man reminded me of some of my Sixth Street Park friends. To make a place to sleep, he had leaned sheets of plywood against two ramen-noodle carts. He accepted a warm rice ball and chatted with us awhile.

Who are the twenty thousand people who live in Kamagasaki? Most are Koreans (the target of much discrimination in Japan). Others are poor Japanese. Many are men who have left their families. In Japan when you apply for a job, the company looks up your family name in the books of family history. If you do not come from a "good family," or if you are Korean, you have a very hard time getting a job. There are no training programs to help these men. Many are alcoholics. If a man can afford it, he rents a tiny room for about 250 yen (one dollar) a night. At the time of my visit, the landlords had recently doubled their profit by splitting the rooms in half. They would build an additional floor to divide each room horizontally, yielding two cubicles just big enough to crawl into.

At midnight we returned to the sleeping center, where by now about one hundred eighty men were sleeping. Another crew arrived shortly after we did, carrying a man in their cart. They checked his eyes with a light. Each time a new man arrived, a member of the day laborers' union would carry a mattress and quilt to a spot on the ground and make up a bed for him. The worker would tuck the man in, make sure he was warm, and say goodnight. I was moved by the physical contact and the personal care. Workers stay there all night, standing guard so that no one can rob or take advantage of the sleeping men, and covering them up if their quilts slip off. I thought again of the people on Sixth Street in San Francisco, wishing the same kind of care were available to them.

We went back to the church and slept until 5:00 A.M., when we returned to the day labor hall. By that time all the bedding had been put away, and a nearby alley was full of minibuses with signs in their windows advertising for workers—ditch diggers, dirt carriers, and so on. But there were not enough jobs, and two-thirds of the men were left milling around.

At breakfast I interviewed one of the regular watch volunteers. He told me that Koreans have always been badly treated in Japan. They were once slaves, and they still do the lowliest work. Counting the street people is important, he said, because the society doesn't want to acknowledge its poor.

On the train back to Kyoto I thought about poor people and tried to envision better ways to get the world's menial work done. If we had a society where everyone was treated well, who would dig the ditches, pick the crops, and clean the buildings? If the United States didn't have a constant stream of immigrants to do that sort of work, who would do it? Are there ways to distribute menial work more evenly, and to value that work?

Everywhere I traveled, there were aspects of the society that I found disturbing. I tried to notice these, and to see whether my discomfort changed over time. For instance, in Varanasi one of the predominant smells is that of burning cow dung. At first I really disliked it. I lost my appetite and wished I could turn off my nose. To put myself at ease with the smell, I studied the cow-dung cycle. I watched people gather the dung, mix it with a little dry grass, and slap it onto a nearby wall. There is hardly a vertical surface that isn't adorned with dung patties clearly imprinted with the hand of the patty-maker. The dung is left to dry and later plucked off and either burned or sold. This is the fuel most poor people use to cook and keep warm. Some patty-makers have a design sense and cover the walls in an artistic fashion; others seem to slap it up without thought or plan. As I became better acquainted with the process, the people, and the city, the smell bothered me less and less until the discomfort finally left entirely.

To this day I cringe at the cultural faux pas I know I've made in my world travels: eating with my left hand in India, touching a Brahman friend on the shoulder as I bade him farewell, losing track of which slippers were for which room in the home of a Japanese host. There must have been dozens of blunders that I still don't realize I made. I have learned to ask my hosts to forgive me for any disrespect I may have inadvertently shown for them, their religious practices, or culture.

When I returned from my world trip, I also returned to my job at Sixth Street Park. In a staff meeting some of the guys asked me to tell them what I had learned. I said I had been struck by the poverty in Japan, Thailand, and India. I told them I had seen people in Bombay living like animals, and people with severe disabilities out foraging for food on their hands and knees. Bird, who was sitting directly across the table from me, looked at me squarely, with a tear in the corner of his eye. He said, "It broke your heart, didn't it?" I could tell that even though he was very poor by the standards of the society around him, he had seen poverty much worse—maybe in the service or the merchant marine—and it had moved him. The park staff talked of their relative good fortune and of the idea of starting an international union of down-and-out people that could go on strike for better treatment.

It used to be that when I thought of India, I'd imagine the outline of the country on a map. I'd think of hungry people, women in saris, wild animals, mysticism, gurus— just floating impressions. Now I know what India looks like, smells like, feels like. I know some Indian people and have seen how their lives work in their own environment. I have a sense of some of the unresolved issues in the lives of individual people there.

This perceptual shift reminds me of going on field trips with my college zoology professor, Dr. Stanford. He would take us to an open field that didn't look special or interesting to us. Then Doc Stanford would say, "Let's take a look at just this one square meter." We'd explore its ecology in detail—the grasshoppers and beetles, the lichens and grasses, the parasites growing on the stalks of plants. Three or four inches below the surface, we'd find worms and a new set of bacteria; further down there were fungi growing on the roots of plants. We'd measure the acidity of the soil and note the kinds of plants it supported. We'd study the wind patterns, the geology, how water percolated down through the soil. We could take hours studying a square meter.

And that's the way I feel about the world now. I used to picture the world as a globe with continents and oceans and countries painted orange, yellow, and pink. Then, when I saw photographs of the earth taken from space, I saw a living whole. Now I see life on that spinning ball: specific places, specific concerns, specific lives.

I'm continually thinking of the people I've met around the world. That couple on the Punjab Mail: Is their granddaughter growing up healthy and strong? How are the street people in Kamagasaki doing? Have the squatters near the One Baht School successfully resisted eviction? In August I think about the monsoons in India. I can see the waters of the Ganges rising.

My listening project is a kind of tuning-up of my heart to the affairs of the world. I hear the news in a very different way now, and I act with a larger context in mind. Conspicuous consumption has become more difficult now that I have met poor people around the world. I hold myself accountable to the people whose lives I have seen. And I work to keep nuclear war from happening to us all.

I carry with me the pain of some of my partners in the world, but it does not weigh me down. Much of my life and environment have been designed to isolate me from this pain, but I have come to see it as a kind of holy nectar. The more I drink, the more I can taste what is happening on this planet.

## Reading Questions

1. Why would Peavey's listening project help to prevent nuclear war?
2. How is her travel different from tourist travel?
3. What seemed to be the major concerns of the people with whom she spoke?
4. Which concerns do you never overhear in American conversations?

## Recommended Reading

Fran Peavey, *A Shallow Pool of Time: An HIV+ Woman Grapples with the AIDS Epidemic* (Philadelphia: New Society Publishers, 1990)

Fran Peavey, *By Life's Grace* (Philadelphia: New Society Publishers, 1993)

For information about Fran Peavey's social change consulting services, "Strategic Listening," write to Fran Peavey, 3181 Mission, #30, San Francisco, CA 94110.

## Recommended Audiovisual Resources

*The Rebuilding of Mascot Flats.* 1992. Produced by Josephine Hayes Dean. A moving story about a group of homeless New Yorkers who set out to renovate an abandoned tenement building. Filmakers Library.

*Women, HIV and AIDS.* 1992. Produced by Hummingbird Films for Channel 4, England. Frank discussion on subjects such as safe sex for straight and lesbian women, health care for HIV-positive women, and advocacy efforts. Filmakers Library.

*Turnarounds: A Pilot Needle Exchange Program.* 1993. Produced by Susan Adler. Documents the successful New Haven legal needle-exchange program that is saving lives. Filmakers Library.

# Yellow Sprouts

## TRINH T. MINH-HA

Trinh T. Minh-ha is an Asian-American filmmaker and author. She is the author of *Woman, Native, Other: Writing Postcoloniality and Feminism* and *When the Moon Waxes Red: Representation, Gender, and Cultural Politics.*

If darkness induces reverie and is the medium of a diffuse eroticism, nighttime remains for many poets and painters of Asian cultures the moment of quiescence necessary to the dawning of new awareness. Both the time when no thought arises and the time when the primal positive energy stirs into motion are called the moon. A ray shining clear through the night with the intensity of a white light burgeoning in an empty room. *Nothingness produces white snow; quiescence produces yellow sprouts* (Chang Po-tuan).[1] When stillness culminates, there is movement. The living potential returns afresh, the cycles of the moon go on regularly, again and again the light will wane. In the process of infinite beginnings, even immortality is mortal.

With each phase a shift has occurred, a new form is attained, several motions interweave within a movement. Crescent, quarter, gibbous, full: an old form continues to mutate between loss and gain, while every growth from and toward voidness invites a different entry into areas of social dissent and transformation. The new moon, as science duly demonstrates, cannot be seen at all. To speak of the thin crescent moon as being new is to forget that only when the dark half faces the earth is the moon truly new. Politics waxes and wanes, and like a lunar eclipse, it vanishes only to return rejuvenating itself as it reaches its full intensity. In the current situation of overcodification, of de-individualized individualism and of reductionist collectivism, naming critically is to dive headlong into the abyss of un-naming. The task of inquiring into all the divisions of a culture remains exacting, for the moments when things take on a proper name can only be positional, hence transitional. The function of any ideology in power is to represent the world positively unified. To challenge the regimes of representation that govern a society is to conceive of how a politics can transform reality rather than merely ideologize it. As the struggle moves onward and assumes new, different forms, it is bound to recompose subjectivity and praxis while displacing the way diverse cultural strategies relate to one another in the constitution of social and political life.

In Chinese mythology, those who first ascend to the moon—the pioneers of the Apollo flight—are the Moon-Queen Chang E who swallows the pill of immortality, the hare which throws itself into the magical fire to feed Buddha, and the Sun-King who comes to visit his wife Chang E on the fifteenth day of every moon. Now that scientists readily speak of the "Old Moon" being extinct with the advent of the "New Moon," access to the world of the moon becomes at the same time more reachable (for some) and more limited (for others). There has been a time when Western science-fiction writers cherished the possibility of using the moon as a military base for building nuclear missiles. The paradoxical idea of "colonizing the moon" with the aim of coming closer to uniting the earth has constituted an argument that some scientists have not hesitated to advance. "The *Eagle* has landed," was the statement symbolically uttered upon North American Man's arrival on the moon. Since then, Apollo has come and gone. But the fact that a dozen men have walked upon its surface does not make the moon one bit less puzzling to the scientists.

Just as new knowledge cannot nullify previous results, different moments of a struggle constantly overlap and different relations of representation across "old" and "new" can be made possible without landing back in a dialectical destiny. Postures of exclusionism and of absolutism therefore unveil themselves to be at best no more than a form of reactive defense and at worst, an obsession with the self as holder of rights and property—or in other words, as owner of the world. In the renewed terrain of struggle and of deterritorialized subjectivities, no moon-lovers can really claim possession of the soft light that illuminates towns, villages, forests, and fields. *The same moon that rises over the ocean lands in the tea water. The wind that cools the waters scatters the moons like rabbits on a meadow.*[2] *The one moon is seen in all waters; and the many-one moon is enjoyed or bawled at on a quiet night by people everywhere—possessors and dispossessed.*

It used to be a custom in many parts of Asia that women, regardless of their classes, all came out in groups to stroll on the night of the Mid-Autumn Festival when the moon is at its fullest and brightest. Also parading through the streets are children from all families who moved together in wavy lines, their songs resonating from quarters to quarters, and their moon lanterns flickering in gentle undulations like so many beads of color on the dragon's body. The moon light walk remains a memorable event, for here in September, the sky is high, the dewdrop clear, the mountains empty, the night lucent. Moon, waves, pearls, and jades: a multitude of expressions founded on these images exists in Chinese poetry to describe feminine beauty and the carnal presence of the loved woman. *Scented mist, cloud chignon damp/Pure light, jade arm cool* ("Moonlit Night," Tu-Fu).[3] Through the eroticization of nocturnal light, she is, as tradition dictates, often all hair and skin: darkness is fragrant, soft, vaporous, moist, mist- or cloud-like, while the glow emanating from her smooth bare arm evokes the sensation of touching jade. Yet, she is not simply night to his day (as in many Western philosophical and literary traditions), she is day in night.

In the realm of dualities where blinding brilliance is opposed to mysterious luminosity, or to use Taoist terminology, where the logic of conscious knowledge is set against the wisdom of real knowledge, she finds no place she can simply dwell in or transgress. Crisscrossing more than one occupied territory at a time, she remains perforce inappropriate/d—both inside *and* outside her own social positionings. What is offered then is the possibility of a break with the specular structure of hegemonic discourse and its scopic economy which, according to Western feminist critiques, circularly bases its in-sights on the sight (a voyeur's *theoria*) rather than the touch. The interstice between the visual and the tactile is perhaps the (nothing-)spiritual conveyed above in the fragrance of mist—at once within and beyond the sense of smell. Within and beyond tangible visibility. A trajectory across variable praxes of difference, her (un)location is necessarily the shifting and contextual interval between arrested boundaries.

She is the moon and she is not. All depends on how the moon partakes of language and representation. Chinese feminists have by now carefully re-read and rewritten the story of goddess Chang E. In their words, the latter was not confined to living solitarily on the moon because she *stole* the pill of immortality from her husband Hou Yi (who later became the Sun-King). Rather, she chose to live on the moon because it was nearest the earth, and she was forced by circumstances to swallow the elixir to *free* herself from the threat of having to belong to a man craving for power and possession who asserted he had killed her husband.[4] As long as the light of the moon is merely spoken of as having its birth in the sun, decreasing in proportion to its distance from the solar ray, and being accordingly light or dark as the sun comes and goes, women will reject Woman. They will agree with feminist writer Ting Lan that: "Woman is not the moon. She must rely on herself to shine."[5] For having occupied such a multiply central role in Chinese arts and culture, the moon has inevitably been the object of much literary controversy. Subjected to a continuous process of re- and de-territorialization, she bears both strong positive and negative social connotations.

Not too long ago, when the fire of the revolution was at its height, some writers decided that to focus on her was to ruin China, therefore the moon had to be liquidated. A person enjoying the mid-autumn moon and eating rabbit moon cakes was either "feudalistic" or "counter-revolutionary." The moon became the property of the conservative leisure class and, again, her sight was thought to be owned by some to the detriment of others. As an ideological instrument in man's manipulative hand, she could easily constitute a means of escapism, hence to sing her praise is, indeed, to "avoid facing reality." Yet, how realistic was it to liquidate the moon? Can women simply leap *outside* the (un-)feminine without falling into the historical model of mastery? The moment was transitional. Today, as the wind keeps on changing direction, the moon can hardly be bestowed with the power to ruin the nation, and again, she proves to be "shared property" among franchised and disfranchised. The moon waxes and wanes in favor of different trends of discursive production, and the war of meaning or what Mao named the "verbal struggle" never really ends. On the social terrain, desire refuses to let itself be confined to the need of ideological legitimation. Whether the moon is scorned or exalted, she continues to be passionately the subject/the passionate subject of discussion. Even when invalidated and stripped bare of her restorative powers, she remains this empty host-center which generously invites its guests to fill it to their own likings without ever being able to arrogate to themselves the exclusive right of a landlord.

*Nothing is less real than realism* (Georgia O'Keeffe).[6] Insubordinate processes of resistance do not lend themselves easily to commodification. A man convicted for seditious conspiracy, and currently serving his sixty-eight-year sentence in prison for having upheld the liberation of Puerto Rico, remarks that "the struggle is also between one fiction and another. . . . We, crazy people always strive toward the kingdom of freedom (Marx), towards our own idea and conception of Utopia." Rejecting the disabling and reductive logic that one should not engage in the so-called luxury of art when people starve every day, or when revolution is in danger, the man further asserts that without art, "revolution will lose its spirit. And the spirit of any revolution is the widening of freedom, collective and individual, and not one or the other" (Elizam Escobar).[7] To disrupt the existing systems of dominant values and to challenge the very foundation of a social and cultural order is not merely to destroy a few prejudices or to reverse power relations within the terms of an economy of the same. Rather, it is to see through the revolving door of all rationalizations and to meet head on the truth of that struggle *between fictions*. Art is a form of production. Aware that oppression can be located both in the story told and in the telling of the story, an art critical of social reality neither relies on mere consensus nor does it ask permission from ideology. Thus, the issue facing liberation movements is not that of liquidating art in its not-quite-correct, ungovernable dimension, but that of confronting the limits of centralized conscious knowledge, hence of demystifying while politicizing the artistic experience.

The moon breeds like a rabbit. She causes the seeds to germinate and the plants to grow, but she exceeds all forms of regulated fecundity through which she is expected to ensure the system's functioning. In the heterogeneity of the feminist struggle and its plurivocal projects, the impossibility of defining once and for all the condition of being sexualized as feminine and racialized as colored does not result from a lack of determination, but rather, from an inescapable awareness of the sterility of the unitary subject and its monolithic constructs. *For language is in every case not only communication of the communicable but also, at the same time, a symbol of the noncommunicable* (Walter Benjamin).[8] The gift that circulates with non-closures offers no security. Here in the all-meaning circle where there is no in no out, no light no shade, she is born anew. This is the third scenario. When stillness culminates, there is movement. Non-alignment paradoxically means new alliances: those that arise from-within differences and necessarily cut across variable borderlines, for "there is no one who is automatically my ally/ because we are the same/ Alliances don't grow wild and unattended/ . . . they grow on two conditions/ that you and I/ both of us/ understand that we need each other to survive/ and that we have the courage/ to ask each other what that means" (Judit).[9]

While the full moon generally represents the conjunction of *yin* and *yang*, of stillness and action, or of beings dear to one another (the cyclic encounter of Hou Yi and Chang E), the autumn Harvest moon connotes more specifically distant presence and desire for reunion. Separated lovers burnt in longing and imbued with the thought of one another, reunite in watching the same moon. *Night follows night, bright luster wanes / Thinking of you, I am like the full moon* (Chang Chiu-Ling).[10] The potential of sharing the seed of a common journey while being apart keeps desire alive; but the lucid tranquility of lunar realizations eventually helps the desirers to find their repose. Lifted in awareness by the light in the calm fragrant night, moon-lovers remain enraptured by its gentle powers while aspiring to quietism in their creations. Such an in-between state of mind does bear the trace of a name: whoever dreams of the simple moon(life) without looking for conscious knowledge is said, in psychoanalysis, to incline toward the "feminine."

*At night inhale the vitality of the moon* (Sun Bu-er).[11] She is the principle of transformation and the site of possibility for diversely repressed realities. With the moon, the Imaginary She is at once centered and de-centered. Access to proper names as moments of transition (the "moon" is a name) requires that "the imagination also [be] a political weapon" (Escobar). For, there is no space really untouched by the vicissitudes of history, and emancipatory projects never begin nor end *properly*. They are constantly hampered in their activities by the closure-effect repeatedly brought about when a group within a movement becomes invested in the exercise of power, when it takes license to legislate what it means to "be a woman," to ascertain the "truth" of the feminine, and to reject other women whose immediate agenda may differ from their own. In undoing such closure-effect one is bound again and again to recognize "that piece of the oppressor which is planted deep within each of us, and which knows only the oppressors' tactics, the oppressors' relationship" (Audre Lorde).[12]

Changes in the color of the sun or the moon used to be signs of approaching calamities. When the moon waxes red, it is said in Chinese mythology that men should be in awe of the unlucky times thus fore-omened. Today, lunar eclipses are still impressive, but scientists find them "undeniably lovely," for the dimming moon often shows strange and beautiful color effects. The old fox sees to it that everything becomes a commodity. Yet between rational and irrational enslavement there is the interval and there is the possibility for a third term in the struggle. *We are what we imagine. Our very existence consists in our imagination of ourselves. . . . . The greater tragedy that can befall us is to go unimagined* (N. Scott Momaday).[13] In the existing regime of frenzied "disciplinarization," such breach in the regularity of the system constitutes the critical moment of disequilibrium and dis/illumination when Buddha may be defined as "a cactus in the moonlight."[14]

# Reading Questions

1. According to Trinh, what are the links between naming, ideology, regimes of representation, and the effort to create social change?
2. What elements of Chinese mythology does Trinh value, and why?
3. Paraphrase, in your own words, Trinh's claim: "Insubordinate processes of resistance do not lend themselves easily to commodification." What are some examples?
4. Of what value for Trinh's understanding of social change is Walter Benjamin's view that language is also "a symbol of the noncommunicable"?
5. According to Trinh, what difficulties accompany coalitions of women when they attempt to "ascertain the 'truth' of the feminine"?

# Recommended Reading

Walter Benjamin, *One-Way Street and Other Writings* (London: Verso Press, 1978)

T. Cleary, trans., *The Inner Teachings of Taoism* (Boston: Shambhala, 1986)

Dexter Fisher, ed., *The Third Woman* (Boston: Houghton Mifflin, 1980)

Emily Honig and Gail Hershatter, eds., *Personal Voices: Chinese Women in the 1980s* (Stanford, CA: Stanford University Press, 1988)

Hsin-Sheng C. Kao, ed., *Nativism Overseas: Contemporary Chinese Women Writers* (Birmingham, NY: State University of New York Press, 1993)

Stanley Karnow, *Vietnam: A History* (New York: Penguin, 1983)

Elaine H. Kim with Janice Otani, eds., *With Silk Wings* (Asian Women United of California, 1983)

Audre Lorde, "Age, Race, Class, and Sex: Women Redefining Difference," *Out There: Marginalization and Contemporary Cultures*, ed. Russell Ferguson et al. (Cambridge: The MIT Press, 1990)

Trinh T. Minh-ha, *When the Moon Waxes Red: Representation, Gender and Cultural Politics* (New York: Routledge, 1991)

Trinh T. Minh-ha, *Woman, Native, Other: Writing Postcoloniality and Feminism* (Bloomington, IN: Indiana University Press, 1989)

# Recommended Audiovisual Resources

For film scripts to accompany her films and interviews that discuss them, see Trinh T. Minh-ha, *Framer Framed* (New York: Routledge, 1992).

*Reassemblage*. 1982. Trinh T. Minh-ha. Women Make Movies. Also available in the Museum of Modern Art Circulating Film Library.

*Naked Spaces—Living Is Round*. 1985. Trinh T. Minh-ha. Women Make Movies. Museum of Modern Art.

*Surname Viet Given Name Nam*. 1989. Trinh T. Minh-ha. Women Make Movies. Museum of Modern Art.

# Notes

## Kimberlé Crenshaw and Gary Peller, "Real Time/Real Justice" (pp. 22–33)

1. 488 U.S. 469 (1989).
2. The critique of this general norm of color blindness has been one of the central projects of "Critical Race Theory" scholars, a group of writers informally organized in 1989 to pursue progressive-oriented studies of race, culture, and law. For a description of the group's aims, see Kimberlé Crenshaw, "A Black Feminist Critique of Antidiscrimination Law and Politics," *The Politics of Law*, ed. David Kairys (New York: Pantheon, 1990), 195. For citations to the group's work to date, see Richard Delgado and Jean Stenfancic, "Critical Race Theory: An Annotated Bibliography." *Virginia Law Review* 78 (forthcoming, 1992). For examples of criticisms of color blindness from within the critical race theory genre, see Neil Gotanda, "A Critique of 'Our Constitution Is Color-Blind,'" *Stanford Law Review* 44 (1991): 1; Gary Peller, "Race Consciousness," *Duke Law Review* (1990): 758; Patricia Williams, "The Obliging Shell: An Informal Essay on Formal Legal Equality," *Michigan Law Review* 87 (1989): 2128.

3. We borrow the term "disaggregation" from Justice Marshall's dissent in *Croson*. See 488 U.S. at 542 (Marshall, J dissenting): "[T]he majority's critique [of the evidence of racial exclusion] shows an unwillingness to come to grips with why construction-contracting in Richmond is essentially a whites-only enterprise. The majority . . . takes the disingenuous approach of disaggregating Richmond's local evidence, attacking it piecemeal, and thereby concluding that no single piece of evidence adduced by the city, 'standing alone,' . . . suffices to prove past discrimination. But items of evidence do not, of course, 'stand alone,' or exist in alien juxtaposition. . . ." For a more extended discussion of the manner in which the Court disaggregated causal factors in *Croson*, see Michel Rosenfeld, "Decoding Richmond: Affirmative Action and the Elusive Meaning of Constitutional Equality," *Michigan Law Review* 87 (1989) 1729, 1761–66.
4. See *Report of the National Advisory Commission on Civil Disorders* (New York: Bantam, 1968), 205–38.

## Wahneema Lubiano, "Black Ladies, Welfare Queens, and State Minstrels" (pp. 34–52)

1. "[T]he narrative takes on its own impetus as it were, so that one begins to see reality as non-narrated. One begins to say that it's not a narrative, it's the way things are." From Gayatri Chakravorty Spivak, *The Post-Colonial Critic: Interviews, Strategies, Dialogues* (New York: Routledge, 1990: p. 19).
2. My mapping of the ways that the black-lady and welfare-queen figures did ideological "work" in this historical moment was informed by Hortense Spillers's "Mama's Baby, Papa's Maybe: An American Grammar Book," *Diacritics*, vol. 17, no. 2 (Summer 1987), pp. 65–81, from which the epigraph that begins this essay is drawn—an analysis of the *Moynihan Report* (Daniel Moynihan, *The Moynihan Report and the Politics of Controversy: A Transaction Social Science and Public Policy Report*, eds. Lee Rainwater and W. L. Yancey, Cambridge: MIT Press, 1967).
3. The television special produced by Bill Moyers, "The Vanishing Family: Crisis in Black America" (CBS Special Report, 1986), is a case in point. It was based on

Daniel Moynihan's *Negro Family: The Case for National Action* (Washington, D.C.: Department of Labor, Office of Policy, Planning & Research, 1965).
4. *The Moynihan Report*, 75.
5. Ibid.
6. Thomas's comments were reported, for example, in the *New York Times* of July 7, 1991: "She gets mad when the mailman is late with her welfare check. That's how dependent she is. . . . What's worse is that now her kids feel entitled to the check, too. They have no motivation for doing better or getting out of the situation." In short, as Avery Gordon (University of California, Santa Barbara) said in response to my argument above, Thomas's remarks paint a picture of Martin as a woman "addicted to" welfare who passes on that addiction to her children; she is the mother of addiction. "Mothering addiction" underwrites the logic of the culture of poverty, a logic that isn't a cultural thesis at all, but a sociobiological thesis (private conversation, January 13, 1992).

7. David Walker, *Appeal, in Four Articles; Together with a Preamble, to the Coloured Citizens of the World . . .* (1829), reprinted in Herbert Aptheker, *One Continual Cry* (New York: Humanities Press, 1965).

8. Avery Gordon extended my argument thusly: "We could not know—since 'we don't know who she is'—that she could really be a woman sexually harassed. Whatever other ideological work the attack on a 'black lady' has to do, it has to ensure that no woman in her position could be seen as sexually harassable; which was why the concept of reasonable doubt had to be deployed in irrational phantasmatic terms. It was easier to suggest that there are no 'knowable' women in her position" (private conversation, January 13, 1992).

9. *Village Voice*, October 22, 1991, p. 25.

10. *New York Times*, October 12, 1991.

11. "Persuasion by congruence" is Raphael Allen's phrase (private conversation, Princeton University, December 29, 1991).

## Andrew Ross, "Cowboys, Cadillacs, and Cosmonauts" (pp. 52–65)

An earlier version of this article appeared in *East–West Film Journal* (Fall 1989).

1. Carey McWilliams describes this appropriation at length in *North From Mexico* (Philadelphia: J. B. Lippincott, 1948).

2. The "denigration" of the genre reached its delightfully campy zenith in Warhol's *Lonesome Cowboys* (1968), where the fun-loving posse, agonizing over hair-styling and ballet moves, wrestles throughout the film with the maxim "We're not out here to raise cain, we're here to raise families."

3. Ralph Brauer and Donna Brauer, *The Horse, the Gun, and the Piece of Property: Changing Images of the TV Western* (Bowling Green: Bowling Green University Popular Press, 1975). Like the TV Western, the dime novel from 1875–1895 and the Hollywood Western from 1937–1957 had both moved through a whole succession of historical inflections of the genre.

4. Rita Parks, *The Western Hero in Film and Television: Mass Media Mythology* (Ann Arbor: UMI Research Press, 1983), p. 163.

5. The suppression of these two histories has not gone completely uncontested in Hollywood—in the case of genocide, by the so-called Cinema Rouge of the 1960s (*A Man Called Horse, Soldier Blue, Little Big Man*) and, in the case of the cattlemen's associations, by neopopulist films from *The Man Who Shot Liberty Valance* to *Heaven's Gate*.

6. The pioneer family was undoubtedly a favored populist model for the countercultural family bent on some degree of agrarian self-sufficiency. But the more politically resonant version of an extended kinship community was provided in the figure of the Native American tribe, more properly egalitarian and thus stripped of the Hollywood Western's historically inaccurate fondness for the absolute sovereignty of the patriarchal "chief." The counterculture's nostalgic "reinvention of the Indian" in the 1960s did not, however, arise solely out of a surplus of white guilt generated by a historical reexamination of the Old West. In most instances the new primitivistic attention to the Native American was articulated within the critical evaluation of the United States' advanced technological intervention in the non-Western world, especially in Southeast Asia. Thus arose a double identification with East and with the prewhite West; the hippie earth mother could carry a papoose and sport "Oriental" cheesecloth without any sense of cultural contradiction. Ironically, this dual identificatory practice reproduced the vestigial association of the Native American with the Orient, perpetuated ever since Columbus' grand navigational/cartographic blunder. It is no surprise, then, that the films of the Cinema Rouge would each come to be interpreted as allegories of the intervention in Vietnam, or that President Johnson would compare the defense of Vietnam to the defense of the Alamo.

7. Marshall McLuhan, "Television in a New Light," in *The Meaning of Commercial Television*, ed. Stanley T. Donner (Austin: University of Texas Press, 1967), pp. 87–89.

8. Andrew Ross, *No Respect: Intellectuals and Popular Culture* (New York: Routledge, 1989), p. 132.

9. Jane Tompkins, *Sensational Designs: The Cultural Work of American Fiction 1790–1860* (New York: Oxford University Press, 1985).

10. For a fuller description of the ideology of conservative familialism, see Michélle Barrett and Mary McIntosh, *The Anti-Social Family* (London: Verso, 1982).

11. The inverted image of this conceit can be found in John Carpenter's *They Live!* (1988), an allegory of aliens as the ruling class, especially the Republican elite, who have taken over the world and are altering the atmosphere through pollution and acid rain in order to make it more comfortable for them to breathe; Earth is their third world to colonize and exploit.

12. Robin Wood, *Hollywood from Vietnam to Reagan* (New York: Columbia University Press, 1986), pp. 162–88.

13. Vivian Sobchak, "Child/Alien/Father: Patriarchal Crisis and Generic Exchange," *Camera Obscura* 15 (1986):7–36.

14. *The Man Who Shot Liberty Valance*, for example,

where the youthful memories of Valance the elder statesman are allowed to flesh out the film's famous parable about the mythical West: "When the legend becomes fact, print the legend."

15. Dale Carter, *The Final Frontier: The Rise and Fall of the American Rocket State* (London: Verso, 1988).

16. Ibid., p. 257.

17. The famous film of the *Challenger* disaster ironically reproduced the kind of special-effects spectacle (like the destruction of the Death Star) that had thrilled *Star Wars* audiences, just as the Zapruder footage of the Kennedy assassination in Texas had recalled a furtive ambush scene in a Western.

18. Carter, *The Final Frontier*, p. 258.

19. A similar gender-coded conflict is played out in *Barbarella* (1968), the Pop fantasy film that features a different kind of space heroine for the 1960s and an earlier discourse around reproductive technologies like the birth control pill, whose recent advent is represented in the film as indicative of a passionless, technocratic future that must be prevented in the name of old-fashioned (male-dominant) pleasure.

## Susan Bordo, " 'Material Girl': The Effacements of Postmodern Culture" (pp. 66–81)

1. Quotations from Trix Rosen, *Strong and Sexy* (New York: Putnam, 1983), pp. 52, 61.

2. "Travolta: 'You Really Can Make Yourself Over,' " *Syracuse Herald*, Jan. 13, 1985.

3. "Popular Plastic Surgery," *Cosmopolitan*, May 1990, p. 96.

4. Tina Lizardi and Martha Frankel, "Hand Job," *Details*, February 1990, p. 38.

5. Jennet Conant, Jeanne Gordon and Jennifer Donovan, "Scalpel Slaves Just Can't Quit," *Newsweek*, January 11, 1988, pp. 58–59.

6. Donahue Transcript #05257, Multimedia Entertainment, Inc.

7. Dahleen Glanton, "Racism Within a Race," *Syracuse Herald American*, September 19, 1989.

8. *Essence* reader opinion poll, June 1989, p. 71.

9. Linda Bien, "Building a Better Bust," *Syracuse Herald*, March 4, 1990.

10. This was said by Janice Radway in an oral presentation of her work, Duke University, Spring 1989.

11. John Fiske, *Television Culture* (New York: Methuen, 1987), p. 19.

12. Michel Foucault, *Discipline and Punish* (New York: Vintage, 1979), p. 138.

13. Related in Bill Moyers, "A Walk Through the Twentieth Century: The Second American Revolution," PBS Boston.

14. Retha Powers, "Fat Is a Black Women's Issue," *Essence*, October 1989.

15. *Discipline and Punish*, pp. 26–27.

16. Susan Rubin Suleiman, "(Re)Writing the Body: The Politics and Poetics of Female Eroticism," in *The Female Body in Western Culture*, ed. Susan Rubin Suleiman (Cambridge: Harvard University Press, 1986), p. 24.

17. Cathy Schwichtenberg, "Postmodern Feminism and Madonna: Toward an Erotic Politics of the Female Body," paper presented at the University of Utah Humanities Center, National Conference on "Rewriting the (Post) Modern: (Post) Colonialism/Feminism/Late Capitalism," March 30/31, 1990.

18. John Fiske, "British Cultural Studies and Television," in *Channels of Discourse*, ed. Robert C. Allen (Chapel Hill: The University of North Carolina Press, 1987), pp. 254–290.

19. Quoted in John Skow, "Madonna Rocks the Land," *Time*, May 27, 1985, p. 77.

20. Ibid., p. 81.

21. Molly Hite, "Writing—and Reading—the Body: Female Sexuality and Recent Feminist Fiction," in *Feminist Studies*, 14; 1, Spring 1988, pp. 121–122.

22. "Fat or Not, 4th Grade Girls Diet Lest They Be Teased or Unloved," *Wall Street Journal*, February 11, 1986.

23. Catherine Texier, "Have Women Surrendered in MTV's Battle of the Sexes?" *New York Times*, April 22, 1990.

24. Susan Bordo, "Anorexia Nervosa: Psychopathology as the Crystallization of Culture," *The Philosophical Forum*, 17; 2, Winter 1985, pp. 73–103.

25. *Cosmopolitan*, July 1987.

26. David Ansen, "Magnificent Maverick," *Cosmopolitan*, May 1990, p. 311.

27. Kevin Sessums, "White Heat," *Vanity Fair*, April 1990, p. 208.

28. Susan McClary, "Living to Tell: Madonna's Resurrection of the Fleshly," *Genders*, Number 7, Spring 1990, p. 2.

29. Ibid., p. 12.

30. E. Ann Kaplan, "Is the Gaze Male," in *Power of Desire*, eds. Ann Snitow, Christine Stansell and Sharon Thompson (New York: Monthly Review Press, 1983, pp. 309–327.

31. E. Ann Kaplan, *Rocking Around the Clock: Music Television, Postmodernism and Consumer Culture* (New York: Methuen, 1987), p. 63.

32. McClary, p. 13.

## Danae Clark, "Commodity Lesbianism" (pp. 82–94)

1. Karl Marx, *Capital*, Vol. I (London: Lawrence and Wishart, 1970) 71.
2. For a recent overview of the literature see Lynn Spigel and Denise Mann, "Women and Consumer Culture: A Selective Bibliography," *Quarterly Review of Film and Video* 11.1 (1989): 85–105. Spigel and Mann's compilation does not so much reproduce as *reflect* the heterosexual bias of scholarship in this field.
3. Jane Gaines, "The Queen Christina Tie-Ups: Convergence of Show Window and Screen," *Quarterly Review of Film and Video* 11.1 (1989): 50. Gaines is one of the few feminist critics who acknowledges gays and lesbians as consuming subjects.
4. Sue-Ellen Case, "Towards a Butch–Femme Aesthetic," *Discourse* 11.1 (1988–89): 56.
5. Roberta Astroff, "Commodifying Cultures: Latino Ad Specialists as Cultural Brokers," Paper presented at the 7th International Conference on Culture and Communication, Philadelphia, PA, 1989.
6. Karen Stabiner, "Tapping the Homosexual Market," *The New York Times Magazine*, May 2, 1982: 80.
7. Stabiner 79.
8. Stabiner 34.
9. Stabiner 34.
10. Stabiner 75.
11. Stabiner 81.
12. Stabiner 80.
13. Stabiner 80.
14. Stabiner 81.
15. Stabiner 81.
16. Stabiner 80.
17. Mary Ann Doane, "The Economy of Desire: The Commodity Form in/of the Cinema," *Quarterly Review of Film and Video* 11.1 (1989): 27.
18. Gaines, "The Queen Christina Tie-Ups," 35.
19. Gaines, "The Queen Christina Tie-Ups," 56.
20. Jane Gaines, "Introduction: Fabricating the Female Body," *Fabrications: Costume and the Female Body*, eds. Jane Gaines and Charlotte Herzog (New York: Routledge, 1990) 12–13.
21. Gaines, "Fabricating the Female Body," 3–9. Also see Kaja Silverman, "Fragments of a Fashionable Discourse," *Studies in Entertainment: Critical Approaches to Mass Culture*, ed. Tania Modleski (Bloomington: Indiana University Press, 1986) 139–152.
22. Gaines, "Fabricating the Female Body," 27.
23. Arlene Stein, "All Dressed Up, But No Place to Go? Style Wars and the New Lesbianism," *OUT/LOOK* 1.4 (1989): 37.
24. Alisa Solomon, "Dykotomies: Scents and Sensibility in the Lesbian Community," *Village Voice*, June 26, 1990: 40.
25. Stein 39.
26. Stan LeRoy Wilson, *Mass Media/Mass Culture* (New York: Random House, 1989) 279.
27. Stein 38.
28. "OUT/LOOK Survey Tabulations," *Queery* #10, Fall 1990.
29. John Fiske, "Critical Response: Meaningful Moments," *Critical Studies in Mass Communication* 5 (1988): 247.
30. Elizabeth Ellsworth, "Illicit Pleasures: Feminist Spectators and *Personal Best*," *Wide Angle* 8.2 (1986): 54.
31. Cathy Griggers, "A Certain Tension in the Visual/Cultural Field: Helmut Newton, Deborah Turbeville and the VOGUE Fashion Layout," *differences* 2.2 (1990): 87–90. Griggers notes that Turbeville's trademark is photographing women (often in pairs or groups) who "stand or sit like pieces of sculpture in interiors from the past in [a] grainy, nostalgic soft-focused finish."
32. Case 64.
33. Case 60.
34. Case 58.
35. Ellsworth 54.
36. Ellsworth 54.
37. Jane Root, *Pictures of Women* (London: Pandora, 1984) 68; Rosalind Coward, *Female Desires* (New York: Grove Press, 1985) 80.
38. John D'Emilio, "Capitalism and Gay Identity," *Powers of Desire: The Politics of Sexuality*, eds. Ann Snitow, Christine Stansell and Sharon Thompson (New York: Monthly Review Press, 1983) 102.
39. D'Emilio 109.
40. David Ehrenstein, "Within the Pleasure Principle or Irresponsible Homosexual Propaganda," *Wide Angle* 4.1 (1980): 62.
41. See, for example, Teresa de Lauretis, "The Essence of the Triangle or, Taking the Risk of Essentialism Seriously: Feminist Theory in Italy, the U.S., and Britain," *differences* 1.2 (1989): 3–37; Diana Fuss, *Essentially Speaking* (New York: Routledge, 1989); Diana Fuss, "Reading Like a Feminist," *differences* 1.2 (1989): 72–92; Carol Vance, "Social Construction Theory: Problems in the History of Sexuality," *Which Homosexuality?* (London: GMP, 1989) 13–34; Jeffrey Weeks, "Against Nature," *Which Homosexuality?* 99–213; Jeffrey Weeks, *Sexuality and Its Discontents* (London: Routledge, 1985).
42. Mark Finch, "Sex and Address in 'Dynasty,'" *Screen* 27.6 (1986): 36.
43. John R. Leo, "The Familialism of 'Man' in American Television Melodrama," *South Atlantic Quarterly* 88.1 (1989): 42.
44. Weeks, *Sexuality*, 200.
45. Dick Hebdige, *Subculture: The Meaning of Style* (London: Methuen, 1979) 93.

46. Roland Marchand, *Advertising the American Dream* (Berkeley: University of California Press, 1985) 186.

47. Judith Williamson, "Woman Is an Island: Femininity and Colonization," *Studies in Entertainment: Critical Approaches to Mass Culture* (Bloomington: Indiana University Press, 1986) 116.

48. Michael Bronski, *Culture Clash: The Making of Gay Sensibility* (Boston: South End Press, 1984) 187.

49. Williamson 109, 112.

50. Laurie Schulze, "On the Muscle," *Fabrications*: 59.

51. Schulze 63.

52. Schulze 73.

53. Annette Kuhn, "The Body and Cinema: Some Problems for Feminism," *Wide Angle* 11.4 (1989): 56.

54. Schulze 68.

55. Schulze 67.

56. John Fiske, *Reading the Popular* (Boston: Unwin Hyman, 1989): 14–17. Fiske cites the research of M. Pressdee, "Agony or Ecstasy: Broken Transitions and the New Social State of Working-Class Youth in Australia," Occasional Papers, S. Australian Centre for Youth Studies, S.A. College of A.E., Magill, S. Australia, 1986.

57. Mike Budd, Robert M. Entman and Clay Steinman, "The Affirmative Character of U.S. Cultural Studies," *Critical Studies in Mass Communication* 7.2 (1990): 169–184.

58. Stein 37.

59. Griggers 101.

60. Jacqueline Bobo, "*The Color Purple*: Black Women as Cultural Readers," Female Spectators, ed. E. Deidre Pribram (London: Verso, 1988) 104–05. See also Stuart Hall, "Race, Articulation and Societies Structured in Dominance," *Sociological Theories: Race and Colonialism* (UNESCO, 1980) 305–45.

61. Williamson 116.

## Barbara Smith, "Between a Rock and a Hard Place: Relationships Between Black and Jewish Women" (pp. 106–120)

Portions of this essay originally appeared in a shorter version, based upon my presentation at the plenary session on "Racism and Anti-Semitism in the Women's Movement" at the 1983 National Women's Studies Association Convention. See "A Rock and a Hard Place: Relationships Between Black and Jewish Women," *Women's Studies Quarterly*, Vol. XI, No. 3 (Fall, 1983), pp. 7–9.

1. Cherríe Moraga, "Preface," *This Bridge Called My Back: Writings by Radical Women of Color*, eds. Moraga and Gloria Anzaldúa (New York: Kitchen Table: Women of Color Press, 1981, 1983), pp. xviii–xix.

2. Bernice Johnson Reagon, "Coalition Politics: Turning the Century," *Home Girls: A Black Feminist Anthology*, ed. Barbara Smith (New York: Kitchen Table: Women of Color Press, 1983), pp. 356–357.

3. Lorraine Hansberry's classic play *A Raisin in the Sun* written in 1958 revolves around this very dilemma of housing discrimination and a Black family's efforts to buy a house in an all-white neighborhood. Cleveland author Jo Sinclair's novel *The Changelings*, which I first read as a teenager, describes the summer when a working-class Jewish and Italian neighborhood begins to change from white to Black. The story is told from the perspective of a pre-teen-age Jewish girl, Vincent, and traces with more complexity and compassion than any work I know what it is that lies between us as Black and Jewish women. Despite my efforts to interest several women's presses in republishing *The Changelings*, it continues to be out of print, but is sometimes available in libraries. Jo Sinclair (Ruth Seid), *The Changelings* (New York: McGraw-Hill, 1955).

4. Barbara Smith, "Introduction," *Home Girls*, pp. xlii–xliii.

5. Elly Bulkin, "Racism and Writing: Some Implications for White Lesbian Critics," *Sinister Wisdom* 13 (Spring, 1980), pp. 3–22.

6. Alice Walker, "Letters Forum: Anti-Semitism," *Ms.* (February, 1983), p. 13.

7. Studs Terkel, "Introduction," *Working* (New York: Pantheon Books, 1972, 1974), p. xviii.

8. Melanie Kaye/Kantrowitz, "Some Notes on Jewish Lesbian Identity," *Nice Jewish Girls: A Lesbian Anthology*, ed. Evelyn Torton Beck (Trumansburg, New York: The Crossing Press, 1981, 1984), p. 37.

9. Cherríe Moraga, "Winter of Oppression, 1982," *Loving in the War Years: Lo Que Nunca Pasó Por Sus Labios* (Boston: South End Press, 1983), pp. 73–74.

10. Smith, p. xliv.

11. Letty Cottin Pogrebin, "Anti-Semitism in the Women's Movement," *Ms.* (June, 1983), p. 46.

12. Deborah Rosenfelt et al., "Letters Forum: Anti-Semitism," *Ms.* (February, 1983), p. 13.

13. Kaye/Kantrowitz, p. 42.

14. Gloria Greenfield, "Shedding," *Nice Jewish Girls*, p. 5.

15. Gertude "Ma" Rainey, "Prove It on Me Blues" (performed by Teresa Trull) *Lesbian Concentrate* (Oakland, California: Olivia Records, LF 915, 1977).

16. "Diana Ross: The White Lady and the Faggot," *The Black American* (New York), Vol. 22, No. 29, July 14–July 20, 1983, pp. 23 ff.

17. See for example the All African People's Revolutionary Party's Educational Brochure Number One, "Israel Commits Mass Murder of Palestinian & African Peoples: Zionism Is Racism. . . . It Must Be Destroyed" (A-APRP, Box 3307, Washington, D.C. 20009).

18. Moraga, *Loving in the War Years*, p. 135.

## María Lugones, "Playfulness, 'World'-Travelling, and Loving Perception" (pp. 121–128)

*Works Cited*

Hans-George Gadamer, *Truth and Method* (New York: Seabury Press, 1975)

Johan Huizinga, *Homo Ludens* (Buenos Aires, Argentina: Emece Editores, 1968)

## Women of ACE (AIDS Counseling and Education), "Voices" (pp. 129–139)

1. Perry F. Smith et al., *Infection Among Women Entering the New York State Correctional System* (1990), unpublished manuscript.
2. All quotations are from the author's conversations with prisoners at Bedford Hills.
3. By Cris Williamson, from the album *The Changer and the Changed*, Olivia Records, 1975.

## Nancy Fraser, "Struggle over Needs: Outline of a Socialist–Feminist Critical Theory of Late Capitalist Political Culture" (pp. 139–158)

Many of the ideas in this paper were first developed in my "Social Movements versus Disciplinary Bureaucracies" (CHS Occasional Paper, no. 8. Center for Humanistic Studies, University of Minnesota, 1987). I am grateful for helpful comments from Sandra Bartky, Linda Gordon, Paul Mattick, Frank Michelman, Martha Minow, Linda Nicholson, and Iris Young. The Mary Ingraham Bunting Institute of Radcliffe College provided crucial financial support and a utopian working situation.

1. Michel Foucault, *Discipline and Punish: The Birth of the Prison*, trans. Alan Sheridan (New York, 1979), 26.
2. In this paper, I shall use the terms 'welfare state societies' and 'late capitalist societies' interchangeably to refer to the industrialized countries of Western Europe and North America in the present period. Of course, the process of welfare state formation begins at different times, proceeds at different rates, and takes different forms in these countries. Still, I assume that it is possible in principle to identify and characterize some features of these societies that transcend such differences. On the other hand, most of the examples invoked here are from the U.S. context, and it is possible that this skews the account. Further comparative work would be needed to determine the precise scope of applicability of the model presented here.
3. For a recent example of the kind of theory I have in mind, see David Braybrooke, *Meeting Needs* (Princeton, 1987). Braybrooke claims that a thin concept of need "can make a substantial contribution to settling upon policies without having to descend into the melee" (68). Thus, he does not take up any of the issues I am about to enumerate.

4. For a fuller discussion of this issue, see my essay "Toward a Discourse Ethic of Solidarity," *Praxis International*, 5 no. 4 (January 1986): 425–29.
5. The expression 'mode of subjectification' is inspired by Michel Foucault, although his term is 'mode of subjection' and his usage differs somewhat from mine; see Foucault, "On the Genealogy of Ethics: An Overview of Work in Progress," *The Foucault Reader*, ed. Paul Rabinow (New York, 1984), 340–73. For another account of this idea of the sociocultural means of interpretation and communication, see my "Toward a Discourse Ethic of Solidarity."
6. The expression 'internally dialogized' comes from Mikhail Bakhtin. By invoking it here, I mean to suggest that the Bakhtinian notion of a "dialogic heteroglossia" (or a cross-referential, multi-voiced field of significations) is more apt as a description of the MIC in complex societies than is the more monolithic Lacanian idea of the Symbolic or the Saussurean idea of a seamless code. However, in claiming that the Bakhtinian conceptions of heteroglossia and dialogization are especially apt with respect to complex, differentiated societies, including late capitalist welfare state societies, I am intentionally breaking with Bakhtin's own view. He assumed, on the contrary, that these conceptions found their most robust expression in the "carnivalesque" culture of late Medieval Europe and that the subsequent history of Western societies brought a flattening of language and a restriction of dialogic heteroglossia to the specialized, esoteric domain of "the literary." This seems patently false—especially when we recognize that the dialogic, contestatory character of speech is related to the

availability in a culture of a plurality of competing discourses and of subject-positions from which to articulate them. Thus, conceptually, one would expect what, I take it, is in fact the case: that speech in complex, differentiated societies would be especially suitable for analysis in terms of these Bakhtinian categories. For the Bakhtinian conceptions of heteroglossia and internal dialogization, see Bakhtin, "Discourse in the Novel," in *The Dialogic Imagination: Four Essays*, ed. Michael Holquist, trans. Caryl Emerson and Holquist (Austin, Tex., 1981), 259–422. For a helpful secondary account, see Dominick LaCapra, "Bakhtin, Marxism, and the Carnivalesque," in *Re-thinking Intellectual History* (Ithaca, N.Y., 1983), 294–324. For a critique of the Romantic, antimodernist bias in both Bakhtin and LaCapra, see my "On the Political and the Symbolic: Against the Metaphysics of Textuality," *Enclitic* 9, nos. 1–2 (Spring/Fall 1987): 100–114.

7. See Kristin Luker, *Abortion and the Politics of Motherhood* (Berkeley, 1984).

8. If the previous point was Bakhtinian, this one could be considered Bourdieuian. There is probably no contemporary social theorist who has worked more fruitfully than Pierre Bourdieu at understanding cultural contestation in relation to societal inequality; see Bourdieu, *Outline of a Theory of Practice*, trans. Richard Nice (Cambridge, 1977). See also Bourdieu, *Distinction: A Social Critique of the Judgment of Pure Taste* (Cambridge, Mass., 1979).

9. Here the model aims to marry Bakhtin with Bourdieu.

10. I owe this formulation to Paul Mattick, Jr. For a thoughtful discussion of the advantages of this sort of approach, see his "On *Feminism as Critique*" (Paper read at the Socialist Scholars Conference, New York, 1988).

11. Included among the senses I shall not discuss are: (1) the pejorative colloquial sense according to which a decision is "political" when personal jockeying for power overrides germane substantive considerations; and (2) the radical political-theoretical sense according to which all interactions traversed by relations of power and inequality are "political."

12. Linda Gordon, *Woman's Body, Woman's Right* (New York, 1976).

13. Throughout this paper, I refer to paid workplaces, markets credit systems, and so forth as "*official* economic system institutions" so as to avoid the androcentric implication that domestic institutions are not also "economic." For a discussion of this issue, see my "What's Critical About Critical Theory? The Case of Habermas and Gender." Chapter 6 [in *Unruly Practices*].

14. The difficulty in specifying theoretically the conditions under which processes of depoliticization are disrupted stems from the difficulty of relating what are usually, and doubtless misleadingly, considered "economic" and "cultural" "factors". Thus, rational choice models seem to me to err in overweighting "economic" at the expense of "cultural" determinants, as in the (not always accurate) prediction that culturally dominant but ultimately disadvantageous need interpretations lose their hold when economic prosperity heralds reduced inequality and promotes "rising expectations": see Jon Elster, "Sour Grapes," in *Utilitarianism and Beyond*, ed. Amartya Sen and Bernard Williams (Cambridge, 1982). An alternative model developed by Jane Jenson emphasizes the cultural-ideological lens through which "economic" effects are filtered. Jenson relates "crises in the mode of regulation" to shifts in cultural "paradigms" that cast into relief previously present but nonemphasized elements of people's social identities; see her "Paradigms and Political Discourse: Labor and Social Policy in the USA and France Before 1914" (Working Paper Series, Center for European Studies, Harvard University, Winter 1989).

15. See Sonya Michel, "American Women and the Discourse of the Democratic Family in World War II," in *Behind the Lines: Gender and the Two World Wars*, ed. Margaret Higonnet, Jane Jenson, and Sonya Michel (New Haven, Conn., 1987), and "Women to Women: The Nineteenth-Century Origins of American Child Care Policy" (Paper presented to the Department of History, University of California, Los Angeles, 28 January 1988). For an account of the current U.S. social-welfare system as a two-track, gendered system based on the assumption of separate economic and domestic spheres, see my "Women, Welfare, and the Politics of Need Interpretation," Chapter 7 [in *Unruly Practices*].

16. See Hannah Arendt, *The Human Condition* (Chicago, 1958), especially Chap. 2, 22–78. However, it should be noted that my view of "the social" differs significantly from Arendt's. Whereas she sees the social as a one-dimensional space wholly under the sway of administration and instrumental reason, I see it as multivalent and contested. Thus, my view incorporates some features of the Gramscian conception of "civil society."

17. It is significant that, in some times and places, the idea of "the social" has been elaborated explicitly as an alternative to "the political." For example, in nineteenth-century England, "the social" was understood as the sphere in which (middle-class) women's supposed distinctive domestic virtues could be diffused for the sake of the larger collective good without suffering the "degradation" of participation in the competitive world of "politics." Thus, "social" work, figured as "municipal motherhood," was heralded as an alternative to suffrage; see Denise Riley, *"Am I That Name?" Feminism and*

*the Category of 'Women' in History* (Minneapolis, 1988). Similarly, the invention of sociology required the conceptualization of an order of "social" interaction distinct from "politics"; see Jacques Donzelot, *The Policing of Families* (New York, 1979).

18. Of course, the social state is not a unitary entity but a multiform, differentiated complex of agencies and apparatuses. In the United States, the social state comprises the welter of agencies that make up, especially, the Department of Labor and the Department of Health and Human Services—or what currently remains of them.

19. For an analysis of the gendered structure of the U.S. social-welfare system, see my "Women, Welfare, and the Politics of Need Interpretation," Chapter 7 [in *Unruly Practices*]. See also Barbara J. Nelson, "Women's Poverty and Women's Citizenship: Some Political Consequences of Economic Marginality," *Signs: Journal of Women in Culture and Society* 10, no. 2 (1984): 209–31; and Diana Pearce, "Women, Work, and Welfare: The Feminization of Poverty," in *Working Women and Families*, ed. Karen Wolk Feinstein (Beverly Hills, Calif., 1979).

20. For an analysis of U.S. social-welfare agencies as purveyors and enforcers of need interpretations, see "Women, Welfare, and the Politics of Need Interpretation," Chapter 7 [in *Unruly Practices*].

21. This picture is at odds with the one implicit in the writings of Foucault. From my perspective, Foucault focuses too single-mindedly on expert, institution-building discourses at the expense of oppositional and reprivatization discourses. Thus, he misses the dimension of contestation among competing discourses and the fact that the outcome is a result of such contestation. For all his theoretical talk about power without a subject, then, Foucault's practice as a social historian is surprisingly traditional in that it treats expert institution builders as in effect the only historical subjects.

22. The point could be reformulated more skeptically as follows: feminists have shaped discourses embodying a claim to speak for "women." In fact, this question of "speaking for 'women' " is currently a burning issue within the feminist movement. For an interesting take on it, see Riley, *"Am I That Name?"* For a thoughtful discussion of the general problem of the constitution and representation (in both senses) of social groups as sociological classes and as collective agents, see Bourdieu, "The Social Space and the Genesis of Groups," *Social Science Information* 24, no. 2 (1985): 195–220.

23. See the chapter "Fundamentalist Sex: Hitting Below the Bible Belt," in *Re-Making Love: The Feminization of Sex*, by Barbara Ehrenreich, Elizabeth Hess, and Gloria Jacobs (New York, 1987). For a fascinating account of "postfeminist" women incorporating feminist motifs into born-again Christianity, see Judith Stacey, "Sexism by a Subtler Name? Postindustrial Conditions and Postfeminist Consciousness in the Silicon Valley," *Socialist Review*, no. 96 (November/December 1987): 7–28.

24. See Stuart Hall, "Moving Right," *Socialist Review*, no. 55 (January–February 1981): 113–37. For an account of New Right reprivatization discourses in the United States, see Barbara Ehrenreich, "The New Right Attack on Social Welfare" in *The Mean Season: The Attack on the Welfare State*, ed. Fred Block, Richard A. Cloward, Barbara Ehrenreich, and Frances Fox Piven (New York, 1987), 161–95.

25. I am indebted to Teresa Ghilarducci for this point (personal communication).

26. In *Discipline and Punish*, Michel Foucault provides a useful account of some elements of the knowledge production apparatuses that contribute to administrative redefinitions of politicized needs. However, Foucault overlooks the role of social movements in politicizing needs and the conflicts of interpretation that arise between such movements and the social state. His account suggests, incorrectly, that policy discourses emanate unidirectionally from specialized, governmental or quasi-governmental, institutions; thus, it misses the contestatory interplay among hegemonic and nonhegemonic, institutionally bound and institutionally unbound, interpretations.

27. Cf. the discussion of the administrative logic of need definition in Jürgen Habermas, *Theorie des kommunikativen Handelns*, vol. 2, *Zur Kritik der funktionalistischen Vernunft* (Frankfurt am Main, 1981), 522–47.

28. See Foucault, *Discipline and Punish*, for an account of the normalizing dimensions of social science and of institutionalized social services.

29. Habermas discusses the therapeutic dimension of welfare state social services in *Theorie des kommunikativen Handelns*, vol. 2, 522–47.

30. In *Discipline and Punish*, Michel Foucault discusses the tendency of social-scientifically informed administrative procedures to posit a deep self. In *The History of Sexuality, Volume I: An Introduction* (trans. Robert Hurley [New York, 1978]), he discusses the positing of a deep self by therapeutic psychiatric discourses.

31. For the sake of simplicity, I shall restrict the examples treated to cases of contestation between two forces only, where one of the contestants is an agency of the social state. Thus, I shall not consider examples of three-sided contestation nor examples of two-sided contestation between competing social movements.

32. For an account of the history of battered women's shelters, see Susan Schechter, *Women and Male Violence: The Visions and Struggles of the Battered Women's Movement* (Boston, 1982).

33. Linda Gordon, "Feminism and Social Control: The

Case of Child Abuse and Neglect," in *What Is Feminism? A Re-Examination*, ed. Juliet Mitchell and Ann Oakley (New York, 1986), 63–85, and *Heroes of Their Own Lives: The Politics and History of Family Violence—Boston, 1880–1960* (New York, 1988).

34. Carol B. Stack, *All Our Kin: Strategies for Survival in a Black Community* (New York, 1974).

35. Prudence Mors Rains, *Becoming an Unwed Mother: A Sociological Account* (Chicago, 1971); hereafter cited parenthetically, by page number, in my text. I am indebted to Kathryn Pyne Addelson for bringing Rains's work to my attention.

36. Frances Fox Piven and Richard A. Cloward, *Regulating the Poor: The Functions of Public Welfare* (New York, 1971), 285–340, and *Poor People's Movements* (New York, 1979). Unfortunately, Piven and Cloward's account is gender-blind and, as a consequence, androcentric. For a feminist critique, see Linda Gordon, "What Does Welfare Regulate?" *Social Research* 55 no. 4 (Winter 1988): 610–30. For a more gender-sensitive account of the history of the NWRO, see Guida West, *The National Welfare Rights Movement: The Social Protest of Poor Women* (New York, 1981).

37. Piven, "Women and the State: Ideology, Power, and the Welfare State," *Socialist Review*, no. 74 (March–April 1984): 11–19.

38. For the view that objectivity is just the mask of domination, see Catharine A. MacKinnon, "Feminism, Marxism, Method, and the State: An Agenda for Theory," *Signs: Journal of Women in Culture and Society* 7, no. 3 (Spring 1982): 515–44. For the view that relativism undermines feminism, see Nancy Hartsock, "Rethinking Modernism: Minority vs. Majority Theories," *Cultural Critique* 7 (Fall 1987): 187–206. For a good discussion of the tensions among feminist theorists on this issue (which does not, however, in my view, offer a persuasive resolution), see Sandra Harding, "The Instability of the Analytical Categories of Feminist Theory," *Signs: Journal of Women in Culture and Society* 11, no. 4 (1986): 645–64. For a discussion of related issues raised by the phenomenon of postmodernism, see Nancy Fraser and Linda Nicholson,

"Social Criticism Without Philosophy: An Encounter Between Feminism and Postmodernism," *Theory, Culture, and Society*, 5 nos. 2–3 (June 1988): 373–94.

39. For a critique of the correspondence model of truth, see Richard Rorty, *Philosophy and the Mirror of Nature* (Princeton, N.J., 1979).

40. The "standpoint" approach has been developed by Nancy Hartsock. See her *Money, Sex, and Power: Toward a Feminist Historical Materialism* (New York, 1983). For a critique of Hartsock's position, see Harding, "The Instability of the Analytical Categories of Feminist Theory."

41. In its first-order normative content, this formulation is Habermassian. However, I do not wish to follow Habermas in giving it a transcendental or quasi-transcendental metainterpretation. Thus, whereas Habermas purports to ground "communicative ethics" in the conditions of possibility of speech understood universalistically and ahistorically, I consider it a contingently evolved, historically specific possibility; see Habermas, *The Theory of Communicative Action*, vol. 1, *Reason and the Rationalization of Society*, trans. Thomas McCarthy (Boston, 1984); *Communication and the Evolution of Society*, trans. Thomas McCarthy (Boston, 1979); and *Moralbewusstsein und kommunikatives Handeln* (Frankfurt am Main, 1983).

42. For arguments for and against this view, see the essays in *Women and Moral Theory*, ed. E. F. Kittay and Diana T. Meyers (Totowa, N.J., 1987).

43. For an interesting discussion of the uses and abuses of rights discourse, see Elizabeth M. Schneider, "The Dialectic of Rights and Politics: Perspectives from the Women's Movement," *New York University Law Review* 61, no. 4 (October 1986): 589–652. See also Martha Minow, "Interpreting Rights: An Essay for Robert Cover," *Yale Law Journal* 96 no. 8 (July 1987): 1860–1915; and Patricia J. Williams, "Alchemical Notes: Reconstructed Ideals from Deconstructed Rights," *Harvard Civil Rights–Civil Liberties Law Review* 22, no. 2 (Spring 1987): 401–33.

44. I owe this formulation to Martha Minow (personal communication).

## Elaine H. Kim, "Home Is Where the *Han* Is: A Korean American Perspective on the Los Angeles Upheavals" (pp. 160–174)

I am deeply indebted to the activists in the Los Angeles Korean American community, especially Bong Hwan Kim and Eui-Young Yu, whose courage and commitment to the empowerment of the disenfranchised, whether African American, Latino, or Korean American, during this crisis in Los Angeles have been a continuous source of inspiration for me. I would also like to thank Barry Maxwell for critically reading this manuscript and offering many insightful suggestions; my niece Sujin, Kim, David Lloyd, and Caridad Souza for their encouragement; and Mia Chung for her general assistance.

1. According to a Semptember 1992 Dun and Bradstreet survey of 560 business owners in Koreatown in South Central Los Angeles, an estimated 40 percent of the businesses damaged during *sa-i-ku* have closed their doors permanently. Moreover, almost 40 percent had no

insurance or were insured for 50 percent or less of their total losses ("L.A. Riot Took Heavy Toll on Businesses," *San Francisco Chronicle*, 12 September 1992).

2. Following quota changes in U.S. immigration laws in 1965, the Korean population in America increased more than eightfold to almost one million. Between 1970 and 1990, Los Angeles Koreatown grew from a few blocks of stores and businesses into a community base for all sorts of economic and cultural activities.

3. Pretense, of course, because I was only passing for Chinese. The temporary comfort I experienced would come to an end whenever it was discovered that I could speak no Chinese and that I had no organic links to Chinese Americans, who frequently underscored both our commonalities and our differences by telling me that everything Korean—even *kimchi*, that quintessentially Korean vegetable eaten at every Korean meal—was originally Chinese.

4. The Black-Korean Alliance (BKA) was formed, with the assistance of the Los Angeles County Human Relations Commission, to improve relations between the Korean and African American communities after four Korean merchants were killed in robberies during the month of April 1986. The BKA sponsored activities and events, such as joint church services, education forums, joint cultural events, and seminars on crime prevention and community economic development. The BKA never received political or financial support from the public or private sectors. The organization had neither its own meeting place nor a telephone. Grass-roots participation was not extensive, and despite the good intentions of the individuals involved, the BKA was unable to prevent the killing of a dozen more Korean merchants in southern California between 1990 and *sa-i-ku*, or to stop the escalation of tensions between the two communities after the shooting of 15-year-old Latasha Harlins by Korean merchant Soon Ja Du in March, 1991. By June of that year, after police declared the killing of an African American man by a Korean liquor-store owner "justifiable homicide," African American groups began boycotting the store, and the BKA failed to convince African American boycotters and Korean merchants to meet together to negotiate an end to the conflict. Nor were the members of the BKA successful in obtaining the help of members of the Los Angeles City Council or the California State Legislature, who might have been instrumental in preventing the destructive violence of *sa-i-ku* if they had had the integrity and farsightedness to address the intensifying hostilities before it was too late. After *sa-i-ku*, the BKA was in disarray, and as of this writing, its members are planning to dissolve the group.

5. According to John Murray, founder of the southern California chapter of Cal-Pac, the black beverage and grocers' association, African American liquor-store owners "sold stores they had bought in the mid-1960s for two times monthly gross sales—roughly $80,000 at the time, depending on the store—for five times monthly gross, or about $300,000." After the Jews fled in the wake of the Watts riots, African Americans were enabled by civil rights legislative mandates to obtain for the first time credit from government-backed banks to start a number of small businesses. But operating liquor stores, although profitable, was grueling, dangerous, and not something fathers wanted their sons to do, according to interviews with African American owners and former owners of liquor stores in African American communities. Former liquor merchant Ed Piert exclaimed: "Seven days a week, 20 hours a day, no vacations, people stealing. That's slave labor. I wouldn't buy another liquor store." When liquor prices were deregulated in 1978 and profit margins shrank in the face of competition from volume buyers, many African American owners sold out to Korean immigrants carrying cash collected in rotating credit clubs called *kye* (Susan Moffat, "Shopkeepers Fight Back: Blacks Join with Koreans in a Battle to Rebuild Their Liquor Stores," *Los Angeles Times*, 15 May 1992).

6. In a newspaper interview, Alberto Machon, an 18-year-old junior at Washington Preparatory High School who had moved to South Central Los Angeles with his family from El Salvador ten years ago, said that he was laughing as he watched every Korean store looted or burned down because "I felt that they deserved it for the way they was treatin' people. . . . the money that we are giving to the stores they're taking it to their community, Koreatown." Thirty-two-year-old Arnulfo Nunez Barrajas served four days in the Los Angeles County jail for curfew violation. He was arrested while going from Santa Ana to Los Angeles to see his aunt, whose son had been killed during the upheavals. According to Nunez, "[T]he ones they've caught are only from the black race and the Latin race. I haven't seen any Koreans or Chinese. Why not them? Or white? Why only the black race and the Latinos? Well, it's racism" (*Los Angeles Times*, 13 May 1992).

7. L. A. Chung, "Tensions Divide Blacks, Asians," *San Francisco Chronicle*, 4 May 1992.

8. *Los Angeles Times*, 5 May 1992.

9. They were also given to gloating over the inability of American authorities to maintain social order as well as the South Korean government can. In an interview, a South Korean diplomat in Los Angeles remarked to me that he was astonished at how ill-prepared the Los Angeles police and the National Guard were for "mass disturbances." They did not react quickly enough, they were very inefficient, they had no emergency plan, and even their communications network broke down, he observed. He could not imagine "riots" getting out of control in South Korea, which was ruled by the military from 1961 to 1987; there, he commented, "the

police are very effective. They work closely with the military."

10. For example, a story about the "black riots" in the 6 May 1992 *Central Daily News* in Seoul listed the writer as Korean-American sociologist Edward T'ae-han Chang, who was astonished when he saw it because he hadn't written it (personal communication).

11. In 1913, a group of Korean-American laborers was run out of Hemet Valley, California by a mob of anti-Japanese whites. The Koreans responded by insisting that they were Korean, not Japanese. What might seem a ludicrous response to racist expulsion has to be viewed in light of the fact that the U.S. sanctioned Japan's 1909 annexation of Korea, closing all Korean delegations and placing Korean immigrants under the authority of Japanese consulates. Since they were classified as Japanese, Korean Americans were subject to the Alien Land Acts that targeted Japanese by denying them the right afforded all others regardless of race, nativity, or citizenship: the right to own land in California and nine other states. Also, foreign-born Koreans were able to become naturalized U.S. citizens only after the McCarran–Walter Act of 1952 permitted naturalization of Japanese. I have heard some Asian Americans equate the Chinese- and Japanese-American use of signs and buttons reading "I Am Not Korean" during *sa-i-ku* with the Korean American (and, not coincidentally, Chinese American) practice of wearing buttons saying "I Am Not Japanese" during World War II. But, in light of the specificities of Korean and Korean American history, this cannot be a one-to-one comparison.

12. In a 23 July 1992 interview, a 50-year-old Korean immigrant woman whose South Central Los Angeles corner grocery store had been completely destroyed during *sa-i-ku* told me, "The America I imagined [before I arrived here] was like what I saw in the movies—clean, wide streets, flowers everywhere. I imagined Americans would be all big, tall . . . with white faces and blond hair. . . . But the America here is not like that. When I got up to walk around the neighborhood the morning after we arrived in Los Angeles from Korea, it was as if we had come to Mexico."

13. John Berger and Jean Mohr, *A Seventh Man: A Book of Images and Words About the Experiences of Migrant Workers in Europe* (New York: Penguin Books, 1975). I want to thank Barry Maxwell for bringing this work to my attention.

14. I am not grappling directly with social class issues here because, although I am cognizant of their crucial importance, I am simply not qualified to address them at the present time. The exploited "guest workers" in Europe described by Berger and Mohr, unlike the Korean immigrants to the U.S., brought with them their laboring bodies but not capital to start small businesses.

Because they are merchants, the class interests of Korean American shopowners in Los Angeles differ clearly from the interests of poor African American and Latino customers. But working with simple dyads is impossible, since Korean American shopowners are also of color and mostly immigrants from a country colonized by the United States. At the same time, it seems to me that class factors have been more important than race factors in shaping Korean-American immigrants' attitudes toward African American and Latino populations. Perhaps because of the devastation caused by Japanese colonization and the Korean War, many Koreans exhibit intensely negative attitudes toward the poor and indeed desperately fear being associated with them. I have often marveled at the importance placed on conspicuous consumer items, especially clothing, in South Korean society, where a shabbily dressed person can expect only shabby treatment. In the 1960s, a middle class American could make a social statement against materialistic values by dressing in tattered clothing without being mistaken for a homeless person. Now that this is no longer true, it seems to me that middle class Americans exhibit some of the fears and aversions that I witnessed in South Korea. Ironically, in the society where blackness and brownness have historically been almost tantamount to a condemnation to poverty, prejudice against the poor brought from Korea is combined with home-grown U.S. racism, and the results have been explosive.

At the same time, I have also noticed among Korean merchants profound empathy with the poor, whose situation many older immigrants know from first-hand past experiences. I personally witnessed many encounters between Korean merchants who lost their stores and African American neighbors in South Central during July 1992, when I accompanied the merchants as they visited their burned-out sites. None of the encounters were hostile. On the contrary, most of the African American neighbors embraced the Korean shopowners and expressed concern for them, while the merchants in turn asked warmly after the welfare of their neighbors' children. Although Korean-African American interaction has been racialized in the dominant culture, the quality of these relationships, like the quality of all human relationships, proved far more individual than that racial schematizing allows for.

15. Every South Korean middle school, high-school, and college student is required to take a course in "National Ethics," formerly called "Anticommunism." This course, which loosely resembles a civics class on Western civilization, government, constitutionalism, and political ideology, emphasizes the superiority of capitalism over communism and the importance of the national identity and the modern capitalist state. From the early 1960s through the 1970s, when most of the Los Angeles Korean immigrant merchants studied

"Anticommunism" or "National Ethics," they were taught that "capitalism" and "democracy" are the same, and that both are antithetical to "communism" or "socialism." According to this logic, criticisms of the U.S., a "democracy," are tantamount to praise of "communism." Such a view left little room for acknowledgement of racism and other social problems in American society. Indeed, the South Korean National Security Law formerly prosecuted and jailed writers who depicted Americans negatively and film makers who portrayed North Koreans as good-looking or capable of falling in love. Today, however, the interpretation of what constitutes antistate activity is far narrower than in former decades, and although the South Korean government maintains that "pro-North Korea" activities are against the law, anti-U.S. sentiments have been common in South Korea since the mid-1980s.

16. I cannot help thinking that these violent baptisms are an Asian American legacy of sorts, for in some sense it was the internment that forced the Japanese Americans to "become American" half a century ago.

17. Many Korean Americans have criticized the *Los Angeles Times* and local television news, and the ABC network in particular, for repeatedly running stories about Soon Ja Du shooting Latasha Harlins (the tape was the second-most-played video during the week of the riots, according to the media-watch section of A *Magazine: An Asian American Quarterly* 1, no. 3,4). They complained that the Los Angeles ABC affiliate aired the store videotape in tandem with the King footage. ABC even inserted the Du–Harlins tape segment into its reportage of the height of the *sa-i-ku* upheavals. Korean Americans have also protested the media focus on armed Korean American merchants. In particular, they objected to the repeated use of the image of a Korean merchant pointing a gun at an unseen, off-camera target. They knew that he was being shot at and that he was firing only at the ground, but they felt that the image was used to depict Korean immigrants as violent and lawless. They argued that by blocking out the context, the news media harmed Korean Americans, about whom little positive was known by the American public. Tong S. Suhr wrote in a Korean American newspaper:

*The Harlins killing is a tragic but isolated case. . . . This is not to condone the Harlins killing; nor is it to justify the death by countering with how many merchants in turn have been killed. Our complaint is directed to the constant refrain of "the Korean-born grocer killing a black teen-ager," which couldn't help but sow the seeds of racial hatred . . . [and make me wonder]: Was there any conspiracy among the . . . white-dominated media to pit one ethnic group against another and sit back and watch them destroy one another? . . . Why were the Korean American merchants portrayed as gun-toting*

*vigilantes shooting indiscriminately when they decided to protect their lives and businesses by arming themselves because no police protection was available? Why wasn't there any mention of the fact that they were fired upon first? Why such biased reporting?* ("Time for Soul Searching by Media," *Korea Times*, 29 June 1992).

I would challenge representatives of the news media who argue that visual images of beatings and shootings, especially when they are racialized or sexualized, are "exciting" and "interesting," even when they are aired hundreds or thousands of times, when compared with "boring" images of the everyday. Three months after *sa-i-ku*, I visited a videotape brokerage company in search of generic footage that could be used in a documentary about the Korean immigrant experience of losing their means of livelihood. Almost every inch of the stringers' footage contained images of police cars, fire engines, and uniformed men heroically wiping their brows as they courageously prepared to meet the challenges before them. Since there were neither police nor firemen anywhere in sight in South Central or Koreatown during the first three days of *sa-i-ku*, none of this footage was of use to me. No doubt the men who shot these scenes chose what seemed to them the most "interesting" and "exciting" images. But if I, a woman and a Korean American, had had a camera in my hands, I would have chosen quite different ones.

18. *Newsweek*, 18 May 1992.

19. The text of King's statement was printed in the *Los Angeles Times* (2 May 1992) as follows:

*People I just want to say . . . can we all get along? Can we get along? Can we stop making it horrible for the older people and the kids? . . . We've got enough smog here in Los Angeles, let alone to deal with the setting of those fires and things. It's just not right. It's not right, and it's not going to change anything.*

*We'll get our justice. They've won the battle but they haven't won the war. We will have our day in court and that's all we want. . . . I'm neutral. I love everybody. I love people of color. . . . I'm not like they're . . . making me out to be.*

*We've got to quit. We've got to quit. . . . I can understand the first upset in the first two hours after the verdict, but to go on, to keep going on like this, and to see a security guard shot on the ground, it's just not right. It's just not right because those people will never go home to their families again. And I mean, please, we can get along here. We all can get along. We've just got to, just got to. We're all stuck here for awhile. . . . Let's try to work it out. Let's try to work it out.*

20. The news media that did cover this massive demonstration invariably focused on the Korean musicians because they looked and sounded alien and

exotic. Ironically, most of them were young, American-born or at least American-educated Korean Americans who learned traditional music as a way to recover their cultural heritage. They perform at many events: I remember them in the demonstrations against the 1991 Gulf War.

21. *Juche sasang*, the concept of self-determination, was attractive to Koreans before the division of the country after the defeat of Japan in World War II. However,

since the term *juche* is central to the official political ideology in communist North Korea, the synonym *jaju* is used in South Korean officialdom.

22. I borrow this image from Walter Benjamin, "Theses on the Philosophy of History," *Illuminations* (New York: Schocken Books, 1969), 256. I would like to thank Shelley Sunn Wong for helping me see its relevance to Korean Americans in the 1990s.

## Leslie Kanes Weisman, "The Private Use of Public Space" (pp. 174–187)

1. Marge Piercy, "An Open Letter," in *Take Back the Night: Women on Pornography*, ed. Laura Lederer (New York: William Morrow, 1980), 7.

2. Yi-Fu Tuan, *Topophilia*, (New York: Columbia University Press, 1990), 220.

3. Lederer, introduction, *Take Back the Night*, 18.

4. John Berger, *Ways of Seeing* (Harmondsworth, England: BBC and Penguin, 1972), 45–47.

5. Nancy Henley, *Body Politics* (Englewood Cliffs: Prentice Hall, 1977); Anita Nager and Yona Nelson-Shulman, "Women in Public Places," *Centerpoint* 3, no. 3/4, issue 11 (Fall/Spring 1980): 145.

6. Nager and Nelson-Shulman, "Women in Public Places," 146.

7. Shirley Ardener, *Women and Space: Ground Rules and Social Maps* (New York: St. Martin's Press, 1981), 33.

8. "British Women Decry Rape Penalties," *New Women's Times*, May 1982, 10.

9. "Rape Victim Jailed in Refusal to Testify Against Defendant," *New York Times*, 26 June 1986, A19.

10. Elizabeth W. Markson and Beth B. Hess, "Older Women in the City," *Signs* 5, no. 3, supplement (Spring 1980): 134.

11. Ibid., 134–35.

12. For more information, write to METRAC at 158 Spadina Road, Toronto, Ontario M5R2T8, or telephone (416) 392-3135.TDD. Also refer to the Fall 1989/Winter 1990 *Women and Environments*, a special issue on urban safety.

13. *Women and Environments* (Spring 1986): 6.

14. Jane Midgley, *The Women's Budget*, 3d ed. (Philadelphia: Women's International League for Peace and Freedom, 1989), 16.

15. "Homeless in America," *Newsweek*, 2 January 1984, 15–17.

16. Jennifer Stern, "Serious Neglect: Housing for Homeless People with AIDS," *City Limits*, April 1989, 12.

17. Midgley, *Women's Budget*, 16.

18. Sarah Babb, "Women's Coalition: New Voices for Affordable Housing," *City Limits*, April 1989, 8.

19. Karin Stallard, Barbara Ehrenreich, and Holly Sklar, *Poverty in the American Dream* (Boston: South End Press, 1986).

20. "Homeless in America," *Newsweek*, 25.

21. Midgley, *Women's Budget*, 17.

22. "Homeless in America," *Newsweek*, 22–23.

23. Ibid., 23.

24. "Bush Budget Funds McKinney, Cuts Housing," *Safety Network, The Newsletter of the National Coalition for the Homeless* 8, no. 3 (March 1989): 3; ibid., no. 6 (June 1989): 1; and Midgley, *Women's Budget*, 16.

25. "Homeless in America," *Newsweek*, 23.

26. Ibid., 21.

27. Patricia King, "The Street Girls," *Newsweek*, 2 January 1984, 24.

28. Alan M. Beck and Philip Marden, "Street Dwellers," *Natural History* (November 1977): 85.

29. Ibid.

30. Babb, "Women's Coalition," 8.

31. Beck and Marden, "Street Dwellers," 81; and Ann Marie Rousseau, "Homeless Women," *Heresies* 2 (May 1977): 86, 88.

32. Senator Manfred Ohrenstein, "Help for the Homeless," *Legislative Report* (1981), unpaginated.

33. "Homeless in America," *Newsweek*, 21–22.

34. Sara Rimer, "The Other City: New York's Homeless," *New York Times*, 30 January 1984, 84.

35. Andrea Dworkin, "Pornography and Grief," in *Take Back the Night*, ed. Lederer, 286.

36. Kim Hirsch, "Guerrilla Tactics at Brown," *Ms.*, October 1983, 61; and Henley, *Body Politics*, 63.

37. Ann-Christine D'adesky, "Peace Camps: A Worldwide Phenomenon," *Ms.*, December 1983, 108.

38. Susan Pines, "Women Tie Up the Pentagon," *War Resisters League News*, no. 228, Jan.–Feb., 1982, 1, 8.

39. "New York City Peace Camp," *New Women's Times* (September 1983): 20; and D'adesky, "Peace Camps," 108.

40. D'adesky, "Peace Camps," 108.

41. Carol Gilligan, *In a Different Voice* (Cambridge: Harvard University Press, 1982).

42. Ibid., 48–49; and Jean Baker Miller, *Toward a New Psychology of Women* (Boston: Beacon Press, 1976).

43. Gilligan, *In a Different Voice*, 38, 164, 174.

44. Sarah Charlesworth, "Ways of Change Reconsidered: An Outline and Commentary on Women and Peace in

Northern Ireland," *Heresies* 2 (May 1977): 78–80.

45. Nell McCafferty, "Daughter of Derry," *Ms.*, Sept. 1989, 73, 76.

46. Elise Boulding, *The Underside of History* (Boulder, Colo.: Westview Press, 1976), 720.

47. Richard A. Cloward and Frances Fox Piven, "Hidden Protest: The Channeling of Female Innovation and Resistance," *Signs* 4, no. 4 (Summer 1979): 657.

48. Virginia Woolf, as quoted in D'adesky, "Peace Camps," 108.

## Cynthia Enloe, "On the Beach: Sexism and Tourism" (pp. 188–205)

1. Paul Fussell, 'The Modern Age of Tourism', excerpted from Fussell's *Abroad: British Literary Travelling Between the Wars* in *Utne Reader*, July/August, 1987, p. 105.

2. Shelly Attix, 'Socially Responsible Travel: How to Prevent the Social and Ecological Damage of Tourism', excerpted from *Building Economic Alternatives*, Spring, 1986, in *Utne Reader*, July/August, 1987, p. 109.

3. Among the sharpest critiques of tourism's effects on local cultures is Afro-Caribbean writer Jamaica Kincaid's description of post-colonial Antigua: Jamaica Kincaid, *A Small Place*, London, Virago, 1988; New York, Farrar, Straus & Giroux, 1988. Cultural Survival, an organization devoted to research related to the rights of indigenous peoples, has published a special issue of its journal *Cultural Survival Quarterly*: 'The Tourist Trap: Who's Getting Caught', vol. 6, no. 3, Summer, 1982. A publication monitoring tourism's impact on Third World societies is *Contours: Concern for Tourism*, published by the Ecumenical Coalition on Third World Tourism, 55 m/173–4 Saranom 2 Village, Thanon Nuanchan, Sukhapibanl Road, Klong-gum, Bangkapi, Bangkok 10230, Thailand. In Britain the address for *Contours* is c/o Roger Millman, 70 Dry Hill Road, Park Road, Tonbridge, Kent.

4. From Richard Montague's *The Life and Adventures of Mrs. Christian Davies*, 1740, quoted in Julie Wheelwright, 'Amazons and Military Maids', *Women's Studies International Forum*, vol. 10, no. 5, 1987, p. 491. See also Julie Wheelwright, *Amazons and Military Maids*, London and Winchester, MA, Pandora Press, 1989.

5. Vita Sackville-West, October 5, 1920, quoted in Nigel Nicolson, *Portrait of a Marriage*, New York, Atheneum, 1973, pp. 109–11. Some Muslim women at this time dressed as men in order to escape the confines of class and gender. On the eve of World War I, Turkish women in the Organization for the Rights of Women launched a campaign to gain for women the right to travel without male consent. One stunt to make their point was a flight in 1913 by Belkis Sekvet, the first Turkish woman to pilot an airplane; she wore men's clothes and meant to demonstrate that women were as brave, and thus as able to travel, as their male counterparts. See Sarah Graham-Brown, *Images of Women: The Portrayal of Women in Photography of the Middle East, 1860–1950*, New York, Columbia University Press, 1988, pp. 142–3.

6. Lisa Wenner with Peggy Perri, 'Pack Up Your Sorrows: The Oral History of an Army Nurse in Vietnam', typescript, Smith College, Northampton, MA, 1986, pp. 15–16. A revised version of this oral history will be published in a volume edited by Peggy Perri and Julia Perez, University of Illinois Press, forthcoming.

7. Mary Seacole, a Black Caribbean woman, is an important exception to the otherwise white Victorian lady travellers. For an account of her adventures in the Crimea and Europe, see Ziggi Alexander and Audrey Dewjee, editors, *Wonderful Adventures of Mrs Seacole in Many Lands*, Bristol, Falling Wall Press, 1984. Two useful guides to the abundant literature written by lady travellers, much of it now in new editions, are: Jane Robinson, editor, *A Bibliography of Women Travellers*, Oxford, Oxford University Press, 1989; Marion Tinling, editor, *Woman into the Unknown: A Source Book on Women Explorers and Travelers*, Westport, CT, Greenwood Press, 1989.

8. Katherine Frank, *A Voyager Out*, New York, Houghton Mifflin, 1986. For a more critical assessment of Mary Kingsley, see Deborah Birkett, 'The Invalid at Home, the Samson Abroad', *Women's Review*, London, no. 6, 1987, pp. 18–19. Also Deborah Birkett, 'West Africa's Mary Kingsley', *History Today*, May, 1987. Deborah Birkett's biography of Mary Kingsley is forthcoming from Macmillan.

9. 'Ladies in the Field: The Museum's Unsung Explorers', exhibition at the American Museum of Natural History, New York, December, 1986. The papers and diaries of Delia Akeley, Dina Brodsky, Sally Clark, Mrs Bogoras and Yvette Borup Andrew are available in the museum's Rare Book Department.

10. Robert W. Rydell, *All the World's a Fair: Visions of Empire at the World Expositions 1876–1916*, Chicago, University of Chicago Press, 1984, p. 2.

11. Ibid., p. 118.

12. Jeanne Madeline Weimann, *The Fair Women*, Chicago, Academy Press, 1981. On the 1876 Centennial Exhibition, see William D. Andrews and Deborah C. Andrews, 'Technology and the Housewife in Nineteenth Century America', *Women's Studies*, vol. 2, 1974, pp. 323–4.

13. Louis Turner and John Ash, *The Golden Hordes:*

*International Tourism and the Pleasure Periphery*, New York, St Martin's Press, 1976, pp. 20–21.

14. Maxine Feifer, *Tourism in History: From Imperial Rome to the Present*, New York, Stern & Day, 1986, pp. 10–11. For more on later European travel, especially by male aristocrats in the seventeenth and eighteenth centuries, see John Tower, 'The Grand Tour: A Key Phase in the History of Tourism', *Annals of Tourism Research*, vol. 12, 1985, pp. 297–333; Judith Adler, 'Youth on The Road: Reflections on the History of Tramping', *Annals of Tourism Research*, vol. 12, 1985, pp. 337–50; Susan L. Blake, 'A Woman's Trek: What Difference Does Gender Make?' in Margaret Strobel and Nupur Chaudhuri, editors, 'Western Women and Imperialism', special issue of *Woman's Studies International Forum*' forthcoming.

15. The principal source of information on Thomas Cook Tours is the Thomas Cook Archives: Edmund Swinglehurst, archivist, 45 Berkeley Street, London W1. The archives hold the collections of Cook's *Excursionist*, launched in 1855, and *Travellers' Gazette*, which made its debut in 1905.

16. Thomas Cook's editorial in the first issue of his *Cook's Exhibition Herald and Excursion Advertiser*, May 31, 1851.

17. Edmund Swinglehurst, 'Miss Matilda Lincolne's Trip to Paris', *Time Traveller*, newsletter of the Thomas Cook Archives, no. 5, January, 1988, p. 2.

18. 'How Four Ladies Visited the Rhine', *Cook's Excursionist and Cheap Trip Advertiser*, August 20, 1855, p. 2. In Boston, abolitionist and anti-war campaigner Julia Ward Howe helped launch the Women's Rest Tour Association in 1891. Its upper-class members, eager to travel abroad without male companions, created a file of practical information about places to stay in Europe suitable for respectable women. Today the association and its files exist as the Travel International Exchange; see William A. Davis, 'Travel Exchange Is Still Marching On', *Boston Globe*, November 15, 1987.

19. 'Across the Class Divide', *The Economist*, January 16, 1988, pp. 47–8; 'Europe's Charter Airlines Love the Summer Weather', *The Economist*, August 1, 1987, p. 57.

20. 'Japanese Tourism: Broadening the Mind', *The Economist*, May 7, 1988, p. 64; Susan Chira, 'It's Official! Vacations Really Aren't UnJapanese', *New York Times*, August 6, 1988.

21. Peter Stalker, 'Going Places: Westerners Invade Paradise', *The New Internationalist*, December 1984, excerpted in *Utne Reader*, July/August, 1987, p. 104.

22. Joseph Treaster, 'Caribbean Savors Tourism Boom', *New York Times*, November 7, 1988. On Gulf and Western's sale of its Dominican Republic sugar lands to Florida's Franjui development company, see Joseph Treaster, 'Is There Life After Gulf and Western?', *New York Times*, May 26, 1985. On Japanese tourism earnings, see *New York Times*, September 12, 1987. On Hawaii's sugar–tourism connection, see Walter Cohen, 'Hawaii Faces the Pacific', *Pacific Research*, vol. 6, no. 2, January–February, 1975; Noel Kent, *Islands Under the Influence*, New York, Monthly Review Press, 1979; Jan H. Mejer, 'Capitalist Stages, State Formation and Ethnicity in Hawaii', *National Journal of Sociology*, vol. 1, no. 2, Fall, 1987, pp. 173–207.

23. *New York Times*, June 5, 1988; Erlet A. Carter, 'Tourism in the Least Developed Countries', *Annals of Tourism Research*, vol. 14, 1987; Linda Richter, *The Politics of Tourism in Asia*, Honolulu, University of Hawaii Press, 1988.

24. In 1988 Fidel Castro announced that Cuba would put into effect policies meant to attract 600,000 foreign tourists by 1992. Although he led a revolution which sought to end the tourist industry's corruption of Cuban society, the fall in the international price of sugar, the country's chief export, left the government with no choice but to pursue the tourism strategy: *New York Times*, September 1, 1988. On Vietnam's tourism policies, see Murray Hiebert, 'Enterprise Encouraged to Invigorate the Economy', *Far Eastern Economic Review*, July 23, 1987, p. 31; Barbara Crossette, 'Vietnam for Visitors', *New York Times*, September 13, 1987; Melanie Beresford, 'Revolution in the Countryside: Report on a Visit to Vietnam', *Journal of Contemporary Asia*, vol. 16, no. 3, 1986, p. 399. On North Korean tourist policy, see Derek Hall, 'North Korea Opens to Tourism: A Last Resort', *Inside Asia*, July–August, 1986, pp. 21–2; Nicholas D. Kristof, 'North Korea Tourism Signals New Openness', *New York Times*, September 20, 1987. On Nicaragua's still tentative moves to develop tourism, see Stephen Kinzer, 'Nicaragua's Ideology of Sun and Surf', *New York Times*, November 23, 1988.

25. Air Lanka advertisement, *Far Eastern Economic Review*, May 1, 1986. See also Jane Clarke and Amanda Hood, 'Hostess with the Mostest', *Spare Rib*, October, 1986, pp. 15–17.

26. Jo Stanley, 'Women at Sea', *Spare Rib*, September, 1987, pp. 26–7. See also Henriette Louise, *Sailors in Skirts*, London, Regency Press, 1980; John Maxtone Graham, *Liners to the Sun*, London and New York, Macmillan, 1985. For reports on the now booming cruise-ship industry, see *New York Times*, September 28, 1987 and August 28, 1988. I am indebted to David G. Enloe for his research on ocean-liner crews.

27. Tom Barry, Beth Wood and Deb Preusch, *The Other Side of Paradise*, New York, Grove Press, 1984, p. 85. See also E. Philip English, *The Great Escape: An Examination of North–South Tourism*, Ottawa, North–South Institute, 1986.

28. Jan H. Mejer, op. cit., p. 199; Phyllis Andors, 'Women and Work in Shenshen', *Bulletin of Concerned Asian Scholars*, vol. 20, no. 3, 1988, p. 27.

29. Veronica M. Fenix, 'Beyond 8 to 5: Women Workers Speak Out', in Pennie S. Azarcon, editor, *Kamalayaan: Feminist Writings in the Philippines*, Quezon City, Philippines, Pilipina, 1987, p. 37. Pilipina's address is: 12 Pasaje de la Paz, Project 4, Quezon City, Philippines. For more on the effects of tourism on women's economic status, see Janice Monk and Charles Alexander, 'Free Port Fallout: Gender, Employment and Migration on Margarita Island', *Annals of Tourism Research*, vol. 13, 1986, pp. 393–413; Shireen Samarasuriya, *Who Needs Tourism? Employment for Women in the Holiday Industry of Sudugama, Sri Lanka*, research project, Women and Development, Colombo, Sri Lanka, 1982.

30. 'Britain: Making History Pay', *The Economist*, August 1, 1987, p. 48; Steve Lohr, 'British Find the Past Enriching', *New York Times*, March 29, 1988; *The Independent*, July 4, 1987; Harriet Lamb, 'The Hamburger Economy', *Spare Rib*, October, 1987, p. 27.

31. The population figures come from a Malaysian journalist, Halinah Todd, in her article 'Military Prostitution: Assault on Women', *The Mobilizer*, Mobilization for Survival, Summer, 1987, p. 8. The figures on business establishments come from Pasuk Phongpaichit, 'Bangkok Masseuses: Tourism—Selling Southeast Asia', *Southeast Asian Chronicle*, no. 78, April, 1981, pp. 15–16.

32. According to South Korean feminist Mi Kyung Lee, the South Korean military government made the service industry, and within it the sexualized entertainment industry, one of the major props of its entire development program. The low pay that women in the industry receive compels them to enter the prostitution subsidiary of that industry: Mi Kyung Lee, speaking at the International Trafficking in Women Conference, New York City, October 22, 1988. For a report of the entire conference, see 'The First US Conference on Trafficking in Women Internationally', *Off Our Backs*, December, 1988, pp. 1–5. To contact the conference follow-up committee: The Coalition on Trafficking in Women, Times Square Station, PO Box 2166, New York, NY 10108. An earlier conference to organize women against prostitution is described in Kathleen Barry, Charlotte Bunch and Shirley Castley, editors, *International Feminism: Networking Against Female Sexual Slavery*, New York, International Women's Tribune Center, 777 UN Plaza, New York, NY 10017, 1984. (A Spanish edition translated by Ximena Bunster is also available.)

33. For a graphic account of international sex tourism, see Joni Seager and Ann Olson, *Women in the World: An International Atlas*, London, Pan Books, New York, Simon & Schuster, 1986, map 36. On Goan women organizing to reverse the Indian government's plans for sex tourism development, see Paola Bacchetta, 'Indian Women Fight Sex Tourism', *Off Our Backs*, January, 1988, p. 12.

34. Quoted in Pasuk Phongpaichit, op. cit. For more on the evolution of the sex-tourism industry in Thailand, see Khin Thitsa, *Providence and Prostitution*, London, Change, International Reports: Women and Society, 1982.

35. 'Thailand Stupefied', *The Economist*, August 1, 1987, p. 82; 'Survey—Thailand', *The Economist*, October 31, 1987.

36. *The Economist*, October 8, 1987, p. 8; Barbara Crossette, 'Fear of AIDS Surfaces in Permissive Bangkok', *New York Times*, November 8, 1987. See also Susanne Thorbek, *Voices from the City: Women of Bangkok*, London and Highland, NJ Zed Books, 1987. I am also indebted to Kari Hartwig for sharing with me her unpublished manuscript, 'The Spread of AIDS in Southeast Asia', International Development Program, Clark University, Worcester, MA, 1988.

37. Niramon Prudtotorn, 'Women in Thailand', in *WRI Women*, vol. 2, no. 1, 1988, p. 9: newsletter of the Women's Working Group of War Resisters International, 55 Dawes Street, London SE17 1EL.

38. Quoted from Deborah Dover, *Prostitution in the Philippines: Political Dependency and Sexual Exploitation*, undergraduate thesis, Department of Political Science, Indiana University, Bloomington, IN, 1987. For a complex analysis of prostitution's causes and effects by Filipino commentators, see *Cast the First Stone*, National Council of Churches in the Philippines, 879 Epifmo de los Santos Ave., Quezon City, Philippines, 1987. See also Linda Richter, *Land Reform and Tourism: Policy Making in the Philippines*, Boston, Schenkman Publishers, 1982.

39. A critique of the raids on Ermita's dance-halls is included in Liza Maza and Cath Jackson, 'When the Revolution Came', *Trouble and Strife*, no. 14, Autumn, 1988, pp. 19–22. For more information on anti-prostitution activism, contact Gabriela, PO Box 4386, Manila 2800, Philippines.

40. Liza Maza and Cath Jackson, op. cit.

41. For a report on the First National Consultations on Japayuki held in May 1988 in Japan, see *Flights*, vol. 1, no. 4, June, 1988, pp. 5–6. *Flights* is the newsletter of the Women's Resource and Research Center, Maryknoll College, Quezon City, Philippines. For more on Asian migrant women in Japan, see Ohshima Shizuko, 'Gathering the Fires of Help', and Yamazaki Hiromi, 'Japan Imports Brides: Can Isolated Farmers Buy Consolation?', and Nakamura Hisashi, 'Japan Imports Brides: From a New Poverty Discovered', all in *AMPO*, vol. 19, no. 4. *AMPO* is a critical Japanese political journal written in English.

## Celeste Olalquiaga, "Holy Kitschen: Collecting Religious Junk from the Street" (pp. 205–220)

1. For a description of contemporary hyperreality see Umberto Eco, *Travels in Hyperreality: Essays*, trans. William Weaver (San Diego: Harcourt Brace Jovanovich, 1986) and Jean Baudrillard, *Simulations*, trans. Paul Foss, Paul Patton, and John Johnston (New York: Semiotext[e], 1983).

2. I would like to thank the following people for allowing me to repeatedly photograph in their stores: Sam and Silvia at Sasson Bazaar, 108 W. Fourteenth Street; Maurice and David at Esco Discount Store, 138 W. Fourteenth Street; and Jamal at Sharon Bazaar, 112 W. Fourteenth Street. Fourteenth Street's internationality can be fully appreciated in these people's polyglotism: most of them speak four or five languages, including English, Spanish, Hebrew, Arabic, and French.

3. Little Rickie is located at 49 1/2 First Avenue (at the corner of Third Street). Thanks to Phillip Retzky for letting me photograph in the store. The prices quoted are from 1987, when this [selection] was written.

4. Available at Hero, 143 Eighth Avenue, and Amalgamated, 19 Christopher Street.

5. Much has been written about the video pope. For his 1984 visit to Puerto Rico see Edgardo Rodriguez Julia, "Llegó el Obispo de Roma," in *Una noche con Iris Chacón* (n.p.: Editorial Antillana, 1986): 7–52. For his 1986 visit to France see the wonderfully illustrated "Pape Show" issue of the French daily *Liberation*, October 4 and 5, 1986: 1–7.

6. Amalia Mesa-Bains, Grotto of the Virgins, Intar Latin American Gallery, New York City, 1987; Dana Salvo, Mary (group show), Althea Viafora Gallery, New York City, 1987; Audrey Flack, Saints and Other Angels: The Religious Paintings of Audrey Flack, Cooper Union, New York City, 1986.

7. Fredric Jameson, "Postmodernism; or, the Cultural Logic of Late Capitalism," in *New Left Review* 146 (July–August 1984): 53–92.

8. "In a vase of Kitsch flowers there is a formal defect, but in a Kitsch Sacred Heart the defect is theological," says Karl Pawek in "Il Kitsch Cristiano," in Gillo Dorfles, *Il Kitsch* (Milan: Gabriele Mazzotta Editore, 1969): 143–50. For another view of religious kitsch see Richard Egenter, *The Desecration of Christ* (Chicago: Franciscan Herald Press, 1967). For kitsch in general see Hermann Broch, "Kitsch e arte di tendenza" and "Note sul problema del Kitsch," trans. Saverio Vertone, in Dorfles, *Il Kitsch*, 49–76, and "Art and Its Non-Style at the End of the Nineteenth Century" and "The Tower of Babel," in *Hugo Von Hoffmannsthal and His Time: The European Imagination 1860–1920*, trans. and ed. Michael P. Steinberg (Chicago: University of Chicago Press, 1984): 33–81 and 143–83. Gillo Dorfles's book is a compilation of essays on kitsch, several of which will

be mentioned throughout this [selection]. See also Matei Calinescu, "Kitsch," in *Five Faces of Modernity* (Durham, N.C.: Duke University Press, 1987): 223–62; Haroldo de Campos, "Vanguarda e Kitsch," in *A Arte no horizonte do provavel* (São Paulo: Editorial Perspectiva, 1969): 193–201; Umberto Eco, "Estilística del Kitsch" and "Kitsch y cultura de masas," in *Apocalípticos e integrados ante la cultura de masas* (Barcelona: Lumen, 1968): 81–92; Clement Greenberg, "Avant-Garde and Kitsch," in *Art and Culture* (Boston: Beacon Press, 1961): 3–21; Abraham Moles, *Le Kitsch, L'Art de Bonheur* (Paris: Maison Mame, 1971). Aimée Rankin's "The Parameters of Precious," *Art in America* (September 1985); 110–17, was brought to my attention after the completion of this [selection]; some of her arguments about the recycling of kitsch coincide with my understanding of it as pertaining to a vicarious sensibility.

9. Hermann Broch, *Hugo Von Hoffmannsthal*, 170.

10. The concept of cultural cannibalism was advanced in a different context by Oswald de Andrade, *Do Pau-Brasil a Antropofagia e as Utopias*, Obras Completas, vol 6 (Rio de Janeiro: Civilizaçao Brasileira-Mec, 1970).

11. For some art theoreticians, this is a "primitive" confusion between referent and representation. See Aleksa Celebonovic, "Nota sul Kitsch tradizionale," in Dorfles, *Il Kitsch*, 280–89.

12. Décio Pignatari, "Kitsch e repertório," in *Informaçao. Linguagem. Communicaçao* (São Paulo: Perspectiva, 1968): 113–17.

13. Gillo Dorfles, *Il Kitsch*, and Clement Greenberg, "Avant-Garde and Kitsch."

14. Hermann Broch spoke of the "kitsch-man" in Gillo Dorfles, *Il Kitsch*, 49.

15. This term was first used by Abraham Moles, *Le Kitsch*, 161–86.

16. For camp sensibility see Susan Sontag, "Notes on Camp," in *Against Interpretation and Other Essays* (New York: Octagon, 1982): 275–92.

17. See Walter Benjamin, "The Work of Art in the Age of Mechanical Reproduction in *Illuminations*, trans. Harry Zohn (London: Jonathan Cape, 1970): 219–53.

18. Ceremony of Memory, Museum of Contemporary Hispanic Art (MOCHA). New York City, 1989. Ironically, this is happening at a time when Hispanics are said to be turning away from Catholicism. See "Switch by Hispanic Catholics Changes Face of US Religion," *New York Times*, May 14, 1989.

19. For a more extensive account of Mesa-Bains's work and of *altares* in general see Tomás Ybarra Frausto's essay "Sanctums of the Spirit—The Altares of Amalia Mesa-Bains," published in the catalog for this show.

20. In his artist's statement for the Pastorale de Navidad show (Nielsen Gallery, Boston, 1987), Salvo describes this exchange: "The Polaroid process quickly dispelled any apprehension or superstition that arose, and the instant image generated an enormous amount of enthusiasm. Soon a crowd of villagers would be about the camera and house. They were moved that their creations were being photographed, and they treasured the Polaroids, displaying the image as part of the altarpiece. . . . Once everyone was accustomed to the photograph they would oftentimes arrange the interiors to better fit the frame. Or, this would encourage others to add small treasures to an altar as it would be seen minutes later in a Polaroid image."

21. Personal interview with Lowery S. Sims, published in the catalog for Flack's Cooper Union show.

22. Gerardo Mosquera, "Bad Taste in Good Form," *Social Text* 15 (Fall 1986): 54–64. For another view on Cuban artistic kitsch see Lucy R. Lippard, "Made in the U.S.A.: Art from Cuba," *Art in America* (April 1986): 27–35. For kitsch in the United States see J Hoberman, "What's Stranger than Paradise?" in "Americanarama," *Village Voice Film Special*, June 30, 1987: 3–8.

23. This is Greenberg's main proposal. See also Miriam Gusevich, "Purity and Transgression: Reflections on the Architectural Avantgarde's Rejection of Kitsch," Working Paper no. 4, published by the Center for Twentieth Century Studies of the University of Wisconsin–Milwaukee, Fall 1986.

24. Walter Benjamin, "Traumkitsch," in *Angelus Novus, Ausgewählte Schriften*, vol. 2 (Frankfurt am Main: Suhrkamp, 1966): 158–60.

25. Jean Baudrillard, *Simulations*, 7–9.

## Gloria Anzaldúa, "How to Tame a Wild Tongue" (222–229)

1. Ray Gwyn Smith, *Moorland Is Cold Country*, unpublished book.

2. Irena Klepfisz, "*Di rayze aheym*/The Journey Home," in *The Tribe of Dina: A Jewish Women's Anthology*, Melanie Kaye/Kantrowitz and Irena Klepfisz, eds. (Montpelier, VT: Sinister Wisdom Books, 1986), 49.

3. R. C. Ortega, *Dialectología Del Barrio*, trans. Hortenicia S. Alwan (Los Angeles, CA: R. C. Ortega Publisher & Bookseller, 1977), 132.

4. Eduardo Hernandéz-Chávez, Andrew D. Cohen, and Anthony F. Beltramo, *El Lenguaje de los Chicanos: Regional and Social Characteristics of Language Used by Mexican Americans* (Arlington, VA: Center for Applied Linguistics, 1975), 39.

5. Hernandéz-Chávez, xvii.

6. Irena Klepfisz, "Secular Jewish Identity: Yidishkayt in America," in *The Tribe of Dina*, Kaye/Kantrowitz and Klepfisz, eds., 43.

7. Melanie Kay/Kantrowitz, "Sign," in *We Speak in Code: Poems and Other Writings* (Pittsburgh, PA: Motheroot Publications, Inc., 1980), 85.

8. Rodolfo Gonzales, *I Am Joaquín/Yo Soy Joaquín* (New York: Bantam Books, 1972). It was first published in 1967.

9. Gershen Kaufman, *Shame: The Power of Caring* (Cambridge, MA: Schenkman, 1980), 68.

10. Hernandéz-Chávez, 88–90.

11. "Hispanic" is derived from *Hispanis* (*España*, name given to the Iberian Peninsula in ancient times when it was a part of the Roman Empire) and is a term designated by the U.S. government to make it easier to handle us on paper.

12. The Treaty of Guadalupe Hidalgo created the Mexican-American in 1848.

13. Anglos, in order to alleviate their guilt for dispossessing the Chicano, stressed the Spanish part of us and perpetrated the myth of the Spanish Southwest. We have accepted the fiction that we are Hispanic, that is Spanish, in order to accommodate ourselves to the dominant culture and colonists' abhorrence of Indians. Hernandéz-Chávez, 88–91.

## Sandra Bartky, "Foucault, Femininity, and the Modernization of Patriarchal Power" (pp. 240–256)

1. Michel Foucault, *Discipline and Punish: The Birth of the Prison*, trans. Alan Sheridan (New York: Vintage Books, 1979), p. 138.

2. Ibid., p. 28.

3. Ibid., p. 147.

4. Ibid., p. 153. Foucault is citing an eighteenth-century military manual, "Ordonance du Ier janvier 1766 . . ., titre XI, article 2."

5. Ibid., p. 153.

6. Ibid., p. 150.

7. Ibid., p. 200.

8. Ibid., p. 201.

9. Ibid., p. 228.

10. Judith Butler, "Embodied Identity in de Beauvoir's *The Second Sex*" (unpublished manuscript presented to American Philosophical Association, Pacific Division, March 22, 1985), p. 11.

11. Marcia Millman, *Such a Pretty Face: Being Fat in*

*America* (New York: W. W. Norton, 1980), p. 46.

12. Susan Bordo, "Anorexia Nervosa: Psychopathology as the Crystallization of Culture," *Philosophical Forum* 17, no. 2 (Winter 1985–86): 73–104 (reprinted in this volume).

13. *USA Today* (Thursday, May 30, 1985).

14. Phrase taken from the title of Kim Chernin, *The Obsession: Reflections on the Tyranny of Slenderness* (New York: Harper and Row, 1981), an examination from a feminist perspective of women's eating disorders and of the current female preoccupation with body size.

15. M. J. Saffon, *The 15-Minute-a-Day Natural Face Lift* (New York: Warner Books, 1981).

16. Sophia Loren, *Women and Beauty* (New York: William Morrow, 1984), p. 57.

17. Iris Young, "Throwing Like a Girl: A Phenomenology of Feminine Body Comportment, Motility and Spatiality," *Human Studies* 3 (1980): 137–56.

18. Marianne Wex, *Let's Take Back Our Space: "Female" and "Male" Body Language as a Result of Patriarchal Structures* (Berlin: Frauenliteraturverlag Hermine Fees, 1979). Wex claims (p. 23) that Japanese women are still taught to position their feet so that the toes point inward, a traditional sign of submissiveness.

19. In heels, the "female foot and leg are turned into ornamental objects and the impractical shoe, which offers little protection against dust, rain and snow, induces helplessness and dependence. . . . The extra wiggle in the hips, exaggerating a slight natural tendency, is seen as sexually flirtatious while the smaller steps and tentative, insecure tread suggest daintiness, modesty and refinement. Finally, the overall hobbling effect with its sadomasochistic tinge is suggestive of the restraining leg irons and ankle chains endured by captive animals, prisoners and slaves who were also festooned with decorative symbols of their bondage." Susan Brownmiller, *Femininity* (New York: Simon and Schuster, 1984), p. 184.

20. Nancy Henley, *Body Politics* (Englewood Cliffs, N.J.: Prentice-Hall, 1977), p. 176.

21. For an account of the sometimes devastating effects on workers, like flight attendants, whose conditions of employment require the display of a perpetual friendliness, see Arlie Hochschild, *The Managed Heart: The Commercialization of Human Feeling* (Berkeley: University of California Press, 1983).

22. Henley, *Body Politics*, p. 108.

23. Ibid., p. 149.

24. Clairol has just introduced a small electric shaver, the "Bikini," apparently intended for just such use.

25. Georgette Klinger and Barbara Rowes, *Georgette Klinger's Skincare* (New York: William Morrow, 1978), pp. 102, 105, 151, 188, and passim.

26. *Chicago Magazine* (March 1986), pp. 43, 10, 18, and 62.

27. *Essence* (April 1986), p. 25. I am indebted to Laurie Shrage for calling this to my attention and for providing most of these examples.

28. Klinger, *Skincare*, pp. 137–40.

29. In light of this, one is surprised to see a 2-ounce jar of "Skin Regeneration Formula," a "Proteolytic Enzyme Cream with Bromelain and Papain," selling for $23.95 in the tabloid *Globe* (April 8, 1986, p. 29) and an unidentified amount of Tova Borgnine's "amazing new formula Beverly Hills" (otherwise unnamed) going for $41.75 in the *National Enquirer* (April 8, 1986, p. 15).

30. ". . . it is required of woman that in order to realize her femininity she must make herself object and prey, which is to say that she must renounce her claims as sovereign subject." Simone de Beauvoir, *The Second Sex* (New York: Bantam Books, 1968), p. 642.

31. The film *Pumping Iron II* portrays very clearly the tension for female bodybuilders (a tension that enters into formal judging in the sport) between muscular development and a properly feminine appearance.

32. Henley, *Body Politics*, pp. 101, 153, and passim.

33. Foucault, *Discipline and Punish*, p. 222: "The general, juridical form that guaranteed a system of rights that were egalitarian in principle was supported by these tiny, everyday, physical mechanisms, by all those systems of micro-power that are essentially non-egalitarian and asymmetrical that we call disciplines."

34. Millman, *Such a Pretty Face*, p. 80. Such remarks are made so commonly to heavy women that sociologist Millman takes the most clichéd as title of her study of the lives of the overweight.

35. I am indebted to Nancy Fraser for the formulation of this point.

36. See my paper "Narcissism, Femininity and Alienation," in *Social Theory and Practice* 8, no. 2 (Summer 1982): 127–43.

37. Millman, *Such a Pretty Face*, pp. 80, 195.

38. Chernin, *The Obsession*, p. 53.

39. Bartky, "Narcissism, Femininity and Alienation."

40. For a claim that the project of liberal or "mainstream" feminism is covertly racist, see bell hooks, *Ain't I Woman: Black Women and Feminism* (Boston: South End Press, 1981), chap. 4. For an authoritative general critique of liberal feminism, see Alison Jaggar, *Feminist Politics and Human Nature* (Totowa, N.J.: Rowman and Allanheld, 1983), chaps. 3 and 7.

41. See, for example, Mihailo Markovic, "Women's Liberation and Human Emancipation," in *Women and Philosophy*, ed. Carol C. Gould and Marx W. Wartofsky (New York: G. P. Putnam's Sons, 1976), pp. 165–66.

42. Foucault, *Discipline and Punish*, p. 30.

43. Some radical feminists have called for just such a deconstruction. See especially Monique Wittig, *The Lesbian Body* (New York: Avon Books, 1976).

44. Foucault, *Discipline and Punish*, p. 44.

45. Michel Foucault, *Power/Knowledge: Selected Interviews*

*and Other Writings, 1972–1977*, ed. Colin Gordon (Brighton, U.K.: 1980), p. 151. Quoted in Peter Dews, "Power and Subjectivity in Foucault," *New Left Review*, no. 144 (March–April 1984): 17.

46. Dews, "Power and Subjectivity in Foucault," p. 77.
47. Foucault, *Discipline and Punish*, p. 138.
48. Ibid., p. 201.
49. Foucault, *Power/Knowledge*, p. 98. In fact, Foucault is not entirely consistent on this point. For an excellent discussion of contending Foucault interpretations and for the difficulty of deriving a consistent set of claims from Foucault's work generally, see Nancy Fraser, "Michel Foucault: A 'Young Conservative'?" *Ethics* 96 (October 1985): 165–84.
50. Dews, "Power and Subjectivity in Foucault," p. 92.
51. See Marcia Hutchinson, *Transforming Body Image: Learning to Love the Body You Have* (Trumansburg, N.Y.: Crossing Press, 1985). See also Bordo, "Anorexia Nervosa."
52. An earlier version of this paper was read to the Southwestern Philosophical Society, November 1985. Subsequent versions were read to the Society for Women in Philosophy, March 1986, and to the American Philosophical Association, May 1986. Many people in discussion at those meetings offered incisive comments and criticisms. I would like to thank in particular the following persons for their critiques of earlier drafts of this paper: Nancy Fraser; Alison Jaggar; Jeffner Allen; Laurie Shrage; Robert Yanal; Martha Gimenez; Joyce Trebilcot, Rob Crawford, and Iris Young.

## Linda Singer, "Bodies–Pleasures–Powers" (pp. 257–271)

1. The term "hegemony" is used frequently in the text, and therefore bears some clarification. As I am using the term, "hegemony" refers to any social construction which has sufficient currency or legitimacy to operate as a naturalized point of orientation for social discourse. Hegemony is not false consciousness, because its organizing and explanatory functions have not been cast in the currency of truth. Rather, the hegemonic apparatus works to provide a context for social struggle by condensing a shared set of assumptions and symbols that set the terms for discursive struggles and for their resolution. I am using the term in this context because I think the language of "sexual epidemic" does not just name an existing state of epidemiological affairs, but it also is a condensation point for a whole set of assumptions about sexuality in terms of which the contours of new sexual-political issues are being framed. By treating the sexual epidemic as a hegemonic construct, I want to emphasize the social labor entailed in its elaboration and circulation, as well as call attention to its strategic function, without denying that the spread of AIDS has reached quantitatively unacceptable proportions, i.e., is epidemic. For a recent discussion of hegemony which has informed my usage, see Laclau and Mouffe.
2. For a discussion of contemporary strategies for re-eroticizing safe sex within the gay community, see Watney, 1–38.
3. For a range of attempts in this direction, see Kroker.
4. This ad campaign was placed in subway stations in New York during the summer of 1987.
5. The initial ruling was subsequently reversed on appeal, restoring Mrs. Whitehead's status as the legal mother. Consequently, she has been granted rights to regular visitation, though the baby will continue to reside with the Sterns.
6. This argument has prompted legislation in several states to outlaw paid surrogacy contracts.
7. This judgment was also reversed on appeal.

### Works Cited

Allen, Jeffner. "Motherhood: The Annihilation of Women." *Women Values: Readings in Recent Feminist Philosophy*. Ed. Marilyn Pearsall. New York: Wadsworth, 1985. 91–101.

Altman, Dennis. *The Homosexualization of America. The Americanization of the Homosexual*. New York: St. Martin's, 1982.

Camus, Albert. *The Plague*. Trans. Stuart Gilbert. New York: Vintage-Random, 1972.

Ehrenreich, Barbara, et al. *Remaking Love: The Feminization of Sex*. Garden City: Anchor-Doubleday, 1986. 103–60.

Firestone, Shulamith. *The Dialectic of Sex: The Case for Feminist Revolution*. New York: Morrow, 1970.

Foucault, Michel. *The Birth of the Clinic: An Archaeology of Medical Perception*. Trans. A. M. Sheridan Smith. New York: Pantheon, 1973.

———. *The History of Sexuality*. Trans. Robert Hurley. Vol. 1. New York: Vintage, 1980.

Kroker, Arthur, and Marilouise Kroker, eds. *Panic Sex in America*. New York: St. Martin's, 1987.

Laclau, Ernesto, and Chantal Mouffe. *Hegemony and Socialist Strategy*. Trans. Winston Moore and Paul Cammack, London: Verso, 1985.

Marcuse, Herbert. *Eros and Civilization: A Philosophical Inquiry into Freud*. Boston: Beacon, 1955.

Patton, Cindy. *Sex and Germs: The Politics of AIDS*. Boston: South End, 1985.

Shilts, Randy. *And the Band Played On*. New York: St. Martin's, 1987.

Watney, Simon. *Policing Desire: Pornography, AIDS & the Media*. Minneapolis: University of Minnesota Press, 1987.

Weeks, Jeffrey. *Sexuality and Its Discontents: Meanings, Myths and Modern Sexualities*. London: Routledge, 1985.

## Ynestra King, "Healing the Wounds: Feminism, Ecology, and the Nature/Culture Dualism" (pp. 284–295)

1. One of the major issues at the United Nations Decade on Women forum held in Nairobi, Kenya, in 1985 was the effect of the international monetary system on women and the particular burdens women bear because of the money owed the "first world," particularly U.S. economic interests, by developing countries.

2. It is one of the absurd examples of newspeak that the designation "pro-life" has been appropriated by the militarist right to support forced childbearing.

3. See especially Murray Bookchin, *The Ecology of Freedom* (Palo Alto, CA: Cheshire Books, 1982). Of the various ecological theories that are not explicitly feminist, I draw here on Bookchin's work because he articulates a historical theory of hierarchy that begins with the domination of women by men, making way for domination by race and class, and the domination of nature. Hence the term "social" ecology. *The Ecology of Freedom* presents a radical view of the emergence, and potential dissolution, of hierarchy. Social ecology is just as concerned with relations of domination between persons as it is with the domination of nature. Hence it should be of great interest to feminists.

4. Sophocles, *Antigone*, trans. Elizabeth Wychokoff, in David Green and Richard Lattimore (eds.), *The Complete Greek Tragedies*, Vol. II: *Sophocles* (Chicago: University of Chicago Press, 1959), pp. 170–1 (lines 335–70).

5. Hans Jonas, *The Imperative of Responsibility: In Search of an Ethics for the Technological Age* (Chicago: University of Chicago Press, 1984), p. 136.

6. See Alison M. Jaggar, *Feminist Politics and Human Nature* (Totowa, NJ: Roman and Allanheld, 1983).

7. Alice Schwarzer, *After the Second Sex: Conversations with Simone de Beauvoir* (New York: Pantheon, 1984), p. 103.

8. Virginia Woolf, *Three Guineas* (New York: Harcourt, Brace & World, 1938).

9. Peter Kropotkin, *Mutual Aid: A Factor in Evolution* (Boston: Porter Sargent, 1914).

10. See the works of scientists Lynn Margolis and James Lovelock, especially *Gaia: A New Look at Life on Earth* (New York: Oxford University Press, 1982).

11. See Cherríe Moraga and Gloria Anzaldúa, *This Bridge Called My Back* (New York: Kitchen Table Press, 1983); Gloria Joseph and Jill Lewis, *Common Differences: Conflicts in Black and White Feminist Perspectives* (Garden City, NY: Doubleday/Anchor 1981); and bell hooks, *Feminist Theory: From Margin to Center* (Boston: South End Press, 1984). Audre Lorde has written eloquently of the problems of attempting to "use the master's tools to disassemble the master's house" and the implicit racism of heretofore definitions of "theory": see Audre Lorde, *Sister Outsider* (Trumansburg, NY: Crossing Press, 1986).

12. Luisah Teish, *Jambalaya* (San Francisco: Harper & Row, 1986).

13. These traditions are complex, and there are critical differences among them. Each has an ancient, and total, cosmology and set of practices, and while it is possible to find commonalities, creating a willy-nilly, random patchwork is not a brilliant new synthesis. That is the problem with the incoherent mush called "new age spirituality" or its slightly more secular version, the "human potential movement." Each religious tradition requires instruction (which may be in an oral or written tradition, or both), study, and the discipline of practice. I also don't know that traditions and cultures that apparently have an antidualistic perspective when it comes to the relationship between human and nonhuman nature are *necessarily* not sexist, xenophobic, or hierarchical in other contexts.

14. See Jean Baudrillard, *The Mirror of Production* (St. Louis: Telos Press, 1975).

15. In raising these issues I am in no way advocating the criminalization of women who market their eggs or wombs. If there is to be criminalization, the purveyors, or pimps, should be penalized, not the women. And obviously, there are critical economic and class issues here.

16. See especially Zillah Eisenstein, *The Radical Future of Liberal Feminism* (New York: Longman, 1981).

17. One exception is Carolyn Merchant, who has written a socialist feminist analysis of the scientific revolution, *The Death of Nature: Women, Ecology and the Scientific Revolution* (New York: Harper & Row, 1979). See also, Carolyn Merchant, "Earthcare: Women and the Environmental Movement," *Environment* 22 (no. 4: June 1981): 38–40.

18. Nancy Hartsock, *Money, Sex and Power* (Boston: Northeastern University Press, 1983); and Alison M. Jaggar, *Feminist Politics and Human Nature* (Totowa, NJ: Rowman and Allanheld, 1983).

19. Cultural feminism is a term invented by feminists who believe in the primacy of economic (as opposed to cultural) forces in making history, but cultural feminists are proud of their emphasis.

20. On the social, mindful nature of mothering see the work of Sara Ruddick, especially "Maternal Thinking," *Feminist Studies* 6 (no. 2: Summer 1980): 342–67; and "Preservative Love and Military Destruction: Some Reflections on Mothering and Peace," in Joyce Trebilcot (ed.), *Mothering: Essays in Feminist Theory* (Totowa, NJ: Rowman and Allanheld, 1983), pp. 231–62.

21. Catherine Caufield, *In the Rainforest* (Chicago: University of Chicago Press, 1984), pp. 156–8.

22. See Edward Hyams, *Soil and Civilization* (New York: Harper & Row, 1976).

23. See Petra Kelly, *Fighting for Hope* (Boston: South End Press, 1984) for a practical, feminist Green political analysis and program, with examples of ongoing movements and activities.

24. I am indebted to ecofeminist sociologist and environmental health activist Lin Nelson for pointing out to me why the feminist health movement is yet to become ecological.

25. See Elizabeth Fee, "Is Feminism a Threat to Scientific Objectivity?" *International Journal of Women's Studies* 4 (no. 4: 1981): 378–92. See also Sandra Harding, *The Science Question in Feminism* (Ithaca, NY: Cornell University Press, 1986) and Evelyn Fox Keller, *Reflections on Gender and Science* (New Haven, CT: Yale University Press, 1985).

26. See, for example, Evelyn Fox Keller, *A Feeling for the Organism: The Life and Work of Barbara McClintock* (San Francisco, Freeman, 1983).

27. The cross-cultural interpretations of personal freedom of anthropologist Dorothy Lee are evocative of the possibility of such an ideal of freedom. See Dorothy Lee, *Freedom and Culture* (Englewood Cliffs, NJ: Prentice-Hall, 1959).

## Carol J. Adams, "The Feminist Traffic in Animals" (pp. 295–310)

Acknowledgments: Josephine Donovan, Greta Gaard, Mary Hunt, Melinda Vadas, and especially Nancy Tuana have been supportive critics as I developed the ideas in this essay. My thanks to them.

1. Claudia Card, "Pluralist Lesbian Separatism," in *Lesbian Philosophies and Cultures*, ed. Jeffner Allen (Albany: State University of New York Press, 1990), 139.

2. Joan Cocks, *The Oppositional Imagination* (London: Routledge, 1989), 223, n.3.

3. Noel Sturgeon, "Editorial Statement," *Ecofeminist Newsletter* 2 (Spring 1991): 1.

4. See excerpts from the 1990 NWSA Ecofeminist Task Force Resolution, *Ecofeminist Newsletter* 2 (Spring 1991):3.

5. Barbara Noske uses the term "animal-industrial complex" in *Humans and Other Animals* (London: Pluto Press, 1989), 24.

6. On government coercion through "meat"-advocacy in the four basic food groups, see my forthcoming "Eating Animals," in *Eating Cultures*, ed. Brian Seitz and Ron Scapp.

7. See Carol J. Adams, *The Sexual Politics of Meat: A Feminist Vegetarian Critical Theory* (New York: Continuum, 1990), 80–81.

8. Emma Goldman, "The Traffic in Women," in *The Traffic in Women and Other Essays on Feminism* (New York: Times Change Press, 1970); Gayle Rubin, "The Traffic in Women: Notes on the 'Political Economy' of Sex," in *Toward an Anthropology of Women*, ed. Rayna R. Reiter (New York and London: Monthly Review Press, 1975), 157–210. See also Janice Raymond, "The International Traffic in Women," *Reproductive and Genetic Engineering* 2, no. I (1989): 51–70.

9. See C. David Coats, *Old MacDonald's Factory Farm: The Myth of the Traditional Farm and the Shocking Truth About Animal Suffering in Today's Agribusiness* (New York: Continuum, 1989); Jim Mason and Peter Singer, *Animal Factories* (New York: Crown Publishers, 1980); John Robbins, *Diet for a New America* (Walpole, N.H.: Stillpoint, 1987).

10. As Eve Kosofsky Sedgwick observes in *Epistemology of the Closet* (Berkeley and Los Angeles: University of California Press, 1990): "The simple, stubborn fact or pretense of ignorance . . . can sometimes be enough to enforce discursive power" (6).

11. Ellen Goodman, "Debate Rages Over Animals: Where Do Ethics End and Human Needs Begin?" *Buffalo News*, December 20, 1989.

12. Nancy Fraser, *Unruly Practices: Power, Discourse, and Gender in Contemporary Social Theory* (Minneapolis: University of Minnesota Press, 1989), 168.

13. Ibid., 168. While a case could be made that animal rights discourse represents a runaway need in accordance with Fraser's analysis of needs, to establish the way in which animal rights follows Fraser's analysis is beyond the scope of this paper. The following argument uses Fraser's analysis of the way that issues become politicized and then reprivatized, but it will not establish a direct match between her categories and animal rights discourse. I wish to thank Nancy Tuana for calling my attention to Fraser's work.

14. Fraser, *Unruly Practices*, p. 168.

15. Nel Noddings, "Comment on Donovan's 'Animal Rights and Feminist Theory,'" *Signs* 16 (1991): 420.

16. Susanna J. Sturgis, "Arsenal of Silencers," *Sojourner: The Women's Forum*, December 1991, 5.

17. On "mass terms," see Willard Van Orman Quine, *Word and Object* (Cambridge: MIT Press, 1960), 99ff. Nancy Tuana pointed out that Quine's explanation of "mass term" was applicable to the cultural construction of animals as edible, and her interpretation of his work has greatly influenced my description in this article.

18. This example is based on an explanation offered by Nancy Tuana.

19. On the way that ontology recapitulates ideology, see

Carol J. Adams, "Ecofeminism and the Eating of Animals," *Hypatia* 6 (1991): 125–45.

20. Zuleyma Tang Halpin, "Scientific Objectivity and the Concept of the 'Other,'" *Women's Studies International Forum* 12 (1989): 286.

21. Caroline Whitbeck, "A Different Reality: Feminist Ontology," in *Women, Knowledge, and Reality: Explorations in Feminist Philosophy*, ed. Ann Garry and Marilyn Pearsall (Boston: Unwin Hyman, 1989), 51.

22. Halpin, "Scientific Objectivity," 287–88.

23. Patricia Hill Collins, *Black Feminist Thought: Knowledge, Consciousness, and the Politics of Empowerment* (Boston: Unwin Hyman, 1990), 172.

24. Elizabeth V. Spelman, "Woman as Body: Ancient and Contemporary Views," *Feminist Studies* 8 (1982): 109–31.

25. Noske, *Humans and Other Animals*, 157.

26. Nancy C. M. Hartsock, *Money, Sex, and Power: Toward a Feminist Historical Materialism* (Boston: Northeastern University Press, 1983, 1985), 302, n. 9.

27. Noske, *Humans and Other Animals*, 125.

28. Ibid., 138.

29. Mary Zeiss Stange, "Hunting—An American Tradition," *American Hunter*, January 1991, 27.

30. Paolo Freire, *Pedagogy of the Oppressed* (New York: Penguin, 1972, 1978), 30.

31. Ibid., 21.

32. See Alison M. Jaggar, *Feminist Politics and Human Nature* (Totowa, N.J.: Rowman & Littlefield, 1988), 6–7. Thanks to Nancy Tuana for her suggestion of Jaggar's text.

33. Ibid., 6–7.

34. Ibid.

35. Ibid.

36. Beverly Harrison, *Making the Connections: Essays in Feminist Social Ethics*, ed. Carol S. Robb (Boston: Beacon, 1985), 255.

37. Ellen Bring, "Moving Towards Coexistence: An Interview with Alice Walker," *Animals' Agenda* 8 (April 1988): 6–9.

38. Stange, "Hunting," 26.

39. Noddings, "Comment," 421.

40. Hartsock, *Money, Sex, and Power*, 9.

41. Noddings, "Comment," 421.

42. Indeed, Nodding's entire response to Donovan on animal rights is contaminated by this refusal to engage the actual issues. While admitting that the greatest difference between herself and Donovan is their position on the eating of animals, she continually strays from that issue. Diversionary issues such as a discussion of whales and dolphins (who are rarely eaten by Americans), and her cats' predatory nature (which has no resemblance to the human traffic in animals), have little to do with the social construction of flesh consumption.

43. See Carol J. Adams, work in progress, "'Physically and Psychically Painless Animal Deaths': A Tolerable Standard for Feminist Ethics?"

44. Luisah Teish, *Jambalaya: The Natural Woman's Book of Personal Charms and Practical Rituals* (San Francisco: Harper & Row, 1985), 92–93.

45. This problem is discussed at length in Adams, *Sexual Politics of Meat*, 63–82.

46. Sally McConnell-Ginet, "Review Article on Language and Sex," *Language* 59 (1983): 387–88, quoted in *A Feminist Dictionary*, ed. Cheris Kramarae and Paula A. Treichler (Boston: Pandora, 1985), 264.

47. Fraser, *Unruly Practices*, 164.

48. Jennie Ruby, Farar Elliot, and Carol Anne Douglas, "NWSA: Troubles Surface at Conference," *off our backs*, August–September 1990, 11.

49. Pat Parker, "To a Vegetarian Friend," in *Womanslaughter* (Oakland, Calif.: Diana Press, 1978), 14.

50. Alice Walker, *Living by the Word: Selected Writings, 1973–1987* (San Diego: Harcourt Brace Jovanovich, 1987), 172.

51. Jaggar, *Feminist Politics and Human Nature*, p. 7.

52. Freire, *Pedagogy of the Oppressed*, 65.

53. Goodman, "Debate Rages Over Animals."

54. Freire, *Pedagogy of the Oppressed*, 29.

55. Ibid., 26.

56. Walker, *Living by the Word*, 182–83.

57. Fraser, *Unruly Practices*, 181.

58. Summarized in the *Ecofeminist Newsletter* 2 (Spring 1991): 3.

59. The recommendation contained twenty-two *whereases*; eleven of them concerned environmental consequences, based on material derived from John Robbin's *Diet for a New America*. For a discussion of the environmental consequences of eating animals, see Adams, "Ecofeminism and the Eating of Animals," and Robbins' book.

60. The health consequences of flesh consumption are reviewed in Robbins, *Diet for a New America*, part 2.

61. See *Ecofeminist Newsletter* 2 (Spring 1991): 3.

## Carolyn Merchant, "Ecofeminism" (pp. 311–328)

1. Françoise d'Eaubonne, "Feminism or Death," in Elaine Marks and Isabelle de Courtivron, eds., *New French Feminisms: An Anthology* (Amherst: University of Massachusetts Press, 1980), pp. 64–7, but see especially p. 25; Françoise d'Eaubonne, *Le Féminisme ou la Mort* (Paris: Pierre Horay, 1974), pp. 213–52.

2. Ynestra King, "Toward an Ecological Feminism and a Feminist Ecology," in Joan Rothschild, ed., *Machina Ex Dea* (New York: Pergamon Press, 1983), pp. 118–29; Janet Biehl, "What Is Social Ecofeminism?" *Green Perspectives*, 11 (October 1988).

3. Alison Jaggar, *Feminist Politics and Human Nature* (Totowa, N.J.: Rowman and Allanheld, 1983); Karen Warren, "Feminism and Ecology: Making Connections," *Environmental Ethics*, vol. 9, no. 1 (1987): 3–10.

4. Karen Warren, "Toward an Ecofeminist Ethic," *Studies in the Humanities* (December 1988): 140–56, quotation on p. 151.

5. Karen Warren, "The Power and the Promise of Ecological Feminism," *Environmental Ethics*, 12, no. 2 (Summer 1990): 125–46.

6. Jaggar, *Feminist Politics and Human Nature*, pp. 27–47.

7. Simone de Beauvoir, *The Second Sex* [1949] (London: Penguin Books, 1972), pp. 95–6; Betty Friedan, *The Feminine Mystique* (New York: Dell, 1963), pp. 11–27, 326–63; King, "Toward an Ecological Feminism and a Feminist Ecology," pp. 121–2; Rachel Carson, *Silent Spring* (Boston: Houghton and Mifflin, 1962), pp. 1–37.

8. Barbara Holzman, "Women's Role in Environmental Organizations," manuscript in possession of the author, Berkeley, Ca.

9. Sherry Ortner, "Is Female to Male as Nature Is to Culture?" in Michelle Rosaldo and Louise Lamphere, ed., *Women, Culture, and Society* (Stanford, Ca.: Stanford University Press, 1974), pp. 67–68.

10. Merlin Stone, *When God Was a Woman* (New York: Harcourt Brace Jovanovich, 1976); Carolyn Merchant, *The Death of Nature: Women, Ecology, and the Scientific Revolution* (San Francisco: Harper and Row, 1980); Carolyn Merchant, "Earthcare: Women and the Environmental Movement," *Environment*, 23, no. 5 (June 1981): 6–13, 38–40.

11. Starhawk, *The Spiral Dance: A Rebirth of the Ancient Religion of the Great Goddess* (San Francisco: Harper and Row, 1979); Carol Gilligan, *In a Different Voice: Psychological Theory and Women's Development* (Cambridge, Ma.: Harvard University Press, 1982); Nel Noddings, *Caring: A Feminist Approach to Ethics and Moral Education* (Berkeley: University of California Press, 1984).

12. Ortner, "Is Female to Male as Nature Is to Culture?" For a recent anthology of varieties of ecofeminism see Irene Diamond and Gloria Ornstein, eds., *Reweaving the World: The Emergence of Ecofeminism* (San Francisco: Sierra Club Books, 1990).

13. Dorothy Nelkin, "Nuclear Power as a Feminist Issue," *Environment*, vol. 23, no. 1 (1981): 14–20, 38–39.

14. Merchant, "Earthcare," quotation on p. 38.

15. Karen Stults, "Women Movers: Reflections on a Movement by Some of Its Leaders," *Everyone's*

*Backyard*, vol. 7, no. 1 (Spring, 1989): 1; Ann Marie Capriotti-Hesketh, "Women and the Environmental Health Movement: Ecofeminism in Action," Department of Biomedical and Environmental Health Sciences, University of California, Berkeley, Ca., unpublished manuscript in possession of the author.

16. Merchant, "Earthcare," p. 13.

17. Susan Prentice, "Taking Sides: What's Wrong with Eco-Feminism?" *Women and Environments*, (Spring 1988): 9–10.

18. Janet Biehl, "What Is Social Ecofeminism?" *Green Perspectives*, No. 11 (October 1988): 1–8, quotation on p. 7.

19. Janet Biehl, *Rethinking Ecofeminist Politics* (Boston: South End Press, 1991), pp. 1–7, 9–19.

20. Friedrich Engels, "Origin of the Family, Private Property, and the State," in *Selected Works* (New York: International Publishers, 1968), p. 455; Engels, *Dialectics of Nature*, ed. Clemens Dutt (New York: International Publishers, 1940), pp. 89–90.

21. Abby Peterson, "The Gender–Sex Dimension in Swedish Politics," *Acta Sociologica*, no. 1 (1984): 3–17, quotation on p. 6.

22. Carolyn Merchant, *Ecological Revolutions: Nature, Gender, and Science in New England* (Chapel Hill: University of North Carolina Press, 1989), p. 14.

23. Irene Diamond, "Fertility as a Sound of Nature: Echoes of Anger and Celebration," Department of Political Science, University of Oregon, Eugene, Oregon, unpublished manuscript in possession of author, p. 14.

24. For examples see Merchant, "Earthcare," pp. 7–13, 38–40.

25. Vandana Shiva, *Staying Alive: Women, Ecology, and Development* (London: Zed Books, 1988), p. 76.

26. Shiva, *Staying Alive*, pp. 55–77.

27. John Farrell, "Agroforestry Systems," in Miguel Altieri, *Agroecology: The Scientific Basis of Alternative Agriculture* (Berkeley: Division of Biological Control, University of California, Berkeley, 1983), pp. 77–83.

28. Wangari Maathai, *The Green Belt Movement: Sharing the Approach and the Experience* (Nairobi, Kenya: Environment Liaison Centre International, 1988), pp. 5–24, quotation on p. 5.

29. Maathai, *Green Belt Movement*, pp. 9–30. See also Lori Ann Thrupp, "Women, Wood, and Work in Kenya and Beyond," *UNASYLVA* (FAO, Journal of Forestry), (Dec 1984): 37–43.

30. Sithembiso Nyoni, "Women, Environment, and Development in Zimbabwe," in *Women, Environment, Development Seminar Report* (London: Women's Environmental Network, 1989), pp. 25–7, quotation on p. 26.

31. Maloba, Robleto, Letelier, Castro, at Managua Conference, June 1989.

32. Chee Yoke Ling, "Women, Environment,

Development: The Malaysian Experience," in Women's Environmental Network, *Women, Environment, Development Seminar Report* (London: Women's Environmental Network, 1989), pp. 23–4.

33. Jeanne Rhinelander, "Crusader in Krakow," *Worldwide News: World Women in Environment*, 8, no. 2 (March–April 1990): 1, 7; Interview with Soviet Environmentalist: Dr. Eugenia V. Afanasieva,

*Worldwide News* (September–October 1989): 1, 5, quotations on p. 5.

34. "Women Meet in Moscow to Talk Environment," *Worldwide News: World Women in Environment* (November–December 1989), pp. 1–2.

35. Olga Uzhnurtsevaa speaking at the conference on "The Fate and Hope of the Earth," Managua, Nicaragua, June 1989.

## Patricia Hill Collins, "The Sexual Politics of Black Womanhood" (pp. 339–351)

1. French philosopher Michel Foucault makes a similar point: "I believe that the political significance of the problem of sex is due to the fact that sex is located at the point of intersection of the discipline of the body and the control of the population" (1980, 125). The erotic is something felt, a power that is embodied. Controlling sexuality harnesses that power for the needs of larger, hierarchical systems by controlling the body and hence the population.

2. Offering a similar argument about the relationship between race and masculinity, Paul Hoch (1979) suggests that the ideal white man is a hero who upholds honor. But inside lurks a "Black beast" of violence and sexuality, traits that the white hero deflects onto men of color.

3. Any group can be made into pets. Consider Tuan's (1984) discussion of the role that young Black boys played as exotic ornaments for wealthy white women in the 1500s to the early 1800s in England. Unlike other male servants, the boys were the favorite attendants of noble ladies and gained entry into their mistresses' drawing rooms, bedchambers, and theater boxes. Boys were often given fancy collars with padlocks to wear. "As they did with their pet dogs and monkeys, the ladies grew genuinely fond of their black boys" (p. 142). In addition, Nancy White's analysis . . . of the differences between how white and Black women are treated by white men uses this victim/pet metaphor (Gwaltney 1980, 148).

4. See Hoch's (1979) discussion of the roots of the white hero, black beast myth in Eurocentric thought. Hoch contends that white masculinity is based on the interracial competition for women. To become a "man," the white, godlike hero must prove himself victorious over the dark "beast" and win possession of the "white goddess." Through numerous examples Hoch suggests that this explanatory myth underlies Western myth, poetry, and literature. One example describing how Black men were depicted during the witch hunts is revealing. Hoch notes, "the Devil was often depicted as a lascivious black male with cloven hoofs, a tail, and a huge penis capable of super-masculine exertion—

an archetypal leering "black beast from below" (1979, 44).

### Works Cited

Andersen, Margaret. 1988. *Thinking About Women: Sociological Perspectives on Sex and Gender*. 2d ed. New York: Macmillan.

Angelou, Maya. 1969. *I Know Why the Caged Bird Sings*. New York: Bantam.

Bart, Pauline B., and Patricia H. O'Brien. 1985. "Ethnicity and Rape Avoidance: Jews, White Catholics and Blacks." In *Stopping Rape: Successful Survival Strategies*, edited by Pauline B. Bart and Patricia H. O'Brien, 70–92. New York: Pergamon Press.

Bell, Laurie, ed. 1987. *Good Girls/Bad Girls: Feminists and Sex Trade Workers Face to Face*. Toronto: Seal Press.

Clark, Reginald M. 1983. *Family Life and School Achievement: Why Poor Black Children Succeed or Fail*. Chicago: University of Chicago Press.

Clark-Lewis, Elizabeth. 1985. *"This Work Had a' End": The Transition from Live-In to Day Work*. Southern Women: The Intersection of Race, Class and Gender. Working Paper #2. Memphis, TN: Center for Research on Women, Memphis State University.

Davis, Angela Y. 1978. "Rape, Racism and the Capitalist Setting." *Black Scholar* 9(7): 24–30.

———. 1981. *Women, Race and Class*. New York: Random House.

———. 1989. *Women, Culture, and Politics*. New York: Random House.

Dworkin, Andrea. 1981. *Pornography: Men Possessing Women*. New York: Perigee.

Edwards, Ann. 1987. "Male Violence in Feminist Theory: An Analysis of the Changing Conceptions of Sex/Gender Violence and Male Dominance." In *Women, Violence and Social Control*, edited by Jalna Hanmer and Mary Maynard, 13–29. Atlantic Highlands, NJ: Humanities Press.

Eisenstein, Hester. 1983. *Contemporary Feminist Thought*. Boston: G. K. Hall.

Fausto-Sterling, Anne. 1989. "Life in the XY Corral." *Women's Studies International Forum* 12(3):319–31.

Foucault, Michel. 1980. *Power/Knowledge: Selected Interviews and Other Writings 1972–1977*, edited by Colin Gordon. New York: Pantheon.

Gardner, Tracey A. 1980. "Racism and Pornography in the Women's Movement." In *Take Back the Night: Women on Pornography*, edited by Laura Lederer, 105–14. New York: William Morrow.

Gilman, Sander L. 1985. "Black Bodies, White Bodies: Toward an Iconography of Female Sexuality in Late Nineteenth-Century Art, Medicine, and Literature." *Critical Inquiry* 12(1): 205–43.

Gould, Stephen Jay. 1981. *The Mismeasure of Man*. New York: W. W. Norton.

Guy, Rosa. 1983. *A Measure of Time*. New York: Bantam.

Hall, Jacqueline Dowd. 1983. "The Mind That Burns in Each Body: Women, Rape, and Racial Violence." In *Powers of Desire: The Politics of Sexuality*, edited by Ann Snitow, Christine Stansell, and Sharon Thompson, 329–49. New York: Monthly Review Press.

Halpin, Zuleyma Tang. 1989. "Scientific Objectivity and the Concept of 'The Other.'" *Women's Studies International Forum* 12(3): 285–94.

Hansberry, Lorraine. 1969. *To Be Young, Gifted and Black*. New York: Signet.

Hoch, Paul. 1979. *White Hero Black Beast: Racism, Sexism and the Mask of Masculinity*. London: Pluto Press.

Jacobs, Harriet. [1860] 1987. "The Perils of a Slave Woman's Life." In *Invented Lives: Narratives of Black Women 1860–1960*, edited by Mary Helen Washington, 16–67. Garden City, NY: Anchor.

Jones, Gayl. 1975. *Corregidora*. New York: Bantam.

Lorde, Audre. 1984. *Sister Outsider*. Trumansberg, NY: The Crossing Press.

McNall, Scott G. 1983. "Pornography: The Structure of Domination and the Mode of Reproduction." In *Current Perspectives in Social Theory, Volume 4*, edited by Scott McNall, 181–203. Greenwich, CT: JAI Press.

Morrison, Toni. 1970. *The Bluest Eye*. New York: Pocket Books.

Murray, Pauli. 1987. *Song in a Weary Throat: An American Pilgrimage*. New York: Harper & Row.

Naylor, Gloria. 1980. *The Women of Brewster Place*. New York: Penguin.

Shockley, Ann Allen. 1983. "The Black Lesbian in American Literature: An Overview." In *Home Girls: A Black Feminist Anthology*, edited by Barbara Smith, 83–93. New York: Kitchen Table Press.

Smith, Barbara. 1983. "Introduction." in *Home Girls: A Black Feminist Anthology*, edited by Barbara Smith, xix–lvi. New York: Kitchen Table Press.

Spelman, Elizabeth V. 1982. "Theories of Race and Gender: The Erasure of Black Women." *Quest* 5(4):36–62.

Tuan, Yi-Fu. 1984. *Dominance and Affection: The Making of Pets*. New Haven, CT: Yale University Press.

Vance, Carole S. 1984. "Pleasure and Danger: Toward a Politics of Sexuality." In *Pleasure and Danger: Exploring Female Sexuality*, edited by Carole S. Vance, 1–27. Boston: Routledge & Kegan Paul.

Walker, Alice, ed. 1979a. *I Love Myself When I Am Laughing, And Then Again When I Am Looking Mean and Impressive: A Zora Neale Hurston Reader*. Old Westbury, NY: Feminist Press.

———. 1981. "Coming Apart." In *You Can't Keep a Good Woman Down*, 41–53. New York: Harcourt Brace Jovanovich.

———. 1982. *The Color Purple*. New York: Washington Square Press.

———. 1988. *Living by the Word*. New York: Harcourt Brace Jovanovich.

Weisbord, Robert G. 1975. *Genocide?: Birth Control and the Black American*. Westport, CT: Greenwood Press.

## Walter L. Williams, "Of Religions and Dreams: The Spiritual Basis of the Berdache Tradition" (pp. 352–361)

1. Joseph François Lafitau, *Moeurs des sauvages americquains* (Paris: Saugram, 1724), vol. 1, p. 52; translated by Warren Johansson in Jonathan Katz, *Gay American History* (New York: Thomas Crowell, 1976), pp. 288–89.

2. Jacques Marquette, "Of the First Voyage Made . . .," in *The Jesuit Relations*, ed. Reuben Gold Thwaites (Cleveland: Burrows, 1896–1901), vol. 59, p. 129; reprinted in Katz, *Gay American History*, p. 287.

3. E. W. Gifford, "The Kamia of Imperial Valley," *Bureau of American Ethnology Bulletin* 97 (1931): 12.

4. By using present tense verbs in this text, I am not implying that such activities are necessarily continuing today. I sometimes use the present tense in the "ethnographic present," unless I use the past tense when I am referring to something that has not continued. Past tense implies that all such practices have disappeared. In the absence of fieldwork to prove such disappearance, I am not prepared to make that assumption, for reasons discussed in Part II on the historic changes in the berdache tradition.

5. Elsie Clews Parsons, "The Zuni La' Mana," *American Anthropologist* 18 (1916): 521; Matilda Coxe Stevenson, "Zuni Indians," *Bureau of American Ethnology Annual Report* 23 (1903): 37; Franklin Cushing, "Zuni Creation Myths," *Bureau of American Ethnology Annual Report* 13 (1894): 401–3. Will Roscoe clarified this origin story for me.

6. W. W. Hill, "Note on the Pima Berdache," *American Anthropologist* 40 (1938): 339.

7. Aileen O'Bryan, "The Dine': Origin Myths of the Navaho Indians," *Bureau of American Ethnology Bulletin* 163 (1956): 5; W. W. Hill, "The Status of the Hermaphrodite and Transvestite in Navaho Culture," *American Anthropologist* 37 (1935): 273.

8. Martha S. Link, *The Pollen Path: A Collection of Navajo Myths* (Stanford: Stanford University Press, 1956).

9. O'Bryan, "Dine'," pp. 5, 7, 9–10.

10. Ibid.

11. Lakota informants, July 1982. See also William Powers, *Oglala Religion* (Lincoln: University of Nebraska Press, 1977).

12. For this admittedly generalized overview of American Indian religious values, I am indebted to traditionalist informants of many tribes, but especially those of the Lakotas. For a discussion of native religions see Dennis Tedlock, *Finding the Center* (New York: Dial Press, 1972); Ruth Underhill, *Red Man's Religion* (Chicago: University of Chicago Press, 1965); and Elsie Clews Parsons, *Pueblo Indian Religion* (Chicago: University of Chicago Press, 1939).

13. Alfred Kroeber, "The Arapaho," *Bulletin of the American Museum of Natural History* 18 (1902–7): 19.

14. Parsons, "Zuni La' Mana," p. 525.

15. Alexander Maximilian, *Travels in the Interior of North America, 1832–1834*, vol. 22 of *Early Western Travels*, ed. Reuben Gold Thwaites, 32 vols (Cleveland: A. H. Clark, 1906), pp. 283–84, 354. Maximilian was quoted in German in the early homosexual rights book by Ferdinand Karsch-Haack, *Das Gleichgeschlechtliche Leben der Naturvölker* (The same-sex life of nature peoples) (Munich: Verlag von Ernst Reinhardt, 1911; reprinted New York: Arno Press, 1975), pp. 314, 564.

16. Oscar Koch, *Der Indianishe Eros* (Berlin: Verlag Continent, 1925), p. 61.

17. George Devereux, "Institutionalized Homosexuality of the Mohave Indians," *Human Biology* 9 (1937): 509.

18. Ibid., p. 501.

19. Ibid.

20. Ibid., pp. 508–9.

21. C. Daryll Forde, "Ethnography of the Yuma Indians," *University of California Publications in American Archaeology and Ethnology* 28 (1931): 157.

22. Ruth Underhill, *Social Organization of the Papago Indians* (New York: Columbia University Press, 1938), p. 186. This story is also mentioned in Ruth Underhill, ed., *The Autobiography of a Papago Woman* (Menasha, Wisc.: American Anthropological Association, 1936), p. 39.

23. John Fire and Richard Erdoes, *Lame Deer, Seeker of Visions* (New York: Simon and Schuster, 1972), pp. 117, 149.

24. Theodore Stern, *The Klamath Tribe: A People and Their Reservation* (Seattle: University of Washington Press, 1965), pp. 20, 24. Theodore Stern, "Some Sources of Variability in Klamath Mythology," *Journal of American Folklore* 69 (1956): 242ff. Leslie Spier, *Klamath Ethnography* (Berkeley: University of California Press, 1930), p. 52.

25. Alice Joseph, et al., *The Desert People* (Chicago: University of Chicago Press, 1949), p. 227.

26. Quoted in Forde, "Ethnography of the Yuma," p. 157. Although he distorted the data on berdache, see also Leslie Spier, *Yuman Tribes of the Gila River* (Chicago: University of Chicago Press, 1933), pp. 6, 242–43.

27. Joseph Quiñones, Yaqui informant I, January 1985.

28. Stephen Powers, *Tribes of California*, ed. Robert Heizer (originally published 1877; reprint Berkeley: University of California Press, 1976).

29. Alfred Kroeber, *Handbook of the Indians of California* (Berkeley: University of California Press, 1953), p. 497.

30. Erminie Voegelin, *Culture Element Distribution: Northeast California* (Berkeley: University of California Press, 1942), vol. 20, pp. 134–135, 228-B note. Ralph Beals, "Ethnology of the Nisenan," *University of California Publications in American Archaeology and Ethnology* 31 (1933), p. 376.

31. Clark Wissler, "Societies and Ceremonial Associations in the Oglala Division of the Teton Dakota," *Anthropological Papers of the American Museum of Natural History* 11, pt. 1 (1916): 92; Powers, *Oglala Religion*, pp. 57–59.

32. Ronnie Loud Hawk, Lakota informant 4, July 1982.

33. Terry Calling Eagle, Lakota informant 5, July 1982.

34. James O. Dorsey, "A Study of the Siouan Cults," *Bureau of American Ethnology Annual Report* II (1889–90): 378. It is unclear from the sources what would happen if a boy tried to get the man's tools and was successful, since the instances cited always have the boy getting the women's tools. If he got the bow and arrow, presumably he would not become a berdache, but would retain the power to seduce men.

35. Nancy Lurie, "Winnebago Berdache," *American Anthropologist* 55 (1953): 708; Alice Fletcher, "The Elk Mystery or Festival: Ogallala Sioux," *Reports of the Peabody Museum of American Archaeology and Ethnology* 3 (1887): 281; Erik Erikson, "Childhood and Tradition in Two American Indian Tribes," *Psychoanalytic Study of the Child* I (1945): 329, based on Erikson's visit to Sioux reservations in the 1930s with anthropologist H. Scudder Mekeel; Robert H. Lowie, "The Assiniboine," *Anthropological Papers of the American Museum of Natural History* 4 (1909): 42; George Dorsey and James Muric, *Notes on Skidi Pawnee Society* (Chicago: Field Museum of Natural History, 1940), p. 108; Alfred Bowers, *Mandan Social and Ceremonial Organization* (Chicago: University of

Chicago Press, 1950), p. 298; George Will and Herbert Spinden, *The Mandans* (Cambridge: Harvard University Press, 1906), p. 128.

36. James S. Thayer, "The Berdache of the Northern Plains: A Socioreligious Perspective," *Journal of Anthropological Research* 36 (1980): 289.

37. Alfred Bowers, "Hidatsa Social and Ceremonial Organization," *Bureau of American Ethnology Bulletin* 194 (1965): 326.

38. Fletcher, "Elk Mystery," p. 281.

39. Alice Fletcher and Francis La Flesche, "The Omaha Tribe," *Bureau of American Ethnology Annual Report* 27 (1905–6): 132.

40. Harriet Whitehead offers a valuable discussion of this element of the vision quest in "The Bow and the Burden Strap: A New Look at Institutionalized Homosexuality in Native North America," in *Sexual Meanings*, ed. Sherry Ortner and Harriet Whitehead (Cambridge: Cambridge University Press, 1981), pp. 99–102. See also Erikson, "Childhood," p. 329.

## Linda Williams, "Fetishism and Hard Core: Marx, Freud and the 'Money Shot'" (pp. 361–379)

This chapter is an expanded version of articles written for the *Quarterly Review of Film Studies* (forthcoming) and for the anthology *For Adult Users Only: The Case of Violent Pornography* (forthcoming). I wish to thank the editors, Susan Gubar and Joan Hoff-Wilson of *For Adult Users Only*, and Beverle Houston of *QRFS*, for their helpful advice. To Beverle Houston, who worked on the manuscript while struggling against cancer, my thank you is unfortunately too late.

1. In any case, *Deep Throat* was the first well-known film to show a penis "in action."

2. Two recent works, both touching on fetishism, have provided me with historical insights into the concept: Mitchell 1986; and Simpson 1982.

3. In her now-classic essay, Rubin (1979, 176) argues that the exchange of women is neither a definition of culture, as Lévi-Strauss says, nor a system in and of itself. A kinship system is an "imposition of social ends upon a part of the natural world. It is therefore 'production' . . . . a transformation of objects (in this case people) to and by a subjective purpose." Rubin's point is that the subordination of women should be seen as a product of the relationships by which sex and gender are organized. It is not a systematic given of all cultural arrangements but, rather, a product of them.

4. See Chapter 6 [of the book from which this article is taken] for a discussion of the waning of the money shot. It is also possible that new (though rarely overtly acknowledged) AIDS awareness may revive reliance on this figure, since the visual spectacle of ejaculation can substitute for the now more dangerous risk of exposure to body fluids.

### Works Cited

Debord, Guy. 1967. *La société du spectacle*. Paris: Buchet/ Chastel.

Foucault, Michel. 1978. *The History of Sexuality*. Vol. 1: *An Introduction*. Translated by Robert Hurley. New York: Pantheon Books. (Translation of *La volonté de savoir*, 1976.)

Freud, Sigmund. [1927] 1963. "Fetishism." In *Sexuality and the Psychology of Love*, edited by Phillip Rieff, 214–219. New York: Collier.

Haug, F. W. 1986. *Critique of Commodity Aesthetics: Appearance, Sexuality, and Advertising in Capitalist Society*. Translated by Robert Bock. Minneapolis: University of Minnesota Press.

Irigaray, Luce. 1985. *This Sex Which Is Not One*. Translated by Catherine Porter and Carolyn Burke. Ithaca, N.Y.: Cornell University Press.

———. 1986. *Speculum of the Other Woman*. Translated by Gillian C. Gill. Ithaca, N.Y.: Cornell University Press.

Kendrick, Walter. 1987. *The Secret Museum: Pornography in Modern Culture*. New York: Viking Press.

Lovelace, Linda, and Mike McGrady. 1980. *Ordeal*. New York: Berkeley.

Marcus, Steven. 1974. *The Other Victorians: A Study of Sexuality and Pornography in Mid-Nineteenth Century England*. New York: New American Library.

Marcuse, Herbert. 1964. *One Dimensional Man*. Boston: Beacon Hill Press.

Marx, Karl. [1867] 1906. *Capital*. Vol. 1. Translated by Samuel Moore and Edward Aveling. New York: Modern Library.

Mitchell, W. T. J. 1986. *Iconology: Image, Text, Ideology*. Chicago: University of Chicago Press.

Rubin, Gayle. 1979. "The Traffic in Women." In *Towards an Anthropology of Women*, edited by Rayna Reiter, 157-210. New York: Monthly Review Press.

Simpson, David. 1982. *Fetishism and Imagination: Dickens, Melville, Conrad*. Baltimore: Johns Hopkins University Press.

Smith, Richard, ed. 1973. *Getting into "Deep Throat."* Chicago: Playboy Press.

Spivak, Gayatri Chakravorty. 1981. "French Feminism in an International Frame." *Yale French Studies* 62:154–184.

Steinem, Gloria. 1986b. "The Real Linda Lovelace." In *Outrageous Acts and Everyday Rebellions*, 274–285.

## Catharine A. MacKinnon, "Crimes of War, Crimes of Peace" (pp. 380–393)

The help and contributions of Natalie Nenadic, Asja Armanda, Susanne Baer, Jeffrey Masson, Jessica Neuwirth, Joan Fitzpatrick, Cass Sunstein, Andrea Dowrkin, Richard Rorty, Kent Harvey, Rita Rendell, and the wonderful staff at the University of Michigan Law Library are gratefully acknowledged.

1. Oliver Wendell Holmes, *The Common Law* (Boston: Little, Brown, 1881), 1. ("The life of the law has not been logic, it has been experience.")

2. Center for Women's Global Leadership, 1991, *Women's Leadership Institute Report: Women, Violence, and Human Rights* (New Brunswick, N.J.: 1992), Appendix C: "Statistics on Gender Violence Globally," 77–80.

3. For a discussion of the killing of women as a systematic practice, see Jill Radford and Diana E. H. Russell, *Femicide: The Politics of Woman Killing* (New York: Twayne, 1992).

4. For the most advanced of Amnesty's efforts, see Amnesty International, *Rape and Sexual Abuse: Torture and Ill Treatment of Women in Detention* (New York: Amnesty International, January 1993). The advance is that rape is noticed; the limitation remains that it is only noticed when women are in official custody, thus, in effect, raped by a state.

5. [Name Withheld] Letter to author, October 13, 1992. Most of this information has since been independently corroborated by international reports and published accounts. See *Mass Killing and Genocide in Croatia 1991/92: A Book of Evidence* (Zagreb: Hrvatska Sveučilišna Naklada, 1992) (documenting genocide); *Human Rights Watch Report* (August 1992) ("A policy of 'ethnic cleansing' has resulted in the summary execution, disappearance, arbitrary detention, deportation, and forcible displacement of hundreds of thousands of people on the basis of their religion or nationality"); Carl Gustaf Strohm, "Serben vergewaltigen auf obersten Befehl," *Die Welt*, October 1, 1992 (30,000 women pregnant from rape); *Večernji List*, September 11, 1992 (20 rape/death camps for non-Serb women); Ibrahim Kajan, *Muslimanski Danak U Krvi, Svjedočanstva zločina nad Muslimanima* (Zagreb: Preporod, 1992) (genocide of Muslims and rape camps must be documented); Women's Group "Trešnjevka": Report (Zagreb, September 28, 1992) ("The existence of rape/death camps must be understood as a . . . tactic of genocide, of a 'final solution'. . . a gender-specific onslaught that is systematic. . . . [T]he tortures include rapes, gang-rapes, forced incest, the draining of the blood of captives to provide blood for transfusions for the needs of the criminals, setting children ablaze and drowning babies"). Given these reports, it is inexcusable that Amnesty International's October 1992 report on human rights violations in this war documents only three rapes, and these from an English newspaper rather than firsthand, as other atrocities are documented. Edith Niehuis, Head of the German Parliamentary Committee for Women and Youth, called the "systematic mass rapes" in Bosnia an "extermination war against women." "Wir machen euch kleine Tschetniks," *die tageszeitung*, December 8, 1992.

6. Universal Declaration of Human Rights, General Assembly Resolution 217 A (III) of December 10, 1948, Preamble ("Whereas disregard and contempt for human rights have resulted in barbarous acts which have outraged the conscience of mankind. . .").

7. An example of formal condonation is the U.S. case in which pornography is recognized as promoting rape, battering, and unequal pay but is protected as free speech. *American Booksellers v. Hudnut*, 771 F.2d 323 (7th Cir. 1985), aff'd 475 U.S. 1001 (1986).

8. For documentation of the use of "reservations" to the major convention prohibiting sex discrimination, see Rebecca Cook, "Reservations to the Convention on the Elimination of All Forms of Discrimination Against Women," *Virginia Journal of International Law* 30 (1990): 632. A lawsuit may be brought to invalidate the ratifications of nations whose exceptions are said to be excessive, voiding their acceptance of the Committee on the Elimination of Discrimination Against Women (CEDAW). "Court Ruling Sought on Women's Convention," *Human Rights Tribune* 1 (1992): 21.

9. Amnesty International says that all parties succeed to the international agreements that Yugoslavia ratified. Amnesty International, *Bosnia-Herzegovina: Gross Abuses of Basic Human Rights, International Secretariat* (London: October 1992). Helsinki Watch says that Croatia and Yugoslavia (the latter apparently referring to Serbia/Montenegro) are parties to the Geneva Conventions and their Protocols, Croatia by contract on May 11, 1992, and Serbia and Montenegro implicitly, by expressing a wish to be recognized as the successor state to what was Yugoslavia. Ivana Nizich, *War Crimes in Bosnia-Herzegovina* (New York: Helsinki Watch, August 1992), 138–39. Bosnia-Herzegovina formally ratified the relevant provisions in 1992. Humanitarian law is customary law, with universal jurisdiction, but human rights provisions require affirmative submission to secure jurisdiction.

10. Addressing the Conference on Security and Cooperation in Europe, U.S. Secretary of State Lawrence Eagleburger said that Serbian leaders were guilty of war crimes against humanity and should be prosecuted, "exactly as Hitler's associates were at Nuremberg." "Legal Commission to Start Investigation of Mass Graves

in Former Yugoslavia," *Agence France Presse,*
December 14, 1992. At the time they were publicly
recognized, the atrocities had been going on for
approximately a year. There is also some discussion of
creating a permanent international war crimes court
whose first task would be to try war criminals from this
war. "U.S., France Discussing Permanent War Crimes
Court," *Reuters,* December 15, 1992.

11. See generally Roy Gutman, "The Rapes of Bosnia,"
*Newsday,* August 23, 1992. A special mission of the
European Council concluded, after a preliminary visit,
that "the rapes [of Muslim women] are widespread and
are part of a recognizable pattern. . . . The general
view expressed by interlocutors whom the delegation
considered responsible and credible was that a horrifying
number of Muslim women had suffered rape and that
this was continuing. . . . The most reasoned estimate
suggested to the delegation indicated a figure in the
region of 20,000 victims. . . . The indications are that
at least some of the rapes are being committed in
particularly sadistic ways. . . . The delegation also
received information strongly suggesting that many
women, and more particularly children, may have died
during or after rape. . . . [T]he delegation frequently
heard . . . that a repeated feature of Serbian atacks on
Muslim towns and villages was the use of rape, or the
threat for rape, as a weapon of war. . . . [D]ocuments
from Serbian sources . . . very clearly put such actions
in the context of an expansionist strategy. . . . [R]ape
cannot be seen as incidental to the main purposes of the
aggression but as serving a strategic purpose in itself."
*Investigative Mission into the Treatment of Muslim
Women in the Former Yugoslavia* (December 24, 1992),
2–4.

12. Among the scores of examples of this seemingly requisite
equalizing of oppressor and oppressed, although it is
among the least egregious, is Amnesty International's
"Bosnia-Herzegovina: Rape and Sexual Abuse by Armed
Forces" (January, 1993), 3: "Reports indicate . . . that
all sides have committed these abuses, but that Muslim
women have been the chief victims and the main
perpetrators have been members of Serbian armed
forces." World War II atrocities against Serbs by
Croatians and Muslims are often cited by Serbs as
historical justification for current Serbian "revenge."
Nothing justifies genocide. There is also historical
evidence that Serbian war losses have been greatly
exaggerated and are being used as a pretext. Phillip J.
Cohen, "Holocaust History Misappropriated,"
*Midstream: A Monthly Jewish Review* (November 1992),
18–20; Phillip J. Cohen, "Exploitation of the Holocaust
as Propaganda: The Falsification of Serbian War Losses"
(unpublished manuscript, July 18, 1992). See also War
Crimes Investigation Bureau, *Fourth Exodus of the Jews:
War In Bosnia-Herzegovina* (Sarajevo, September 1992).

Alain Finkielkraut comments on this in his *Comment
peut-on être croate?* (Paris: Gallimard, 1992), 50: "La
Serbie falsifie le passé en disant que les Croates étaient
tous nazis et les Serbes tous résistants, falsifie le présent
en disant que les Croates restent un 'peuple génocidaire',
et mène à l'abri de cette double falsification la première
guerre raciale que l'Europe ait connu depuis Hitler.
Pour le dire d'un mot: *les nazis de cette histoire ont
voulu se faire passer pour les Juifs.*" ("Serbia falsifies the
past by saying that the Croatians were all Nazis and the
Serbs all resisters, falsifies the present by saying that the
Croatians remain a 'genocidal people,' and carries out,
in the shadow of this double falsification, the first racial
war that Europe has known since Hitler. To put it in a
word: *the Nazis of this story are trying to pass themselves
off as the Jews.*")

13. A. Kaurin, *Večernji List,* "War Crimes Against Young
Girls" (September 11, 1992) ("They are even conducting
orgies on the dead bodies of the torture victims, who are
after that thrown [out]").

14. In addition, when the dead are counted, their rapes are
not. When raped women are counted, their rapes are
not.

15. Asja Armanda, *The Women's Movement, Feminism, and
the Definition of War* (Kareta Feminist Group, October
1992).

16. "A Pattern of Rape," *Newsweek,* January 4, 1992, 34:
"In his own defense, one attacker told Rasema, 'I have
to do it, otherwise they will kill me.'" According to *Die
Welt,* a rapist told his victim: "'We have to do it,
because our commanders ordered it, and because you
are Muslim—and there are too many of you Muslims.
We have to destroy and exterminate you, so that the
heroic Serbian people can take over the reins in this area
again.'" "Serben vergewaltigen auf obersten Befehl"
(Serbs rape on highest orders), *Die Welt,* October 1,
1992.

17. Roy Gutman, "Mass Rapes in Bosnia," *Newsday,*
August 23, 1992 (reports on rape as a tactic of war,
where victims were told by Serbian forces they were
under orders to rape them); John F. Burns, "A Serbian
Fighter's Trail of Brutality," *New York Times,* November
27, 1992 (an indicted Serb terrorist says "he and other
Serbian fighters were encouraged to rape women and
then take them away to kill them").

18. S. Džombic, "Go and Give Birth to Chentiks," *Večernji
List,* November 25, 1992.

19. The prior analysis and the facts underlying it are based
on my reading of firsthand accounts provided by victims.

20. Many firsthand accounts report this. See Center for
Anti-War Activities, *Save Humanity Report* (Sarajevo:
July 7, 1992), 6; Roy Gutman, "Victims Recount Nights
of Terror at Makeshift Bordello," *Newsday,* August 23,
1992. It is unclear whether the brothels simply organize
serial rape or whether some men are being paid or

receiving other benefits in exchange for access to the women.

21. Z. Džombic, "Go and Give Birth to Chetniks," *Večernji List*, November 25, 1992. My testimonies further support this.

22. Evidence indicates that Jewish babies born in concentration camps were drowned. See *The Trial of German Major War Criminals* (London: HMSO, 1946), Part 5, 188. No Jewish women were documented to have been impregnated, then released, to "bear German babies." However, the Nazis required special permission to be obtained before the fetuses of Eastern European women and German men could be aborted. For discussion of this, see *McRae v. Califano*, 491 F. Supp. 630, 759 (1980).

23. [Name Withheld] Letter to author, October 13, 1992. See also "Schwere Vorwürfe gegen UN-Soldaten in Bosnien, *Die Welt*, October 6, 1992.

24. "Investigation Against General MacKenzie," *Večernji List*, November 25, 1992. According to an interview with Ragib Hadžic, head of the Center for Research on Genocide and War Crimes in Zenica, Bosnia, General MacKenzie visited the "Sonje" restaurant in Dobrinja, which was a brothel and had become a wartime rape/death camp. He reportedly loaded four Muslim women in his UNPROFOR truck, and drove away. The women have never been seen again. "Vergewaltigungen als eine Taktik des Krieges," *Die Welt*, December 2, 1992.

25. Nazis documented many atrocities with photographs, including those shown in *The Trial of German Major War Criminals*, Part 7; 99–101: "these naked women are being taken to the execution ground. Condemned to death, these women have been forced, by the same Obergruppenführer, to pose before the camera" (photographs presented by Soviet prosecution team). See also Helke Sander, *Befreier und Befreite* (Munich: Verlag Antje Kunstmann, 1992), 131–34 (German photographs of dead raped German and Russian women). On the point of media manipulation, my correspondent from Croatia ([Name Withheld] Letter to author, November 28, 1992) notes: "The manipulation of film documentation of atrocities in which Muslim and Croatian victims of Serb aggression have fallaciously been presented as Serb victims of Muslims and Croatians has been a notable strategy of the war against Croatia and Bosnia-Herzegovina." See also A. Kaurin, "War Crimes Against Young Girls," *Večernji List*, September 11, 1992 ("pictures and videotapes of the concentration camps exist"); *Mass Killing*, 234 (dead Croatian boy presented as dead Serbian boy); "Villages in Croatia Recount Massacre by Serbian Forces," *New York Times*, December 19, 1991; Ibrahim Kajan, *Muslimanski Danak U Krvi, Svjedočanstva zločina nad Muslimanima* (Zagreb: Preporod, 1992), 31–34, 51–52.

26. "MacKinnon's central point is that 'a woman' is not yet the name of a way of being human." Richard Rorty, "Feminism and Pragmatism," *Michigan Quarterly Review* 30 (1991): 234.

27. Isaiah Berlin, "Two Concepts of Liberty," in *Four Essays on Liberty* (Oxford: Oxford University Press, 1969).

28. *Belgian Linguistics Case*, ECHR, 1968, Series A, No. 6, 832.

29. Inter-American Court of Human Rights, *Velasquez-Rodriguez v. Honduras* Judgment of July 29, 1988, Series C, no. 4.

30. Lori Heise, quoted in Center for Women's Global Leadership, *Women, Violence, and Human Rights*, 17.

31. For illuminating background, see M. Tardu, *Human Rights: The International Petition System*, vol. 1 (Dobbs Ferry, N.Y.: Oceana Publications, August, 1985), 45 ("The potential of [divisive postwar] UN debates for conflict escalation was so obvious that all governments became fiercely determined to keep the process under their own control through rejecting individual complaint systems"). See also Louis B. Sohn, "The New International Law: Protection of the Rights of Individuals Rather than States," *American University Law Review* 1 (1982): 32.

32. For an example of the inability to see a violation of a woman's human rights to the degree the abuse is deemed "personal," see *Lazo-Majaro v. INS*, 813 F.2d 1432 (9th Cir. 1987) (dissent).

33. See Tardu, *Human Rights*, vol. 1 (German-speaking minorities used as a propaganda base in other countries by insisting on minority rights); Alessandra Luini del Russo, *International Protection of Human Rights* (Washington, D.C.: Lerner Law Book Co., 1971), 32 (nations realized that individual protections cannot be left solely to states).

34. Elizabeth Spelman, *Inessential Woman* (Boston: Beacon Press, 1988); Eva Kuehls, *The Reign of the Phallus* (New York: Harper & Row, 1985).

35. This is discussed further in my *Toward a Feminist Theory of the State* (Cambridge, Mass.: Harvard University Press, 1989), chap. 12.

36. John Stuart Mill and Harriet Taylor, "On the Subjection of Women," in Alice Rossi, ed., *Essays in Sex Equality* (Chicago: University of Chicago Press, 1970).

37. Susan Moller Okin, *Women in Western Political Thought* (Princeton, N.J.: Princeton University Press, 1980); John Locke, *The Second Treatise of Government*, ed. J. W. Gough (Oxford: Blackwell, 1966); Thomas Hobbes, *Leviathan*, ed. M. Oakeshott (Oxford: Blackwell, 1946).

38. This point is made unintentionally by Theodor Meron in his attack on CEDAW for conflicting with existing notions of human rights in various areas. Theodor Meron, *Human Rights Law-Making in the United Nations* (Oxford: Clarendon Press, 1986).

39. "Court Ruling Sought on Women's Convention," *Human Rights Tribune* 1 (1992): 21.

40. Art. 6, CEDAW; Convention for the Suppression of Traffic in Persons and the Exploitation of the Prostitution of Others, 1949. See also the draft, "U.N. Convention Against Sexual Exploitation," reported in *Ms.*, September/October 1991, 13.

41. In 1966, Thailand enacted the Service Establishments Act which gives specific legal status to "special service girls." The women had to turn to the establishments for protection from prosecution under prostitution laws, which exempt customers but not the women. Thanh-Dom Truong, *Sex, Money and Morality: Prostitution and Tourism in Southeast Asia* (London: Zed Books, 1990), 155. In another sense, wherever prostitution is legalized, the state is trafficking in women.

42. U.S. State Department, *Country Reports on Human Rights Practices for 1991* (Washington, D.C.: USGPO, 1992) ("Physical compulsion to submit to abortion or sterilization is not authorized, but continues to occur as officials strive to meet population targets. Reports of forced abortions and sterilizations continue, though well below the levels of the early 1980s. While recognizing that abuses occur, officials maintain that China does not condone forced abortion or sterilization, and that abuses by local officials are punished. They admit, however, that punishment is rare and have yet to provide documentation of any punishments" [818–19]).

43. An intelligent discussion of these provisions can be found in Karen Engle, "International Human Rights and Feminism: When Discourses Meet," *Michigan Journal of International Law* 13 (1992): 517.

44. E. M. Adams, *The Metaphysics of Self and World: Toward a Humanistic Philosophy* (Philadelphia: Temple University Press, 1991).

45. Simone de Beauvoir, *The Second Sex* (New York: Alfred A. Knopf, 1952).

46. Jacques Maritain, *The Rights of Man and Natural Law*, trans. Doris C. Anson (New York: Scribner, 1951; France, 1942). "[The] human person possess[es] rights because of the very fact that it is a person, a whole, a matter of itself and of its acts . . . by virtue of natural law, the human person has to have the right to be respected, is the subject of rights, possesses rights. These are things which are owed to a man because of the very fact that he is a man" (65).

47. Herbert C. Kelman, *Crimes of Obedience* (New Haven: Yale University Press, 1989); M. McDougal, H. Lasswell, L. Chen, *Human Rights and World Public Order* (New Haven: Yale University Press, 1980).

48. Mortimer Adler, "Robert Bork: The Lessons to Be Learned" (comments on Robert H. Bork, *The Tempting of America*) *New York University Law Review* 84 (1990): 1121.

49. Max Solomon, *Der Begriff der Gerechtigkeit bei Aristoteles* (Leiden: A. W. Sijthoff, 1937), 26; E. W. Vierdag, *The Concept of Discrimination in International Law* (The Hague: Nijhoff, 1973). See page 8 regarding Aristotle, and page 26 for the Third Reich and the proposition that "equality in the sense of complete equality is identity: one and the same thing." Illustrating equality thinking during the Nazi period, leading constitutional scholar Ulrich Scheuner states in 1939 that the substance of the equality right is "Artgleichheit" of Aryans (page 267). From the "völkisch" tenets of contemporary German law, see page 267, "[daraus] folgt notwendig die Absonderung der artfremden Elemente, insbesondere der Juden, aus dem deutschen Volkskörper, und ihre . . . differentielle Behandlung" ("follows necessarily the extraction of elements of alien blood, particularly Jews, from the body of the German people, and their . . . differential treatment"). How the Jews were treated is thus rendered "differential treatment." See also the use of the Aristotelian principle at page 260. Scheuner cites the U.S. Supreme Court with approval with regard to racial segregation and miscegenation laws, noting that this leads to "Benachteiligung" (disadvantage) of people of color, which is exactly what is intended, at pages 265–66. He also notices the Court beginning to weaken in its defense of segregation. "Der Gleichheitsgedanke in der völkischen Verfassungsordnung," *Zeitschrift für die Gesamte Staatswissenschaft* 99 (1939): 245.

50. Andrea Dworkin, *Right-Wing Women: The Politics of Domesticated Females* (New York: Putnam, 1983).

51. Art. 2, Universal Declaration of Human Rights, General Assembly Resolution 217 A (III) of December 10, 1948.

52. Part I, Art. 1, CEDAW, adopted December 18, 1979.

53. General Recommendation No. 19, Violence Against Women, Committee on the Elimination of Discrimination Against Women, CEDAW/C/1992/L/1/ Add. 15, January 29, 1992. This document goes very far in recognizing the scope of the problem and in adapting sex equality as a concept to addressing violence against women. For a useful discussion, see Charlotte Bunch, "Women's Rights as Human Rights: Toward a Re-Vision of Human Rights," *Human Rights Quarterly* 12 (1990): 483.

54. Many other human rights documents, notably Art. 3 and Art. 26 of the International Covenant on Civil and Political Rights, December 16, 1966, guarantee sex equality. This covenant stands out in allowing, through an Optional Protocol, complaints by individuals as well as state parties, but only applies to those who have accepted it specifically. Yugoslavia did not. Enforcement includes denunciation of violators.

55. These movements are well documented. See Robin Morgan, *Sisterhood Is Global: The International Women's Movement Anthology* (Garden City, N.Y.: Anchor Press/Doubleday, 1984); Center for Women's

Global Leadership, *Women, Violence, and Human Rights*. See also Marilyn Waring, *If Women Counted* (New York: HarperCollins, 1990) (economic discrimination against women including exclusion of women's work from international accounting systems). The reference to Canada is to the "Montreal Massacre," in which fourteen young women were murdered by a man screaming he hated feminists. Jane Caputi and Diana E. H. Russell, "Femicide: Sexist Terrorism Against Women," in Radford and Russell, *Femicide*, 13–14.

56. In this sense, equality is derivative in virtually all legal systems. See Art. 14, Convention for the Protection of Human Rights and Fundamental Freedoms, 213 U.N.T.S. 221, E.T.S. 5, U.K.T.S. 71 (1953) (September 3, 1953), which has been held to permit no complaints on its own, but merely refers to equal access to other rights. *X and Y v. The Netherlands*, ECHR, 1985 Series A., No. 91, para. 32.

57. *The Law Society of British Columbia v. Andrews* [1989] 1 S.C.R. 143, 171–182.

58. *Jane Doe v. Board of Commissioners of Policy for the Municipality of Metropolitan Toronto* [1989] Ont. L.J. LEXIS 115.

59. *Fanzen v. Platy Enterprises* [1959] 1 S.C.R. 1252 (sexual harassment is sex discrimination under the Manitoba human rights code).

60. *Brooks, Allen and Dixon v. Canada Safeway* [1989] 1 S.C.R. 1219 (pregnancy discrimination is sex discrimination).

61. *Norberg v. Wynrib* [1992] 2 S.C.R. 224.

62. *K.M. v. H.M.* (1992) 142 N.R. 321 (S.C.C.).

63. *Regina v. Lavallee*, 76 C.R. (3d) 329 (1990).

64. *The Queen v. Canadian Newspapers Co.* [1988] 2 S.C.R. 122.

65. *R. v. Seaboyer* (August 22, 1991) (S.C.C., Rep. Serv. 2nd ed. 1991 cases [Digest 1713]).

66. Less positive results occurred in the prostitution cases, *R. v. Skinner* [1990] 1 S.C.R. 1235, and in statutory rape, *R. v. Nguyen and Hess* [1990] 2 S.C.R. 906. No serious sex equality argument was made in either instance.

67. *Daigle v. Trembley* [1989] 2 S.C.R. 530.

68. On women's rights in childbirth: See *The Queen v. Sullivan and LeMay* (March 21, 1991), Doc. 21080, 21494 (S.C.C.).

69. *Keegstra v. The Queen* [1991] 2 W.W.R. 1; *The Queen v. Butler* [1992] 2 W.W.R. 5577 (S.C.C.).

70. Women's Help Now and Kareta, "Who Are We? Where Are We?" (leaflet, October 2, 1992, Zagreb); Natalie Nenadic, "How do you get rid of the guns?" *Everywoman*, July–August 1991, 19; Katja Gattin for Kareta, "Where have all the feminists gone?" (unpublished paper, January 20, 1992, Zagreb). ("In 1991/1992, Croatia is a woman.")

71. A useful review is Yougindra Khushalani, *Dignity and Honour of Women as Basic and Fundamental Human Rights* (The Hague: Nijhoff, 1982).

72. Art. 77(1), Protocol I, Protocol Additional to the Geneva Conventions of August 12, 1949 (victims of international armed conflict protected against "rape, forced prostitution and any other form of indecent assault"); Art. 4(e), Protocol II, Protocol Additional to the Geneva Conventions of August 12, 1949 (victims of noninternational armed conflicts protected against "outrages upon personal dignity, in particular humiliating and degrading treatment, rape, enforced prostitution and any form of indecent assault"). Murder and torture are prohibited under many international conventions, with additional protections against doing so on ethnic grounds.

73. *In re Yamashita*, 327 U.S. 1 (1945). Courtney Whitney, Brigadier General, U.S. Army, *The Case of General Yamashita: A Memorandum* (1950), 5–16, contains detailed excerpts from the record of the trial, revealing many rapes. The U.S. Supreme Court upheld the decision of the military tribunal. See also Richard L. Lael, *The Yamashita Precedent: War Crimes and Command Responsibility* (Wilmington: Scholarly Resources, 1982), 83–84; L. C. Green, *Essays on the Modern Law of War* (Dobbs Ferry, N.Y.: Transnational Publications, 1985), 227–28; Arnold Brackman, *The Other Nuremburg: The Untold Story of the Tokyo War Crimes Trials* (New York: Morrow, 1987), 179–80. Brackman discusses the death sentence of General Iwane Matsui, who was convicted of "failing to take adequate steps to secure the observance and prevent breaches of conventions and laws of war in respect of prisoners of war and civilian internees" in the mass rapes that were called the Rape of Nanking (419; see also 180 and 409).

74. Lael, *Yamashita Precedent*, 83. All that is distinguishable in the Japanese war accounts is the pornography and the intention to create pregnancies.

75. Joan Fitzpatrick, "The Use of International Human Rights Norms to Combat Violence Against Women" (unpublished manuscript, 1992). This is a lucid, informed treatment. On the rapes in Bangladesh, see Susan Brownmiller, *Against Our Will: Men, Women and Rape* (New York: Bantam, 1976), 78–87.

76. *The Trial of German Major War Criminals*, Part 6, 303 (evidence of Soviet prosecutors); Part 5, 159, 325–27 (evidence of French prosecutors).

77. *The Trial of German Major War Criminals*, Part 1, 24: "One hundred and thirty-nine women had their arms painfully bent backward and held by wires. From some their breasts had been cut off, and their ears, fingers and toes had been amputated. The bodies bore the marks of burns." (Russian women's bodies in Stalingrad region after German expulsion).

78. Opening statement by Justice Jackson, *The Trial of German Major War Criminals*, 53. One exhibit of a

Soviet official documenting "revolting acts of rape" by the German invaders observed this: "Unquestionable facts prove that the regime . . . did not consist of certain excesses of individual undisciplined military units, or individual German officers and soldiers. Rather does it point to a definite system, planned far in advance and encouraged by the German Government and the German Army Command, a system which intentionally unleashed within their army the lowest animal instincts among the officers and men." *The Trial of German Major War Criminals*, Part 7, 26 (notes of V. M. Molotov, National Commissar for Foreign Affairs in USSR, Exhibit USSR 51, dates as early as January 6, 1942). The Nuremberg trial was conducted under the common law of war, even though the violations of the Geneva Conventions under which the Nazi leadership was charged had not been made a specific penal offense. See Howard S. Levie, *The Code of International Armed Conflict* (London: Oceana Publications, 1986), 862.

79. "Consistent pattern of gross and reliably attested violations of human rights and fundamental freedoms" violate Resolution 1503 (XLVIII) of the Economic and Social Council authorizing the establishment of a subcommission on Prevention of Discrimination and Protection of Minorities. It is empowered to appoint a group to determine violations and bring them to the attention of the subcommission and it enables the U.N. to interfere in "domestic" matters. See Ermacora, "Human Rights and Domestic Jurisdiction," *Recueil des Cours* (1968): 124, 375, 436.

80. Bogdan Tirnanic, quoted by Michael Moorcock, "Working in the Ministry of Truth: Pornography and Censorship in Contemporary Britain," in C. Itzin, ed., *Pornography: Women, Violence, and Civil Liberties* (Oxford: Oxford University Press, 1992), 536. As Moorcock then asks, "Have sex crimes dropped in Serbia?" (550).

81. It should be noted that the Serbs consider the Serbian-occupied areas of Croatia and Bosnia-Herzegovina to be Serbian states, parts of the United States of Serbia. So the Serbian military forces, in addition to being state actors under orders from Belgrade, function under color of official authority of the self-declared Serbian ministates within and against the established governments of Croatia and Bosnia-Herzegovina. In addition, the local Serbian irregulars, termed *chetnicks*, provide yet another layer of actual and apparent state authority.

## John Stoltenberg, "How Men Have (a) Sex" (pp. 410–419)

1. My source for the foregoing information about so-called sex determinants in the human species is a series of interviews I conducted with the sexologist Dr. John Money in Baltimore, Maryland, in 1979 for an article I wrote called "The Multisex Theorem," which was published in a shortened version as "Future Genders" in *Omni* magazine, May 1980, pp. 67–73 ff.

2. Dworkin, Andrea. *Woman Hating* (New York: Dutton, 1974), p. 174.

3. Dworkin, *Woman Hating*, p. 183 (Italics in original).

## Patrick D. Hopkins, "Gender Treachery: Homophobia, Masculinity, and Threatened Identities" (pp. 419–433)

1. I want to thank Larry May for his encouragement and editing suggestions throughout the writing of this paper. I also want to make it clear that although I think some of this essay is applicable to hatred and violence directed against lesbians (sometimes called lesbophobia), for the purposes of a volume specifically on masculinity I have deliberately (though not exclusively) focused on males and hatred and violence directed against gay males. Even with this focus, however, I am indebted to work on homophobia by lesbian researchers and theorists. In a future, more comprehensive project I will explore the oppression and marginalization of a wider variety of gender traitors.

2. Although the scope of this essay prevents a lengthy discussion, it should be pointed out that many male teachers and coaches call their students and team members "girls": to be playful, to be insulting, or to shame them into playing more roughly.

3. It should also be pointed out that gay men often use the word "girl" to refer to each other. In these cases, however, signifying a lack of masculinity is not registering insult. Often, it is expressing a sentiment of community—a community formed by the shared rejection of compulsory heterosexuality and compulsory forms of masculinity.

4. I deliberately sidestep the philosophical debate over the existence of "self" in this discussion. While I am quite skeptical of the existence of a stable, core self, I do not think the argument in this paper turns on the answer to that problem. "Self" could simply be

interpreted as a metaphor for social situatedness. In any case, I do not mean to suggest that subverting gender is a way to purify an essential human "self."

5. For work on Native American societies that do not operate with a simple gender binary, see Walter L. Williams, *The Spirit and the Flesh: Sexual Diversity in American Indian Culture* (Boston: Beacon Press, 1986) and Will Roscoe (ed.), *Living The Spirit: A Gay American Indian Anthology* (New York: St. Martin's Press, 1988).

6. For works on the social construction of gender and sexuality see: Judith Butler, *Gender Trouble: Feminism and the Subversion of Identity* (New York: Routledge, 1990); Michel Foucault, *Herculine Barbin: Being the Recently Discovered Memoirs of a Nineteenth Century French Hermaphrodite* (New York: Pantheon, 1980); Michel Foucault, *The History of Sexuality: Volume 1. An Introduction* (New York: Vintage Books, 1980); Montique Wittig, *The Straight Mind and Other Essays* (Boston: Beacon Press, 1992).

7. In the United States and many other countries, if a baby is born with anatomical genital features that do not easily lend themselves to a classification within the gender/sex system in place, they are surgically and hormonally altered to fit into the categories of male or female, girl or boy.

8. I am grateful to Bob Strikwerda for pointing out that none of these characteristics taken by itself is absolutely necessary to be perceived as masculine in contemporary U.S. culture (except perhaps heterosexuality). In fact, a man who possessed every characteristic would be seen as a parody.

9. I borrow the insightful term "gender treachery" from Margaret Atwood. In her brilliant dystopian novel, *The Handmaids' Tale* (Boston: Houghton Mifflin, 1986), set in a post-fundamentalist Christian takeover [in] America, criminals are executed and hanged on a public wall with the name of their crime around their necks for citizens to see. Homosexuals bear the placard "gender traitor."

10. It doesn't matter if this rejection is "deliberate" or not in the sense of direct refusal. Any deviant behavior can be seen as treacherous unless perhaps the individual admits "guilt" and seeks a "cure" or "forgiveness."

11. Someone might ask: But why those people most *thoroughly* sexed rather than those most insecure in their sexuality? My point here is a broad one about the categories of gender. Even those people who are insecure in their sexuality will be laboring under the compulsory ideal of traditional binary gender identities.

12. "Queers"—the name itself bespeaks curiosity, treachery, radical unidentifiability, the uncategorized, perverse entities, infectious otherness.

13. See Gregroy M. Herek, "On Heterosexual Masculinity: Some Psychical Consequences of the Social Construction of Gender and Sexuality," *American Behavioral Scientist*, vol. 29, no. 5, May/June 1986, 563–77.

14. For all these terms except "homohatred," see Gregory M. Herek, "Stigma, Prejudice, and Violence Against Lesbians and Gay Men," pp. 60–80, in J. C. Gonsiorek and J. D. Weinrich (eds.), *Homosexuality: Research Implications for Public Policy* (London: Sage Publications, Inc., 1991). For "homohatred," see Marshall Kirk and Hunter Madsen, *After the Ball: How America Will Conquer its Fear & Hatred of Gays in the 90's* (New York: Penguin Books, 1989).

15. See Jacob Smith Yang's article in *Gay Community News*, August 18–24, vol. 19, no. 6, 1991, p. 1. The brutal July 4 murder of Paul Broussard sparked an uproar in Houston's queer community over anti-gay violence and police indifference. To "quell the recent uproar," Houston police undertook an undercover operation in which officers posed as gay men in a well-known gay district. Although police were skeptical of gays' claims of the frequency of violence, within one hour of posing as gay men, undercover officers were sprayed with mace and attacked by punks wielding baseball bats.

16. See Kirk and Madsen, p. 127. They mention the case of Rose Mary Denman, a United Methodist minister who was a vocal opponent of the ordinations of gays and lesbians until she eventually acknowledged her own lesbianism. Upon announcing this, however, she was defrocked. Kirk and Madsen quote a *New York Times* article that states: "In retrospect, she attributed her previous vehement stand against ordaining homosexuals to the effects of denying her unacknowledged lesbian feelings."

17. See John Money, *Gay, Straight and In-Between: The Sexology of Erotic Orientation* (Oxford: Oxford University Press, 1988), pp. 109–110.

18. See Suzanne Pharr, *Homophobia: A Weapon of Sexism* (Little Rock, AR: Chardon Press, 1988) and also Kirk and Madsen, *After the Ball*. The stereotypical story is one I have elaborated on from Kirk and Madsen's book, chapter 2.

19. See Herek, "On Heterosexual Masculinity . . .", especially pp. 572–73.

20. One can think of the typical scene where one boy challenges another boy to do something dangerous or cruel by claiming that if he does not do so, he is afraid—a sissy. Similarly, boys who are friends/peers of homophobes may be expected to engage in cruel physical or verbal behavior in order to appear strong, reliable, and most importantly of all, no faggots themselves. They know what happens to faggots.

21. See Herek, *On Heterosexual Masculinity*, p. 573.

22. See Celia Kitzinger, *The Social Construction of Lesbianism* (London: Sage Publications, Inc., 1987).

23. For example, in my own area of the country we have Rev. Don Wildmon's American Family Association, headquartered in Tupelo, Mississippi—an ultraconservative media watchdog group dedicated to the elimination of any media image not in keeping with right-wing Christian morality. Also, in Memphis, Tennessee, there is FLARE (Family Life America for Responsible Education Under God, Inc.), a group lobbying for Christian prayer in public schools, the elimination of sex education programs, and the installation of a "Family Life Curriculum" in public schools that would stress sexual abstinence and teach that the only form of morally acceptable sexual activity is married, heterosexual sex.

24. I borrow the term "boogeyfag" from David G. Powell's excellent unpublished manuscript, *Deviations of a Queen: Episodic Gay Theory*. Powell deconstructs California Congressman Robert Dornan's claim that "The biggest mass murderers in history are gay."

25. Gary David Comstock, *Violence Against Lesbians and Gay Men* (New York: Columbia University Press, 1991), p. 172.

26. For this analysis of masculinity and performance, I owe much to insights garnered from Judith Butler's article "Imitation and Gender Insubordination," in Diana Fuss, *Inside/Out: Lesbian Theories, Gay Theories* (New York: Routledge, 1991).

27. I use the term, "monster" here in a way similar to that of Donna Haraway in her essay "A Cyborg Manifesto: Science, Technology, and Socialist-Feminism in the Late Twentieth Century," reprinted in her book *Simians, Cyborg, and Women: The Reinvention of Nature* (New York: Routledge, 1991). Haraway says: "Monsters have always defined the limits of community in Western imaginations. The Centaurs and Amazons of ancient Greece established the limits of the centred polis of the Greek male human by their disruption of marriage and boundary pollutions of the warrior with

animality and woman" (p. 180). I loosely use "monster" in referring to homosexuality in the sense that the homosexual disrupts gender boundaries and must therefore be categorized into its own species so as to prevent destabilizing those boundaries.

28. Aquinas, for example, viewed the "vice of sodomy" as the second worst "unnatural vice," worse even than rape—a view echoed in contemporary legal decisions such as Bowers v. Hardwick (106 S. Ct. 2841, 1986), which upheld the criminal status of homosexuality. See Arthur N. Gilbert, "Conceptions of Homosexuality and Sodomy in Western History," in Salvatore J. Licata and Robert P. Peterson (eds.), *The Gay Past: A Collection of Historical Essays* (New York: Harrington Park Press, 1985), pp 57–68.

29. On the creation of homosexuality as a category, see Foucault, *The History of Sexuality*.

30. In this sense: The repressive hates the species "homosexual," but nonetheless desires the body "man." It is only an historically contingent construction that desiring a certain kind of body "makes" you a certain kind of person, "makes" you have a certain kind of "lifestyle." Unfortunately, it is also true that being a certain "kind" of person can carry with it serious dangers, as is the case for homosexuals.

31. See Comstock, p. 55.

32. See Comstock, p. 59.

33. This is not to say that gays and lesbians are not often treated as a minority; good arguments have been made that they are. See Richard D. Mohr, "Gay Studies as Moral Vision," *Educational Theory*, vol. 39, no. 2, 1989.

34. In fact, I very much enjoy studies in applied mythology, particularly the work of Joseph Campbell. However, I am extremely skeptical about any application of mythology that characterizes itself as returning us to some primal experience of masculinity that contemporary culture has somehow marred or diminished. There is always the specter of essentialism in such moves.

## Thomas W. Laqueur, "The Facts of Fatherhood" (pp. 433–446)

1. For an account of these industrial narratives see Catherine Gallagher, *The Industrial Reformation of English Fiction, 1832–1867* (Chicago: University of Chicago Press, 1985).

2. Gayle Rubin, "The Traffic in Women: Notes on the 'Political Economy' of Sex," in Rayna Reiter, ed., *Toward an Anthropology of Women* (New York: Monthly Review Press, 1975) pp. 179–180.

3. *Philosophy in the Bedroom* (New York: Grove Press, 1965) p. 106.

4. William Harvey, *Disputation Touching the Generation*

of Animals, trans. Gweneth Whitteridge (Oxford: Oxford University Press, 1981) pp. 182–183.

5. Sigmund Freud, *Moses and Monotheism* (1939), in *The Standard Edition of the Complete Psychoanalytical Works*, ed. James Strachey (London: Hogarth Press) vol. 23, pp. 113–114; I have altered the translation slightly based on the standard German edition. Aeschylus, *The Eumenides*, trans. Richmond Lattimore, in David Greene and Lattimore, eds., *Greek Tragedies*, vol. 3 (Chicago: University of Chicago Press, 1960) pp. 26–28.

6. Isidore, *Etimologias [Etymologiarum]*, ed. and trans.

with facing Latin text by J. O. Reta and M. A. Marcos (Madrid: Biblioteca de Autores Christianos, 1983) 6, 4.

7. *Ibid.* 5, 5, 4. On blood, see 4, 5, 4.

8. See Thomas W. Laqueur, *Making Sex: Body and Gender from the Greeks to Freud* (Cambridge: Harvard University Press, 1990), for more extensive discussion of these points.

9. William Cowper, *Anatomy*, introduction, n.p.

10. David Hume, A *Treatise of Human Nature*, ed. L. A. Selby-Bigge (Oxford: Oxford University Press, 1965) 2, 1, 9, p. 303.

11. Civil Case no. A-027810. I am grateful to Donna Hutchins, Esq., of San Francisco for making available the various depositions, briefs, and other court papers on which I base the following discussion.

12. Roberta Achtenberg, ed., *Sexual Orientation and the Law* (New York: Clark, Boardman, Co. Ltd., 1889) section 1–70.

13. Anne Taylor Fleming, "Our Fascination with Baby M," *New York Times Magazine*, March 29, 1987, p. 87. There were at the time of this article about one thousand known "surrogate mothers."

## Trinh T. Minh-ha, "Yellow Sprouts" (pp. 479–484)

1. *The Inner Teachings of Taoism*, T. Cleary, trans. (Boston: Shambhala, 1986) p.6.

2. Gerald Vizenor, *Griever: An American Monkey King in China* (New York: Illinois State University and Fiction Collective, 1986), p. 227.

3. Quoted in Francois Cheng, *Chinese Poetic Writing*, D.A. Riggs and J. P. Seaton, trans. (Bloomington: Indiana University Press, 1982), p. 71.

4. See *Women in Chinese Folklore* (Beijing: Women of China, 1983), pp. 29–43.

5. Ting Lan, "Woman Is Not the Moon," in Emily Honig and Gail Hershatter, eds., *Personal Voices: Chinese Women in the 1980's* (Stanford: Stanford University Press, 1988), p. 329.

6. Quoted in Elizam Escobar, "The Fear and Tremor of Being Understood: The Recent Work for Bertha Husband," *Third Text*, Nos. 3–4 (Spring–Summer 1988): 119.

7. Quoted in Bertha Husband, "A Deep Sea Diver in the Phantom(ly) Country: Art and Politics of Elizam Escobar," *ibid.*, pp. 113; 116.

8. Walter Benjamin, *One-Way Street and Other Writings* (London: Verso, 1978; rpt. 1985), p. 123.

9. Judit, "Alliances," *Companeras: Latina Lesbians*, ed. Juanita Ramos (New York: Latina Lesbian History Project, 1987), pp. 245–46.

10. Quoted in *Chinese Poetic Writing*, p. 108.

11. Sun Bu-er, "Ingestion of the Medecine," *Immortal Sisters: Secrets of Taoist Women*, ed. and trans. T. Cleary (Boston: Shambhala, 1989), p. 47.

12. Audre Lorde, "Age, Race, Class, and Sex: Women Redefining Difference," *Out There: Marginalization and Contemporary Culture*, ed. Russell Ferguson, et al. (New York: The New Museum of Contemporary Art and M.I.T. Press, 1990), p. 287.

13. Quoted in Gerald Vizenor, "Socioacupuncture: Mythic Reversals and the Striptease in Four Scenes," *Out There*, p. 419.

14. Soseki, *Oreiller d'herbes*, R. de Cecatty and R. Nakamura, trans. (Paris: Editions Rivages, 1987), p. 137.

# *Audiovisual Resources*

The following are the addresses and phone numbers for some of the audiovisual resources listed thoughout the book:

AIDS Film Initiative, 732 West Nedro Avenue, Philadelphia, PA 19120. Telephone 251-224-4934.

California AIDS Clearinghouse, P.O. Box 1830, Santa Cruz, CA 95061. Telephone 800-258-9090.

The Cinema Guild, 1697 Broadway, New York, NY 10019. Telephone 212-246-5522.

Filmakers Library, Inc., 124 East 40th Street, Suite 901, New York, NY 10016. Telephone 212-808-4980.

Films for the Humanities & Sciences, P.O. Box 2053, Princeton, NJ 08543-2053. Telephone 800-257-5126.

Gay Men's Health Crisis, Videotapes/Publications Distribution, 129 West 20th Street, New York, NY 10011. Telephone 212-337-3558.

Insight Media, 121 West 85th Street, New York, NY 10024. Telephone 212-721-6316.

Ms., P.O. Box 57122, Boulder, CO 80321-7122.

The Museum of Modern Art Circulating Film Library, 11 West 53rd Street, New York, NY 10019. 212-708-9530.

The National Breast Cancer Coalition, P.O. Box 66373, Washington, DC 20077-6302.

National Film Board of Canada, 1251 Avenue of the Americas, 16th Floor, New York, NY 10020-1173. Telephone 800-542-2164.

Women Make Movies, 225 Lafayette Street, Suite 211, New York, NY 10012. Telephone 212-925-0606.